The Autobiography of Ozaki Yukio

The Autobiography of Ozaki Yukio

THE STRUGGLE FOR CONSTITUTIONAL

GOVERNMENT IN JAPAN

TRANSLATED BY FUJIKO HARA
WITH A FOREWORD BY MARIUS B. JANSEN

PRINCETON UNIVERSITY PRESS

PRINCETON AND OXFORD

Library of Congress Cataloging-in-Publication Data

Ozaki, Yukio, 1858–1954.
[Gakudo jiden. English]
The autobiography of Ozaki Yukio: the struggle for constitutional government in Japan /
translated by Fujiko Hara; with a foreword by Marius Jansen.
p. cm.
Includes index.
ISBN 0-691-05095-3 (alk. paper)
1. Ozaki, Yukio, 1858–1954. 2 Statesmen—Japan—Biography. 3. Japan—Politics and
government—1868–1912. 4. Japan—Politics and government—1912–1945. I. Hara, Fujiko.
II. Jansen, Marius B. III. Title.

DS885.5 O9 A3 2001
328.52′092—dc21
[B]   00-065211

This book has been composed in Times Roman typeface

The paper used in this publication meets the minimum requirements
of ANSI / NISO Z39.48-1992 (R1997) (*Permanence of Paper*)

www.pup.princeton.edu

Printed in the United States of America
3   5   7   9   10   8   6   4   2

• C O N T E N T S •

following page 216

1. Ozaki in his prime. Photograph of September 1, 1937.

2. Ozaki with his wife, Yei Theodora, and daughters Shinaye and Yukika. Photograph taken at Karuizawa summer home, 1922.

3. Ozaki with dogs at his Zushi residence, 1935.

4. Ozaki speaking in the Imperial Diet, February 7, 1937.

5. Ozaki addressing a Shimbashi crowd, April 18, 1947.

6. Ozaki addressing a Shinjuku crowd in support of his long-time associate Tagawa Daikichiro during the Imperial Rule Assistance Association elections ordered by the Tōjō government in 1941. Later in the campaign Ozaki was arrested and briefly imprisoned, but not convicted, on charges of lèse majesté.

7. Ozaki, ninety years old and invited to America by the American Council on Japan, at a New York banquet held in his honor in 1950. On his right is Joseph Grew, U.S. ambassador to Japan from 1932 to 1941.

I HAVE BEEN privileged to complete the translation of my grandfather's autobiography with the generous collaboration of two men I greatly respect, Professor Marius Jansen and my husband, Martin Blakeway. It is with deep sorrow that we have learned of the death of Marius Jansen, just a few months before this book which owes so much to him is due for publication. We join with his colleagues and students and his dear wife Jean in lamenting our loss of this great scholar and universally loved gentleman. Professor Jansen, who was Professor Emeritus at Princeton University and America's foremost authority on Japanese and East Asian studies, fielded my lapses of scholarship, clarified historical inconsistencies, added the helpful footnotes, and honored our work with his foreword, while Martin, in whom I see so much of my grandfather's spirit and vision, gallantly reworked my English. Without them the book would not have reached the press.

The most significant thing to me about Ozaki's autobiography is the relevance of his views even today, especially as they apply to Japan. Ozaki was deeply misunderstood by his countrymen during his lifetime because he was half a century ahead of them. As he picks his way with almost self-defeating uprightness across the unmarked political terrain of the young modern state, his one unwavering purpose was to serve Japan with all his might. This led him eventually to the conclusion that the survival of his beloved country and the happiness of its people were inseparable from achieving the same for the whole world of which it was a part. This meant, as he saw it, bringing justice and democracy to bear universally even as he strove to assure them for Japan.

The secret of Ozaki's enduring relevance is partly to be found in his exceptionally objective turn of mind, coupled with an ability that never left him to grow in wisdom and, without changing his faith, to change his mind. He recalls his first trip abroad in 1888 (an opportune use of his sentence of three years' exile from the capital for belonging to a group agitating for the revision of the "unequal treaties"). Emulating the Chinese statesmen, he had kept a book of "rewards and reprisals," including the names of people he felt deserving of one or the other. But the loss of the book in a storm off San Francisco that swept away his belongings with those of his fellow passengers freed him from past injuries. From then on, he felt he could devote his whole attention to building a modern state and parliamentary democracy.

The experience that did more than any other to shake him out of the narrow nationalism of his early years was a visit to the battlefields of Europe in the aftermath of the Great War. He saw in the heaps of rubble and twisted iron that had once been great buildings and the homes of innocent people the folly of men who obediently wrought destruction on each other and killed and died for what?— for "nations."

It provoked a catharsis in him that motivated him to fight for suffrage and disarmament for the rest of his life. And when his struggle failed to keep Japan out of the senseless war that followed and another even more terrible loomed, he sought to use the resources the country would save from spending on arms for the study of world peace. Just as the air, the sun, and the oceans belonged equally to all peoples, he believed that the land too should be regarded as the common heritage of humankind to be wisely managed by custodial governments.

We are most grateful to The Japan Foundation for their generous help in funding the preparation of this book.

I dedicate this book to Ozaki Yukio's youngest daughter, Sohma Yukika, my mother, who has selflessly devoted her life to great causes, national and global, and to my two sons, Naomichi and Nobumichi, and their wives, and to my daughter Makiko.

Fujiko Hara
Tokyo 2000

THERE ARE numerous occasions where Ozaki in dictating his reminiscences introduces or reintroduces topics out of chronological sequence. Where a modest degree of editorial license does not impair the logic or intention of the author's words, we have sometimes taken the liberty of changing the order of thoughts or paragraphs. In other places, where we have not attempted this feat, it is hoped that the attentive reader will make sympathetic allowance for any apparent lapses of continuity.

Also, in seeking to convey Ozaki's true character and the spirit of his words, which were often redundant or stilted in the original Japanese, we have sought to interpret proverbs, figures of speech, and other locutions that are not readily conveyed in English in a manner which we believe corresponds closely to Ozaki's meaning. We have held throughout to the Japanese practice of putting family names before personal names.

FH/MBJ

THE AUTOBIOGRAPHY of Ozaki Yukio (1858–1954), translated here by his grand-daughter, provides Western readers with the initial opportunity to explore a first-hand account of the struggle for democracy in modern Japan. Ozaki's leading role in that story throughout a long career makes his account a personal history of constitutional government in Japan, the subtitle under which the book was origi-nally published in Japan.

Ozaki's account is unusual, indeed unique. The members of the oligarchy from the domains of Chōshū and Satsuma, who created the Meiji (1868–1912) state, left few personal accounts. Saigō Takamori, Kido Takayoshi, and Ōkubo Toshimi-chi, who dominated the first decade, died as it ended, Saigō in rebellion, Kido of illness, and Ōkubo through assassination. Their successors—Itō Hirobumi, Yama-gata Aritomo, Matsukata Masayoshi, and Ōkuma Shigenobu—led longer lives, but their careers were so closely intertwined with the life and aura of the Emperor Meiji that it would have been difficult to provide a personal account that did not affect the aura of the ruler in whose name every action had been taken without endangering his primacy. Because they were founding fathers of the imperial state, their letters and biographies were carefully edited and quietly screened by panegyrists eager to protect and enhance their reputations.

Those farther from the power center could be more frank. Foreign Minister Mutsu Munemitsu left a full account of his stewardship during the Sino-Japanese War of 1894–1895, though its publication was long delayed, and he also provided biting commentary on many of his chiefs, though not over his own name.

Ozaki, on the other hand, outlived the men he worked with and could be free with judgments. His Matsukata is a dullard, Itō is childlike, Yamagata a crafty schemer, and Ōkuma, long his mentor, ends as a garrulous figurehead able to take both sides of any issue. These and other pen portraits with which the book is studded go far to make it interesting and important.

The enduring value of Ozaki's account, however, lies in the light it casts on Japan's experience with representative government as seen in the career of its foremost parliamentarian. Ozaki's life encapsulates a century of government in modern Japan. Born the son of a stern samurai who, thanks to the patronage of a Restoration loyalist, became an official in the new Meiji government, Ozaki stud-ied in the Keiō academy of Fukuzawa Yukichi, the foremost educator of that generation. With Fukuzawa's recommendation, he became the editor of a newspa-per in Niigata on the coast of the Sea of Japan, but soon returned to the capital and a government post with the sponsorship of Yano Fumio. The ouster from the government of Yano's powerful associate, Ōkuma Shigenobu, plunged Ozaki into political wars against the Chōshū-Satsuma clan monopolists, and that struggle became the center of his life.

At the dawn of the Meiji era, the boy emperor had issued a pledge, largely designed to reassure the feudal elite, that, in the future, matters would be settled on the basis of public discussion carried on in deliberative assemblies. In less than a decade this promise found echo in the complaints of dissident members of the leadership who demanded a greater say in government decisions. That demand soon struck a responsive chord with other outsiders and local notables, and by 1881, the year Ōkuma was driven from his post, the governing oligarchy found it wise to have the young emperor, now approaching thirty, promise a constitution with a parliament that would meet at the end of the decade. The populace was counseled to be patient while a constitution was prepared, but nevertheless the emperor's pledge made politics legitimate, for now opposition figures could argue that insufficient attention to popular opinion constituted betrayal of the emperor's intent and wish.

Ozaki now threw himself into political battles against the clan oligarchs. He began as a lieutenant of Ōkuma Shigenobu, a former Saga clan leader who shared prominence with Itagaki Taisuke, the Tosa samurai whose 1874 petition had sparked the movement for a constitution. The government recognized Ozaki's importance by banishing him from Tokyo in 1887; the young writer found himself with a police guard as he left the capital; he would not have such protection again until he was a cabinet minister.

By the time the constitution was promulgated in 1889, Ozaki had returned from a trip to the West. He stood for election to the first Diet as a candidate from Mie Prefecture and won a seat in the first parliament to be convened in Asia. He was to retain that seat in the House of Representatives for sixty-three years through twenty-five elections until 1953, a record that made him Japan's, and probably the world's, longest-serving parliamentarian. To the talents of a journalist's pen, he added powerful oratory. His electoral base remained invulnerable through changes in which the electorate, in response to efforts in which he played a leading role, grew through the gradual lowering of tax qualifications until universal manhood suffrage was enacted in 1925. Support groups named for his pen name, "Gakudō," developed in and beyond his constituency. In the capital he became so well known that a visit to a demonstration he hoped would go unnoticed found enthusiastic crowds surrounding him and demanding that he mount a monument and speak.

As this suggests, Ozaki's was usually a voice of protest. The issue that most concerned him was the manner in which prime ministers were selected. The Meiji Constitution was centered around a powerful emperor, but gave few specifics about the cabinets through which his rule would be exercised. In practice, the clan oligarchy maintained a monopoly over the process by which the imperial command was handed down to a prospective prime minister. It was the center of Ozaki's life to free that office from Satsuma-Chōshū control and base it instead on the selection of the prime minister by a popularly elected House of Representatives. Consequently, he was usually in opposition to the government, except on the few occasions when the selection of his one-time mentor, Ōkuma, as prime minister seemed to indicate movement toward his goals. For the rest, he conceived it his duty to overthrow successive cabinets by introducing motions of nonconfidence in the hope that the oligarchs would come to recognize the necessity of working through responsible political parties in the lower house.

Incredibly, Ozaki doubled as mayor of Tokyo for a decade from 1902 to 1912. This contributed to his future internationalism. It brought him into personal contact with world leaders who visited japan, and it was as mayor that he proposed and carried out the gift of cherry trees to Washington, D.C. It also acquainted him with the problems surrounding modernization of the infrastructure of that metropolis during a period of rapid growth.

The most memorable occasions of Ozaki's Diet career center around speeches in which he impeached governmental arrogance. A fiery denunciation of Katsura Tarō for the manipulation of the throne in 1913 led directly to the fall of that government, and he notes other occasions on which nervous governments dissolved the Diet rather than risk the sting of his rhetoric. He was a central figure in organizing coalitions to "Protect Constitutional Government," as they were called, in 1913 and again in the 1920s.

Ozaki was twice a cabinet minister under Ōkuma, in 1898 and again in 1914, and he worked closely with Itō Hirobumi for a few years after 1900, but for the most part he stood in opposition alone or with a small group of like-minded followers.

In the 1920s, political party leadership seemed finally to be becoming the normal path to control over the executive. Politicians and governments sensed the need to curb rising radicalism by granting electoral concessions, and by 1925 universal manhood suffrage, sharply resisted a few years before, became law almost without controversy. Future threats to democracy would come from the armed services instead of the Satsuma-Chōshū oligarchs.

Ozaki began his career as a strong nationalist. In this he reflected the atmosphere of his times, for the movement for representative government had begun with discontent over the government's failure to challenge Korea in 1874, and the political agitation that brought on Ozaki's banishment from Tokyo in 1887 had its origins in the government's failure to demand full equality with Western powers in treaty reform. As the Meiji empire took form with the occupation of Taiwan and Korea, however, Ozaki moderated his stand and ended as a firm internationalist. A visit to Europe at the end of World War I convinced him of the futility of arms races that ended in ever larger wars. He now wanted his country to lead, instead of resisting, calls for naval arms limitations. Here again he stood alone against an unpersuaded Diet and a hostile military. In speaking tours in which he distributed postcards in a crude attempt to poll public sentiment, he found that he was closer to the popular perception than were his timid and unimaginative Diet colleagues who had voted against his resolutions. Events proved him correct. Japan received little credit from the democracies for its reluctant acceptance of naval ratios worked out at Washington in 1922 and London in 1930. Had it instead taken the lead in proposing such limitationsm, the history of the twentieth century could have been quite different.

Unfortunately as political parties found themselves closer to power, internal struggles between factions intensified instead of easing. To Ozaki's dismay, party politicians now turned to powerful figures in the armed services and bureaucracy in a search for funds and leadership. Bureaucrats and generals in turn saw affiliation with the parties as a path by which to carry out their financial and political programs. Meretricious politicians were as prepared to sell out to militarists as they had been to be co-opted by the Meiji oligarchs.

Ozaki had a sharp eye and tongue for such betrayal, and some of the most poignant passages of his autobiography detail his lament for the lack of what he considered true parties in Japan. He abhorred the pretense of the wartime Imperial Rule Assistance Association, but when party activity resumed in post-surrender days, he proposed the dissolution of all parties and the formation of a national unity government instead.

Ozaki's sturdy independence was not without its dangers. He was several times a target of would-be assassins, and carried farewell death poems with him when he spoke against Japan's rash military masters. A speech in which he pointed to the proverbial tendency of third-generation heirs to squander the accumulation of their forbears brought him charges of lèse majesté and a night in Sugamo Prison. Typically, he insisted on a formal trial with the demand for severe punishment if the charge should be sustained. His respect for the Meiji emperor is clear throughout the book, but Hirohito, Emperor Shōwa, is less clearly sketched. Ozaki was granted an audience shortly after the end of the war, but found the emperor had little to say; he, in turn, said little because he was "not sure how much he would understand."

As one might have expected, Ozaki, now in his late eighties, maintained his independence after World War II. He approved of Occupation reforms and of the new constitution, but found it intolerably humiliating that such advances toward democracy had to come from foreign hands. Worse, the reconstituted political parties seemed no better than the old; at this point Ozaki considers that his countrymen's political immaturity is reminiscent of the Meiji years in which his career began.

Ozaki's account is a rich resource for reflections on Japan's political culture. Readers accustomed to thinking of courteous resolution of differences and of Japan's as a society of consensus will be astonished by the crudity and violence of early Meiji politics. Meetings could turn into brawls, sometimes with lethal consequences. Accounts of violence in the Diet itself serve to remind one that Meiji Japan was still a developing country. It was not for nothing that governments monitored such groups, but it must be remembered that they had their own, more discreet, forms of violence. As Ozaki was ushered out of Tokyo after being banished in 1887, the policeman who arrested him told him that he had been given instructions to cut Ozaki down immediately if there was the slightest sign of resistance. After the promulgation of the Meiji Constitution in 1889, governments repeatedly resorted to intimidation of electors by gangs of ruffians. Then, as governments resorted to money instead of violence, public violence gave way to private threats as tempers rose. The politician's life was not an easy one. Military men, Ozaki notes, could vaunt themselves on risking danger for the sake of their country, but in fact politicians ran greater dangers. In the military, higher rank brought greater safety, but with politicians it was just the opposite. The fates of Ōkubo, Hoshi Tōru, Hara Takashi, and Ozaki's long-time associate Inukai Tsuyoshi underscore the point.

The Ozaki memoir is not without its relevance for the student of contemporary Japanese politics. The author's accounts of party formation, division, and reconsolidation, and of factional groupings and financial manipulation often have a familiar ring. Nevertheless we are unlikely to find a future parliamentarian with the consistency, integrity, and courage of the author of this history.

Small wonder that Ozaki was honored at home and abroad. He was given a warm welcome by the United States Senate on a final visit to America in 1950. In 1953, now ninety-four and confined to his bed, Ozaki stood for election a last time. When that bid failed, the Japanese House of Representatives immediately voted him an honorary membership and installed a bronze bust of him within the Diet building. The Tokyo Metropolitan Government made him its first Honorary Citizen. An Ozaki Yukio Memorial Foundation was established with private donations that included a token ten yen contribution from every primary- and secondary-school child in Japan. Ozaki Yukio has thus come to stand as the symbol and spokesman of constitutional government in Japan.

THE BOOK AND THE TRANSLATION

The book translated here occupies all 791 pages of Volume 11 of Ozaki's 12-volume *Works, Ozaki Gakudō Zenshū* (Tokyo: Kōronsha, 1955), where it is subtitled *Nihon kensei shi o kataru* (The History of Constitutional Government in Japan). It is greatly amplified and far more detailed than a shorter account he published shortly after the end of World War II in 1947.

Throughout the book names are given in Japanese order, with family name before given name. In the Japanese original Ozaki often gives people the title they received in the new nobility the Meiji government created in 1884. Men's titles changed, however, as their careers progressed, and the chosen few, like Itō and Yamagata, ended as "Prince" or "Duke" (*Kōshaku*). We have decided to avoid confusion by omitting virtually all such titles; to do so may jar the Japanese reader, but to include them risks confusing Western readers for whom this translation has been prepared.

Macrons have been provided for all personal names but not for well-known place names like Tokyo and Osaka. Romanization follows *Kenkyūsha's New Japanese-English Dictionary*, 4th Edition (1974). For readings of names and dates, we have followed *Kadokawa Nihonshi jiten*, 2d Edition (Tokyo: Kadokawa, 1976).

We are grateful to a number of people who have been extremely helpful in preparing this book for publication. Daniel Botsman, now of Cambridge, and Yukio Lippet of Princeton were particularly helpful in verifying names and smoothing the flow of Ozaki's account. We owe particular thanks to three colleagues who have seen the manuscript through the press. Ralph L. Meyer of Princeton helped with editing and contributed his mastery of computer mysteries, and Robert E. Brown and Jill Harris of Princeton University Press proved skilled and helpful editors during early and final stages of our work.

Marius B. Jansen
Princeton 2000

The Autobiography of Ozaki Yukio

The Birth of Constitutional Government in Japan

IN SETTING OUT these recollections of Japanese constitutional government, it is not my intention to write an academic study. There are enough scholars for that. This is to be a personal memoir. I shall tell the story of constitutional government in Japan through my own experience, how it germinated and evolved, where it is today, and where it should be going.

Ever since the Movement for Freedom and People's Rights (*jiyū minken undō*) was launched in the first years of the Meiji era, I never stopped working to promote the development of constitutional government in Japan. From the very first assembly of the newly founded national parliament, the Diet, in 1890, I have held a seat in the House of Representatives without a break. My entire life has been dedicated to the development of constitutional government. These memoirs, therefore, should be instructive in some degree for people today as well as for later historians. It was with the establishment of the Progressive Party (*Kaishintō*) under Ōkuma Shigenobu in 1882, that I first became directly involved in the mainstream of Japanese constitutional government. However, I would like to begin by briefly outlining the circumstances of my birth and the development of constitutional government in Japan prior to that date.

SON OF A SAMURAI LOYALIST

I was born in the Sagami hills, in a village by the name of Matano in the county of Tsukui.[1] Here, the pure streams that gushed and trickled from the green Musashino, Kai, and Sagami mountains gathered into the Sagami river, famous for its *ayu* trout fishing. This makes it sound rather idyllic, but in reality it was an unremarkable and remote place where one's dreams would be trapped in the skirts of the pressing hills. My family members were apparently long-term residents of Matano, and the Buddhist mortuary tablets and graves of successive generations of my ancestors are to be found in the Shōsenji temple in Ōsawa, about one *ri* [2.44 miles] away. We are descended from Ozaki Kamon-no-kami Yukinaga, an important official in the pre-Tokugawa government. In Matano one can still see what remains of Fuukumaden Castle, where he is believed to have lived, and below the castle ruins there is a field by the name of Ozaki. Nothing, however, is known about what he did or where he came from. The mortuary tablets at Shōsenji suggest that he died in 1622 and was followed by his wife in 1628, but apart from

---

[1] Matano village is today a hamlet within the boundaries of Tsukui town in the district of the same name in Kanagawa prefecture.

this there is not a single record pertaining to him. The year 1622 came toward the very end of the reign of the second Tokugawa shogun, and the third shogun, Iemitsu, acceded the following year. The shogunate was thus still only newly established, and it may have been the case that my ancestor retired to Matano to live a secluded life after having fallen into disfavor for rebelling against the Tokugawa. In any event, the wording on his mortuary tablet indicates that he was a man of considerable status, although "Fuukumaden Castle" can only have been a modest structure on the top of the hill, nothing like what would ordinarily be thought of as a "castle."[2] The area is on the border of the Kai and Sagami districts, where there had been frequent warfare between the Hōjō and Takeda families, and so it may have been that a watchtower of some sort was built there. Either way, it certainly is a tale shrouded in mystery.

When I was about three years old a fire destroyed our home and everything in it, including all the family records. Later I learned from books published in the Tokugawa era that the Ozakis were an "old family." Beyond that, however, I could discover nothing more about my ancestry. I hold no particular sentiment regarding the provenance of my family, and it matters little to me whether we are descended from apes or men. In this sense, I am not at all bothered by our lack of a family tree. I was aware, though, that my family was given special treatment in the village, and I do recall that my parents treated ordinary people in the village as if they were their retainers.

I was born in November 1859.[3] This was the year of the notorious Ansei Purge, which was followed the next year by the assassination of the Shogun's Chief Minister, Ii Naosuke, outside of the Sakurada-mon gates. Six years earlier Commodore Perry had sailed his "black ships" into Uraga Bay, and ten years more would bring the Meiji Restoration. It was thus a time in which the crises of the late Edo period were building to a climax.

My father, Yukimasa, had been adopted into a family from the Mineo family of Sanda village in Hachiōji. I was his first son. It was difficult for a small child to understand what was happening at the time, but riding the tide of history, my father seems to have become involved with loyalist activists from an early stage, and he travelled the country to promote their cause. He was hardly ever home when I was a child. I vaguely remember the day when we received news of his death. We were soon informed that the report had been incorrect, but it seems that at the time of the Restoration he led a troop of Kōshū *rōnin* [masterless samurai] called the "Dan-kin-tai," which had joined Itagaki Taisuke's expeditionary army when it set out to subdue the recalcitrant Aizu clan in the Restoration War of 1868. I never heard much about the details.

---

[2] In the original text, Ozaki specifically notes the use of the word "Inden" in the Buddhist mortuary tablet of his ancestor as an indicator of his high status. The full Buddhist names of Ozaki Kamon-no-kami Yukinaga and his wife are recorded on p. 4 of the original.

[3] Ozaki was born on November 20, 1858. For unknown reasons the entry on the family register records his birth as being in the following year, 1859. For most of his life Ozaki consistently used the date as officially recorded in the family register and did so in the dictation of his memoirs. His reasons

One of the interesting men with whom father was closely associated in those days was Ochiai Naosuke. He was both a very good friend and a relative of my father's. He came from a village called Komagino, across the river from Matano, in the Bushū country at the foot of the Takao mountains. From early childhood Ochiai had been trained in the Motoori and Hirata schools and was an ardent loyalist. He was the father by adoption of Ochiai Naobumi, a well-known literary figure in the Meiji period.

Ochiai Naosuke was a resourceful and determined man. On a number of occasions he conspired to bring down the Tokugawa shogunate, at one point with Kiyokawa Hachirō, and at another with Fujimoto Tesseki. In 1867 he had been plotting with the Satsuma forces to incite an insurrection in Edo, but before any of these plans could achieve their purpose he was found out by the shogunate, and forced to flee. Chased by a warship with orders to take his life, he managed to escape safely to Satsuma, where he linked up with Saigō Takamori and Iwakura Tomomi and went on to render meritorious service in the campaign to restore Imperial rule.

With my father away like this, our household was very poor, and we lived a truly lonely existence up in those mountains. Around us there were a number of families with the surname Wakō, who were all said to be descended from former retainers of my family. Yet, by this point, as a result of the mysterious fire, our home had been completely destroyed and only the godown was left standing. In this situation and with father absent, the Ozaki household teetered on the brink of extinction and came to know utter poverty. There was only my mother and myself, and although we had some relatives, they lived far away and were of no help to us.

To make matters worse, I did not have a strong constitution as a child. From infancy I was tormented every day by headaches. And, as if this were not enough, my entire body was plagued by itchy boils. My childhood was quite miserable. My mother apparently worried less about educating me than keeping me alive. Later I shared her attention with my brother and sister, but in my early childhood my health and well-being were her sole concern.

As for my education, there were no schools or teachers in the mountain areas in pre-modern Japan. I recall on those rare occasions when father was home that he taught me verses from an anthology of T'ang poems. Even now I can remember thinking to myself at the time how difficult and incomprehensible "scholarship" was! This is of course understandable, for imagine the shock it would cause today if first-year elementary school textbooks began with T'ang poetry. In any case, I received only the roughest of educations. I was taught Chinese characters by my parents but never had to practice writing very much. This was how I spent my childhood, without any proper education, in a mountain village forgotten by the world.

---

may have been both of vanity and as an expedient to avoid complications in official documents. Much later, he gave his real age and often wrote it in the calligraphy he produced.

Eventually the Tokugawa shogunate fell and Imperial rule was restored. My father, like the other samurai loyalists who had been constantly on the move in their struggle to bring this about, now found himself in the employ of the Meiji government. In the first year of the new Meiji era he became a civil servant and was assigned to Tokyo. I was ten years old by the Japanese way of counting.

THE FIVE ARTICLES OF THE CHARTER OATH

In that same first year of Meiji that I accompanied my father to Tokyo, a solemn ceremony to proclaim the Charter Oath took place in Kyoto.[4] On April 6, in the Hall of State Ceremonies, Emperor Meiji read out the following covenant before the gods of heaven and earth:

1. Deliberative assemblies shall be widely established and all matters decided by public discussion.
2. All classes, high and low, shall unite in vigorously carrying out the administration of affairs of state.
3. The common people, no less than the civil and military officials, shall each be allowed to pursue his own calling so that there may be no discontent.
4. Evil customs of the past shall be broken off and everything based upon the just laws of Nature.
5. Knowledge shall be sought throughout the world so as to strengthen the foundations of imperial rule.[5]

These five articles of the Charter Oath laid the foundation for constitutional government. Following the wishes of his forefathers, Emperor Meiji had graciously enunciated the basic principles of the nation and in so doing had clearly defined the noble objective of building a constitutional government in a most unprecedented manner. On that same day, Saigō Takamori and Katsu Kaishū had been in Edo (present-day Tokyo) to negotiate the surrender and evacuation of Edo Castle. My young heart filled with emotion to think that on that historic day the course of national policy had been given to posterity by the emperor himself.

Needless to say, the ten-year-old boy that I was then hardly appreciated the historical significance of the Charter Oath. Later, when I became involved in the movement for constitutional government, words could not express the strength we were able to draw from the covenant. It meant more to us than having a million allies. A clear national policy had been set. Devoting our energies to the cause of constitutional government was to obey the Imperial will and serve the empire. The belief that anyone who obstructed the realization of a constitutional govern-

---

[4] The Charter Oath was designed to reassure the old elite that the new regime would take their opinions into consideration. It was read for the emperor, who was a boy of sixteen, by Sanjō Sanetomi to an assemblage of nobles and feudal lords.

[5] This translation of the articles of the Charter Oath is from Ryusaku Tsunoda, William Theodore de Bary, and Donald Keene, eds., *Sources of Japanese Tradition*, Vol. 2 (New York: Columbia University Press, 1964), p. 137.

ment was a traitor to the people and an enemy of the throne gave us courage to stake our lives on the cause.

With the oath the emperor also released a letter declaring his intention to promote the welfare and honor of the nation. In it he stated: "At this time of national renewal, if any person shall be unable to realize his full potential it shall be deemed Our own failure. Therefore, we are conscious of Our duty to fulfill our mission and be worthy of Our people, as we hold ourselves accountable for the achievement of Our objectives, being the first to face adversity, following faithfully the wisdom of the sages, and promoting good administration throughout the land." He further encouraged the people: "You shall enjoy happiness in life by fulfilling our wishes, elevating each other and setting aside personal interest for the public good. Assist us in Our enterprise, defend the integrity of Our divine land, and thus console the spirits of Our Imperial ancestors." Who would not be moved in his heart and stirred to great deeds by these words? As loyal subjects we had no choice but to follow the Imperial will and dedicate ourselves body and soul to achieving true constitutional government.

Its fundamental principle, as surely as the sun is in the sky, was established by the first article of the Charter Oath: "Deliberative assemblies shall be widely established and all matters decided by public discussion." The other four articles also concerned themselves with constitutional government.

Article 2 states: "All classes, high and low, shall unite in vigorously carrying out the administration of affairs of state." Communicating the minds of the leaders to the people and theirs to those who lead them is the essence of constitutional government. A true debate can only be had if there is effective communication.

Article 3 states: "The common people, no less than the civil and military officials, shall each be allowed to pursue his own calling so that there may be no discontent." In the despotic feudal age the bureaucracy and military did not live up to their mandate and citizens were unable to fulfill their aspirations so that in the end they no longer supported the government of the shogun. The rest can be easily imagined.

Article 4 states: "Evil customs of the past shall be broken off and everything based upon the just laws of Nature." Of all the transgressions of the autocratic government that had but lately been overthrown, the worst was that the lives of the common people were at the mercy of the samurai. People were treated like animals and their rights to life and property ignored. To treat humans as they ought to be treated was the foundation of constitutional government as well as the path of justice.

Article 5 states: "Knowledge shall be sought throughout the world so as to strengthen the foundations of Imperial rule." The political history of civilized countries teaches us that constitutional government is the supreme form of political institution. With such a government in place, love of one's country and loyalty to the emperor would join to promote the highest good for our land.

The Five Articles of the Charter Oath laid the foundations of Japan's constitutional government. The challenge lay in building a fitting edifice on this sure foundation. This was a grand venture that the people of Japan should undertake together in compliance with the Imperial will. My own life was totally given to this momentous purpose. I felt immense pride in the fact that the first page of the history of constitutional government in Japan was graced with the emperor's inexpressibly grand oath.

THE NEW MEIJI GOVERNMENT

After coming to Tokyo with my father in the first year of Meiji we lived for some time with the Yasuokas at their Surugadai residence. A loyalist, Yasuoka Yoshitaka was a country samurai from Nakamura village in the county of Hata in Tosa domain (today's Kōchi Prefecture). He was trained in the Hioki school of archery and the Otsubo school of horsemanship. He had also practiced the martial arts with sword and spear under Hijikata Kenkichi and studied artillery with Tadokoro Sayoji. In addition to these skills, he was well versed in literature as a distinguished student of Kamei Tetsutarō of Chikuzen (northern Kyushu). He was, in short, a man of both martial and literary excellence. His outstanding background stood him in good stead when he joined the Restoration forces in the campaign to subdue the eastern clans. After the Restoration he was chosen to occupy important government positions, first as an official in the judiciary (*danjō-dai daichū*) and then the Deliberative Assembly (*shūgi'in hankan*) and the Ministry of Civil Affairs (*minbu shōkyoku*). My father served as a government official under Yasuoka for about ten years.

Until I came to Tokyo I had hardly received any education to speak of. Now I studied the Confucian Analects and the teachings of Mencius and sat in on Mr. Yasuoka's lectures on the Seven Books of Classical Chinese. Among my classmates were Kōno Toshikama, Obata Mine, and Ōtsuka Narumi, who were as old as my parents. After two years or so we moved to Bancho (Chiyoda-ku) and I continued my study of the classics at Hirata Academy. My teacher there, Mr. Hirata, was the son of the famous *kokugaku* scholar Hirata Atsutane, and I seem to recall that he had also presented lectures to Emperor Meiji. Among my memories of the Hirata Academy were three or four occasions in which I blacked out while playing with my friends, turned deathly pale, and fell senseless to the ground. Perhaps because of this unusual tendency I came to develop certain views, if not firm convictions, about the soul.

The most disagreeable part of my journey to school each day was the harassment I received from boys who threw stones and shouted insults at me. This experience gave me an unfortunate sense that all strangers were my born enemies. I could not understand why I should be the target of abuse and stone-throwing when other boys seemed perfectly able to escape such ordeals. Perhaps there was something about me that encouraged them to pick on me. Had I been physically strong I would certainly have taken them on, but since I was timid anyway I knew better than to fight. I did not flinch from this wretched treatment but simply endured it in silence as I made my way with a heavy heart each day. This tendency to be disliked by others continued for a long time after this. In my mid-teens I was called a snob and accused of being affected, and this persisted even when I was thirty. I cannot exaggerate how much I suffered because of whatever it was in me that made me so disliked. I suspect that I am not free from it even today, but after forty it has bothered me less.

In the meantime, the new Meiji government gradually strengthened its foundations. At first it seemed to me that the government took the will of the people seriously, respecting the intention of the Five Articles of the Charter Oath and attempting to develop a system of governing based on public debate. One of the reasons for the downfall of the Tokugawa shogunate was that it had lost the support of the people. The obstinate feudal system presented an obstacle to the recruitment of bright young men into the service of the central government. The government of the shogun and the life of the people had become disconnected. Government officials had no way of fathoming the desires of the ordinary people, who in turn had no way of channeling their yearning for political reform. Officials were blind to the forces stirring beneath them. As rulers and ruled became increasingly alienated, the fall of the shogunate became inevitable. The new government of Meiji was painfully aware of this. This was what inspired the rediscovery of the ancient device of appointing a *Dajōkan*, or Council of State, and filling it with princes, aristocrats, loyalist clan chiefs, and samurai.[6] The government also established a new system to recruit able people from the rank and file. Men known as *chōshi* were recruited from among the best of the clansmen and the public, and assigned as councilors or directors in the government departments. They were normally to serve a term of four years. It was decided, however, that the most meritorious of them might serve for an extended period to be decided by public discussion.

There was no particular limit to the number of those who would be recruited as *chōshi*. Naturally, however, there was a limit to the number of posts to be filled at councilor and other senior levels. To ensure that a greater number of capable men could be recruited, a second, parallel system was instituted. This second type of recruit, known as *kōshi*, was equivalent to the present-day elected representatives. The head of a clan was invited to pick the brightest of his clansmen, and they then served in a "Lower Assembly" (*kagijisho*). It was decided that major clans would appoint three such men, middle-sized clans two, and small clans one. When it was established, it was stated that this Lower Assembly was to be an "office for public debate and for gauging public opinion in the realm." This was the first time that the terms "public debate" and "public opinion" (*kōgi yoron*) had found their way into official documents. In addition to the Lower Assembly, the *kōshi* also had their own "Policy Office" (*kōshi taisakusho*), through which they could make policy recommendations to the government and be asked by the government for their views on specific proposals.

In some respects then, this Lower Assembly where representatives of the clans debated could be compared to the later House of Representatives. Naturally, the

---

[6] Ozaki here and later refers to the feudal lords who ruled the 260-odd domains into which Japan was divided in Tokugawa times as "clans."

organization was underdeveloped and its authority extremely limited. Nonetheless it was a sure step toward constitutional government insofar as it recruited from among the people wise men who would devote themselves to national business, allowing them to engage in public debate and play an effective, if qualified, role in government. This is impressive evidence of the expeditious manner in which the Meiji government promoted public debate and opened its ears to public opinion.

The institutions of *chōshi* and *kōshi* were established in February of the first year of Meiji, on the eve of the promulgation of the Five Articles of the Charter Oath. In April of that year, the government reintroduced the ancient *Dajōkan* system, while also instituting a separation of legislative, administrative, and judicial functions for the first time. Within the *Dajōkan*, departments were established for legislative and administrative matters, and for religious, accounting, military, foreign affairs, and the judicial system. Legislative officials represented the legislature, criminal judges oversaw judicial affairs, and the remaining five offices constituted the administrative branch.

Members of the legislature were divided into two tiers. The upper tier was composed of persons holding the positions of senior councilor (*gijō*) and councilor (*sanyo*), while the lower tier accommodated the *kōshi*.[7] Thus, what was now created was a bicameral system in which the upper tier was analogous to a House of Lords while the lower served as a House of Commons. This was not, however, a bicameral system in the evolved sense because the authority of the two houses was unequal, with the lower house expected merely to deliberate if and when it was required by the upper house.

It can be seen then that through the appointment of recruits from each domain, the Meiji government sought to encourage broad public debate and deliberation. In fact, however, often times the recruits would aimlessly pursue useless debates, and they were criticized as being incapable of dealing with the practical business of government. At this point, the Meiji government decided that there was a pressing need to first unify the debates going on in each of the domains, and to promote mutual understanding between upper and lower elements of society. A new system of domanial administration was thus settled upon, with executive, administrative, and deliberative officials appointed to serve as a link between the various regions and the central government. In other words, within each domain the deliberative officials were to make sure the policies of the central government were thoroughly understood, while at the same time, within the central government, they served as members of a Deliberative Assembly (*kōgisho*), presenting the issues that were of particular concern in their domain. This Deliberative Assembly was the lower chamber of the government's legislature, the *Gijōkan*, and the structure described here was more or less in place by the early months of 1869.

---

[7] Robert A. Wilson suggests that while the *gijō* were more senior than the *sanyo*, "The functional distinction between the two groups is not readily apparent. Both titles may be translated as 'council-

In the spring of the same year, an Ombudsman's Office (*taishō-kyoku*) was set up in Tokyo to collect petitions from all across the realm. Since there was inevitably a limit to the number of *chōshi, kōshi*, and members of the Deliberative Assembly, this marked yet another attempt to gain access to public opinion.

Towards the middle of 1869, canvassing (*tōhyō kōsen*) for various important public offices took place. As a result, Sanjō Sanetomi was selected as chief minister (*hoshō*), and Iwakura Tomomi, Tokudaiji Sanenori, and Nabeshima Naomasa were selected as the three senior councilors. Higashikuze Michinobu, Kido Takayoshi, Ōkubo Toshimichi, Gotō Shōjirō, Soejima Taneomi, and Itagaki Taisuke were elected councilors. The successful candidates were all predictable winners. What was remarkable was that an attempt had actually been made by the Meiji government to appoint government officials through public elections. However, public participation in the election of government officials was discontinued after this first attempt.

A few months later, another major reform of the *Dajōkan* was undertaken, and the legislative and executive functions that had been clearly separated earlier were united once more. The upper and lower tiers of the legislative organ were also abolished. The government, however, still recognized the need for an organ in which public opinion could be aired, and in their place a National Assembly (*shūgi-in*) was established. It provided for debate by officials appointed from among senior figures representing the various regions of the country.

This development was still a variation of the constitutional system, and one could say that it marked yet another step toward the establishment of proper constitutional government. This much is clear from the official duties assigned to the National Assembly in its rules: "The Assembly shall be for the wide ranging consultation of public opinion and, respecting the Imperial will which laid the foundations of national government, it will be a place where the energies of the multitude are harnessed. Thus, it is necessary that proceedings will show respect for the Imperial rescript, be united in purpose with the *Dajōkan*, take the fundamentals of government to heart, judiciously address matters which arise, and act to ensure that unity within the country is not compromised."

In the latter part of 1869, the Emperor Meiji paid a visit to the National Assembly and observed a session attended by the chief minister, Sanjō Sanetomi, the three senior councilors, Iwakura, Tokudaiji, and Nabeshima, and other lords and councilors. Originally, the plan had been for the emperor to receive all of the members of the assembly in a single audience, but this was not possible due to the lack of adequate space, and each member was presented with a gift from the emperor in compensation.

One can see then how zealous the emperor Meiji was in his efforts to "conduct the government of the people with the people."[8] We can also see that at this point the new Meiji government was striving sincerely for the development of

---

lor.' " See his "Genesis of the Meiji Government in Japan, 1868–1871," *University of California Publications in History*, 56 (1957):12.

[8] Imperial Message, September 27, 1869.

government based on public debate, and thus remained faithful to the first article of the Charter Oath: "Deliberative assemblies shall be widely established and all matters decided by public discussion." The attitude of the Meiji government changed abruptly, however, with the introduction of the *haihan-chiken* (abolishing clans and establishing prefectures) policy in 1871.

I Witness Torture and Executions

With the inception of *haihan-chiken* and the setting up of new administrative districts in place of the former feudal fiefdoms, Yasuoka Yoshitaka was appointed Governor (*daisanji*) of Takasaki Prefecture. My father accompanied him.

The abolition of the clans was the most sweeping of all the changes that had occurred since the Restoration of Imperial rule. For all practical purposes it dealt a death blow to the feudal system in Japan. It is understandable then that there was an atmosphere of trepidation throughout Japan at this time. The Jōshū region (where Takasaki Prefecture was located) was, however, a particularly rough place, and even though I was only a child I remember constantly hearing of rowdy local samurai making trouble by attacking the prefectural office that the Meiji government had established, or killing government officials. I expect that it was because Yasuoka was such an accomplished man, with both literary and military training, that he had been dispatched to this area to quell the disturbances.

My own recollections of this period include witnessing torture, beheadings, and ritual suicides (*seppuku*). Since administrative and judicial powers were no longer separate, my father was often required to serve as a judge in addition to carrying out his responsibilities for school affairs. When he conducted torture himself, he would call me to watch secretly from behind a sliding screen. When criminals were to be executed he would take me, together with the students from school, to the scene of the beheading. In Tokyo too the bodies of people who had been executed or who had disemboweled themselves were sometimes to be seen lying out in the streets, and I remember my father urging me to look at them. Why should my father have wanted me to see such things? I suspect he was trying to cure my timidity by shocking me with these gruesome scenes, but the result was quite the opposite. It not only failed to cure me of the cowardice I was born with, but every time I was taken to a beheading I felt terribly sick. I barely glanced at the disemboweled bodies I was told to look at. My classmates, however, proved more stout-hearted, some even stirring the spilled bowels with a stick. Such boys were praised later while I was harshly scolded. At times when we saw many heads roll and I smelled the stench of blood I could hardly eat my lunch. I was reproved for being a coward. What would boys living under a democratic government today feel to see such horrors? Disregard for human life and property was a vice inherited from the despotic feudal age. It is at the very core of the principles that inspire constitutional government to destroy such appalling customs and treat people as human beings. I did not, of course, understand such things as a boy, but I hated the bloodcurdling experience of having to watch torture and beheadings.

In Takasaki I was enrolled for the first time in a school and learned English. The head English teacher was Koizumi Atsushi, who enjoyed a high reputation for his command of the language.

I have since lost contact with most of my schoolmates, but one of them was Arai Ryoichirō, who was later to become active in US-Japan relations as an exporter of silk yarn.[9] Arai was a handsome boy, while I was as ugly as sin. My teeth protruded and my nostrils opened to the sky. People made fun of me and told me to hold my head down so the rain would not go up my nose. My mother was much pained by this. I resolved to try hard to do something about my unsightly features, and with Arai as my model, I was able to improve greatly the way I looked.

With the disturbances in Takasaki successfully suppressed, Yasuoka was transferred to Ise, another area racked by disorder. Since father was again transferred with him, we all moved to Doai Prefecture (part of today's Mie Prefecture). This was the beginning of my lifelong relationship with Ise.

At the time of the transfer, my father, mainly in consideration of my weak constitution, requested a month's leave to take his family to the Kusatsu hot springs. Some time during the thirty days we spent there I was completely freed of my persistent headaches. My skin improved too. I recall with horror the famous thermal bath. It has since become much more respectable, but in those days it was extremely filthy, and consisted only of a roof over the crowded bathers, among whom were many with advanced cases of syphilis and lepers with deformed limbs and no noses. Told that only cowards shied away from taking these renowned waters, I gritted my teeth and shared the bath with them a couple of times, fervently hoping that I would escape infection.

The Doai prefectural office was in Yamada city in Ise district. Mie Prefecture with which Doai was later merged had its office, as I recall, in Tsu. In Yamada there was a library called Miyazaki Bunko near the Outer Shrine of Ise. Attached to the library was an English school, and Mr. Koizumi from the school in Takasaki was invited to join the teaching staff. Some of my friends from this school, such as Motoba Chū and Ōi Saitarō, went on to earn doctoral degrees at Kogakuryō (now Tokyo University) and make important contributions to the country in their own fields.

Father took me to see beheadings in Ise as well. Young as I was, I soon discovered that there was a considerable difference between criminals here and those in Takasaki. On the way to the execution ground in Takasaki the condemned men often hummed a tune. Some even dared to taunt their executioners, admonishing them to take extra care with their sword, and warning them that their necks had muscles of iron so that no half-hearted cut would do the job. The ultimate pride of an executioner was to sever the head but leave it dangling by a single piece of skin. This was no easy task, and even a veteran might miss after being harassed in this way. In contrast to those in Takasaki, most of the victims I saw at Ise were

[9] Arai's rise as a silk merchant and exporter is chronicled by a granddaughter, Haru Matsukata Reischauer, in *Saumrai and Silk: A Japanese and American Heritage* (Cambridge, Mass.: Harvard University Press, 1986), pp.170 ff.

so paralyzed with fear that they could barely walk, let alone hum a tune. Indeed, they already appeared half-dead before they even reached the execution ground. I do not know whether their abject appearance was to be accounted for by the treatment they had suffered in prison, or whether the people themselves were of a different grade: Ise men were submissive and weak, while those from Jōshū were inheritors of the area's proud tradition of popular rebelliousness. In any case, whatever the cause, there seemed to me a great deal of difference between the two groups of men in their last hour.

After we had been at Ise for a year or so, I began to yearn to study in Tokyo. There were two reasons for this. Accompanying my father in the course of his peripatetic career as a teacher and low-ranking local government official, I had become infatuated with the widespread fame of a school in Tokyo called Keiō Gijuku. Keiō Gijuku was considered to be the best in Japan, enjoying a far higher reputation than any government school. I thought that if I was to pursue my education then I should have the best the country could offer. The other reason I wished to go to Tokyo was that as much as I enjoyed being with my parents I also longed to be independent. I very much resented their well-intentioned interference and I heartily wished to escape from it. I begged my father to let me go, and at last received his permission in the summer of 1874. With my ten-year-old brother I left for Tokyo to enroll at Keiō Gijuku. I was sixteen.

So it was that I came to attend Keiō Gijuku, which was considered to be in the forefront of liberal democratic ideas in the early Meiji years. It was an event that had a large impact on my life. At this point it will be appropriate to resume the story of the nation's political development following the abolition of the domains and the impact it had on the evolution of constitutional government in Japan.

THE GENESIS OF CLAN CLIQUE GOVERNMENT

While the Tokugawa shogunate itself fell with the Meiji Restoration, the three hundred or so regional clans at first continued to rule their own areas of the country as they had always done. This meant that the Restoration of Imperial Rule was a reform in name only, with the mechanisms of feudal government essentially unaffected. Consequently, a second convulsion, to which I have already alluded, soon took place. Called *haihan chiken*, it would involve the abolition of feudal fiefs and the establishment of new administrative districts known as *ken* or prefectures. The abolition of the clans proved to be a formidable undertaking.

When the Tokugawa family returned their power to the throne, it was argued that they should also return its land and people. By the same argument it was held that other clans should do the same, return their fiefdoms and privileges as local rulers, so that all the lands and peoples of Japan might be unified under their emperor. There could be no question that this was the right thing to do. Nonetheless it was not done, since the main forces responsible for the Meiji Restoration were the major clans of Satsuma, Chōshū, Tosa, and Hizen. Only when the *haihan chiken* was carried out in the latter months of 1871 did the foundations of the feudal system finally collapse.

The *haihan chiken* was a bold decision on the part of the Meiji government, and it resulted in two major changes affecting the work of laying foundations for constitutional government in Japan. One was the blatant backsliding on the government's part regarding its commitment to constitutional rule. The other was that the ambitions of the Satsuma, Chōshū, Tosa and Hizen clans to usurp the powers of government were no longer covert.

With the introduction of *haihan chiken*, a major reform took place in the structure of the central government involving the establishment of three new "boards" (center, left, and right). Ministries were administratively distinct from the three boards as branches of the Dajōkan. The "Central Board" with the prime minister and other ministers advising the emperor and conducting all the affairs of state, looked very much like today's cabinet. Ministers of the right and the left were directly responsible to the prime minister. There was no restriction on the number of councilors of state (*sangi*) appointed to serve the administration and assist the three ministers. Thus the prime minister, the ministers of the left and the right, and the councilors were the principal officials advising the emperor and wielding the actual power of the government. The "Left Board" was where members of parliament enacted law, with a speaker assisted by a councilor. The "Right Board" was where heads of ministries and their deputies discussed administrative business. For the sake of appearances, the establishment and abolition of rules and regulations was officially to be done within the Left Board after public deliberation. On the surface, therefore, it seemed that the Left Board had the right to legislate; however, in reality the authority of the so-called legislature to participate in the process of legislation was limited to the ability to seek the judgment of the Central Board. Actual authority to adopt or disregard legislation thus resided solely in the Central Board. In short, legislative powers were all but absorbed by an omnipotent Central Board, relegating the "legislature" to the position of a mere bureau taking orders from above. As a matter of fact, when the rules for the Central Board were revised in 1873 it was clearly stated that "legislative affairs (were) the prerogative of the Central Board. Its officials (should) deliberate on their merits and priority, reach consensus, and submit them to lower officials for implementation." Soon after this, the National Assembly, which had continued to maintain some semblance of its role as a bureau for consulting public opinion, was also abolished and merged into the Left Board. With this, the constitutional system that had been developing since the first year of Meiji disappeared completely.[10]

At the beginning, the new Meiji government had been disposed to respect public opinion and debate, but as its foundations firmed, especially when the transition from the old clan system to the new prefectural system went smoothly and

---

[10] These developments are analyzed in Albert M. Craig, "The Central Government," in *Japan in Transition from Tokugawa to Meiji*, ed. Marius B. Jansen and Gilbert Rozman (Princeton, N.J.: Princeton University Press, 1986), pp. 36–67.

it felt more assured of its own base, the government began to show less and less respect for public opinion. Even when institutions such as the National Assembly and the Ombudsman's Office (where petitions were received) had existed, the government had done no more than make a symbolic effort to listen to opinions emanating from the people and in practice left it up to the arbitrary discretion of the administrator to decide whether action would be taken. In this sense, these institutions had never been able to fulfill the promise of their names, and now that the Assembly had been formally abolished as a concomitant of the *haihan chiken*, the Japanese constitutional system had clearly begun to retrogress.

It is a truism of *realpolitik* that for those in power there is nothing more convenient than arbitrary despotism. Therefore, in countries where a constitutional system has but lately been established, it is tempting for the government to revert to autocratic rule and neglect public opinion as soon as it is confident of its foundations. As noted above, the second of the changes that followed the abolition of the feudal fiefdoms was the emergence of clan cliques as a dominant force on the surface of the political scene. The smooth implementation of the abolition of the fiefs itself was a result of the united support of the four most powerful clans; and, to go further, it was common knowledge that they were the main forces behind the collapse of the Tokugawa shogunate and the successful Restoration of Imperial Rule.

At this time, Ōkubo Toshimichi wrote that "in judging the current balance of power, we see that Satsuma and Chōshū have greater power than the court. The two, however, do not use their power to assist the court but rather each one stores up what they have for their own selves. Rather than advance, they retreat. This is why the court is feeble." At the time of the abolition of the fiefdoms the four major domains lent their weight to the cause of national integration, which boosted the strength of the central government. A not unintended corollary of this was that the influence of the clan cliques within the central government became unshakable.

As I have intimated, it was an unchallenged fact that already Satsuma, Chōshū, Tosa, and Hizen had wielded real power within the Meiji government from the first days of the Restoration. In the beginning, however, they did not allow this to be too conspicuous, at least not at an official level. Thus, for example, all of the important offices at the Court, such as the *fuku sōsai*, *hoshō*, and *hohitsu*, were filled by court nobles and feudal lords, as were the important positions of minister of state (*dajō daijin*), minister of the left, minister of the right, *nagon*, and all of the headships of the various government departments. At the same time, samurai from the four clans were restricted to such posts as "advisor" to a ministry (*sōsai-kyoku komon*), "councilor" to an administrative official (*gyōseikan sanji*), the deputy headships of various departments, or else prefectural governorships. In fact, the clansmen were hesitant even to take up the deputy headships of departments, and were content to hold the position of secretary (*hanji*), or lower. Following the reform of mid-1867, these samurai became eligible for appointment to the new position of councilor of state (*sangi*), but the nobility and feudal lords continued to head the ministries and agencies, and clansmen could not aspire to any post in government above that of their deputy.

Following the institutional reform that was carried out at the same time as the *haihan chiken*, members of the four major clans began to infiltrate the political system and were even appointed as heads of ministries. At the same time, the court nobles and feudal lords were gradually eased out of the main offices of the central government, and thereafter did not hold important posts other than those of minister of state, ministers of the left and right, *Nagon*, and one or two others.

In the cabinet reshuffle that accompanied the *haihan chiken*, four councilors of state were appointed: Saigō Takamori (Satsuma), Kido Takayoshi (Chōshū), Itagaki Taisuke (Tosa), and Ōkuma Shigenobu (Hizen).[11] Thus, each of the four big clans now had a representative through whom to consolidate their influence in the cabinet. After this, the number of councilors of state was gradually increased so that in the end all of the heads of ministries and agencies held this position. Moreover, they were all selected from Satsuma, Chōshū, Tosa, and Hizen. Thus, the councilors of state came to include men such as Gotō Shōjirō of Tosa who was also the president of the left board (*sain gichō*); Ōki Takatō, the education minister; Etō Shinpei, the justice minister; and Soejima Taneomi, the foreign minister, all of whom were from Hizen, and Ōkubo Toshimichi, the finance minister, who was from Satsuma. In this way the core of the government came to be occupied solely by representatives of the four clans, and their ambitions to conduct autocratic government with the aid of their cliques were now becoming obvious.

PETITION FOR A POPULARLY ELECTED PARLIAMENT

The rupture that occurred within the cabinet over the proposed Korean expedition shook the basis of the Meiji government.[12] The government was thrown into a panic. Opinion within the cabinet swung from one day to the next. It was impossible to know what its decision would be. When Saigō Takamori realized that his recommendations were not going to be acted upon, he thrust a letter of resignation at his colleagues and stormed back to his native town in Satsuma. Four of his sympathizers—Itagaki Taisuke, Gotō Shōjiro, Soejima Taneomi, and Etō Shinpei—followed his example and quit their posts. Imperial Guard officers from Satsuma also resigned their commissions. The whole country, sensing imminent conflict, fell into a state of confusion.

With the resignation of the five councilors of state, the government was left without teeth. The cabinet was hastily reformed around Iwakura Tomomi and Ōkubo Toshimichi. Ōki Takatō added the ministry of justice to his responsibilities, Itō Hirobumi was made a councilor and minister of industry, the former vassal of the Tokugawa shogunate, Katsu Kaishū, was asked back as councilor and minister

[11] Although Japan is not usually said to have had a British style cabinet until 1885, Ozaki does specifically use the term "cabinet" (*taikaku, naikaku*) here.

[12] In 1873, while a mission led by Iwakura Tomomi was touring the Western world, Saigō, the leading member of the government left behind, urged a "punitive expedition" against Korea to avenge the Korean government's blunt refusal to institute modern diplomatic relations with Japan. When the Iwakura group returned the decision was overturned, leading to a split in the Restoration coalition.

of the navy, and Terajima Munenori was also recalled as councilor and minister of foreign affairs. Shimazu Hisamitsu, the erstwhile lord of Satsuma, was appointed government advisor (*naikaku komon*), a new post that was created in an attempt to mend the damage which had been done in the crisis. Yet, the restlessness that resulted from the split over the ill-conceived Korean enterprise could not be pacified by these half-hearted, makeshift measures.

Soon, insurrections broke out in various places in the Southwestern part of the country, first in Saga, then in Kumamoto, Akizuki, and Hagi, and finally in Kagoshima, where a major uprising took place in 1877.[13] All these convulsions were rooted in the deep controversy that surrounded the proposed expedition to Korea, fomented by people discontented with the clan clique (*hanbatsu*) government and conspiring its overthrow.

Yet, the movement to do something about the evils of the Meiji government did not consist solely of persons who sought to do so with military force. There were also those who saw that at a fundamental level the problem with the government was that it was controlled exclusively by the clan cliques, and thus a movement now emerged that sought to eradicate the evils of clique government through the establishment of a genuine constitutional system and an approach to politics that was truly based upon the nation's people. This was the Movement for Freedom and People's Rights (*jiyū minken undō*). Thus, the upheavals created by the planned invasion of Korea unexpectedly provided a major opportunity to promote constitutional government in Japan.

It happened that just at this time Komuro Nobuo, Furusawa Tsujirō, and others had newly returned from abroad, where they had been much inspired by the development of democracy in western countries. They forcefully presented the advantages of the parliamentary system to their fellow intellectuals. Itagaki Taisuke, who was indignant over developments within the autocratic Meiji government, was deeply stirred by the report. On January 18, 1874, he submitted a recommendation to the Board of the Left requesting the establishment of a popularly elected parliament. The recommendation was co-signed by eight men—four councilors who had resigned earlier: Itagaki, Gotō, Soejima, and Etō, together with Komuro Nobuo, Furusawa Urō, Yuri Kimimasa, and Okamoto Kenzaburō.[14] It began:

> When we humbly reflect upon the quarter in which the governing power lies, we find that it is not in the Imperial House above, nor the people below, but in the officials alone. We do not deny that the officials revere the Imperial House, nor that they protect the people. Yet, the manifold decrees of the government appear in the morning

---

[13] The uprising in Kagoshima in 1877, generally known in English as the Satsuma Rebellion, was led by Saigō Takamori himself.

[14] The translation given here is taken from W. W. McLaren, ed., *Japanese Government Documents, 1867–1889* (Tokyo: Asiatic Society of Japan, 1914), pp. 426–32. Some changes were made to the original translation in keeping with the abridged version, which appears in Ryusaku Tsunoda, et al., eds., *Sources of Japanese Tradition* (New York: Columbia University Press, 1958), Vol. 2, pp.176–78.

and are changed in the evening, the administration is influenced by private considerations, rewards and punishments depend on personal favor or disfavor, the channel by which the people should communicate with the government is blocked, and they cannot state their grievances.

After enumerating the inequities of the bureaucracy, the petition went on to declare:

Unable to resist the promptings of our patriotic feelings, we have sought to devise a means of rescuing [the country] from danger. We find this means to consist in developing public discussion in the empire. The means of developing public discussion is the establishment of a council-chamber chosen by the people.

It continued:

The people whose duty it is to pay taxes to the government have the right of sharing in their government's affairs and of approving or condemning. Since this is a universally acknowledged principle, it is not necessary to waste words in discussing it. . . .

Declaring the right of the people to vote refuted every argument put forth by those who were of the opinion that it was too early for a parliament. The petition thus provided the following rejoinder to those who said "Our people are wanting in culture and intelligence, and have not yet advanced into the region of enlightenment. It is too early yet to establish a council-chamber elected by the people":

If things really are as they say, then the way to give to the people culture and intelligence and to cause them to advance swiftly into the region of enlightenment is to establish a council-chamber chosen by the people. For in order to give our people culture and intelligence and to cause them to advance into the region of enlightenment, they must in the first place be induced to protect their rights, to respect and value themselves, and be inspired by a spirit of sympathy with the griefs and joys of the empire, which can only be done by giving them a voice in its concerns. It has never happened that under such circumstances the people have been content to remain in a backward condition or have been satisfied with their own want of culture and intelligence.

To those who argued that "to establish a council-chamber at once would be simply to assemble all the blockheads in the empire," the petition dealt a crushing blow:

What shocking self-conceit and arrogant contempt for the people this indicates! No doubt there are among the officials men who surpass others in intelligence and ingenuity, but how do they know that society does not contain men who surpass them in intelligence and knowledge? Whence it may be inferred that the people of the empire are not to be treated with such arrogant contempt. If again they deserve to be treated with arrogant contempt, are the officials themselves not a part of the nation, in which case they also are wanting in intelligence and culture?

It went on, sharpening its attack:

> Between the arbitrary decisions of a few officials and the general opinion of the peo-
> ple, as ascertained by public discussion, where is the balance of wisdom or stupidity?
> We believe that the intelligence of the officials must have made progress as compared
> with what it was previous to the Restoration, for the intelligence and knowledge of
> human beings increase in proportion as they are exercised. Therefore to establish a
> council-chamber chosen by the people would promote the culture and intelligence of
> the people and cause them to advance rapidly into the region of enlightenment.

It was a well-reasoned line of argument. Finally, it urged the establishment of
a strong and above all legitimate government:

> How is the government to be made strong? By the people's being of one mind. . . .
> The establishment of a council-chamber chosen by the people will create community
> of feeling between the government and the people, and they will unite into one body.
> Then and only then will the country become strong.

When the petition was published in the daily news journal *Nisshin shinjishi*,[15]
public opinion was inflamed, and the pros and cons were debated throughout the
nation. When I too read the petition while attending class at the English school
in Yamada, I was jolted as if I had received an electric shock, and I felt that my
course in life had been set. It was then that I resolved to become a politician.

The rupture over the Korean invasion fracas brought about two major changes
in the political scene in Japan. First, one of the four pillars of the alliance that
had supported the Meiji government collapsed, and with the complete disappear-
ance of Tosa from the central government it in effect became a Satsuma-Chōshū
operation. True, Ōkuma Shigenobu of Hizen and also Ōki Takatō remained in the
cabinet to defend their ground, but they gradually succumbed to pressure from
the clan cliques of Satsuma and Chōshū. As I shall discuss further below, Ōkuma
was eventually to resign during the political crisis of 1881, leaving the government both in name and in practice under the unchallenged control of Satsuma and
Chōshū.

Second, the controversy over Korea ironically provided the impetus for the
eventual establishment of a constitutional government. Prior to this, voices had
been heard among the people calling for democracy, but it was only after the
petition for a popularly elected parliament that these isolated voices were converted into a mass movement throughout the nation.

It was a portentous coincidence for me that it was at this very time that I moved
to Tokyo to take up my studies at Keiō Gijuku , which was one of the centers of
the movement for democracy. What sort of a place was Keiō Gijuku ? Permit me
to turn now to some personal reminiscences.

[15] The *Nisshin shinjishi*, one of Japan's first newspapers, was founded in 1872 by the Englishman
John Reddie Black.

KEIŌ GIJUKU AND FUKUZAWA YUKICHI

Although it is called Keiō, the school was in fact established in the fifth year of Ansei (1858), seven years before the beginning of the Keiō era. It is, of course, the oldest existing institution of higher learning in Japan. In the social field it stood for the eradication of all the evils of the old system, while in the political arena it advocated the establishment of constitutional government.

There were two principal schools of political thought that inspired democratic ideals in Japan. One was the French school of liberty and equality, and the other was the English school of people's rights.

It was the members of the French school who first rose against the autocracy of the Meiji government, proclaiming human rights and equality. Some compared the Japanese situation to that of pre-revolutionary France and argued that the means to redress the abuses of the government must be learned from the French revolutionary leaders. Among this group was Nakae Chōmin, who opened a French school and taught political philosophy. He lectured on Jean-Jacques Rousseau's idea of the "social contract", and taught basic political principles through publications such as his *Seiri sōdan*. Excited by its theories of liberty and civil rights, hot-headed young people embraced the notion of a social contract, sang revolutionary songs, and turned increasingly to radical tactics. The later Liberal Party (*Jiyūtō*) belonged ideologically to the French school.

By contrast, those who were affiliated with the English school had a more realistic agenda. Rather than indulging uselessly in theory, they argued that the most effective way of extending freedom and people's rights was to establish a pragmatic English-style parliamentary government. Among the educational institutions advocating this line of thinking were Seki Shinpachi's "Kyōritsu Gakusha" and Nakamura Masanao's "Dōjinsha;" but Keiō Gijuku was indisputably the leader among them. The later Progressive Party (*Kaishintō*) drew its ideology mainly from this school of English thought.

Fukuzawa Yukichi, the founder and headmaster of Keiō, had been a brilliant student at Ogata Kōan's Tekijuku school in Osaka.[16] When the shogunate dispatched a warship to the United States in 1860, he was sent as an assistant to Kimura, Lord of Setsu, the government's naval magistrate (*gunkan bugyō*). And when the shogunate sent a mission to Europe in 1862, he again went as a member of the delegation. His observations and experiences on these missions were compiled in his book, *Conditions in the West* (*Seiyō jijō*) published in 1867. It was this book that for the first time made knowledge of western civilization and the situation in the outside world widely available in Japan. The whole nation, including men in government and opposition alike, all read the book.

At the time of the Restoration, the number of students at Keiō, which had previously been around one hundred, dropped for a time to as few as eighteen.

---

[16] Fukuzawa's autobiography, which he dictated toward the end of his long life, has been translated as *The Autobiography of Fukuzawa Yukichi*, which is available in several editions. See also Carmen

The headmaster was not the least daunted by this, however, and indeed, it is said that on the day that the battle of Ueno was being fought he continued to instruct his eighteen students from a recently acquired economics text by an American named Wayland, as if nothing unusual was happening.[17]

Fukuzawa, as I have mentioned, had been abroad twice during the old régime and was painfully aware that the waves of civilization were washing at the shores of Japan. It was not enough for the shogunate to return the government to the imperial court. The lives and values of the people had to be totally reconstructed if they were to be able to compete on equal terms with the Western countries. He believed that the evil traditions of the feudal era must be completely abolished. Without such sweeping reforms, he reasoned, a new civilization could not be built. He set himself to this task by means that were considered radical and eccentric by the standards of his day. He threw away his two swords, which were considered the soul of the samurai, wore his hair in a knot like a common man, wore an apron (as do merchants), and went about proudly calling himself "commoner Yukichi of Edo (Tokyo)." It was the custom then for married women to have their eyebrows shaved and their teeth blackened. To put an end to this barbaric practice, Fukuzawa published a story book called *Deformed Girl* (*Katawa musume*). It was a time when few people were willing to give their lives for the emperor, but samurai were expected to die for their lords. In public, Fukuzawa dared to call his lord, the Daimyo of Nakatsu, a dullard. At a time when the movement to restore imperial rule was flourishing and the name of Kusunoki was associated with heroism, he also likened the death of Lord Kusunoki at the battle of Minato-gawa to the beheading of a servant.[18] There was no end to these daring acts of the master. What does not seem exceptional today could well have cost him his life then. On one occasion, in fact, Asabuki Eiji, a junior man from Fukuzawa's home town, came to Edo on a secret mission to assassinate him. He lived every day with this ever-present threat.

Fukuzawa was perpetually misunderstood by his contemporaries. He not only failed to explain or apologize for his deed, for some reason he also had a strange inclination to downplay his achievements and flaunt behavior that was sure to be criticized. I once had the temerity to call him a "false villain." I suspect that he was so disgusted by the many "false heroes" around him that out of disdain for them he played a reverse role. Some of his contemporaries considered him to be too interested in money, but the charge was completely unfounded. Some time around 1897 one of the clever young men at Keiō Gijuku published a small book

---

Blacker, *The Japanese Enlightenment: A Study of the Writings of Fukuzawa Yukichi* (Cambridge: The University Press, 1964).

[17] In 1868, when the Meiji armies advanced to take control of Tokyo (then known as Edo), one group of Tokugawa retainers disobeyed the shogun's orders to surrender peacefully and set up camp at Ueno, in the middle of the city. Eventually a fierce battle was fought and the Tokugawa forces were routed. This was the battle of Ueno referred to in the text. The American book on economics referred to is Francis Wayland's *Elements of Political Economy*.

[18] Kusonoki Masashige (? –1336) was held up as a paragon of loyalty for his valor in fourteenth-century warfare by nationalists, but there is little evidence to support that legend.

titled *Money Worship* (*Haikin shū*). It was simply a translation of an American booklet with a similar title, but without ever reading the book some people concluded that it somehow reflected the master's thought.

Fukuzawa was exceptionally versatile and resourceful, and he certainly had great ability in business matters. It would have been easy for him to make a fortune for himself had he wished to do so, but the fact was that he was almost totally indifferent to his own financial situation. He gave others ideas as to how they might make money, but for himself he was never interested. He exhorted his pupils to "save well and spend well" and he lived by the same maxim. He was also fond of saying that it was foolish to spend money without good reason. Yet, at the same time, I am sure that the amounts he gave to students, friends, and acquaintances, and to Koreans and Chinese seeking asylum in Japan must have been very large.

His contribution towards building a new civilization in Japan was enormous. He took the lead in advocating the promotion of sericulture, the construction of a national railway system, support for people's rights legislation, the opening of parliament, the assertion of national power, the expansion of the navy, the improvement of the status of women, revision of the tax system, and the development of commerce and industry. He was the first to organize public speaking events and parliamentary-style debates, and enterprises such as the Maruzen foreign book store, the Meiji Life Insurance Company, various private banks, and the *Jiji Shinpō* newspaper were all projects of his, which he gave to former students to manage. The greatest of all his projects was, however, Keiō Gijuku. A great builder must also be a great destroyer. Fukuzawa was a man of extraordinary accomplishments who had the greatness to destroy and to build at the same time. His prodigious contribution to the nation outshone that of all others who lived at the time of the Meiji Restoration. In my eyes he had no peer.

Having had the immense good fortune to study under this great man, I was nonetheless unable to fully comprehend his greatness until after his death, and constantly defied him while he lived. It is too late to regret my shameless behavior, which I can now see was like a small insect attacking the Imperial carriage. It was of course terribly thoughtless on my part, but it was due in part to the special circumstances of my first days at school in Tokyo. Let me explain.

I Pretend to Be Dumb

It was the summer of 1874 when I sailed with my little brother from Ise to Yokohama by steamship (for there were no railways in those days) and arrived at last in Tokyo, where we both enrolled at Keiō Gijuku. I was sixteen by the Japanese way of counting (though no more than fourteen the western way). My long-held dream of studying in Tokyo had come true, and I was happy, but at the same time extremely anxious. I supposed that a school as famous as Keiō would have many excellent students. Believing with a heavy heart that it was my fate to be disliked, I dreaded the thought of being treated with disdain and rejected. From childhood

I must have been extremely proud for I could not bear to be scorned. Worrying over how I could avoid being reproached or treated as a fool, I tossed sleeplessly in my bunk each night during our voyage from Ise. After mulling it over, I came up with a solution—I would play dumb. At the time I thought it was an extremely fine idea. My lack of education and ability would be exposed as soon as I opened my mouth. It followed that if I avoided saying anything then I would never betray my intellectual shortcomings, and no one could ever reproach me for them. I believe my classical Chinese education had something to do with this decision to live the life of a mute. It had taught me to despise speech and men of many words, and to revere the ancient art of writing. Since I was brought up in this Chinese way of thinking, it was not surprising that I looked down on speech and spoke very little. At the same time, however, even though I worked very hard at my writing and was bent upon becoming a good writer, I could never manage to be any better than second rate. In any event I grimly resolved not to say a word unless I had to.

When I entered the school I was enrolled in the lowest possible class, just as I had expected. I was sixteen years old, and yet the class I was in was only one small step up from my ten-year-old brother's. This greatly increased my misgivings about being ill-treated, and I resolved more firmly than ever to remain silent. On arriving for the first day of school among my noisy classmates, whose ages ranged from thirteen down to ten, I kept my mouth closed tight as a clam. Once in the classroom, however, I quickly found that the other children were asking trivial questions that even I could answer. My apprehensions were somewhat eased when I realized that I actually knew more about some things than they. Of course, this was to be expected since I had been put in a class with much younger children. The teacher must have realized it too, and in less than a month I was promoted to a higher class. In those days the school held tests every month, and promotions and demotions were made on the basis of the results. In this way I was able to move up every month, and sometimes even twice in a single month. Before long I was in the highest grade but one. Nevertheless, I continued all this time to avoid speaking more than I could possibly help; in fact, if anything, I was more determined to keep it up than ever.

A child's psychology is strange. At first I stayed silent because I was afraid of the other students, but as soon as I realized I was better than they were arrogance took over, so that now I would not speak to them because they were not worthy of my attention. Inevitably they called me smug and snobbish, and I made few friends during my schooldays. Some of my classmates at Keiō whom I remember fondly were Hatano Shōgoro, Inukai Tsuyoshi, Katō Seinosuke, Yoshida Karoku, Morita Bunzō, Miyake Yonekichi, Minoura Katsuto, and Fujita Mokichi. Yano Fumio is another, but he was in a senior class. Most of these in fact became my close friends after we left school, and while I was there it was really only Hatano, Miyake and Yoshida that I had relations with. Miyake was a boy of few words too, and he would spend the whole day sitting opposite me in my room without saying much. Strange as it may seem, this was what he enjoyed and why he came to visit me.

I had never been a talkative boy at the best of times, and with my resolve to remain silent I became a total mute. While I was attending the school, which was located in Tokyo's Mita district, I suffered from chronic beriberi and had to go to Hakone every year for treatment at a hot spa. The Fukuzumi Inn had long been frequented by Master Fukuzawa, and as a favor it gave special treatment to his pupils from Mita. Public hot springs were usually a good place to make friends, but even there I did not make any. I used to stay in Hakone for thirty or forty days at a time, but apart from asking the maid to make my bed or bring my meal I kept to myself and just read books in my room. Later I learned from a friend that the people at the inn were quite concerned about their eccentric guest. In those days I played dumb not just to my schoolmates but to everyone. I was a poor communicator anyway, but I only made myself worse.

In spite of my obsession, however, when it suited me to torment my teachers I could speak well enough. My behavior was so terrible that I burn with shame today and feel the need to confess to it in order to absolve my guilt. I remember thinking that if the teachers were promoting me when I behaved well, they would be all the more anxious to move me into the next class if I behaved badly! My strategy was to buy books that were more advanced than those that were being used in the class. Armed with superior knowledge, I would then deliberately ask questions in order to harass the teachers. To my great satisfaction, they were usually unable to answer. So they took it in turns to advance me to higher grades, partly to avoid embarrassment and partly because they overestimated my academic abilities. Not surprisingly, though I was not aware of the fact then, I was soon put on the blacklist.

Among the teachers at the school there were two who had answers to all my questions and took no nonsense from me. As I recall, they were Kadono Ikunoshin, and Gotō Makita. They were among the youngest of the teachers and I admired them greatly. In the end, I decided that being impressed was not enough, and I strove to emulate their intelligence and scholarship. It gave me quite a shock later when Mr. Kadono turned up as my rival for a seat in the House of Representatives. Kadono Ikunoshin was the elder brother of Kadono Jūkurō, who became a prominent businessman.

Keiō Gijuku had three dormitories to which one was allocated according to age. There was one for adults, another for teenagers, and the third for children. I was put in the one for teenagers, but all my classmates lived in the adult dormitory. Perhaps for this reason when an additional dormitory for young adults was created later, I was hastily moved there.

Those who were transferred with me to the new dormitory, including one or two who were younger than I, were all notorious troublemakers, if not delinquents. I was extremely displeased and took it as an insult to be lumped together with this disreputable group. Until then my sins were limited to such improprieties as harassing teachers, but otherwise I apparently enjoyed a fair enough reputation and was accorded good treatment. Now, however, I was feeling quite discontented and I began to make trouble not just for the teaching staff but also for the administrators. There was another motive for my consistent rebelliousness at this time, but I shall leave my discussion of it for later.

I Decide to Leave School

In 1875, the year after I entered Keiō, I turned seventeen (by Japanese counting) and made up my mind that the time had come for me to travel the world to broaden my knowledge. I decided I had better start by going all over Japan, but first I should learn as much as I could about the country's geography, fauna and flora and so on. Before I was ready to start out, my father was transferred to Kumamoto with Mr. Yasuoka and, deciding to make the most of this, I planned to use my summer holidays to tour Kyushu. So I set off for Kumamoto with my brother.

In the end I did not make the planned tour due to a couple of disheartening accidents that befell me en route. They were nothing much really, but they seemed major events to me at that age.

The best way to reach Kyushu in those days was by boat, and the fare was very reasonable as an American steamship company and Mitsubishi were in keen competition for passengers. In fact, the fares were so low that even an impecunious student could afford a first-class ticket. The group my brother and I were traveling with boarded an American steamer as first-class passengers. One of the boys in the group lost his ticket, so when a purser came to check our tickets he could not produce one. It was a serious matter. We tried hard to explain, but we were not successful in communicating with the American and did not know what to do next. Somehow I managed with a combination of body language and writing to satisfy the purser. I reasoned that if inquiries were made in Yokohama it would quickly be proved that the ticket had been purchased, in which case there would be no reason to impose a penalty. If not, then I was prepared to pay for the other boy. The truth of the matter was that I did not have enough money. Fortunately, the purser agreed to wait until we got in touch with Yokohama, and our friend was allowed to disembark. This was a relief, but for a while the incident had caused us great anxiety.

Our friend left the boat at Shimonoseki, and my brother Yukitaka and I sailed on to Nagasaki, where we spent the night at an inn. It was here that the second of my misadventures occurred.

The inn was undergoing renovations while we were there, and a large number of carpenters were thus staying there. Somehow, from the moment we arrived I had a premonition that there might be dubious characters among them. Sure enough, suddenly waking in the middle of the night I found the bag that I had placed by my pillow was missing. Then I heard someone cry out "Stop thief!" and a great deal of commotion downstairs. I guessed that one of the carpenters had taken my bag and was now pretending to chase the thief. Eventually I found the bag on the roof, forcibly opened and with its contents missing. Fortunately, I had taken the precaution of dividing what little money I had, leaving part of it in the bag and keeping the rest on me. We were therefore able to make it to Kumamoto even with that portion in the bag lost. It had given me quite a fright though.

Unlike today, the trip from Nagasaki to Kumamoto was not an easy one at that time. We boarded a small Japanese boat at Nagasaki and made calls at Amakusa and many other ports on the way. Thinking back on things now, it was a daring trip for a boy of my age to make with a small brother. I must admit that I was a little daunted by my recent experiences and I had begun to realize that traveling required more than I had bargained for. So, with half my money lost, I gave up my bold plan to tour Kyushu and instead spent the next month with my parents.

In Kumamoto there was an English school that had been established at the time of the Restoration by the former daimyo Hosokawa, where a dedicated and religious retired American soldier by the name of Janes was now teaching.[19] There was also a medical school, which included a German on its staff. Both were small schools but had brilliant instructors. Yokoi Tokio, Ebina Danjō, Kozaki Hiromichi, and Tokutomi Iichirō all studied at the English school. Doctors such as Ogata Masaki and Kitazato Shibasaburō received their instruction at the medical school. My father passed on to me some papers written by the best students at the English school. I found many were impressively written. Some were so excellent, in fact, that I felt I would never be able to match them.

My return trip passed without untoward event and I reached Yokohama on the same boat as Yokoi Tokio. This was the beginning of my association with him.[20]

After my return from Kumamoto I still continued to play dumb. The only difference was that I was now more rebellious than ever because of my resentment at the circumstances in which I had been moved to the young adults' dormitory. I had always been a timid boy and never dared to quarrel. Worse than that, as I have told, I was often tormented by those who were more aggressive than I. Even as a child I was conscious of the need to change myself if I were one day to be a leader. In an effort to conquer my timidity, I pretended to be brave by rebelling at every opportunity. Over the years this habit became part of me, but my bravery has always been a sham.

At Keiō I found that most of the teachers were convenient butts for my newfound rebelliousness, but after being transferred to the young adults' dormitory I was even defying the school directors.

Apart from lecturing us occasionally on good learning habits when we were assembled together, Mr. Fukuzawa did not do very much teaching. Instead he picked out those of us who showed promise with the pen and made us write papers for him. I once turned in a paper titled something like "The Independence of Scholars." At that time, most educated men went to work for the government as

---

[19] There is a biography of Janes by F. G. Notehelfer, *American Samurai: Captain L. L. Janes and Japan* (Princeton: Princeton University Press, 1985).

[20] Yokoi (1857–1927), eldest son of the Restoration figure Yokoi Shonan, became a leading intellectual as pastor, president of Dōshisha, and member of the House of Representatives in the Imperial Parliament.

bureaucrats. Young as I was, I thought this was wrong, and criticized their office-hunting. I thought that scholars should be independent, and this was what I wrote about. My paper was returned with a comment written either by Fukuzawa or his deputy, I forget which. It said something to the effect that my idea was laudable, but it was too bad that so few carried it out. Most probably the comment was not meant to be sardonic, but I took it to be a way of chiding me that I was all words and no action. I took my pen and promptly wrote another pompous paper saying that I intended to do exactly as I had written. Though I had written the piece on impulse, I felt by then that I had no choice but to go through with my declared intention. For some reason I felt that I had put myself in a position where I now owed it to my teacher, Fukuzawa, to study a subject that would give me independence and a livelihood. Law, economics, and political science, the kind of subject taught at Keiō Gijuku, gave one no chance but to work in government or some other equally stultifying bureaucracy. Racking my brains, I decided to become a dyer.

Looking back now, it seems to me that this was a thoroughly irrational urge, but I did have a motive. I had learned from a book I read around that time that British and French soldiers fighting in the Crimean War fell ill because of the bad dye used in their stockings. I had read somewhere else that Japan was importing low-quality dyes from the West, and that not only did cloth dyed with them fade easily but that they were rumored to be toxic. Improving dyes, I concluded, was a major enterprise that would be a service to the country and a means for my own independence. The best course, it seemed to me, was to quit Keiō and enroll in the national Technological Institute (kanritsu no kōgaku ryō). At about this same time, I had mounted another challenge to the school directors and student supervisory board over the question of morality and discipline. I claimed that the bad manners of our students were a disgrace to Fukuzawa and destructive of the fine reputation of the Mita school. By this point the directors had decided that I was too much of a nuisance, and they secretly contacted my guarantor. The school authorities felt sorry for me and did not want to expel me, but it was hoped that I would quietly leave. They were prepared to expel me if I did not do so. Thus, I withdrew from Keiō Gijuku and entered the Technological Institute. I believe this was early in 1876.

AROUND THE OSAKA CONFERENCE

While I was absorbed with finding my way, the world around me was shifting with great speed. At the heart of it all was the movement demanding the establishment of a parliament. In January 1874, when Itagaki, Soejima, Gotō, and Etō submitted their petition for the establishment of a popularly elected parliament, public opinion in favor of the proposal spread to the farthest ends of the country like ripples from a stone hurled into a pond. Among those who opposed the petition were Katō Hiroyuki, Mori Arinori, and Nishi Amane; outstanding among the supporters were Tsuda Mamichi, Nishimura Shigeki, and Nakamura Masanao.

Since Katō Hiroyuki had published important works on constitutional government even before the fall of the shogunate, people were truly astonished that he should now stand at the forefront of the movement opposing the proposal.

Itagaki, Soejima, and Gotō, of course, busied themselves fighting against such opposition, while Ōi Kentarō and others used pseudonyms to engage in heated debates, which soon flooded the newspapers. To support the petition Itagaki formed a political organization that he named the Aikoku kōtō or Patriotic Public Party. He gave it this name because he believed that the new party's goals of establishing a constitutional government and destroying the clan cliques represented a true expression of patriotism and loyalty to the emperor. Its pledge began, "Heaven, in creating our people, has endowed them with certain inalienable and universal rights." After proclaiming the rights of the people, the document addressed the urgent need for removing the remaining evils of the feudal system that regarded people as slaves: "If the ways of the government are not reformed, our longing for the enhancement of our nation's honor and the increase of the people's wealth will be to no avail. Roused by our sense of loyalty and love of our country, we pledge with like minded colleagues that we will proclaim the universal rights of our people and thus preserve heaven's blessings. This is the correct way to demonstrate our love of our ruler and our country."

Charging that the national government had become the private fief of one or two clan cliques, it asserted: "Government must be for the people. . . . The monarch and his subjects should be as one in sharing prosperity and adversity and whatever befalls our nation. It is only in this way that our Japanese empire can be maintained and prosper."

Unlike today's political parties, the Aikoku kōtō did not publicize its guiding principles or policy platform and it did not recruit members. Nevertheless it could be regarded as a kind of embryonic political party. Only a few days before its formation was announced, however, Iwakura Tomomi, the minister of the right, was ambushed by Takeichi Kumakichi and nine other men from Tosa who had had an argument with him earlier in the Akasaka area of Tokyo. As a result of this, the government considered the very existence of the Aikoku kōtō to be extremely dangerous.[21] So many different steps were taken to suppress it that before long it simply dissolved itself.

Once lit, however, the fire of the freedom and people's rights movement could not be put out merely by the dissolution of one Aikoku kōtō. When the former councilors (*sangi*) filed their petition for a popular parliament, men of like mind rose throughout the land, organized political societies, and demanded the establishment of a popularly elected assembly. The momentum increased by the day to the point where the reluctant government could no longer resist its force. At this time, Ōkubo Toshimichi had come to be the single most prominent figure in the government. Although it is usual to speak of the dominance of the four clans of Satsuma, Chōshū, Tosa, and Hizen, I have already discussed how, after the split that occurred over the Korea issue, the influence of Tosa and Hizen in the

---

[21] Itagaki, like the men who attacked Iwakura, was from Tosa.

higher echelons of government had been completely destroyed. Chōshū's power also suffered a blow when Kido Takayoshi resigned from the government in April of 1874 because his views about a proposed expedition to attack Taiwan did not fit with the dominant opinion. Popular demand for a genuine parliament was thus gaining momentum just as the ruling clique was going through a phase of self-destruction. The petrified clan government tried to bolster its position by inviting back the various elder statesmen of the Restoration who had resigned since the split over the Korea issue. This took place at the historic Osaka conference, which was convened in January, 1875.

The conference was organized by Inoue Kaoru, who was then in Osaka. From the government side there were Ōkubo Toshimichi and Itō Hirobumi, while those that had left the government were represented by Kido Takayoshi and Itagaki Taisuke. Inoue served as moderator. Saigō Takamori, whose presence had been most desired, rebuffed the invitation, saying that if Kido and Itagaki were to be in the government there was no need for him. Soejima Taneomi too voiced exception and declined to attend.

As soon as the conference got under way, Itagaki put forward his long-cherished dream of a representative parliament, insisting that it was the only way to fulfill the grand purpose of the Restoration. Kido had already submitted a statement of his position to the government in September of 1873, and was in agreement with the principles of constitutionalism. He felt, however, that given the circumstances and the level of the people's political sophistication, the sudden introduction of a representative parliament would have adverse effects on government. He thus preferred an evolutionary approach, and argued that for the time being regional administrative officials could be expected to represent the popular will. Then, as a first step, local assemblies (*chōsonkai*) could be established to enable people to learn about democracy. Next, prefectural assemblies would be formed, and this would eventually lead to the creation of a national assembly. Ōkubo was the most conservative of all, but not even he was completely against reform, admitting that a popular parliament would have to be set up eventually, while maintaining that now was not the time.

Soon, the ice was broken and a start was made towards compromise. None of the participants opposed constitutionalism in principal. The only differences were to do with questions of method and timing. With a good deal of give and take on both sides a compromise was reached on a general plan to establish a *Genrō-in*, or senate of senior statesmen, a *Daishin-in*, or supreme court, and to organize a conference of regional administrative officials. Kido and Itagaki agreed to return to the government as councilors and to cooperate in the completion of the new political system. In April of 1875 an Imperial rescript was issued confirming the separation of powers and endorsing the idea of constitutional government: "Building now upon Our wishes as proclaimed in the Charter Oath, We hereby establish the Genrō-in to enact laws for the Empire, and the Daishin-in to consolidate the judicial authority of the Courts. By also assembling representatives from the various provinces of the Empire, the public mind will be best known and the public interest best consulted, and in this manner the wisest system of administration will be determined."[22]

The first conference of regional administrative heads was held in June of 1875. Regional heads (*chihō chōkan*) had already been called to the Ministry of Finance (*Ōkurashō*) as early as April of 1873 to submit their recommendations on government and finance, and this had proved extremely productive. Thus, taking heed of the strength of public opinion, the government decided to use a conference of these same regional heads in place of a popularly elected assembly. Members would then come to develop an understanding of parliamentary government, and eventually this would lead to the establishment of a full fledged constitutional system. On May 2, 1874, the government promulgated rules and regulations concerning the parliamentary constitution (*gi'in kempō*). One part of the assembly rules that were included in this document stated, "While the main business of the governors who have been appointed to each region of the country lies in their role as governors, when in the assembly they must nevertheless strive to serve as representatives of the ordinary people." In other words, these government-appointed officials were expected to represent the will of the people but only when they were in the assembly. This was unabashed sophistry, but such was the original design for the conference of governors. This abnormal agency, which pretended to represent the people, could not be expected to function properly. Before long, it simply followed the will of the central government and, at best, served as a forum in which the views of individual governors could be questioned. It was respected by neither officials nor the people.

Considering the domestic situation at this time, we should note that Etō Shinpei's Saga Rebellion had taken place in February of 1874, and that by October of 1876 the Shinpūren rebellion had broken out in Kumamoto. It was during this latter rebellion that Governor Yasuoka, my father's superior, was killed, together with the commander of the Kumamoto garrison, Major Taneda. A geisha from Tokyo, who had become Major Taneda's mistress and was in Kumamoto at the time, sent a brief telegram to her mother in Tokyo informing her of the tragedy: "Patron dead. I am wounded." It went the rounds in the capital causing a great deal of hilarity, and inspiring the line: "What will you do now?"

The rebellion in Kumamoto left a large number of people dead or wounded and, left alone in Tokyo, I was quite concerned abut the fate of my family. As it turned out, my father had been attacked, but miraculously escaped injury, and my mother Sadako, I learned to my immense relief, had escaped with the three children, Yukitaka, Yukitake, and Masa. After this incident my father resigned his position and left Kumamoto to retire in the vicinity of Yamada in Ise, where he had earlier acquired a piece of land.

At about the same time yet another rebellion broke out, this time led by Maebara Issei in Hagi (Chōshū). With uprisings like this occurring one after the other, a mood of alarm had begun to spread in the country, but when they were all suppressed without difficulty people realized that radical means were not the way

---

[22] Adapted from the translation in McLaren, ed. *Japanese Government Documents*, p. 42.

to achieve their goals for the nation. Political societies that had sprung up sponta-neously throughout the nation now converged to mount a single offensive against the government to demand direct representation in a parliament.

The most powerful of these political societies was the Risshisha of Tosa, which had a membership of more than one thousand. The Risshisha had opened a private school, like the one run by Saigō in Satsuma, to teach the public about govern-ment, and it used an old manor house located in Obiya-machi in Kōchi as a public hall and organized for speeches to be given there. When Itagaki resigned from the government for the second time, his reputation was widely respected through-out the Inland Sea area, and since many of the advocates of popular parliament were inspired by him, the Risshisha of Tosa was at the center of the national parliamentary movement.

In Awa, there was another political group called the Jijosha or Self-Help Soci-ety. Nakamura Masanao's translation of Samuel Smiles's *Self-Help* was then sweeping the country under the Japanese title *Stories of Self-Made Men in the West, or a Treatise on Self-Help* (*Saikoku risshi hen-Jijoron*), and anyone with ambition to be part of the new civilization competed to read it. It was for this reason that Itagaki named his Tosa group the "Risshisha," or the Society of Self-Made Men, and why the group in Awa was called the "Jijosha," or Self-Help Society.

It was during this time that I entered the Technological Institute. I was already eighteen and I could not help but be affected by the developments in the country.

WRITING TO NEWSPAPERS INSTEAD OF STUDYING

The Technological Institute became the foundation of the engineering sciences in Japan. Later it was renamed the Engineering University (*Kōbu daigakkō*) and today it is the Engineering Department of the University of Tokyo. The college was founded when Itō Hirobumi was the minister for industry, for the purpose of encouraging practical learning from the West. The management of the college and even the academic direction were left entirely up to foreigners. The teaching faculty were all Westerners, and lectures as well as all other activities were con-ducted exclusively in English. I had learned a little English previously, but since my lessons at Keiō Gijuku consisted entirely of written translation, I could not speak or understand a word of the spoken language. My shortcomings were not only in English. Up until this point I had studied almost no mathematics, which was of course necessary at the engineering college. Given all of this I was hardly qualified for admission to the engineering college, so I first enrolled myself in something along the lines of a preparatory school[23] to study English and mathe-matics. Even this proved to be a formidable challenge for me.

---

[23] Ozaki's recollections here are inexact. The Kōgakuryō was established within the Ministry of Industry (or Engineering) in 1871 and renamed the Kōbu daigakkō several years later. Dyer, who had

At that time an English missionary by the name of Shaw lived within the grounds of Fukuzawa Yukichi's estate. This was the man who later developed the small hill town of Karuizawa as a summer resort. It was from him that I learned English and advanced mathematics. Mr. Shaw happened to be a friend of Mr. Dyer, who was the de facto president of the engineering college, and through his introduction, undeserved though it was, I was soon enrolled in the college. The college was then located in Tokyo's Toranomon district. Later, the building came to be used by one of the Imperial offices (*goryōkyoku*) and then the Toranomon Women's School. The official president of the college at the time of my enrolment was, I believe, Ōshima Keisuke but, as I have mentioned, the teaching staff were all Westerners. Henry Dyer, who held the real power, was a Scotsman, so everything from food and dress to housing were all done in the Scottish manner. The college doctor was a foreigner and the toilets were imported from the West. Come to think of it, it was quite a radical arrangement. On returning home, Mr. Dyer became president of Glasgow University and stood as a candidate for parliament.

The teachers were all up-and-coming figures fresh out of British universities. Apart from Mr. Dyer, there were many others who went on to become world-renowned scholars, including the seismologist, Milne, and the architect, Josiah Conder.

My intention was to study chemistry there, and after graduation to become a dyer in the Nishijin quarter in Kyoto. Had things worked out according to plan my life would have been entirely different from what it is today. But that was not to be.

From the very moment I first entered a chemistry laboratory at the college I began to suffer headaches, and the smell of the malodorous chemicals every time an experiment was conducted soon became unbearable. I tried different classes but did not like anything that was taught.

I did not have a strong constitution, and although the spa in Kusatsu had helped a little I was far from enjoying normal health. The college would have turned me down for health reasons had Mr. Dyer not intervened. On top of being such a weakling, having to study subjects I did not like was not helpful. In the end I became quite ill. Of the approximately one year I was at the college, I probably spent half that time in the infirmary.

I regretted my decision to go there. I had never liked chemistry anyway, and now I was trapped by this odious curriculum. I reproached myself bitterly. I hardly studied during class. Mr. Dyer personally oversaw the study period every evening when all the students were gathered in the big dining room. Whenever I was not in the infirmary I had to be there. The study period was usually two to three hours, and one could not just sit and do nothing, so to kill time I thought I would write to the newspapers. Mr. Dyer did not understand what I was doing. He would come around and commend me for studying so hard. Was I doing some translation, he

---

headed a technological school in Glasgow, was recruited as its head. A lower school (Shōgakkō) was developed as part of the college and lasted from 1874 to 1877.

would ask. I could not continue for very long like this. It was impossible for me to keep up with such disagreeable subjects, so before the year was out I left the college.

One of the pieces I wrote during these study periods was entitled "Conquer Satsuma!" (*Tō Satsu ron*). At that time, Satsuma was practically an independent country and it openly defied the power of the central government. Saigō Takamori built a private school, kept a private army, and did as he pleased. Satsuma was a special case and was treated accordingly; the government could not do anything about it. With the Restoration, the class system was formally abolished and on the surface the former samurai warriors, farmers, artisans, and merchants were considered to enjoy equality. In fact, however, the leaders of Satsuma and Chōshū continued to act in the old autocratic manner and ruled their governments as they always had. Even as a youth I felt indignant at their insolence and it was thus that I wrote an article calling for the conquest of Satsuma. I was secretly proud of my thesis, and as a mark of my gratitude and respect for my old master I presented it to Fukuzawa. All he said, however, was that I could be arrested for writing such things. I did not welcome the thought of going to prison, but I felt I could not ignore my convictions and just do nothing. Although Fukuzawa did not approve, I mailed the piece to the *Akebono Shinbun* which, together with the *Nichi-nichi*, the *Hōchi*, and the *Chōya*, was one of the big four newspaper of the day. This was my first association with the newspapers. Before long, Saigō Takamori raised the standard of revolt, provoking the Satsuma Rebellion of 1877. This made me feel that my own call for the "conquest of Satsuma" had been heeded, and I was very pleased.[24]

POLITICS IN WORKERS' JACKETS

My formal education ended when I left the engineering college. I had attended classes at the Hirata school, at English schools in Takasaki and Yamada, at Keiō Gijuku, and finally at the college, but my year and a half at Keiō was about the longest I spent at any of these institutions, and thus, my time as a student in fact totaled no more than five or six years.

At this point I decided not to try and enter any other institution, and so now with free time on my hands, I spent my days reading or writing to newspapers and doing translations. It was during this period that some friends and I decided to revive a magazine called the *Minkan zasshi*, which had been started by Fuku-zawa, but had been out of print for some time. Our first issue was published in April, 1877. At first it was a monthly, but from March, 1878, we began to publish daily.

The financial side of the magazine was the responsibility mainly of Asabuki Eiji, and with Kowatari Norihide, Katō Seinosuke, Hatano Shōgorō, Honda Ma-

---

[24] Saigō was a complex figure; his career and image are the subject of Charles L. Yates, *Saigō Takamori: The Man Behind the Myth* (London: Kegan Paul International, 1995).

goshirō, and Motoyama Hikoichi on the writing staff it did remarkably well. It was Asabuki who suggested that since we were publishing a magazine for the people we should wear workers' jackets instead of the formal Japanese *haori* and *hakama* or the Western suits that men of politics seemed to favor. I agreed it was an excellent idea. But the jacket did not suit me at all. I was too stiff in my speech and posture, and the others had a good laugh at my expense.

Eventually, my friends were taken away from Tokyo by their work and we all went our separate ways. On top of this, when Home Minister Ōkubo was assassinated in Tokyo's Kioizaka quarter in May 1878, the magazine carried an editorial headed "Bad Luck for the Home Minister!" and urged the government to remain calm. This displeased the authorities, who demanded that the magazine publish an acknowledgment that it would not write the same sort of thing in the future. Fukuzawa was greatly offended and again discontinued the magazine.

While I was searching for ways to pass my time after leaving the engineering college, I accepted an invitation by the Kyōkan Gijuku at Yushima in Hongō to give a series of lectures on English history. The school was considered to be one of the three most reputable at the time, along with Fukuzawa's Keiō and Nakamura Masanao's Dōjin-sha. I was asked because the son of the president was a classmate of mine at both Keiō and the engineering college. My lectures, I believed, were easy to understand, but the students obviously did not think so. Many of them were older than me and they ridiculed me for my "ghostly" lectures. Japanese ghosts have no legs, so what they meant by this was that the ends of my sentences were unclear. They showed their disapproval by boycotting my lectures, so after half a dozen I quit. Later, I was often criticized in parliament for my affected speech, in particular because of the way I overemphasized the ends of sentences. This must have been due to an unconscious effort on my part to correct my "ghostly" diction.

I lived the life of a poor student for some time after my failed lecture series, and my translations of works such as "Western Fault-Finding" (*Seiyō anasagashi*) and "Speaking in Public" (*Kōkai enzetsu hō*) were products of this period. It was also around this time that I visited Fukuzawa to ask his opinion about my writing. He glanced at me sideways while picking at his nose hair, and asked me who exactly it was that I expected would read what I wrote. I was offended by his manners and the way he posed the question. Attempting to control my feelings, I solemnly replied that I was writing for the educated reader. With this, he erupted in anger. "You fool!" he shouted. "You have to write for monkeys! That's what I do." And then he smiled at me the way he always did when he was charming people. I was confused and did not know whether to take his words as scorn or praise. Nevertheless, his attitude was so galling that I did my best to avoid visiting him from then on. I was wrong. He had shown me the secret of practical writing.

For a while I went to Katō Ōrō, a teacher of Chinese learning (*kangaku*) in Surugadai (Tokyo) to study Chinese poetry and prose. He was a master of ancient Chinese music, and maintained that those who studied poetry should study music as well. This meant learning to play such instruments as the Chinese flute, the *koto*, the *hichi*, the *ritsu*, and the *shō*. I never mastered any of these, but I did learn the basics of how to play the koto. Certain of my friends found this quite amusing and insisted that my hands were better suited to plows and spades than delicate musical instruments. The pen-name I used during this period of my life was "Kinsen," the characters for which suggested a combination of the sound of the koto and the water from a spring.

It was, I think, towards the end of 1877 that Hatano Shōgorō, Kirino Sutezō, Katō Seinosuke, and I founded a group called the *Kyōgi-sha* to organize public debates and speeches and to write letters to the newspapers. In competition with our group was an organization called the *Yūkō-sha*, which had formed because we were too conceited! The leader of the *Yūkō-sha* was Inukai Tsuyoshi, but at this stage I was yet to get to know him.[25]

It was to Fukuzawa that I, who had hardly spoken at all during my time at Keiō, owed my ability to speak before the public. Fukuzawa had set up a hall for public speaking in Mita, where he taught by example. It was not enough to lead people by the pen, he said; one must be able to teach by word of mouth. He therefore sought to encourage public speaking. At first I took the rostrum with great reluctance, but soon I was invited to speak in many places. I accepted these invitations, but I had no ambition to be an orator. In my heart I still despised speaking, so I never became very good at it. I spoke not to perform, but to communicate my thoughts.

Of all the speeches I gave in those days the only one I still remember was titled "Shōbu-ron" or "Militarism." This speech was given, if I remember rightly, in the spring of 1879 in the corner of a temple in Shiba that housed something along the lines of a naval officers' club. This club, which I believe was probably the predecessor of today's *Suikō-sha*, would, from time to time, invite various people to address them. Through an intermediary, Hasegawa Sadao, a naval officer and later member of the House of Peers, had asked me, despite my young age, if I would speak, and it was thus that I came to give my speech on the virtues of militarism. In it, I used examples from history to argue that the rise and fall of nations depended on whether or not the spirit of militarism had been developed. When this speech came to be published it was warmly received and provided opportunities that changed the course of my life.

EDITOR-IN-CHIEF AT TWENTY-ONE

One day in the winter of 1879 I received word that Fukuzawa wished to see me. I hurried over to see him, and he told me that Kowatari Norihide, who had recently been appointed as editor-in-chief of the regional newspaper, *Niigata Shinbun*, had taken ill and died. He explained that he had been asked to find a replacement, and

---

[25] As the reader will see in the following chapters, the two men later became closely linked in parliamentary causes. Even their pen names were similar, with Inukai's Bokudō corresponding to Ozaki's Gakudō.

asked if I would be interested. Kowatari had been at Keiō after I left, but he was older than me in years and an exceptionally talented writer. Niigata itself is, of course, a long way from anywhere, but at that time the *Niigata Shinbun* was one of the leading regional papers of the day, rivaling the big newspapers in Osaka, and so I promptly accepted the offer.

There was, of course, no train to Niigata then. It was still only recently that rickshaws had been introduced, and the trip was a very long one. I stopped overnight at Kumagaya, Honjō, Takasaki, and Karuizawa, and on the sixth day I reached Nagaoka, where I embarked by river boat for Niigata.

In Niigata, people had turned out on the docks to welcome their new editor-in-chief. When I disembarked from the boat they quickly sized me up and asked me if Mr. Ozaki had arrived. When I told them they were looking at him, they inspected me dubiously and welcomed me with obvious misgivings. Later when they had gotten used to me they told me that at first they were shocked by the realization that the man they had thought was a secretary was actually Ozaki himself. They had felt cheated by Fukuzawa for sending such a youngster, and they were deeply apprehensive about my ability to head their newspaper. Given that I was only twenty-one, small, and physically unimpressive, I could scarcely blame them for having these doubts.

Fukuzawa Yukichi's Letter of Recommendation

(Addressed to Mr. Suzuki Chōzō, owner of the *Niigata Shinbun*, dated September 18, 1879)

Dear Mr. Suzuki,

On that matter of someone to help you with your newspaper, I am very pleased to recommend Mr. Ozaki Yukio, who is a former student from Keiō Gijuku.

Mr. Ozaki was at Keiō Gijuku for some years and is a gifted writer. It is possible that Mr. Nishiwaki would also know him. I am confident that he will be able to carry out the duties required of him. Recently he has been invited to speak by the army. He has also been in contact with the Osaka Shinbun and up until this morning had not yet made up his mind as to what he should do. However, I have just now succeeded in prevailing on him to go to Niigata. After I hear from you by telegram that you have agreed among yourselves to accept this recommendation, I will see to it that he leaves for Niigata as soon as he is ready.

As to what you might give Mr. Ozaki by way of remuneration, I would judge, since in my opinion he is certainly no less capable than Mr. Kowatari, that a salary of fifty yen per month would be in order. With regard to travel expenses, whatever you offer will of course be acceptable.

Please forgive me that being rather pressed at this moment I have referred only to the matter in hand.

Yours sincerely,

Fukuzawa Yukichi

At that time, the *Niigata Shinbun*'s main office was in Igaku-cho, where today's printing shop is. It was there that I wrote the paper's editorials. From the beginning, my editorials were quite popular. Subscriptions increased, the employees were happy, and my reputation within the company was good. In fact, my efforts had little to do with the paper's success, since subscriptions to newspapers everywhere were increasing greatly due to a surge in people's sense of civic responsibility and general enlightenment on the part of their readers.

For me, writing was one thing, but speaking with people was another matter altogether. As editor-in-chief of the newspaper I was visited by all sorts of country folks and was often invited to be their guest. I was not a good socializer, though, and the best I could usually manage by way of conversation were the short ambiguous syllables so beloved of inarticulate Japanese. I found it difficult to make even the usual mundane remarks about the weather. Anyway, I considered it the height of silliness to say what everybody knew already: "Warm today, isn't it!" "Yes, isn't it!" "Turned a little cold, hasn't it!" "Yes, it has, hasn't it!"

Some time after I arrived in Niigata I was invited in my capacity as a journalist to a dinner co-sponsored by the government and private business. Governor Nagayama of Niigata was the main guest. When I arrived I found I had been seated at the end of the table. I was young and unimportant, so I suppose it was not out of order for me to be given this inferior place. But I had heard that in America journalists were held in high regard and were treated as uncrowned kings wherever they went, so I took the organizer aside and complained that this was not the way to treat a journalist, and asked for a better seat. The organizer was unsympathetic, but I would not give up, spurred by the conviction that the custom of always putting government officials above private citizens had to be changed. Governor Nagayama overheard us. "That's interesting," he told the organizer. "Put him next to me." As a result of this my request was finally answered and I found myself sitting next to the governor. I was not pleased by the tone in which the governor had spoken, however, and later in the meal, after I had begun to feel the effects of the *sake* I made my feelings known. Grabbing the carefully arranged flowers from a vase behind the governor, I then proceeded to shower him with petals and said, "Accept these with my compliments!", before storming off home.

In those days a governor was a very powerful figure and the petty officials present were enraged. They swore not to let Ozaki get away with this outrageous performance, and they meant it. Governor Nagayama must have been an extremely tolerant person, however, because he remained completely unruffled throughout and showed no sign of anger at all. I was ashamed of my behavior, which was inexcusable even for an excitable youth. Governor Nagayama, I thought, must be a really exceptional person.

Newspapers then, unlike their successors today, considered the editorial to be their most important feature, and consequently, editorial writers wielded considerable power. The head of the editorial committee was called editor-in-chief and it was his responsibility to oversee the editing of the entire newspaper. The title of "editor-in-chief" was not enough for me, however, and from the start I referred to myself as "premier" (*sōri*) of the *Niigata Shinbun*. I even had the presumption to assert my authority over the financial side of operations and went so far as to have the company president, who is, after all, the representative of the shareholders, replaced. Most young men do tend to be arrogant, but even so, it is a wonder that there were no complaints at the time. Several decades later, the son of the owner of the *Niigata Shinbun* showed me a letter that helped to explain why this had been the case.

The letter had been written by Fukuzawa to the owner of the newspaper at the time that I took up my new appointment. It seems that Fukuzawa was more than a little concerned about the possible behavior of the stubborn, egotistical young man he had recommended for the job, and he thus felt it necessary to describe my character in some detail to my new employer and to offer pertinent advice on how I should be handled. Fukuzawa certainly knew me well! Little did I know or appreciate this when I was at Keiō and even afterwards, and to this day I regret the fact that I kept my distance and sometimes rebelled, thus failing to fully avail myself of the opportunity to learn more from my teacher while he was alive.

In fact, just before leaving Tokyo for Niigata, it dawned on me that I had only just left school and completely lacked the experience necessary to take on the job of editor-in-chief of a newspaper, and so I visited Fukuzawa to ask him how I could best contribute to society in my new profession. He told me that I should devote myself to fostering the knowledge and experience of the local people, and that I should not just write in the newspaper, but also organize public speeches and lead the world around me by appealing to both their eyes and their ears. He also wrote a few directions on a scroll of paper to remind me, for example, of the importance of educating people in the ways of commerce and of the need to assist in the establishment of a prefectural assembly.

Following Fukuzawa's instructions I forced myself to speak in public a great deal in the Niigata region, and as a result of this I found that though I was not good in group discussion I did possess a certain gift for reasoned argument. Compared to some of my contemporaries who had also graduated from Keiō Gijuku I was a very poor speaker, but it seems I was able to hold an audience because what I said made sense.

With regard to the development of commerce, I gained the cooperation of powerful businessmen in Niigata to help organize the Northern Japan Society for the Promotion of Commerce (*Hokuetsu kōshōkai*), whose general purpose was to provide opportunities for commercial education and eventually to build a school. I was not able to see to the establishment of the school since I was to leave Niigata as suddenly as I came. However, plans were drawn up with the help of a group of volunteers, and in December of the year I left the school opened. This was the predecessor of today's Niigata Prefectural School of Commerce (*Kenristu Niigata shōgyō gakkō*).

I also started a poetry society called the *Issui-ichigin-sha* (Have-a-drink, Read-a-poem Society) in which we practiced writing and reading poetry under our teacher Sakaguchi Gōhō. In actual fact, we spent more time drinking than writing poetry. Nonetheless, most of the poems later included in my *Poems by Gakudō* were written at this time.

Sakaguchi had been an outstanding student of Mori Shuntō, who was well known in Tokyo, and his *Short History* was read all over the country. Despite his achievements and fame, at the time he still was a handsome young man of only twenty-two or so years. He worked for an important local businessman at the rice exchange, yet still found time to produce poems and calligraphy that were of the same quality as the work of veterans and masters. He really was an amazing person. Sakaguchi did not talk politics in those days, but as time went by he became leader of the Progressive Party (*Shinpotō*) in the Niigata region. Later he served for some time as a member of parliament and was a most helpful colleague.

I Lead the Niigata Prefectural Assembly

With the issuing of prefectural assembly regulations in July 1878, it was announced that assemblies were to be convened stage by stage beginning in March of the following year. This was in accordance with the decision taken by the Osaka conference to pursue a gradual approach to popular participation in government according to which prefectural assemblies would first be convened before proceeding to the creation of a national parliament. The opening of an assembly in Niigata Prefecture had been delayed and there was none in existence when I arrived. Since this was the first time that such assemblies had been created in Japan, no one was conversant with the rules of parliamentary procedure. I therefore helped with the opening of the assembly as it was one of the things Fukuzawa had wanted me to do.

With the assembly at last about to open, it was ruled that since my official title was secretary (*shoki*) my seat should be placed below that of the speaker. I was not pleased at this since I had assigned myself the role of "teacher." I insisted that if I was to be able to lead the assembly then I should be seated beside the speaker. Finally, I did get a table and chair at his side.

The speaker, Matsumura Bunjirō, was an affable gentleman with high moral standards, but he was completely unaccustomed to the responsibilities of his office. He was too easy-going to manage the assembly, and it was often the case that in my self-appointed role of advisor I had to help him carry out his duties. There were times when debate got out of hand and I would advise the speaker to stop the proceedings and dismiss the assembly. On occasion, it actually adjourned. At other times, when the speaker did not listen to me, I myself declared the assembly adjourned, stopped taking notes, and simply left. Minutes of those meetings that I kept as a curiosity contain comments in my hand, such as "Stupid argument not worth listening to!" or "This proposal unfit for adoption!" The following year I had every intention of continuing as the assembly's so-called secretary, but the affable Mr. Matsumura resigned from office and was replaced by Yamaguchi Kenzaburō. Yamaguchi was much sterner than his predecessor, so knowing that my presumptions of authority in the assembly would no longer be indulged as before, I strategically resigned my post as soon as he was appointed speaker.

The years 1880 and 1881 witnessed a great surge in the movement for freedom and people's rights in Japan. For me, though, buried in the tall grasses of Echigo, far from the center of politics and with no adversary at hand, life was rather dull. This changed with the appearance of a powerful foe in Nagaoka. This was Ōhashi Sahei, founder of the Hakubunkan publishing house and father of Ōhashi Shintarō. He was a man of great ability, and had decided to found a newspaper company in Nagaoka. Niigata was, however, the center of the region, and the *Niigata Shinbun* had a history with which its young rival could not normally hope to compete. Ōhashi therefore set about looking for someone who would be able to generate more popular interest than I was able to. He was prepared to spend however much was needed to attract such a person, and in the end he chose Kusama Tokifuku.

In terms of both his age and his academic background, Kusama was my junior, but he had become quite famous in Tokyo as a result of his having given speeches and worked with men such as Numa Morikazu.[26] Ōhashi thus invited him to challenge me and my more established newspaper. The going salary for a newsman of that rank in those days ranged from fifty to eighty yen, but it was rumored that Kusama had been offered as much as one hundred and fifty or even two hundred yen. This can be taken as an indication of just how much enthusiasm Ōhashi had for his new project. Kusama arrived confident that he could easily humble the paper that I was writing for. He had also been to Keiō Gijuku, but though I knew him by sight I had never made his acquaintance. I knew of his reputation, however, so I welcomed the challenge presented by his arrival and wrote editorials that I hoped would keep him in his place. Despite my enthusiasm, however, I eventually ran out of issues to write about in my editorials. Then I remembered my speech on "Militarism" and published it in fifteen daily installments under the same title. It was received so warmly in this form that I decided to publish it as a book in 1880. It sold very well and I received quite a few orders from Tokyo.

As the cry for freedom and people's rights rang ever louder throughout the country, the mood even caught on in Niigata. My own ambitions burned inside me as I felt the pull of the changing times and watched the situation evolving in the capital. After a year and a half in the country I yearned to return to Tokyo. Just then, out of the blue, I received a letter from Yano Fumio, telling me that parliament would soon meet and that it had been decided to bring capable people into government to investigate related matters. Prominent young men from Keiō would be assigned to the task and I had been nominated to join the group. Would I come to Tokyo? I was looking for an opportunity to return to Tokyo anyway, so I gladly accepted.

Yano had been my senior at Keiō and I might even have studied under him at some point, but I remembered him only vaguely. After he left Keiō I heard only that he had become a correspondent for the *Hōchi Shinbun*. There had been no

---

[26] Numa Morikazu (1843–1890) was an important figure in the Movement for Freedom and People's Rights in the early Meiji period. He later became a member of the Progressive Party and managed the Tokyo-Yokohama *Mainichi Shinbun*.

communication between us and I supposed that he had heard as little of me as I had of him. It was entirely as a consequence of my essay on militarism that he now wrote to me. I learned later that another Keiō graduate of his acquaintance had been impressed by the essay and recommended me to Yano, who decided on the strength of it to include me among the new recruits for government.

When I resigned from the *Niigata Shinbun*, I recommended that Tsuda Kōji be appointed as editor-in-chief in my place. He had been a classmate of mine, and later in life attained a high position in Mitsui. Tsuda was succeeded by Minoura Katsundo, and he in turn by Yoshida Karoku. All three were recommended by me at the request of the paper. At one point, the *Niigata Shinbun* was discontinued temporarily as a result of unfortunate trouble with the political parties, and since resuming business it seems never to have regained its former reputation.

At any event, here I was at twenty-two, a former editor-in-chief and ecstatic at the prospect of venturing into real politics. Around the time of the Restoration in Japan, men were considered to have come of age at fifteen and women at thirteen. Everyone was precocious and I was no exception. I had been discussing politics from childhood, and by the time I went to Niigata, as it was with anyone who had ambitions to be in politics, I wanted to be part of the struggle to destroy the system of autocratic clan government. This, I thought to myself, would require me to have a loyal following of my own. One's own children would surely be the most loyal of followers, and if mine were to be politicians they would have to be boys. I dreamt therefore of having as many boys as possible before I became old and impotent. This ambitious plan had its origins in a story that I had believed to be true as a child in which a grand old lord from Mito had sired some fifty sons and had them installed as feudal lords all over the country, thereby greatly increasing his power and influence. Taking my inspiration from this story, I wasted no time getting married and rejoiced at the prompt arrival of a son in Niigata. I felt that I was well on my way to emulating the old lord, but I had not understood the economics of fatherhood, which in no time spoiled my plan. My salary was barely enough for my own modest needs, but now with a wife and child (nowhere near fifty!) my fantasy of fathering large numbers of sons was shattered overnight.

In those days public-spirited men were like monks. We were poor but we had great dreams and never thought about our own welfare. Faced with reality, though, I quickly came to understand the inconveniences of poverty. Among my other useful discoveries during this period was the unprofitability of having relations with other women and all the problems that that invites. Despite these things, I still cherished the dream of committing my life to a great cause together with those I trusted. It was on account of this that I ended up wronging my brother. I shall speak more of this later.

In Preparation for a National Parliament

ATTEMPTS TO PRESENT A PETITION TO THE THRONE

As mentioned in the previous chapter, the Satsuma Rebellion of 1877 marked a major turning point in the campaign for a new national parliament. The fact that even Saigō Takamori, with all of his power and influence, had failed to overthrow the Meiji government with military force, made it clear that it was indeed impossible to do so, and thus the popular forces that sought to destroy the system of clique government now turned away from the possibility of armed uprisings. Instead, energies came to be concentrated in the movement to have a national parliament established, and the power of public opinion was used to mount a frontal attack on the forces of clique government. It was decided that efforts should instead be concentrated on pushing for the opening of a national parliament and on fighting the influence of the dominant clans by enlightening the opinion and the conscience of the people. The central figure in the struggle was still Itagaki Taisuke.

The new push for a national parliament began when Kōno Hironaka traveled all the way down to Kōchi from Fukushima to urge Itagaki to resurrect the Aikoku-sha (Patriotic society). Soon he was followed by others such as Sugita Sadaichi from Fukui, Kurihara Kyōichi from Mie, Takeuchi Masashi from Okayama, and Tōyama Mitsuru from Fukuoka. With all of these men gathered together in Kōchi, it was resolved that they would work together to rebuild the Aikoku-sha. This was in April of 1878. The group then published a pamphlet explaining their decision, and young emissaries were sent throughout the country to enlist like-minded men to their cause. Everywhere political societies were organized in spite of measures taken by the government to tighten its control over the formation of discussion groups.

In the north-eastern region the Sekiyō-sha and Sanshi-sha set up by Kōno Hironaka were followed by other groups such as the Nishū-kai of Iwate and Iwaki, the Jinsei-sha in Sakata, the Kyūga-sha in Morioka, the Kakumei-sha in Sendai, the Hokushin-sha in Sōma, the Kōfū-sha in Iwaki, and the Aishin-sha in Aizu. In Kyushu, there were groups such as the Kyōai-sha of Fukuoka, the Kyōben-sha in Kurume, the Gōitsu-sha in Toyotsu, and the Sōai-sha in Kumamoto. In the western district of the main island were the Shōshi-sha of Izumo and the Kyōritsu-sha of Tottori, while the island of Shikoku had the Gōritsu-sha and Nanzan-sha in Tosa, the Kōritsu-sha in Iyo, and the Kōkyō-sha of Matsuyama. In addition there was the Jigyō-sha in Rikuzen, the Chōrai-sha in Hitachi, the Kōshin-sha in Mikawa, and in Nagoya, the Kiritsu-sha. All of these groups issued statements of their objectives and strongly urged the establishment of a national parliament.

In March 1879, the Aikoku-sha held its second convention at Edobori in Osaka. At its third convention in November of the same year it adopted a resolution that marked the start of a coordinated campaign for the opening of a national parliament. Men from twenty or so Aikoku-sha affiliated societies blanketed the country to rally support. It was after this that public opinion became most vocal.

When the fourth Aikoku-sha convention was held in March 1890 at the Kitafukutei restaurant in Osaka's Kita Kyūhōji-chō district, 114 people attended, representing 87,000 members of twenty-seven affiliated societies from twenty-four prefectures. It was at this convention that a formal request (*seigansho*) to the throne for the establishment of a national parliament was finally drafted, and Kōno Hironaka and Kataoka Kenkichi were chosen to travel to Tokyo to present it. It is representative of the enormous changes that had occurred in the intervening six years that whereas the 1874 petition (*kenhakusho*) for a popularly elected assembly had been addressed to the government, this time the request for a national parliament was being made to the emperor himself.

On April 17, Kōno and Kataoka presented themselves at the Council of State and requested permission to submit the people's request directly to the throne. They were refused. Matters relating to legislation, they were told, must be submitted to the Genrōin, the senate of senior statesmen, which had been created in 1875. It made no difference whether the document was called a request (*seigansho*) or a petition (*kenhakusho*), the government clerk said; the procedure was the same. So the two men went to the *Genrō-in*, which refused the document because it was not called a petition. Kōno and his partner then went back to the Council of State and asked to see Chief Minister Sanjō. Their request was impatiently rejected. With both the Council of State and the senate of senior statesmen having refused to accept the request in this way, the two men gave up the idea of presenting it directly to the throne and instead wrote a detailed report for the benefit of their colleagues. The episode, needless to say, enraged the public. Undeterred, other committed men continued to journey to Tokyo to petition the government, but all was in vain. Arguments between the petitioners and government officials went something like this:

OFFICIAL: "There is no rule that allows people to make direct representations to the throne where matters of politics and government are concerned. Therefore you cannot do it. The rules state that should any citizen desire to present a petition, it must be addressed to the senate of senior statesmen."

PETITIONER: "Does this mean that the people have no right to petition the throne?"

OFFICIAL: "They do have the right."

PETITIONER: "If that is so, since there is no law that takes away that right of the people, the government should accept the petition. In fact, there is a precedent for the government accepting petitions in the past."

OFFICIAL: "Well, the opening of parliament is a matter which concerns the whole empire and as such it should not be a subject for petitioning by one group of people from one particular region."

PETITIONER: "Would the government accept the petition if it represented the united will of the whole nation?"

OFFICIAL: "It would be entirely up to the emperor himself to decide whether to accept it or not."

PETITIONER: "And how is the will of the emperor to be known if the petition cannot be presented to him?"

OFFICIAL: "The government is not obliged to explain any further."

Following a heated exchange of this nature, petitioners were simply turned away. The government was determined to use any and every means to suppress petitions for the establishment of a parliament.

Yet, the government could not ignore the growing national movement for the establishment of a parliament indefinitely. In fact, even within the government there were some who felt that the opening of parliament was simply a matter of time. This group, spearheaded by Ōkuma Shigenobu, was already preparing secretly for the inevitable and, as it turned out, the Statistics Office (*tōkei-in*), to which I was appointed, was one part of these preparations.

On my return to Tokyo from Niigata I had gone directly to see Yano Fumio, who explained that the point of the new Statistics Office was not really to collect statistics, a task for which the pre-existing government bureau had been more than adequate. He told me that the progressive mood of the times meant that even within the government the argument for opening a national parliament had been made. Ōkuma and his associates were aiming to establish such a parliament in 1883 and had already begun to make preparations. Yano also explained that if a parliament were to be opened, it would require large numbers of government officials who were capable of explaining national affairs. For this reason, it had been decided to bring talented private individuals into government posts and give them two years of training in government business.

I had always detested the traditional bureaucratic ideology of "revere the government, despise the people" (*kanson minpi*). As a result, I had not once thought of government employment, and I had even harbored a secret contempt for people who did. Now, however, I was being asked to become a civil servant to help prepare the way for a parliament and I could find no reason to refuse. Just as Yano had suggested, when I showed up for work at the Statistics Office I was told that as one of those who would be working with the national parliament in the future I should spend my time preparing for this task. I was informed that I need not waste energy on compiling statistics, and that I should instead direct my efforts at gaining a complete understanding of matters of government.

Thus it was that in July of 1881 I took up my appointment as a junior secretary (*kenshō shokikan*) in the Statistics Office. At this point I was still just twenty-three years old, and my only significant achievement was to have been editor of a country newspaper. When my record was being reviewed in the Council of State it was noted that no one so young had ever been appointed to a permanent government post before, and there seems to have been quite a bit of skepticism about it. Inukai Tsuyoshi, who was appointed to the same post as I, was not only older than I, but had also been involved with various newspapers and magazines in Tokyo, and had already made something of a name for himself.

EARLY INVOLVEMENTS WITH ŌKUMA SHIGENOBU

The directorship of the Statistics Office was one of Ōkuma Shigenobu's responsibilities.[1] After the assassination of Ōkubo Toshimichi in 1878, Ōkuma had more or less appointed himself as his successor and one of the things this meant was taking over responsibility for that office. In those days, the Council of State and the government ministries were separate. The most powerful statesmen participated in the Council of State as councilors (*sangi*), while second-tier politicians were left to head the government ministries. Each councilor was then given responsibility for supervising the activities of two or three of the ministries. At the time I joined the Statistics Office, Ōkuma was in charge of four ministries: foreign affairs, finance, justice, and agriculture/commerce.

Before the Restoration, Ōkuma had not been prominent in national affairs, but he was propelled to power with recognition of his skill in negotiating with the British minister, Harry Parkes, over the issue of the treatment of Christians in Kyushu. In an anti-Christian campaign carried out in the first year of Meiji by Inoue Kaoru, who was then an assistant to the governor of Nagasaki, Christians were imprisoned for ostensibly violating Japanese law and were forced to abandon their faith.[2] The diplomatic corps in Tokyo headed by Parkes made a protest to the government. Parkes's name carried a good deal of weight, and his nononsense attitude toward the Meiji government intimidated many. Negotiations were conducted in the annex of the Hongan-ji temple in Osaka. Opposing Parkes were representatives of the Japanese government headed by Prince Yamashina, who was then the chief official in charge of foreign affairs. When Parkes protested that freedom of religion was the inalienable right of all human beings and that the Japanese government had no justification for persecuting Christians as heretics, let alone for treating them as if they were lowly animals, not one of the officials there knew what to say. Then Ōkuma, who for lack of seniority occupied a seat at the end of the room, spoke up. Religion was an internal matter for each country, he said, and no foreign power had any business to interfere.

---

[1] Ōkuma (1838–1922), who figures importantly in Ozaki's career, was a principal Saga leader in late Tokugawa politics and a leading figure in the early Restoration government. After his expulsion from that government in 1881, he founded a political party, a school that would become Waseda University, and served twice as prime minister under the Meiji Constitution.

[2] The issue of the "hidden Christians" (*kakure kirishitan*) arose in 1865 when villagers who had concealed but retained their faith through two centuries of persecution made themselves known to the French priest of a church newly established in the foreign section of Nagasaki. Tokugawa and Meiji government leaders responded with alarm and, in 1870, some 3,000 adherents, of whom 660 died, were subjected to harsh exile in other provinces.

Parkes was furious, recognizing the junior status of the man who dared to challenge him. "I beg your pardon," he said. "A young junior officer does not have the authority to negotiate with Her Majesty's minister plenipotentiary. This is an insult to Great Britain."

"If you represent Her Majesty's government," Ōkuma shot back, "then I represent the government of His Majesty the Emperor. If you insist that you cannot negotiate with me, it will be taken as a serious affront to His Imperial Majesty and to the Japanese Empire. Is this your intention?"

Parkes and Ōkuma were engaged in single combat, and Ōkuma would not accept defeat. Each time Parkes threw a few words at Ōkuma, Ōkuma reciprocated in kind. Thinking quickly on his feet, Ōkuma managed to overcome his opponent, or at least to fight his way through successfully. It seems that the logic of his arguments was occasionally somewhat strained, but at that time there was no one else in Japan with the knowledge of Western practices, which enabled Ōkuma to take this kind of action.

The incident marked the beginning of Ōkuma's rise, and not long afterwards he had been appointed a councilor in the new government. He had a large mansion in the Tsukiji district of Tokyo. Next door was the home of Itō Hirobumi, while Inoue Kaoru is also said to have lived in one of the tenements on Ōkuma's estate. The estate came to be known as Tsukiji's Ryōzanpaku (Ch: Liang Shan Po)— after the famous fort where the Chinese hero Sung Chiang and his band had gathered[3]—for it was here that those in the Meiji government who were in favor of opening a parliament met to plan their strategies. It was also the place where the three men, Ōkuma, Itō, and Inoue, would come to consult with each other about all manner of things. The Satsuma clan was at this time the main force in the government, controlling the army, the navy, and the police. This caused considerable uneasiness in the Chōshū camp. Generally, Satsuma was thought of as more militaristic while Chōshū was regarded as advocating the power of speech, which they probably saw as the only weapon they could wield against the military might of Satsuma. Nevertheless, the two clans, strained as they were within the government, were sure to combine their forces against the people's rights movement when it challenged their power.

The opening of the parliament would give fighters for people's rights powerful leverage against the clan government of Satsuma and Chōshū. It is not surprising then that Ōkuma, who was himself from the Saga clan, and thus outside of the Satsuma/Chōshū clique, gave strong support to their cause. In addition, Inoue and Itō, who were the most progressive of the Chōshū men, joined forces with him to resist the conservatism of the Satsuma faction.

Of the three men, Inoue was the first to have held a government position, having worked under Ōkubo to help manage the financial affairs of the nation. With his

[3] The story of Sung Chiang and his band was immortalized in the Chinese literary classic *Shui Hu Chuan* (Jp: *Suikoden*). C. P. Fitzgerald has suggested that Sung Chiang is a figure not unlike Robin Hood, and thus it might be helpful for readers more familiar with European folklore to think of Ōkuma's estate as being described as a version of "Sherwood Forest." See C. P. Fitzgerald, *China: A Short Cultural History*, 5th ed. (London: Cresset Library, 1986), pp.507–12.

fiery disposition, however, he had attracted his superior's disfavor and had been out of office for some time. It was Ōkuma who, after Ōkubo had passed away, rediscovered Inoue and gave him an important post in the government.

I always thought Inoue to be a rough sort of person and perhaps even evil, but Ōkuma liked him and always defended him even when Inoue later became his political foe. Inoue may do wrong, Ōkuma used to tell me, but he is not an evil man. There was no logic in it, but Ōkuma would often get away with this sort of thing. While Ōkubo was alive, Ōkuma and Itō served at different times as his chief secretary. Ōkuma, however, was the older of the two and always occupied the senior political office. It was perhaps because of this earlier relationship that whenever the two met, Itō always seemed to treat Ōkuma with respect while Ōkuma overpowered Itō with his strong personality.

I once saw the two men play a game of chess together, and it was very interesting for what it revealed about each of their characters. Ōkuma was an amateur but skilled player and Itō could only compete against him with the help of a three-move handicap. Itō approached the game with deep concentration while Ōkuma seemed to play in a more relaxed manner, seemingly placing his pieces without much thought. Only when he found himself in a tight corner did he sit with folded arms thinking about what his next move should be. Then, being a resourceful man, he would find some way of getting out of the difficulty. Itō was cautious, used conventional moves, and rarely made a mistake. Whereas Ōkuma drew on his own deeper resources only when he was forced to do so, Itō took great care to avoid falling into difficulty in the first place. This was the difference between the two men. Ōkuma was a genius but his boldness often betrayed him and he ended up losing.

Ōkuma was very intelligent, but he also had a remarkable memory. He never forgot anything that he had heard once. While at the finance ministry it was rumored that he had completely memorized the whole budget. Of course the national budget then was much simpler than it is now, but even so, the foreigners all talked about him as the man who was able to keep the entire budget under his hat. He always knew all of the details of such things as the population of each of the prefectures and the production statistics for various commodities.

Before I visited China in 1884 I went to see Ōkuma to say goodbye. He advised me what to see in Shanghai and the hotel I should stay at without ever having been there himself. In fact, although he had never been out of the country he knew everything there was to know about London and Paris too.

In his old age, though, Ōkuma became forgetful and would sometimes be caught giving the same information to the man from whom he had learned it in the first place. Another thing which is famous about Ōkuma is that he hated writing and had supposedly never once used a calligraphy brush in his entire life. Ōkuma's childhood name was Yatarō, and the story goes that when his mother asked him to write a letter inviting relatives to a memorial service for his father, little Yatarō refused to do so and instead sprang to his feet and ran all the way to inform them directly. Later, as a student studying away from home in Nagasaki, they say that he employed two assistants to write his letters for him. Ōkuma sometimes asked me to write a brief on some subject or other which he would then correct. To such a ridiculous extent did he abhor using his brush that he would edit my text by taking a small knife and cutting out phrases from the page rather than by running a line through them with brush and ink.

I once asked him why he had such a phobia about using his brush, but he never gave a convincing answer. I rather suspected that he had written badly as a child and had either been ridiculed by his schoolmates or scolded by his teacher. Given his disposition, it is quite possible that such an incident caused him to have sworn never to write again.

As minister of foreign affairs, however, he naturally could not avoid signing letters that were sent abroad in his name. And as prime minister he also had to put his signature to documents recording decisions by the cabinet. On such occasions he would steal quietly away and sign them where no one could see him. I remember on one occasion I had some business to discuss with Ōkuma and I surprised him by suddenly showing up at his hideaway just as he was in the process of affixing his signature to some official documents. I caught a glimpse of his handwriting at this time, and as you might expect, it was quite awful.

When I first met Ōkuma he had just returned to Tokyo from a tour of the northeastern part of Japan. Yano Fumio introduced us. It was generally said that councilors who served as cabinet ministers were mere decoration and did not have real power; it was their chief secretaries who made the important decisions. Yano, who was Ōkuma's chief secretary, had previously been a reporter for the *Hōchi shinbun* newspaper and had already made a name for himself as a front-line correspondent during the Satsuma Rebellion. During this time he had also had some dealings with the elder statesman Kido Takayoshi (who had died in 1877). After entering the government he came to be thought of as Ōkuma's "brain" and principal strategist. I did not find this hard to believe and thought that much of the credit for Ōkuma's high reputation should really have gone to his outstanding strategist. For me it seemed that Yano must be the real teacher and that Ōkuma was the student. Yet the student held high office, while the teacher was in a lowly position. I was very curious to see how the two people who found themselves in this situation would behave in front of a third party, and thus I found myself looking forward to our meeting quite eagerly. In fact when we did meet, I found Ōkuma, the one I supposed to be the pupil, looking very much like the teacher, and Yano, whom I expected to be the teacher, with his head held low and acting with great deference toward him. I was puzzled, but suspected that they must be performing some kind of act in order to make Ōkuma look good. To tell the truth, I felt quite baffled. While I was at Ōkuma's home the head of a certain ministry paid him a visit. And Sano Tsunetami, the powerful minister of finance, also dropped in. These two visitors spoke to Ōkuma with even more humility than Yano, I thought, and behaved extremely reverently towards him. At first I could not make sense of it all, but gradually I realized that Ōkuma was a truly great man.

So it was with Ōkuma at the helm that some of us dreamed of carrying out our great design. An unexpected turn of events, however, confounded all our hopes. This was the political upheaval of 1881.

ŌKUMA'S SO-CALLED SECRET SUBMISSION TO THE THRONE

It was in 1880 that the three-man team of Ōkuma, Itō, and Inoue had begun to lay plans for the opening of a parliament at their meetings at the so-called Ryōzan-paku estate in Tsukiji. Naturally, the conservative forces from Satsuma and elsewhere who dominated the government were sternly opposed. Given this situation, other government officials obviously could not be relied on for assistance. Promising young men had to be found from among the general public, and the best strategy for doing this seemed to be to recruit the brightest of Fukuzawa's former students. This was how Yano, Inukai, and myself all came to work for Ōkuma at the Statistics Office. Inoue also recruited Nakagamigawa Hikojirō and Ushiba Takuzō in a similar fashion.

At the time, Ōkuma was Ōkubo's heir presumptive and as the chief of the councilors he occupied a position analogous to that of a present-day prime minister. Itō and Inoue served as his able lieutenants. Yet, for all this, Ōkuma still did not have the strength to match the combined forces of the clan conservatives. He and his allies were thus painfully aware that they had no choice but to turn to the power of the people if the autocratic government was to be overthrown and a parliamentary system put in its place. Late in 1880, therefore, Ōkuma, Inoue, and Itō called on Fukuzawa and urged him to publish a newspaper that would serve as a mouthpiece for democratic principles. Inoue was a passionate man who would pursue an objective single-mindedly once he had set his mind to it. So it was he who explained to Fukuzawa exactly what they had in mind. In the process he revealed that Ōkuma, Itō, and himself were all secretly committed to the establishment of a parliament. The clan government could not hang on forever, he insisted; if it tried to do so, the change might well end up being imposed at gunpoint. Inoue explained that having committed themselves to the creation of a national parliament, the three men were also prepared to hand over the reins of government to whichever political party was able to win over the hearts of the people. For this reason, they wished to see the establishment of a newspaper that would report to the people in a fair and honest fashion. Inoue admitted that within the government of the day it was still only the three of them that were committed to this plan, and that others such as the councilor from Kagoshima (Kuroda Kiyotaka) seemed unlikely to accept talk of parliaments and the like. Still, he insisted, if they continued to press forward it would not be long before these others too became convinced of the need for change.

Fukuzawa knew well how politicians from the clans could argue one day on one side of an issue but then change their minds the next day when things turned against them. He therefore wished to make doubly sure that the three men were of the same opinion. Inoue reassured him that they were indeed of the same mind, and had sworn themselves to the cause. Hearing this Fukuzawa was finally persuaded to begin preparations for publishing the new newspaper.

The details of this exchange can be ascertained by examining the letters Fukuzawa later sent to Itō and Inoue asking for confirmation of their plans. Judging from the date of Inoue's reply to Fukuzawa, it can be concluded that at least until the spring of 1881 Ōkuma, Itō, and Inoue continued to be united in their efforts to work from inside the government for the opening of a parliament.

What then were the opinions of the three ministers who were at the center of the Council of State? Leaving aside the question of Chief Minister Sanjō Sanetomi's views for the moment, it was the Minister of the Left, Arisugawa Taruhito,[4] who was most in favor of creating a parliament. The Minister of the Right Iwakura Tomomi was most extreme in his opposition. He was opposed even to the opening of prefectural assemblies, let alone a national parliament. Such assemblies were, in his opinion, signs of out and out insubordination.[5] He insisted that they must be firmly resisted if the government was to regain its power and prestige and contain the rebelliousness of the people. The power of the armed forces and the police should be strengthened and the common people treated sternly so as to strike fear into their hearts. According to Iwakura, there were numerous examples in our history of heroes rising up to impose military rule for the purpose of maintaining order. Thus, while the imposition of such policies now might cause some subjects to be disgruntled for a period, this could hardly be accepted as a sufficient reason to desist.

It should be noted here that the Emperor Meiji himself had a profound understanding of the movement to establish a national parliament. Already, in 1876, His Majesty had ordered Arisugawa, then the president of the senate of senior statesmen, to compile a national constitution. So when there arose a movement demanding a parliament, the emperor showed special interest and ordered each councilor to submit his opinion through Arisugawa, who had now been appointed as the minister of the left.

Accordingly, in 1880, the councilors submitted their written opinions, none of which was overtly opposed to the idea. Though each proposed different approaches or sequences of measures leading up to the creation of a parliament, the majority converged on the need first to draft a constitution. Most, however, were lukewarm in their attitude and little more than supportive in abstract terms.

Ōkuma, who was the most committed to the opening of parliament, was alone among the councilors in failing to submit an opinion. Prompted by Arisugawa, Ōkuma stated that he wished an imperial audience, at which he would directly submit his opinion to the throne. The wish was not granted, however, and, when

---

[4] Arisugawa (1835–1895), an Imperial Prince, named commander of the imperial forces in the Restoration war and again in the Satsuma Rebellion, was the highest-ranking noble involved in late Tokugawa and early Meiji political and military affairs.

[5] The author uses the term *gekokujō* here, which literally means "those below striking those above," and is generally used to describe periods of upheaval. Ironically, it was Prince Iwakura (1825–1883) who led the great embassy around the globe in 1871–1873 in search of foreign models as fulfillment of the Restoration pledge to "seek wisdom throughout the world."

asked again, Ōkuma finally submitted his opinion in written form, together with a draft constitution.

Ōkuma's submission was somewhat lengthy, but in the main contained the following points: first, an official statement should be made to announce in advance the year and month of the opening of the national parliament; second, appointment of government officials should reflect the will of the people; third, permanent officials appointed by the government should be distinct from those appointed by political parties; fourth, the constitution should be promulgated with the blessing of the throne; fifth, an election should be held toward the end of 1882 and the parliament opened early in the following year; and sixth, a set of basic principles of government should be firmly established.

Ōkuma's opinion was modeled after the British parliamentary system as was his draft constitution. Of course, the thing which caused the greatest surprise was his proposal to hold an election as early as the end of 1882 and to open the parliament in the spring of the following year. Knowing the views of other councilors and fearing that his opinion would cause havoc when it was made public, Ōkuma begged Arisugawa to keep it in strict confidence until it was seen by the emperor. This was the basis of what became known as the "secret submission" incident. Despite Ōkuma's request, Arisugawa, who was surprised by the radical nature of Ōkuma's opinion, secretly showed it to Chief Minister Sanjō and Iwakura, the minister of the right.

Iwakura, who was particularly shocked by Ōkuma's proposals, confronted him about it. Ōkuma responded calmly and explained that staying at the forefront of change was the best way to govern people. "In the current situation," he continued, "it is as if a large crowd of people is gathered outside the gateway into a garden, trying to get in. If the gates are kept shut, then it can only lead to havoc and confusion, but if they are thrown wide open, then it will simply be a matter of watching them enter."

Minister Iwakura then took Ōkuma's submission to Itō and demanded to know if he was of the same opinion. Itō found himself in an awkward position, but after examining the submission he wrote Iwakura a strongly worded letter stating that he found Ōkuma's opinion to be unexpectedly extreme and that he could not follow such a foolish proposal. In conclusion, Itō wrote that although he felt a great deal of regret about it, he could see no other course for himself but to resign his post. Why did Itō, a long-time colleague of Ōkuma, suddenly change his attitude in this way? Apparently, Itō was furious with Ōkuma for breaking the bond between the three men who had been working hand in glove since the death of Ōkubo, and he could not forgive Ōkuma for secretly attempting to submit a personal petition to the throne without first consulting him. He swore that he would never again work with such an unprincipled man.

Arisugawa as well as Sanjō and Iwakura were all much disturbed by this development and tried to mediate between the two men. For his part, Ōkuma went out of his way to visit Itō in order to explain his actions, and eventually Itō relented and withdrew his earlier decision to resign from the government. Even so, the rift between the two men was never fully mended, and the conservative elements from Satsuma and Chōshū skillfully turned this to their advantage.

It was at this critical juncture that a serious dispute over the sale of government assets in Hokkaido took place. Development of the northernmost of Japan's main islands had commenced in the first year of Meiji, and after ten years and an investment of fifteen million yen it was time for the project to be handed over to the private sector. The problem lay in the price of the assets to be sold. It was perfectly obvious to everyone that they were worth at least ten million yen, but in spite of this they were to be sold for a mere thirty thousand yen payable over thirty years without interest. The offer was tantamount to giving the assets away. Not unexpectedly it became a controversial issue within the government, but no one dared speak up lest he incur the displeasure of Kuroda Kiyotaka, who was director of the Hokkaido Development Agency.

In the end, Ōkuma decided to speak out. It was a reasonable protest and once the scandal was exposed public opinion exploded in indignation. Intellectuals and other men of high purpose rose with one voice denouncing the despotic government and demanding the introduction of parliamentary democracy at the earliest possible date. Newspaper editorials focused on the issue and thousands of people thronged to public meetings called to protest the government's corrupt plans. The demand for a national parliament was once again loudly proclaimed throughout the land.

Ōkuma presumably did not foresee the consequences that speaking out against the government's wrongdoing would have. As it turned out, the people were enthusiastic in their support for him and his views and were not satisfied until he made a personal appearance at protest gatherings. Ōkuma was at the height of his popularity. It was almost inevitable that he should become a target of hatred for the Satsuma-Chōshū alliance, which had by now been joined by his erstwhile co-conspirators Itō and Inoue.

I never quite understood why Itō and Inoue had betrayed their long-time friend and colleague. It is true that Itō had provided an excuse for himself, citing Ōkuma's "secret submission," which obviously still rankled. Yet, by the time of the Hokkaido scandal, the dispute between them had supposedly been settled. Perhaps the strength of the Satsuma-Chōshū coalition's opposition to the opening of a parliament simply caused them to lose their nerve, and led them to suddenly back away from their earlier plans. In any case, whenever the clan government found itself in a difficult position it was able to strike back with a truly formidable show of unity. Thus, in spite of all the popularity he seemed to enjoy, Ōkuma found himself abandoned by his political allies and suddenly thrown out of the government.

THE COUP OF 1881

It was in July, just before the summer holidays, that I began my work at the Statistics Office. During the summer Ōkuma was away in the northeast with the emperor, and Yano was off on leave in the western part of the country. For a brief period the office was left in the hands of a few like myself who had recently joined the staff. Towards the very end of the summer vacation, however, a strong push to expel Ōkuma from the government suddenly erupted. This was the so-called coup of 1881. In its political dimensions the coup was even more far-reaching than the disruption caused by the 1873 split over the plan to attack Korea. Ōkuma's dismissal had been planned during the two months of his absence from Tokyo, so that neither he nor the emperor had any idea of it until they returned to the capital. The public was also caught unprepared. There are many ways one might try to account for the incident, but the most likely underlying cause was the jealousy felt by the Satsuma and Chōshū clansmen over Ōkuma's prominence. He was after all not one of them, yet he was powerful enough to have won over the likes of Itō and Inoue, who came from their own ranks. So when they found Ōkuma alone and deserted by Itō and Inoue they seized the moment to undo him.

The imperial tour of the northeast began on 28 July, 1881 with Ōkuma and Kuroda Kiyotaka accompanying His Majesty. While the two councilors were away from the capital the Satsuma and Chōshū men planned to oust Ōkuma by accusing him of having conspired with Fukuzawa Yukichi and secured funding from the founder of Mitsubishi, Iwasaki Yatarō, to organize a political party which would overthrow the government. They argued that he represented a threat to social order, and criticized him once again for his "secret plan" to submit to the throne his radical opinions regarding the establishment of a parliament. A special hearing was arranged upon the emperor's return to Tokyo, at which it was advised that three measures should be implemented: First, Ōkuma was to be dismissed from the government; second, the plan to sell government assets in Hokkaido was to be suspended, and, third, a national parliament was to be established in 1890.

Emperor Meiji showed extreme concern at the proposed dismissal of Ōkuma, and, according to the diary kept by Sasaki Takayuki, after hearing what the various ministers and councilors had to say, he asked them whether the Satsuma and Chōshū forces were not simply joining together to have Ōkuma removed. He also asked whether there was any actual evidence of his involvement in the alleged plot. Iwakura then responded that the advice proffered to the emperor represented the consensus of all concerned and that His Majesty's demand for evidence could be taken as a show of distrust of Satsuma and Chōshū, which would mean the breakup of the government. According to the diary, the emperor then said that if the case against him was clear then there was nothing to be done to help him, but that it would not be appropriate to dismiss Ōkuma without giving a clear explanation for the decision. He therefore suggested that someone should be sent to confront Ōkuma with the charges laid against him.

The emperor then questioned his ministers on the proposed sale of the government assets in Hokkaido. In response to this questioning, Sanjō suggested that Kuroda would not object to calling off the sale provided that Ōkuma was made to resign. Upon hearing this, there was an abrupt change in the emperor's countenance, and he demanded to know what connection there could be between the sale of government assets and Ōkuma's dismissal. Sanjō promptly offered his apologies for the unwarranted suggestion and reassured the emperor that Ōkuma's resignation and the sale of government assets were indeed two separate issues. With this the emperor was finally appeased.

Later that evening Itō Hirobumi and Saigō Tsugumichi were given the task of calling on Ōkuma to request his resignation. Ōkuma replied that he would respect the decision of the emperor's special hearing, but that he wished to tender his resignation directly to the emperor. The following morning he quietly donned formal attire and headed for the palace, but the government had moved too quickly for him and the palace gates were firmly closed. When Ōkuma called out his name and said he wished to pass, the gate keeper reluctantly replied that he was under orders to deny him entry.

Ōkuma turned and made his way to Arisugawa's residence, but here too he was not allowed to pass the gate. As it turned out, that day the Tokyo army garrison was ordered to prepare for possible mobilization, and the chief of police personally led his officers in patrolling the metropolitan area, exactly as if civil war were about to break out. Later when Ōkuma recalled this episode he said that he felt like a Meiji version of Sugawara no Michizane, and that if it had not been for the emperor's own expression of support for him, he might well have lost his life in the incident.[6]

Thus the Satsuma and Chōshū forces succeeded in eliminating Ōkuma from the government, but aware that they still had to quell popular unrest they decided to cancel the sale of government assets in Hokkaido, and to set a definite date for the opening of parliament. These decisions were made public on the day following Ōkuma's ouster, and an imperial rescript was issued announcing the opening of a parliament in 1890. In this way, ministers and councilors who only a year earlier had expressed lukewarm and non-committal opinions to the throne on the issue of a parliament, now suddenly decided they were fully in favor of opening one. This was directly due to the pressure of public opinion which had been inspired by the petition that cost Ōkuma his political life. Clearly then Ōkuma's petition made a significant contribution to the establishment of constitutional government in Japan.

The coup of 1881 also meant that the Meiji government was entirely purged of Tosa and Hizen influence, and it now became the exclusive preserve of the two powerful clans of Satsuma and Chōshū. In ancient Japan, the ruling Taira family had boasted that no one counted unless he was a Taira. Now, those from Satsuma and Chōshū were to have their turn, and from this time onwards the clan-dominated government did not even attempt to conceal its abuse of power.

Fukuzawa was bitterly angry over Ōkuma's dismissal and wrote scathingly of Itō and Inoue. He accused them of weakly succumbing to pressure from Satsuma and Chōshū and of seeking to win their way back into favor by presenting them with the severed head of their former colleague. Fukuzawa considered that Inoue in particular owed him an apology and he even had the driveway up the hill to

---

[6] Sugawara no Michizane (845–903) was a famous statesman of the Heian period, who was the victim of a plot by his rivals at the imperial court.

his residence in Mita repaired so that Inoue's horse-drawn carriage would be able to reach it.

When Ōkuma was dismissed, those of us in the bureaucracy who were seen to be his followers handed in our resignations one after the other. Among the more prominent persons who resigned at this time were Kōno Toshikama (the minister for agriculture and commerce), Maejima Hisoka (the director of railways), Kitabatake Harufusa (a judge), Nakagamigawa Hikojirō (first secretary in the Ministry of Foreign Affairs), Ono Azusa (accounts inspector), Mutaguchi Gengaku (first secretary in the Ministry of Agriculture and Commerce), Tanaka Kōzō (second secretary in the same ministry), and Morishita Iwakusu (second secretary in the Finance Ministry).

Yano Fumio, who was serving as secretary to the Dajōkan, as well as head of the Statistics Office, also resigned at this time, as did all of the others whom he had recruited for the Office including Ushiba Takuzō and Inukai Tsuyoshi. Needless to say, I too resigned. It had only been two months since I took the position, and, just as I had suspected, the bureaucracy was not where I was to find my role in life.

The coup had other consequences for me as well. The most immediate was conscription. I had become eligible for military service the previous year but had been given a year's grace due to ill health. Then it had been waived temporarily when I entered government service. Now that I was out of the civil service as a result of the political crisis, I received instructions to report directly to the Tokyo Metropolitan Office. It was sometime late in October or early in November, as I recall, when I showed up for my physical examination. By that time, of course, the weather was getting cold. I was immediately told to take all my clothes off, and was disgusted to be put in line with others who, to judge from the boils and pimples all over their bodies, seemed to be suffering from every kind of nasty condition. I considered myself a distinguished citizen who deserved better treatment.

I am slight in build but had no other outward defects, and I dreaded the thought of picking up some venereal disease from one of the others being inspected. So, when one of the doctors tried to open my mouth with his fingers after having just handled the private parts of those who were in front of me I instinctively stepped back and glared at him. He saw my indignation and seemed to lose interest in continuing with the examination. Then, however, he began to dictate something to the junior medic seated next to him. I was curious to see what was written on my card, so I stole a glance at it out of the corner of my eye. It described me as being of fair complexion and slightly overweight—both of which were the exact opposite of the truth. I realized then that he was simply writing things down without conducting a proper examination. At the bottom of the card he had written "A+."

This differed dramatically from the result of an examination I had been given by a Meiji Life Insurance doctor, who had informed me that I was not eligible for standard life insurance and would have to pay an extra premium because of my poor physical condition. He assured me at the same time that I had no chance of passing the physical for military service. But here I was with a grade of A-plus. In those days, however, the system in Japan allowed a conscript to escape service with a payment of three hundred yen. That was a great deal of money then, but I considered it necessary under the circumstances and managed to borrow the sum from my friends. This marked the beginning of a period of chronic indebtedness which for years caused me to be victimized by unsympathetic money-lenders.

The fact is I have had a weak constitution all my life. I almost failed to get into the Engineering College due to my poor showing in the physical examination and I had the same problem when I tried to buy life insurance, but I am still alive, while so many of those who were physically fit in those days are long dead. How can one explain this? It is because those who were fit then lived recklessly and overdid everything: alcohol, tobacco, women, even their studies. Too much of these things shortened their lives. The way most people live is slow suicide.

Because I was dogged by illness as a child I learned from an early age to be careful about my health. I remember how much I loved persimmons but resisted the temptation to eat them since I knew they would upset my stomach. As I wrote earlier, forcing myself to study subjects that I was not interested in at the Engineering College almost ruined my health. My body has never been able to tolerate excess of any kind. Knowing this has been the single most important reason for my longevity. Once I set my mind to give something up I have no trouble doing so, regardless of whether it is alcohol or tobacco or anything else. No doubt this is because I was brought up to be able to forgo eating even those things which I liked the most.

There are many people in the world who will tell you how they were able to give up drinking but were simply unable to give up smoking. When I was in my forties, however, I broke the habit with ease, despite the fact that up until then I had always been a smoker, and of strong cigars at that. There was also a time when I might have drunk as much as a bottle of saké at one sitting, but toward the end of the war I had reduced this down to only a half a glass or so, and then, to mark our defeat, I gave it up completely.

I have heard that humans could live five times as long as it takes us to grow to maturity, in other words to the age of a hundred and twenty-five, if we did not kill ourselves prematurely with our reckless living. Advances in science might one day extend even this biological limit so that humans can simply go on living forever in the way that trees and plants do.

THE LIBERAL PARTY AND THE PROGRESSIVE PARTY

I have already discussed how the Satsuma-Chōshū alliance against Ōkuma resulted in an imperial rescript promising the opening of a parliament. This had a tremendous effect on us. Although it was not to be as soon as we had hoped, we had been promised a parliament within ten years, and the knowledge that a date had now been firmly fixed gave us new strength.

Members of the Alliance for the Attainment of a National Parliament (*kokkai kaisetsu kisei dōmeikai*) realized only too well that in their existing form they could not hope to oppose the clan government effectively. The new political organizations that had mushroomed up all over the country were also too fragile to be able to withstand any pressure put on them by the bureaucracy. Everyone involved had long been aware that stronger political parties would have to be organized at some point, but the imperial rescript now provided the necessary impetus for their realization.

Thus it was that on October 17, five days after the rescript had been issued, a large social gathering took place at a restaurant named Yaomatsu-rō in Ureshino-mori and on the following day a conference meeting was held at the Ibusemu-rarō restaurant in Asakusa to discuss the organization of a political party. On October 29 a charter and party rules were decided upon, the president and other party officials were elected, and the Jiyūtō, or Liberal Party, was born.

The Liberal Party was based largely upon the earlier Alliance for the Attainment of a National Parliament. The Alliance itself had been formed as the successor to the Aikoku-sha which, of course, had its origins in the Risshi-sha of Tosa. Thus, the fundamental strength of the Liberal Party derived from the original Risshi-sha, and the natural person to head Japan's first real political party was the Risshi-sha's founder and president, Itagaki Taisuke. Itagaki, however, refused to be considered for the position, arguing that he was, by nature, a stern man, and thus unlikely to achieve popularity with the people. In deference to other aspirants, followers of Itagaki from Tosa also decided not to push for their leader to take the job, and so it was that the party officially elected Gotō Shōjirō as its first president. Gotō, however, would not accept the nomination, knowing that in fact it was Itagaki who most people wished to see as leader. Eventually, Itagaki was persuaded to change his mind and it was agreed that he would be the leader of the new party after all.

From then on, the Liberal Party's new president and other officers canvassed the country tirelessly organizing public meetings and recruiting members. It was during one of these trips while in Gifu that an attempt was made on Itagaki's life. He was stabbed near the heart by a would-be assassin as he made his way back from a gathering at the Chūkyō-in. The story has it that after being stabbed Itagaki looked straight at his assailant and said the famous words, "Itagaki may die, but liberty never!" In competition with the Liberal Party, we founded the Kaishintō or Progressive Party, with Ōkuma as its president. When Ōkuma left the government with his young supporters after the coup of 1881, the whole country wondered what he would do. There was, of course, the precedent of Saigō, who had left the government after his proposal to lead an expedition against Korea was rejected, and ended up losing his life after raising an army of rebellion. There was also Itagaki who had become the main leader of the Freedom and People's Rights Movement against the government.

Ōkuma showed no bitterness towards the government over what had happened and continued to live a life of leisure at his mansion, where he received visitors each day. "Just wait and see what I will do next," he would tell people. "Whether

I am in government or out, I will not change my principles. Even great men often betray their principles when out of government, but I intend to set an example for all loyal servants who find themselves out of office."

When it was learned that Ōkuma was about to organize a new political party, the Satusma and Chōshū leaders were shocked, believing that Ōkuma, like Saigō and Itagaki before him, was about to involve the public in a conspiracy against the government. When he was accused of this, Ōkuma replied that he had meant what he said when he swore that he would remain true to his principles. Itagaki had left the government on account of the defeat over the Korean expedition, and only then began campaigning for the opening of a popularly elected parliament—which was not at all in keeping with his views up until that time. This was not Ōkuma's way. When still in government he had advocated the establishment of a constitutional government based on political parties and it was as a result of this that he had been driven out. Thus, it was entirely consistent with his earlier views for Ōkuma to organize a political party when out of government. Certainly there was nothing underhanded about his intentions. They were perfectly honorable.

The impetus for the creation of a new political party grew rapidly and, on March 16, 1882, the Progressive Party was born. Ōkuma, as I have noted, became its president, with Kōno Togama as vice-president. Recruiters were promptly dispatched throughout the country to gather support. I left for the Kansai region with Yano, while Ono Azusa toured the Kantō and Ōu regions. As a result, local branches of the Progressive Party were created in Aichi, Hyōgō, Oita, Toyama, Akita, and Niigata. Japan now had two major political parties.

There were three organizations which, as it took shape, came to form the core of the Progressive Party. One was the Ōmei-sha, which was a group centered around Numa Morikazu and mainly known to the public through the *Mainichi shimbun*. Shimada Saburō, Koezuka Ryū, and Tsunoda Shinpei belonged to this group. The second was the Tōyō Gisei-kai, the so-called Mita group, which was organized by Yano Fumio at the center, together with Fujita Mokichi, Minoura Katsuto, Inukai Tsuyoshi, and myself. Our main mouthpiece was the *Hōchi shimbun*. The third was the Ōto-kai led by Ono Azusa, and organized by graduates of the Imperial University, including Takada Sanae, Amano Tameyuki, Yamada Kinosuke, and Ichijima Kenkichi.

The Progressive Party was composed of these three groups plus certain former government officials who had served under Ōkuma, such as Kōno Togama, Maejima Hisoka, Kitabata Hirofusa, and Mutaguchi Gengaku. The most outstanding person in the Progressive Party was Yano Fumio. Virtuous, gracious and knowledgeable, he excelled in every way. Unfortunately he died young without fulfilling his ambitions. I never understood why, with all his gifts, Yano was unable to achieve his goals. Perhaps he was just too well brought up. He was not the sort of Oriental hero who drank a great deal and behaved roughly. Rather, he seemed somewhat inaccessible at times, like a great feudal lord. This may have been one factor that contributed to his lack of success.

Yano had virtue, grace and refinement as well as common sense and powerful observation skills. His speeches were sometimes good, sometimes not, and in general were not as well regarded as those of men such as Shimada Saburō. At the founding of the Progressive Party, however, he gave a marvelous speech, which was even better than Shimada's. As Yano mounted the rostrum that day my attention and curiosity were caught by the foot-long scroll he carried. Holding it in his right hand as he spoke, he used it to gesture with in a way that impressed me with its dignity. I have heard many speeches in my time, but none to my mind has surpassed Yano's that day. The white paper scroll was a clever prop, which I imagine was more than a casual accessory. In any case, it certainly added to the effect of the speech. Fujita Mokichi wasted no time in copying Yano's style, but when he proceeded to beat the podium with the scroll he ended up looking like a comical street entertainer.

The Liberal Party and the Progressive Party had competing political philosophies. The Liberal Party was based on the movement for people's rights in Tosa, which had its origins in the Aikokukōtō. Nakae Chōmin, Baba Tatsuo, and Matsuda Masahisa joined it, advocating liberty and equality in the French tradition and a single-chamber parliament, which would give equal voting rights to all nationals. The Liberal Party thus represented a radical idealism. The Progressive Party, in contrast, was modeled on English-style parliamentary government and stood for a more practical and moderate approach. As a result of these different philosophies, those who joined the Liberal Party tended to be the hot-blooded and radically inclined former samurai who were not from Satsuma and Chōshū. In the Progressive Party, on the other hand, we recruited men with knowledge, property, and distinguished reputations, and we also attracted members of the commercial and industrial classes, which were gradually gaining strength. This basic difference in composition between the two parties existed to the end.

While members of the Liberal Party enjoyed making radical speeches and sought to bring about innovation and reform as quickly as possible, the Progressive Party sought to bring about change in measured stages and tried to achieve its objectives in a moderate manner. Due to this difference it was customary for us to criticize the Liberal Party men for their naivete and lack of pragmatism, while they in turn rebuked us for what they called our timidity and excessive caution. We mocked them for their lack of education and property and their crudity and roughness, and they chided us for our apathy and incompetence and said they could not work with us. The two parties could not see eye to eye. Unfortunately, these conflicts played into the hands of the clan government, affording them a weapon with which to blunt the strength of the peoples' parties.

In addition to the two major parties, another called the Teiseitō, or Imperial Party, was also created. It was established to serve the needs of the government by ministers from the Chōshū faction, such as Itō Hirobumi and Inoue Kaoru. It was not very popular from the start and was derisively known as the "three-man party," since its main supporters were Fukuchi Genichirō of the Tokyo *Nichinichi shinbun*, Mizuno Torajirō of the *Akebono shinbun*, and Maruyama Sakugaku of the *Meiji nippō*. We called it the "Party in Government Service" and did not take it seriously. As far as we were concerned, our only competitor was the Liberal Party.

Newspapers of the Day

With the birth of the Progressive Party, Yano took over the *Hōchi shinbun* and made it our party newspaper. Fukuchi's *Nichi-nichi Shinbun* was clearly the best-regarded newspaper of the day, but the *Hōchi shinbun* was second. Next came Numa's *Mainichi shinbun*, then the *Chōya shinbun* of Narishima Ryūhoku and the *Akebono shinbun* of Okamoto Takeo. These were the five big papers of the day. In fact they were the only papers. It was only later that smaller ones such as the E-iri *Chōya shinbun* and the *Yamato shinbun* were established.

When the *Hōchi shinbun* became our party newspaper, I joined it with Inukai and Minoura. This was, I believe, around early 1882. Fujita Mokichi worked on the paper full-time, while five of us, Yano, Fujita, Inukai, Minoura, and I took turns writing the editorials.

Fukuzawa had long argued that the press had as its mission the development of culture, and he seems to have placed a great deal of faith in it. Quite a few of his pupils went into the newspaper business, including Minoura, Fujita, and Inukai. As I have already explained it was also at his recommendation that I had originally gone to work for the *Niigata shinbun*.

Fukuzawa used to ask his best students to take down his commentaries while he dictated them orally. I was never asked to do this myself, but Minoura, Fujita, and Inukai had. I have actually never taken dictation for anyone, but I suspect it can be even more challenging than writing one's own article. It is said that half such an article probably reflects the speaker's thoughts, and the other half the writer's. Among the Mita elite, Minoura was considered to be the most accurate in his transcriptions of Fukuzawa's dictation. Inukai sometimes produced writing that improved on the original, but at other times he is said to have taken too many liberties. As if to bear out the old adage that the personality we develop by the age of three determines what we will be at a hundred, Minoura was always a leader of great fairness while Inukai never lost his unflinching ego.

It was usual for newspapers to have a circulation of about five thousand, and if they ever topped ten thousand the occasion was marked with a special celebration. We had heard that in the West newspapers enjoyed circulations of hundreds of thousands, but none of us thought that possible in Japan. Journalists in those days considered themselves the eyes and ears of society and the great leaders of the age. As a result of this, no matter how difficult their financial situation became they would never do anything to compromise their dignity. The newspaper ordinance was quite draconian, and any paper that dared to criticize or cast even the slightest aspersion on the government or bureaucracy could be banned or have its editors imprisoned. All newspapers, therefore, employed men for the exclusive purpose of taking those punishments. They were known as the "jail house editors." Significantly, even these most lowly of employees took great pride in their association with the newspapers.

Writing staffs of that period were constantly involved in skirmishes with those responsible for the commercial operations of newspapers, because they refused to consider how things would affect sales and stressed only the importance of honest reporting and serious argument. This was particularly true of those in our group. Editorial writers in those days were for the most part ambitious patriots rather than ordinary political commentators. There were so many enthusiastic young men, all ready to take over the reins of government as soon as a chance arose. As a result, our editorials were full of self-importance and had a real air of arrogance.

Being the organ of a political party, the *Hōchi shinbun* suffered from a great deal of official pressure and its publication was often suspended. Circulation decreased to three thousand, and it was hard to keep it at even that level. In spite of this we editorial writers still all maintained our own rickshaws, and Numa of the *Mainichi* paper often chafed at the extravagance of our row of black cabs parked in front of the *Hōchi* office.

One might have expected to find newspaper companies at the leading edge of progress, but back then even they were bureaucratic. Even at the *Hōchi shinbun*, the editorial bureau was divided in to upper and lower sections with the editorial writers occupying the upper section while general writers and translators were in the lower.

When I joined the paper one of the first things I thought of was the name of Hara Takashi, whose editorials I had quietly come to admire while at the *Niigata shinbun*.[7] I looked for Hara in the upper section of the bureau but could not find him, and I soon learned that he was in fact a French language translator in the lower section who only helped with the editorials in his spare time.

Knowing his talent, I thought he should belong to the upper section. Yano and others in the upper section were against the idea, however. They suspected him of being in secret communication with the government and were considering letting him go. I did everything I could to save him, but without success. My colleagues insisted that he did not belong with us. They said that he made trips around the country with the likes of Watanabe Kōki and that he was on the side of the government. It was a great pity but I did not have the resources to prevail in his defense. Hara eventually left the newspaper of his own accord and moved to Osaka, where he worked for the *Daitō Nippō*, which was an organ of the Imperial Party.

It was Yano who was mainly responsible for Hara leaving the *Hōchi shinbun*. Later, when Itō Hirobumi organized the Seiyūkai Party, Hara served as its secretary-general. By then Yano had tried his hand at various things, all of which were largely unsuccessful. Eventually the *Osaka Mainichi shinbun* expressed an interest in taking him on. Motoyama Hikoichi, manager of the *Osaka Mainichi*, was a good friend of ours who had much respect for Yano. Motoyama must have had it in his mind to make Yano the chief editor of the paper. Hara Takashi, who

[7] Hara (1856–1921), after newspaper posts that brought him closer to the government, entered the Foreign Ministry and went on to hold several cabinet posts, becoming the central figure in parliamentary politics. In 1918, he became the first political party leader to win the post of prime minister. He was assassinated in 1921.

had once worked in the editorial section of the *Osaka Mainichi*, had maintained contact with the paper, and Motoyama seems to have consulted him about Yano's proposed employment. Soon afterward Hara took great delight in telling Itō and a group of others that he had decided to make sure that Yano did not get the job.

I thought to myself then that Hara could in fact have exacted his revenge on Yano in a splendid fashion by making every effort to help him get the job, and thus demonstrating his own moral superiority. It was a heaven-sent opportunity, but Hara was not man enough to seize it. "Those who are unable to be generous have not yet learnt what it means to be an adult," was how I summed it up to myself. Of course everyone has his own style. Hara was entitled to do things his own way, and there was nothing anyone could do about it. Had he the capacity to behave differently, however, he may have avoided being assassinated at Tokyo Station.

The Government Pressures

As soon as the Liberal Party and the Progressive Party were born on the wave of enthusiasm aroused by the imperial rescript concerning the opening of parliament, the government considered them subversive organizations and tried to destroy them. Its justification was that it was treasonous to resist the government that enjoyed the sovereign's trust. A political party in opposition was of course no different from the government in power insofar as its services to His Majesty, the nation and the people were concerned. The government, however, would not accept that the only difference between the opposition and itself lay in the principles and methods chosen to achieve their objectives.

Those in government did not understand that we were challenging them politically through the power of speech, since the only way they knew was war. A group of the Satsuma-Chōshū coalition bosses swore publicly that they would never relinquish the power they had won with the sword to those challenging it with pens and abacuses. Nothing was mightier than the sword. In June, 1882, the government announced a revision of the assembly ordinance (*shūkai jōrei*). It was remodeled along the lines of the laws in Germany designed to suppress the Socialists, and in England to curb support for the Irish Party. If the old law of assembly was strict, the new one was far worse. Before permission could be obtained to form an organization for the purpose of discussing politics it was now required to register at one of a number of listed police stations the name and address of the proposed organization, its rules and regulations and a list of its members. If one wished to hold a public political meeting it now became mandatory to obtain prior authorization after notifying an approved police station three days in advance of the date and place of the planned meeting, together with the proposed agenda and the names and addresses of the speakers.

There was also a provision which stated that "Parties shall neither advertise nor encourage the public to attend political meetings through the dispatch of party officials or the distribution of publications, or establish branches or communicate with other like-minded associations." It was also stated that, "The home minister may prohibit the formation of associations or the convening of assemblies if he deems it necessary in the interests of national security."

We naturally opposed all such measures.

The repressive regulations in Germany and England were enforceable for seven and five years, respectively, and limited to the duration of the national crisis. Moreover, each included procedures that would nullify the law automatically on the expiration of its term. In our case, the government had made no such distinction between an emergency law and an ordinary one, which created a much more serious and dangerous situation. I was particularly opposed to the government's actions for the following reason: any political party would necessarily seek to mobilize millions of people, but unless every village had some sort of registry it was virtually impossible to produce a list of members as the government had demanded. The very nature of a political party required that people should be free to join or leave according to their principles and convictions. Members could easily change their position too, and become friends or foes depending on the party's policies. It was therefore not practical to attempt to create a membership list. It was such an outrageous requirement, in fact, that I maintained there was no point in even trying to observe it. However, the majority of the party seniors argued in favor of a more moderate approach, being of the view that as citizens of Japan we were obliged to obey the law even if we found it objectionable. As this was the opinion of the majority, it was decided that we should go ahead and register as a political organization.

In my view, a political party and a political association were two different things and should be kept distinct. However, because we submitted to the unreasonable ordinance, in effect what was created was a political party with a list of registered members. Ever since then, Japanese political parties have been organized as though they were political associations and have kept membership registries more like fraternal organizations, in fact, than true political parties.

As a result of the revision to the law of assembly, political activities were greatly restrained. It affected us particularly, since when public speeches were planned we were obliged to notify the police three days in advance, thus submitting our intention to the discretion of local police officers who would either give or refuse permission as they saw fit. Because of this, political parties constantly clashed with the police, and the Liberal Party frequently came close to bloody confrontation with the authorities. This excited the crowds and drew large audiences.

This was not the government's only strategy in its endeavors to root out political parties. Shinagawa Yajirō, a powerful figure in the clan government, and his group, believed that the only way to protect national security was to stamp out political parties altogether, treating their members as traitors and suppressing defenders of the people's rights for their resistance to the imperial government.

On April 16, 1883, the newspaper ordinance too was revised, dealing yet another blow to our party newspapers. Even before the revision, the government had expanded the paper which printed its official line, at the expense of those related to political parties whose publications were often banned. After the revision, the oppression was so severe that many papers were driven out of business. At first the clan government tried jailing journalists who worked for the opposition papers, but this did not prove effective. The reasons for this were twofold. Firstly, if a well-known journalist was jailed his popularity soared and with it that of the paper for which he wrote. Secondly, as I have mentioned, since the newspapers could not afford to lose such journalists if they were imprisoned, they kept in their employ students and proofreaders who would go to jail in the event the paper was found guilty of some infraction by the government. As a result, the government changed its tactics and frequently banned publication altogether.

As the organ of the Progressive Party, the *Hōchi shinbun* was considered the flag-bearer of the anti-government forces and an enemy of the state. I made use of my capacity as an editorial writer to advocate parliamentary government, but the more I fought against official oppression the heavier it became, to the point where the paper was often banned on the embarrassing pretext of subverting national security. When this happened, not only were we unable to publish our views but the paper suffered economic loss. Initially the bans were imposed for five to ten days, but the ten days would usually be extended to fifteen and then twenty, and in the end we were often prevented from publishing for as long as four weeks. A ban of this length caused the sales division to complain bitterly. It made it impossible to manage the paper.

Throughout such times the government paper never failed to publish and to deliver copies to our readers. After a month or so, some people, though at first reluctant, became used to reading the government paper and continued to subscribe to it. In this way we continued to lose subscriptions and the odds against us increased.

The main justification for banning our paper lay in our alleged attack on the clan government, but this attack was never more extreme than to demand a prompt opening of parliament. Our criticism of the autocratic government centered on in its exercise of favoritism. We demanded that the parliament be opened so that this wrong could be addressed. Today this would be considered quite reasonable, but as soon as we put it into print the paper was banned.

The other reason given for banning us was what the government called "insulting the bureaucracy." There was in existence a libel law, which included the phrase "regardless of whether or not (the allegation) is true." So if we criticized a bureaucrat we could be sent to jail regardless of whether the criticism was factually correct or not. Thus, for example, if a bureaucrat took a bribe and we reported that he had done so this would be enough for us to be jailed. If we wrote that a bureaucrat had overexcited himself at a geisha party this too was enough for us to be jailed. Of course if an allegation had no basis in truth then punishment was to be expected, but when it could be clearly proven it was absurd that publishing it should be treated as a crime. And so we demanded that the clause stipulating that it did not matter whether an allegation was true or false be struck from the books. This, however, simply led to more bans on publishing! It really was a no-win situation.

The government continued in this way to harass those who championed the people's rights. We needed to keep sales up in order to survive, but the frequent bans on our paper made it increasingly difficult for us. The government's next tactic was to offer dissident writers other opportunities for employment, sometimes even in the government itself. As a result many champions of the people's movement defected to the government side.

I called this operation "taming the Indian tiger." A tiger deprived of food snarls and scratches at first, but it becomes hungrier and hungrier until when it is eventually fed it becomes as tame as a house cat. This was the government's trick. Other men have starved to death rather than give in. We did not starve, but we were not fully alive either. As we were going through this ordeal, Inukai left Tokyo to assist with the establishment of the Progressive Party in Akita in the north east. There he remained for some time as a writer for the *Akita shinbun*, and after his return to Tokyo he left the *Hōchi* and worked for the *Chōya shinbun*. Yano wrote his famous *Keikoku bidan*, for which he received acclaim, and then left for Europe to study, inter alia, the management of newspapers and political parties.[8] Minoura was invited to become chief editor of the *Niigata shinbun* at my recommendation. That left Fujita and myself at the *Hōchi* to try to do the work of the original five, but the difficulties had multiplied and the newspaper was gradually being driven into a corner.

The government must have assumed that if they dealt with the political parties and their affiliated newspapers they could suppress national opinion. In those days there was a popular song which went, "Try as they will to sew up all the pieces, the mouths of men will never be sewn!" The government tried in vain to gag us. The tactics employed were outrageous, and it was not rare for members of the political parties to be jailed or even killed.

Itō Hirobumi had formidable lieutenants in Inoue Kowashi and Ozaki Saburō. They assumed important posts in the government and were thought to have been the real authors of the infamous libel law and newspaper ordinance. The *Chōya shinbun*'s Narishima Ryūhoku attacked them in an article, intentionally mixing up the two men's names. "Once upon a time," he wrote, "there were a couple of cunning bureaucrats whose names were Ozaki Tsuyoshi and Inoue Saburō" Narishima was jailed for this, and I believe that it was also because of some connection with the article that Suehiro Tetchō was put in jail around the same time.

Actually, for people such as Suehiro and Narishima, being "put in jail" in those days did not mean being sent to an ordinary jail, but rather entailed confinement in a special room. Even this must have been a very annoying and inconvenient experience. Those confined in this way were given the freedom to write, however, so the two men wrote constantly, reporting their circumstances in detail.

---

[8] Because of government oppression, many political party strategists followed the example of Disraeli and other Victorians by writing political novels in which leading characters could hold forth on the virtues of constitutional government. Yano Fumio's *Keikoku Bidan*, "A Noble Tale of Statesmanship," is a historical romance based on the life of Epaminondas of Thebes, which set him as a model for aspiring youth in Japan. It was enormously popular.

One of the articles they wrote while being confined was about cleaning their chamber pots. They not only described the exercise but called the job one of the most enjoyable he had during their confinement. It was the only time that they were allowed outside of their small, stuffy room to breathe fresh air. One can only imagine what unpleasant conditions they had to endure if they looked forward to going outside to clean their chamber pots!

Inukai and Shimada suffered kicks and bruises during this same period. Even a gentle person like Minoura was thrown in jail. Being an extremely stubborn man myself and a spearhead of the attacks upon the government, a role that came to be expected of me, I was often the target of their hatred. I have run many risks in my life, but fortunately I managed somehow to avoid being jailed at that time.

As the government stepped up its suppression of political parties, resentment against it filled the nation. The government, which has the responsibility of protecting the people, had become the target of their extreme anger and bitterness. As a poem by the Dowager Empress Shōken puts it, "Just as the shallowest mountain stream will overflow if dammed, so too will the hearts of the people." Unfortunately, the government's oppressive policies not only obstructed the sound development of national opinion, but also resulted in frequent national disturbances.

With the government's imposition of the harsh new regulations governing the right of assembly and the oppressive newspaper ordinance, some of our men, deprived of the freedom to express their convictions and indignant at the intimidating behavior of the local police, began to turn to violence to carry out their objectives.

In August 1882, Kōno Hironaka, who had clashed with the then governor of Fukushima, Mishima Michitsune, organized a meeting of like-minded men to make a pledge that they would "rise against the autocratic government which is the enemy of freedom and elect a government of the people". When a group of ruffians attacked the Kitakata police station in November of the same year, the Fukushima prefectural assembly saw it as an excellent opportunity to destroy the opposition. Kōno was promptly arrested and accused of having plotted the vicious attack. He and fifty other men were subsequently sent to the Tokyo High Court and tried for treason. It was also in November 1882 that a member of the Liberal Party in Niigata prefecture named Akai Kageaki drew up a statement of purpose and rules for a group called the Tenmatsu-tō, and with his comrades began plotting to assassinate several important government ministers. The plot was eventually exposed, and Akai was arrested in April of 1883.

Then, in June 1883, Mishima Michitsune, the governor of Fukushima, moved to Utsunomiya to double as governor of Tochigi, and again clashed with local citizens. As a result of this incident, Kōno Nobemoto (Hironaka's nephew), decided to kill the governor. By chance a gala reception to which all of the important government ministers were invited had been scheduled to mark the opening of a new prefectural government office in Utsunomiya. Kōno and his co-conspirators decided that this was a perfect opportunity to strike, and they pledged that if they were unable to carry out the assassination, they would change their tactics and try to form an army. Thus, when the assassination plot was exposed, sixteen of the group gathered in the Kabayama mountains and attacked the Machio police station with bombs.

In March of 1884, Muramatsu Aizō, Sakurai Heikichi, and a group of followers in Iida city in Nagano prefecture conspired to bring down the government, but this plot was also exposed and they were found guilty of planning an insurrection in November 1885.

It was also in 1884 that Okumiya Takayuki and other members of the Liberal Party began plotting to overthrow the government. They hoped to persuade troops of the Nagoya garrison to join with them and then build a larger force. When a group of them attempted to rob a wealthy mansion along the Gifu Kaidō to procure funds to purchase military provisions, the plot was uncovered. The group was finally convicted in 1892.

From around April of 1884, Yuasa Rihei, Shimizu Shōzaburō, Inoue Momonosuke, Hibi Son, and others became impatient with the self-appointed champions of freedom and civil liberties, whom they claimed only talked of constitutional government. They thought there had been enough idle talk and it was now time for action to arouse the people from their sleep, and they succeeded in mobilizing thousands of men from among the ranks of gamblers, sumo wrestlers, and hunters. The group wielded considerable strength, although it was only for a brief period.

In Shizuoka in 1884, Yamaoka Ototaka, and others organized yet another group which sought to assassinate political figures, because they believed that they could not trust the government with the establishment of a parliament. The plot was discovered in June of 1886 and resulted in many arrests. The series of incidents in Fukushima, Takada, Kabayama, Iida, Nagoya, Gunma, and Shizuoka were all plotted by members of the Liberal Party. Naturally the nation was not sympathetic to these armed uprisings and we too took every opportunity to condemn them. It must not be forgotten, however, that it was government oppression that drove these men to such desperate means.

"Slaying the Sea Monsters"

Apart from the visible oppression meted out against budding political parties, the government also employed insidious means to induce their self-destruction. The sinister hand of the government stretched out first to the Liberal Party. In November of 1882 representatives of the government talked the party's two leaders, Itagaki Taisuke and Gotō Shōjirō, into taking a trip abroad. This was a crucial time for political parties as the opening of the parliament drew nearer. Many members of the Liberal Party had become impoverished after putting their lives and property on the line, while others had had to resort to government employment to make ends meet. It was a time of crisis for the Liberal Party. The rank and file of the party members were unhappy and critical of their leaders for choosing this time to go abroad, leaving the rest to suffer. There were also disturbing rumors about the source of their traveling funds. It was said that the government had paid the expenses of Itagaki and Gotō's trip so as to bring about the self-destruction of the Liberal Party and thus isolate Ōkuma.

Having lost its leaders, the Liberal Party men split between those who supported their leaders' overseas trip and those who opposed it. Ōishi Masami, Baba Tatsui, and Suehiro Tetchō, who had tried in vain to talk Itagaki out of it, decided to leave the party together once they knew the majority were against them. Meanwhile, the government was working on the Progressive Party through what came to be known as the Mitsubishi issue. The Satsuma-Chōshū coalition monopolized the powers of the army, navy, police forces and even private enterprise with the one exception of the shipping industry, which was in the hands of the Mitsubishi group. I did not know what connection there was between Ōkuma and Mitsubishi, but the government suspected that Mitsubishi had grown to its formidable strength under the patronage of Ōkuma while he was in the government and that the Progressive Party's funding came from Mitsubishi. Accordingly, the government embarked on a campaign to crush Mitsubishi, thinking that cutting the logistical line would trap Ōkuma.

Shinagawa Yajirō and his group were particularly important in all of this, and they decided to establish a steamship business called the Kyōdō Transportation Company, and secured a government subsidy to help them do so. Fierce competition erupted between Kyōdō and Mitsubishi, and caused both companies to suffer greatly. Eventually, under the guidance of the government, it was decided that the two should merge. This sounds absurd by today's standards but it took place because the Satsuma-Chōshū coalition still equated political battles with military ones. The initial objective was to take away Mitsubishi's shipping rights, but the government ended up using the incident to drive a wedge between the Progressive Party and the Liberal Party.

Once the government began to mount its attack on Mitsubishi, the Liberal Party seized the opportunity to assault its political rivals, crying "Down with these treacherous businessmen! Down with the pseudo-party!" Because the Progressive Party's connections to the shipping industry were at the center of all of this, the Liberal Party described their campaign against us as "Slaying the Sea Monsters." We were challenged to take up the gauntlet. Fully aware that the government had masterminded the plot to engage the two political parties in a dogfight and knowing only too well that we were being manipulated to play its game, we fought back fiercely.

As one of the *Hōchi shinbun*'s editorial writers, I had just started my political career with the Progressive Party and promptly involved myself in this battle. I fought it with my pen and with my mouth. Unfortunately, my gifts as a speaker were as feeble as ever. Whenever I was invited to speak in public I would always accept but my speeches would usually flop. I rarely received any applause and my words were often summarily dismissed. To my chagrin, those whom I secretly despised often made brilliant speeches. Even then I was not motivated to improve my skills. On the contrary, I despised speech-making, and rather than trying to do something about my appalling lack of talent I stuck to my dreadful style, telling myself that what mattered was not the art of oratory but simply saying what was on my mind.

In March 1883, I went on a speaking tour of the Tōkaidō with Yano. Transportation was inconvenient and slow in those days and we spent the first night in Kanagawa, traveling on to Odawara the second day in rickshaws. We took our time as we made for Kyoto, speaking on the way and enlisting new members into our party.

It was a leisurely trip but we had to remain vigilant as interference from the Liberal Party might await us at every spot. Our speech meetings were low-key, as those attracted to the Progressive Party were generally well off and well read and therefore men of moderation who disliked trouble. Eventually we reached Nagoya, where we put up at an inn that doubled as a restaurant. There we met with local leaders, through whom we sought to enlist supporters for the Progressive Party. One day a notorious leader of the Liberal Party, Naitō Rōichi, arrived with a mob of thirty or so men and demanded to see us. Naitō was skilled at jūdō or kendō, and when the attempt was made on Itagaki's life in Gifu he was reputed to have picked up the would-be assassin and thrown him across the room. When he approached us he squared his shoulders and demanded to know why the *Hōchi shinbun* did not attack Mitsubishi, a plague on the nation. It looked as if we would be in for some trouble if we did not give the right answer.

Yano began by expressing his condolences on the misfortune that had befallen the Liberal Party's president, and told the ruffian that he had sent Itagaki some gifts. He then assured the man that his question would be looked into as soon as we returned to Tokyo. If the accusations he made turned out to be true then the newspaper would carry an appropriate article. Since Yano had the manners of a gentleman, Naito and his men were satisfied that their purpose had been served. Next they turned to me to make sure that I had concurred. I had only to say "absolutely" and it would have ended there. But I did not. I was disgusted at the way Naitō had blackmailed us by turning up with his group of thugs, and so I said I was not in agreement. It was none of his business who our newspaper chose to attack. I did not have any kind of weapon on me, I never do, and sometimes it proves better not to have one. Sure enough, the group turned on me, shouting, "Throw him out of the window! Beat him to death!" Naitō controlled them, however, saying that as long as they had Yano's word they need not bother with a young fellow like Ozaki. Among his men were some who were later involved in the Nagoya and Kabayama incidents and who even committed murder. I suppose we were lucky to get out of the situation as we did.

Following this encounter, they continued to make a nuisance of themselves during our whole stay in Nagoya. If we went out for a walk they would make a scene on the road and when we organized public meetings they came to disrupt them. Naitō's brother was a rascal as well and came to our speeches with a big bamboo stick with which to frighten Progressive Party men away. At that time the Naitō brothers were known and feared by all of the roughnecks around Japan.

PARTIES DISBAND AND REORGANIZE

In June 1883 the Liberal Party's president, Itagaki, returned to Japan. His countrymen welcomed him back, anxious to know what the man said to be a "god" of the movement for liberty and people's rights had learned in Europe, where the ideas he championed had originally come from. Half a year abroad had changed Itagaki's thinking. The change disappointed other members of the Liberal Party, however. He explained that his observations of Europe led him to conclude that the progress which had been made there in improving social conditions was so great that political developments could hardly keep up. In Japan, on the other hand, progress had been made in politics alone, while the level of social development remained low. Man needed to learn how to live before he needed government, Itagaki said, and he pointed to the situation in Europe as evidence of this natural law at work. He regretted the situation in Japan where the cart was put before the horse. People's lives were being neglected at the expense of politics. The road ahead for Japan, Itagaki argued, lay in improving people's lives rather than political reform. In other words, he admonished members of the Liberal Party for their impatient radicalism, telling them that they should not neglect the need to nurture the strength of civil society.

It was inevitable that the young and ambitious Liberal Party men should be greatly disappointed at the change that had come over their leader. It was regrettable that as a result of this the extremists within the party resorted to suicidal measures responsible for the violent outbreaks described earlier. Frequent violent outbreaks by Liberal Party men earned the unanimous condemnation of the nation. The government took advantage of the situation and increased its oppression. The Liberal Party, already suffering from difficulty in raising funds, found it difficult even to stay in existence. Eventually its leaders came to the conclusion that it was wiser for them to dissolve the party and attempt to reform it at a later date than to let it die a slow death. Accordingly, at its convention in Osaka in October 1884, the Liberal Party dissolved itself. It had been in existence for just three years.

The dying embers of the Liberal Party sent a disheartening spark over to the Progressive Party, which was experiencing administrative troubles of its own at the time. It was Kōno Togama who took the lead in advocating the dissolution of the party. I took the opposite view, urging the need to maintain it at all costs. Severely restricted as we were by government suppression, it was an extremely discouraging time and those in favor of dissolution were in the majority. A directors' meeting for the purpose of coming to an official decision was held by those us who were in Tokyo.

All of this took place in 1884. In spite of the fact that it was a vital meeting to decide the fate of the party, fewer than thirty people attended. I could not but lament the sad fall of our movement. Nonetheless, though a minority, there were quite a few among our party members who shared my conviction that we should keep going. While they were not officially qualified to attend the meeting there were several others who asked to be allowed to sit in as observers. There were about eight young men among them who were just fresh out of school, including Sakamoto Moritoku and Edamoto Nagatatsu. It was by no means a small matter that they should be allowed to be present, but the chairman, Kōno Togama, made a special exception for them, and they took their seats in one corner. Kōno was from Tosa and had held a cabinet post at one time. He was an interesting person but a man of harsh words at times as well. He began the meeting by welcoming the observers and members present.

We debated the question of dissolution hotly. Kōno was adamant and so was I, reinforced by Numa, who for some unknown reason was now on my side. The meeting was inconclusive and ended with a resolution that responsibility for making the final decision over the fate of the party should be given to its president, Ōkuma. Kōno, on behalf of those who favored dissolution, Kitabatake Harufusa, for those opposed, and Maejima Mitsuru, for those who remained neutral, were chosen to visit Ōkuma together.

Shortly after that the three men called on Ōkuma in the house he then occupied in the Waseda district of Tokyo. They reported to him on the course of our meeting and asked for his judgement. I never was able to ascertain exactly what Ōkuma said to them, but the three were satisfied that he had conveyed to them the decision that they would present to us at a meeting to be held two days later. It was a strange report indeed, for while Kōno informed us that Ōkuma had judged in favor of dissolution, Kitabatake said he had decided against it and Maejima said he did not quite know which was right. The three had heard Ōkuma together and each had interpreted his words differently.

Listening to them, I was amazed at the wide discrepancy between their versions of what had transpired. Ōkuma was a grand old man. I guessed that he had treated Kōno, Kitabatake, and Maejima as if they were small children. Whatever the old man told them made each of them happy. The ability of the three men to understand what he had said in as many ways puzzled me so much that for a time this absorbed me more than the question of the party's future.

After several months I realized that, notwithstanding any peculiarities of his own which might help to account for Ōkuma's mixed message, the district of Saga where he came from had certain peculiar ways of communication. People there used ambiguous terms that satisfied all of their listeners while making none angry. It was this Saga style of communication that Ōkuma occasionally employed. At the time of that infamous dispute over the proposed Korean expedition, Ōkuma's attitude became an issue, and Itagaki in particular became extremely cross at what seemed to be Ōkuma's double-talk. I eventually realized what had happened. Ōkuma must have pulled out his secret weapon from Saga.

Saga, of course, is not entirely exceptional in this regard and there are other regions with a similarly ambiguous manner of speaking, but the people of Saga seem to be especially good at it. Many years later, in 1892 or 1893, I was a member of a committee looking into the question of government interference in a recent election, and I went with Nakano Takeo to interrogate the incumbent home minister, Ōki Takatō. I recall bluntly questioning the minister as to whether he had interfered in the election or not, but I never received a firm answer one way or the other.

Then there was Matsuda Masahisa who was also notorious for being ambiguous and habitually noncommittal. He was in fact extremely bright and was perfectly able to express himself quite categorically whenever he wished to do so. In any case, Saga style or not, there was nothing to be done so long as the party was unable to make up its mind. Some of us decided to stir things up a bit. We were not ready to let the party dissolve just when we were so close to the opening of the parliament. We even said there was no need for the special school at Waseda, which we had established for the purpose of instilling our ideas into young men and training like-minded fighters. We might as well set fire to the school. This finally drove mild-mannered Ōkuma in to a rare fury.

Ōkuma was extremely cheerful by nature, and not at all easily annoyed. I had had a long association with him and had never once seen him betray a moment's anger. But this time was the exception. I had not said anything to him directly, but I was told that he was enraged at what I had said in public. This was very unusual. Normally, as I say, he never showed anger, which was no doubt one of the reasons for his longevity.

Some of us still adamantly insisted on holding on to the party even at the risk of again incurring his wrath. We could not let the matter rest unresolved any longer and decided that we must hear directly what Ōkuma had to say. It was then that Ōkuma took the initiative. He declared that with the party split beyond remedy he would resign from it with the other senior members, Kōno, Kitabatake, and Maejima. And he left what remained of it to those of us who wanted to keep it alive. I realized then that if he had decided on resigning from the party he was after all neither for dissolution nor against it.

It was now December of 1884. Numa Morikazu, Shimada Saburō, Nakano Takeo, Fujita Mokichi, Minoura Katsutō, Koezuka Tatsu, and I met at the Progressive Party office in Tokyo's Kanda Naka Sarugaku-cho district and decided to remain with the party and rebuild it. It was an uphill battle. Even when it was under the big umbrella of Ōkuma the party had had a hard time managing itself. Now suddenly left without its head, the party was in a worse situation than ever. Government pressure increased still more and our hands and feet were tied. Few people came to our public meetings, the newspaper subscriptions continued to fall off, and more members resigned.

Political parties, as we have seen, were to all intents and purposes unable to operate as a result of government oppression, so we decided to create a club which we called the Meiji Kyōkai, and looked for weak-minded people who would not join a political party, but were willing to join a non-political social club. This did not work either. The club hardly existed except in name. These were hard times for political parties.

The Men of the Progressive Party

Earlier I mentioned that the core of the Progressive Party consisted of Numa, leader of the Ōmei-sha, Yano of the Tōyō Gisei-kai, and Ono Azusa, who dominated the Ōto-kai. Ono was a man who was easily on a par with Yano and Numa, but he was, if anything, too hard -working and literally worked himself to death. Had he lived longer, he would have made a great contribution to the country. It was a tragic loss.

Ono was not only a capable activist but a fine academic as well. His collected works, which were published after his death, show that he managed to write in his diary every day in spite of his busy life. We learn from the diary that each evening he gathered a group of young people at his home and lectured to them. It was Ono's efforts that created the basis of what became today's Waseda University. Although Yano, Numa, and Ono were all Ōkuma's followers, there were some slight areas of friction between them. Numa was the most powerful among them. In contrast to Yano who was a gentleman, he was known for his arrogance and lack of courtesy. He was a talented man though, and while he had two brothers who were also very capable, he was clearly the brightest in the family.

Numa began his career as a student of military tactics and was an instructor in the army of the Tokugawa Shogunate before the Restoration. During the Restoration war, he served as an officer in the Shogunal forces and led a group of his trainees into battle against the forces headed by Itagaki at Nikkō Imaichi. Itagaki was impressed with his young adversary and invited Numa to Tosa as an instructor in Western-style military drill and training. This episode tells us something about Itagaki's character, but it also suggests that Numa was a person of ability from very early on. Numa's arrogant personality did not go down well with the soldiers, however, and it is said that they in fact rebelled against him and forced him to flee.

Numa was later recruited by the new Meiji government as a bureaucrat. Even while he held a government post he earned fame as a campaigner for people's rights, and after he resigned from the government he founded the *Mainichi shimbun*, established the Ōmei-sha and continued to champion the movement for freedom and people's rights.

He had his idiosyncrasies too and managed his financial affairs in an unusual way. He was, to put it bluntly, a miser. He took home the left-overs from the cheap lunch box provided in the Tokyo municipal assembly, and though among the richest of the politicians, he never kept his own ricksha, but called one when he needed it. He was proud of picking the most run-down rickshaws pulled by old men with whom he haggled over the price of the ride. Prices were low in those days. A banquet in Shimbashi or Yanagibashi cost less than three yen a head. When it was Numa's turn to make the arrangements he would settle for a charge of one yen or one and a half yen per person even with a geisha present. His secret was to walk in the geisha town until he spotted one who was obviously without work, then ask her to come over without charging as she had the time to spare. Numa could get away with this because he had the resources as well as a name, and no else was able to imitate him.

There was one occasion when Numa and I left together for Ibaragi prefecture to speak on behalf of the Progressive Party. One night we stayed at a temple, and in the middle of the night I was startled when he climbed into my bed. It was not that long after the Restoration and the evil practices of male-male love were still quite common. Suspecting that he harbored unwelcome intentions I hit him with my fist. With a moan he tumbled onto the floor and back to his own bed. The next morning I confronted him and said that he had behaved in an unacceptable fashion. He apologized, but then showed me how his nightshirt was muddied and explained that while he could not remember anything now he seemed not only to have climbed into my bed, but also to have fallen into the garden during the night! So, along with his other peculiarities, it turned out that Numa was a terrible sleep walker!

Shimada Saburō and Koizuka Ryū both belonged to Numa's group. Together they were a powerful faction within the Progressive Party. Over time, Inukai and I, who both belonged to Yano's group, argued with them on many issues. Shimada was the most impressive of them all, and it was not long before I had my clashes with him. No doubt partly because of my own immaturity, I had a tendency to clash with people who seemed impressive to me. If I had collaborated with Shimada, it would probably have made the Progressive Party much stronger, but I chose instead to make him a rival. Thinking back on things I realize that when Inukai and I were junior officials in the government, Shimada had already risen several grades higher up in the bureaucracy. In this sense, if I had been a more respectful person, my relationship with him should really have been that of a subordinate. Bowing my head was never my style, however, so it was probably inevitable that we should end up arguing with each other.

When I stood up to Shimada, Inukai, who was like a brother to me, naturally took my side. Other members likewise took their places either in the Shimada faction or the Ozaki faction. Those in the Ono faction threw their support behind Shimada but later the members of his own faction moved over to my side. In any case, the conflict with me certainly had an adverse effect on Shimada's career. Later, out of guilt for what had happened I befriended Shimada, and when he was appointed Speaker I did what I could to help him behind the scenes. In the end, however, the appointment did not go well for him.

Shimada had many strengths and should certainly have been able to achieve more. He spoke well and made a name for himself as an orator long before I did. He eclipsed the rest of us in speaking up for reason and justice and calling a spade a spade. Unlike many of his colleagues in the Ōmei-sha he never used a cooing voice or affected gestures. His speech gave one the impression of a wide flowing river. He wrote extremely well too, in a style that reminded one of the T'ang dynasty Lu Hsüan-kung. Shimada's popularity as a speaker lost its allure in the eyes of the public because of Inukai's powerful criticisms. Inukai made an art of derisive language and sarcasm, and was extremely good at finding colorful ways to cut people down. He was the first to make fun of my old pen-name "Kinsen," which he said sounded like something a female artist or masseur would use. I had to agree that Kinsen was a weak name so I changed it to "Gakudō." When Inukai criticized my choice by noting that it was the word for school in Chinese, I was able to get the better of him by pointing out that his pen-name "Bokudō" meant a shed for storing wood in Chinese—and was thus much more absurd. Playing on Shimada's first name, Saburō, Inukai used to call him "Shaberō," which means a fellow who talks too much. It was a sharp way of lampooning Shimada's eloquence, but it certainly took the shine off the flowing oratory which he had once used to impress his audiences.

The other person who could rival Shimada in his reputation as a speaker was Baba Tatsuo. Baba had recently returned from abroad with Kaneko Kentarō, and spoke with confidence on a wide range of topics. He was not in Japan for long before leaving again for America, however. Apart from these men, the Ōmeisha had some impressive speakers in Tsunoda Shimpei, Koezuka Tatsu, and Taguchi Ukichi. Taguchi spoke haltingly but moved his audience because he was very clear about what he wanted to communicate.

By contrast, our group, the Tōyō Giseikai, had little popular appeal because none of us were particularly good speakers, and that included Yano, Fujita, Inukai, Minoura, and myself. Among us the most amusing was Minoura. Speaking once in summer in a hall that had been opened on all sides because of the heat, the text of his speech, which he had with him on the rostrum, was blown away by a sudden gust of wind. He calmly told the audience they would have to wait until his notes had been gathered up, as if this were an entirely normal thing.

If the same thing had happened to me I would have improvised somehow without the text, but Minoura had a different style. Much later I happened to attend a meeting in England at which Gladstone, in the course of a speech before a crowd of thousands, also lost part of his notes. The prime minister stopped talking altogether and waited in silence until someone brought the errant pages back to him. I immediately remembered Minoura, and thought to myself how similar some things could be in East and West.

I Go to Shanghai as a Correspondent

In 1884, with China and France at loggerheads over Annam and amid fear that war might break out at any time, I went to Shanghai to cover the story for the *Hōchi shinbun*. The Japanese worship of China at the time was feverish, and went well beyond our present day worship of the West. Of course, even then worship of the West was quite common. I personally disliked both tendencies and thought that a war between China and France would afford an excellent opportunity to observe the true worth of each.

Traditional *Kangaku* or "Chinese Studies" was a discipline established by the Chinese back in an age of barbarism, when they believed their country to be at the center of the world, and the Japanese had simply accepted this view without questioning it. The Chinese called their own country the "Middle Flower" or the "Middle Kingdom" and the inhabitants of foreign lands "barbarians." The Japanese, true to form, imitated them, and called the people of England, America, and France "distant barbarians" too. Japanese scholars like Ogyū Sorai were even so shameless as to refer to themselves as "Eastern barbarians." It was as a result of this kind of thinking that we Japanese learned Chinese characters before our own language, and had to use Chinese characters for whatever we wanted to write.[9]

Considering that even today we cannot express ourselves in writing without using Chinese characters, one can readily imagine how pervasive was the worship of China among the young in a period when learning meant mainly the study of Chinese. There were a few who had studied English but only as a secondary subject in addition to those traditionally required in Chinese studies. In my case too, as recounted earlier, I began by studying Chinese, followed by Japanese studies and then English subjects. Even during the period of transition from shogunal rule to the restored monarchy, students in Edo (Tokyo) who came from the southwestern regions were the envy of their peers when they headed home for the vacations, for they would be traveling in the direction of the "land of the masters." This, of course, meant China, birthplace of Confucius and Mencius. Literary meetings in those days were always being organized around visiting diplomats from China.

As I had been raised on Chinese studies myself I could not expect to be completely free of Chinese thought, but I felt that the fever of China worship needed to be cooled down. Before departing for Shanghai I wrote as follows in the *Hōchi*:

> It cannot be denied that when Japan began its history of intercourse with Korea and China the civilization of these two countries excelled our own. Today, however, the positions have been reversed. We have become the most advanced country of the Orient whereas China and Korea have fallen far behind. . . . It is now our turn to take the initiative to guide these two countries, free them from their obstinate habits, and develop their knowledge. While this will serve to repay all that we have benefitted from them in the past sixteen hundred years, it is at the same time in the interest of our own country to do so. This is the weighty mission that the author expects this country and all scholars of Chinese studies to undertake.

I also wrote that it was most disagreeable to see our Chinese scholars demean themselves with their worship of China:

> Our Chinese scholars wave their flag of surrender at China without even doing battle. If they do not actually call themselves the eastern barbarians they fall into the same obsequious trap when they call China by such fawning names as "Middle Flower" and "Middle Kingdom." I cannot but lament this excessive adulation on their part.

[9] Ozaki here overlooks the fact that there was no way of writing Japanese before the entry of Chinese characters, which provided the base for the phonetic syllabary of Japanese. For a discussion of Ogyū and other Tokugawa scholars, see Marius B. Jansen, *China in the Tokugawa World* (Cambridge, Mass.: Harvard University Press, 1992).

In any case, I firmly believed that the war between France and China would provide an opportunity to assess China's real strength, and it was with this in mind that I left Yokohama for Shanghai by boat on August 26. Besides myself, the other reporters on board were Honda Magoshirō of the *Jiji Shimpō*, Nagano Kazue of the *Asahi Shinbun*, and Mori Jōta of the *Hokushin Nippō*. Also with us were Watanabe Yutaka from the postal service and Komuro Nobusuke of the Liberal Party.

In those days the Japanese knew little about the West, so a trip to Shanghai was something to boast about when one returned. Progressives like Yokoi Shōnan also went there to broaden their knowledge.[10] At that time it was usual for visitors to Shanghai to return with Western-style suits they had had tailored there. As soon as Japanese visitors arrived, tailors would call on them at their hotels and flatter them into ordering suits, saying that "those who had suits made there made good" when they returned to Japan.

Reasoning that it would be impossible to learn all about China in the course of a short trip, I resolved to learn as much as I could before my departure. Accordingly, I called on everyone I could find who had lived in or frequently visited China. Once there, I decided, I would learn as much as possible about the present situation from those who were already there ahead of me. I studiously did as I had planned.

However, after a month or so in Shanghai I began to feel that much of what I had learned might have been misleading. Conscious of the fact that I had only been there a few weeks and had not yet had time to learn how to judge things for myself I tried to dismiss my suspicion that people who had lived there for three or four years might be wrong. As the weeks passed though, I felt more and more that my fears were well founded. After two months the conviction was stronger than ever. I learned too that the saying "seeing is believing" did not apply to observing something as huge as a country. One's eyes could easily deceive one.

The truth of this became increasingly clear to me in the course of subsequent trips abroad. There were those who found fault with everything they saw in the West and became ultra nationalists, and there were also those who marveled at everything in sight and became overly zealous imitators of all things Western. In order to see things as they truly are, however, it is necessary to discard all prejudices. This is a challenge for us Japanese, as we tend to be very one-sided.

Anyway, on my arrival in Shanghai I found the city in great confusion as the Chinese army prepared to march. I was amazed at what I saw. Many of the soldiers carried guns that were rusty. Some carried their guns upside down. Others carried them on their backs together with umbrellas and lanterns and miscellaneous pieces of equipment. Flagbearers and drummers carried them. The men were in good spirits, but not fit for war. At their head was a general, perhaps seventy years old, riding in a fine palanquin. Behind him came a succession of other palanquins.

---

[10] Yokoi (1809–1869), who was assassinated by an anti-foreign zealot shortly after the Tokugawa fall, was a leading reformer intellectual of the 1860s. He himself did not, however, travel to China.

When I asked who was in them I was told that it was his mistresses. This appalled me. Even a civilian like myself could tell that China was unprepared for war.

That day a local newspaper carried a report on the battle in Fukien written by two of the Chinese ministers. It was hideously warped and not worth reading. Indeed, the most creative writer of fiction could not have concocted such rubbish. The articles were obviously not based on fact, but were sheerly products of the imagination of the writers. They were further examples of the same Chinese predilection for hyperbole that describes a twelve-inch beard as being three thousand meters long.

With their highly developed literary gifts, the Chinese are skilled at describing places and objects in a flowery and aesthetic manner far removed from the real thing. A six-foot-wide path becomes an avenue, a small bridge over a ditch is transformed into the Northern Flower-Perfume Bridge or some such thing, and a shack by a pond metamorphoses into the Mid-Lake Tea House. This is how the Chinese always dress up facts with a copious use of rhetoric. Nor does it end with descriptions of scenes and objects. The same kinds of exaggeration are liberally applied to people and events as well.

My stay in China led me to conclude that in order to cure the Chinese of the arrogance they maintained in spite of their lack of real power and their state of disorder, and to cure the Japanese of their excessive veneration of China, the two countries would have to fight it out. I suggested this to various people I met, but none took me seriously. Among those with whom I discussed my idea was General Fukushima Yasumasa, then a lieutenant or colonel, who happened to be returning to Japan on the same ship as myself from a field survey in northern China. His reaction, however, was simply one of surprise. He might well have been a Sinophile like so many others, but whatever the reason he had not reached the same conclusion as I had, even after his fact-finding mission.

The war between France and China that I had hoped to observe ended abruptly, and the only real fighting took place when a French warship launched an attack on a shipyard in Fukien province. This meant I had hardly any opportunity of performing a comparative study of the national strength of the two countries as I had intended. Under the circumstances, it was not much use staying there, so I packed my things and started back for home.

I had allowed my brother Yukitaka to accompany me to Shanghai, thinking that it would be an excellent opportunity for him to broaden his experience and knowledge. My ulterior motive in permitting this was that I had hoped he would one day serve as my secretary. It was my considered opinion that a good statesman had to have a first-class secretary, a secretary who could be trusted. Who could be better suited for such a job than one's own brother? Being in Shanghai made it possible to observe to both Eastern and Western learning better than when one was in Japan. My brother seemed more gifted than I and quickly picked up English. He was to remain in Shanghai after my return home to train himself to be a good secretary. Unfortunately, his elder brother remained a poor journalist and could not afford to employ a secretary. So, Yukitaka had no job to come back to after all.

I RECOMMEND THE CONQUEST OF CHINA

By the time I returned home in early November my theory had grown into a conviction that China must be conquered. No sooner had I got back than an armed uprising erupted in Seoul, which rapidly developed into a hostile confrontation between Japan, Korea, and China. The root cause of the incident was the conflict between the progressives and conservatives within Korea.

The Korean progressives were led by Pak Yong-hyo, Kim Ok-kyun, and So Kwang-yong. These three had all studied in Japan where they witnessed the development of modern institutions. After returning to their country they had urged upon the government the need for change. The conservatives in power, however, with China as their patron, rejected the idea of reform.

The clash between the two Korean factions, which took place on December 7, was quickly carried to the Japanese legation, which was surrounded by a mob of conservatives and set on fire. Minister Takezoe escaped with the legation staff, troops and other Japanese citizens, to the consulate in Inchon. As soon as the incident was reported by telegraph to the Japanese government and then out to the nation, opinion split over how the situation should be dealt with.[11]

Previously I had been of the opinion that China, Korea, and Japan should jointly prepare for the aggression of the West. As a result of my trip to China, however, I had changed my mind. Having observed the apathy and corruption of the Chinese people, I felt collaboration was now out of the question. Japan should take it upon itself to assist Korea to achieve complete independence. One way to achieve this, to my mind, was to negotiate the return of the Korean regent, Taewon'gun, from China where he had been detained. This was the subject of one of my editorials.

Taewon'gun was a close relative of the Korean king, who wielded considerable political power. He had been incriminated as an instigator of an uprising in July 1882, however, and had subsequently been arrested and detained in China. In spite of this, he continued to enjoy wide popularity and those in Korea who most wished to see him returned to power were those who disliked Japan. Negotiating the release of Taewon'gun on behalf of the Korean government, I argued, would be welcomed not only by the progressives but by the conservatives too, all of whom longed for his return. This would help win for Japan the confidence of the whole Korean nation. The Korean problem was deeply related to the Chinese problem, and I wrote a number of essays with titles such as "Our National Policy towards China and Korea" and "War and Peace" in which I argued for an aggressive policy vis-à-vis China.

With regard to Japanese policy towards China and Korea I argued as follows, "If we are to take the initiative and have the countries of the East compete with the West, it is imperative that we first form an alliance with China and Korea and guide them, and second, that they should not be left to the mercy of the Western

---

[11] For a better account of these events, see "The Japanese and the Korean Reform Movement," in Peter Duus, *The Abacus and the Sword: The Japanese Penetration of Korea, 1895–1910* (Berkeley, Cal.: University of California Press, 1995), pp. 51–60.

powers." I examined Japan's relations with our two neighboring countries and their respective political situations and concluded that Japan should assist Korea, but fight China.

It was my view that the Koreans were alert and observant, and capable of judging developments both domestically and internationally. They knew their weaknesses and were willing to learn from the strength of others. If the Japanese dealt with them at both official and private levels with courtesy and kindness, they would develop a deeper respect for Japan as their society progressed. It would not be so difficult to assist Korea to gain its independence. All that was needed was to expand our Korean policy sufficiently to nurture the gratitude of the Korean court and people.

As far as China was concerned, however, I argued that while there were some Chinese who recognized the vigor of our people and feared the bravery of our armed forces, the great majority of Chinese, who were uneducated and obstinate, remained arrogant and ignorant of developments outside their country. Such persons had nothing but contempt for Japan simply because of our small land area and population. Those who had studied here and were in a position to explain the developments in our country had learned what they knew from Japanese devotees of Chinese studies who were poorly informed about national affairs. Mingling with them, Chinese students were exposed to a terrible jumble of stories about financial troubles and abandonment of "the Way" and thus came to the conclusion that there was only chaos and confusion in Japan, and further reinforced their scorn for our nation. For this reason, I urged all Japanese with a clear sense of vision to abandon the fantasy of helping China, see that it was not able to be helped, and set the course of our national policy accordingly. The Western powers had already begun to dismember China, and in order for Japan to seize the opportunity afforded by developments there, I argued for the conquest of China.

At the time, the Japanese government was negotiating with the Koreans who had the power of China behind them. In this situation, an aggressive stance on the part of Japan could develop into a war with China over Korea. I was of the view and continued forcefully to argue that since Japan was likely to win such a war, we should not be fearful of provoking it and should therefore press for resolution of the Korean issue. The government dispatched Inoue Kaoru as ambassador plenipotentiary to negotiate with his Korean counterpart, Kim Hong-jip. As a result of these negotiations, the Koreans agreed to pay the cost of reconstructing our legation as well as providing compensation to the Japanese who had been evacuated. Other details were settled, the agreement was signed, and the Inoue returned to Japan on January 19, 1885.

I was the only person who advocated taking a hardline posture vis-à-vis the Chinese government over the Korean incident. As a consequence of talking and writing about this as much as I did, gradually the national opinion was awakened and people criticized the Inoue mission for returning from Korea without negotiating with the Chinese side. Yet, the government could not avoid negotiating with China for long and it soon dispatched a special mission headed by none other than Itō Hirobumi. The mission left Yokohama on February 28, 1885 and arrived in Beijing on March 21. From there they traveled to Tientsin, arriving finally on April 1. In Tientsin, negotiations took place with the Chinese viceroy and ambassador plenipotentiary, Li Hung-chang. In the end, both sides agreed to withdraw their troops from Korea.

It was just around this time that Yano returned to Japan. This was something I had been looking forward to eagerly. After having lived for two years in the West he brought many new ideas with him and promptly embarked on a major reform of the *Hōchi shinbun*. My hopes and expectations were quickly betrayed. Yano cut the size of the paper to make it more appealing to a mass readership, saying that it must sell. The *Hōchi* had always been a large paper—large enough to use as a floor mat—but now was reduced to one-third or even one-quarter of its original size. Yano wanted to turn it into a small tabloid newspaper. Also, it had been the rule for major newspapers to print Chinese poems, but Yano decided to cut them now in favor of the more popular Japanese haiku and senryu. Major newspapers also prided themselves on having an educated readership that did not need Japanese *kana* glosses alongside Chinese characters to be able to read them, but Yano decided that such aids should now be employed for all Chinese characters. This was his contribution to making newspapers more accessible to ordinary people.

At the same time, Yano was also responsible for the creation of a press agency. The Teikoku Tsushin-sha or Imperial Press Agency, which was the first press agency in Japan, was created by Takemura Yoshisada at Yano's suggestion. Yano was also involved in publishing something along the lines of a weekly pictorial magazine.

In any case, Yano's reforms at the *Hōchi* proved successful, and the newspaper, which had suffered in his absence, was revitalized and enjoyed great success. In spite of this, however, I was unhappy. I was something of a purist, devoted to guiding society with debates and argument, so I had spoken up against Yano's management philosophy, saying that a newspaper should not sacrifice its self-respect by playing down to its readers. Yano would not listen because he was determined to put his newly acquired knowledge into practice. As a result, the paper lost its magic for many of us. It was Fujita who first left the *Hōchi* to become a freelancer, and eventually I went too. Even so, I still kept up a relationship with the *Hōchi* as an occasional contributor. Meanwhile, at Inukai's invitation, I went to work for the *Chōya shinbun*.

After the death of its founder, Narishima Ryūhoku, Suehiro Shigeyasu had taken over as editor of the *Chōya*, but the paper was not successful as it had been under Narishima. In addition to Suehiro the staff writers there were Inukai, Machida Tadaharu, Takimoto Seiichi, and myself. A little later we were joined by Yoshida Karoku, who had just returned from abroad. It was an impressive team, who continued to advocate with zeal the need for parliamentary government.

The *Chōya shinbun* gradually gained in popularity, but because it was the spearhead of anti-government forces it was frequently banned for what it had printed.

Each time, it cost the paper several thousand yen. Repeated bans, therefore, were enough to plunge the newspaper into economic difficulty.

Political literature was quite popular in those days. With a national parliament still unrealized and freedom of speech severely limited, many political activists found an outlet in writing fiction. I have already mentioned Yano's *Keikoku Bidan*, which sold extremely well. I too followed the trend and wrote a political novel called *Shin Nippon* or *New Japan*. The main character in my story was a brilliant, young, beautiful woman. It was not a bad story, as far as it went, but the heroine's conversation was uncompromisingly political, and Inukai commented that she was a very strange woman who seemed much more like a man. My style of writing was too earnest and Inukai's jab was only to be expected. It really was a waste of time. I continued to work for the *Chōya shinbun* until 1888, when I was "banished from Edo" for violating the security ordinance.

NUMA AND I BATTLE IN THE TOKYO ASSEMBLY

In 1885, I was elected to the Tokyo Metropolitan Assembly from the district of Nihonbashi. The assembly had first met in 1879 but eligibility was limited to those over the age of twenty-five so I had had to wait until I was old enough.

The Tokyo assembly included among its members Hatoyama Kazuo, Masujima Rokuichi, Ōoka Ikuzō, Tsunoda Shinpei, Takagi Masatoshi, and Inukai Tsuyoshi—a formidable list. Another member who was particularly strong, was Numa Morikazu. He was an "old hand" in the assembly, having held a seat from October of 1879, and because a large number of the members were his supporters, his influence was strongly felt. After a scandal forced Fukuchi Genichirō to resign as speaker of the assembly, Numa had taken over, and this had further strengthened the position of his faction, who made life extremely difficult for any outsiders. The financial contribution of rural county areas to the assembly's budget was quite small, and so members for such areas in particular were dismissed as if they were no better than beggars.

Numa and his faction were our rivals within the Progressive Party, and although they could be counted on to join us over national issues and to fight as loyal comrades, nonetheless within the metropolitan assembly I became embroiled in a major battle with Numa. I could not stand his arbitrary and arrogant ways and so, in spite of the fact that I was still a newcomer, I refused to take notice of anything he said. Taking the side of the rural county members, I began to argue with him. This, of course, pleased the county members no end, and I'm sure they wished to make me leader of the "anti-Numa faction." After the next election, anti-Numa members from county and other areas joined together to ensure that people from their group were elected to one of the assembly's standing committees. I was one of those elected in this way.

Numa, who had had unchallenged power in the assembly in the past, was furious over the election of three new faces to the standing committee. He promptly plotted to oust me from the group and contrived to engineer the resignation of

nearly all the other members of the committee including even Inukai. He calculated that with all the powerful members of the committee resigning the rest of
us would be forced to follow. I would not resign, however, and said that I could
even handle the business of the committee single-handedly if necessary. Kōno
Togama also refused to resign. Having worked with Numa in the general assembly, he did not think that it was consistent for Numa to refuse to work with him
now in the standing committee. Since Kōno was an important member of the
Progressive Party and senior to Numa, his plan was temporarily foiled. Eventually, however, the Numa group did somehow manage to convince Kōno to resign.
Even then, I refused to do so.

Numa and I could not come to terms and he took it out on me in many different
ways, which only strengthened my determination to resist. On one occasion the
county members were being attacked on tax issues. I took their side and argued
against Numa who swore at me and finally, shouted that someone such as myself
who was not even capable of calculating how much interest was due to be paid
on his loans, had no business speaking on a local tax matter.

Numa's accusations were not groundless. My life was at its lowest ebb and I
was practically destitute. I had left the *Hōchi shinbun* by then for the *Chōya
shinbun* but my salary was very small. The little that I earned had to support my
wife and child and a couple of secretaries, and my involvement in politics was
causing my family severe hardship. I remember one New Year's holiday, perhaps
that of 1887, when my wife, brother, and the two secretaries had wanted to play
cards. There was not a pack of cards in the house, so I said that one of them
should go out and buy a pack, but we did not have enough money in the house.
A pack of cards would have cost a mere fifty sen or at most one yen, but we did
not have even that much between us. I had never felt so miserable over such a
little thing. I had been used to living in penury for so long that I had become
hardened to it, but on this occasion for some reason I felt real pain.

Then there was another time when I stayed up all night to listen to the bells
ring in the New Year and the lamp ran out of oil. I had to sell some of my books
to buy more oil. I remember thinking ironically then that whereas in the old days
people sold their swords to buy books, now they had to sell their books to buy
the oil which they needed to read them. In any case I was always fighting off my
creditors. In fact, there was one New Year's holiday in which my family shared
some cheap sake just to celebrate the fact that I was still alive.

Be that as it may, Numa really had gone too far when he made a mockery of
my situation. Eventually I became so enraged that I started thinking of ways that
I might be able to have him locked up in a lunatic asylum.

By then Numa was drinking too much and often went about with a bag of ice
on his head while arguing with all and sundry. For a long time he still enjoyed
unchallenged dominance in the metropolitan assembly and his arrogance continued to grow. He was unteachable and boiled in fury at the slightest criticism.
When he was angry, however, he drank, and this just muddled his brain up even
further. I thought that if I continued to harass him constantly for a while, he might
even be driven to lose his wits altogether. With this in mind I decided to seize

every opportunity to challenge and infuriate him. Before three more meetings of the assembly had been called, however, I was banished from the capital for violating the security ordinance, and as a result I never succeeded in driving Numa to madness. This was fortunate for him—and for me too, no doubt, in that I was prevented from doing such a calculated and evil thing.

Although Numa and I were engaged in this vicious battle in the Tokyo assembly, we got along fairly well in other respects. Later, after his death, I learned that he had actually told his colleagues at the time that I was quite an interesting young fellow.

Around the Time of the Security Ordinance

THE "ROKUMEIKAN ERA"

Political parties atrophied under the government suppression and the newspapers were gagged. I defended what was left of the Progressive Party and kept up a bitter struggle, but the political fire had gone out just as the government had hoped.

Meanwhile, the government was preparing the way for constitutional government on its own terms. In 1881, not long after the imperial rescript on the opening of the parliament was issued, the government established the *Sangi'in*, a kind of House of Councilors, and also established a bureau for the reform of laws. Itō Hirobumi was appointed head of the new organization.

In February of the following year, it was decided that Itō would be sent to Europe to gather information in preparation for the drafting of a constitution. Itō left for Europe with a merry contingent of the best and brightest in government employ including Yamazaki Naotane, Itō Miyoji, Kawashima Jun, Hirata Tōsuke, Yoshida Masaharu, Miyoshi Taizō, Saionji Kinmochi, Iwakura Tomosada, and Hirohashi Kenkō.

After studying the constitutions of the European countries, the group returned to Japan in August 1883. Once back, Itō established a research bureau for the purpose of drafting a constitution, with himself at its head. It was also decided that an integrated cabinet would replace the earlier *Dajōkan* system, which was divided into ministerial committees. In December 1885, the Chief Minister (*Dajō daijin*) Sanjō Sanetomi advised the throne that the design of the proposed body was complete and begged to be relieved of his post.

Sanjō was now made lord keeper of the Privy Seal, the traditional *Dajōkan* offices were abolished, and new ministers were appointed to a cabinet intended to oversee the various ministries under a prime minister. This was the beginning of today's cabinet system. It was the most radical institutional change since the Meiji Restoration.

The first cabinet was formed by Itō Hirobumi. Itō was a novelty-seeker; he liked to be the first. In fact, he enjoyed appointing himself the first head of anything. When the conference of local officials was created in 1874, he had become its first speaker. He was the first head of the bureau of legislation when it was established in 1875. In 1881 he became the first head of the councilors and, having proved his appetite for being the first this and the first that, he became the first prime minister as soon as the first cabinet was installed. He continued to be true to his love of being "the first," and became in turn the first speaker when the House of Peers was founded and the first president of the Privy Council. He also became the first resident-general of Korea. He simply relished being in at the beginning of things, even when the models for most of the bodies he set up were borrowed from other countries. Of all his firsts, probably the proudest moment for Itō was when he was named to head the new cabinet as prime minister in 1885.

The first Itō cabinet had to face numerous problems. Home Minister Yamagata Aritomo wrestled to complete the local government system, Minister of Finance Matsukata Masayoshi addressed fiscal issues, Army Minister Ōyama Iwao, and Navy Minister Saigō Tsugumichi oversaw military expansion, Minister of Justice Yamada Akiyoshi supervised the compiling of a code of law, Education Minister Mori Arinori tackled the educational system, Minister of Agriculture Tani Kanjō and Minister of Transport Enomoto Takeaki grappled with the development of industry and transportation. But the greatest problem was that of revising foreign treaties, which came under the jurisdiction of Foreign Minister Inoue Kaoru.

Inoue embarked on the challenge with tremendous enthusiasm. It seemed simple enough to him, that with his fame and power he would be able to convince foreign emissaries of the need to revise the unequal treaties that had been forced upon Japan. The matter had been high on the national agenda since the Restoration. However, it did not turn out to be as easy as Inoue at first thought. Foreign diplomats held us in contempt and did not seem as ready as he anticipated to come to terms in spite of the many compromises we made.

Inoue came to the conclusion that the difficulty lay in the enormous differences which existed not only in the institutions but also in the national sentiments and customs of Japan and Western countries. He decided that Western manners had to be copied and made our own. Without this, he considered, it would be difficult to revise the treaties and raise the standing of Japan to that of equality with the powers. This led him to embark on a radical program of Westernization.

Traditional customs were abandoned, the manners of Western countries, even women's fashions and hair styles, were adopted, and both men and women were encouraged to travel abroad. These were the more reasonable things, but some Japanese also advocated international marriages in order to improve our racial stock, while others went so far as to recommend making Japan a Christian country. This was the beginning of the so-called "Rokumeikan Era."[1]

The infatuation with "Westernization" became more pronounced as the spring of 1887 approached. The prime minister's and foreign minister's residences became scenes of unrestrained merry-making, dragging the whole nation down with them into hedonism. More perhaps than any other occasion, the fancy-dress ball held by Prime Minister Itō on April 20th, which was attended by four hundred ladies and gentlemen from Japanese society together with members of the international community, was rumored to have been a scandalous event.

---

[1] The era was named for an imposing Western-style building, designed by Josiah Conder, reserved for special Western-style social events staged by the governing elite; it gave its name to the period from its completion in 1883 to the end of Inoue's tenure as foreign minister in 1887.

Now, what is dancing? It is nothing more than Western *bon odori*. While prohibiting our traditional *bon odori*[2] as vulgar and unrefined, these people had no shame in enjoying Western *bon odori*. As if they imagined that dancing would solve the problem of the Unequal Treaties, the dignified Yamagata and Saigō, the self-proclaimed country gentleman, danced the night away in fancy costume. This was not just ridiculous but pathetic.

This is what I wrote about it:

> The affair was rightly enough called a ball, as elegant as any event of the kind in the foreign land it came from. It is not to be wondered at that in times when things Western are feverishly sought after it is said that learning to dance is a necessary accomplishment of gentle folk. In essence, though, it is hardly different from our own *bon odori*. Their demerits are likewise matched. The Rokumeikan[3] has high doors and thick walls, but sometimes scandalous rumors manage to leak through them. Yet it is the very same people who prohibit our traditional *bon odori* who eagerly bring in these undignified dances from abroad.

Eventually, even in government circles, there were those who took exception to these disgraceful excesses and who spoke out against Foreign Minister Inoue's humiliating strategy for resolving the matter of the Unequal Treaties. Minister of Agriculture Tani, on returning from a fact-finding tour of the West, was enraged at the turn of events and resigned as minister, expressing himself in the most scathing terms. That was in July 1887. Even as early as May Katsu Kaishū had made representations to the government on the subject, and in August Itagaki Taisuke too voiced his opposition to what was turning out to be a source of national shame. Even Monsieur Boissonade,[4] who was then an advisor to the ministry of justice, also presented a memorandum warning that this sort of conduct compromised national independence.

As the substance of the proposed revision of the treaties became known to the public, conservatives as well as the progressive-minded like ourselves were of one mind in condemning the development.

Not only in the capital, but throughout the country opinion flared in overwhelming opposition to Inoue's proposed revisions. There were many secret publications. Submissions by Tani, Itagaki, and Katsu, and Boissonade's memorandum, as well as a draft constitution, were printed in secret and disseminated nationwide. There was no man of consequence who did not possess them. These subversive documents, to use contemporary terms, littered the country, and a flustered government dispatched secret agents in an attempt to control the situation.

[2] Buddhist communal festivals held in August to honor the dead.

[3] Construction on the Rokumeikan had begun in 1881. Its name was taken from an ancient Chinese poem expressing the pleasure of greeting guests from afar. See Dallas Finn, *Meiji Revisited: The Sites of Victorian Japan* (New York: Weatherhill, 1995), pp. 93ff.

[4] Gustave Emile Boissonade de Fontarabie (1829–1910), an important figure in the development of a new legal code for Japan.

While opposition to the government's policy was gathering momentum, there was no political force, in the absence of credible political parties, to guide it. The Progressive Party, particularly, manned almost single-handedly by myself with a little help from Numa's group, was unable to put up an adequate fight.

There was little hope in these circumstances of winning the battle. We needed a solid leader who would unite the various fronts against the government. Our search for a suitable candidate led us to Gotō Shōjirō, who was like a tiger in adversity.

Calling on Gotō to provide the leadership we needed dramatically revitalized the party. Immediately, opposition to the way the government was handling the Unequal Treaties issue spread like wildfire.

WE ASK GOTŌ TO TAKE THE LEAD

Gotō was all that one would imagine a truly great man to be. He possessed an extremely manly and openhearted nature. He was the most agreeable man I had ever met. There was a characteristic magnanimity in his speech and behavior that was most appealing. On top of all these attributes, he wrote skillfully in the *Kaiso-ryū* style. There was probably none among the towering figures of the Restoration whose brushwork excelled his.

"How are you able to write so well?" I once asked.

"Well, I was lucky and had a different way of studying," he replied. "I was taught by human hands. Most people learn from paper bugs." I understood what he meant. Old calligraphy text books are worm-ridden and full of holes.

Students just copy the characters worm-holes and all, and that wasn't the way to learn, he said. What happens then is that you learn the shapes of the characters but not the spirit of the writer. Without learning the spirit you can never become a really good writer.

There was something else that distinguished Gotō from others. He never spoke of the past. Those with great hopes for the future, I was once taught, did not speak of the past. Itō had far-reaching schemes for the future but he also loved to talk about the past. Ōkuma and Gotō rarely spoke of the past. Gotō, especially, probably hated to do that.

One evening, a few close friends were at Gotō's house in Takanawa. We agreed to try to get him to talk about his past, and after a few rounds of sake I raised the subject of how it had been possible to get the shogunate to relinquish power. It was almost unthinkable that anyone would dare to demand that the Tokugawa shoguns, who had ruled the nation absolutely for two hundred and fifty years, should restore supremacy to the throne overnight. It was Gotō who had proposed it and seen it through. It was surely the most glorious page in his eventful life.

Even a man who normally detested to talk of his past would surely be tricked into sharing his most exalted memories, I thought. But Gotō gave me a polite answer and went on to some other topic. He did not make a scene out of refusing; he simply did not take the bait. There would have been no shame in talking to us of those momentous days, but he preferred not to. He really was a very unusual man.

Gotō was very poor in those days. Thinking that there would be a need for funds if he wished to be a force in politics, Gotō had resigned from the government early on and gone into business. But being a samurai, he was not a successful businessman. Apparently he had established a trading firm called Horai-sha near Shimbashi and tried his hand at international trade as well as at managing a coal-mining company in Nagasaki, but everything had failed and he had accumulated huge debts.

It was rumored in those days that any millionaire who happened to be sailing in the same ship as Gotō between Tokyo and Nagasaki was sure to end up lending him money. It was even said that it was impossible to complete a journey with Gotō without his borrowing money from you. Yet every time Gotō did so he somehow succeeded in leaving his benefactor with a pleasant memory. There is no doubt that he possessed an extraordinarily attractive personality.

In the historic days of the Restoration, Gotō was quite senior to Ōkuma. In fact, at the end of the shogunate, Inoue and Yamagata must have been more to him than little boys. It was this great senior statesman I marked out to head our declining party, and I asked Suehiro Tetchō to accompany me to negotiate with him.

Gotō was out of Tokyo traveling in the Hokuriku region on the Japan Sea at the time, and our meeting with him had to await his return. Gotō was happy to oblige and agreed readily. "I like the idea," he said. "I will be happy to work with you people even if it is to be my swansong." He went so far as to say "I would go through fire and water to support a cause championed by Ozaki and Suehiro." It was the first time I had heard words like this from such a great man and I was enormously encouraged. I put my whole heart into elaborating our plans, and Gotō agreed to everything. Until then I had always worked under instructions from superiors, so this was a heady experience.

Our little group of two was joined around this time by Ōishi Masami, who had returned from Britain. Thereafter the three of us planned everything together. Then there was a talented young fellow by the name of Yoshida Masaharu, who was either the son or grandson of Yoshida Tōyō of Tosa.[5] Yoshida had been in the entourage of Itō when he traveled to Europe to study the constitutions of the various countries. Gotō introduced Yoshida to us, saying that he was a relative who was working as his secretary and that he wanted the lad to be part of the conspiracy.

While there were quite a few others, including Hayashi Yūzō and Hoshi Tōru, who also frequented the Gotō residence in those days, Gotō had promised us that he would be guided by the advice the four of us provided, including the gentle Yoshida who said very little.

---

[5] Gotō entered Restoration politics as a disciple of Yoshida Tōyō (1816–1862), a leader of reform in Tosa before his assassination by radicals. See Marius B. Jansen, *Sakamoto Ryōma and the Meiji Restoration* (Princeton, N.J.: Princeton University Press, 1961), for these tangled politics.

It was agreed that on October 3 at the Sanroku-tei restaurant in Shiba, Gotō would make his maiden speech as the head of the party before seventy opposition leaders. He addressed them as follows:

Gentlemen, may I ask how you see the present circumstances of our nation? Externally, we hardly deserve the dignity of being called an independent country; internally the sweat and blood of the people are almost used up. We have allowed the legendary forces of loyalty and patriotism, which are the foundation of our country, to sink from view. Gentlemen, today our ears are covered, our eyes are blindfolded, and our tongues are tied. If we do nothing to alter this frightening and lamentable situation, what will become of the empire?

It was a great speech, resonant with indignation and stirring the audience with its passion. After returning to his seat, Gotō continued to speak of the need to challenge Satsuma and Chōshū resolutely with all the resources at hand. The next day, a joint meeting of the Progressive Party and Liberal Party was held at the Ibuson-rō restaurant. This was to be followed by a joint public meeting on October 9 and 10.

A VIOLENT BRAWL AT THE IBUSON-RŌ

Up to this time, the Progressive Party and Liberal Party had been bitter rivals. But here were the two adversaries meeting together as allies with the single aim of jointly organizing a major rally to challenge the clan government over the mishandling of the Unequal Treaties. The effect on the country was electrifying.

At the same time, it was not possible altogether to dissolve the long-accumulated hostility of the two groups in a single night's conviviality. There was a need for caution lest a small disagreement develop into a major row.

Knowing I was the focus of the Liberal Party's antagonism, I was constantly on the alert. Hoping that the evening would pass without incident, I was leaning on a pillar from where I could watch people as they filed into the big hall. Suddenly I saw a huge man coming directly toward me with his hand pointing straight at my head. Being small and weak I knew I had no chance if I went for his arms, but I had learned when threatened to grab an attacker's thumb. If one grasped the thumb firmly one could control most men. This I now did, and it worked. The man backed away and bowed his head in apology. I learned later that he wanted to see the bill posted on the pillar behind my head, to check where his seat was. I thought he was going to try to embarrass me by tweaking my ear. Unfortunately, my natural cowardice has often led me to make a fool of myself like this.

This was the only trouble I experienced personally that night. But to avoid any untoward developments we declared the meeting officially closed as soon as it was polite to do so after the dinner had been placed before the guests on lacquered trays and a few cups of sake had been drunk. I left the hall with Gotō. I went home and was soon asleep, satisfied that the evening had passed peaceably. But violence had broken out after we left.

Numa of the Progressive Party and Hoshi Tōru and his group of Liberal Party men did not leave the hall with us. Numa and Hoshi were both well established as Western scholars around the end of the shogunate, but of the two, Numa came from a better family. Hoshi was not yet independent economically and lived with his mother in Ōmori, and Numa took every opportunity to belittle him, calling him "the peasant from Ōmori." That night, after drinking quantities of sake, Numa behaved boorishly as usual. Thrusting his sake cup toward Hoshi, Numa taunted him, shouting, "Here, peasant, take my cup!"

Hoshi was no less arrogant and conceited, and years of political enmity had combined with his long dislike of Numa to make him retort, "What, drink with a lout like you?"

"You heard me! I said to drink with me!"

"With the likes of you?" shot back Hoshi . . .

Immediately, the lights were switched off and ruffians in Hoshi's pay surrounded Numa and beat him with the brass candlesticks that were on the table. Hoshi blocked the staircase to prevent the police from intervening. He had every intention of beating Numa to death and throwing him out of one of the upper windows into the Sumida River. Luckily, the police arrived and rescued Numa from the brink of death.

When I learned of this later that night I was incensed. At this critical juncture when the two parties had put aside their rivalry to stand together against the "*hanbatsu*" (Satsuma-Chōshū) government, any quarrel among them would spoil the whole plan before it got under way. This was precisely why we were careful and had agreed among ourselves to leave the gathering while it was still light. Even the younger members had left as agreed. I was baffled that Numa, one of our own leaders, could so lose control of his emotions and provoke this deplorable incident.

I visited Numa to see how he was doing as well as to raise the issue with him. His body was bruised and swollen all over and he was unable to move. After expressing my sympathies, I said to him, "Sympathy is one thing, but after all we agreed, what if the alliance breaks up because of this? You must come to the joint meeting today at any cost to make up for the damage. You must be there even if you have to be carried in on a stretcher, to show that there is no change in your commitment to working with the rest of us for the national cause."

Others who were present were understandably furious at me for being so cold-blooded, but Numa understood. "You're right," he said. "I am terribly sorry for letting myself get carried away like that. I will come to the meeting if it kills me." He did not make it to the meeting, however, as his doctor would not permit it. This was not unreasonable, Numa did in fact die afterward because of the beating he had taken.

The immediate sequel to the incident was that members of the Progressive Party reacted with such bitter animosity toward the Liberal Party for their rough treatment of Numa that they felt quite unable to work with them and decided officially not to send a representative to the joint meeting.

But I was determined not to give up. A row was a row; but it should not be allowed to cause a rift among the forces allied against the clan government. I went to the meeting accompanied only by Yoshida Kiroku. In my speech to the joint meeting, I told them, "Numa's behavior was a personal matter and had nothing to do with national affairs. Whatever other members of the Progressive Party may say, I am ready to continue the alliance even if I am the only one. My participation at this meeting on behalf of the Progressive Party should be allowed to have some impact in rallying the people to our cause." My statement was welcomed by the Liberal Party people, and the crowd showed their approval with resounding applause.

GOTŌ GOES TO THE PALACE

The political alliance looked as though it would hold in spite of its turbulent beginning. But now people were warning me to beware of the possibility of Gotō's backing out. The last thing I wanted was for this man above all to let us down at a time of crisis, as some were suggesting he would. I thought that to be on the safe side I had better test the strength of his commitment.

At one point I suggested that we might do as in England where aristocrats have the privilege of presenting petitions to the monarch in person. Although there was no such tradition in Japan it was a desirable custom. As Gotō was now a peer it ought to have been possible for him to approach the throne directly on a matter of national importance. With the endorsement of other members I therefore brought the subject up with Gotō, who thought it was a good idea. So we dusted off Gotō's old morning coat and bought him a pair of gloves, and saw him off to the palace. I recall that it was December 2, 1887.

Gotō drove to the imperial household ministry and requested an audience, but was refused. It appeared the decision came from the minister, Hijikata Hisamoto. On his return home, we told Gotō that a veteran statesman of the Restoration like himself could not accept no for an answer; he had to keep trying until he was granted an audience. Gotō took it very well and set out again, but returned home after being once more rejected. It was decided finally that a written petition would be presented via the minister. This incident assured us of Gotō's sincerity and we all felt encouraged about the future.

It was one thing to have Gotō's commitment but quite another to find ways of carrying out the objectives of our grand alliance. We analyzed Gotō's failure to get an imperial audience and decided it was due to the lack of visible national support. As a last resort we decided to assemble three thousand men from around the country. Gotō would lead these men to the palace and line them up in front of the double bridge and beg for the discontinuance of the negotiations on the Unequal Treaties. Three thousand men protesting themselves before the palace should get some result. With this in mind we went about the logistics of getting these men to Tokyo. Also, Hayashi Yūzō of Tosa, who was a resourceful man, heard of our intention and offered to send three hundred men from Tosa.

I had up my sleeve an exceptional young man by the name of Saitō Shinichirō who hailed from Aomori. Saitō, though not strong physically, was a brilliant student who was earning money to pay for his studies at Waseda by selling bottles of milk. He was well versed in Chinese learning and his Chinese poetry was as good as any professional's.[6] He turned up without even a letter of introduction. He wore shabby clothes but quickly demonstrated that he had discerning opinions and a resourceful nature. We became good friends and through him I established good relations with other young men like Sakuraba Tsunei of Hirosaki and Hikita Nagasuke of Akita. They all impressed me with their exceptional intelligence. But among all the promising young men I worked with, Saitō and Hikita possessed the most outstanding qualities. It was these young men who argued with the bureaucrats at the foreign ministry, often even daring to raise their fists to make a point. With their help my opposition to the government's handling of the Unequal Treaties gained visibility.

It was around this time that the term "sōshi" became popular. Men of consequence had long been called "yūshika," but seeing that the word was beginning to lose its original aura I replaced it with "sōshi," meaning "brave men." For some reason Inukai was not part of this movement, but when he heard of the new use of "sōshi" he immediately made fun of it, saying it should be written not with the character meaning "brave men" but with a homonym meaning "miserable men," because many of our men, including Saitō, were thin. Strangely, the use of "sōshi" seemed to give us strength.

Bringing three thousand men to Tokyo was easier said than done. By the day they were meant to assemble few had yet made it to the capital. We were obviously better at making speeches than at logistics, and it was unfortunate that at a time when transportation was still primitive this could not really be helped. Some groups arrived too soon while others were late. Some who got to Tokyo early could not meet their bed and breakfast expenses and came to us for help. We consulted Gotō, but he was not much help. Those were the days when it was said he kept a ferocious dog to ward off his creditors.

Our supporters from out of town were becoming unhappier by the day as their expenses mounted. We were at a loss. There came a point when three hundred men had made it to Tokyo. This was less than perfect, but the country was watching our every move and the consequences could be significant.

I AM BANISHED FROM THE CAPITAL

The three hundred men from outside Tokyo had to be taken care of, and the government appeared to be on the point of revising the treaties. Feeling extremely

---

[6] Chinese verse (*kanshi*) was an accomplishment on which the Meiji generation prided itself, and it was not uncommon to consult a specialist.

pressed, we assembled at the Gotō residence in Takanawa on December 24, 1887. We picked our brains anxiously for ideas, but the more desperate we became, the fewer ideas we had. We were achieving little but helping ourselves to sake and squandering the night with useless discussion. At length I said in jest, "If no one else has a bright idea, I have! Tosa's suicide squad is a sham. Of the three hundred Hayashi promised, fewer than ten are here. But we should at least have enough men to start a good fire. Get thirty or forty to place cans of oil in key locations. Then light them and, wind willing, Tokyo will be a sea of fire. Cabinet ministers will rush to the palace, where they will be sitting targets for assassins. Anyone short of money can rob the vaults in the ministry of finance." Everyone was amused by the absurdity of the idea and drank to it. It was around midnight when we took our leave and dispersed to make our separate ways home. I had not dreamed that this silly joke would be the cause of such a stir later.

Two days later on the morning of December 26, I left home to attend the Tokyo metropolitan assembly. One of the committee members brought me a copy of a special government gazette announcing a new security ordinance. I said to the man, "What can be the purpose of such an ordinance in a time of peace?" After attending the standing committee meeting I made as I always did for the *Chōya Shinbun*. On my way I noticed that the Marunouchi district was fenced off by wire and I had no idea that it was the army that had strung the wire.

That evening I attended a party at a house in Yanagibashi. It was a congenial occasion with pleasant talking and drinking, and I went home around midnight. I was taking a nap in the ricksha when I was rudely awakened by a voice crying "Stop!" and the shock of the ricksha jolting to a stop right in front of my own gate. Even with my bleary eyes I could tell that the man clad in black who had stopped the ricksha was a policeman. He asked my name and handed me a piece of paper which he took from his inside pocket.

In the dim lamp of my gate all I could discern were the characters of the Ogawa-chō police station. Dismounting from the ricksha and reading the paper directly under the light at the entrance, I read: "Report immediately to this police station."

Involved as I was in a political campaign against the government, I knew that one day I would end up in prison. This did not cause me too much concern as I had always been careful to avoid any radical action of which I might be found guilty. The only thing I feared was compromising my health if they kept me in jail for weeks on end. With the order to report immediately to the police, it looked for certain as if I would be sent to prison.

The police station was noisy and animated, even at that late hour. An officer showed me politely to the office of the station chief. They were evidently in no hurry to put me behind bars. As I was about to ask why I had been summoned the police chief handed me a form which was in his desk. It read: "In accordance with Article 4 of the Security Ordinance, you are hereby ordered to remain beyond three *ri* from the Imperial Palace for a period of three years beginning 3 p.m. on the 31st of December."[7]

---

[7] There had been a Tokugawa precedent, in banishment from Edo. "Edo barai."

There were many things I wanted to ask, but the police would not talk to me, and I left the police station with the order in my breast pocket. I had been prepared to live in confinement, and instead they had freed me to travel anywhere in the wide world. I thanked my lucky stars. I had been feeling that there was nothing more one could do in Tokyo at that point. I was being given an opportunity to realize the trip abroad that I had been dreaming of for some time. It did not take a split second for me to make up my mind.

Nonetheless, I was taken by surprise. Little did I suspect that the special government gazette I had read that morning applied to me. I now changed the Chinese characters of my pseudonym Gakudō, from "the hall of learning" to "the hall of amazement." Later I changed the reading again by taking away the prefix of mind when I felt I had become weaker with old age.

Armed with the writ of the security ordinance, the police knocked on the door of all political activists who were known to be opposed to the government and ordered them to report to police stations. According to the ordinance, married men with wives and families were given three days; those without families twenty-four hours to leave the imperial capital. Six hundred people were thus ordered out.

In addition, fearing an uprising, the government summoned medical doctors to the army hospital and deployed special police to ministries and the residences of ministers and in all munitions depots and armories, thereby putting the capital under a total state of emergency. They even saw to it that each activist was escorted outside the three *ri* radius from the palace and handed over to local police, who in turn took him to his designated residence. The meticulous care with which the police carried out the letter of law was simply staggering.

There were a dozen or so men, one of whom was Kataoka Kenkichi, who had come up from Tosa to join us and who had all been staying at the Kinko-kan in Kanefusa-cho Shiba. When they were summoned they were escorted by police and special police guarding them front and rear so that it looked more like soldiers conducting prisoners of war. Kataoka refused to submit to the order, claiming that he was completely at a loss as to what was happening, and demanded to know on what account he had been ordered out of the capital, but he too suffered the same fate as the rest of the group.

He was not the only one to be flabbergasted by this sudden turn of events. Little could I have imagined that my own silly joke after drinking at the Gotō residence would develop into this disaster. I was aghast to learn later that a report by a secret agent who had been hiding under the floor of the Gotō residence had caused the government to panic and take this reckless course of action. It was a costly lesson in staying away from mindless jokes.

At first the policeman who had been assigned to keep an eye on me treated me like a criminal, but gradually began to call me respectfully by my pseudonym. As time passed we developed great camaraderie and he confided some alarming things to me. "The night you were arrested in front of your gate, did you notice anything strange?" he asked.

"Well, no, nothing exactly strange," I replied, "but you made me jump when you suddenly appeared from the shadows."

"Didn't you see my right hand on my saber when I grabbed your ricksha with my other hand?" he asked.

"Not really. Why was that?" I answered.

"I was under secret orders to kill you then and there had you resisted," he told me. "You see, the police expected you to put up a fight when you were ordered to give yourself up."

In any case, the midnight joke at the Gotō residence had been taken seriously by the government, who were convinced that we had been planning to start fires and commit other acts of violence. Expecting that we might resist arrest, they had issued orders for us to be killed on the spot if we did. This accounted for the barbed-wire barricades manned by soldiers I had seen in the Marunouchi district, and the orders the government had given for the Tokyo division to guard the vaults at the finance ministry and for the imperial guards to protect the palace.

A POLICE GUARD MAKES ME FEEL LIKE A CABINET MINISTER

The abruptness of the security ordinance certainly caught the government unprepared and resulted in some tragicomedies. On hearing a rumor that a three-hundred-man suicide squad from Tosa was on the way, the government banned all Tosa people from the capital. A fourteen-year-old relative of Gotō had arrived to attend school in Tokyo a few days before the security ordinance was proclaimed, but was ordered out of the city simply because he was from Tosa.

Then there was the street vendor who was driven out of the city for the crime of selling dried skipjack from Tosa instead of from Satsuma. So absurd were the lengths to which the government went that even secretaries and grooms were not spared if they happened to come from Tosa. One poor young Tosa student failed to meet the deadline to leave the city as he hurried about trying to borrow money for the trip, and ended up behind bars.

Amusingly, there were some who nevertheless managed to escape the dragnet. Ōishi, Suehiro, and Yoshida were in the same boat as I; in fact, with me, they were at the core of the strategy of the alliance, and by this fact alone should have suffered the same fate. They were even with me at the Gotō residence on that fateful night. I do not know how Yoshida got away with it, but Ōishi and Suehiro, both of whom were known to Prime Minister Itō, were spared the ordeal when he struck their names off the list of deportees. "These men are all right," he is reported to have declared. "These are no arsonists!" I suppose he saw in me a potential pyromaniac. Be that as it may, the three of us, Hayashi Yūzō, Hoshi Tōru, and I, were given the severest penalty. We were exiled from the capital for three years.

Having decided that I would make the most of this opportunity to travel abroad, I then realized I had no money. Parents, it is said, are the best prophets of their children's future, and my father had confided while at Ise to the father of Kadono Ikunoshin, "Yukio will be poor all his life." He was right. Even Inukai assured me that I was not the kind to make money even if I tried. There was no way I could finance my trip. The great idea was fast becoming history. Then I had the idea to talk it over with Asabuki Eiji. I was still in Tokyo, and I went to see him the following morning.

Asabuki had helped me out in matters of finance before, such as tiding me over my loans or fighting off loan sharks. When things were not going so well and he was unable to help he listened to my woes and gave me his sympathy. Unfortunately, this was one of those times. But when I explained what had happened and the hope I had of traveling abroad he agreed in spite of his circumstances that it was a good idea.

I had been given three days to leave Tokyo, and I wanted to take leave of my friends. On the afternoon of December 27, I went over to the *Chōya Shinbun* to clean out my desk. While I was there I wrote a note which I asked to be delivered to other newspapers with the request that they would carry it. It was very short, merely reporting that I had been "banished from Edo" and begging to be spared the customary obligation of sending year-end and new year's greetings.[8]

Since being officially served the order to leave Edo I was accompanied at all times by two policemen. When I went to say good-bye to Gotō, I told him in jest that the police escort made me feel like a cabinet minister. The only difference was that I rode a ricksha instead of a horse-drawn carriage. Gotō had a hearty laugh at this and said he would lend me his carriage so that I could see how it was to drive around like a cabinet minister. When I shared with him my plans of studying in the West, he did not hesitate. "I know you are not exactly wealthy," he said. "Tell me what you need. I would like to help." It was generous of him, but I knew that he himself was reduced to fighting off loan sharks by keeping a ferocious dog, so I did not take him up on his offer. "Friends help each other in good times and bad," he insisted. "I would be offended if you did not ask me." I remembered how he had earlier pledged to support me through fire and water, and now once again he would stand by me. I was very grateful.

I left Gotō's residence in his carriage and greatly enjoyed myself riding aimlessly around the city. The poor ricksha man following with the two policemen could not keep up, so I sat the policeman on the driver's seat and continued to visit friends.

Seeing me with a police escort, some people even saluted. At the Ōkuma residence, Suehiro Tetcho who arrived after me saw the carriage and the policemen at the gate and thought a cabinet minister was visiting. Eventually, of course, I would be the real thing, but the three days of playing cabinet minister was a lot of fun.

Visiting so many people was tiring, so I drove over to the Yanagibashi Kamekiyo house for a quick drink. The geisha were suspicious at seeing me with a police escort, so I told them what had happened. They were all very sympathetic at the misfortune that, as they put it, something like this should have befallen someone so dignified. Each in turn performed her best in dance and song to make me feel less downhearted. The evening passed very pleasantly and, as it happened,

---

[8] *Edo barai*, "Banished from Edo," was standard Tokugawa terminology.

I had more than one drink. On my return home late that night, I composed a
Chinese-style poem:

> Smiling at my own folly
> I sought to console myself with drink.
> The young girls comforted their guest.
> Their gentle courtesies gave me rest.

The three days of grace passed quickly and the 31st, the day I had to leave
Tokyo, arrived. I visited Asabuki at his home in Kiba-chō to bid him good-bye.
It was lunchtime and he invited me to eat with him. He had them serve me a
whole sea bream, head and all, but I saw that his own tray did not have one. The
household had plain food.

By 2:30 in the afternoon I had said good-bye to my family and had left Tokyo
from Shimbashi. My first destination was Hakone, where I lodged at the Fukuzumi Inn in Tōnosawa. Kadono had also booked into the inn for the new year
holidays, so we spent ten days together. We took walks in the hills and by the
river, read novels and poems, and played *go*. In the evening we played cards with
the maids, and the loser had his or her face painted with ink. Occasionally the
police sent their men to check the inn and once my own escort appeared with his
face smeared with ink, which caused considerable merriment.

Used to being chronically pressed for time, I found my unsought new year
holiday at Hakone rather boring. On the other hand, my plans for the trip abroad
were maturing and I had much to look forward to. Even so, I could not help being somewhat melancholic, and on sleepless nights sometimes wrote short poems
in Chinese, such as this:

> 'Neath blue-black sky and dark green hills
> I dream of rain by window tight.
> All's calm, and cold the rushing rills
> While melancholy fills my night.

I MEET HOSHI TŌRU

With preparations for my journey now complete, I moved to Yokohama on January 10, 1888. where I stayed with Nishimura Shinshichi in Benten Street. There
I was visited by such a stream of friends and acquaintances that it was not much
different from being in Tokyo. But whenever I went for a walk in Yokohama with
friends, the police escort aroused the curiosity of passers-by. They invariably
looked to see who was the prisoner, pointing to one or other of my friends. No
one ever seemed to point his finger at me. Perhaps I did not look sufficiently
criminal; somehow or other I did not qualify.

One day, in the course of a visit to meet some Westerners who were staying in
Yokohama, an Englishman asked me why Prime Minister Itō was behaving like
Napoleon III in driving out the activists. "I don't quite know why," I replied. "But

if he sees himself as Napoleon III, then I'll be Victor Hugo." We had a good laugh.

The *hanbatsu* clique, having driven their opposition from Tokyo with this outrageous security ordinance, must have realized that the momentum building against them was now unchallengeable, and they seemed to be looking for a way to strike a compromise with Ōkuma.

With activists of all stripes chased from the capital, the new year of 1888 opened in an unnatural calm. But beneath the stillness volcanic forces were moving. The government too must have sensed the storm clouds rising. Unless measures were undertaken promptly to relieve the pressure, the constitution which was soon to be promulgated would no longer have the impact expected of it. Kuroda Kiyotaka convinced Prime Minister Itō that the only way to avoid a fateful clash with the opposition was to invite one of their representatives to sit in the cabinet. It was Kuroda who thus acted as a mediator between Itō and Ōkuma.

Ōkuma and his wife came down to Yokohama and held a farewell party for me at the Fūki-rō restaurant on January 26. Yano, Fujita, Mutaguchi, Inukai, and Asabuki also came from Tokyo for the occasion. At one point Ōkuma called me aside in a separate room and told me, "There is soon going to be a cabinet reshuffle with Kuroda as prime minister. I am expected to join the cabinet. It is still a secret, but I am letting you know because you are going away."

The reason for our opposition to the treaty revision was to protect national honor and not expressly to bring down the Itō government. I was deeply gratified to think that our campaign had served as the hound that brought the government to bay and resulted in the appointment of Ōkuma, my mentor, to the government.

Not long after I left Japan Ōkuma replaced Inoue as foreign minister. In reality, this amounted to his being prime minister in all but name. Kuroda, held that post in name, but he considered himself above the details, and left everything to Ōkuma in whom he had complete trust. From this foothold Ōkuma's power expanded throughout the ministries so that in effect the Kuroda cabinet afforded Ōkuma the opportunity to dominate the cabinet on his own.

The same evening that Ōkuma gave me the farewell party Asabuki brought me the vital funds that Gotō had promised. Asabuki had handed me the bulky package wrapped in newspaper, and since it was far too big to carry on me I had placed it in a corner of the room. As I was leaving ahead of the rest, feeling quite mellow with drink, the owner came running after me with the precious package in her hand. I had been so carried away by the party that I had completely forgotten it. I suspected that Mrs. Ōkuma had sent the hostess after me with it.

The following day I received word via Itō Jintarō, from Hoshi Tōru, who had also been a victim of the security ordinance, that he and his other similarly banished friends from the Liberal Party wished to give me a send-off also. The Liberal Party and I differed at the ideological level, but personal relations were another matter. I accepted their friendly gesture with pleasure, and offered to join them wherever they wished. The party was held at the Kaiko-rō, in Aoi-chō.

There were twenty or so Liberal Party men there, including Hoshi Tōru, Yamada Taizō, Hayashi Homei, and Suzuki Shōji. In general, Liberal Party members were known to be a pretty rough lot, but these men, who had been ordered out of Tokyo, were ruffians by any standard.

One of them, wearing a padded kimono and sitting with his legs crossed in Turkish fashion, was leaning on a pillar in front of a *tokonoma* alcove when I arrived and was shouting rudely to those around him. Suddenly, he turned brusquely to me, without even so much as a bow, and called out, "You there, you must be Ozaki. I'm Hoshi." For a moment I was quite startled. He looked more like a gangster than a politician.

This was the first time I had met the man, although his name had been familiar to me since my student days at Keiō Gijuku. I had often found myself in the opposing political camp in the newspapers and at public meetings. Hoshi Tōru was famous as the only barrister in the country at the time who had studied in Britain, so I expected him to look like a real gentleman scholar. I could not possibly have expected to recognize him in this guise.

As we parted, Hoshi told me he would also be coming to England, as indeed he did. One day he dropped in to see me at my lodgings in London and asked me about books. "I know you like to read," he said, "so I thought you would be the best person to ask about new books." He seemed an entirely different person from the one I had met in Japan.

As a courtesy I paid him a return visit. His room was full of books. It seemed that he asked publishers for catalogues in which he checked the titles he ordered and received. I decided that there was more to the man than met the eye.

First Impressions of America

The steamship *Peking* was due to sail for San Francisco on the twenty-ninth, but its departure was delayed for two days, so I let my friends who had promised to come to see me off know by express mail and telephone of the delay.

At 10:30 one morning I received a visit from Gotō, who had had the courtesy to come all the way to Yokohama to inform me of his wish to resign as head of our coalition. I appreciated this very much, and all the more when I learned that his daughter was to be married that same evening and he was of course extremely busy. I also learned that until recently important visitors to Tokyo would unfailingly knock at his door, so it was said his residence was always jostling like a marketplace. But to the dismay of many, since the brouhaha over the security ordinance and the expulsion of activists he had had few visitors.

At 9 o'clock on the morning of 31 January I boarded the steamship accompanied by many friends. One well-wisher who had come to see me off remarked, "You've certainly chosen a long way from the capital to retire to."

"The farther the better," I replied. "I am going all the way to Europe to make the government leaders feel safe."

In life one never really knows what brings happiness or unhappiness. If it had not been for the events that led to my expulsion, it would have been very difficult for me to fulfill my wish to travel abroad. The funds that now made it possible had materialized, it seemed almost of their own accord, because friends were sympathetic over my misfortune at having to leave Tokyo.

Also, Hoshi, who with me was one of the three to suffer the heaviest penalty, had already made his name, as I have remarked above, even while I was still a student at Keio. And Hayashi, the other, having been active since the early Restoration days, had acquired experience and fame far beyond any comparison with mine. My being treated with the same severity as Hoshi and Hayashi gave me the visibility that an upstart of no more than thirty years of age could not otherwise have dreamed of. Being linked in this way with the two veterans undoubtedly gave a thrust to my political development. This sort of thing happens to nations just as it does to people. Most people see happiness and unhappiness as separate phenomena and never realize that they are juxtaposed, or that there can be a causal relationship between them that leads directly from one to the other.

The *Peking* was a small boat and she vibrated terribly. Not a good sailor at the best of times, I spent the better part of the first week at sea in my bunk. It was an uneventful trip. I read gluttonously day and night and in a short time had devoured all the books I had brought with me. The rest of the time I devoted to writing a book titled "Diary of an Exile."

After nineteen days at sea we at last arrived in San Francisco. Bored by the long voyage we were all waiting eagerly to disembark when we learned that a Chinese among the lower deck passengers was caught with a pox and the ship was ordered by the quarantine authorities to stand off for two weeks. There are no words to describe the boredom of being confined to a ship with one's port of disembarkation right before one's eyes. When we were just about halfway through the required period of quarantine another Chinese was found to have the same affliction. It seemed there would be no end to this. So the first-class passengers appealed to the shipping company to separate them from the third class. The company obliged and sent the *Alice Garlett*, a small three-decked steamship, to take the first-class passengers on board.

The ordeal seemed over and our cheerfulness had returned, but no sooner had we transferred to the steamship than we were plunged into a ferocious storm. In spite of being moored inside the harbor, the small ship pitched and rolled as if we were still in mid-Pacific. I was wakened early next morning by the sound of the lifeboats being lowered. The gale-force wind and high waves had snapped the anchor chain and the ship was being blown against the wharf.

The passengers were terrified and women and children were in hysterics. I was on the second deck watching the commotion, and just as the ship slammed into the wharf I jumped from a height of six feet.

It was a great relief to be on solid land again, although all I had with me was a cigarette in my mouth and nothing in my hands. Without worrying about my belongings I struggled through the storm until I found a wagon, which I directed to the Palace Hotel that I had been told of, and thus managed to avoid the quarantine.

The ship was severely damaged, and while by good fortune the passengers were all safe our luggage had been lost. Among my possessions there were some things that were dear to me, among which was a goose-skin notebook to which I had given the title "Record of Obligations and Scores to Settle." In my childhood I had read an outline account of Chinese history, in which someone had said that he was scrupulous about paying his obligations and avenging wrongs done to him. At the time I thought that was an admirable idea, and had since faithfully recorded all the instances of gratitude and revenge I felt I owed my seniors and peers. Unless it was a special case that I had committed to memory I had then forgotten about the incident after entering it in my notebook. To reproduce the record from memory held little promise of the thoroughness that I liked and I regretted losing the book. Then a thought struck me: it was the instinct of a small man to want to pay back every obligation and avenge every slight. Anyone with the ambition of being a big man must possess higher thoughts. To forget both obligation and revenge is one choice; another and more virtuous one is to record all obligations, but to forget the wrongs that are done one. This should be the way of a right-minded and chivalrous person. There and then I discontinued the habit of keeping such records. I believe this episode was providential and helped my personal development. Three days later, my cabin trunk was washed ashore. I was able to recover the contents, but most was of no further use after having been soaked in seawater for three days and nights. I never saw my book of "Obligations and Scores to Settle" again.

One of the first things that struck me after going ashore in San Francisco was the popularity of the newspapers. Shoeshine stands kept two or three papers for clients to read while their shoes were been polished. Restaurants kept papers on each table. The newspapers were not necessarily of the highest caliber, but it surprised me to see everybody reading them regardless of their station in life.

Newspapers and editors, having checked the guest list at the hotel, wasted no time in sending journalists to interview me. They were not the kind of people for whom a few words sufficed. Rather, they heard me say a few words and then made up the rest. Articles appeared about me with big headlines and embarrassing fictions. Newspaper A would say I was a person of remarkable talents, and then paper B would describe me as a dashing and courageous man. Another paper likened me to an oriental Garibaldi while yet another, not to be outdone, called me the Victor Hugo of the Orient. Before long I was reincarnated as a man of extraordinary gallantry and wit.

At this rate, I smiled to myself, by the time I reached England I would be no less than a handsome and outstanding statesman. A friend of mine advised me before leaving Japan that since I could read books anywhere, I should make a point of traveling as widely as possible and observing for myself everything I could during the three years I would be away. I resolved to do exactly as he said and after arriving in America took every occasion to travel. But I could not help thinking that I was getting little out of it, considering the expense. For about two months I stayed in San Francisco, using it as a base for visiting other places nearby. Among the impressions I came away with were the power of women, which was beyond anything I had heard, and the high salaries, which I thought must pose difficulties when hiring qualified personnel.

I was especially distressed by my fellow-countrymen. At first I expected them to be highly motivated compared with students in Japan, for after all they had left their country because they were dissatisfied with it. However, most of those who had come to America to work and study were inferior academically and many had not even bothered to learn the rudiments of English. Among the two thousand or so of my compatriots whom I met, only a few of the most enterprising young people were enrolled in universities. Not even three hundred were studying in primary schools. The other sixteen or seventeen hundred were happy to find their next meal and quite content to remain cooks and maids. At this rate, there would be an even greater number of these unworthy people in the future, and the thought that the Japanese would come to be regarded as a nation of maids and menial servants horrified me, thinking of the harm it would do our country.

The U.S. Congress Disappoints Me

On April 5, I left San Francisco for New York and arrived there on the fourteenth, having enjoyed the spectacular scenery of the Rockies and Niagara Falls on the way.

Reports of Europe were inviting and I had an urge to cross the Atlantic as soon as possible, but I thought better of it and decided to take advantage of my stay in the US and went to Washington to study American politics.

Congress was in session, and the two houses were in the midst of a grand debate over whether or not to reduce tariffs. Congress was the first Western parliament I had seen in action, and I was greatly disappointed by what I saw. Some members had their feet up on the desks, others smoked cigarettes or gnawed at apples. And when a member at the back of the chamber spoke, those in the front rows swung their chairs round, turning their backs on the Speaker. There were stands and sofas and chaise lounges around the chamber. Members took turns leaving the floor to go to these corners to smoke or chat, and there was even one who was fast asleep and snoring loudly. I could not help but think this behavior rude for members engaged in matters of state. I mentioned this to an American woman, whose comment was striking. "It is not surprising," she said, "considering that members of the House of Representatives come from all over the states and some of them are quite uncouth. In fact, just the other day one of them staying at a hotel did not know how to turn off the gas and almost killed himself when he tried to blow it out like a lamp."

One day I learned that a leader of the Republican Party in the Senate was going to speak in response to accusations made earlier by a prominent Democrat. I cut short my lunch and rushed to the Capitol. The Senate gallery was already crowded and overflowing into the corridors, but I managed to squeeze myself into the gallery. The senator had already begun his speech. He spoke for two hours. Usually, many seats were left empty as Democrats left the floor when a Republican was speaking and vice versa. That day most seats were occupied. A large number of members from the lower house were also in attendance, notwithstanding their own debate. Nevertheless, except for the crowd outside in the corridors, people listened attentively to the senator, who occasionally caused loud laughter with his clever abuse and mockery, to the point where the Speaker had to remind the audience to keep quiet.

After the long speech was over and the legislator had returned to his seat to thunderous applause, it was the turn of the Democrat to reciprocate the derision that had been heaped upon him. In the best tradition of oratory, the more heated his words became the cooler he appeared. Then the Republican lost no time in sharply answering every new accusation with facts. At length the Democrat was driven to undisguised anger and railed at his opponent with unbecoming words such as liar, traitor, and outlaw.

It was said that the vehemence of the debate was the worst to have been heard in Congress since the Civil War. I could well have imagined that in France it would have developed into a duel. The Americans did not go so far, but it was unseemly of them nonetheless.

When I returned to the hotel, a woman who was also staying there asked me if I had been in the Senate that day. Yes, I had, I answered. "I heard a very heated debate."

"I was there too," the woman said, "but I am ashamed that we had to show our visitors such an undignified performance."

Congress was somewhat of a disappointment, but my visit with the president was a surprise in its own way too. I had expected that a courtesy call on the president, the head of state of a great nation, would involve a rigid procedure, but he made himself available quite easily. Workers and tourists were milling about freely in parts of the White House that were open to them. Such casualness was unthinkable in Japan, where bureaucrats lorded over ordinary citizens as their masters. Here I was, after all, in the country that gave birth to Lincoln. Not the least thing to impress me was what I saw of government offices. They had far fewer bureaucrats, lower remuneration, and many more female clerks than in Japan.

Toward the end of April, the weather in Washington suddenly became oppressively warm. I returned to New York, but it was hot there too, which made it difficult for me to sleep. I have always suffered from the heat and could not bear this for long. I therefore decided to cross the Atlantic alone, leaving my younger brother Yukitaka in New York.

Even as an exile I took my brother with me because I had not abandoned the idea of training him to be a good secretary. But once we reached America Yukitaka, however, decided that he would rather indulge his love of literature rather than conform with the ideas I had for him. Perhaps he saw the writing on the wall and abandoned ship thinking his brother would never become a great politician who could afford a secretary.

In any event, Yukitaka remained in America, pursued his love of literature and eventually joined a theatrical group and performed on stage. Whenever I visited America he came to see me at my hotel, but when I inquired after him during my 1950 visit I was told that he had died during the war.

I Am Impressed by the Character of the English

It was a relief to leave humid New York behind and board a ship that would take me across the ocean. Although I normally hate to travel by ship, this time it was different. I was not seasick and was among the first in the dining saloon for every meal. During the voyage it was cold enough to warrant a coat. On the eighth day we saw land in the hazy distance, and to celebrate the joy I felt I wrote these Chinese verses:

> Ten thousand *ri*
> Across the vast and surging sea
> Wind colder than my dreams
> A world of water without land
> For seven nights and seven days till dawns the eighth
> When in the haze, beyond the blue, in awe
> I make out Ireland's green and pleasant shore.

I was simply overjoyed when at last I set foot in England. Compared to the voyage across the Pacific it had been a relatively short passage, so I was not even seasick.

Not having gained an altogether favorable impression of America as a nation, or of its inhabitants, I was elated to think that at last I had come to the country where Pitt once lived, and now Gladstone. It gave me a *frisson* of anticipation. On my arrival in London from Liverpool I found lodgings in a quiet neighborhood in the north of the city. The house where I boarded was quite large and had a greenhouse as well as a small garden. It always had two or three boarders. The couple who owned it did not depend exclusively on it for their living, as the husband was in business and left home every day for his office. His wife was a cheerful person who liked to have people around. These family-run boarding houses were quite common in those days.

I was on my best behavior because I did not want to be looked down upon as a traveler from an uncivilized country. This earned signal attentions from my landlady, who took me sightseeing in a carriage she hired for the occasion and sometimes served me special dinners. As time passed she would even ask me for my opinion on family matters. She had only graduated from high school, but she had the quality and common sense of a middle-class woman.

In those days I loved to smoke cigars and always had one in my hand. Normally one was not allowed to smoke in the dining rooms and drawing rooms of English homes, but my landlady made an exception of me. Eventually she also took up smoking, and she would sometimes get into an argument with her husband over this. One appreciates being treated kindly in these little ways when one is in a strange country and far from home.

At a hundred degrees Fahrenheit, the temperature in New York was almost unbearable, but in England one needed a coat to go out. Apparently it was an unusual year—unusually hot in America and excessively cold in England.

I had noted that most homes in American cities had a garden but the plants were not very aesthetically arranged. In England they were most elegantly set out, and many homes had their third- and fourth-floor windows pleasingly decorated with potted flowers. Big homes and mansions were usually given thoughtful names, which were posted at their gates. I thought this was a charming and practical custom.

Of course, when it came to conveniences of everyday life, things were far better in America. Most homes there, for example, had running water even on the fourth and fifth floors. In English towns maids had to carry water to fill jugs in each room every day. Most American hotels had installed lifts and electric or gas lamps, but in England even some major hotels lacked these facilities. Trains were commonly used in America, whereas in England transportation was mainly by buggies and carriages.

Americans had more machines, probably because they wanted to be independent, not wishing to work for others as servants. Also, because things were expensive, they had thought of ways to use manpower sparingly. In comparing the two countries, I thought that England had more poor people, and American cities were more orderly... English buildings, however, were all solid and well built. Probably these differences stemmed from differences in their national character. What impressed me deeply about the English was their unique spirit and sense of morality.

First, there was their notion of a gentleman. In England, the qualification for being called a gentleman is not wealth, but deeds. It is not how a man dresses, but what he is. Thus, it is often said that so-and-so may be a member of the upper classes, but that he is no gentleman. Shopkeepers and their assistants who speak well and refrain from rough or impolite manners are considered fine gentlemen. It is this notion of gentlemanliness that sustains morality among the English and does much to elevate the grace of their society.

Second, I was impressed with their sense of fairness. Englishmen abhor unfairness, cowardice, and cheating. An uneducated child will correct himself if he is accused of any of these things. On one occasion a Japanese student was called unfair and scorned by his English classmates for using judo techniques to win in a fight. Later when they learned that judo was a martial art some began to practice it themselves. For those who did not know it judo was seen as a kind of cheating because it involved misleading the opponent into believing that one had lost, and then defeating him with an unexpected move.

I ran into this characteristic of the English many times. I was once taken to visit Hampton Court, which lies twenty miles up the Thames from London. On the way there we took the train, and had planned to return by river. We were negotiating with one boat-owner when another approached and tried to butt in. The first boatman brushed the newcomer aside, but the latter became furious and challenged our man to a fist fight. He did not suddenly spring on him, however, but waited until our fellow was ready, and only then did they set to. After they had exchanged a few blows he was felled by a punch to the face and was pinned to the ground, momentarily dazed.

Having previously had no experience of other than Japanese brawls, in which it was not unusual for the man on top to beat his opponent senseless, I was afraid

I might have to intervene. But to my surprise our boatman let his opponent get up without further punishment and even helped him to his feet. I kept watching, fascinated. Once on his feet and without even waiting to wipe the blood from his face, the interloper immediately braced himself to continue the battle. The first boatman had no choice but to do likewise and after a short time dealt another blow to the man's face, knocking him to the ground as before. But again he did not take advantage of him and made to help him up as he had the first time. The other took his time, but as soon as he was on his feet he again squared up to his foe. This time he was punched on the nose, so he went to the river bank to wash the blood from his eyes and mouth. Helplessly, I watched him return to the fight for the fourth time, with the same painful result. But this time he staggered to the river, and did not come back for more.

Our man appeared quite prepared to take on the other fellow if he dared to challenge him again. He waited where he was, but when he realized that the fight was over he walked slowly back to where we were and asked politely, "May I be of service, gentlemen?" His expression, his tone of voice and language, none of these betrayed the slightest emotion.

During my stay in the country I witnessed many such fights among the lower-class Englishmen, but they all followed the same unwritten rules. The Englishman does not take advantage of his opponent's weakness nor does he take him by surprise. I was struck by the similarity between their code of honor and that of the old samurai. The English nature is also seen in the way in which the women view the opposite sex. They seem to find robust, well-built men the most hand-some—in sharp contrast to Japanese women, who see handsomeness in pale and sickly actor types. Another thing I observed in England was that the sons of aristocrats and the wealthy excelled their counterparts in the middle and lower classes in intelligence as well as in physical strength.

Looking back on those days when I hardly knew how to eat or dress naturally in the English manner, I realize that I must have presented a comic sight to my hosts, but I was never ridiculed for it. This was in complete contrast to the contemptuous way our own people looked down on students from China.

I Celebrate the Promulgation of the Constitution from Afar

While I was far away in exile, preparations for the constitution were making steady progress. It was April of 1888 when Prime Minister Itō completed the draft text and presented it to the emperor. On receipt of the draft His Majesty convened a Privy Council composed of those who were considered the most learned men in the realm to study each article of the document. The Privy Council, with Itō as its first president, was formally inaugurated on May 4. The council first met on May 8, 1881, and thereafter, weekly, and sometimes biweekly, until December 17 of the same year, to deliberate on the Imperial Family Code, the Constitution, and laws governing the parliament and elections to its two houses. Meetings took place twice a day, in the morning and afternoon, and His Majesty was present at each session. Only once on the morning of October 12 did the emperor miss for reasons of health, but in the afternoon he returned despite still not feeling well. I was deeply moved to learn to what extent the Emperor Meiji had been personally involved in this long task and how profoundly committed he was to proclaiming the constitution.

I would like to quote from the informal diary of Kaneko Kentarō, who was charged with keeping daily minutes of the meetings:

> The emperor sat in an armchair but never once did he lean back to rest, remaining erect without once moving his head or body to left or right. I could not help but be impressed.
>
> To this day I am overcome by awe as I recall November 12, the day His Imperial Highness Prince Michihito (Aki-no-miya) passed away. A flustered chamberlain entered the room where we were meeting and whispered into the ear of Chairman Itō. A certain councilor was eloquently making a point. Itō left his seat and quietly conferred with the emperor. None of us was aware of what had happened. Only when the meeting was over for the day and His Majesty had withdrawn to his chambers did Itō share with the other members the news of the death of the emperor's son. Itō had asked His Majesty if he wished to suspend the conference, but the emperor had instructed that the meeting should continue until they had finished working on the article under study. We therefore continued until everyone was in agreement, and only after the day's agenda had been completed did His Majesty withdraw. We were deeply awed to learn the truth.

The emperor must have reasoned that his son's death was an imperial family matter, and therefore of less importance than the conference on the constitution, which was an affair of state. I am convinced that there can be no other monarch who is so concerned about his nation.

This incident movingly illustrates the Emperor Meiji's unsparing personal participation in the work of the council to finalize the constitution. On February 11, 1889, a date chosen to coincide with National Foundation Day,[9] the Constitution of the Empire of Japan was promulgated at a grand ceremony. To mark the occasion the following Imperial Rescript was issued:

> It is Our heart's greatest desire that Our nation enjoy prosperity and Our people be blessed with happiness, and by virtue of the authority inherited from Our illustrious imperial ancestors We now proclaim this supreme and fundamental law for the benefit of Our people present and their succeeding generations.
>
> Our venerated imperial ancestors have with the faithful support of the forefathers of Our subjects built Our empire and made it unequalled to others. We have inherited its glorious history due to the virtues of Our revered ancestors and to the steadfastness and courage of Our subjects and their unfailing devotion to Our country. Recalling that Our subjects are the sons and daughters of the faithful subjects of Our imperial ancestors We do not doubt but that that they will make Our wishes and endeavors

[9] 660 B.C. was the date ascribed to the accession to rule for the legendary Jimmu, the first emperor.

theirs and that in a harmonious spirit of understanding and cooperation they will share with Us the loyal burden to make the honor of Our empire known at home and abroad, and to enshrine in perpetuity the glorious undertakings of Our imperial ancestors.

On this auspicious day, when the imperial constitution was promulgated, I was still living in the lodgings in London that had been my temporary home since my arrival as an exile from the imperial capital under the public security ordinance. Sixteen years had passed since the petition had been filed in 1873 for the establishment of a popularly elected parliament, and eight years since the imperial rescript of 1881 had promised the opening of a national parliament. At last the constitutional government we had been fighting for all these years was assured. My emotions were all the more deep-felt because I was celebrating this great moment so far from home.

On the same day, all Japanese citizens were invited by the Japanese legation in London to join in a fitting celebration. This was on Monday, and the day before, Sunday, the tenth, it had started to snow after lunch; the snow had still not stopped when night fell. It was an unusually heavy snowfall for London and few pedestrians or carriages ventured onto the streets. However, the next day was fine, and the sun shone on a pure blanket of snow. It seemed to me that the gods were celebrating the occasion by purifying heaven and earth.

Unused to so much snow, Londoners were slow to clear the streets, which delayed the resumption of normal traffic. It was feared that Japanese who lived in the outskirts of the capital would not be able to make it to the legation, but by nine in the evening fifty-six of my countrymen had gathered after somehow overcoming the difficulties of travel. Counting the members of the legation, there were sixty of us Japanese celebrating the proclamation. Only a few who lived hundreds of miles out had had to excuse themselves.

After the crowd had all settled down at their tables, the acting minister, Mr. Okabe, spoke briefly, saying that this was the day all Japanese had been waiting for and that it was an unprecedented celebration in the annals of Japan. He praised the illustrious virtues of His Majesty and shared with those present a cable received only a few hours earlier from the foreign minister, which read: "His Imperial Majesty has in person promulgated the Constitution of the Empire of Japan amidst the great enthusiasm of the people." All those present cheered spontaneously and cried "Long live the Emperor!"

After dinner, entertainments were held in the hall. Some volunteered their *Nō* songs and dances, others performed a Western-style skit and yet others displayed their skill as *rakugo* raconteurs. I was amazed at the amount of talent to be found among the Japanese community.

Under normal circumstances I did not care much for such playfulness. This evening was different. Elated to be present at this once-in-a-thousand-years, historic celebration, I found myself enjoying the evening and quite forgetting how the time was slipping by. It was four the next morning by the time I got back to my rooms. I suspect that not a few of my compatriots remained at the mission drinking until the sun came up.

Of the numerous historic achievements of the forty-five-year reign of Emperor Meiji, the greatest and the one which bequeathed the widest and most long-lasting benefits to our country and its people was the promulgation of the constitution. No doubt our victories in the wars with China and Russia were illustrious national achievements, but with the passage of time they would be relegated to the status of mere historical events. The promulgation of the constitution, however, protecting the lives and safeguarding the property of the people and ensuring the Japanese the same level of rights and obligations due the citizens of all nations, would not be forgotten even for a day as long as the state existed and the people lived.

More than any other national accomplishment the constitution would endure and would not fade into oblivion even after thousands of years. As long as the Japanese breathed and possessed property and did not lose awareness of their rights and obligations, this great legacy of Emperor Meiji which ensured their very survival would live eternally in the memories of the people. It was the responsibility of the whole nation, not just the government or the people, to go on seeking to perfect the Meiji Constitution.

The qualities required of those responsible for perfecting the constitution were numerous, but the most important were to develop political knowledge and morality. This meant that all those dedicated to carrying out the imperial will, government and private citizens alike, must be faithful to their commitment. The clan politicians, however, so used to their old autocratic ways, not only tried to delay the implementation of constitutional government but constantly acted to impede the development of political thought and morality. They most probably did not intend to be disloyal to the emperor, but by their actions they hurt his grand design. We had fought for years to change the minds of these people and to bring down institutions created for the purpose of perpetuating clan government and to establish constitutional government under the monarchy, but we had not stamped them out.

Only when its implementation was perfected and the constitution was universally respected would the people of Japan be freed from the past. Only when the *hanbatsu* were finally overcome and the people enjoyed true equality under the law would there be fair competition. With fair competition, excellence would prevail over mediocrity. This was the righteous way in heaven and on earth, and our objectives would only have been achieved when the way was guaranteed. It could not be helped that some would win and some would lose.

Even after the imperial constitution was promulgated on February 11,, the Satsuma and Chōshū clansmen retained their places and power at the center of the government, and even accumulated more. As long as the fundamental law was infringed upon from left and right, we were determined to keep up the political pressure.

THE BREAKUP OF OUR ALLIANCE

Even after the constitution came into being, the ruling clans hardly changed their attitude toward the existence of political parties. They suppressed without apology political parties, which were attempting to articulate national opinion, and, on the other hand, tried to subvert them by infiltrating their ranks to reduce their cohesion and effectiveness.

The very day after the promulgation of the constitution, Prime Minister Kuroda, speaking at a meeting of prefectural governors, made a so-called declaration of "transcendentalism" or supra-party government. The declaration in part stated:

> It should be clearly understood that the constitution is not a license for divisive opinions. While one cannot escape the tendency for political parties to exist by consolidating like-minded people who have divergent views on matters of governance, the government must always indicate a certain direction, stand transcendental to political parties and remain on the path of justice. Respected governors should remind themselves of this and address the people from a nonpartisan attitude, and with their support and cooperation endeavor to assist the government to ensure national prosperity for all.

On February 15, Itō Hirobumi, while still president of the Privy Council, spoke thus to heads and elected representatives of prefectural assemblies:

> The emperor governs the nation and the prime minister offers advice to the emperor in his mission. In dispensing the responsibility of advising the throne, there must be recognition of different roles and stations. The monarch reigns above the people and outside political parties. The government must maintain its unbiased independence, wary of benefiting one party to the disadvantage of others. It is extremely destabilizing if the government is constantly influenced left and right by the whims of political parties. While political factions will inevitably form in the private sector it must be seen that they exceed their role when they seek to influence the government.
>
> In the future, when the national parliament comes into being and public opinion is invited to determine political matters, it is most dangerous to expect the immediate establishment of parliamentary government, in other words the organization of cabinets by political parties.

Such opinions were representative of the *hanbatsu* leadership, and this kind of thinking controlled the clan government for many years to come. Their favorite terms were "transcendentalism" and "unbiased independence," but what these men had in mind was simply to build a fortress to protect clan domination of government. Political parties supported by public opinion would be the most formidable opponents of the *hanbatsu* coalition. The clan leaders probably thought that if they could only defend themselves from this threat they would be able to hold the reins of autocratic government in perpetuity.

In those days it was the movement spearheaded by our alliance that the *hanbatsu* government feared most. The movement had evolved from the one that we started with Gotō Shōjirō prior to our expulsion under the security ordinance. Gotō was exceptionally committed to the cause of the alliance. The day before I was to leave the country, he asked me to name a person who could be trusted just as much as I. I replied that if there was any one person who was perhaps most to be trusted among my good friends, it was Inukai, and I asked Gotō to trust him as he trusted me. Inukai had for some time been a good friend of Ōhishi's and I thought they would get along well together. This apparently had not proven to be the case, according to a letter Ōhishi sent me reporting that things were difficult because Gotō did not trust Inukai. And Inukai, for his part, had written to me saying in effect, "Just wait and see whether I get the political organization or whether Gotō does." No wonder the two did not get along well. Gotō apparently complained that "Inukai was through and through an Ōkuma man and could not be counted on as a team member, while Ozaki was one of us even though he was an Ōkuma man." In any event, Gotō evidently could not bring himself to trust Inukai. On the other hand, it is possible that Inukai might actually have been trying to get control of the alliance for his own purposes.

It was very unfortunate that Gotō and Inukai could not get along well, but the movement initiated by the alliance had an enormous impact throughout the country nevertheless. Gotō had been traveling from one speaking engagement to another since the previous year, 1888. "In its international relations, Japan has compromised its independence and sovereignty," he would say, "while at home, people have been deprived of civil liberties and burdened by excessive taxation, which has driven 400,000 to 500,000 to abandon the country every year. This is a time of serious national crisis. The only way to salvage the situation is to come together in a grand alliance, setting aside small differences and bringing local organizations to the center to bring their collective pressure to bear on the government." He lectured widely in Nagano, Tōhoku (the northeastern region), Tōkai (Nagoya), and Hokuriku (the Niigata area), in all of which political societies had sprung up in his wake. By the spring of 1890 there was enough momentum to organize the alliance of which he spoke.

It was the turn of the *hanbatsu* government to be surprised. They feared that left unattended a competitive counterforce could develop. With the opening of the national parliament imminent they must have reasoned that it was in their interest to bring their opponents into the fold rather than fight them. Through an intermediary they begged Gotō to join the cabinet. The move was known as an attempt to set up an "all-inclusive cabinet of loyal servants."

Three men in public favor at this time were Ōkuma Shigenobu, the head of the Progressive Party; Itagaki Taisuke, president of the Liberal Party; and Gotō Shōjirō, the initiator of the alliance. Ōkuma was already in the cabinet, and the clan leaders must have calculated that if they were able to get Gotō too they would not have to fear the political parties even if Itagaki remained in opposition. Pursuing this course, they succeeded in convincing Gotō to join the Kuroda government.

Being out of the country, I had no idea what Gotō's motive was in accepting a cabinet portfolio. There were many among our colleagues, I learned, who condemned Gotō for his disloyalty in selling out his friends, compromising his principles and accepting a position of power. Gotō apparently took little notice and even declared with arrogant indifference: "I am simply obeying an imperial order. There is not the slightest difference in realizing the objectives of the alliance, whether they are pursued in opposition or from within government."

Gotō's apparent defection to the cabinet caused a great turbulence within the alliance. In the first place, the alliance was nothing more than a loose collaboration among heterogeneous political forces that had rallied around the old Liberal Party, part of the Progressive Party, and some conservatives. Finding itself suddenly without its central figure, it was only to be expected that the alliance would fragment again. As feared, a schism developed between those who thought the alliance should evolve into a political organization and those opposed to the idea. Members of the former group created the Daidō (grand alliance) Club while its opponents created the Daidō Kyōwa-kai (association).

Immensely disheartened by this development, Itagaki, the former head of the Liberal Party, traveled to Tokyo to mediate between the two groups, but to no avail. While the alliance continued to exist on paper it really did so only in name, and the so-called Mintō, the People's Party, was forced to fight the first general election as divided as ever.

ŌKUMA ATTACKED

In mid-March I received a letter from a friend in Tokyo informing me that a general amnesty had been announced to coincide with the promulgation of the constitution. Those detained in jail for their part in the struggle for the cause of constitutional government since 1882 were all declared free. I too was pardoned.

I thought of returning home immediately to prepare for the first election, which, it was announced, would take place the following year, but decided to delay my departure until mid-May to complete some unfinished business. I booked passage on a French steamer due to sail on May 19 via Greece, and Italy. At Cook's Travel Agency I bought myself a ticket for the voyage and was in the process of preparing for my departure from London on April 3. By chance, however, I made the close acquaintance of an Englishman, and, on his introduction, was invited to a number of clubs and meetings. This was much more interesting to me than traveling to lands whose languages I did not understand, so with the help of my new friend I was able to sell my ticket to a third party and decided to stay in London. I stopped being a hermit and went out to meet people at all times of the day and night. Sometimes I traveled outside London too in search of information and experience that might possibly come in useful.

Suddenly I found myself busy both socially and with sightseeing. I explored the north of England in July and then returned to London before crossing the Channel to the Continent. I twice visited Paris, also Cologne, Hamburg, Berlin, and Frankfurt, and even took a boat down the Rhine. After touring the Continent I came back to London to make final preparations for my return to Japan when I received the terrible news that my good friend, Ōkuma, had lost a leg in a bombing incident on October 18.

Since joining the cabinet Ōkuma had been saddled with the unenviable task that he had inherited from his predecessor, Foreign Minister Inoue, of negotiating the revision of the Unequal Treaties. Until then, Japan had sought to negotiate with all other treaty powers as a bloc. Ōkuma decided instead to tackle them country by country. If the negotiations with the United States succeeded, then he expected the other powers would follow suit. The method was certainly more resourceful.

The *London Times* carried Ōkuma's proposed treaty revision, which faced fierce opposition back home because of two items: permitting the appointment of foreign judges, and mixed residence of foreigners.[10] Opposition came from a Liberal Party–affiliated alliance group, which was inimical to the Kaishintō as well as from middle-of-the-road conservatives under Torio Koyata and the neoconservatives led by Tani Kanjō, who jointly attacked the proposed treaty revision as "treason." The opposition forces increased in strength when Kumamoto's Shienkai and Fukuoka's Genyōsha joined the bandwagon.[11]

Undaunted, the stiff-necked Ōkuma pushed ahead with the negotiations until he encountered opposition from within the ranks of his own cabinet. Itō Hirobumi, the president of the Privy Council, formally declared his opposition, tendered his resignation to the throne, and left the capital on October 11. Agriculture Minister Inoue Kaoru followed suit and returned to his home on the pretext of illness. Prime Minister Kuroda alone kept his trust in Ōkuma and stood by his foreign minister. But on October 15, in the face of the increasing difficulty of the situation, Ōkuma requested a conference at the palace to beg His Majesty's intervention.

At the meeting, Ōkuma reported the details of the negotiations and explained the central importance for the country of the revision. The most controversial issue was the appointment of foreigners as judges, and Ōkuma explained that, in his view, this was not unconstitutional, since the foreigners in question would be naturalized Japanese citizens. Gotō Shōjirō, the minister of postal services, led the opposition against Ōkuma. Home Minister Yamagata Aritomo, it was afterwards learned, assailed him with extremely biting questions, while Finance Minister Matsukata Masayoshi criticized his proposals from the financial point of view. The meeting ended inconclusively, and another cabinet meeting was called on October 18. It was on his way home after this meeting that Ōkuma was struck by a bomb thrown at his carriage by a Genyōsha man, Kijima Tsuneyoshi.

---

[10] Ōkuma saw the use of foreign judges in Japanese courts as a step away from the extraterritoriality of the Unequal Treaties, but his opponents saw this as a continuation of the present system. Again, under the Unequal Treaties, foreigners were restricted to treaty ports, but reforms that put an end to "treaty ports" would, in consequence, give foreigners unrestricted travel and residence throughout Japan. Many Japanese were afraid that would impair national sovereignty and bring economic domination by the intrusive foreigners.

[11] The Genyōsha later spawned the *Kokuryūkai*—Amur River, or "Black Dragon" Society, a strong force in Japanese ultranationalism.

The incident drove Kuroda and all other ministers to resign en masse, taking responsibility for the division within the cabinet. Sanjō Sanetomi, the lord keeper of the Privy Seal, briefly doubled as interim prime minister. In due course, Yamagata Aritomo was named prime minister, and presented his cabinet on December 24.

These events I learned after my return, since cables received in London from abroad brought only sparse information. It was hard to know Ōkuma's condition after he lost his leg. His survival had an enormous bearing on my own future political life, and I worried myself to exhaustion. Three eminent London surgeons whose advice I sought all had more or less the same thing to say of Ōkuma's prognosis. Whether one lived or died following such an injury had much to do with the place of severance, in other words whether the amputation was below the knee or above. The outcome was influenced also by the age and responsibilities of the victim. The greatest number of fatalities from among those who lost their legs occurred during the American Civil War. Young soldiers usually survived even when their legs were severed at the thigh. They were only glad to be alive and looked forward to meeting their parents and family. Commissioned officers, on the other hand, had more to worry about, such as how differently the battle would have turned out had they not been wounded, and, as a result, many faced a greater risk of death. More generals were sure to die from such injuries since their responsibilities were heavier. Ōkuma was already fifty-two and held an important post in the cabinet with concomitant responsibilities. Even with one leg severed his chances of survival were rated slim, with odds of one in ten.

It was with a leaden heart expecting never to see Ōkuma again that I set out for home. The return voyage took me eastward across the Indian Ocean. In those days, there was not much difference in the length of the trip whether one traveled via America or Asia. All the way I prayed for Ōkuma's life, and after about forty days we finally docked back in Japan. It was the end of 1890. I found Ōkuma packing his belongings at the foreign minister's official residence to return to his own home in Waseda. "I'm fine now," said Ōkuma. I was immensely relieved. Remembering what the doctors in London had told me I wondered how Ōkuma had survived his traumatic injury. It must have been due entirely to his characteristic optimism. Ōkuma's leg was amputated under anesthesia, and when he regained consciousness and was told that he had lost his leg the first thing he said to the anxious doctors was, "I should be healthier now that the blood that went to my leg will be circulating in other places." Before his narrow escape from death, I learned, he occasionally fainted, perhaps due to overwork, during cabinet meetings. He seemed too thin and bloodless, though with his leg gone Ōkuma could joke that he would now have enough blood to keep him healthy. This was the way his mind worked. Not for a moment did he despair or lose courage. It was this inner strength that got him through a brutal operation and gave him many more years of life.

It was extremely lucky that Ōkuma lost just one leg, but it was his own generosity that saved his life. When the bomb was thrown, the two guards, one on either side of Ōkuma, were so shaken that neither could later recall exactly what happened. According to the coachman, as the carriage was passing through the gates of the foreign ministry, he saw the stranger before the guards did and lashed his horse. The quickened pace of the horse prompted the stranger to throw the bomb in haste. Had he been able to aim better, the result might have been fatal, but the quick action of the coachman had saved Ōkuma's life.

The coachman had been in the employ of Ōkuma for some time. He was an engaging individual but sometimes drank too much, and when he did he became violent. At times he had threatened others with a knife, and the butler had on many occasions tried to dismiss him, but each time Ōkuma would not have it. "Let it pass," he said. And this was the coachman who saved Ōkuma's life.

On returning to Japan from my study of constitutional government in England, I received frequent visits from powerful local leaders and heads of prefectural assemblies, who asked me how elections were conducted and many such things. The fact that they were so keen to learn, even from a youngster like myself, reflected the eagerness with which the people wished to make constitutional government a reality.

Throughout my absence I had continued as their overseas correspondent to send back pieces I had written to the *Chōya Shinbun*, and I continued to write for the paper after my return. Subscriptions increased, but the situation remained very tight financially, and within less than a year, the paper went bankrupt. After the *Chōya* collapsed in January, 1891, I established a daily newspaper called *Minpō* (People's Daily) together with Inukai and others, but this too went bankrupt. By this time, Inukai and I had gained quite a reputation as "masters at ruining newspapers".

The Early Days of the Parliament

Japan's First General Election

The first general election to be held in Japan took place on July 1, 1890. The Yamagata government took great pains to maintain its "transcendental" position above political parties. It dispatched the following instructions to local governors: "The implementation of the Constitution is imminent. As we await this great national event, it is unavoidable that there will be controversial debate and that political parties will quarrel. The power to govern resides in His Majesty the Emperor and is delegated by him. Therefore, those who are assigned the responsibility of discharging this mandate should stand outside political parties, abjure every kind of partisanship, adopt the way of justice, and faithfully discharge the duties that are entrusted to them."

It is a clear instruction, and had successive clan governments carried out this policy the election process might have been spared the corruption that was to mar it. However, as I shall describe later, the government itself intervened flagrantly soon afterwards, planting the seeds of corruption in the electoral process of its own accord.

The first election, in which the government did not dare intervene, at least blatantly, was conducted in a relatively calm manner. While the political awareness of the common citizen had as yet had little chance to develop, there was hardly any resort to the atrocities that would later be committed.

For myself, I was not sure from which region I should stand for the first election. Although I was born in Kanagawa prefecture I had only spent several years of my early childhood there and had since had very little connection with the area. There was only an empty plot at the site where our house once stood in Matano village and I knew no one who could help me to run an election.

With the encouragement of enthusiastic friends I had secretly made up my mind to run from Saitama prefecture with the help of Katō Seinosuke and others, when my father Yukimasa, who had settled on his retirement in the outskirts of Yamada city, suggested that there was a good chance of winning the election if I stood for Mie prefecture instead.

My father, who worked for the government in Mie prefecture while promoting business and industry, covered a large area, often staying with other government officials, and he had developed a wide circle of acquaintances. I had spent some years of my boyhood with my parents in Yamada city, so in a sense Mie prefecture was my second home. It was rather quickly decided that I should stand for Mie.

From an historical point of view, it was a memorable election that started me off on my sixty-odd years of parliamentary life, but my own experience was unexciting. Mie was a two-seat electoral district. However, there was hardly any competition to speak of from my opponent, Kitagawa Kuichi, and I was elected with a safe margin, collecting 1,172 votes out of a total of 1,919.

All the same I was quite pleased with myself, and as soon as I returned to Tokyo I paid my respects to my old *sensei*, Fukuzawa. I thought that I at least deserved a word of congratulation rather than the usual reprimand. Instead of complimenting me, however, he took up a brush and jotted down this verse:

> Ambition begins as a hobby
> But you're quite mad to become an M.P.
> You'll end up pawning your family fields
> For eight hundred yen a year. You'll see.

In those days the yearly stipend for a member of parliament was eight hundred yen.

In contrast to my own easy victory, the Kaishintō suffered a dire setback. As mentioned earlier, Ōkuma's proposed treaty revision was attacked from all sides, from the Jiyūtō on the left to all shades of conservatives on the right. Although Ōkuma did not officially belong to the party, he had guided the Kaishintō as its de facto president. But having supported the Ōkuma treaty revision the party was everywhere opposed for allegedly endangering the independence of the country, much as we had earlier brought down the Ito government ourselves. Some called the party the "treacherous subject" party, playing on another word that sounded like Kaishintō. Had the general election taken place before Ōkuma's injury the Kaishintō would probably have gained a considerable majority. As it was, however, only fourteen of us who publicly associated ourselves with the Kaishintō were successfully elected. Others ran without burdening themselves with the Kaishintō platform.

As mentioned earlier, Gotō's abrupt defection to the clan government having caused the collapse of our alliance, the first general election was fought among a number of small parties. However, after the election, Yamada Taketoshi, Yoshinobu Ujifusa, Taketomi Tokitoshi, and Haseba Sumitaka of the Kyushu Kaishintō took the initiative to push for the amalgamation of the Jiyūtō and what remained of the Kaishintō. The plan gained considerable support and came close to succeeding. Even the name of the new party had been decided. It was to have been called the Rikken Jiyūtō (Constitutional Liberal Party), taking the Rikken from "Rikken-Kaishintō" and attaching it to "Jiyūtō."

I was opposed to the idea of the merger. While the Kaishintō was suffering from the misfortune of having inherited the failed treaty revision, the Jiyūtō, on the other hand, had been able to pull itself together after the collapse of the alliance and even increased its strength. A merger in these circumstances would not give the two parties equal status. It seemed to me at the time virtually inevitable that such a union would disintegrate almost as soon as it formed. I objected particularly to the use of "Jiyūtō" as part of the new party's name. It signified surrender, I said, not merger, and I opposed it with all my might. On the Jiyūtō side as well, there was an undercurrent opposing fusion with the Kaishintō, so in the end the Kaishintō stayed out.

The few of us who had been elected decided on September 1 to dissolve the party temporarily, so as to study the workings of government and prepare ourselves for action within the House. We did, however, reserve a meeting place for ourselves.

Meanwhile, the Aikoku Kōtō (Patriotic Party), the Daido Club (Grand Alliance Club), the Saiko-Jiyūtō (Reborn Liberal Party) and the Kyushu Dōshikai (Like-minded Kyushu Group), all of which were affiliated to the Jiyūtō, met at the Yayoi restaurant in Shiba park on September 2 to establish the Yayoi Club.

Although the Yayoi Club was ostensibly to be a meeting-place for all members of parliament, in reality those who used it were exclusively members of the Jiyūtō and the Kaishintō. The Yayoi Club affiliated with the Jiyūtō boasted the largest membership with 130 members, while those who belonged to our group were a mere 41. The combined membership of 171, all of whom belonged to opposition parties, thus constituted an absolute majority out of the total of 300 seats in the House. By contrast, the formal government party, the Kokumin Jiyūtō (National Liberal Party) had a membership of only five. However, they were able to bring together a sufficient number of conservatives and independents to organize what they called the Taiseikai with a total membership of seventy-nine. Collectively, this was the government party.

I had secretly hoped that a few dark horses might find their way into the House as a result of the election. But looking around me, I was disappointed that hardly any potential new stalwart was to be seen. Indeed, most of the honorable members were frankly of less than third-class material. In the circumstances, Taketomi Tokitoshi alone seemed to stand head and shoulders above the rest. It did not take long for him to prove his prowess in the House and to earn much respect from the public as well. Later, Taketomi displayed his ability as a cabinet secretary. In my opinion, of the successive cabinet secretaries, no one proved more excellent than Itō Miyoji, Taketomi Tokitoshi, and Inoue Kowashi.

Taketomi was usually silent, but his mind was clear. Kōmuchi Tomotsune used to carry budget documents in a *furoshiki* wrap. He also had a methodical mind when it came to discussing the budget. "Kōmuchi Tomotsune certainly is well informed when it comes to the budget, isn't he?" I remarked one day. "Well, let us say he is seldom parted from it," corrected Taketomi. Taketomi was himself well versed in budgetary matters, so Kōmuchi Tomotsune must have appeared to him to be the sort of man who liked carrying papers around.

Apart from Taketomi there was no other outstanding person among the newly elected members. Having said this, there were many fine men who nevertheless enjoyed high local repute. They were mostly young. Of the 300 members, 136 were in their thirties, 114 in their forties, 36 in their fifties, and 14 in their sixties or above. Their average age was forty-two years and four months. After ten general elections, younger members below the age of forty accounted for only one-tenth of the House.

RECOLLECTIONS OF THE FIRST DIET

The first Diet (November 1890–March 1891) was convened on November 25, 1890. It was after all the very first session, but the lack of experience of parliamentary procedure and the incompleteness of House rules resulted in a great muddle over the election of the president. Much of the confusion was due simply to unfamiliarity with the election process, but matters were not improved by the ill-advised observation of Sone Arasuke, the House secretary in his capacity as acting president, when he announced: "Let us break for fifteen minutes to give you time to cool off!", which resulted in a comic scene in which he was forced to apologize publicly for his remark. I recall that we spent several hours just electing the president, during which Acting-President Sone had no opportunity to escape to the men's room.

Finally, the House elected Nakajima Nobuyuki of the Yayoi Club as president and Tsuda Masamichi of the Taiseikai as deputy-president. Had we been better prepared in parliamentary procedures and united among the opposition, we would not have lost the post of deputy-president to the Taiseikai, a member of the coalition. But there was nothing we could do about it.The confusion did not end with the election of the president. There was much ado about nothing, even in matters of general parliamentary procedure, which wasted a great deal of our time.

Members were generally earnest and hardworking. In particular, we had Abe Yoshihito, who was an expert in fiscal matters and who drew up a draft proposal to cut government spending, in our group. Abe had been a member of the Kaishintō from the time of its founding, but had left the party in midstream to work as a bureaucrat in the ministry of finance in order to gain greater knowledge of fiscal matters. He had stood successfully in the election for Fukushima prefecture and had a seat in our block.

Then there was also Hikida Nagasuke of Akita prefecture who had been my invaluable assistant since we mounted our opposition against Foreign Minister Inoue's proposed treaty revision. During my absence from the country he had done an excellent job of listing areas of the administration where reform was needed. On my return he presented the result to me, saying it was what he had done during the two years I had been away. I took Hikida's administrative reform plan to the Diet first, followed by Abe's proposal for reducing government spending.

The principal matter of business for the first session of the Diet was the budget. The government could carry on with its work even if legislative bills failed to pass the House, but not the budget. When we presented our revised budget proposal based on Abe and Hikida's recommendations, it gained great support both in the budget committee as well as the plenary session and became the rallying point of opposition against the government.

The first Diet was dominated by the initiatives of the Kaishintō although the party commanded no more than forty-one seats. With these numbers it was not very visible but it impressed the public by its tactics. I was proud of our achievement and felt that I had got my political career off to a reasonably good start.

The national budget in those days, including the ordinary and special accounts, was a mere 80 million yen, which was an insignificant amount compared with today's budget. Nevertheless, we managed to cut it by 8 million. Our revised budget was known as "*satei-an*" (the revised plan). The parliamentary battle was fierce from the beginning, and the popularity of our proposed revision was such that in the Mukōjima district of Tokyo, for example, a newly-opened *shiruko* (a sweet bean soup) shop even adopted the name '*satei-an*.' Some members of the "people's parties," as we called ourselves and our allies, and other members of the House went out of their way to visit Mukōjima for a bowl of that mediocre sweet bean soup. I was one of them.

The government fought back in an attempt to save the budget from being thus slashed by one-tenth. Prime Minister Yamagata tried to refute the reasons for our proposed cut by explaining national policy since the Restoration and listing all the reasons why the budget as originally presented was necessary to implement the government's grand strategy for achieving its avowed objectives. We refused to budge. Yamagata was enraged. "Parliament should not obstruct government!" he cried. Finance Minister Matsukata went so far as to imply a threat to dissolve the House. Still we did not give in. Both the Kaishintō and the Jiyūtō were fully committed to cutting the budget, having fought for so many years for "less government spending and more money in people's pockets." Eventually our *satei-an* was adopted by the budget committee and seemed certain to win in the plenum with the support of the allied forces of the opposition. The government struck a deal at the eleventh hour. Prime Minister Yamagata, who must have wanted very much to ensure the passage of the budget without dissolving the Diet, succeeded in persuading twenty-eight of the Tosa men from the Jiyūtō to change sides. Because of this, we lost the absolute majority and had to compromise with a reduction of 6.5 million yen.

The upshot of this incident was that the twenty-eight Tosa men seceded en bloc and the de facto president, Itagaki, also submitted his intention to leave the party to take responsibility for the actions of his men. In the end, they ate their words and were restored to the party roll. The incident, however, marked the beginning of political party corruption, and in particular of the oft-repeated politics of compromise. Nakae Chōmin was quickly disillusioned and resigned his seat, citing alcoholism as an excuse.

THE MATSUKATA GOVERNMENT AND THE SECOND DIET

While Yamagata was able to contain the budget cut at 6.5 million yen by buying off part of the opposition, the cut dealt the government a heavy blow. As was well known, Yamagata was the giant of the *hanbatsu* and the most committed to defending the clan government. From the beginning, however, he found the opposition of the people's parties to be a bigger thorn in his side than he had anticipated, and he did not take long to tire of having to manage this fractious assembly. The defeat over the budget had caused disquiet within the cabinet too, and Yamagata took the opportunity offered by the conclusion of the first session to resign.

The *genrō* (elder statesmen) convened to decide on Yamagata's successor. The *genrō* were not formally appointed by law nor was their mandate constitutionally assigned, but it was customary for them to be responsible for certain important decisions. We used to call their meetings "*kuromaku kaigi*" (mastermind meetings).

In those days the Satsuma and Chōshū clans tried to maintain a balance of power between them. It sounds ridiculous today, but the first government was headed by a Chōshū man, Itō, the second by a Satsuma man, Kuroda, and the next by Chōshū's Yamagata. And when the Yamagata government fell, the immediate problem was to find a suitable successor from Satsuma. The mastermind meeting agreed to call on Kuroda Kiyotaka again, but he rejected their appeal. They then tried to convince Saigō Tsugumichi, but he too declined. In the end they apparently had no other choice but to call on Matsukata Masayoshi, who had little power to organize a cabinet.

The opposition forces were united against the government. Seeing that the Kaishintō, rallying under its de facto president, Ōkuma, and acting in complete unity, controlled the House of Representatives with just forty-one men, there were those within the Jiyūtō, led by Matsuda Masahisa, Hoshi Tōru, and Kōno Hironaka, who felt the need to have a properly elected president. However, there was difficulty in getting their candidate, Itagaki, accepted. The Kyushu faction led by Kawashima Jun and the Kanto faction led by Ōi Kentarō had to be convinced. It was Matsuda who took the initiative and successfully talked them into accepting Itagaki as the party president. The appointment was confirmed at their Osaka convention in March of 1891.

The long-standing mutual antagonism that had existed between the Jiyūtō and the Kaishintō had mollified when the two fought together against their common foe during the first election, and although there were deserters at the last minute, the experience of fighting on the same side had done a great deal to thaw their hard feelings. Now there was a growing impetus to forge an even stronger unity in order to fight against the Satsuma-Chōshū coalition in the second Diet. The man who led this momentum was Nakae Chōmin, who, though a member of the Jiyūtō, had many friends within the Kaishintō. He successfully staged a summit meeting between Ōkuma and Itagaki.

On November 8, Itagaki rode his horse to visit Ōkuma at the latter's residence in Waseda and apologized for their long estrangement. The friendship between the two men was renewed, and this had an enormous impact on the current political situation. The government panicked and, alleging misconduct on the part of a member of the privy council for meeting with the head of an opposition party, dismissed Ōkuma. This brought the two parties closer together still, and Ōkuma, now freed from his official obligations, formally assumed the chairmanship of the Kaishintō.

In order to protect itself by rallying its own members and forging closer ties with members of the Kokkentō (National Rights Party) and sympathetic ex-bureaucrats, the Taiseikai (the government party) founded the Kyōdō (Cooperative) Club. At its founding, led by such men as Suematsu Kenchō, Inoue Kakugorō, Ōe Taku, and Suehiro Shigetaka, the club boasted a membership of eighty, but as the true story was exposed the members drifted away, until November when the club was forced to disband.

At the same time as the Kyōdō Club was founded, those who were not happy with Taiseikai being party to the ruling coalition, together with some independent members, organized the Dokuritsu (Independent) Club. The club had a membership of nineteen and was also referred to as the Chūsei-ha (or justice group). Meanwhile a hard-core group within the Taiseikai got together with some members of the Jiyūtō and organized the Pari (Paris) Club. It had a separate platform and was in favor of collaborating with the opposition "people's parties." It had a membership of seventeen.

This was how the members of the House were deployed as we went into the second Diet (November 21–December 25, 1891).

The second Diet had an extensive agenda, which included nationalization of the railroads and emergency relief in relation to the recent major earthquake in the Nagoya area. This generated fierce clashes between the government and opposition forces on many more fronts than in the first Diet.

From the first Diet, the Matsukata government inherited the public promise of "administrative reform and spending reductions." To satisfy these expectations the government undertook cosmetic reforms and effected limited reductions in personnel expenses to the tune of a mere 600,000 yen, which gave us ammunition for attack.

It was at one point during this session that Navy Minister, Kabayama Sukenori, who was honest to a fault, lost his temper with the opposition and retorted: "Have you forgotten the achievements of the navy in the last twenty years? You criticize Satsuma and Chōshū for their autocratic ways but who do you think carried out the great achievement of the Restoration? Is it not to the Satsuma and Chōshū power that you owe the security of your life and property?" To this I responded: "I too would like to see the Japanese navy expanded. But what Japanese navy are we talking about? All I see is a Satsuma navy. Enomoto Takeaki is a Japanese who has studied naval affairs at a professional level. He cannot set foot in the naval ministry. Yet any amateur, so long as he happens to come from Satsuma, can become minister."

Just as during the first Diet, we decided to challenge the government on the budget. We again fought for a major reduction of 8 million yen, defeated the government on its plan to purchase private railways, and won approval retrospectively of the money already spent on the Nagoya earthquake relief. Again victory went to the people's parties. The Matsukata government, like its predecessor was forced to the wall.

Yamagata had resources to draw on and Itō had a talent for warding off opposition attacks, but not the dullard Matsukata. All he did was to confront his opponents head on by waving the imperial authority at them.

In the end, Prime Minister Matsukata decided to dissolve the House, giving the lame reason that he could not run the government with a recalcitrant House of Representatives. On December 25, he announced the dissolution in the name of the throne.

This marked the beginning of gross disrespect on the part of the government for the democratic foundations of parliament.

ELECTION INTERFERENCE BY HOME MINISTER SHINAGAWA

The first and second Diets both witnessed a frontal crash between the government and parliament, which resulted in extreme confusion of the political world. I learned that Emperor Meiji was seriously concerned at these developments and had said to the prime minister (Matsukata), who had recommended the dissolution in His Majesty's name that "Under the circumstances perhaps dissolution cannot be helped." But he advised that great attention should be given to the general election, since if the same sort of people were re-elected there was not much point in dissolving the House. He told the prime minister that "Efforts must be made to improve the quality of members of parliament and to ensure that good citizens will be elected to represent the people." I of course could only guess what the Emperor meant by "good citizens." The Matsukata government simply considered that those who were on their side were "good citizens" and those who opposed them were rioters, and in this way justified the use of the official police force to intervene in the election. As a result, there was unprecedented confusion. However much loyalty and patriotism one had, without the backbone of constitutional government there was no way one could obey His Majesty's wish.

Shinagawa Yajirō, in particular, who was home minister and reputed to be the bravest general in the clan government, held the view that anyone who opposed the government, which enjoyed the emperor's confidence, was by definition the enemy of the empire. During the Restoration War he had led an army against the enemies of the new government and loudly sang "Death to the Foe," which he had composed himself, with the same fervor with which he approached the election. In fact, the home minister had secretly let governors of prefectures know his mind, suggesting that "since the dissolution of parliament was an imperial command, re-election of incumbents was against the imperial will."

When I returned to my own district I found myself pretty unpopular, as I had more or less expected. In spite of this, Doi Mitsuhana, who represented an adjacent district, greeted me at Matsuzaka with banners and placards. However, finding himself soon after that under threat from the government, he too turned against me. It was he who gave me the nickname "chokkan giin" (imperially- repudiated member), since I held my seat at the time the House was dissolved in the emperor's name. The nickname circulated around the prefecture and added to my unpopularity. On top of this, my own voters, who were lobbying for the revision of land tax assessments, had wrongly accused me of opposing their interests, so from my point of view the second election looked much more uncertain than the first.

For some time, the revision of official land tax assessments for the purpose of taxation had been a local issue in the affected areas, of which Mie was one. I had been crusading for a nationwide land tax cut, as I felt that this was necessary in addition to reducing the official land prices for tax-assessment purposes in certain areas, which were out of tune with the rest of the nation. The Mie voters who were in favor of revising land prices argued that I was compromising the interests of the prefecture, since my two-pronged approach would necessarily result in a tax shortfall, as a result of which the government would be discouraged from going through with the land price revision. This was also instigated by the government to obstruct my election. However, those who were not parties asked by the government, but were interested in revision of land tax assessments, were convinced that I had to be defeated in order for their cause to win. They therefore deployed lobbyists from organizations throughout the district around to work actively to defeat me in the election.

Fierce government intervention as well as the land tax assessments issue continued to haunt me throughout this election. Not only did I find myself immensely unpopular with many of my constituents but no one had even suggested that I stand for re-election. Those mayors of villages and towns who had supported me in the first general election were almost without exception against me now. Men whom I considered fellow-fighters vacillated and were unwilling to help. Even my own chief of staff dared to advise me against running. "Please take a rest, just this once," he said. "There's no chance whatever of winning." It was depressing but I could not allow myself to be defeated. So I decided to go it alone and announced my intention at a gathering of ex-supporters. "I won't ask you to help me," I told them. "I am going to do this on my own." It is a strange thing but no sooner had I made my announcement than a few ventured to work with me, and as the days passed a few more. Still, it was a pitifully small team.

I toured the constituency and was not surprised to find myself a most unpopular object. The Kishu district was particularly determined not to show hospitality to a rebel. No inn offered me a room, nor did any hall provide a place where I could hold a meeting. When I finally found a place and tried to hold a meeting, a ruffian in the pay of the government broke in with drawn sword, and the police, as, I suspected, part of his plan, ordered the meeting closed because they were unable to manage the situation.

The government used street louts and any rough character who could carry a sword or a pike to threaten my campaigners, even in broad daylight. Once when I retired to rest in an upstairs room they used a spear to beat on the ceiling of the room below.

One day I was campaigning in Shima when I was told that a mob was waiting in ambush at a certain pass. In spite of the warning I plucked up my courage and went ahead as planned. At the pass I found a large group of men wearing surcoats emblazoned with dragons, and brandishing pikes and naginatas (halberds). It was obvious to them that we carried no arms, yet we walked past them and to their merit they did not lay a hand on us. However, since they had informed us in no uncertain terms that they would get us on our way back, we decided to take precautions. On our return, therefore, we asked some boar hunters with guns to walk in front of us, and the mob scattered like baby spiders.

The inhabitants of Ise were renowned for their gentleness. People might go so far as occasionally to resort to fisticuffs with each other if greatly provoked, but the sword was considered excessive. When they did use one, it was to cut off the heads of dogs and pigs. My chief of staff was the owner of an inn, and our political foes stuck a bleeding pig's head on a bamboo stick, which they posted at the entrance. This was very bad for business and it annoyed him a great deal. Those who campaigned for me were sure to get a kick or two, so I was given a wide berth even by my own helpers.

After a desperate campaign, I somehow managed to win re-election and returned to Tokyo. As soon as I could, I hastened to the home of Ōkuma to give him a detailed report of the battle. Rather unexpectedly, he asked how big my electoral district was. I said it was probably about fifty ri (122 miles) wide and stretched from one end of Ise across Shima to the far end of Kii. Ōkuma, with a fierce expression, snarled, "We'll buy up the whole place! Then the government won't dare to intervene!" As it happens, he was at this time involved in oil exploration in Echigo (now Niigata), from which he was expected to emerge very well off; nonetheless, his offer to purchase three provinces and five counties was overdoing it a bit. It was said in jest, of course, but I was tickled by its audacity. Apparently, on passing through Kōbe as a boy and being told that it was going to prosper as an open port, Ōkuma had precociously declared that he would therefore invest in a few square ri of land in the vicinity. It seems he had a fondness for grand ideas from an early age.

I barely won the election thanks, ironically, to the government's failure to resort to extreme measures on the strength of a secret report of the home ministry, which had branded me a sure loser due to my extreme unpopularity. In other districts things were far worse.

The worst barbarities were committed in Kōchi prefecture, Itagaki's home and the birthplace of the Jiyūtō. Policemen and hired ruffians working hand in hand overran districts contested by candidates from the people's parties, at times drawing their swords as they surrounded and sometimes violated the homes of powerful opposition candidates by forcing their way in without taking off their shoes as was the custom. The more hot-blooded Jiyūtō men did not sit idly by either, but met sword with sword, and sometimes blood was spilled.

Realizing that the local police were not strong enough to suppress the opposition by themselves, the government enlisted the military police and regular units of the army. This was done ostensibly to put down an insurgency, but what happened in fact was that the government mobilized His Majesty's army to put pressure upon the people's parties and duped young men into using cold steel against their fathers and superiors. Then, seeing that their swords and rifles still did not quite do the job, the government ordered cannon brought up to fire on the homes of their opponents. Ten people died. Sixty-six were wounded.

On the day of the election, people who were victims of police intimidation and gamblers and other unsavory characters in the pay of the government voted for the official party or abstained against their will. In the second district of Kōchi prefecture, the mob stole the ballot box so that the voting process had to be repeated.

Saga, Ōkuma's native prefecture and the home ground of the Kaishintō, did not fare much better than Kōchi. The chief of police, for example, personally instructed his own men and paid miscellaneous scoundrels and toughs off the street to threaten citizens. He gave them instructions to draw their swords without hesitation on people who did not vote for the official party. *Shizoku* (former samurai) who sympathized with the people's parties took up their own swords, and countless local battles were joined.

Police looked the other way when *shizoku* turned in or accused rioters. Ruffians roped and dragged to police stations were reported as behaving "like fish in water;" when they saw a policeman, they would say, "Sir, I am on the side of the bureacracy." In Saga too, where military police and units of the army were also deployed, eight civilians died and ninety-two were wounded. In Saga's third district the voting had to be postponed due to the violence. Even when it was held later two-thirds of the voters abstained. Ishikawa, Toyama, and Fukushima prefectures followed in the degree of atrocities they experienced.

It is unthinkable that such a thing should occur today, but in some places policemen told voters who to vote for and threatened them if they failed to cast their ballot as instructed. In one county all police, county, and local officials in all its municipalities were out campaigning for the government party, leaving their offices empty and their duties unattended. Intimidation and bribery were routine. Government party campaigners resorted to every kind of foul play under its protection, brandishing their swords, firing guns, setting homes on fire, and murdering anyone who did not support their purpose of obstructing the people's candidates from winning the election. The authorities themselves announced that during the election campaign 25 people were killed and 388 wounded. Since these were the numbers officially admitted, there can be no doubt that the true figures were far worse.

In spite of the appalling lengths to which the government went to support the ruling party, it remained extremely unpopular. For the first four years or so after the Imperial Diet was opened in 1890, it was considered so shameful to be identified with the government party that in some country schools children whose parents were known to support it were so badly teased and ridiculed that they begged their parents to change their party affiliation.

The object of the government party's dastardly intervention was to make sure they won a majority in the House, and it must be acknowledged that especially when it came to ensuring the defeat of their leading opponents they left no stone unturned. As a result, eminent popular party leaders lost their election bids in districts where their opponents would have had no chance without the intervention.

For example, among the Jiyūtō men, Ōi Kentarō lost in Osaka, Naitō Roichi in Aichi prefecture, Kataoka Kenkichi and Hayashi Yūzō in Kōchi prefecture, Matsuda Masahisa in Saga prefecture, and Yoshinobu Ujifusa in Kumamato prefecture. Among the Kaishintō men, Kusumoto Masataka and Takagi Masatoshi lost in Tokyo, Abe Yoshihito in Tokushima prefecture, and Taketomi Tokitoshi and Amano Tameyuki in Saga prefecture. They all lost by wide margins. What was worse, they lost mostly to unknown candidates.

THE POISON OF POLITICAL CORRUPTION

The electoral interference by the Matsukata government not only left a major blot on the early days of constitutional government in Japan but poisoned its operation. In retrospect, the first general election went relatively well, we can now see, notwithstanding the unfamiliarity of both candidates and voters alike with such events. By contrast, government intervention in the second election set a deplorable precedent by corrupting the electoral process and extorting enormous campaign funds to support their candidates. In this election was born the government's bad habit of blackmailing restaurants, inns, antique dealers, and pawn shops known to support opposition candidates by placing them under undue surveillance, while protecting the campaign staff of candidates running for the government party and facilitating the giving and taking of bribes. Criminal acts committed by or on behalf of the ruling party were glossed over, while any trifling misdeed of the opposition was heavily penalized. Pretexts were even found for arresting people who had done nothing wrong at all. At other times, an opposition candidate's campaign manager would be detained or members of his staff followed to intimidate and harass them. In some places the government put fear into the people by employing gamblers to harass the elderly or blackmail voters. From the voters' perspective, their lives and property were often placed at risk if they sided with opposition candidates, but protected whatever they did if they supported the government party. In fact, they were often paid to do so. One does not need to guess most what people would do in these circumstances.

Later, many bureaucrats were among those who hurled accusations of political corruption against the parties and voters, little knowing that it was their own predecessors who had established the practice and were its first exemplars. In this art, bureaucrats have been the teachers from the start, while the political parties have been their students and learned it from them. Prefectural governors were appointed government officials, and by that token as instructed by the first Yamagata government they should never have involved themselves in political wrangling of any kind. But if the government instructed them to intervene in the election, it was only to be expected that the process would become corrupt.

The poison did not stop at the election process, but spread within the walls of parliament itself. In those days, violence became common, so that it was not unusual to be attacked by a mob even inside the House. It was not unusual to see members arriving at the Diet all bandaged up. Inukai was wounded in the head. Shimada Saburō was attacked a couple of times and badly hurt. Takada Sanae was cut down with a sword from behind and the blade almost reached his lungs; he would have died on the spot had he not been obese. Kawashima Atsushi, Ueki Emori, and Inoue Kakugorō were all attacked at different times and came wearing bandages. Suematsu Kenchō was hit by horse manure thrown from the gallery. Members often even got into fist fights on the floor of the House, which became a rather rough place to be.

Seats were lined up not in party blocks as today but usually by prefectures so that the people's representatives and government representatives were seated side by side rather conveniently if one wanted a brawl. It was while the House was in session during the second Diet, I recall that when the proceedings were interrupted by a desperate voice calling "Help!" We all jumped to our feet to try to find the owner of the scream, but none was to be seen. Eventually, Inoue Kakugorō emerged from under his own seat. He had been awarded the nickname "General Crabshell" because his face was square and pockmarked. "The 'Hage-man' hit me and pushed me under my seat!" he expostulated. "Hage-man" is Japanese for a bald man. The culprit was Suzuki Manjirō from Fukushima prefecture, who, though the youngest representative to win his seat in the first election, had earned his name by being completely bald.

When Inukai was punched in the face by Nakamura Yaroku, Inukai himself was not without blame. This also occurred during the second Diet. We had all delivered speeches attacking the government and the president had ordered the doors closed for vote-taking. Nakamura, who was in the cafeteria if I remember rightly, and had failed to cast a vote in the important ballot, rushed in as soon as the doors were reopened. Inukai, as I have told, was known for his careless and sometimes hurtful remarks, but the hurt was seldom intended. Seeing Nakamura rush in, he called out, "How much did you get?" meaning how much had he taken in bribes from the government to stay out while the vote was taken. Nakamura flared, grabbed Inukai and punched him in the face. But instead of fighting back Inukai quickly apologized for what he had said. I was impressed, and I decided then and there that Inukai had shown greatness of character in behaving as he did. I would not have reacted like that. It was wrong to have made the silly joke, but he hardly deserved to be punched in the face for it. I would have at least resisted. Here is a man I could throw in my lot with, I thought to myself.[1]

That was the sort of minor unruliness we quite often experienced. Other incidents were more serious. Takada Sanae, for example, suffered a deep sword cut from behind as he was addressing the House and calling for the impeachment of the president, Hoshi Tōru, on a matter to which I shall refer later. There were few

---

[1] And so he did. Inukai and Ozaki were comrades in many a parliamentary battle. Even their pen names, Ozaki's Gakudō and Inukai's Bokudō, reflected this.

among us, even the mildest and least offensive, who escaped being attacked at least once or twice.

Strangely enough, I was one of the exceptions. I did have an encounter with a ruffian on my way to the Diet one day, though. I was alone and without a bodyguard at the time, and while many others carried arms in those days I did not even have a walking stick. But I had rehearsed in my mind what I would do if I found myself in a situation like this. Before running away I would walk straight up to the person threatening me and look him in the eye. I liked to ride horses so I knew that if I looked a horse in the eye it would not do me any mischief. I tried this out now, and it must have unnerved the fellow for he did not lay a hand on me.

I recall one time when I was present at a lecture meeting in Naoetsu. I was quietly smoking a cigar, a favorite habit of mine in those days, when suddenly a man came at me, obviously intending to harm me. When he came close enough to strike I raised my cigar-hand to defend myself, but the cigar must have touched and burnt his arm because he promptly ran away. Cigar-smoking was quite uncommon then, so my assailant, seeing that I had not budged, must have thought that I possessed some new and fearful weapon.

Another time, Shimada Saburō was struck with an iron pipe in a guest room at the Diet. His attacker had asked to see me first, but I sensed that he had something under his *hakama* (loose, pleated trousers for formal wear), so I kept him the other side of the table and out of mischief. Shimada met him directly afterward and was immediately assaulted. Shimada might have been more daring than I. Be that as it may, it would seem that it is worth one's while to be prepared.

Speaking of violence, Inoue Kowashi, who was later made a viscount and minister of education, comes vividly to my mind. It was around 1885. After reading my article in the *Hōchi* newspaper about the Berlin Conference, Inoue asked to see me. He was then chief cabinet secretary in the first Itō government. They were engaged in a campaign of administrative reform at the time, as a result of which many redundant staff members had been dismissed. Inoue was considered to be its architect and was shadowed by assassins wherever he went. Rumor had it that they were out to set fire to his house. Inoue confided to me that he had no martial training and that he would undoubtedly be murdered if there were an attempt on his life. He could not sleep without a sword beside his pillow. Knowing only too well that having a sword at his bedside would do little to save his life, he said he still needed it for peace of mind, and he was ashamed for his lack what he called a cultivated mind. Inoue then spoke of Yokoi Shōnan, who was a master of both literary and martial arts, as an example of such a cultivated mind. It appeared that Yokoi was once staying at an inn in Kyoto when a small group of would-be-assassins crept up on him with drawn swords. When he heard men creeping up the stairs in the middle of the night. Leaving his long and short swords where they were, Yokoi wound a towel round his head the way farmers do, and saying, "Excuse me, sir. Excuse me, sir," walked past his would-be-assassins and down the stairs to safety. Yokoi's quickwittedness and courage had saved his life and were an example to all. Inoue confessed there was no way he could emulate him.

It is my belief that while violence always had to some extent been part of the scene, it was a matter of fact that, whether or not it was due to the electoral intervention during the Matsukata government and the personal experience every member had had of being involved in one way or another with swords and guns, it had become more disorderly than ever before and members now resorted to violence even within the walls of parliament itself.

THE MATSUKATA GOVERNMENT CRUMBLES

Having waged a brutal campaign against the people and meddled shamelessly in the election, what did the Matsukata government gain? It managed to gain a few more seats in the House but failed to break the majority held by the people's representatives. The composition of the third Diet (November 1892–March 1893) was as follows: the Yayoi Club (Jiyūtō) had won 94 seats, the Giin Shukaijo (Members' Meeting Place), (Kaishintō) 38, and the Independent Club 31, bringing the three people's parties' total to 163. In contrast, the ruling Taiseikai having been disbanded with the dissolution of the second Diet, those who had been re-elected now sought to rebuild it. However, with only 28 members re-elected of their 52 before the dissolution and with one having defected to the Independent Club, it was an impossible task. They had therefore decided to organize a new group and, under the initiative of Suehiro Kenchō, the Chūō kōshō-bu, or "Central Negotiating Section," was organized. With 95 members and an additional 42 from the Kinki (District) Club and others, the government could count 137 in the ruling coalition.

The general situation still favored the opposition parties. Most of the members of the opposition who had been treated harshly or unfairly during the election nursed a thirst for revenge and were determined to show their strength.

The Matsukata government was already weakened at its foundation even before the third Diet had begun. Within the ranks of the cabinet, Mutsu Munemitsu, the minister of agriculture and commerce, was totally opposed to Home Minister Shinagawa's election interference, and together with Communications Minister Gotō Shōjirō, exerted constant pressure on Shinagawa and his allies. When the results of the election revealed that in spite of the corrupt and violent interventions of the government the absolute majority of the opposition parties was still secure, the latter were heartened and raised their anti-government campaign to a more determined level than ever. Minister Shinagawa for his part felt no guilt because he saw nothing wrong in what he had done. Shinagawa was an honest man. He was convinced that unless the influence of the people's parties was decisively broken the nation was at risk. All means to break the opposition were therefore justified. In fact, in the course of a lecture tour Shinagawa declared publicly: "The second Diet had to be dissolved because destructive elements in the House had attempted to undermine the imperial prerogative by resorting to unreasonable arguments. When the special election was called I, as home minister, did all in my power to support the election of loyal men at the expense of those elements who if re-elected would do great harm to the maintenance of national security. And if ever during my time in office a similar situation occurs again, I swear to heaven that I will do whatever is needed to defeat the forces of destruction." No one was able to convince him otherwise.

The cabinet was divided between those who criticized the election meddling and those who supported Home Minister Shinagawa. To the first group belonged Agriculture Minister Mutsu and Communications Minister Gotō, while Army Minister Takashima Kuranori and Navy Minister Kabayama Sukenori belonged to the latter.

Then out of the blue dark clouds gathered over the privy council. Itō Hirobumi could not sit idly by and watch the constitution he had drafted under imperial command violated as a result of election fraud committed by the Matsukata government. Itō had on a number of occasions admonished the government during the election, but had gotten nowhere in the face of opposition from the strong-willed Shinagawa. Apparently, Shinagawa had threatened Itō to the effect that he would have to be disciplined by a decree if he were too extreme in his views. Itō, it was told, shot back at Shinagawa: "Not even the home minister would dare to discipline me." The relationship between the two deteriorated still further after the election. Prime Minister Matsukata was thus forced to convene a meeting of the *genrō* at his official residence on February 22 in order to find a way out. Matsukata must have done his best to defend the government position, but Itō was not satisfied. The government could not treat Itō's criticism the way it shrugged off questions on the floor of the House. Two days later, on February 24, Itō presented a letter of resignation as chairman of the privy council and prepared to return to Odawara. The government was embarrassed and did everything in its power to persuade Itō to reverse his decision, but nothing would make him change his mind.

On March 11, the Matsukata government finally forced the resignation of Home Minister Shinagawa and replaced him with Soejima Taneomi. The government, however, did not remove Shirane Senichi, the vice-minister under Shinagawa, who was if anything even more ferocious than the minister in carrying out his policy. Seeing that he owed no further loyalty to the government which, having dismissed Shinagawa, retained Shirane, Mutsu too tendered his resignation on March 14. Mutsu and Shinagawa were the two pillars of the Matsukata government. Having lost the resourceful mind of Mutsu and Shinagawa's dauntless courage, the government faced the third Diet looking weaker than a tiger with no fangs.

Matsukata's appointment of Soejima to succeed Shinagawa as home minister was in itself a success. Soejima was a loyal and virtuous man and much respected by the public. Although not well versed in the new field of constitutional government, Soejima was a scholar of Chinese statecraft, which armed him with knowledge of the art of ruling with justice. He believed it was his mandate to love and lead the people, abhorred the use of cruel or oppressive means of governing and considered bribery contemptible. He was a close friend of Ōkuma, having come from the same town, and of Itagaki ever since the latter had written the petition for a popularly elected parliament. Assuming the post of home minister, Soejima often met with Ōkuma and Itagaki and tried to unite the government and the people's parties. This was only possible because of the sincerity of Soejima Taneomi. When we attacked the government for the high-handed manner in which it had obstructed the election he did not attempt to justify its behavior, but seemed truly sincere in his acceptance of our criticism. However, as Mutsu had forseen, the change of minister made no fundamental difference so long as Shirane remained as his vice minister. Shirane Senichi was not the least affected by the cabinet reshuffle and carried on with his usual argument, even with his own minister. Soejima was too much of a gentleman to descend to this level, and, soon realizing that he did not have the means to manage his deputy and blaming himself, resigned while the parliament was in session. There was no hope for a cabinet that could not allow a gentleman like Soejima to stay.

We battled on against the Matsukata government, continuing to attack it on the grounds of its wrongdoing in the election. The House of Peers, which had not been involved in the election, passed a resolution impeaching the government:

"The bureaucracy having intervened in the election has incurred the wrath of the people and as a result blood has been shed. This is now public knowledge and a source of public complaint. Throughout the country people are enraged at the bureaucracy's intervention in the election and regard it with hostility."

In the House of Representatives we could not keep silent. On May 12, the first item on the opposition agenda was a draft memorial to the throne on the impeachment of the government. While it was defeated by a close call of 146 to 143, this was because some members, though not denying the wrongdoing, were too embarrassed to have it formally reported to the throne. We therefore immediately presented the draft again in the form of a resolution:

"Considering, it is clearly evident before the people without any room for defense that the government officials abused their authority and violated the right to vote during the general election for the House of Representatives which took place in February, the House must now accept this as given fact. Be it resolved that cabinet ministers all undertake soul searching and in the light of their given mandate take appropriate actions. Without it the outline of the constitutional government will be lost."

The resolution was adopted with a majority of 154 to 111. With these unequivocal statements tantamount to impeachment adopted by both houses, it was clear that the cabinet had lost the confidence of parliament. Ordinarily there were but two choices, to dissolve the House and go to the nation or to resign en masse. Prime Minister Matsukata did neither, reasoning that "The ministers of state enjoy the confidence of the throne and should not lightly resign merely on the strength of a parliamentary resolution." Instead, he called for a seven-day recess. When pressed for an explanation, he replied that the suspension of parliament was within the purview of the imperial prerogative and therefore the government was in no position to offer an explanation to parliament. There is little one can say about it but that it was a hopeless government indeed.

Though mortally wounded, the Matsukata government survived the extraordinary session and lasted another two months, shamelessly hanging on to power. The attitude of Matsukata, offering neither resignation nor a bold offensive, offended quick-tempered members. Army Minister Takashima called Matsukata abusive names and presented his resignation as did Navy Minister Kabayama. Matsukata apparently searched for suitable successors but none could be found. With this realization the government faltered and fell as if dying in the street. The void was filled by the so-called *genkun* or senior statesmen headed by Itō.

RISING DEBATE FORCES THE GOVERNMENT TO RESIGN

The Itō government appointed Inoue Kaoru as home minister and Yamagata Aritomo as minister of justice. Kuroda Kiyotaka, Ōyama Iwao, and Nirei Kagenori were respectively assigned communications and the army and navy portfolios. It was almost a full team of clan players. Both the Yamagata and Matsukata governments had fallen in the face of opposition attacks. It appeared to us that the *hanbatsu* were now playing their last high card, Itō, and were deliberately lining up a formidable array of clan giants for a decisive battle against the people's parties. The new government even approached former prime minister Matsukata to assume the post of minister of finance. But Matsukata did not have the nerve to accept, and his deputy Watanabe Kunitake took it on in his place. Gotō Shōjirō and Kōno Toshigama stayed in the cabinet, retaining their agriculture and education portfolios, and Mutsu Munemitsu assumed the post of foreign minister.

This was almost the best possible array of men a clan government could hope for at the time. For our part, we welcomed an enemy credible enough to be worth fighting. And we were enormously stimulated to think that if we managed to crush this last government we would succeed forever in putting an end to clan government. On their side, men who had managed to be elected with government help in the last election organized what they called the Kokumin-kyōkai, or National Association, with Saigō Tsugumichi and Shinagawa Yajirō as their leaders.

Misfortune befell the fourth Diet (November 1892–March 1893) from the very beginning. Prime Minister Itō fell from his carriage only two days after the session had opened and could not attend debates. Taking his place and doubling as acting prime minister was Home Minister Inoue.

In those days ordinary people were considered less than government officials, and prefectural governors, who considered themselves to be very important ones, behaved like feudal daimyō. In some prefectures people were required to prostrate themselves on the ground to greet their governors. Ministers were considered above human beings altogether and held in great awe, so few elected representatives dared to challenge them on the House floor on an equal footing. Under the circumstances, I feared that, unless the people learned that ministers were not superhuman, or otherwise different from the rank-and-file members of parliament they had elected, we would not be able to carry out our calling in the newly established parliament.

When the fourth Diet opened, all the ministers from the acting prime minister down were present. It seemed an excellent opportunity to take them on, and in preparing my speech I made sure that I had a question for each minister. I had an axe to grind, so I made a rather obvious point of avoiding the polite forms of address and other expressions of deference normally accorded to people of such eminence.

In this round of our war of words I felt the only enemy worthy of my respect was Watanabe Kunitake. He had just been appointed finance minister, but from the first Diet he had impressed me most among those who had held vice-ministerial posts. He made no attempt to conceal his fondness for Zen and spoke in the paradoxical and enigmatic manner of a Zen master whenever he had an opportunity. On one occasion when he was accused of contradicting himself he got out of it by saying, "Well, my second remark was just a fleeting thought and so was my first!" Whenever he reversed himself on what he had just firmly asserted he put it down to a change of mind. He knew the art of debate.

In addition to his skill with the Zen spoken word, Watanabe wrote poetry and prose. He must have been trained in swordsmanship too, since he called himself the swordsman of lost opportunities. It was even rumored that on moonlit nights he played the *koto* (Japanese harp). He remained a bachelor all his life, and spent most of his spare time reading. It was said of him that he had studied English, French, and German, as well as classical Latin and Greek.

With this unusual combination of interests, Watanabe was something of an eccentric and his speech and manners were enough to excite the curiosity of younger people. His fame had traveled far even before the opening of the parliament.At one time it was widely reported that the Tosa clan, one of the four that propelled the Restoration, was plotting with Saigō Takamori to betray the Meiji government. In fact, it was more than a rumor. Hayashi Yūzō and others were working together with Mutsu Munemitsu of Wakayama to advance the plan. To suppress this crisis, Watanabe was sent to Tosa as governor, though he must still have been only in his twenties. I learned from Kataoka Kenkichi that, on hearing of Watanabe's appointment, certain hot-headed young bloods in Tosa conspired to raise an armed force to attack his entourage. But Watanabe arrived alone to take office in an uncertain land without even a bodyguard. And every time spies looked to see what he was up to they found him alone, sitting bolt upright and reading. It seems his enemies were unable to find the right opportunity to attack.

One would not have expected a man of Watanabe's extraordinary character to be a good administrator. But as vice-minister of finance he proved himself a shrewd and practical bureaucrat and I could not help but admire him. On all accounts I thought him a foe worthy of my steel. He parried my blade well. I could see that beneath his cool air there was intense concentration, but in the cut and thrust of our verbal duel I had the feeling that I would win. In the end, he had to admit to having stated that he was unwilling to cut even a *sen* from the proposed budget. It was hailed by poets of the day as the "one-*sen* debate that distressed the crown."

Agriculture Minister Gotō was not cooperative in response to my questioning. After all, I reminded myself, I had once worked for him and he had been kind enough to let me have the use of his horse-drawn carriage when I was seized and exiled under the security ordinance. Remembering that he had served in the past as minister of communications I asked him some questions on postal policy, thinking that it could not be difficult for him to answer. He did not respond at all, however, claiming that the affairs of that ministry no longer belonged within his mandate. "It may not be within your mandate," I badgered him, "but as a minister of the cabinet you are obliged to attend meetings and therefore must be acquainted with its affairs. In any case, you do not wish to end your career as a mere minister, do you?" It was a tactic I employed to grill ministers by asking questions which were hard for them to answer. My final sally before I left the rostrum was: "There is nothing to be gained by asking further questions of this minister." I had to admit, nevertheless, that the Itō government was a first-class government for its time. As for us, we then decided to engage them on the matter of the budget. The government had proposed a budget of 83.7 million yen, but by disputing the way it was assessed we succeeded in slashing it by 8.8 million yen in the budget committee.

A progress report presented to the plenary session by Kōno Hironaka, the chairman of the budget committee, was received with resounding applause. And when the government invoked Article 67 of the Constitution to express its disapproval of the budget committee's report, Kōno refuted the government's objection with passion and confidence. "No review of the revised budget is necessary. I again request the government to assent to the revisions agreed upon by the committee."

Kōno was regarded with the highest esteem within the Jiyūtō before Hoshi Tōru gained power. Kōno, unlike Hoshi, possessed a gentle nature. He had handsome features as well as a commanding posture and a virtue to which people readily submitted. He reminded one of Sung Chiang-ming in the *Shue-hu-chüan*, (*The Water Margin*).[2] He seemed able to see things from above, but hardly said a word and fought with none. In defeat he simply wept.

Kōno did not have the quick and crafty mind needed to fight over the budget with the cunning Itō cabinet. His speech actually focused not so much on airing opposition to the budget itself but on the ills of clan government. When he could escape the world of concrete facts and dwell on matters of principle he had no match. The government did not budge. We therefore resolved to give them five days to decide on one of three courses of action: to resign en masse, to recommend a dissolution or to agree to our assessment. We had put a dagger to the throat of the government which was now forced to give a clear-cut response. But the government took no action, and the people's parties had no choice but to fall back

[2] As noted earlier, a classic Chinese novel long popular in Japan, variously translated as *All Men Are Brothers* and *The Water Margin*.

on their last resort: to place a motion on the table for the impeachment of the cabinet.

On January 23, when Kōno Hironaka stood to read from a prepared text, like a bolt from the blue an imperial rescript announcing a fifteen-day recess was issued. It looked to me like a government ploy to gain time to appease the opposition during the recess.

The Itō government had a significant asset in Foreign Minister Mutsu Munemitsu, who through his subordinate, Okazaki Kunisuke, was in a position to manipulate politicians from Wakayama. Moreover, Hoshi, who held sway over the Jiyūtō, was considered a younger brother of Mutsu. In addition, Mutsu had many close contacts with members of the Tosa faction. Thus through him the Itō government commanded numerous channels to the Jiyūtō.

My "Fight to the Death at Minatogawa" Speech

When the session resumed on February 7, Prime Minister Itō appeared in bandages to oppose the motion for impeachment. In spite of this the House of Representatives passed the draft memorial by a vote of 181 to 103. Hoshi, the president, presented the memorial to the throne on the following day. We recommended that all members remain in their seats to await the emperor's decision. But it seemed that the Jiyūtō had already been softened up and had decided to recess until the judgment was received. On the morning of February 10, an imperial rescript was handed to all government ministers and members of the Imperial Diet. His Majesty commanded that the government and the parliament work harmoniously together.

> While it is our wish to entrust to the ministers of the cabinet the responsibility for making decisions on matters of import, at the same time We have no doubt that the elected representatives of the people should share Our daily concerns. The provisions of Article 67 of the Constitution are already guaranteed by law and are not a matter for debate today. We do therefore instruct Our ministers to conduct the government of Our Empire according to their mandate, subject to appropriate and sufficient deliberation and our approval.
>
> In matters pertaining to the national army and defense, a day of indulgence may bring a hundred years of regret. We shall reduce the expenses of Our court and pledge 300,000 yen a year for the next six years and command the ministers of the civilian and armed services, with the exception of those who are under special circumstances, to donate one-tenth of their annual remuneration to augment the cost of building battleships.
>
> It is Our wish that the ministers of the cabinet and the parliament shall build the constitutional machinery, each exercising with moderation the authority with which he is invested, and by way of peace and conciliation, assist Us successfully in Our grand endeavor.

The imperial rescript, which was conveyed to the parliament by the president, was received with much emotion and gratitude for the wisdom of His Majesty's judgment. A negotiating committee was promptly set up to ensure that the government would commit itself to carrying out the emperor's wishes. The committee consisted of Kōno Hironaka, Haseba Sumitaka, Ishida Kannosuke, and Yamada Tōji for the Jiyūtō, Shimada Saburō, Nakano Takeei, and myself for the Kaishintō; Kawashima Atsushi and Shiba Shirō represented the Dōmei Club. Of these men Kawashima Atsushi left the most memorable impression.

Kawashima was from Satsuma and was said to have been a spirited youth. The story goes that when he came to the Sekigahara fields on his way to the capital with the Satsuma forces he stamped his foot with excitement, that he was at last about to avenge two hundred years of tyranny.[3] This charismatic young man was expected to bear the future of the Kagoshima clan on his shoulders. Kawashima always had a sense of his own destiny. While it is normal for boys born into great houses to be groomed for leadership from their early days, those born in Chōshū and Satsuma appeared to be born with particularly high aspirations. Kawashima appeared to think that the future of Japan depended on him and those like him. Those born outside these big clans, unless they possessed exceptional overconfidence, would not think such thoughts. What impressed me particularly about Kawashima was that while there was no issue of importance to the national interest that he had not researched and deeply considered, he was always willing to study and learn more. Nevertheless, he had come to the realization quite early that the future of Japan could not be built on a clan foundation. By 1890, when the first parliament met, he was speaking publicly of the need to destroy the clan cliques or at the very least to build them on a national foundation. He joined a political party, and when the Kyushu Kaishintō proposed that opposition parties should join forces in a grand coalition, he was one of the foremost advocates of the plan.

Along with the qualities mentioned, Kawashima unfortunately had an explosive temper and the physical strength to go with it. He was easily provoked to violence and it was reported, possibly with exaggeration, that very few escaped his punches while he was in Europe. For all his high ambition and ample knowledge, he was not able to manage people because of his quarrelsomeness. Nor was he able to realize his political aspirations. At one time he was considered Kagoshima's most promising son, but gradually his fame waned and, regrettably, he died with his hopes unfulfilled. His last post was as minister for Hokkaidō. For all that, I remember him as an exceptional and delightful individual.

Now let me pick up where I left off, with the formation of a committee to mediate between the House and the government. Even the government put its cards on the table this time. However, since the future was at stake for both the Itō government and the parliament, it was hard to find enough common ground on

---

[3] In 1600, Tokugawa Ieyasu's victory at Sekigahara over a coalition that included Satsuma and Chōshū armed forces opened the two and one-half centuries of Tokugawa rule.

which to base a compromise. One evening, after several inconclusive rounds of talks, we were together in a room in the House. It was winter and we were warming ourselves in front of a stove, and as our negotiations had stalled and no resolution seemed near we were chatting informally. Prime Minister Itō began talking about the trip he had made to Europe to study national constitutions. Strangely enough, Kawashima, the fiery man from Kagoshima, suddenly became quiet. This was quite an interesting development. Since Kawashima was representing the parliament, he and the rest of us, when we were engaged in formal negotiation for that matter, bargained with the prime minister on an equal footing. Once the talk turned casual, however, he became so docile that I feared he would not have as much clout as before once we returned to negotiation. It was not that one was master and the other vassal, because the only relationship the two men had had previously was when Kawashima accompanied Itō on the latter's trip to Europe as a member of his staff. This did not in itself give Itō more authority in this situation, but it was fascinating to watch the sensitive interplay of personalities.

That same evening, Prime Minister Itō was warming his back at the stove muttering something like: "These are hard days. The kindest thing would be for some assassin to kill me and get it over with." And at that instant a man burst into the room. Itō looked very alarmed, though actually it was not unusual for ill-bred members to break noisily into a room uninvited. It was amusing, nonetheless, to see the prime minister's reaction when only a moment before he had practically invited someone to murder him.

The government side was represented mainly by Itō, Mutsu, and Watanabe. This was the first time I had found myself across the table from Mutsu. When he saw me, he said diplomatically: "You and I should be negotiating over more important matters of state. Isn't it ridiculous for us to be wasting our time over such a trifle as the budget?" I found him to be extremely prickly. Negotiating with him was like walking in a field of thorny rose bushes in a delicate silk robe. No matter what direction I turned I would get scratched. And Mutsu, like the thorny patch, was difficult to pass. At the same time, however, I thought his scratch was never deep enough to be fatal.

The negotiation ended in victory for the government. But the so-called imperial rescript on harmonious collaboration relating to affairs of state, which had been countersigned by every cabinet member from the prime minister on down, was in fact tantamount to an acknowledgement by the Itō government that it was accountable to the petition made to the throne. At least this was what we claimed. Particularly embarrassing to the government was the fact that it had lost the confidence of the parliament on the basic principle of governance, and as a result was not able to win the appropriation it demanded for defense. This notwithstanding, the government resigned itself to accepting from the emperor as graciously as it could his offer to reduce the palace expenses and to donate 300,000 yen annually toward the cost of building battleships. Having endorsed the rescript, the Itō government should thenceforth in obedience to the Constitution have been accountable to the parliament. We in the Kaishintō kept our side of the bargain by refusing to compromise. But the Jiyūtō had already given in and the budget was to pass the House with a cut of only 2.72 million yen. I held out to the end even in the plenary session of the Diet where I submitted a revision on the revised budget urging an additional cut of half a million yen.

If we are so afraid of a difference of opinion, if we are ready to withdraw once the government voices its disagreement, we should not have considered submitting a counter-budget in the first place. It would have spared us the inconvenience of clash- ing with the government. Have you forgotten that we have submitted our own draft of the budget ever since the first parliament because we believed it was in the interest of the nation and the happiness of the people? It was because of this that the govern- ment called for a dissolution. It was because of the resulting deadlock that we had reluctantly to petition the throne.

This parliament must respect its own integrity. If we admitted to the public that we were willing to cast away the draft budget we have fought for over the past three years, we would lose the confidence of the people. They would say that their parliament lacks the courage of its convictions. Without the confidence of the public what grounds does the parliament have to function at all?

We gave in to the government on the cost of warship construction. We gave in on the appropriation for civil service personnel. The parliament ignored the rescript and surrendered without shame. We conceded meekly on every point. Now we should demand that the government concede on a matter unrelated to the rescript and accept our draft budget. Then we could honestly say we had a harmonious and collaborative relationship.

The imperial rescript urging harmony and collaboration was not just addressed to the parliament. It was addressed equally to the parliament and the government.

Vacillating on convictions, temporizing on results and spineless surrender are not the way to achieve true harmony and collaboration.

My argument fell on deaf ears since it was considered that the issue had already been settled. My revision was therefore promptly aborted and the Itō government was able to ride out the fourth Diet without trouble.

The public must nevertheless have appreciated that I fought on their behalf until the very last. They called it the "uchijini (fight-to-the-death) speech," citing the old legend that tells how the hero, Kusunoki Masashige, fell while fighting at Minatogawa.

Responsible Cabinet and Independent Diplomacy

Having lost our battle over the budget due to the softening up of the Jiyūtō, we decided to pursue the government on diplomatic issues.

Sassa Tomofusa, Kōmuchi Tomotsune, Ōi Kentarō, Suzuki Shigeto, and Abei Hane had established the Dainihon Kyōkai (Great Japan Association) to promote the full implementation of international treaties. Japan was still handicapped in exercising its sovereignty because of the "Unequal Treaties" signed in 1858. The government, however, curried favor with the Western powers and failed even to exercise rights guaranteed by treaties, let alone seek to revise them. Treaties in place were needless to say extremely disadvantageous to Japan, but there were provisions which, if implemented, would impose restraints upon the powers too. The objective of adopting a hard line diplomacy was to persuade the powers to reconsider the revision of existing treaties by insisting on the strict implementation of the provisions they already contained.

The Great Japan Association invited the Kaishintō to collaborate with them. Negotiations between us went quite smoothly, because taking a strong position in foreign affairs had long been our own policy and we more or less shared their views on full implementation of the treaties. The one obstacle was that the central figures of the association were conservatives. Bearing this in mind, we proposed to work with them on condition that they agree to a party cabinet system. After further negotiation it was mutually decided to call party cabinet "responsible cabinet" and treaty implementation "independent diplomacy." Strangely enough, diplomatic issues became the bridge between ourselves and the Kokumin Kyōkai, whom we normally regarded with great hostility, so that we could temporarily work together against the Itō government.

There is another side to this story. As told earlier, Shinagawa was chased out of the Matsukata cabinet by Itō, who was then out of government, and by Mutsu from within. Shinagawa consequently held a grudge against the Itō cabinet, which included Mutsu as foreign minister. So when Saigō Tsugumichi, the head of the Kokumin Kyōkai, was appointed to succeed Navy Minister Nirei, Shinagawa took the opportunity to attack the government for its weak-kneed diplomacy, calling himself a true man of the people.

As far as the Kaishintō was concerned, we would have liked to have the Jiyūtō, our long-standing comrades-in-arms, at our side. However, the Jiyūtō became increasingly and overtly pro-government as the fourth Diet drew to a close. Members of the Independent Club did their best to maintain unity among the three people's parties, and for our part we in Kaishintō also persevered patiently. However, by then Mutsu and Hoshi were closer than we had realized, and the Jiyūtō left our ranks.

The Independent Club joined our people's alliance in working for "responsible government and independent diplomacy," while the Jiyūtō went its own way and took a quasi-government party attitude. The first victim to be sacrificed was the Speaker, Hoshi Tōru.

THE IMPEACHMENT OF SPEAKER HOSHI

Hoshi had studied in England in the early years of Meiji and had returned with a law degree. It was, if I remember correctly, the first such degree earned by a Japanese, and he gained a certain fame calling himself Barrister Hoshi. He became a lawyer attached to the ministry of justice, and since he was the only one, his popularity increased all the more. His law practice prospered and in a short time he became quite rich. At first politics did not interest him, but he joined the Jiyūtō at its birth and poured his money into it. It was said of Hoshi that he was astute as a lawyer but naive and honest to a fault in politics. Anyway, he spent all he had. In the process of getting to know him personally, I discovered that he had no one to blame but himself for the hundreds of thousands of yen he gave away. He was not really interested in money. He wanted power.

Hoshi rose within the ranks of the Jiyūtō, and from the third Diet on he became the Speaker of the House. However, his headstrong personality and the skeletons he was rumored to keep in his closet made him disliked by some in his own party. Feeling against him grew until at the beginning of the fifth Diet the impeachment of the president was on the agenda.

Just at that time it was rumored that Hoshi had had a secret meeting with a businessman with political connections. Abei Hane, a senior member known for his scrupulous honesty, reacted by tabling an urgent motion asking the Speaker to resign. "This House," he said "cannot place confidence in its Speaker, Mr. Hoshi Tōru. Since the House does not wish the said member to remain in the position of Speaker, it hopes that the said member will take it upon himself to resign." In response, Hoshi said he had absolutely nothing to be ashamed of and had no reason to resign even if the resolution were to be adopted. However, he was willing to withdraw from the floor of the House as a matter of honor and asked the Deputy Speaker, Kusumoto Masataka, to preside. After deliberation the resolution was passed by a vote of 166 to 119.

This was how the curtain rose on the impeachment of President Hoshi, a stormy scene in the history of the Diet remembered to this day. The other leading actor was Vice-President Kusumoto. He too was an uncommon but interesting personality. Kusumoto had attracted a certain amount of attention to himself since the Restoration. He sometimes displayed a rather embarrassingly girlish disposition but at other times he bore himself with the perfect composure of a mature man. The public did not quite know what to make of him and called him "manu dan" for his somewhat dull, lordly appearance that conveyed the idea of a half-witted Kabuki Danjūrō.

This reputation was not entirely deserved, in fact, for although he may have been circuitous on details he was sharp in his general observations. With a few glasses of *sake* under his belt he would make fun of me: "General Ozaki looks imposing seated on his campstool," he once taunted, "but look closely and you will see he has a drawn sword at his side. When a general sits on his stool in camp on the battlefield it is more fitting for him to hold a baton of command. In any case, it is wrong to carry your sword unsheathed." Remarks like this made me feel ashamed of myself and yet respect the man for his shrewd observation.

Kusumoto considered himself one of the three musketeers, along with Itō and Ōkuma. "Don't you worry," he used to declare to us, "Japan is going to be all right because the three of us Itō, Ōkuma, and I have an agreement between ourselves."

Everyone took it for granted that once he had removed himself Hoshi would stay out. After all, the vote of no confidence had been passed and the mood of the House was quite hostile. On top of this, the media had been denouncing him severely. Oddly, in spite of this, I felt he just might appear. So I spoke to Kusumoto and urged him to tell Hoshi to stay away even if he had to use the pretext of feeling ill, as I feared that if he came back it might rouse members even more and make matters worse. Kusumoto promised to pass on the message. I received the following reply: "I told him what you said. He will not attempt to take the chair." Here was the Deputy Speaker telling the Speaker what to do. It was his style.

In spite of the Deputy Speaker's warning, Hoshi did return, to all appearances unperturbed, as soon as the debate on the resolution was over. To our amazement, he walked calmly over to the Speaker's chair and attempted to proceed with the agenda where he had left off. We were compelled to recess for the day, if only to call for grave reflection on Hoshi's part. When the session resumed the following day, again, to add insult to injury, Hoshi calmly took the Speaker's chair. We were flabbergasted. Again the session was recessed by an urgent motion.

On the third day Hoshi returned once more to the Speaker's chair. There was nothing else to do but to fall back on the last resort and send a memorial to the throne. It read: "Your Majesty's subjects in accordance with Article 3 of the Diet Law recommended Hoshi Tōru to be appointed president. Due to lack of insight on our part we beg to inform Your Majesty that we have advised the throne wrongly."

Through the minister of the imperial household the emperor returned the following question: "Is it the object of the memorial to have us dismiss the Speaker? Or is it merely to apologize for negligence on your part as members of our parliament? We ask you to deliberate and inform us." The House promptly sent the following reply: "Your Majesty, the purpose of the memorial was to apologize for our negligence caused by ignorance. We beg Your Majesty to accept our deep regrets for the ambiguity of style which prompted your question. Your Majesty's most humble subjects."

With all that had occurred there was nothing we could do except to refer the case to the disciplinary committee. Hoshi's statement made on the twenty-ninth that he was not obliged to respect the resolution of the House presented substantial grounds for this course. The statement was a blatant disregard of the will of the House and a disgrace to its honor. As a consequence, the House passed a resolution suspending Speaker Hoshi for one week.

Though the resolution merely called for a week's suspension, we all believed that this would dismiss him forever. To our horror, no sooner had the week passed than Hoshi was back in the Speaker's chair attending to parliamentary business. We therefore brought a charge of disrespect for the decision of the House against him and moved that the matter be referred back to the disciplinary committee.

On that particular day Hoshi must have made up his mind in advance. He was resolute. He not only refused to step down from the chair, but declared that the House should first debate whether the attendance of the Speaker could be a matter for disciplinary action. This was the last straw, fists flew and a free-for-all erupted on the floor.

Hoshi had no intention of changing his mind and declared once again that the House should consider first things first. Not a single member was willing to respond. In the end Hoshi opened the door to the chamber himself and let himself out. The disciplinary committee decided on Hoshi's expulsion and the House in turn resolved with a majority of 185 to 92 in favor of striking his name off the members' list.

As soon as the question of a motion of no confidence against Hoshi was brought up, some among the Jiyūtō, unhappy at Hoshi's high-handed manners and particularly uneasy about his drawing close to the government through Mutsu, spoke in favor of dismissing him and reestablishing the openness of the party. A majority of the party members, however, saw Hoshi's impeachment as a matter of private revenge on the part of their rivals. On the grounds that the party's prestige had to be protected, a resolution was proposed and adopted in support of Hoshi. The fourteen men who belonged to the first group then left the party and organized the Dōshi Club (club for the like-minded), which later joined us in the coalition of opposition parties.

Elated by the successful removal of the Speaker, the opposition coalition turned their attention to the government. The underlying purpose of removing Hoshi was all along to purge the House of obstacles in preparation for enforcing discipline on the officials of the government.

Simultaneously, a scandal had flared concerning the exchange. It was rumored that Agriculture Minister Gotō and his Vice Minister Saito were frequent guests at parties organized by businessmen who had special interests in the exchange. It was suspected that they were taking bribes and that Saitō in particular was frequenting a house of assignation in connection with behind-the-scenes political deals.

On December 4, the House passed a memorial to the throne and in these words impeached Gotō Shōjirō, the minister of agriculture: "A minister of Your Majesty's cabinet has failed to bear himself in a manner befitting his station. He has frequented disreputable places and engaged in unlawful dealings with felonious persons, allowed himself to be entertained, and caused a senior official in his ministry to accept bribes. The scandal is public knowledge and ill repute fills the streets. The dignity of the government is impaired and the minister has fallen into discredit." Gotō was thus forced to resign.

However, the expulsion of Hoshi and Agriculture Minister Gotō were but curtain-raisers. The main objective of the opposition coalition was to challenge the Itō government on the related issues of enforcing treaties and adopting a firm attitude in foreign relations. Accordingly, on December 19, the opposition introduced the following motion as a prelude to impeaching the government: "The House of Representatives, recognizing that the government in implementing the current treaty is permitting the legal interests and dignity of the Empire to go unheeded, hereby resolves that the government be urged to clarify the rights and obligations of the parties to the said treaty and strictly enforce them." Only a few minutes had been allowed for presenting the case for the motion when a rescript was received suspending the Diet for ten days.

After the ten-day recess we were back in the House with the motion concerning the enforcement of treaty rights. Foreign Minister Mutsu took the floor to state his opposition to the motion. No sooner had he finished speaking than we received yet another rescript recessing the Diet, this time for fifteen days. And without warning on the following day yet another imperial rescript arrived calling for the dissolution of the House. Thus the fifth Diet (November–December 1893) ended without offering any opportunity for debate on our prized treaty bill.

Later we heard what had happened. As soon as it was learned that the House was being presented with a bill on treaty enforcement, emissaries of the foreign powers put pressure on the ministry of foreign affairs by threatening that they would have to request their governments to strictly enforce their treaty rights should Japan decide to enforce its own. Intimidated, our government apparently decided to take no chances. We were not to have an opportunity to say a single word on the subject.

Strenuous Election

The third general election took place on March 1, 1894. The Itō government, professing constitutionalism, was careful not to employ the same tactics as the Matsukata government. The election was conducted peacefully throughout the country, but to me this was the most memorable election of all. I have fought many elections in my time but this was the hardest. After the dissolution of the Diet I returned to my constituency only to learn most unexpectedly that Kadono Ikunoshin would stand against me in the election. It was an awful shock.

Unlike myself, a wanderer from other parts, Kadono was born into a distinguished local family in his constituency of Toba. When I was a student at Keiō he was a young and successful teacher whom I wished to emulate. I was troubled. Kadono's campaigners exploited this to their advantage, letting it be known that "Kadono was Ozaki's teacher." This hurt me. The prospects were not good. In desperation I asked my audiences, "Who was the teacher of Hidari Jingorō? Important men all become greater than their teachers. A man is of no use if he cannot excel his teacher." After a number of these speeches the effect began to show and people started agreeing with me. Then the Kadono side offered a compromise. Our district was a two-seat constituency. I was pairing with Morimoto Takuya, while Kadono's running mate was Okuno Ichijirō, a Jiyūtō orator. The offer was for both camps to agree to field a single candidate instead of two; then both Kadono and I would easily win. Some of my own colleagues thought this a good idea.

I took to the road again. "If you want medicine, choose medicine. If you want poison, so be it. But a cup of medicine and a cup of poison together makes no sense. Those who do not want to vote for Morimoto, don't vote for me either!" I fought the Jiyūtō with this line from one end of the constituency to the other. The result was better than expected, and Morimoto and I both gained votes. In jubilation I wrote this poem in the Chinese style:

> A worthy foe and well-matched strife to put me to a
>   sterner test!
> Who'd want to use a butcher's knife to slice a tender
>   chicken's breast?

In reality, my opponent was no spring chicken. He was a much respected senior from my alma mater whom I secretly held in awe. The poem is convenient for the purpose of bragging a little.

While I am on the subject of elections, let me recount some episodes from the earlier ones. Those were rough elections, but though there was no lack of physical violence one saw hardly any of the corruption that so detestably stained the later ones. Thuggery was used instead. The thugs were young volunteers, but not necessarily common hooligans. They were sent out from both camps to intimidate voters, chase them away from ballot boxes or use unloaded guns to frighten them, using tricky tactics as if they were combatants in little wars. An election in a particular constituency developed all too often into a contest between these bands, and the side that employed them most effectively usually won.

Generally speaking, the Jiyūtō enlisted rougher characters, while the Kaishintō fielded more cultivated types and many from the lower echelons of local merchants and farmers. Unfortunately, our fellows almost always lost to the Jiyūtō's. In order to prevent voters from being scared away from the polling places, some districts, on the pretext of giving them free accommodation, locked them up for a few days preceding the election. It was a terrible thing to do, but it was done in desperation.

In the countryside, warehouses always had a room attached. Campaign meetings were often held in well-to-do citizen's warehouses. Voters were invited to come and listen to so-and-so speak while eating from lunch boxes provided free by the organizing party, and, when they were busy eating, the doors were padlocked from the outside. This was to prevent the voters from being driven away by rival thugs. Box meals were brought regularly for the prisoners, and the campaign manager would make reassuring visits from time to time. Invariably, among the detained would be men who needed to attend to their businesses, but they too were inveigled and cajoled into staying until the election. And when the day came, they were all escorted in a group to the ballot-box. Under the circumstances, any rumor about the party ruffians, as, for example, whether one side commanded scores of them or hundreds, affected the outcome of an election. There were cases where ordinary men were dressed in rough clothes and transported by train merely to intimidate the public.

In addition to campaigning on my own behalf I have also campaigned for friends. One such occasion that I still vividly recall was when I traveled to Tokushima to campaign for Abe Yoshihito. His rival was Ōkubo Bentarō from the Jiyūtō. Itagaki was there to campaign for him, and rough characters from neighboring Tosa were in every hamlet and village. These Tosa men were about as bad as their counterpart from the three Tama districts on the outskirts of Tokyo. They were notorious for their ruthlessness at intimidating the countryfolk, and our candidates hesitated to campaign in the villages for fear of the ruffians in their rival's employ.

We had to find an clever way of dealing with these louts. My thought was to pretend to be planning an attack on the residence of the rival candidate, Ōkubo. This should be a signal for him to pull his troublemakers from the villages. But when I gave instructions to our men to this effect, Iizuka Chōjirō, a gallant and resourceful man from Ibaragi prefecture, came forward. "Leave it to me," he declared. "I'll scare the rascals away single handedly." I was curious as to what his ruse could possibly be. Iizuka wasted no time. He rented a two-story farmhouse in Ōkubo's neighborhood and requested the farmer to supply enough rice balls to feed fifty men, whom he was expecting shortly. The owner accepted the order, but rice balls for fifty men was an unusually large number and he wanted to be sure who they were for. "I am from the Kaishintō," Iizuka told him. "A force of fifty men are arriving from Tokyo to make sure Mr. Ōkubo makes no trouble in the election." As Iizuka had planned, the farmer promptly reported this to Ōkubo. Learning that fifty rival toughs were due to arrive in his own neighborhood, Ōkubo immediately dispatched messengers to recall his own men.This gave our side undisturbed freedom to work in the hamlets and villages. And it only cost us five or six yen, since we were able to cancel the rice balls, saying that the plan had changed.

Another time, I was in Miyagi prefecture to campaign for a colleague in a by-election. Itagaki himself was there to support the opposite side. Morikubo Sakuzō was there too with a group of scoundrels from the three Tama districts. Shimada Saburō arrived to lend support to our man and a fierce contest loomed. Eloquent orator that he was, Shimada of course was a valuable president, but he worried excessively over every trifle. He was always the first at our local office to become agitated the moment there was a report of the arrival of a couple of dozen ruffians. This did nothing to improve the morale of our team, and some complained that with his constant apprehensiveness he was doing more harm than good. No one dared, naturally, to tell him to his face that we really would prefer him to be somewhere else. I felt too sorry for him to do it myself.

Within the district there was a small county called Kisennuma. It lay along a remote stretch of seashore dotted with fishing villages which could perhaps scrape together a couple of hundred votes. So far as the election was concerned, it was evident that the fate of Kisennuma mattered little, and it occurred to us that we might be able to kill two birds with one stone if we could contrive to remove Shimada and Itagaki from the more vital parts of the district where each in his way was having too much of a negative impact. Based on what we knew of the sympathies of the voters I drew up a plan of campaign and gave it to Shimada, saying, "As you can see, we are running more or less neck and neck. It looks as though victory will go to the side that wins Kisennuma." "If it's that important, I'll be there," said Shimada, and off he went in high spirits. Itagaki also made for Kisennuma on learning that it was to be crucial to the outcome of the election. There both sides engaged in a furious battle. With the leader of the opposing camp and our wet blanket Shimada safely out of the way in a remote part of the constituency we were immensely relieved and marched to a landslide victory.

SIX "PEOPLE'S PARTIES" VERSUS THE ITŌ GOVERNMENT

In the wake of the general election the sixth Diet (May–June 1894) was convened on May 12, 1894. The "people's coalition" of six parties commanded a total of 130 seats: 48 from the Kaishintō, with 5 from the Chūgoku Shinpotō (Chugoku Progressive Party), a flying column of the Kaishintō led by Inukai; 26 from the Kokumin Kyōkai (National Association), which now called itself the Kokumin Seisha (National Political Society) in accordance with the law regulating political organizations; 37 from the Kakushintō (Renovation Party), which was the result of a merger between the Dōshi Club founded by Haseba Sumitaka and Taketomi Tokitoshi, who had earlier split from the Jiyūtō on the question of President Hoshi's expulsion, and the Dōmei Club led by Hashimoto Masataka and Kawashima Atsushi; there were also 5 from the Zaisei Kakushinkai (Financial Reform Society) created by Taguchi Ukichi and others; and 9 from the former Dainihon Kyōkai (Great Japan Association). The "people's coalition" as we called ourselves then challenged the government to take a firm stance on foreign policy issues.

On May 8, the people's coalition held a get-together at Nakamura-rō restaurant in Tokyo's Kōtō ward and adopted the following resolution: "This meeting has been called to ratify our commitment to fighting for a hard-line foreign policy and responsible parliamentary government. We affirm that this meeting represents the will of the majority of the Japanese people, and that we are therefore determined to ensure that the Imperial Diet recognize these same principles in the making of its laws and that the government observe them in all matters pertaining to the administration." With 1,500 representatives gathered there that day, we were elated at the prospect of battling the government on two fronts: responsible government and independent foreign relations . The government could count on 119 votes in the House from the Jiyūtō and 20 compliant independents. The two sides were nearly evenly matched. The Jiyūtō was under the influence of the government and could be considered in practice a quasi-ruling party. It was an extremely awkward position, however, as the party could not very well openly admit to being patronized by the government.

Directly after the new Diet convened, the people's coalition presented a memorial to the throne impeaching the government in strong terms, but it was defeated by five votes. At this, the Jiyūtō presented its own memorial. It was lukewarm in tone and avoided any reference to foreign relations, merely calling to the attention of the throne the need for administrative reform and requesting the throne to remonstrate with the ministers to carry out their duties. It was a hollow artifice carefully worded so as not to deal a fatal blow to the government if adopted. It would kill two birds with one stone by giving the Jiyūtō an alibi as an opposition party and at the same time undermining the strongly worded coalition memorial.

The coalition in turn presented a revision of the Jiyūtō memorial, since the draft memorial, apart from mildly criticizing the misdoings of the government, had no clause prompting the government to take corrective measures. We extracted from our draft the harsh wording censuring the government for its mishandling of both domestic and foreign affairs and artfully inserted a paraphrase of the same indictment into the text of the Jiyūtō sponsored memorial. "Particularly in areas of foreign policy," our contribution began, "the government, fearing the loss of foreign favors, has adopted a humiliating policy of temporization and lost all sense of priority and balance." This was followed by a strong expression of no confidence in the government: "Ministers of the cabinet, being in constant betrayal of the way of harmony and collaboration, have prevented the elected members of the people from carrying out our mandate of assisting governance. We are therefore of the opinion that we cannot possibly have confidence in this administration." With these passages inserted, the lukewarm memorial changed to a strongly worded impeachment of the government. What was more, the revised memorial was adopted with the support of the independents despite frantic efforts by the Jiyūtō. The government was deeply embarrassed. At the end of its resources, it petitioned the throne for another dissolution and the Diet was again dissolved on June 1; one dissolution after another.

The Itō government had been in the midst of negotiating treaty revisions, and I suspected that it had determined to give no opportunity for the people's parties to speak up. From our point of view, the treaty revision talks had failed in the past since they were drafted by the government without the support of the people. We advocated a firm foreign relations posture because we felt strongly that the government must be persuaded to forfeit its feeble policy in order to achieve truly equal treaties. The government obviously wanted to be left alone. It not only issued an order prohibiting all newspapers and magazines from printing articles and editorials on the subject of treaty revision but forbade all public debate of the issue, thus silencing orators and preventing information from reaching the people.

What concerned us most was the Korean issue. Already there was trouble simmering between China and Japan that could be touched off at any moment, and the country was being led by an Itō government notorious for its weak-kneed diplomacy. We therefore advocated a strong foreign policy, afraid that the government might agree to terms that would jeopardize the interests of the country over the long run.

As things developed, even the feeble Itō government was now compelled to make a crucial decision. On August 1, war was declared against China and we sprang to the new task of supporting the war on the somewhat unaccustomed basis of national unity.

JAPAN'S WAR WITH CHINA BRINGS A POLITICAL CEASE-FIRE

Immediately on the outbreak of war we entered a period of political armistice. At the same time, since the coalition's recommendations for a hard-line foreign policy were an expression of our united and profound love of the country and our commitment to democracy, we could not but feel some satisfaction in having been instrumental in fostering the conditions for the decision to go to war with China. The fourth general election was conducted on September 1 very calmly and without incident. The outcome in terms of the number of seats held by the various parties and factions was more or less the same as before the election.

In the interests of national unity all political parties put aside past favors and grudges to face the common enemy and adopted a resolution to support whatever expenditure was required to achieve a successful outcome to the war. For our part, the members of the people's coalition decided that until further notice there would be no opposition, no government party, no hardliners, and no critics, but that we would work together and in unity with the government to consolidate the foundations of a just peace in the orient. The seventh Diet (October 18–21, 1894) was convened at the imperial headquarters in Hiroshima and all members were asked to collaborate in the important matters facing a nation at war. The Diet trusted the government's programs, passed all government-initiated bills and endorsed without hesitation a military budget of 150 million yen.

In the face of a foreign enemy there would be no domestic dissension. This is our national feature. It was said that Li Hung-chang and Yuan Shih-k'ai waged war on Japan thinking that, with our people's coalition at odds with the Itō government, the country would be too preoccupied with domestic strife to dispatch troops abroad. If that is really what they thought, it was certainly a pitiful miscalculation. In Japan, too, the clan bureaucrats behaved as if they had a monopoly on loyalty and patriotism and treated us as if we were traitors. Seeing the performance of the Diet during the war, however, they must have realized how wrong they had been. The reason we had fought so hard for political principles was because we all believed it was in the best interest of the nation. It was clear from the start of the war with China that the reason for contesting political principles in peacetime is to prevent an enemy from holding us in contempt in wartime.

I felt personally vindicated in a way, because the war with China seemed to substantiate the thesis I had held for ten years. Since publishing my thesis "On Conquering China" in 1884 I had often been treated as if I were insane. Now that we were finally at war with China I was last proved to have been of sound mind after all.

The Japanese, in public and private life alike, held China in awe even when we were at war with it because of our not-easily-broken fifteen-hundred-year habit of revering it as the most advanced country in the world. In contrast, the Chinese despised Japan as their small and backward neighbor.

Once we were at war, as I had predicted, our army and navy won every battle as easily as cutting down dead trees. I was feeling very optimistic about the outcome, but one could not afford to be careless until it was all over. It was for this reason that during the eighth Diet (December 1894–March 1895) we passed an additional military expenditure of 100 million yen in order to bolster the war effort, even while a peace envoy from China was actually being received in Japan.

Peace talks were held from March to April of 1895 at Shimonoseki. We were naturally anxious about the progress of the talks and planned to go down to Shimonoseki with a group of party leaders to lend encouragement to the government negotiators. By then, however, things were going so well that they had become too cocksure, holding in disdain not only the enemy China, but their own political parties in Tokyo as well. As if they had forgotten that the reasons for our convincing victory over China were the bravery of our loyal soldiers in the field and the united support of the people back home, the members of the Itō government had become so arrogant that they had no ears for what we as the people's representatives had to say. When a man becomes arrogant and contemptuous of others he courts disaster. The Itō government did just that. At the eleventh hour it struck a major snag: none other than the so-called Triple Intervention.

A Speech to Go Down in Parliamentary History

The Triple Intervention and the retrocession of the Liaotung peninsula enraged the Japanese people. Their anger against the three countries (Russia, France, and Germany) turned against the Itō government, which meekly succumbed. When I realized that the government had yielded to the Triple Intervention, I abandoned my support and prepared to attack. I immediately wrote a couple of treatises, in addition to one to that I gave the title "Inquiry Addressed to Loyal and Patriotic Citizens on Current Events," challenging the statement of the government spokesman that there was no alternative but to return the Liaotung peninsula. The government responded predictably by fettering freedom of speech and public discussion, cracking down most severely on anyone who criticized it for coming to terms with the Tripartite Intervention. One of the treatises I wrote at that time could not be published until two and a half years later. In it, I pointed out that the government should not have succumbed to the unjust demands of the three powers, "blinded by fear of their bluff." The weak-kneed diplomacy of the government only "made the public and the nation afraid of the West, which would encourage the insidious custom of self-imposed servility." "Without any recourse to subterfuge all we needed to do was resolutely to refuse the unjust demand. This would have been enough to cause the triple alliance eventually to break up."

The government not only barred discussion but held many a banquet celebrating the war victory and peace so as to drown national resentment. We did not, however, forget our indignation. We had been united in our support of the Itō government in the war with China, putting to rest all our differences for the time being. And what had the government being doing all that time? The Triple Intervention did not come out of the blue. Those powers had been increasing their forces in the East in broad daylight. What measures had the government taken against this provocation? Had the government been unable to predict the intervention, it would have been guilty of boundless stupidity. Had it predicted it but failed to take needed measures, then its inaction was inexcusable. The government should have been made accountable for having committed this colossal blunder. How could it still hang on to national power without being ashamed of this?

A memorial addressed to the throne impeaching the government for the part it played in the Triple Intervention and the retrocession of the Liaotung peninsula was presented to the House on January 9, 1896. I was the first to take the floor on behalf of the hardliners. As I delivered my speech impeaching the government on the Triple Intervention and the Queen Min incident[4] I felt the anger of the nation surge up my spine. It was this speech that people said would go down in parliamentary history. I was more than a little surprised because, as I mentioned earlier, my talents as an orator were notoriously feeble. The speeches I made outside the Diet were so bad they could not by any stretch of the imagination be compared with the first-class oratory of men like Inukai and Shimada. This was not my style. Instead, I worked hard at convincing my audience and winning battles of words with my opponents. Perhaps the effort was beginning to pay off.

In other countries, as I had seen, a good orator in parliament did not necessarily make a good speaker outside. It took quite different skills, and the same could be said of speakers in Japan. I was a case in point. Nevertheless, in spite of the fact that my speech in the House was received unexpectedly well, its main object of impeaching the government was a miserable failure.After the war, the Jiyūtō had drawn even closer to the Itō government under the auspices of Mutsu, and during the ninth Diet (December 1895–March 1897) it had become a party completely patronized by the government. The Kokumin Kyōkai too had betrayed its original raison d'être and changed sides to defend the government. It was no wonder that the impeachment bill was killed.

While the bill itself was unsuccessful it did indirectly fell the government. The government just managed to hang on to power through the ninth Diet with the help of the Jiyūtō, but when the session was over the party sought to exact the price of its service: namely, a cabinet post for its president, Itagaki. The Jiyūtō justified its demand by saying that using a political party without giving it a share of the power was tantamount to reducing it to the role of a mercenary. Home Minister Itō yielded and gave Itagaki the home minister's portfolio. A cabinet seat for Itagaki raised a storm of opposition among the members of the privileged clans. The privy council and the peers were also against it. They maintained that for a bureaucrat and politician to shake hands with a political party was a major affront to the clan clique. Prince Yamagata, using abusive language, called Itō a national traitor.

The Kokumin Kyōkai which had once changed sides to support the Itō government now began to turn its back on it, in part out of jealousy at the favorable treatment the Jiyūtō was receiving. The departure of the Kokumin Kyōkai took from the government its last chance of commanding a majority in the House, even with its alliance with the Jiyūtō firmly in place as a result of Itagaki's promotion

---

[4] Sensing opposition to Japanese control from members of the conservative groups around Queen Min in Seoul, Japanese representatives cooperated with Korean and Japanese ruffians who invaded the palace and murdered Queen Min in October 1895, prompting an international incident.

to the cabinet. But none of this could conceal the diplomatic blunders of the Itō government. As the government became increasingly unpopular the public began to see that the best solution would be for Ōkuma of the Shinpotō (Progress Party) and Satsuma's Matsukata to come together. The idea was circulated mainly by Tokutomi Sohō's *Kokumin Shinbun*. Thinking that a combination of Matsukata's confidence and Ōkuma's resourcefulness would make a fine government I put in my share of effort to realize this.

The Shinpotō had by now formally come into existence, and, with Ōkuma as our leader, our maneuverability had increased. Until this time we had challenged the government as a coalition, but a coalition of small political parties was a handicap when it came to making swift political moves. Besides, the government had brought in a law to restrict the freedom of action of political associations. Under the circumstances, toward the end of the ninth Diet we dissolved all parties and most of us came together to form a single major party, the Shinpotō.

Almost all political parties with the exception of the Jiyūtō and the Kokumin Kyōkai joined. Among the main participants were the Kaishintō, the Kakushintō, the Zaisei Kakushin Club, the Chugoku Shinpotō, and the Ōte Club affiliated with the Dainihon Kyōkai and the Echisa-kai, which was a part of the Kokkentō (National Rights Party) of Niigata. We said farewell forever to the Kaishintō, which had given us so many memories, but needless to say it was the mainstay of the Shinpotō. In fact, one could say, to put it the other way around, that the Shinpotō was a much strengthened extension of the Kaishintō. The establishment of the new party gave us almost 100 members in the House. We now had a major political party that enabled us to compete credibly in numbers with the Jiyūtō.

From the Matsukata-Ōkuma Government
to the Ōkuma-Itagaki Government

THE MATSUKATA-ŌKUMA COALITION GOVERNMENT IS BORN

By the time the ninth Diet (December 1895–March 1896) was drawing to a close, as we saw in the previous chapter, the second Itō government found itself friendless. To make matters worse, the "razor-sharp minister" Mutsu, as he was called, resigned from his post as foreign minister, on account of ill health. Finance Minister Watanabe Kunitake, too, let it be known that he wished to leave due to his inability to control the country's runaway spending.

It seemed inevitable that the Itō government would collapse. But, as might have been expected of him, when worse came to worst, Itō turned to the enemy camp to rescue his government from its difficulties. Thus he attempted to fill the yawning gaps in his eroding cabinet by inviting his great opponent, Ōkuma Shigenobu, to fill the post of minister of foreign affairs, and the Satsuma clan's magnate, Matsukata Masayoshi that of finance.

In the end, however, Itō was replaced by a government headed by Matsukata that included Ōkuma, who, as head of the Shinpotō, was Itō's avowed enemy. Itō's greatness lay in his attempt to include the two enemy generals in his own cabinet. However, the suggested appointment of Ōkuma was squarely opposed by Itagaki, the home minister. "Ōkuma is the government's enemy," he said. "To invite such a person into the cabinet is against the principles of constitutional government. We cannot possibly cooperate with the Shinpotō for long. I cannot remain in the government with this man." Itagaki stood firm and Itō was forced to invite Matsukata alone. But by then Ōkuma and Matsukata had been in contact, and Matsukata sent Itō his regrets saying that he could not accept the invitation to join the government without Ōkuma. And so it was that Itō was finally forced to resign. The *genrō* conference convened and decided to recommend Matsukata and Ōkuma. On May 18, 1896, Matsukata received the imperial command to head the government.

Ordinarily, by virtue of his capacity and experience, Ōkuma would have been the natural choice for prime minister, but because of clan politics it could not be done. As in the Kuroda cabinet, similar circumstances now dictated that Ōkuma could only wield the actual power if Matsukata were publicly named prime minister.

Matsukata chose his cabinet cautiously because of the manifest presence of Ōkuma. He did not have to be reminded of their relationship. In the first year of the Meiji period, Ōkuma was the finance minister and Matsukata was the third-ranking official in the ministry, a post below that of vice-minister. Because of their long-standing superior-subordinate relationship, and because the two men were of different caliber, Matsukata probably felt the need to establish a firm foothold in the cabinet that he was to head. The natural thing to do would have been to consult Ōkuma as soon as he received the imperial command. Matsukata first named a couple of ministers and only then convened a meeting.

Ōkuma, true to form, launched into an instructive policy speech on internal and external matters as if he himself had been named prime minister, and this before he had even been given a cabinet portfolio. He started with the grand principles of constitutionalism, then the need to respect human rights, the duty to listen to the wishes of the people, the accountability of ministers of the cabinet as a group, and the need to streamline the administration so as to rebuild the basis of the national finances. He spent over an hour wading through these topics like a professor lecturing his students. Everyone was astonished. "Excuse me, sir, you are not the prime minister," someone finally remonstrated. "It is imprudent of you to speak against the views of the great statesman," thundered Kabayama, silencing the speaker.

The meeting was troubled from the start. Feeling disgusted, Ōkuma complained of a toothache and went home. I was at his residence with some other supporters when he arrived. "I give up," he said. "It's no use doing anything with those people." Ōkuma went straight to bed. We did not know what to do. We had gone too far to back out now from entering the coalition with Matsukata. We did everything we could to urge Ōkuma to join the cabinet. After all, Matsukata had accepted the premiership strictly on the condition that he would have Ōkuma with him. We were too deeply indebted to Matsukata's people as well as a great many others to withdraw now. I cared only about the obligations we owed the Matsukata group. "We have come too far for us to back out now," I flared. And then, pleading angrily with Ōkuma at his bedside, "If you do not want to join the cabinet, so be it. You will leave us no choice. We shall have to break away from you politically and support the Matsukata cabinet." He remained adamant and refused to budge. I left Ōkuma's bedside in despair but with my mind made up. On the way out Ōkuma's wife called me aside. I was a little surprised at this for my relations with her had not been very good. "Is he still refusing?" she asked.

"Yes," I replied, "he is quite determined to step down. We have no choice but to stand by Mr. Matsukata."

"Now, don't be too hot-tempered," the woman advised me. "Just give me a little time. As soon as his toothache is better I shall talk to him. Leave this to me."

I was desperate, so I agreed. Eventually I received this message from her: "Ōkuma has consented to join the cabinet." I don't know what magical powers she had, but she certainly knew how to get around her husband. Ōkuma had never been known to eat his words once he had made up his mind. This time he did, though. In September, 1896 the Matsukata-Ōkuma coalition government was formed. Matsukata doubled as prime minister and finance minister while Ōkuma took the foreign ministry. The central figures of the Satsuma clan were Takashima

Tomonosuke and Kabayama Sukenori. The army and colonial ministries went to Takashima, while Kabayama, the most powerful figure in the clan, took the Home Ministry, Saigō Tsugumichi was made naval minister, Enomoto Takeaki, minister of agriculture, who was basically nonpolitical. Communications Minister Nomura Yasushi, Minister of Justice Kiyoura Keigo, and Minister of Education Hachisuka Shigeaki appeared to have joined the government to keep an eye on things for the *genrō*. From the beginning, it was clear that they were merely figureheads and could be expected to contribute little. Rather, they could be counted on to take a conservative and temporizing attitude and were constantly in the way of getting things done. It was to this clan-dominated government that Ōkuma, the outsider, now attached himself. Behind him, however, was the Shinpotō with a force of one hundred in the House. As soon as the coalition government was in place, Takahashi Kenzō and Kōmuchi Tonotsune were appointed chief cabinet secretary and director general of the cabinet legislation bureau respectively. They were to serve as liaison between the cabinet and us. Takahashi was a graduate of the imperial university and had worked in the government. At one time, he had served as director-general of the official gazette. Later, he left the government and worked as a correspondent for the *Osaka Asahi Shinbun* and was quite an activist. He was versed in politics as well as in literature. His particular talent where politics was concerned was in negotiating behind the scenes. Whenever there was a major national issue he was always passionately involved. Since the days when he worked for the *Nihon Shinbun*, his outspokenness and unyielding spirit were respected by men of learning and character. Takahashi and Kōmuchi were close friends and had worked with us for a strong foreign policy since the early days of our campaign. Both had streaks of conservatism in them, but were extraordinarily passionate in their love of the country and their countrymen and worked tirelessly to serve them. During the campaign, Kōmuchi had proved himself extremely fair and selfless and had earned the deep respect of us all. We asked these two men to watch over Matsukata. Since as chief cabinet secretary and director-general of the cabinet legislation bureau they would be near the prime minister day and night we decided to ask them to keep a close watch on him.

A SHABBY ROOM AT THE FOREIGN MINISTRY

Once the coalition was in place we pressed the government to establish the office of parliamentary vice-minister in line with the British system. The government did not welcome the idea but could not very well refuse and created a position called councilor to be appointed by the emperor. I became the first councilor. But since the government had been reluctant to create the post in the first place, I was given no work. It was a completely useless job. It may have been only because the foreign ministry did not have large premises in those days, but I was assigned a small and shabby room by the stairs. Of all the imperially appointed councilors I had the worst room. With no work to do I spent my time in my squalid room reading diplomatic documents one after the other in an attempt to extract wisdom from them. The most interesting and the most amusing was the record of the communications that passed between Mutsu Munemitsu and Aoki Shūzō in 1888. At the time, Inoue Kaoru was the foreign minister and Aoki was appointed to represent us in Germany. Mutsu, assigned to London, had to take instructions from Aoki. But subsequently, their positions were reversed; Mutsu became foreign minister in the Itō cabinet, and Aoki, named minister to Germany, returned to Berlin. Now, in reporting to his chief, he found it difficult to accept this reversal of status, and, in his correspondence, Aoki continued to maintain the same dignity he had always shown as Mutsu's superior. He even maintained it in the telegrams he dispatched to his minister from Berlin, for every time Mutsu responded to Aoki he added, "No more instructions, please."

Of particular interest was the exchange of communications between them toward the end of the war with China. Mutsu, anxious to know if there would be intervention by the powers, sent telegrams to ministers of Japanese legations in Europe asking for their observations. Aoki replied to the following effect: "Rest assured that while I am assigned here I shall never let Germany stand in opposition to Japan." But soon afterward, in spite of Aoki's assurances, it was Germany that took the initiative in the Triple Intervention. Mutsu immediately sent back the jeering message: "Now just what did you mean by your previous telegram, 'Rest assured Germany will never oppose Japan'?"

I also read through every diplomatic document that had passed between Japan and China since the first year of Meiji. In diplomacy I felt that the Chinese were constantly getting the better of us, perhaps because of their facility with language. We prevailed because we were committed to taking up arms if all else failed. In talks we did not seem to do very well.

Soejima's famed negotiations with Peking were long considered a great success, but I felt that there was more to his apparent success than we had been made to believe. Indeed, behind the scenes there moved the figure of General Charles William Le Gendre (1830–1899).

General Le Gendre was an American consul stationed at first in Amoy. Passing through Japan on his way back to the United States he met with Foreign Minister Soejima. The general urged Soejima that as a matter of urgency Japan should annex Korea to the north and Taiwan to the south, so that it would stretch its arms in the shape of a half-moon toward the Asian continent. He warned that Japan's security would be enormously threatened if Russia occupied Korea and England or France occupied Taiwan. Soejima was convinced by Le Gendre, as was Saigō Takamori in turn through Soejima. It was said that Saigō's later strategy to conquer Korea had its origins here.

The general was an ardent Japanophile and worked in many ways to help the Meiji government. If I recall correctly, he also accompanied Soejima as an advisor on the latter's trip to Peking. Earlier, while the general was stationed as consul in Amoy, a certain Chinese official secretly broke into the foreign settlement and put poison in the well. He was probably motivated by xenophobic sentiments and intended to poison all foreign residents in China. However, he was caught in time by the general, who then let him go. Le Gendre probably had an intimation that the man might serve a useful purpose at some time in the future. On accompanying Soejima to Peking, Le Gendre found that the would-be poisoner had now become a high official in the Chinese ministry of foreign affairs. The general apparently let him know that unless he made himself useful to Japan his old secret would be exposed, and as a result the official contributed materially to the success of Soejima's talks with Peking. I learned this directly from the general, but I never found anything of the sort in the foreign ministry archives.

The American general became a close friend of Soejima and Ōkuma but did not make friends with other government officials. There was a time when he returned in disillusionment to the United States, but having lived long in the Orient he was not comfortable in his own country. He later returned to Japan and took up residence in Sashigaya in Tokyo's Koishikawa district.

It was about that time that I first got to know him. I was then in the midst of opposing Foreign Minister Inoue's treaty revision plan. The general too was against the proposed revision. He was a resourceful man and contributed considerably to my action program.

To my mind, Le Gendre was an unforgettable player in Japan's diplomatic history. He was the author of "An account of the Conquest of Taiwan" and other books, and there was much to learn from his opinions on China. On being invited by the Korean government to serve as an adviser, he moved to Seoul, where he died. Miss Sekiya Toshiko, a famous vocalist, was his daughter.

TANAKA SHŌZŌ, GUARDIAN OF TOCHIGI

Many amusing incidents occurred during my days at the foreign ministry. Although I was a councilor appointed by the throne it did not stop me from frequenting party headquarters as a leader of the Shinpotō. The young fellows in the office treated me with respect and never failed to address me by my proper title. One evening a man came into the office and called out, "Is Ozaki here?" The junior official on duty thought this very rude and shot back, "And who are you, sir?" "Army Minister Takashima Tomonosuke," the man answered. Hearing the name, the young man was doubly shocked. In all the time the Shinpotō had been in opposition, its offices had never before been visited by such an important member of the government.

That story reminds me of the frequent visits I received from Foreign Minister Ōkuma and his vice-minister, Komura, in my shabby office at the ministry. The young men at the ministry often wondered why the minister and his deputy would visit someone who occupied such a dingy room. They were even more surprised when "Totsuchin sensei" came to see me.

"Totsuchin," an abbreviation of "Tochigi chindai" (defender of Tochigi), was the nickname of Tanaka Shōzō, an unpredictable character who devoted his life to fighting pollution caused by the Ashio copper mines.[1] He was a great friend of Shimada Saburō and often stayed at his place overnight. Each time he did so he left a trail of lice behind him. When his host's wife and maid complained, he had the nerve to scold them roundly: "Don't you know lice are the decoration of a man with a cause?"

Tanaka was known to abuse people in a loud voice and to strike his friends. One day he came to see me about the copper poisoning. I could not agree with him on every count. Unfortunately, another of his regrettable habits was that he considered anybody who did not agree with him a mortal enemy. So, on that particular day, he was unhappy that I did not eagerly agree with all he had said, and he denounced me loudly enough to be heard throughout the ministry.

The ministry of foreign affairs was a decorous place, since it was frequented daily by foreign diplomats. Its dignified halls seldom echoed with abusive language. Tanaka's trumpeted abuse was probably the first that had been heard there since the founding of the ministry.

All things considered, Tanaka and I were good friends, but we had a few collisions in our time. Once, during a meeting he became quite angry and declared that he was going to hit me during the reception which was to follow. I was determined not to be his victim, and though I knew perfectly well it was not the right thing to do, I was prepared to hurt him so badly he would never forget it. I even fancied that it would be almost an honor for him to be able to say that I had crippled him and given him an even better decoration than his lice. What in the world could I have been imagining? I was certainly no match for him with my small fists. If he should try to strike me I would stick my thumb in his eye so he would never see with that eye again. I was sure that if I went for his eye I could fight him with a single finger.

We retired to the reception, and after a while when it had become quite merry, Tanaka came up to me much the worse for drink. This was the moment I feared. I thought he would strike any moment. But he did not. He must have seen the secret determination in my eyes. Just then Moriya Kōnosuke, who was standing next to me, said something or other to Tanaka. It was a perfectly ordinary remark, and nothing at all to get angry about. "You scoundrel!" bellowed Tanaka, and struck Moriya with his fist. The poor man was left wondering what had hit him. No wonder Moriya was astonished. Tanaka had come over to make trouble with me, but as he had to forego his plan he simply struck the nearest person instead. Violent as he was, he had the presence of mind to hold back when he sensed that his quarry was prepared to defend himself.

Later, his speeches became famous. He was an eccentric and often used totally unexpected words. Yet if he had to repeat the same speech he would work on it to improve it every time. I must say I admired him for that.

---

[1] For a study of this crusader, see Kenneth Strong, *Ox Against the Storm: A Biography of Tanaka Shozo: Japan's Conservationist Pioneer* (Vancouver: University of British Columbia Press, 1977).

THE TENTH DIET AND THE NEWSPAPER ORDINANCE

The Shinpotō pledged itself in these words to three major policies:

> We adopt the following platform in order to profess our commitment to the nation's progress, to ensure the prosperity of the imperial house, and to strengthen the rights and happiness of citizens. We are resolved to:
>
> 1. Undertake political reform so as to create a genuinely responsible government.
> 2. Redesign our foreign policy and achieve greater sovereign rights for the nation.
> 3. Streamline finance the better to assist the development of the people.

Soon after its inauguration, the Matsukata-Ōkuma coalition government made an almost identical policy statement. That there was little difference between the government's policy and the Shinpotō platform did not come as a great surprise in view of the fact that half of the responsibility for the government's policy lay with Ōkuma, who was, after all, still the de facto head of the Shinpotō. The Shinpotō therefore adopted the following resolution in the tenth Diet.

It began: "The platform of the Matsukata government in all matters of importance hardly differs from our party's policy. Therefore, our party will support the full implementation of its provisions. But our party believes rhetoric must be accompanied by action. We are conscious therefore of the obligation to denounce the government if it does not act as it has pledged." The remainder of the resolution was of less importance. As we shall see, not long afterwards we were forced to keep our promise.

No sooner had the Matsukata government formed, than it presented to the Diet a barely disguised rehash of the previous government's budget. The Jiyūtō consequently found itself deprived of its biggest target. Because the Jiyūtō had been the ruling party in the previous government and voted for the budget, it could not very well oppose the present government. It looked as though the tenth Diet (December 1896–March 1897) would be able to proceed with unaccustomed smoothness.

However, in the eyes of the Jiyūtō's members, Ōkuma had been their avowed enemy for many years. It galled them to see Ōkuma as head of the foreign ministry, and they attacked him with a vengeance on matters of foreign policy at every opportunity.

Ōkuma had been in politics since the Restoration. He was a veteran. He described the true circumstances without dissembling, presented his policies for dealing with them with clarity, and then bore the brunt of the Jiyūtō's criticism without flinching. We were elated to see for the first time since the first Diet a foreign minister worthy of a constitutional country.

For a very petty reason the Matsukata-Ōkuma government fell prematurely, having done very little work. The one important exception was the revision of the newspaper ordinance, which had been such an impediment to truly democratic government.

People's failings were often in another sense their strength. We considered Chōshū men to be untrustworthy, but they could also be cautiously considerate. By comparison, Satsuma men were simple and naive. This made us feel less uncomfortable about forming a coalition government with Satsuma men rather than Chōshū men. If the Satsuma men were simple and naive enough, by providing them guidance we could find them to be partners in our search for constitutional government. Unfortunately, all too soon this would prove to have been wishful thinking.

The leading figures in the Matsukata government were the two admirals Kabayama and Takashima. Admiral Takashima by nature was considered extremely outspoken and capable of anything. He could reverse himself and think nothing of it. House Minister Admiral Kabayama, on the other hand, was considered strong and straightforward, someone who always kept his word. Since the Sino-Japanese war he had been dubbed the Nelson of the Orient; his repute was considered second only to that of Saigō Takamori.

Thinking that in collaborating with the Matsukata cabinet the man most to be trusted was Admiral Kabayama, we hoped that he would represent the cabinet in our negotiations with them. For this reason we were greatly reassured when Prime Minister Matsukata agreed to this arrangement.

The Shinpotō was represented by Ōhashi Gitetsu, Inukai Tsuyoshi, and myself. The most important issue at the time was human rights, and a firm commitment was reached between Home Minister Kabayama and ourselves on the matter of guaranteeing freedom of speech and assembly. In particular, we received a firm promise from Kabayama that he would be lenient with regard to enforcing ordinances under which newspapers had been banned so frequently.

In those days there was a magazine called *Twenty-Sixth Century* published by Takahashi Kenzō in Osaka. That it was an unapologetically nationalistic was apparent from the fact that it used as its calendrical starting point the sixth-century B.C. date for the accession to rule of the legendary Emperor Jimmu rather than that of the Western calendar. The magazine had then begun publishing an article titled "On the Imperial Household Ministry," citing facts to support its denunciation of the corruption that had developed in that ministry under the Itō Government. It became so popular that the *Nippon Shinbun* in Tokyo and other papers republished it to encourage national debate. It was to be expected that this sort of denunciation would meet with opposition from among the old Chōshū clansmen, and we heard a rumor that the minister of the imperial household had demanded suspension of the *Twenty-Sixth Century* and the newspaper "*Nippon.*" It was also rumored that the figurehead ministers, Justice Minister Kiyoura, Communications Minister Nomura, and Hachisuka were demanding at cabinet level that these publications be disciplined. If the government decided to ban publication after we had left Tokyo on the campaign trail it would be enormously disadvantageous to our campaign. So we went to Minister Kabayama to beg that he would stand by his promise. The admiral, tapping at his neck with his hand, said, "You can be assured that there will be no ban, even at the risk of my own neck. I will keep my promise." His words were more precious to me than rivers of gold, and, with further assurances from Minister Kabayama, whom I trusted implicitly, we took off on our campaign. At a meeting in Ibaragi, speaking in support of the Matsukata-Ōkuma government, I announced that it had fully guaranteed freedom of speech and assembly. It was during this same campaign that we received a telegram from the Shinpotō headquarters in Tokyo informing us that the government had banned the *Twenty-Sixth Century* and suspended the *Nippon*. I was speechless with shock. I therefore cut short my campaign and promptly returned to Tokyo, where I questioned Admiral Kabayama on the devastating turn-about. He did not appear particularly troubled and sought to pacify me with lame excuses. It was then that I realized the error of collaborating with the Matsukata cabinet and regretted that I had not obeyed the conviction of Ōkuma. I immediately suggested that we should sever our collaboration with the government, but my opinion was defeated by a small margin as there were those who wished to continue the arrangement.

By this time a crack had already appeared in the Matsukata government. Interestingly, we had not expected much from Admiral Takashima, who was reputed for his trickery and a propensity for going back on his word, but he had kept his faith with us. It was Kabayama, who had a reputation for keeping his word who had gone back on it. I was young and impetuous, so after we broke with the government I assailed Kabayama, saying that such a faithless man should be banished from the political world. I do not think I had anything to do with it, but Kabayama, who had been so popular with the public at first as a sort of political reincarnation of Ōkubo, lost his good name in a matter of less than a year.

I Agitate Against the Government While in Its Employ

We were greatly disillusioned by Home Minister Kabayama, who had proved so untrustworthy. Worse still was our disillusionment with the prime minister. To be quite frank, we did not think him to be a man of stature at all. Had he not been from Satsuma he would not likely have become prime minister.

Mutsu Munemitsu had a gift for seeing through people and a disrespectful manner to go with it. According to him, "One can be sure to find one or two men of Matsukata's stature in any village office." I would say, however, that Matsukata had a certain insight and did a reliable though not outstanding job while in the ministry of finance. Since all his superiors had died one after the other, his turn to represent Satsuma came through no particular merit of his own. In this sense he was fortunate.

He carried himself well enough, but was extremely dull-witted. There is an interesting story about him in this regard. In an informal moment, Emperor Meiji asked Matsukata how many children he had. Matsukata, who had sired many children, could not give a definite reply. He tried counting on his fingers, but gave up and said sheepishly "I shall check on it, Your Majesty." Emperor Meiji was greatly amused by this and from time to time would ask him the same question: "Now, how many children did you say you had?" to which he would invariably respond, "I shall give you an answer, Your Majesty, after I have it checked." It became a standing joke among members of the foreign diplomatic corps.

We had assumed Matsukata to be trustworthy, if only because of his slowness, which bordered on stupidity, and we thought the cunning Chōshū people would easily be able to cheat us, but not Matsukata, who was simple and honest to a fault. But he proved us wrong.

Every time we asserted ourselves strongly, Matsukata congenially followed our bidding, allowing us to think we had settled the matter for good, but the moment Home Minister Kabayama or Takashima stormed in, he vacillated. So we had to go back to reclaim his loyalty, but we were never sure of him. Like the man in the Chinese saying who changed his mind three times in the morning and four times in the evening, no one was more unreliable than Matsukata.

As it happened, it was Cabinet Secretary Takahashi and Director-General of the Cabinet Legislative Bureau Kōmuchi, whom we had appointed our unofficial Matsukata-watchers, who were the first to despair and give up. "We have had enough," they said and turned in their resignations. "We can keep an eye on him during the day," they complained, "but Matsukata changes sides during his sleep. He never keeps his official promises. We'll have to recruit women to watch him." Matsukata always agreed with the last person in to speak to him. This was where he earned the nickname "Last-in-Man." It was the reverse of the idea that a first impression is the lasting impression; in Matsukata's case the last impression was the one he never forgot.

With Takahashi and Kōmuchi deserting, we were at a loss. It was decided that there was nothing else to do but to bring down the government from within. At the outset, we had supported the coalition government in order to promote our principles through a collaboration between the Shinpotō Party and the Satsuma faction. But, for the reasons explained, we could not depend on Matsukata. I was still a palace-appointed councilor in the foreign affairs ministry, but, as a leader of the Shinpotō Party, I naturally participated in the resolution to overthrow the government. This became an issue within the government, and I was warned that unless I immediately resigned my post, I would be discharged on disciplinary grounds. To me, there was no difference between resignation and dismissal. The person who warned me whispered that disciplinary dismissal could be an obstacle to any future appointment to government office. As I did not tender my resignation, in the end I was dismissed.

As a member of the coalition government, Ōkuma fought to right the fiscal situation, demanding reform of the monetary system, along with strict banning of unconstitutional acts and the dismissal of time-serving ministers, but none of these measures was accepted. In the meantime, our party announced its resolve to "sever partnership with the government, which on all present evidence appears to lack the will to carry out its earlier declarations." We also asked Ōkuma to resign since we were getting nowhere. "Has it taken you this long to come to your senses?" he laughed. "I told you from the beginning, but it was you people who wanted me to get into the government. Now do you know better?" and he tendered his resignation. This was January 6, 1898.

DISSOLUTION AND RESIGNATION EN MASSE

With the Shinpotō's departure and Ōkuma's resignation, the Matsukata government had, to all intents and purposes, fallen. Among our men who had supported the government, some now abandoned ship without delay while others stayed on. Haseba Sumitaka and Tokutomi Iichirō remained with the government and parted from us, but most of the Shinpotō members who had joined the government at my persuasion now left it with me. Munakata Sei, however, did not. He wrote me a letter saying that he would go to Dan-no-ura with the government to keep his promise of collaboration. This episode earned him the nickname "Governor of Dan-no-ura."[2]

Members of the Satsuma clique, from their experience of successfully manipulating political party members during the first Matsukata government, apparently believed that they could tame political parties no matter what their principles and affiliations. We were wary of this from the start, of course. Learning from the fact that once the Jiyūtō and the Kokumin Kyōkai had become part of the ruling party, they had developed scandalous financial relations with the government, we were particularly careful on this point. During our coalition with the government we therefore restricted contact with them to Inukai and myself alone, and strictly forbade other party members from frequenting the homes of government officials. In spite of this, the government tried indirectly to tempt Takahashi and Kōmuchi with offers of material benefit. Honest men that they were, they accepted nothing, nor did any person from among our ranks. Later we learned that the government considered us a rather strange lot.

With relations with the Shinpotō severed, the government people now approached the Jiyūtō in search of support in the Diet. The collaboration between the Jiyūtō and the Itō government had come about as a result of the efforts of Mutsu and Hoshi, and as such its main strength lay with the Tosa and Kantō factions. Within the Jiyūtō, however, there were elements that were dissatisfied with this arrangement. It was this group that secretly negotiated with the Matsukata government at the invitation of Admiral Takashima Kakuhei. Dozens of hoodlums calling themselves renovationists broke in during a Jiyūtō convention and attempted to force the adoption of a resolution calling for collaboration with the government. The unsolicited attempt failed, and the government failed also in its plan to appease the Jiyūtō. The party convention, with a vote of 85 to 40, adopted a resolution calling for the submission of a vote of no confidence at the start of the eleventh Diet. Five men, including Okumiya Takenori, were expelled on presentation of sufficient proof that they had been bought by Admiral Takashima.

Representatives of the Shinpotō met with those from the Jiyūtō, the Kokumin Kyōkai, the Dōshi-kai, and the Jitsugyō Dōshi Club (Businessmen's Club) at Isekan in Minami Nabe-chō to strengthen the unity of the people's parties and to

---

[2] Dan-no-ura was the conclusive battle in which the Minamoto defeated the Taira in 1185; Munakata was promising to fight to the death.

discuss submission of a vote of no confidence in the government. Unity among the people's parties was achieved and we were ready and eager to go into the eleventh Diet (December 24–25, 1897) with colors flying.

On December 25, 1897, at the start of the plenary session, just when the parliamentary secretary began a reading of the proposed budget and other government-sponsored bills, Suzuki Shigeto interrupted the secretary and submitted the following resolution: "Be it resolved that this House does not have confidence in the present cabinet." The sentences were simple, straightforward, and powerful. But when Suzuki proceeded to explain his motion, the house was ordered to dissolve immediately.

We were astounded. What was even more extraordinary was that Prime Minister Matsukata, having dissolved the House, immediately presented himself to the palace and submitted the resignation of his cabinet. If the prime minister had asked the throne for a dissolution, he should have done so with the intention of challenging the people's parties. If on the other hand he wanted the cabinet to resign, he had no business dissolving the House. It was a strange ending to a strange government.

All our efforts to bring together our leader Ōkuma and Matsukata into forming a government fell apart in this meaningless way. During the coalition government there was, however, one very moving episode. On April 10, 1897, Sasaki Takayuki was granted an audience with Emperor Meiji. As they were discussing political developments, His Majesty turned to Sasaki. "Matsukata too was complaining about party politicians," said the emperor. "He felt that leading a constitutional government was easier said than done." Sasaki, thinking he had a sympathizer, replied, "The constitution of Japan, unlike other European laws, has its origins in our unique national polity . There is no need for us to be wedded to the European type of parliamentary democracy. If the parliament does not respect the purport of the constitution bestowed by the throne and becomes a nuisance in its pursuit of parliamentary government, Your Majesty may deem it fit to suspend constitutional government at an appropriate time." His words betrayed the wish to suspend the constitution that was still harbored by some of the former clansmen. The emperor, somewhat surprised at this, apparently told him, "I had merely remarked that constitutional government was a challenge. I did not say it should be abolished, nor have I any intention of abolishing it in the future. I responded to your complaints by acknowledging that constitutional government is indeed a difficult proposition." He made it clear so that there would be no misunderstanding. This commitment of the emperor was of inestimable encouragement to us.

THE ITŌ GOVERNMENT AND THE JIYŪTŌ

Asked to take the helm again following the collapse of the Matsukata government, the first thing Itō Hirobumi did was to meet with Ōkuma to discuss the latter's participation in the cabinet. Itō's thought was to deal with their difficulties by forming a coalition between the Satsuma and Chōshū clan leaders and the political parties. Ōkuma appeared quite tempted.

We had had enough of coalitions with the clan leaders. Perhaps we were being overly cautious, but we were afraid that an Ōkuma-Itō coalition would produce the same results. Ōkuma was an optimist by nature and he might have felt that it would go well with Itō.

Itō and Ōkuma had been avowed political enemies since the political coup of 1881, but in their hearts each had always had a place for the other. The two men had common traits and their political views were not very different. They became foes by accident. That was on the surface; underneath they were the best of friends.

Their discussion about collaborating at this time bore no fruit. After Itō failed to interest the Shinpotō in a coalition, it was the Jiyūtō's turn. A meeting at the Imperial Hotel between Itō and Itagaki, Jiyūtō's president, went well. Home Minister Itagaki reported to his party's general assembly on the successful talks, and the assembly in turn unanimously decided to leave the final decision to Itagaki and policy affairs director Kataoka Kenkichi.

Eventually the Jiyūtō announced its support of the Itō government, but this did not, as might have been expected, signal an immediate invitation to the party's president to join the cabinet. The excuse given was that "with the general election slated for March 15, it is not wise to give the home minister's portfolio to the chief of a political party. Even assuming the election is conducted fairly, we will be criticized for having intervened if we win, and we will incur the wrath of the ruling party if we lose." Apparently Itō broke the news to Itagaki something like this: "I shall do my utmost to complete the establishment of constitutional government. I believe you should remain outside the cabinet and lead the Jiyūtō to become a model for political parties under the constitutional government." His statement could easily be taken as manipulating the Jiyūtō with sweet words.

As the result of the general election, the Jiyūtō won 98 seats, the Shinpotō 91, the Kokumin Kyōkai 26, the Yamashita Club 48, the Dōshi Club 14, and Independents 23. There was little change in the political map.

After the election the Jiyūtō insisted on a place for Itagaki in the cabinet. At a cabinet meeting on April 13, Prime Minister Itō took up the subject very casually. "Hayashi Yūzo has asked that Itagaki be given a seat in the cabinet," he said, "but I see there is no vacancy. If he were to be invited in, one of us would have to be sacrificed, and that would be too cruel." Then one of the ministers commented: "That would be more difficult than the recent demand on Dairen and Lushen." With this, the members of the cabinet laughed and the subject was buried.

When the Jiyūtō realized that their leader was not being given a seat, they became defiant and served notice of abandoning their support for the Itō government on two counts of failure on the part of the government: 1) to open the way to a party cabinet, and 2) to conduct an active fiscal policy in managing the postwar economy. Having severed its relationship with the Itō government, the Jiyūtō had but one choice, which was to collaborate with us in the Shinpotō. When the twelfth Diet (May–June 1898) opened on May 18, 1898, the people's parties vetoed the government's fiscal program and voted down its tax increase plan by 247 votes to 27. The government did its level best to pass the tax bill by threatening to suspend, extend, or even dissolve the Diet. On June 10, the government delivered an imperial rescript of dissolution.

ITŌ PLANS TO ORGANIZE HIS OWN POLITICAL PARTY

When presented with the notice of severance by the Jiyūtō on April 16, 1898, Itō rose to announce his intention to organize his own political party. "Mercenaries are not dependable," he declared. "One needs one's own troops." This was not the first time Itō had planned to organize a political party. Once before, clearly seeing the dangers posed by inimical relations between the government and the parliament and realizing the essential role of political parties in implementing constitutional government, he had attempted to organize one himself. Mutsu Munemitsu, who was considered Itō's mastermind, backed him up, saying, "If you will organize a political party, I will resign my ministerial post and work with you."

Itō's plan to organize a political party that first time is described in detail in a work titled *Emperor Meiji and Constitutional Government* by Watanabe Ikujirō. According to this source, when we were fighting the Matsukata government in the winter of 1891, Itō returned to his home town in Yamaguchi prefecture and quietly consulted his political colleagues about organizing a party. On returning to Tokyo in January of the following year, he advised the throne of his intention through Chief Chamberlain Tokudaiji and sought imperial permission. "Political parties are essential to constitutional government. I therefore beg to be relieved of the presidency of the privy council in order to organize a political party as an unencumbered citizen. Incompetent as I am I believe it would not be too difficult to gather as many members as Ōkuma's Kaishintō. I wish to lead such a party to assist the government."

Emperor Meiji, having listened to Itō's petition, is reported to have said that there were parts he was unable to understand and therefore he could neither approve nor deny the request. Itō followed up by asking for an audience on January 22, which was granted, and then explained his plan to the emperor in person: "The purpose of the political party I wish to organize," he said, "is not to destroy the government but to assist it." The emperor, according to Watanabe's book, replied, "I don't understand. You have constantly criticized Matsukata, charging that he was unsuitable for the prime ministership. You have also attacked the cabinet, saying none of the ministers is worthy of mention. If those words were not false, whom do you wish to assist by organizing a political party yourself? What is needed today is not to create another political party, but to reshuffle the cabinet you have. Unless you remake the cabinet into one that you can trust, you will not be able to assist it. If you formed a political party under the present circumstances, it would oppose the cabinet and prove that it is no different from the Jiyūtō and the Kaishintō. You should suspend your proposal."

This took place during the gross election interventions of Home Minister Shinagawa when the whole nation was in a state of ferment, but Itō did not give up his idea of leading his own political party. On February 23, he arranged a meeting at Prime Minister Matsukata's residence with the genrōs, Kuroda Kiyotaka, Yamagata Aritomo, Saigō Tsugumichi, Inoue Kaoru, and Ōyama Iwao, present and shared with them his thoughts on political party organization. Every genrō opposed Itō's plan and demanded that he change his mind. Although he had undoubtedly made up his mind to go through with his plan, Itō was, after all, not so determined as to ignore both the concerted opposition of the genrō and the emperor's disapproval, so his party remained but a dream. Seven years now had passed since that incident. Having failed to get the Shinpotō to collaborate with him and having been deserted by the Jiyūtō, Itō again sought to organize a party from among his own followers.

The story of Itō's efforts to organize a political party is detailed in *A History of Japanese Political Parties* by Hayashida Kametaro, who served as the central figure in establishing the new party. According to the *History*, Itō had English, German, and French political parties researched in order to design a model political party for Japan. The base would be composed of politicians close to Itō, flanked by university graduates on one side and the wealth of businessmen on the other. According to the plan, with Watanabe Kōki in charge of finding university graduates, and Inoue Kaoru the businessmen, the total would be sufficient. But Itō still lacked adequate funds. Learning of this, Magoshi Kyōhei offered to provide what funds were needed, promptly putting up three hundred thousand yen and promising to consider more if this were not enough. Itō was greatly encouraged by this, and setting up an office in the finance minister's residence he quickly embarked on organizing a political party.

With his preparations in place, Itō officially reported to the cabinet meeting on June 19 and asked support for his plan. At first, according to the cabinet proceedings documented in Watanabe's literature, no one, it appears, commented one way or the other. The ministers stared into space without saying anything. At length, Kaneko Kentarō, the minister of agriculture and commerce, rose and said, "Your humble colleague already spoke about the need for creating political parties even at the time the constitution was promulgated. If Your Excellency is as devoted as he tells us to the idea of organizing one himself, it is a great step forward and a matter of congratulations for the state." After this, every member of the cabinet approved the idea without dissent. Kuroda, the president of the privy council, who was present offered, "If Mr Itō organizes a political party I will stump the country with my *hamabishi* walking stick." So it was decided that the matter be taken up, and it was left to Suematsu Kenchō, the communications minister, to draft a declaration.

That evening, Shibusawa Eiichi, Masuda Takashi, Ōkura Kihachirō, and a dozen or so prominent businessmen met at the Imperial Hotel to discuss the proposed political party. The next day, the twentieth according to Hayashida's memorandum, they met with Sassa Tomofusa, Motoda Hajime, Ooka Ikuzō, and Wada Hikojirō from the government side to reach agreement on details.

THE KENSEITŌ IS BORN

While Itō was proceeding step by step to organize his own political party, our opposition forces were forging an alliance. The Jiyūtō, having abandoned the Itō government, was now eager to have closer relations with the Shinpotō, having no choice but to set aside the years of enmity and to forge a common front for the annihilation of the clan clique government. The Jiyūtō's first move was to send Ōe Taku and Takeuchi Tsuna to Ōkuma to solicit his opinion.

As far as the Shinpotō was concerned, we had also learned from our sorry experience with the Matsukata government that the next collaboration would have to be with the Jiyūtō. Ōkuma welcomed the idea. It was Hiraoka Kōtarō who rose to the occasion. He was a Shinpotō member elected from Kyūshū's Fukuoka prefecture.[3] Ever since he had earned a name for bravery in the Satsuma Rebellion of 1877, he had lived for the national cause. Realizing that funds were needed for political activities he had started a mining business. His big gamble paid off handsomely, especially after the war with China (1894–1895), and with his enormous new-found wealth he propelled himself into politics. He was not highly educated and had only a shallow understanding of constitutional government, but from his readings in the Chinese classic, *The Romance of the Three Kingdoms*, and military tales of the warring states, he had learned to cloak himself with the dignity of an oriental hero. "In order to triumph over the Satsuma-Chōshū government, we must learn from their own strategy when they destroyed the Tokugawa shogunate. We must replace the Satsuma-Chōshū coalition with a Jiyūtō-Shinpotō alliance. Is there anyone else who can play the role of Sakamoto Ryōma in forming this new alliance?[4] I have many thousands of yen to spend on my colleagues in need. When that is all spent I can always mine as much as they want from the infinite bounty of the earth beneath us." He applied himself to the new enterprise with a mixture of irrepressible zeal and clever bluff. Hiraoka took it upon himself to negotiate between the two parties and, on the last day of the Diet, June 7, he called the negotiating partners to his residence where conditions for an alliance were worked out. On the tenth, at a meeting of former elected representatives following the last dissolution, both parties in turn accepted the draft terms of the alliance, which was duly approved. The following day, at an informal gathering at the Kinkikan, Kataoka Kenkichi solemnly announced the creation of the alliance. The convergence of the two political parties was thus dramatically accelerated.

It was obvious for all to see that when the Jiyūtō and the Shinpotō were divided, the clan government prospered, but whenever the two parties joined forces the cabal was eclipsed. However, due to a tendency for one party or the other to play the government hand periodically for tactical reasons, or due to jealousies among

---

[3] Hiraoka was a leading proponent and patron of ultranationalist causes. See Marius B. Jansen, *The Japanese and Sun Yat-sen* (Cambridge, Mass.: Harvard University Press, 1954), pp. 36ff.

[4] On whom, see Marius B. Jansen, *Sakamoto Ryōma and the Meiji Restoration* (Princeton,N.J.: Princeton University Press, 1961).

their rank-and-file members, the two people's parties had come close to alliance, but had always gone their own ways again.

Hoshi Tōru constantly obstructed their union. For some reason Hoshi detested Ōkuma and never missed an opportunity to attack him. Ōkuma on the other hand was above that sort of thing and, probably trying to mend our relations with Hoshi, often reprimanded us, saying, "You should not speak so badly of Hoshi." In fact, when Hoshi was serving as minister in the Japanese legation in Washington, Ōkuma, who during that period was twice foreign minister, showed us Hoshi's reports in order to commend him. "Look," he would say, "Hoshi is learning his lessons."

It made no difference to Hoshi, who hated Ōkuma all his life. That Hoshi was away from the scene at his post in America was fortunate for the emerging alliance. In these circumstances the negotiations proceeded with unexpected dispatch so that, by June 17, we were able to hold a mass rally of the opposition coalition at the Nakamurarō restaurant in Kōtō ward. Both Ōkuma and Itagaki were present and spoke to the audience of five hundred. It was the first time they had met since 1892.

On June 22, the Kenseitō (Constitutional Government Party) held its inaugural ceremony. There were two thousand in the audience at the former Shintomiza hall, with Kataoka Kenkichi acting as chairman. Hiraoka Kōtarō stated the purpose of the meeting and moved the adoption of the declaration, party platform, and party rules.

The tentative and often fragile alliance of the past between the Jiyūtō and Shinpotō had now at last given way to a major new party. The Kenseitō was born. The Declaration of the Kenseitō was as follows:

"It will soon be ten years since the promulgation of the constitution and the establishment of the parliament. During this time the House has been dissolved five times and the fruits of constitutional government have not been reaped. Political parties have been unable to function effectively. Under the circumstances, clan forces have united and there has therefore been neither harmony nor collaboration between the government and the opposition, a situation that has resulted in a loss of national strength. This is a matter of grave concern for loyal and patriotic men. With due regard for circumstances within and without the country, we declare the dissolution of the Jiyūtō and Shinpotō, unite all like-minded men, organize a single major political party, and with new spirit dedicate ourselves to completing the introduction of constitutional government."

ITŌ AND YAMAGATA ENGAGE IN A GRAND DEBATE

Formation of the Kenseitō sent a shock wave through the Satsuma-Chōshū clique. Equally if not more surprising was the fact that Itō was attempting to match the Kenseitō with a party of his own.

Yamagata and his followers were among the most shocked of all. Katsura, minister of the army at that time, who was considered Yamagata's heir-apparent, demanded abrogation of the constitution and squarely opposed Itō's plan to organize another political party. On June 23, Yamagata, Inoue, and Saigō, the minister of the navy, gathered at Katsura's residence to confer. Katsura, in the words of his own autobiography, recalls the position he took on this occasion: "The need for sound management of the postwar economy was clear. It was most unfortunate that Itō had made such a decision. One choice was to do nothing and let events take their course. An alternative would be to get the *genrō* to organize a cabinet. In that case I would be ready to step down as army minister in favor of General Ōyama and serve as his deputy. All other ministerial positions should likewise be assumed by *genrō* with all juniors serving as deputies. With this deployment in government we should have nothing to fear from the peoples' parties. The postwar economy has to be managed if this arrangement is agreed upon. And if they resist we shall respond by dissolving the House. Even at the cost of the extreme expedient of suspending the constitution the economy cannot on any account be allowed to get out of control."

Suspension of the constitution was an outrageous thought for any loyal subject. That Katsura should have been driven even to suggest it was a measure of the state of panic Yamagata's group was in. It was hardly unnatural in the circumstances for a major clash to occur within the clan clique before the *genrō* conference on June 24.

I stated earlier that Itō and Ōkuma were outwardly enemies but at a deeper level were really good friends. Exactly the opposite characterized the relationship between Itō and Yamagata. Both were senior leaders of the Chōshū clan and pillars of the Meiji government and they were seemingly inseparable, but there existed a constant tension and competitiveness between them. Underlying their apparent rapport Itō and Yamagata possessed very different characters and unaccommodating views on many, particularly political, matters.

Strange are the ways of men. Ōkuma and Itō, who were alike in so many ways, became avowed enemies, while here were two men with deeply contrasting characters who ended up being on the same side. Itō and Yamagata were forced to collaborate by force of circumstances, so, while they were in the same camp, they still regarded each other as enemies and remained suspicious of the other until death. It is said that there is no deeper gulf than that between estranged, angry brothers. The relationship between Itō and Yamagata was something of that sort.

Later, when I had the opportunity to discuss the developments of this period with Yamagata, he kept using with great emphasis such expressions as "it was not his pleasure" or "it was not to his liking." I thought Yamagata was referring to Emperor Meiji, but, when I asked him, I found he had been referring all the time to Itō. He might have used the polite terms in a jocular way but it certainly did not sound like that. Yamagata must have been competing intentionally with Itō. Every time reference was made to Itō his attitude betrayed tension, and his manner was defiant throughout.

The suppressed friction between the two clan chiefs surfaced at the *genrō* conference of June 24. The developments at the meeting as recorded in Hayashida's *"A History of Japanese Political Parties"* unfolded as follows.

At the *genrō* conference Itō explained how political changes had taken place since the last *genrō* conference. He had no choice but to organize a political party. Yamagata immediately opened fire in unequivocal opposition. "I suppose political parties are a necessary part of the parliamentary system. We are not necessarily absolutely opposed to political parties. But you happen to be a prime minister, and you are gathering like-minded men to establish a party. This would only aggravate political strife between the government and the people. In terms of policy this cannot be said to be wise. All the more so because the government must be above all political parties. If the prime minister heads a ruling party the government could not help but forfeit nonpartisanship. I urge Itō to abandon his cause."

Itō, offended, replied: "I have already made up my mind. If it is your view that I should not organize a political party while in office I shall resign and organize a political party as an ordinary opposition member of the House."

Yamagata did not relax his attack: "Even if you say you will resign from office I cannot refrain from expressing my views. Itō, you are above all a *genrō*. A *genrō* serves His Majesty and assists him in important matters of state. As a *genrō* heading a political party, can you honestly say that you would be able to rise above favoring one party or one faction over others? I shall resolutely oppose Itō forming a party."

This made Itō all the angrier. "You tell me I cannot form a political party as prime minister. And you tell me that if I resign, I still cannot because I am a *genrō*. Are you telling me I can never form a party? Then I shall return my peerage and decorations and do it as a plain citizen. There is absolutely no need for me to consult the *genrō* as long as I organize a party as an independent citizen." Itō made his point quite clearly.

Yamagata did not give up.

If you are so decided, what more can I say? Let me, however, say the following as a personal friend. Itō, when you returned from your study of European constitutions, you reported on the advanced state of science in Germany and on its political organization. We listened to you advocating that our ministers should report only to the emperor in person and that the only reference Europe offered for our national polity was the German model. The Imperial Constitution was drafted in this belief and we have also guided the parliament accordingly. This notwithstanding, Itō, do you still plan to organize your own political party, work with the masses and open the way to a parliamentary cabinet? Parliamentary government will mean the destruction of the national polity. You are relegating this perfect empire into being a simple democracy. I find it difficult to justify your change of mind, and as a friend hope that you will still reconsider your plan.

Yamagata probably spoke his true mind. At first he played lip service to political parties by admitting that they were a necessary part of the parliamentary system, but in the end he absolutely denied that parties had any role in government. Itō was undaunted and contined to argue with Yamagata, but when he realized that Yamagata was completely obdurate, he left the meeting to go to the palace, where he had other business to attend to. Returning from the palace, he convened a meeting of his ministers and told them what had passed at the *genrō* meeting, including his offer of resignation.

The following day Itō formally submitted his resignation and begged the throne to permit him to return the prime minister's seal as well his peerage and decorations. He wished to follow the dictates of his conscience as plain Mr. Itō.

Emperor Meiji did not, however, grant his wish. "Your peerage and decorations," the emperor was reported to have said, "were given for services previously rendered. They are not related to your work as prime minister. Let them be a reminder to posterity of your services."

The struggle between the two was very similar to the rift that occurred over the proposed Korean expedition of 1873. In that episode, Saigō and Ōkubo were leading figures of the Satsuma clan. This time, ironically, Itō and Yamagata came from the Chōshū clan. In both cases the rift was between those who espoused civilian rule and those who were militarists. This time, the militarists won.

Nevertheless, Itō had still not given up his plan to create a political party. Because of the implacable opposition of Yamagata he was forced to discontinue his efforts temporarily, but in his recommendation for the government that would succeed him, he stood resolutely by his convictions about the nature of constitutional government. He had made up his mind quite early about recommending Ōkuma and Itagaki.

THE FORMATION OF THE ŌKUMA-ITAGAKI CABINET

The *genrō* conference was reconvened on June 25, but nothing was settled. Itō had not expected more. He proceeded with his own plan, therefore, and invited Ōkuma and Itagaki to a private meeting, at which he shared with them his intention of recommending them jointly to succeed him.

This was ostensibly an outcome of the fierce argument Itō had had with Yamagata the day before. I suspect, however, that there must have been a strong calculation on Itō's part, rather than fighting the Kenseitō alliance frontally, to give the two men a government before the alliance had had a chance to develop into a full-fledged major party, thus giving him an easier task to defeat it.

At first, on hearing Itō's proposal, Ōkuma and Itagaki were at a loss for words. Itagaki was the first to speak. "While the Jiyūtō and the Shinpotō have joined forces to build the new Kenseitō party, I have only just been reunited with Ōkuma. We have not even had an opportunity to exchange notes on our political views." He was very hesitant. Ōkuma too. "You should have let us know your thoughts before your resignation," he said. "I am indeed sorry for you and for the country that the person who has made such a vast contribution to establishing constitutional government is to be deprived of his prime ministerial responsibilities just as we are about to see the establishment of a party cabinet."

Itō, however, persisted. "The Kenseitō is already in place, and now that there is a political party that represents the majority of the people. For men who command that organization to form a cabinet is clearly the best way to promote the national interest. This should be in line with the wish of the throne. I wanted to organize a new party and fight a great battle with you, but instead I ended by resigning. I have no other wish now than to see a new government organized by the two of you as early as possible. Please do not take me into account but promptly prepare to organize a cabinet." Ōkuma and Itagaki withdrew, promising Itō that he would have their considered response.

The recommendation to name the leader of the largest political party to head the new cabinet met with fierce opposition from Yamagata and his group. Emperor Meiji, however, accepted Itō's recommendation and invited Ōkuma and Itagaki to the palace on June 27th. "As Itō Hirobumi has tendered his resignation out of respect for the wish of the people, I have accepted his request and command the two of you to organize a new cabinet. The domestic and external affairs of the state must not be delayed for a single day. The two of you should consult with each other and organize a cabinet with the least possible delay." They did as the emperor had commanded and immediately prepared to form a cabinet.

Ōkuma Shigenobu, they decided, would be prime minister and foreign minister. Although the party had been officially inaugurated it was still new, and maintaining a balance of power between the Shinpotō and Jiyūtō factions was a major concern. From the Jiyūtō group, therefore, Itagaki Taisuke was given the home minister's portfolio, while Matsuda Masahisa became minister of finance, and Hayashi Yūzō post and telecommunications minister. From the Shinpotō group, Ōhigashi Yoshitetsu became minister of justice and Ōishi Masaki agriculture and commercial affairs minister. I became minister of education.

Inukai Tsuyoshi was my senior in terms of career and age. It would have been natural for Inukai to be given a cabinet post before me, but Inukai always let me take the front seat so he could use me from behind the scenes. When the Kenseitō was formed Inukai had recommended me to manage its general affairs. It was subsequently decided that the four of us heading the general affairs section of the new party would assume cabinet posts in the Ōkuma-Itagaki coalition, which explains why I became a minister before Inukai.

Thus from the erstwhile Jiyūtō, Itagaki, Matsuda, and Hayashi were given ministries, and from the Shinpotō group, Ōhigashi, Ōishi, and myself. On the face of it this seemed to be a balanced distribution. In fact, the ratio of cabinet seats was three to five, respectively, as Ōkuma was to head the cabinet and double as minister of foreign affairs. This caused some muttering among members of the Jiyūtō group. However, the home minister had authority over the prefectural governors and commanded real power as the deputy prime minister, while the post of minister of finance was also of great importance as it sustained the life of the whole cabinet, and the post and telecommunications ministry employed the largest staff of any government offices. The Jiyūtō group was finally pacified on being convinced that their three cabinet seats were of far more importance than the peripheral offices of agriculture, justice, and education.

In this way seven cabinet posts were filled, but the difficult choice of whom to head the two service ministries still had to be made. No means or precedent existed for finding men for these jobs outside the Satsuma and Chōshū clans, and certain members of the clans seized on this as an excuse to abort the Ōkuma-Itagaki coalition. When the matter was confided to Emperor Meiji, His Majesty solved the dilemma by graciously offering to "directly name the army and navy ministers and in this way assist the formation of the cabinet," and he reappointed from the preceding cabinet Saigō Tsugumichi as navy minister and Katsura Tarō as army minister. The two ministers respectfully obeyed his wish. That was how the first party cabinet was born. The major immediate challenge facing the cabinet lay not outside, but within it. In other words, instead of fighting the *hanbatsu* our priority was to find ways of forging internal unity. Their newfound coexistence in the Kenseitō did not automatically dissolve the long-standing strife between its constituent parts from the Jiyūtō and Shinpotō. Knowing this, the *hanbatsu* leaders turned to a strategy of not attacking the cabinet but rather of waiting for it to destroy itself from within. On that point the Ōkuma-Itagaki coalition was definitely vulnerable.

When the members of the cabinet got together at the prime minister's residence on our way back from the cabinet accreditation ceremony at the palace, Itagaki was the first to speak up. "There is an important matter I wish to discuss with Ōkuma at this time," he began. "All ministers may attend and listen." We had no idea what was to come. "I want to affirm that the new cabinet formed today is a double household composed of former members of the Jiyūtō and Shinpotō," he continued. "These parties were at odds with each other for many years, and there is a risk that we might face division in the future as a result of competition for power between the old adversaries. Ōkuma and I will never be part of that. I give my solemn word that even if one day we were to abandon our followers we will always keep our pledge to work together. I want this promise to be signed in blood, as once it would have been." I greatly admired the deep conviction with which Itagaki spoke.

Itagaki was a passionate man, but at the same time he possessed highly developed powers of reason. Generally speaking, those who have passionate natures have little ability to reason and those who excel in the latter tend to be cold. Itagaki had the strong qualities of both types. At times when he was given to passion he would flare up and become unreasonable, but ordinarily he would not hesitate to yield to an argument that he logically saw was right. It was for this reason that he initiated a movement to open the parliament and left an indelible mark on the history of Japan's constitutional government.

First in the Kaishintō and then the Shinpotō I had held positions far removed from Itagaki and rarely had any opportunity to be directly associated with him. My father, however, fought with Itagaki during the turmoils leading to the Restoration. They participated together in the expedition to quell the recalcitrant domain when my father was with the Dankin-tai association organized mainly by Kōshū rōnin (free samurai from around today's Yamanashi prefecture). My father admired him greatly. As a child I often heard Itagaki's name at home.

Many years later, listening to Itagaki's bold and upright pledge before his new cabinet, my respect for him grew even more. After that, we developed an especially close relationship in the cabinet. I believe that he was kindly disposed towards me.

MY FIRST CABINET POST

Ten years after the police guard assigned to get me out of Tokyo made me look like a cabinet minister, I had become a real one. By then I was beginning to be counted as one of the powerful politicians in the country, but my state of poverty had not improved. One day, long before this, an insurance agent visited me and tried to persuade me to take out life insurance and my funeral expenses to cover my family. I thought the man was rather rude, but in jest I told him not to worry, my family would not have to pay—when I died my funeral would be paid for by the state. The story of Ozaki's national funeral was still told mockingly long after the incident. When I became minister of education in the Ōkuma-Itagaki cabinet, a sympathetic friend congratulated me. "Well, congratulations!" he said cheerfully. "You're getting closer to your state funeral!" He meant well, I suppose, but I did not think too much of his sense of humor.

At first Ōkuma wanted to give me the justice portfolio and Ōhigashi Yoshitetsu that of minister of education. But Ōhigashi balked, because he thought he would not be able to handle scholars. I tried to talk him into it. "I don't want to be in the cabinet," Ōhigashi told me. "But I have come to the conclusion that the ministry of justice should be abolished. So if it is agreeable I would not mind particularly joining the cabinet as minister of justice." "I don't mind which ministry I have," I answered. "We can discuss the switch of portfolios with Ōkuma. I cannot promise to abolish the ministry of justice right here and now, but you can submit a proposal once you are in the cabinet. If the plan is good I will not only support it myself, but I will get others to support it as well. But the first thing is for you to join the cabinet." Ōhigashi agreed to join.

In those days the ministry of justice was filled with Yamagata's men, and Ōhigashi's idea probably derived from that. He did not file a plan to abolish the ministry after he became minister, though. "Why don't you table your proposal?" I urged him, but the bill to abolish the ministry of justice never came. However, there was a bill to reduce the number of agencies such as the prosecutor's office. I expected Ōhigashi to support it, but he did not. What had become of his idea to abolish the justice ministry? Stranger still, he was noticeably slow to support any bill that was aimed at cutting down government bureaucracy, so for a while he became a bit of a joke.

I learned a lesson myself at this time. Once you are put in charge of a department you find you are surrounded by those who want to maintain the status quo. In the end you are corrupted by them and hesitate to obey your own convictions. It is too easy to fall into the trap of wanting to keep things as they are.

As soon as I was installed as minister of education a group from the Imperial University headed by President Kikuchi Dairoku paid a courtesy call on me. I thought that Ōhigashi must have hesitated to take the post because of people like these, so I said to them, "I hear you like to frighten ministers by posing difficult questions. What have you for me?" President Kikuchi reassured me that that was not true, and we chatted while the others sat around. Suddenly, Yamakawa Kenjirō said, "If there is nothing for me to do, I would rather take my leave." Mr. Kikuchi stopped his small talk and gave Yamakawa his place. This must be a professor among professors, I thought. Later Yamakawa became a highly respected president of the university.

Hiraoka Kōtarō came to see me one day to ask me to take on Kashiwada Moribumi as my deputy. He was an experienced educator and would be a good right-hand man. Kashiwada was considerably older than I, but we had been in the same class at Keio Gijuku and he wrote well. He had been elected to the Diet in the 1892 general election, the one that was so notorious for the government. Kashiwada walked onto the political scene as though he owned it. For a time, he commanded respect as a representative of the Satsuma group, but he was one of those who persisted in supporting the Matsukata cabinet when it was already a lost cause. After the cabinet fell he was politically destitute.

I sympathized with Hiraoka's friendship for Kashiwada and called on him at his home. He seemed quite surprised at my sudden visit. He was even more surprised when I asked him to be my deputy, and for a moment seemed lost for words. After a pause, he managed to say, "Are there any conditions attached?" "Nothing much," I answered. "But as a vice-minister you won't be allowed to follow young men around." It was a clumsy remark, I suppose, but it was meant in good humor. I had not been aware that I was one of them, but while a student at Keio, like most of the Satsuma boys, he sought out young men, and I was apparently one of them. I recalled those days, and seeing that he was worried about this new development I wanted to put him at his ease.

Quarrels within the Ōkuma-Itagaki Cabinet

The Kenseitō was born with the purpose of felling the Satsuma-Chōshū clique in government. It was not the product of a complete consensus of political ideas. Consequently, it was inevitable that differences of opinion would arise between members of the two former parties. When the cabinet was formed, a new ad hoc policy research bureau was instituted to guard against these differences, among other things, with Itagaki, the home minister, as its chairman.

This did not put an end to the clash of opinions over every issue. The Jiyūtō group were in favor of nationalizing the railways, but we were opposed to this. In turn, we were for the abolition of the police agency, to which the Jiyūtō group objected strongly. Concerning appointments to the civil service we were in favor of a restricted appointment system while the Jiyūtō group wanted a free appointment system. Such differences of opinion led to fierce strife between the groups.

The sixth general election took place on August 10, 1898. The Kenseitō scored a major victory by winning 243 of the 300 seats in the House, but by then the bad feeling within the party had become unmanageable. If it had been merely a matter of differences over policy matters we might have found a way to harmonize our views after much discussion. But the years of emotional discord together with disagreements and jealousies over personnel appointments made relations between the groups progressively more bitter as each side attempted to occupy preferred positions. It had become a shameless state of affairs.

The strife within the cabinet was an open secret to the resentful clan leaders, who meddled wherever they could to make matters worse. Navy Minister Saigō and Army Minister Katsura were not members of our two groups, and they were well situated to act as secret agents of the clans. Of the two, Saigō was closer to us in the Shinpotō group, whereas Katsura tended to be closer to the Jiyūtō group. Saigō did not meddle actively, but Katsura would take Itagaki aside to another room during a cabinet meeting for a secret talk. He appeared to be fanning the emotions of the Jiyūtō group in order to exacerbate the strife.

My first encounter with Katsura was around the time of the first Diet. He was then vice-minister of the army and sat on the government benches in the House. He rarely said anything. Although he was a military man, I learned he was adept at political negotiation and always put his word in whenever the occasion permitted. At that time, Katsura was commander of the Nagoya division. When a major earthquake struck the Nobi plains he sent in his troops to maintain security and rescue victims of the disaster. His excellent handling of administrative matters made Katsura's reputation soar.

In the war with China, however, he was forced into a difficult battle situation, in the course of which he was surrounded by troops of General Sung Ching. For a time his whereabouts were unknown. He apparently was not very good at war, but his administrative skills stood him in good stead when he did a fine job of maintaining security and order in the occupied territory.

It was only during the Ōkuma-Itagaki government that I came to know Katsura well. It was immediately apparent to me that he was an unusually gifted man, although he did not impress me much when I heard him speak in the cabinet. He once said, "The block I lived on was called 'Success Block' because of my record of successes." This kind of silly boasting made me think he was a small man. He was most proud of his experience during his period of study in Germany. Apparently one of his seniors advised him that the coming age was not going to be conducive for the enjoyment of power by a military man, and that he should instead study political science. Katsura boasted he had stuck to his original purpose and returned to his country having studied military matters. "Today I am both a general and a minister," he liked to say. It was difficult for us to have any respect for such a man.

A person of such worldliness was apt to provoke strife among his colleagues in the party. After all, Katsura shared the clan clique view that a political party cabinet was too dangerous to be allowed in Japan. He just did not say so openly. In fact, after Katsura's death, his autobiography and letters made it clear that he remained as minister of the army for the sole purpose of bringing down the party cabinet, thinking that it was easier to do so from within than by assailing it from without. The Ōkuma-Itagaki cabinet, therefore, was a big lion with a deadly worm inside its body. On top of this, Hoshi Tōru, who had been serving as minister in the Japanese legation in the United States, returned to Tokyo on August 15. No official instruction to do so had been sent him, but details of that sort did not prevent Hoshi from filing his wish to return and acting on it without further ado.

With Hoshi back in the country the pressure on the government intensified. Prime Minister Ōkuma still doubled as minister of foreign affairs, and Hoshi believed that he only had to return home to be given the post. He had even told his friends and acquaintances back in America that he was returning to head the ministry. It is true that Ōkuma had repeatedly said that he wanted Hoshi to take the post. I was against it. "If you let Hoshi into the cabinet there will be trouble," I cautioned. "He likes to quarrel. He will make trouble if he is in the cabinet and he will make trouble if he is outside. But it will be worse if he is inside. He should be kept out." Ōkuma was his usual optimistic self. "If we let him in," he said, "it will discourage him from quarrelling." However, I still stuck to my conviction that it would not be good for the cabinet to bring Hoshi in. Someone must have misinformed Ōkuma about my intentions, because he then said to me, "Why don't you become foreign minister yourself and be done with it?" I had no such ulterior motive. I refused, but again urged Ōkuma to rethink Hoshi's case.

Apparently there were enough within the Jiyūtō group too who opposed Hoshi's joining the cabinet, and it became clear that there would be no Foreign Minister Hoshi. Being the sort of person he was, Hoshi now embarked on an effort to bring the cabinet down. "If the cabinet does not want me it will have to go," he averred. Its foundations already weakened by its internal feuds, the government could not survive much longer with Hoshi doing all he could to destroy it. Most unfortunately I added my bit to the process with what came to be called my "republican speech."

THE TRUTH ABOUT MY "REPUBLICAN SPEECH"

On August 22, I was invited to speak at an all-Japan primary-school teachers' study meeting. In my speech I warned against the current materialistic trend. "A recent development in Japan is to respect the power of money to the detriment of principles and justice. If this is allowed to continue the future of the empire will become a matter of deep concern. Those responsible for education must correct this." I spoke against the worship of money and the importance of upholding moral standards. To illustrate my point, I said that while the Japanese are apt to think of the United States as the birthplace of money worship, no one ever became president just because he had money. Most American presidents, in fact, were quite poor.

"In Japan," I continued, more or less to this effect, "there is no danger of having a republican government. Even after thousands and tens of thousands of years there will be no republic. But just for the sake of argument let us imagine that I dreamt of a republican government. Most likely, Mitsui and Mitsubishi would become presidential candidates." The Tokyo *Nichi-Nichi Shinbun*, which was a de facto organ of the *hanbatsu*, took up my speech and declared that I was republican in my political beliefs. This afforded ammunition not only to the clan cliques but to the members of the Jiyūtō group in the cabinet to attack me.

Needless to say, I did not advocate a republican government. Quite the contrary, I spoke to promote moral values. As a matter of record, the five or six hundred educators who heard me that day all applauded my speech. The aspersions leveled against me in the paper were groundless, but our political foes had twisted my words to destroy the cabinet. "If there is criticism that a member of your cabinet made an inappropriate speech," I told Ōkuma, "you should as prime minister send a responsible person to check on what I said. If it is found that I in fact spoke out of turn then I should of course be admonished."Fortunately, my speech had been taken down by a stenographer, and the transcript was kept under lock and key at the Imperial Education Association. When a cabinet secretary accompanied by a stenographer went to the Imperial Education Association to check the text as I had urged, nothing could be found in it to support the allegations of our enemies.

My opponents then claimed that I had had the transcript rewritten. This opened the way for me to take the offensive. There was little or nothing I could do about the article itself, but now that I was accused of having rewritten the transcript I had to speak up to defend my honor. I counter-attacked vigorously against those who claimed that I had fabricated the record. The opposition could make all the noise they liked, but they dared not make a major issue of the matter since the whole thing was fabricated. Eventually the attack subsided, the archers put down their bows, and other pretexts were found for blaming the cabinet.

Then it was Itagaki's turn to put his foot in it by antagonizing the Buddhists. Up to that point no one except Buddhist monks concerned themselves with the education and rehabilitation of prisoners. Itagaki, acting on well-intentioned advice, decided to employ Christian ministers for the job as well. Buddhist monks abetted by meddlers rose in opposition to his plan. The issue was an easy weapon to use against the government. A man by the name of Ishikawa Shundai of the Ōtani sect of Honganji Temple called Itagaki, "the enemy of Buddhism," a label that was widely circulated. Itagaki lost his temper at the cabinet meeting and complained about the monk for criticizing the incumbent government. Some were of the opinion that it would be better to let the matter rest, but Itagaki took action in the name of the home minister and this consequently became another public issue.

At the same time the newspaper *Yorozu chōhō* carried an editorial entitled "Pseudo-loyalists, Pseudo-patriots." The editorial criticized false loyalty and false patriotism. It certainly did not criticize loyalty or patriotism per se. But certain members of the imperial household ministry and of the government, misunderstanding this and taking it as disparaging loyalty and patriotism, let it out that the article was written on Ōzaki's instruction and under his guidance.

A certain government bureaucrat argued that I had had the *Yorozu chōhō* publish the article as a quid pro quo for the criticism of my republican speech. Next, an official in the imperial household ministry demanded that I, as minister in charge of national decency, should check on such inappropriate statements. I had at first not read the editorial of the *Yorozu chōhō*. I had it brought over. There was nothing in it that posed any problem. I sent the official away, saying I could see nothing provocative about the article. If there was a need for action it was for the home minister to decide, not the education minister. The man then went to Itagaki, who also read the article and said there was nothing wrong with it. This too became an issue.

These irritations arose one after another to harass Itagaki. A man of delicate disposition, he was flustered. There were also in the government ranks some officials who blamed Itagaki for alienating the Buddhists. This caused him additional anxiety. Someone evidently whispered in his ear that it would be extremely disadvantageous to fight back publicly on the Buddhist issue. He should play it down as much as possible, and instead divert attention back to Ozaki's republican speech. It would be better for him to be seen to take a stand against Ozaki and say he could not share the cabinet with the man who had made that speech. This should make the Buddhist problem fade naturally. So Itagaki took this recourse as a way out of his predicament, and the controversy over my republican speech was set to flare up again.

ITAGAKI BETRAYS ME TO THE THRONE

One day, as the cabinet meeting was breaking up, I prepared to leave, as I usually did, with Itagaki. I sometimes accompanied Ōkuma, as he had difficulty with stairs because of his artificial leg. But he was a large and heavy man and I was small and not very stable support for him. So Saigō Tsugumichi went with him instead.

It was customary for me to have a friendly talk with Itagaki on the way out together. But that day was different. All the other ministers had left, but Itagaki, instead of saying "Well, let's go," paced up and down the cabinet room looking worried. "Shall we go?" I called to him. "No," he answered, "I must go to the palace." Itagaki had been a veteran statesmen at the time of the Restoration and was close to the throne. However, he kept his distance out of respect for the emperor, and whenever there was something he wished to discuss with His Majesty, he would always take someone along. That day he asked no one. He seemed to be behaving rather strangely. "Well then, excuse me if I go ahead," I said, and left without him. After I had gone, Itagaki went to the palace and informed the emperor that he could no longer work with me. Itagaki certainly had reason to behave strangely that day. He was acting on another person's advice to use a comparatively good friend as a scapegoat in an effort to deflect criticism from himself.

Of course, I had no idea what had taken place. Nor had I any reason to think that I had not won a complete victory over the authors of the unjust criticism directed against me for my 'republican speech.' The visit I now received at my official residence from Iwakura Tomosada, the emperor's senior chamberlain, came as a bolt from the blue. Iwakura briefed me on what Itagaki had told the emperor, and communicated His Majesty's decision: "Your senior colleague Ita-gaki feels that he cannot work with you. Regardless of the basis for this, his junior colleague Ozaki should resign to save the cabinet."

I replied as follows: "I apologize most abjectly for troubling His Majesty, and shall willingly submit my resignation if he so desires. But if it is his wish that I should be held accountable for the so-called republican speech, I humbly request that the matter be disposed of by law. This would be a better lesson for posterity than if I were only to resign. It would, I respectfully submit, be more salutary for the country and more appropriate a reprimand."

Iwakura clearly and repeatedly said, "This has nothing to do with the republican speech. It is simply because your senior Itagaki said he could not continue to work with you." There was only one thing left for me to do. I had made it a habit to carry a letter of resignation with me at all times. I now took it out and showed it to the chamberlain. "As you see," I said, "I am prepared at all times. I shall follow the wish of the emperor and resign in favor of my senior."

I decided to submit the letter of resignation and called on Prime Minister Ōkuma. "Our political enemy is attacking me as a strategy to take the horse before he takes the general. He is not after me but you. You must be prepared to defend yourself." The prime minister with his customary optimism replied, "As long as you back out quietly things will be all right." I did not think so, but there was nothing I could do if the prime minister was of that mind. I handed my resignation to Ōkuma on October 22, recommending Inukai as my successor.

This was how my relationship with Itagaki came to an end. Even then, I could not nurse any ill feelings towards him, and I remained as ready as ever to work for him if I could be of help. His most urgent problem was his domestic finances. He was pure and poor. On a number of occasions I reasoned with the minister of the imperial household that it was wrong for the country to do nothing to assist the heroes of the Restoration. He would agree, but nothing was done.

When the first Katsura cabinet was sworn in in 1901, I brought this up again with Minister Katsura whose anger I did not fear in the least. "Leaving Itagaki without assistance could have bad repercussions for the throne. If the government does nothing to recognize the merit of past services, I will have to go public about this rather than working behind the scenes as I have tried to do until now." "That will not be necessary," the prime minister said. Katsura had been giving thought to the matter. "What you say is true. Ōkuma was awarded the First Order of Merit, but he has not received any since then. This must be put right. I shall see what I can do." It was not long before Ōkuma was awarded the Grand Cordon of the Paulownia and Itagaki received money from the imperial coffers. There must have been others who had worked for the same cause, but I was among those who had persisted in trying to see that Itagaki, whose character I still respected, should receive due recognition.

With regard to the republican speech, it was the attitude of the educators that bothered me as much as anything at the time, and still does today. Most if not all of those six hundred educators greeted my speech with applause. They were of the same mind then. And they were of the same mind once again, it would seem, when I was the object of groundless criticism and the same speech was called lèse-majesté, a speech of the disloyal, and there was not one among those educators who would speak up. In private, there were some who said they were shocked at the slander. It saddened me that not one, to my knowledge, even among those, spoke up publicly against this injustice. They thought, if they thought at all, of the advantages and disadvantages of doing so and were afraid of the consequences. Educators who were responsible for teaching others what is right and wrong should have spoken up for justice and said what they had heard. I was sure that if the incident had taken place in Europe or America there would have been any number of people who would have spoken the truth and protested the baseless accusations. I knew of many such instances.

For twenty years I did not speak about this for fear that I would be misunderstood for soliciting the educators' support. I was sad for the country that its children should be taught by people who had no commitment to put right what is wrong, if necessary at risk to their own lives, for the cause of justice.

THE GREAT SPLIT

I resigned as minister of education in order to forestall the collapse of the Ōkuma-Itagaki cabinet. I was pessimistic about the cabinet's chances of survival, but the ever-optimistic Prime Minister Ōkuma seemed perfectly confident.

My resignation was followed by a fierce argument within the cabinet with regard to my successor. The Jiyūtō group recommended Hoshi Tōru and Etō Soroku as their candidates, maintaining that, in the interest of maintaining a balance, my successor should come from their camp. But the Shinpotō men would not compromise. The successor to one of their own should come from among them.

Home Minister Itagaki recommended Aoki Shūzō, who had not belonged to either of the former political parties. However, Prime Minister Ōkuma felt that Aoki leaned too much to the side of the Jiyūtō group; if a successor free of any former party affiliation was sought, he felt that Konoe Atsumaro was more appropriate. But Itagaki was resolutely opposed, as he felt Konoe's preference lay with the Shinpotō group.

The question of a successor was carried over to the cabinet meeting the following day, but again no solution was found. At one time it was suggested that Finance Minister Matsuda take on the job. This was not acceptable. After every other possibility had been tried, in desperation someone suggested that Navy Minister Saigō and Army Minister Katsura be asked to find a candidate, but Prime Minister Ōkuma was adamant that as long as he had the imperial mandate to head the cabinet he would not transfer that mandate to any other. He would choose a successor for the education portfolio himself and make a direct recommendation to the throne. In none too good a mood, he then left the cabinet meeting for the palace, where he reported the latest developments to His Majesty and recommended that Inukai Tsuyoshi take over as education minister. The recommendation was accepted and the following day Inukai received his appointment.

Secretly I feared that Inukai would not be accepted. The ease with which the appointment was approved made me feel that I was still unfamiliar with matters of the political world. Ōkuma obviously had a better eye for it than I. My resignation, I was comforted to believe, would give the Ōkuma cabinet a new lease of life. I was to be proved wrong.

Hoshi's foiled attempt to grab the vacant education ministry exposed him for what he really was. In his pique at being passed over he resorted to measures that only he would dare. The very day after the official appointment of Inukai as minister, the Jiyūtō group's general affairs director made a formal proposal to his counterpart in our Shinpotō group to dissolve the Kenseitō. When our side rejected the offer, notice was given to all members of the Jiyūtō group in the name of the Kenseitō to attend an ad hoc meeting at Kanda's Kinkikan restaurant. As soon as the meeting opened it was declared a Kenseitō party convention, and then promptly passed a resolution dissolving the party.

It then tabled a proposal to establish a new Kenseitō organization and proceeded at great speed to adopt its platform and party rules and regulations. The whole business was decided at the speed of lightning. It was a breath-taking magic show by Hoshi.

Naturally we protested at the hijacking of the Kenseitō. But the Kenseitō headquarters in Shiba was occupied physically by the Jiyūtō group's men and access was strictly controlled. And since the home minister and the chief of the police agency were both in the Jiyūtō group we knew we would have no chance in a showdown.

We naturally rejected Hoshi's deceitful dissolution of the party and continued to act in the name of the Kenseitō. This meant therefore that for a time there were two parties with the same name. However, it did not take long for the following notice to be served in the name of Home Minister Itagaki Taisuke banning our Kenseitō: "The political organization whose headquarters is located at 3-1 chome, Uchisaiwai-chō, Kōjimachi-ku, Tokyo city and which calls itself the Kenseitō is deemed to be an obstruction to public order. It is, therefore, banned herewith in accordance with Article 29 of the Assembly and Political Society Law." Under these circumstances, the best thing we could do was to reorganize ourselves as the Kensei Hon-to (the authentic Kenseitō) to challenge the Jiyūtō group's Kenseitō.

The merger of the people's parties with all its expectations had lasted a feeble half-year and now was split again into the old Jiyūtō and Shinpotō. The names were now Kenseitō and Kensei Hontō but in reality little else had changed.

With the old Kenseitō breaking apart, Minister Itagaki submitted his resignation along with the Jiyūtō group's Finance Minister Matsuda and Communications Minister Hayashi. But Ōkuma, an optimist to the end, apparently believed that with the Jiyūtō group gone he could form a new cabinet from members of the Shinpotō group. He therefore submitted to Emperor Meiji a report on the recent split, with a plan to appoint a cabinet composed only of these men. His Majesty merely told him to "reunite with Itagaki in accordance with the former order for Ōkuma and Itagaki to organize the cabinet,", and offered no suggestions as to the composition of a reshuffled cabinet. Meanwhile, groups within the bureaucracy were attempting in so many ways to overthrow what remained of the old cabinet that Ōkuma finally had to face the unpalatable truth and tendered his resignation on October 31.

In view of the fact that my resignation had been intended from the start for the sole purpose of maintaining the Ōkuma-Itagaki coalition, it might have been better after all if I had recommended one of the Jiyūtō group to succeed me as they wished. Since Itagaki's complaint was that he found it impossible to work with Ozaki, not with Ōkuma, my resignation followed by the appointment of a Jiyūtō man as my successor might have saved the day.

At the time, however, believing without a doubt that the object of the assault on me was the overthrow of the Ōkuma government, I adopted, in resigning, what I thought was the best strategy. The next priority, I felt, was that we should fight for our cause without showing weakness by accepting an easy compromise. It was with this reasoning, if with a little uncertainty, that I recommended Inukai to succeed me.

As prime minister, with the survival of his government foremost in mind, Ōkuma should have refused my recommendation and picked a Jiyūtō man in order to remove the major cause of strife within the cabinet. However, Ōkuma, with his born optimism, at first believed he could suppress the Jiyūtō faction and then that he could rebuild the cabinet solely from members of the Shinpotō faction. He fell in the end because he was wrong on both counts.

I believe one of Ōkuma's miscalculations was in his understanding of Saigō, the navy minister. Saigō was a gentleman of polished manners and courteous disposition. As navy minister in the Ōkuma government he was always most polite to his senior, the prime minister, and gave every indication of being deeply respectful of Ōkuma. One can see why Ōkuma took it for granted that Saigō could be counted as one of his own men.

Therefore, when Itagaki and the two other Jiyūtō group ministers tendered their resignations and he faced the decision of whether to reshuffle the Ōkuma-Itagaki coalition rump to produce a simple Ōkuma cabinet or to dissolve it, Ōkuma calculated that while Katsura would go along with the Jiyūtō faction, Saigō could be counted on to support him. It is human nature to believe one is in the right, and as the Shinpotō men did not now believe otherwise they expected impartial people to side with them, and anticipated until the last minute the support of the fair and just Saigō. These things never happened and the government collapsed. A few years later, when I had occasion to visit Katsura, we talked of his position in the Ōkuma-Itagaki government. The following is, in part, what he told me: "As we were leaving the palace together the day after Saigō and I had decided to remain in the Ōkuma-Itagaki government, Saigō stopped me and said, "The cabinet will soon start quarrelling. When that happens the Jiyūtō group will seek your support and the Shinpotō group mine. Let us decide now not to support either. We must not let ourselves get caught up in other people's quarrels." And he laughed in his usual carefree way."

It was thoughtless of me to expect Saigō to support us, without realizing that the farsighted man would already have made up his mind as indeed was later proved when, as home minister, he aligned himself with Itagaki at the expense of Ōkuma's party.

Be that as it may, Saigō Tsugumichi was one of the most outstanding personalities of his time. His older brother Saigō Takamori's greatness lay in his unlimited capacity to empathize with others and in the chivalrous instinct to lay down his life for them. He did not bother himself with trifles. He was able to see the large patterns of events and was willing to face them at the risk of his life.

Saigō Tsugumichi had neither Takamori's great heart nor his resolute spirit, but he had a clear mind and a wonderful sense of humor. He was afraid of nothing. In 1877, when his elder brother was persuaded by the young turks of Satsuma to raise the flag of rebellion against the new government, the entire nation watched Tsugumichi's behavior. Not in the least disconcerted by his brother's action, he declared, "I shall now have to meet my brother on the battlefield." The easy-going young man showed that when the occasion demanded he was gifted with rare qualities of leadership. Their cousin Ōyama Iwao was also endowed with the fine characteristics of the Saigō family. The general was calm and composed by nature and never lost his fair and selfless mind.

I often wondered how the Saigō family came to be blessed with sons of such distinction. Was it the way they were brought up, or something passed down to them by their forefathers? I have always wanted to know their secret but I have yet to find it.

The Birth of the Seiyūkai

After the collapse of the Ōkuma cabinet, the usual *genrō* conference was held as was customary. Following its recommendation, the imperial mandate fell on Yamagata and not Itagaki, contrary to expectations. Itō was in China when he learned of the crisis facing the Ōkuma cabinet and immediately headed back to Japan in order to support Ōkuma. It was November 7, 1898 when he finally reached Nagasaki.

Yamagata was in desperate haste to form his cabinet in order to complete the process before Itō could return and threaten his plan. The chief strategist in the whole process was Katsura, who had worked behind the scenes to bring down the Ōkuma cabinet. Although Yamagata publicly opposed a party cabinet, he knew that running a government could be very difficult without the assistance of a political party. Therefore he let Katsura negotiate with Itagaki. Two cabinet seats were offered as concessions but those appointed would have to renounce their party affiliation. For their part, the Kenseitō asked for at least four cabinet posts with their men retaining party membership. The two sides were too far apart, however, and the negotiations broke down.

Yamagata decided to proceed alone and organize a cabinet composed strictly of ex-bureaucrats who belonged to his old clan. He had decided to ignore political parties, probably with the conviction that he could manipulate the Kenseitō once the cabinet was in place. The Yamagata cabinet was completed on November 8, just in time to get the better of Itō. Learning of the development, Itō was furious. "Until today it was customary for a new cabinet to be formed after consultation among the *genrō* and endorsement by the throne," he fulminated. "Knowing very well that I have arrived back in Nagasaki, it is inexcusable for Yamagata to organize his own cabinet without consulting me." Thereafter, the schism between Itō and Yamagata steadily widened.

Although the first attempt at negotiation between Yamagata and the Kenseitō had failed, Yamagata wanted to try again. He delayed the opening of the Diet, using as an excuse his absence from the capital while he accompanied the emperor to watch large-scale army maneuvers, and arranged to meet with Kenseitō members in Osaka. At the meeting the government was represented by Prime Minister Yamagata, Home Minister Saigō, and Army Minister Katsura. The Kenseitō sent its president, Itagaki, with Hoshi Tōru and Kataoka Kenkichi. However, like the earlier meeting, it produced no results.

It appeared that negotiations between the government and the Kenseitō were leading nowhere, but the government knew only too well that without some form of alliance with the Kenseitō it would quickly find itself in difficulty once the Diet was convened. It was clear on the other hand that in spite of its uncompromising stand in their negotiations so far, the Kenseitō secretly wanted a working arrangement. In the end it was resolved, with a number of ambiguous provisions, that the Yamagata government would adopt the Kenseitō political platform.

The thirteenth Diet (December 1898–March 1899) at last held its opening ceremony on December 3, some twenty-seven days after it was convened. The strength of each political party was as follows: our Kensei Hontō held 123 seats, the Kenseitō 119, the Kokumin Kyōkai 19, and the Hiyoshi Club 12; the remaining 27 were independents.

During this Diet the Yamagata cabinet submitted a bill on a land tax increase. The land tax bill had been a cancer eating at successive governments. Even within the ranks of the Kenseitō, there was opposition to it. National opinion veered against the bill and a powerful anti-land tax increase union was formed. Our Kensei Hontō collaborated with it to fight against the government.

The government panicked and ordered the union dissolved, and, applying its usual carrot-and-stick method of judicious distributions of money and applications of pressure, attempted to bulldoze the bill through the Diet. The government also used the well-tried tactics of mobilizing police power to suppress national opinion, and arrested or placed activists and helpless farmers under supervision. It suspended freedom of speech and assembly and ordered the cancellation of meetings organized by our colleagues throughout the country. This led, as before, to violent incidents and the threat of far more serious consequences.

At the time there was a certain profiteer who had filed an application to the home ministry asking for permission to reclaim land off Yokohama Honmoku-chō. Seeing that the government was under duress over the proposed land tax increase, he secretly visited Hoshi and proposed that he would find ways to get opposition members to betray their party and switch sides to support the government. As a quid pro quo if he was successful, he asked Hoshi to use his good offices to secure a permit for the reclamation. Hoshi promptly agreed with the proposal, and with the express understanding of the government the man dispensed money to buy opposition members. This was how the land tax increase bill passed the Diet.

During this Diet the Kenseitō was little more than a rubber stamp for the government. It did not complain when the one *sen* postcard rate was increased to 1.5 sen or when a two *sen* letter rate was increased to three *sen*. Moreover, it played its game of facilitating the passage of all tax bills for the government.

The true nature of the relationship between the government and the Kenseitō at this time did not escape the general public. "The Diet is a slave market," it was said, "where its members are animals to be sold at market price." Under the first and second cabinets, and now under Yamagata's, this assessment was not too inaccurate.

Hoshi had not given his support to the Yamagata government for nothing. He demanded his price as soon as the Diet opened. Again it was to demand the appointment of Kenseitō members in the cabinet. However, Yamagata had foreseen that Kenseitō members would be clamoring for cabinet seats and had taken countermeasures in the form of revisions of the civil service appointment ordinance, civil servant status ordinance, and discipline ordinance.

THE KENSEITŌ'S PRIORITY: GREED RATHER THAN POWER

Until this time, successive cabinets had followed a more or less progressive path. In contrast, Yamagata's was a reactionary cabinet. Yamagata and his henchmen appeared at first to be confident that a party cabinet would never emerge. So they were rudely surprised when the Ōkuma-Itagaki cabinet, helped by timely changes in the political climate, was formed with unexpected ease. The second Yamagata cabinet therefore attempted to turn the clock back so as to ensure that there would never be another party government, and installed every mechanism to protect their power base from being damaged if there were.

Accordingly, they restricted the appointment of army and navy ministers to generals and lieutenant generals on active duty; they revised the ordinance regulating the appointment of civil servants so as to limit that of vice-ministers and directors-general to those with certain qualifications; and by revising the civil servants' status ordinance they guaranteed the status of all employees of the state. In these ways they made certain that if ever a political party were to form a cabinet in the future, none of the party élite would penetrate the inner circles of government.

Until then, under the existing civil service appointment ordinance, candidates for posts other than those directly appointed by the imperial court could be chosen freely. The system governing the appointment of service ministers had allowed men such as Katsu Kaishū (Awa) to become navy minister, and Kabayama and Saigō, both originally army men, to be appointed navy ministers. (Kabayama, a colonel in the Imperial Army, was made a rear admiral in the war with China and chief of the navy general staff. He was Japan's first admiral and founder of the Japanese navy.) Although there were no naval men who became army ministers, there was nothing to prevent them from doing so. The Yamagata cabinet now restricted these appointments through the civil service ordinance, and in another move they distinguished military orders from imperial orders, making the former unaccountable to the prime minister by not requiring his signature.

Even Hoshi had not expected things to be taken this far. In the wake of the thirteenth Diet, when the revised civil service appointment ordinance—the guarantee of civil servants' positions—and the disciplinary ordinance became effective, leaders of the Kenseitō demanded a full explanation by the government, asserting that these new measures were intended to alienate the party. As far as the Yamagata cabinet was concerned, it had pulled through the session securing the desired tax increase and at least for the time being had no future use of the Kenseitō.

The cabinet rejected all demands by simply threatening to "resign if the Kenseitō intervened in measures taken by the cabinet," or "criticized it." The party had already sustained serious wounds with the collapse of the Ōkuma-Ita-gaki cabinet and the fracturing of the old Kenseitō. Yamagata's latest measures and subsequent intransigence dealt the weakened party a further succession of crippling blows. For these reasons the consequences of the Kenseitō's decision to support the Yamagata cabinet amounted to little short of political suicide from the party's perspective, and the effective elimination of interference from political rivals from the point of view of the hanbatsu clique. For some time afterwards no political party was able to expand its effectiveness due entirely to these measures taken by the Yamagata cabinet. The Kenseitō's support of it thus helped to erect a serious obstacle to the advance of parliamentary democracy in Japan. The Yamagata cabinet destroyed the political parties with one blow of its iron mallet and put in place a system to perpetuate the reign of the *hanbatsu*. To be fair, it may also in the long run have had some salutary effects, but on balance it exerted a deeply baneful influence on the development of party government.

The Kenseitō must have received some sort of compensation, for it continued to support the Yamagata cabinet despite the ill treatment it had received. It now switched from demanding cabinet posts to harvesting gains of other kinds. The Yamagata cabinet's strategy, having built impermeable defenses against the party's aspirations for office, was to keep it compliant by meting out other rewards in many cunning ways.

With Hoshi as the intermediary, it was this government that gave the city of Tokyo permission to build a municipal railroad. It is an example of how the government manipulated political parties. The price we paid was enormous. As compensation for cutting off the very roots and raisons d'être of the political parties and for slamming the door to cabinet entry shut, the Yamagata ministry magnanimously opened another door to corruption and manipulated the parties through the distribution of benefits. The damage remains to this day.

Scholars years hence analyzing our political history will have no difficulty concluding that during the Meiji era it was the Yamagata cabinet that did the nation the greatest disservice and that the Kenseitō helped it to do so. Even the damage done by government intervention in general elections was not as fundamental as this. The poison of election intervention caused only superficial injury, whereas the poison administered by the Yamagata cabinet penetrated every part of our body politic.

SMALL RIPPLES MARK THE FOURTEENTH DIET

When the fourteenth Diet (November, 1899–February, 1900) was convened on November 20, the Kenseitō declared its intention to maintain its alliance with the government. Our Kensei Hontō, the avowed opposition, challenged the government by submitting a revised budget bill.

The bill was voted down. I then took the floor on behalf of our party and voiced our opposition to the entire budget. All parties with the exception of ours formed a swift alliance on the grounds that "the budget includes expenses for the imperial family. Anyone opposing the budget is committing lèse majesté," and passed a resolution to trap me. Since this was not long after the clan clique and the bureaucrats had succeeded in victimizing me unjustly over my "republican speech" our rivals probably now thought it would be most effective to attack me on grounds of disloyalty to the throne. The resolution was submitted by Hoshi Tōru for the Jiyūtō, Sassa Tomofusa for the Teikokutō (Imperial Party), and Motoda Hajime as the leader of a bureaucratic faction. The draft resolution if it had been put to a vote would easily have passed.

As soon as the intent of the draft resolution was explained, I took the floor and pronounced that those who submitted the resolution "appear to understand neither the constitution nor the budget.". I then pointed out that the imperial household expenses were not subject to parliamentary surveillance. Article 66 of the constitution stated that the imperial household expenses did not require endorsement by the Diet. Any item that did not require parliamentary approval was not formally part of the budget. The item in question was listed only as a matter of consistency and could only be referred to as a separate item but not on the list for deliberation.

My speech lasted less than five minutes, but I was conscious of the enormous effect it produced. As I walked to the podium I sensed the sneers of the members. I could feel their cold smiles piercing me, almost as if daggers were pressing at my throat. I spoke only the truth, of course, but with it I poured out my anger against the insidious ways of the opposition parties. My intense feelings appeared to have moved my listeners, for after I had spoken a few sentences there was considerable restlessness. When I finished, a few leaders gathered and talked quickly together. Then Motoda Hajime mounted the podium and, without giving any good reason, declared a postponement of the debate on the draft resolution. In my long parliamentary life there was no other time that such a short speech of mine had such an impact.

The following day the political party alliance submitted a motion effectively saying that "Ozaki's statement was after all not unreasonable" and attempted to withdraw their earlier resolution. Immediately, Shimada Saburō took the floor on our behalf pointing his finger at the government for its "inappropriate use of the name of the imperial family with the object of fomenting political strife" and demanded the draft resolution to be put to a vote. As a result, the resolution was rejected 157 to 114. Those voting against it included members of the parties in the political alliance who as a matter of conscience had changed their minds.

Encouraged by this turn of events, the Kensei Hontō submitted a motion of impeachment against the cabinet for abusing the powers of government, citing the bribing of politicians to support the passage of the government's land tax increase bill and reciprocating by granting permission to reclaim land in Yokohama, and meddling in prefectural assembly elections. Again I took the floor to state our reasons for the impeachment. I cited facts to prove each case. This vexed the ruling party to the extent of driving Inoue Kakugorō to shout, "Ozaki must be punished for fabrication of facts and contempt of members of this House." This time the ruling party displayed strong unity and our impeachment bid failed.

The Yamagata cabinet somehow managed to survive the fourteenth Diet with the help of the Kenseitō, which had, in effect, become a government party. After the session closed, the Kenseitō again brought up the long-pending subject of securing posts in the cabinet. The Yamagata cabinet, without bothering to reply, simply threatened to resign en masse. At this, the Kenseitō finally decided to part with Yamagata and sought to collaborate with Itō. There were members within the Kenseitō who had wished for some time that Itō would lead them. Now that the party had broken with the Yamagata government, the four officers responsible for general party affairs, Hoshi Tōru, Kataoka Kenkichi, Matsuda Masahisa, and Hayashi Yūzō, officially approached Itō to be their president. Itō reserved his answer that day, but invited Hoshi, Hayashi, Matsuda, Suematsu, and Kataoka to visit him at his residence, "Sōrō-kaku," in Ōiso on July 8, and in that relaxed setting explained why he would not accept.

"I am afraid I am not in a position to accept your offer at this time. I am glad, however, to share your hopes for the improvement of the political party system. I look forward to the day when I make my views public concerning the achievement of genuine constitutional government. I hope it will be to our mutual happiness if at that time circumstances will permit me to work with you and walk on the same path."

While Itō refused the offer, it was clear from his reply that he already had plans to organize a political party. The political world was suddenly animated. Itō refused to head the Kenseitō only because it would be inconvenient for him to provide leadership to so many sections of the nation at once. Itō wished to create a political party entirely unlike those that already existed, that he could use as a vehicle to uphold his own ideals and keep under his own complete control.

PRINCE ITŌ AND I

I have already related how Itō had twice tried to organize a political party. On each occasion his plans failed, but his ambition did not. All this time he had been working steadfastly to realize his dream. He studied Western political parties. He traveled throughout the nation to explain the nature of constitutional government to the public and mobilize their support. He worked daily to find talented men to man various posts in his political party. One historian has concluded that Itō's contribution to the development of constitutional government was greatest at this time.

Observing the public's dislike of political parties, the villainous ways in which Yamagata manipulated them, and the resulting corruption of the government, Itō was determined to build a genuine political party. Having been approached by the Kenseitō, he now decided to go ahead and organize the new party he had dreamed of.

I was of course deeply dissatisfied with the Kenseitō, but not wholly happy with the Kensei Hontō either. Neither of them was a genuine political party committed solely to the good of the nation. They were both private parties whose members were connected by relationships based on personal loyalty or obligation and mutual interest. I felt the need to bring together like-minded men who were committed to advancing the good of the nation as well as of its people and to vanquishing the abuses of the existing parties. I knew sadly that I did not have the resources to do it.

It was then that I learned of Itō's intention to organize a new party, and I wanted to hear what he had to say. Itō was after all, along with Yamagata, a leader of the Chōshū clan and our sworn enemy of many years. For Itō to establish his own political party was a step in our direction. In a sense he had surrendered to our convictions. My own idealism dictated that as a statesman I should not obstruct any other person from working for the same cause just because he had been a long-time enemy in the past.

Japan's relations with Russia had deteriorated to the extent that a clash seemed inevitable. I thought a war with Russia was extremely undesirable from Japan's point of view and had been studying ways to avoid a clash without compromising our position. Indirectly I learned that Itō also nursed similar thoughts.

As far as domestic politics was concerned, I felt I should assist the leader of the *hanbatsu* to become a true party man now that this accorded with his own aspirations. On foreign relations, I felt it was my duty in the interest of the state to support those who favored resolving our differences with Russia without going to war. For these two reasons I decided I should put the past behind me and try to work with Itō. I therefore approached him with this in mind.

Talking with Itō directly, I confirmed that he and I shared the view that a breakdown in relations with Russia at this time would be against the interests of the state. He appeared uncertain, however, as to how relations could be settled without going to war and how to deal with public opinion. "A major decision has to be made," I said. "We must take great risks for the sake of the nation. In these circumstances public opinion might have to be ignored." I cannot, of course, take credit for it but Itō did decide that Japan's differences with Russia must be resolved by peaceful means.

Regarding a reorganization of the political parties, I proposed the following: "First of all, a major political party should be formed combining three groups: the Kenseitō with the former Jiyūtō; the Kensei Hontō with the former Shinpotō; and bureaucrats with eminent individuals from the private sector. In this way each would serve as a check on the others and would in turn be restrained from acting arbitrarily. If you remain manifestly impartial you will be able to bring it off."

Itō seemed not to disagree with this suggestion, but Hoshi of the Jiyūtō group campaigned vigorously against members of the Shinpotō group, apparently with the sole exception of myself, being included in the new party. A problem for Itō was that the inclusion of the Shinpo group necessitated collaboration with Ōkuma. Itō still seemed uneasy about Ōkuma and could not bring himself to include the whole of the Kensei Hontō. While my own proposals with regard to the organization of the new party were met with many objections, I did not surrender my conviction that all the members of the Shinpotō group should be included.

In this way I became deeply involved in Itō's development of the political party. My original intention was to make sure of Itō's intentions and then to consult my colleagues, so I did not at first consult Ōkuma or anyone else. In my mind, as this was a major undertaking which had to be carried out even at the risk of my own political career, I was going to go ahead with it with or without the consent of my colleagues. In my earnestness, I did not consider the procedural matter of whether to consult my colleagues before or after meeting with Itō or afterwards an issue.

When someone disclosed my action to my colleagues they felt betrayed, and were of the impression that I had got the better of them and surrendered to Itō. So when I met with Ōkuma, Inukai, and Ōishi Masami at Ōkuma's residence, I had no sympathy from any of them, however hard I tried to explain myself. If they could have kept an open mind they might have understood, but since they had already decided that I had betrayed them, no one listened. Ōishi was the only one who said he was prepared to go along with the other two if they believed my story. Ōkuma spoke to me sternly. "You misjudge Itō," he said. "How do you think he can succeed where we failed?" Then, raising his voice, he said, "Please stop what you are doing!" This was the first and only time that I saw anger on Ōkuma's face. I was told that Ōkuma was actually furious at what I said earlier regarding the dissolution of the Kaishintō, but that time he did not show it. I do not know whether he was really furious or just pretending, but Ōkuma, who was known not to betray his anger, not only showed it now but raised his voice as well.

Even then, I stuck to my guns. "I cannot stop what I am doing," I retorted, "because this is what I think is best for the country. If I stopped now, it is the country that I would be betraying." As I firmly believed in the rightness of my actions, I took steps to muster my own party members who resided in Tokyo to explain my convictions to them and ask their support.

However, many of my countrymen still believed that I had betrayed my colleagues by siding with Itō for my personal advantage. It was even alleged by some that I had approached Itō in order to regain the confidence of the throne after my notorious "republican speech." Even some of my own colleagues were of this opinion. Nonetheless, I wished to share my thoughts with them and solicit their support for the sake of our country. I presented myself at the Kensei Hontō headquarters on schedule.

It appeared that Inukai had tried his best to resolve the issue in an amicable manner and had sent the following letter to Ōkuma: "With regard to the Ozaki case, I have talked with many people in the last few days. The matter seems to have been more or less settled, but the man is quite headstrong. The leading members of the party have been invited to headquarters to hear Ozaki tell us plainly what he has in mind. Whatever difficulties there might be, the matter should be settled amicably. I shall report to you on the details in person later."

However, it was too late. Even Inukai could not contain the resentment of my critics, who in the heat of the moment expelled me from the party. I was not even given a chance to state my views. That was how I came to part ways with my seniors and old friends and to participate alone in Itō's new party. If I had called, I was sure that thirty or forty Kensei Hontō members would have joined me. But I thought I would stand a better chance of eventually winning over the entire party if I set out alone at first rather than taking thirty or forty of the fellows with me. For this reason I was welcomed by all of the Itō crowd and found it easy to work with them.

Since the Kensei Hontō did not throw in its lot with the new party, Itō formed it around Hoshi's Jiyūtō group. As I had feared, the Jiyūtō group came to enjoy a dominant position within the party and eventually caused Itō much grief, as I shall recount.

The New Party Receives the Imperial Sanction

Under Hoshi's leadership the Kenseitō acted with unity throughout. When Itō refused to be the Kenseitō's president, Hoshi took a drastic step, just as might have been expected of him. His idea was to dissolve the Kenseitō and offer it up to Itō, ostensibly as a gift. This was based on a well-thought-out political strategy. Hoshi was a realist to his bones and did not put great stock in titles. He believed that in a political party the man who had the real power won. If Kenseitō members accounted for the majority in the new party, the latter would necessarily owe itself to Kenseitō. In contrast, Itō believed in his own strength. He believed that since the Kenseitō had come begging, as long as he held the reins of the government, which he intended to run with exclusive powers vested in himself as party president, he would be able to mold the party to his own design. Therefore he accepted Hoshi's offer against powerful voices of opposition.

Developments proceeded apace, and on August 25, 1900, the inaugural committee meeting of the Rikken Seiyūkai (Friends of Constitutional Government) Party was held at the Kōyō-kan in Shiba, Tokyo. At the meeting, the Seiyūkai publicly adopted a declaration and a political platform that contained some important concepts. Parties of the past, be they Jiyūtō or Kaishintō or any of the others that came and went under different names inserted, had the objective of destroying the Satsuma-Chōshū *hanbatsu* by mobilizing popular forces to challenge them. Itō had no need either to destroy the *hanbatsu* or to scheme to seize the government. From his own experience with the Diet he knew both the strengths and the weaknesses of political parties. And now he was organizing his own new party, whose majority he would command, to complete the process of establishing constitutional government in the service of the throne.

Accordingly, the party declaration included a new interpretation of the imperial prerogative: "Appointment of ministers belongs within the purview of the imperial prerogative as stipulated in the constitution. Their selection and appointment may be made from among members or non-members of political parties. The prerogative lies within the discretion of the head of state."

Itō assailed the view held by Yamagata, Matsukata, and others of their persuasion that it was unconstitutional to form a cabinet with members of a political party, while at the same time he disparaged extremists who maintained that all cabinets must be party cabinets. Furthermore, in attempting to correct the errors of conventional political parties that gave more importance to seizing power than to attending to the affairs of the nation, it was stated: "Once chosen to fulfill the task of assisting the throne by carrying out the imperial mandate, no one, be they party members or friends, should be allowed to intervene in the full exercise of that task." In other words, it was made clear that a political party should be an organ to lead the people, but not a tool for power-mongering.

To be sure, some members of the Kenseitō were unhappy at this, but they did not dare to complain lest they lose Itō. Hoshi, being a pragmatist through and through, suppressed their complaints at being obliged to participate in the creation of the Seiyūkai.

With his ambition close to being achieved, Itō requested an audience with Emperor Meiji and, secretly requesting His Majesty's endorsement, explained to him in detail how political parties were essential to constitutional government and how his own political party differed from conventional parties. The emperor not only expressed no opposition, but, when Itō resigned his position in order to form his party, he granted him 100,000 yen in recognition of his long years of service. It is said that Itō used this money for the establishment of the party. The Seiyūkai thereafter prided itself on being the party with the imperial blessing.

Itō did not forget to communicate the imperial will to Yamagata Aritomo and Kuroda Kiyotaka to preclude their possible interference. Yamagata apparently tried behind the scenes to obstruct the new party, but not visibly this time. Kuroda was bedridden when he received a special envoy carrying Itō's message, and was said to have replied, "Three years ago when we met at the palace you talked of the need for a solid major party in order to put right the ills of the political world and be at the heart of a genuine constitutional government. At the time I did not have the foresight and rejected your argument, but I now see your intentions. I respect you for your praiseworthy efforts. If you act on your laudable convictions, I, Kiyotaka, will assist you with all my strength." It was indeed what the open-minded Kuroda would have been expected to say. He never left his sickbed again, however, and died not long afterwards.

As the preparations for the inauguration of the Seiyūkai went steadily forward, Itō, fearing lest his association with a political party bring any harm to the palace, submitted to the throne through Minister Tanaka of the imperial household ministry his resignation from all major imperial household positions—adviser to the crown prince, president of the imperial household research bureau, and adviser to the imperial household economy. It was on September 9.

On September 14, the emperor granted Itō's wish and released him from the three posts. Iwakura Tomosada, a senior chamberlain, was dispatched to Itō's residence with 20,000 yen and two rolls of crêpe de Chine, one red and one white, and the following imperial message: "I endorse your petition and grant your wish. I have much trust in your loyalty. It is my earnest wish that you should at all times assist me in governing." It was as if Itō had finally received the vaunted imperial blessing on the organization of his political party.

On the following day, September 15, the inauguration of the Rikken Seiyūkai took place at the Imperial Hotel. In spite of drizzling rain, carriages and rickshaws arrived one after the other with guests who filled the hall. No fewer than fifteen hundred people attended the inauguration, and more than six thousand congratulatory telegrams were received.

At the ceremony the chairman of the inaugural committee, Watanabe Kunitake, delivered an opening address. This was followed by a statement from the president of the party, Itō Hirobumi, who urged: "Political parties should set aside all personal interest and serve the country. It is my wish that the Rikken Seiyūkai be the model of such a party." Under President Itō a general affairs committee was established, charged with the management of party business. I became one of its members.

Thus was born the Rikken Seiyūkai. Its strength in the House of Representatives was 152, of whom the majority of course belonged to the Jiyūtō group led by Hoshi. Apart from this group there were just 41 who joined: 9 from the Kensei Hontō, 5 from the Teikokutō, 2 from the Dōshi Club, 5 from the Hiyoshi Club, and 20 independents.

The newly-born Seiyūkai was dominated inevitably by the Jiyūtō faction, and contained too few loyal to Itō. This was the main internal reason for the failure of Itō's political dream. It was exactly as Hoshi had predicted.

The ringing applause of the inauguration had hardly died when Itō began to suffer from the high-handedness of Hoshi's group. On almost every issue, Hoshi blackmailed Itō, saying: "My people couldn't possibly go along with that," or "You may have my agreement, but I cannot speak for others." Things did not develop as Itō had hoped. As they went from bad to worse, he often wrote me letters lamenting the fact. It seemed that he was consoled by sharing his disappointment with me. With pressure from Hoshi's group within the party and obstruction from Yamagata without, Itō was in distress from the very birth of the Seiyūkai.

THE FOURTH ITŌ CABINET

No sooner had the Seiyūkai come upon the scene as the express enemy of the government, than Prime Minister Yamagata suddenly submitted his resignation, recommending Itō as his successor. And on the same day, September 26, he retired to his residence "Chinzansō," in spite of the need to attend to government business following the outbreak of the Boxer Rebellion in North China.

Barely ten days had passed since the Seiyūkai was born. Yamagata's strategy was clear. Before the Seiyūkai was able to put itself into solid shape, Yamagata wanted Itō to fall into difficulty with the tribulations of putting a cabinet together. Under the circumstances, when he was so little prepared, it was difficult even for Itō to take on the premiership. He tried in every way he could to refuse, but in the end when the *genrō* intervened he was forced to form a cabinet. Although he complained that "this was the art of war in true Yamagata-style—to ambush the enemy before his troops are in position," it was exactly what Itō had himself done to cause us grief as soon as the Kenseitō was born by resigning in favor of Ōkuma and Itagaki.

Receiving the imperial mandate on October 7, Itō immediately set about forming a cabinet, but his ship was already foundering. Vice-Premier Watanabe Kunitake, who had served as chairman of the inaugural committee, sent Itō a letter suddenly severing relations with him and resigning from the party in protest against Hoshi's authoritarianism, which to his mind invalidated the rationale for Itō's earlier refusal to join the Kenseitō and the principles on which Itō claimed to have founded his own party, the Seiyūkai. Whatever Watanabe's motive, a traitor among the ranks of the party executive compromised the unity of the party. Many men intervened, and after a few days Watanabe knocked at Itō's door to apologize for his rash behavior and returned to the fold. Then he unabashedly appointed himself minister of finance, saying simply that he had had a change of heart while taking a walk in the suburbs.

It was now the turn of the Jiyūtō faction to complain. Since it was rumored that Watanabe had insisted on the finance portfolio as his price for returning to the party, the Jiyūtō faction now demanded Watanabe's expulsion. The incident was settled by dismissing Watanabe from the party's general affairs committee. By October 19, the fourth Itō cabinet was complete. However, it was malformed from the beginning.

The cabinet was composed entirely of Seiyūkai members, with the exception of Army Minister Katsura Tarō, Navy Minister Yamamoto Gonnohyōe, and Foreign Minister Katō Takaaki. The remaining cabinet posts were filled by Suematsu Takasumi as home minister, Watanabe Kunitake as finance minister, Kaneko Kentarō as justice minister, Matsuda Masahisa as education minister, Hayashi Yūzō as agriculture and commerce minister, and Hoshi Tōru as communications minister.

Soon after the cabinet was in place, Saionji paid a surprise visit to my home in Shinagawa. I was not aware then of any reason for the prince to visit me, and even to this day I do not quite know what brought him. We had a nice chat before he left, and I vaguely supposed he must have come on some business or other that had eluded me. On reflection, my guess was that Itō, perhaps feeling that I should have been asked to join the cabinet though the circumstances did not actually permit it, might have sent Saionji as his envoy to tell me he was not neglecting me. To tell the truth, I did think at the time that there would be an offer for me to join the cabinet, but I had no reason to complain if there was not. Possibly Saionji came to console me but realized there was no such need, and therefore did not broach the subject and left after a little small talk. He was extremely bright and quick to understand others' feelings.

No sooner was the new Itō cabinet appointed than Communications Minister Hoshi became the object of public outrage for his involvement in the scandal over the land reclamation and city train projects. Hoshi, "the public thief," was now the target of attacks that undermined his credibility. The Yamagata group in the House of Peers seized the opportunity to threaten the cabinet with impeachment. It had not taken long for the government to find itself in distress.

I checked with officials in the ministry to ascertain Hoshi's reputation. All said without hesitation that of all the ministers they had worked under he was the most outstanding. Most ministers placed their seal on documents prepared by their subordinates, but Hoshi checked them all and took little time doing it. Documents were usually presented to him by directors-general or their deputies, but Hoshi was never satisfied with their explanations. He would demand to see the authors. It was unusual in any ministry for a minister to want to listen to what lower civil servants had to say, and those invited were greatly honored at being called. Such occasions also gave Hoshi an opportunity to demonstrate his competence.

After listening to low-ranking officials, he made decisions on the spot. If the man appeared useful, Hoshi would invite him to his home, but when he respectfully turned up at Hoshi's residence there was usually no particular business waiting for him. "I am busy today. Please come back another time," Hoshi would say. "Take this. It may be of use to you." It was customary for Hoshi to hand his visitor an envelope containing money. If he refused, Hoshi shouted at him, "I told you to take it, do you hear?" The visitor soon realized it was better to take the proffered envelope than to suffer Hoshi's ill will. Then, when he had accepted the envelope, Hoshi would say nicely, "Be sure to come back." And so the man would return another day, when once again he was given money. After this, he would find himself asked to do certain things for the ministry and also for Hoshi on a private basis. It was a blatant case of mixing official and private affairs, but this was how Hoshi developed his own power base.

As the leader of a political party Hoshi held a stick in his right hand and money in his left. If money did not work to bend a person to his will then Hoshi used the stick. With this method he conquered one after another, and within a short period he became a powerful figure. Not surprisingly, he needed money. It was more likely than not that he did things to arouse public disdain. To be sure, Hoshi's objective was not money itself, but power.

When Hoshi became minister of communications, however, his luck ran out. His way of doing business as chairman of the Tokyo municipal council, which gave him overall control of the administration of the capital, led to the arrest of many of his underlings in the city assembly and the city council for alleged irregularities. Since all those who were arrested named Hoshi as the main culprit, public criticism of him soared rapidly. Prime Minister Itō had little choice but to urge Hoshi to resign to protect the integrity of the cabinet. Hoshi struck back. "Was it not you, Your Excellency, who personally recommended me to the throne? If my continued presence, as you say, would undermine the integrity of the cabinet, you should resign with me. The allegations are pure fabrication and rumor. I have nothing to be ashamed of. I can be arrested just as well in office as not. If I am forced to, I shall vindicate myself in court." He stuck it out just as he had when he was impeached as president of the House. But just then the climate in the House of Peers turned so severely against Hoshi that the prime minister had no alternative but to talk him sternly into resigning. This incident greatly provoked Hoshi.

Hara Takashi, who succeeded Hoshi, was the secretary-general of the Seiyūkai and a hard worker like his predecessor. By this yardstick it was difficult to judge between them. It was equally hard to say which of the two was superior in terms of intelligence and boldness, or in the capacity for playing dirty tricks. By coincidence, both came to terrible ends. Hoshi met his death rather soon after this incident, but Hara was just beginning to make his mark on the political scene.

HOSHI AND I

When it came out that I was thinking of joining Itō's group, Ōkuma, as I have recounted, advised me against the move in no uncertain terms, saying that Itō could hardly succeed with his political party when we had tried and failed. I joined the Seiyūkai anyway, telling Ōkuma, "You may be right. On the other hand, while you have failed, he has not yet done so. It does not necessarily follow he has to fail as well." Ōkuma proved right in the end.

There were some incorrigible villains among Hoshi's men. Once, as we were returning from a party gathering at the Kōyō-kan, a notorious ruffian by the name of Kawakami Yukiyoshi appeared. "If the president wants to know who is boss, I'll show him," he jeered. Then he went right up to Itō and urinated on him. Kawakami was a notorious murderer who had killed to avenge his father's death. Later he came to work for me and remained loyal until his own death. This was the kind of man Hoshi kept in his fold. The Jiyūtō faction was too formidable for bureaucrats to cope with, and President Itō's authority was often not strong enough to keep its members in line.

Itō must have thought that no man with a bureaucratic background could possibly be a match for Hoshi. At the very first session following the organization of the Seiyūkai, therefore, he named Hoshi and myself as majority whips.

Without telling us what was ailing him, Hoshi claimed sickness and locked himself up in his villa in Koyama in Tochigi prefecture. Itō, troubled, consulted me. I said, "You don't have to worry about Hoshi's health. I'll see to it that he gets well," and I resigned as majority whip. As soon as Hoshi heard this, he returned to Tokyo and managed the party in the House alone.

Hoshi had many men at his beck and call whom he had trained over the years, but I was alone in the enemy camp and there was no way I could fight him. Concluding that discretion was the better part of valor, I therefore kept well clear of the administrative affairs of the party.

The impeachment seemed to be a big blow to Hoshi. "I cannot think that to have once held ministerial rank is all I am good for. If I am made to resign because of the way I do things, then I will have to change my ways." He was an intelligent man and he must have meant what he said. From that time on he made efforts to approach me. Itō said to me, "I want you and Hoshi to get along well together. Why don't you two talk things over?" Then one evening Itō invited Hoshi and myself, and the three of us spent a leisurely evening at Itō's private residence at

Reinanzaka. Matsuda Masahisa, Suematsu Kenchō, and Kaneko Kentarō, who were Itō's closest colleagues, were not even invited. I suspected that there might be something behind this, but neither Itō nor Hoshi talked of anything meaningful. We just chatted and ended up talking about books. A love of books was something we all had in common, and we talked until late. Whether this was Itō's idea or Hoshi's I did not know, but I suspected that they both hoped for a reconciliation between Hoshi and myself.

Hoshi sent one of his men to tell me that he wanted to work with me. I sent the man back to Hoshi, saying that I could not work with a man of different principles. But after a while he returned and said he had passed on my message to Hoshi, who then promised that if I would work with him he would adopt the Ozaki style instead of his own. The formula sounded like Hoshi all right, but I was not convinced that the man really represented him and I refused Hoshi's offer of collaboration.

Hoshi's apparent capitulation, I thought, gave me all the more reason to keep my distance. Every man should have his own style and do things his own way. If Hoshi were to switch to mine he would be betraying weakness. In all novels and plays a repentant villain usually comes to a sticky end. If he is not murdered, then he is sure to be at least arrested. If Hoshi were truly to change his style, that would spell his political downfall. It was no use working with a man who was fated to fall.

In those days Hoshi's style was popular with young people and many emulated it. "It will get him nowhere in the end," I remarked more than once. "It may take him to certain heights but he will not do great things.'

I was invited by the Teachers Training College in Ochanomizu to give a speech on June 21, 1901. On the subject of Hoshi, I referred to the fact that he seemed to have many admirers. While I too thought Hoshi was a man to reckon with and his technique of holding money in one hand and a stick in another had indeed got him a cabinet seat, that was all it would get him. The fact that he had had to resign his post almost as soon as he was given it was proof enough. I even went so far as to say that if Hoshi did not change his ways he would end up assassinated or in jail. At an intersection at the bottom of the Ochanomizu hill on my way home after the speech, I stopped the rickshaw to buy a special edition of the newspaper I saw was on sale. Hoshi had been assassinated.

It was a dreadful shock to learn of his murder less than thirty minutes after my warning. It certainly put an end to our relationship. Later, I was to learn that in the days before his death Hoshi really had been serious about wanting to work with me. I shall discuss this more in a later chapter.

THE ITŌ CABINET FALLS

During the fifteenth Diet (December 1900–March 1901) the Seiyūkai had little to worry about in the House of Representatives, where it commanded an absolute majority, but the House of Peers remained a bastion of conservatism. Yamagata's group worked on its members so effectively that they were deeply hostile towards Itō's formation of a political party. At first the Upper House appeared intent on fighting the government over Hoshi's bribery scandal, but, robbed of their cause because of Hoshi's resignation, they chose to mount an unreasonable assault on the government over the proposed tax increase to finance our military commitments in northern China.

Itō took the floor in the Peers to solicit their understanding, but Yamagata and his followers would not give in. Itō felt compelled to seek a ten-day recess, at which the Peers became even more aggressive. The government then, having tried every other recourse, finally sought the advice of the throne. This was what Itō usually did when driven to the wall.

The imperial rescript that followed was accepted by the Peers, who rested their objections and passed all the government's tax increase bills without amendment. To its great relief the Itō government thus managed to pull itself through the fifteenth Diet, but almost before it could catch its breath, Itō faced a rift within the cabinet.

Finance Minister Watanabe, concerned over excessive spending, was secretly determined to carry out a spending cut. Accordingly, he advocated suspension of government projects financed by public debt for fiscal 1901 on the grounds that yearly financing of public works by public debt undermined the foundation of national finance. He attempted to adopt the same measures for the fiscal 1902 budget as well.

Five ministers from the Jiyūtō group who hated Watanabe united themselves in opposition to his proposal, alleging that suspending public works was against the interest of national development. Watanabe, however, true to his belief, did not give an inch to his opponents, maintaining that his budget was fundamental to sound management of the Empire's finances.

The conflict that had erupted within the cabinet, fueled by the emotional estrangement of the protagonists, proved to be quite serious. After less than six months after its formation, the cabinet was in danger of collapse, but in a cabinet meeting at the end of April, thanks to the mediation of Navy Minister Yamamoto Gonnohyōe and Foreign Minister Katō Takaaki, all members agreed under the circumstances to cooperate.

The controversy over the suspension of public works was not difficult to understand, and the issue was public knowledge to anyone attentive to national finance. However, since his youth Itō had always left financial matters to Ōkuma and Inoue, and had little knowledge of them. It seems he was not even aware of the rift within his cabinet until it became serious. "Why didn't you let me know about it earlier?" he apparently complained to Watanabe.

Having no idea that the issue had been settled at the cabinet meeting, I called on the prime minister with the intention of advising him of the undesirability of a cabinet rift over fiscal matters. But Itō only complained to me about the state of national finance and criticized the finance minister. "Well, it's all your fault and you must take responsibility," I dared to say to him. "You have neglected finance since this cabinet was formed and now you complain of fiscal difficulties, which, by the way, is public knowledge. Don't tell me you are shocked to have learned about it from Watanabe. That is more shocking. The prime minister should at least be versed in matters affecting the military, foreign relations, and finance and have enough knowledge to give appropriate instructions. You don't qualify as prime minister if you have to complain like this."

Itō listened with disappointment, and the following day, May 2, suddenly submitted his resignation. I found out afterwards that until the previous evening the whole cabinet had decided to pull together. My attempt to encourage the prime minister by the use of harsh words had backfired, prompting him to change his mind and resign. Perhaps there were other causes too, but as one minister put it: "It had been decided among us in favor of maintaining the cabinet. Your uninvited intervention is responsible for his resignation."

With the prime minister's resignation, other ministers were obliged to follow. Finance Minister Watanabe not only was alone in his refusal to resign, but asked Itō to withdraw his decision. When this proved unsuccessful, he submitted to the throne something like the following: "Itō may resign but your subject Kunitake remains. I beg Your Majesty to rest assured." Emperor Meiji did not grant Watanabe his wish, so that in the end he was dismissed in spite of all his exertions to abide by what he believed was right. This was the last time the fearless Watanabe enjoyed such prominence.

Following Itō's resignation, Saionji Kinmochi was ordered to act as prime minister and take over the finance ministry while the other eight ministers remained in charge of their portfolios. The five ministers in the Jiyūtō group, happy at the successful ousting of Watanabe, dreamed of retaining their posts with Saionji properly installed as prime minister.

The Childlike Itō

It was around this time that my relationship with Itō was closest. The first impression I had of him following his resignation was that he still retained his childlike guilelessness, which was perhaps one reason why to his death he was never disliked by the public. Itō, with his unaffected and almost childlike innocence, wholeheartedly enjoyed praise and was often distressed over small matters when things did not go as he wished. To some people this would not seem of very great importance. Even after attaining a most respectable position and a peerage, he would play the clown by wearing a Japanese towel around his face like a thief, sitting at official functions with the end of his kimono tucked into his belt like a commoner, or talking while tapping his knees, which gave the lie to his usual serious countenance. He never lost this engaging playful characteristic even in his old age.

Itō was, perhaps more than one might have expected, a very fair person. In addition to Saigō, Ōkubo, and Kido, the three great men of the Restoration, I have had the opportunity of meeting most men of the times, each of whom has left a distinct impression on me. Ōkuma Shigenobu was generous-minded, Yamagata

Aritomo scrupulous, Saigō Tsugumichi big-hearted, and Gotō Shōjirō broad-minded and magnanimous. Itō was above all just. Needless to say, each had his strengths and weaknesses, but compared to current leaders they seemed to possess higher and greater virtues.

As I said, Itō was a fair man. I had grown up being told he was our political enemy, and therefore I had at first a bad impression of him. But, as my own ability to judge people developed, and I learned to distinguish right from wrong, I realized that while Itō might commit errors like anyone else, he was neither selfish nor malevolent in his intentions. It was clear that he managed the affairs of the state as fairly and justly as he could. He had his weaknesses, to be sure, but he deserves to be called a fine statesman for having served his country unswervingly on the basis of fairness.

At the same time, in a certain way, Itō was also indifferent towards others. He never allowed himself to be too indebted to people. He therefore employed officials whom he regarded as useful to the state, but he had no compunction about abandoning them when they were no longer of use. He welcomed those who came and did not pursue those who left. On one occasion, a person close to Itō ventured, "Inukai and Hoshi have quite a few men around them whom they can count on to serve them for life," implying that this was not one of Itō's virtues. Itō replied: "I am exactly the opposite. My strength lies in not creating followers." That may well have been true. Itō Miyoji, who was considered the closest and indeed only protégé of Itō, saw their relations cool in later years. I don't know whether it was intended as a spiteful gesture, but Itō Miyoji enrolled his son in Ōkuma's school. If that were so, it was more like an act of war than an act of an indebted friend. Itō Miyoji, who had been named a count, was said to have declared, using the language of a merchant, "I've paid him off." He meant that while he had felt indebted to Itō, his debts had been paid and he owed Itō no further obligation. Itō Miyoji's statement gave one a glimpse of the true nature of their relationship.

By contrast, Yamagata and Inoue made strong personal commitments. Especially Yamagata. Once he had decided to take someone under his wing, it was for life. Inoue was similar. If Inoue gave a person his protection in political life, he thought he had to look after that person's kitchen as well. But under emotional pressure Inoue was capable of breaking with someone whom he had once favored. Yamagata was not that fickle.

Consequently, Yamagata had a party of faithful followers, which Itō lacked. There was never an Itō faction, only admirers. Itō recruited without prejudice anyone from anywhere whom he considered good for the country, but he never had anyone as devoted to him for his own sake as had Yamagata. What was more, he was proud to live by this principle.

The difference between the two princes was evident from their residences. In affairs of the state Itō was scrupulous and cautious, but in personal and domestic matters he was careless and utterly indifferent. His villa in Ōiso, known as Sōro kaku, was impressive only in name. The gardens and the house itself were both simple and without any taste or decoration. In complete contrast, Yamagata's residences, Chinzansō, Kōki-an, and Murin-an, were richly and tastefully furnished, and in the splendid gardens with their charming pavilions every tree and stone was specially selected and artfully placed. The particular beauty of the running streams was a mark of Prince Yamagata's exquisite taste that made visitors gape with wonder.

I have seen what appears to have been Itō's last will and testament. It was written before he took office as resident-general of Korea in consideration of what dangers he might encounter, including possible assassination. It ordered his son and heir to give a hundred thousand yen to his widow. A hundred thousand yen in those days was a great deal of money. Where on earth did Itō keep all that money, I wondered to myself. The prince owned no property besides his simple residence. Leaving his widow a large amount of money could not have more vividly demonstrated Ito's lack of economic sense. Yamagata would never have done anything of that sort.

THE KATSURA CABINET

Although Itō had to step down, he still seemed to have an appetite for government. He had resigned, but he knew he had a major political party behind him. He must have calculated that no one would dare to challenge the Seiyūkai by trying to field a rival cabinet and that eventually his time would come again. This would give him an opportunity to reshuffle his cabinet and make a clean start.

So to start with, Itō recommended Yamagata as his successor. As expected, Yamagata did not accept. Instead, he encouraged Saionji to succeed Itō. Saionji and Yamagata had a providential sort of relationship. During the Boshin War, Saionji was the governor-general and Yamagata was a staff officer when they went to subdue the Nagaoka clan. The Nagaoka clan had a brave warrior by the name of Kawai Tsugunosuke, who put up formidable resistance and sent Saionji running for his life. Yamagata described their experience in this poem:

> In our foes' dark fort, the shadows of their torches,
> The night wind chill. Then the summer day that scorches.

It must have been a desperate battle.

Saionji was an uncommonly orderly person, but in his flight, no doubt flustered and frightened out of his wits, he dropped his diary. Last year, in the Nagaoka Museum, where it is preserved to this day, I read the entry he had made on the day Yamagata visited him: "Today Kyōsuke came for an audience." Kyōsuke, the name Yamagata used as a young man, was written in Saionji's diary, however, with the characters meaning "crazy boy." One should not try to read too much into this, but it would be a bad mistake to write in one's diary that someone by that misspelled name had come for an audience. I guessed that Saionji must have made the slip by accident, as ever since boyhood he was used to being at the palace, where he was a page to Emperor Meiji, and accustomed to receiving people in audience.

My first meeting with Saionji was around the time of the formation of the Seiyūkai. I was visiting Itō at his Ōiso villa, Sōrō kaku, when Itō suggested I should also meet Saionji, and sent a messenger to call the prince, who had a villa adjacent to Itō's. The prince appeared in his morning coat. A table and chairs were set out in a tatami room, where we sat after having taken off our shoes, but Saionji entered the house from the garden and kept his shoes on when he joined us in the tatami room. It was a sight to remember. There was no pretense about him, but still he had the natural bearing of a prince. This sort of thing could only come from his upbringing.

Itō introduced Saionji, saying, "This man is Japan's Rosebery." Lord Rosebery was an English statesman of extreme generosity and unselfishness who had married a Rothschild girl, became prime minister, and whose horse won the Derby— a triply lucky man.[1]

Saionji was without a rival in his sagacity and wisdom. When it came to putting his finger on the weakness of another and prevailing with one powerful word he had no equal. So when Yamagata encouraged him to organize a cabinet he saw right through him and asked, "Are you saying this on His Majesty's orders?" When Yamagata replied that he was acting of his own accord, Saionji put him on the spot. "In that case," he said, "I must decline. One should not discuss such matters unless ordered by the throne." Yamagata was an exceptionally ceremonious person in such matters, so it must have been terribly embarrassing to him when Saionji so adroitly drove a dagger right into his weak spot. Few if any except Saionji could put in his place a man as scrupulously cautious as Yamagata. Apparently this was not the only occurrence of this sort. Saionji frequently got the better of him, it seems, so Yamagata often complained of him to his men as "that scoundrel!"

Since the wise and observant Saionji had cleverly evaded taking the government, the succession to the premiership was passed along among the genrō, but none offered to accept the post for fear of Itō. A promising candidate was at last found in Inoue Kaoru, a good friend of Itō's. Inoue apparently was keen to try his luck and began to consult people with a view to putting a cabinet together.

Even from our perspective Inoue was not really prime-minister material. Ōkuma, for some strange reason, perhaps because they were similar in some ways, made it a point to defend Inoue even when they found themselves in the arena as enemies. On the other hand, most damning of all, perhaps, was Ōkuma's faint praise: "Inoue may make mistakes sometimes," he said patronizingly, "but he is no villain." According to Ōkuma, a person who committed wrong knowingly was to be blamed, but since Inoue was never aware of the fact that he had done wrong he was not a villain.

The first time I met Inoue was during the time of the notorious opposition we put up to his planned revision of the Unequal Treaties. Inoue was energetic and sharp, and full of an intrepid spirit, which showed between his eyes with ominous features in his forbidding glare. Observing his behavior over the years, I realized

---

[1] Rosebery was also an admirer of Japan. Sensing a contrast between England's performance in the Boer War and Japan's endurance in the Russo-Japanese War, he sponsored a "Learn from Japan" movement.

that his passionate loyalty to the country far outweighed what we had seen as a political obstacle, having sacrificed his whole life in the interest of the nation. Straightforward and ardent by nature, his passions seemed to intensify with advancing age. He was born a Chōshū man, but he had the disposition of an Edokko (Tokyoite)—single-minded, that is, and a man who could not be trusted to control himself when angered. On every count he seemed unfit to lead the cabinet.

Despite his efforts, as it happened, Inoue could not put a cabinet together and gave up the attempt. The crown was still being passed around the genrō like a hot potato until finally it came to Katsura. He seized on the opportunity that his seniors had shunned. Itō had not been expecting this. Katsura had a fierce warrior of a follower by the name of Sone Arasuke, who had been hounding him to "snatch at the chance if it comes your way, if only to surprise Itō." Also among Katsura's followers was Kodama Gentarō, a man of great resourcefulness who schemed to set the stage for Katsura's bid.

Itō was predictably unhappy about this turn of events and took off for Europe. Japan's relations with Russia were deteriorating rapidly, and Itō was entrusted with the grave mission of negotiating an understanding between the two empires. He left for Russia with Emperor Meiji's approval on September 18, 1901. By then Hoshi had already died, and as the Diet was scheduled to open shortly, Itō instructed Matsuda Masahisa and myself to act jointly as majority whips, and departed leaving everything to us.

OUTPLAYED BY KATSURA

Itō left for Europe without issuing any instructions with regard to the political tug-of-war that would occur during his absence. I took that as a carte-blanche power of attorney. Itō should have known that I had consistently taken an aggressive attitude towards every cabinet. If he wished Katsura to be helped, he should have left appropriate instructions. I interpreted Itō's silent departure as an order to bring down the Katsura cabinet during his absence. If this was not what he expected then it was not conceivable that he would leave without saying so. I took it, therefore, that he was leaving the country while I did the dirty work of finishing off the Katsura government, as his presence might be an impediment.

For me to lead the Seiyūkai's assault did not bode well. Hoshi was already dead, but our party was still dominated by the old Jiyūtō people. It was, after all, the party against which I had fought for the last twenty years. By then my own old colleagues were with the Kensei Hontō. However, the party had atrophied and its attitude toward the government was ambiguous. I was resolved, however, to bring Katsura down before Itō returned to the country and launched an attack before even half a year had passed since his cabinet was formed.

The Katsura cabinet was a young cabinet, to put it kindly, but it was also called a "second-rate cabinet" or "vice-minister cabinet." It was a completely unaffiliated cabinet to which not a single member of a political party belonged. The cabinet ministers were all junior men from the Yamagata group and were completely isolated in the Diet. Behind it, however, stood Yamagata. From my previous association with him I had nothing but contempt for Prime Minister Katsura, but his cabinet contained Sone Arasuke and Yamamoto Gonnohyōe, of whom I thought highly. In the cabinet, Yamamoto held the naval post while Sone doubled as minister of finance and foreign affairs.

When the sixteenth session (December 1901–March 1902) began, I chose Finance Minister Sone as my first target. The government had compiled a budget based on incorporating into the general account war reparations from China, but we were opposed to this and I questioned the government on three points. Unexpectedly, the finance minister was unable to offer a single convincing answer, quickly plunging the government into difficulty. The Katsura cabinet's back buckled. Encouraged by this successful strike, I was pressing my advantage when the prime minister, maintaining a low personal profile, offered a compromise.

We regarded the Katsura cabinet with disdain when Sone, whom we thought to be more of a man, surrendered for the government without putting up a fight. We set two conditions to their offer to compromise. We demanded that since the thrust of our position was financial, Sone should not be present as he was ill-versed in the field. We also said we would meet them at the Imperial Hotel rather than our having to go over to the prime minister's residence. We honestly did not expect Katsura to accept our rather unreasonable ultimatum, but to our surprise he agreed to both our demands. The government was represented by the prime minister and Naval Minister Yamamoto, while for the Seiyūkai there was Matsuda Masahisa and I.

Had I been more thoughtful I might have realized that the prime minister would not have accepted our demands so meekly if he did not have something up his sleeve. It is written in Sun tzu's *Art of War* that "those who keep a low posture and make preparations will advance." It is wrong, the master stated, to assume that polite words from an enemy signal his retreat; on the contrary, they must be seen as a sign of an imminent advance.

With my sense of importance and arrogant mind I did not think. I imagined I only needed one last blow to finish Katsura off. His manner was gentle and his words soft, but he did not accept our main demands. Apparently at the request of the government, Inoue Kaoru attempted to mediate between the two parties, but the principal figure in all this, Katsura himself, pleading illness, failed to come to the meeting Inoue had arranged. I realized for the first time that Katsura had no regard for Inoue.

No sooner had we realized that things were not going according to plan, than opposition rose within the ranks of the Seiyūkai even as we were negotiating with the government. The dissident members stayed away from our headquarters and set themselves up in an office in Hama-no-te restaurant in Karasumori, often frequented by the elite of both the government and of the opposition during the early years of the Meiji era.

This rebellious group included Den Kenjirō, Inoue Kakugorō, and Ogawa Hei-kichi—powerful men within the party. They were for striking a compromise with the government, and while Matsuda and I negotiated on behalf of the Seiyūkai, twenty or thirty members of this group were simultaneously carrying out secret negotiations with the government. It was a clever tactic for Katsura to play his hand in this way, knowing about this group that was waiting to ambush us. He must have calculated that the more high-handed he allowed me to appear, the more sympathy he would gain from those willing to compromise within my own party.

With my own shaky base there was little I could do. I expelled the dubious members from the party and continued to negotiate, but the number of defectors at the Hama-no-te increased all the time and eventually I lost control of the situation.

Following our first meeting with Katsura at the Imperial Hotel another was arranged at the prime minister's official residence, but we were steadily losing ground. The traitors had got in through the back door before us and were already talking with the government. What with mutineers leaving the party and fire breaking out behind us, I had walked into a trap of my own making.

At length a cable reached me from Itō in Russia: "Do not push too hard." According to one source, Itō Miyoji had reported to Itō that I was being unreasonably pushy. The telegrams we sent to the prince went through Inoue. Inoue forwarded them in the coded language of the ministry of foreign affairs and the replies came back via the ministry in the same code. This meant that before we received our telegrams the government already knew their contents.

I was defeated, forced to sound the retreat with dishonor, to compromise with Katsura, and await the return of Itō. Matsuda occupied a higher position than I within the party and was probably in a better position to know what was on Itō's mind, but he had left things to me from the beginning and did not intervene. Katsura had certainly outplayed me. I was completely outmaneuvered by this man, whom I thought I could handle, and I alone was responsible for the Seiyūkai's first fiasco.

Though it is little consolation now, I was not the only person to be outdone by Katsura. Itō himself was another. At the time, as I have mentioned, Itō was in Russia negotiating to improve relations. Quite out of the blue and contrary to Itō's plans, the possibility of an alliance with Britain had come up and talks in that direction were already far advanced. Itō was of the opinion that an alliance between Japan and Britain anticipated war with Russia and therefore was against the national interest. I was of the same opinion, but I was not in a position to do anything to check the progress of Japan's convergence with Britain.

Britain had shown little interest in concluding an alliance with Japan, which was then generally regarded as a second- or third-rate power. But quite by accident the British secretary for the colonies, Joseph Chamberlain, learned of Itō's attempts to negotiate an agreement with Russia and proposed a British alliance with Japan to forestall a possible Russo-Japanese alliance turning against Britain.

It was rumored that Prime Minister Katsura and Foreign Minister Komura used Itō, in spite of his feelings on the matter, to conclude an alliance with Britain. It was only natural that Itō should have disclosed to the emperor the purpose of his journey to Moscow and likewise should have communicated it fully to Katsura. The unexpected emergence of a possible Japanese alliance with Britain thrust Itō into a difficult position, forcing him to leave Russia for Berlin under cover of darkness.

Katsura was proud of his achievement in forging the Anglo-Japanese Alliance and often said to me later that nothing had given him greater satisfaction. He was implying that Emperor Meiji had rejected Itō's view and found Katsura's suggestion of an alliance with Britain more to his liking. Since Katsura had in fact merely reacted to a British initiative, there was no real reason for him to be so pleased with himself. Still, he no doubt wanted to boast that he rather than Itō enjoyed the greater confidence of the emperor.

On the conclusion of the alliance with Britain all the members of the Japanese cabinet were awarded peerages or elevated to higher ranks. No one in Britain was so honored. Later, when the alliance became the object of criticism in Japan, those who had received rewards might in retrospect have felt a little embarrassed. At the time, however, the fact that the Katsura cabinet was able to take credit for having accomplished an alliance with Britain, which was then considered to be a country above our station, had promoted it from one of 'vice-ministers' to respectability, at least in its own eyes.

COMPROMISE

Although I had suffered at the hands of Katsura, I was determined to harbor my strength and wait for my next chance. In the seventeenth Diet, which convened on December 6, 1902, the Katsura cabinet submitted, in addition to the land tax increase bill, a naval expansion bill. My strategy, with the backing of the majority of Seiyūkai members, was to support the government bill for the naval expansion, but to oppose the land tax increase.

By then our Seiyūkai head, Itō Hirobumi, had returned and we were able to fight with renewed unity. The Kensei Hontō also expressed its opposition to the tax increase, and Katō Takaaki accepted the main responsibility for bringing Itō and Ōkuma together again. At his invitation the two met at Katō's residence, reaffirmed their friendship, and agreed to wrestle jointly against the government. The Teikokutō and the 1901 Group declared their opposition to the government too. The government and the political parties had now completely parted company, leaving the Katsura cabinet totally isolated.

But the government stuck to its guns in the face of a hostile parliament and on the very first day of the new Diet submitted its naval expansion and tax increase bills. The budget committee refused to listen to the government's arguments, however and, ignoring its blandishments and attempts at pressure, rejected the tax increase bill by a vote of twenty-seven to three and referred it for deliberation to the joint committee.

The government, with the support of most of the ministers, had tried in vain to protect its original bill, and now there remained little or no hope that it could regain its lost momentum. With no other course left open to it the government asked the throne for a five-day recess, during which it sought to buy and tempt as many politicians as it could reach and otherwise destroy the unity of the opposition parties. This did not work either. The government therefore asked for another week's recess. This time, as a last resort, Army Minister Kodama Gentarō visited Itō in Hakone where he was staying to ask him to mediate a compromise solution, but Itō refused.

The reconciliation between the leaders of the two main parties, Itō and Ōkuma, left the Katsura government without any means of escape, and it took the last possible step of dissolving the House just before the vote was to be taken on the controversial tax issue. Katsura often boasted afterward that he had unflinchingly stood up to the two great statesmen, Itō and Ōkuma. He was referring to his decision to dissolve the house.

A general election was held on March 1, 1903. The government did everything it could to influence the outcome, but the public would not accept its planned tax increase and gave the opposition a resounding victory. The result was 193 seats for the Seiyūkai, 91 for the Kensei Hontō, and 18 for the Teikokutō, with the remaining 73 distributed among the minor parties and independents.

It seemed that the Katsura cabinet's fate was sealed. At the last minute, however, Katsura appealed to his sponsor, Yamagata, to make a final attempt to broker a compromise and begged Itō to come to his rescue. Itō, whatever his reason, sent word without even consulting us, the leaders of his own party, that he would accept a compromise solution. When I learned what had happened I insisted that we could not possibly give away what we had steadfastly opposed even at the risk of dissolution, and that we must fight to the end, but it was to no avail. A compromise had indeed been struck between President Itō and Prime Minister Katsura. A new term for compromise—"dakyō"—coined by Itō at this time has since entered popular use.

Feeling uneasy, perhaps, over what he had done, Itō invited me and some others to a dinner as a gesture of apology and recounted to us what had happened. I was not in the least mollified, however, and rather curtly said, "We cannot let you keep getting away with this sort of thing. It has been a blow to our honor." This rubbed Itō the wrong way and he turned on me angrily and asked if I knew the saying "It is the mark of a small man to utter only words which can be trusted and do only that which brings results." He was quoting one of the sayings of Confucius which taught that it was the mark of a small man, like a small stone, obstinate and inflexible, to believe that promises must be honored regardless of circumstances. Afterwards, some friends who had overheard my heated exchange with Itō told me that I had come out of it relatively unscathed. In my place, they said, they would have been reprimanded more severely.

I said earlier that Ōkuma never lost his temper, but Itō did and quite often. He did not conceal his emotions. In this respect he was a child. During the short period I was close to him I saw him lose his temper frequently.

Some time after that last incident, at a large gathering for members of the Seiyūkai at the Kōyō-kan, Mochizuki Kōtarō, in the course of a speech, made fun of Itō's weakness for compromise. Itō exploded with fury, and, while Mochizuki was still speaking, shouted, "How dare you, Mochizuki! I have made my way through drawn swords. I will not let brats like you make a laughing stock of me. Bring your sword. I'll show you how to use it!" I was sitting only a couple of seats away from Itō and could hardly keep a straight face. The Kōyō-kan had a stage. There were undoubtedly plenty of wooden swords and daggers somewhere.

I tried to catch Mochizuki's attention. "Backstage, backstage!" I hissed as loudly as I dared, but he did not hear. With Itō so close, the best I could do was gesture to Mochizuki to fetch swords from behind, but I could not make him understand. In the end Mochizuki offered his apologies and the issue was closed. It would have been amusing, though, if he had accepted Itō's challenge to a duel, then gone backstage for two wooden swords. Some of the young party members with bureaucratic souls spoke encouragingly to Mochizuki afterwards. "We really envy you for catching it from Itō," one of them said. "One would have to be really close to him to be treated like that. If only we could have such a close relationship!" It was what palace maids would have said. This is the way the mind of a bureaucrat works.

I WITHDRAW FROM THE SEIYŪKAI

I was disgusted at the compromise the Seiyūkai had struck with Katsura. The more I thought about it the more uncertain I was as to what course I should now take. I decided to leave the party.

Readers may think that a compromise over a tax increase, and a small increase at that, did not justify my resignation. But my honor as a politician was at stake. When I tendered my resignation to Itō, he spent a full two hours at the party headquarters trying to get me to change my mind. To be sure, he had to confront the Yamagata/Katsura alliance, which defied him in the House, and things were not going all that well within the Seiyūkai either. He must have been in a very tight spot because he tried every way he knew to persuade me not to go. But I would not reverse my decision, so I left him and went home.

The next day Itō sent his son-in-law Suematsu Kenchō to get me to change my mind. He repeated the same things over and over so many times that I lost patience with him. "It will make no difference to my decision however many times you repeat yourself. Now, be kind enough to leave." Suematsu appeared quite shaken. "Please excuse me for saying this," he said rather pitifully, "but Itō wants you to know that he is willing to look after your expenses for the rest of your life if you will stay." This was more than I could stomach. I took great offense and replied furiously: "Is that so! I thought Mr. Itō would have known better than to imagine that I of all people would change my mind for such an offer. I am extremely indignant at him, as well as at myself for my own lack of judgment in allowing myself to work with such a person." At that time I was as poor as always and had mountainous debts. But since I hated bowing my head to anyone, my debts were all owed to usurious moneylenders from whom I could borrow without abasing myself. I suppose the offer was made with good will on Itō's part, but from that day I lost all respect for him.

When I left the party, Kataoka Kenkichi said he would resign too. I had been closer to Kataoka than any other person in the Seiyūkai. He could see things objectively, and he knew the difference between right and wrong. He was a virtuous man, and as president of the House he said little, but performed his function well. For many years we had been political foes, but never once had he shown me any animosity. When at last we found ourselves on the same side in the Seiyūkai we instinctively trusted each other. When we left the capital to go campaigning, Kataoka always asked to come with me, so we had traveled together to Kyūshū, Hokkaido, and Shikoku. "Come and help me campaign back home," he once asked me. When I agreed he arranged for welcoming arches to be erected on the road where his district began. I had never once received such a welcome on a campaign tour. And Kataoka was not the sort of man to have any ulterior motive, so I took it simply as a sign of his feeling for me.

We were good friends now, but when Kataoka told me of his intention to resign with me from the party, I felt I should advise him to reconsider as his position was different from mine. He was in rather poor health in those days, but he said there was no hope for the party without me, and left. Thirty other men followed him. This was the biggest blow to the Seiyūkai in its whole existence. I left the party entirely over the issue of the land tax. But since there was no disagreement on other issues, I continued to support it even after my departure. I had created a small organization of my own, but on most issues I stood by my old party.

ITŌ IS APPOINTED TO THE PRIVY COUNCIL

The Katsura cabinet, given a new lease on life as a result of the compromise struck with Itō, managed to manipulate the Seiyūkai and survive the eighteenth Diet. Its position, however, was extremely precarious as it did not have a single man in the House of Representatives.

Itō still constituted a potential menace to the government, though, because he not only was a close confidant of the emperor as a *genrō*, but wielded great power as president of a huge political party. When the session closed, Katsura took advantage of his senior Yamagata's unquenchable hatred of Itō for leading a political party, requested a meeting with Itō and Yamagata and asked Itō to step down either as *genrō* or party president. Itō emphatically rejected Katsura's request. "I was given the title of *genrō* by His Majesty because of my long years of service, and this cannot be withdrawn. The presidency of a political party is my mission, and I am dedicated to completing the establishment of constitutional government in this country. This I shall definitely not renounce."

Prime Minister Katsura's next strategy was to announce his own decision to resign. "Today, when our diplomacy with Russia demands stern resolution founded on strong national unity, this is hardly possible so long as Itō wields a two-edged sword as *genrō* and head of a political party. The attitude of the Seiyūkai during the eighteenth Diet is proof of this. I shall therefore withdraw from my position and ask that the empire's greatest statesman head the cabinet so that he may without hesitation, address the pressing issues of the nation."

On July 1, 1903, Katsura submitted his resignation. However, at a time when there was a need to adopt a strong policy towards Russia and to be prepared for war in case Russia refused to accept our demands, it was considered not in the interest of the nation to change the cabinet. Accordingly, Yamagata and those around him schemed that the only thing to do under the circumstances was to let Itō walk the red carpet to the privy council as its president, from which elevation he would be in a position to assist the Katsura cabinet and so materially help to create national unity. The best way to achieve this was to plead with Emperor Meiji to order it.

Yamagata was soon summoned to the palace with Matsukata, and when His Majesty inquired what was to be done as a result of Prime Minister Katsura's resignation, the two princes promptly advised him as follows: "The present circumstances do not permit an unstable cabinet. It is desirable therefore that incumbent ministers be retained in their posts. However, if Itō Hirobumi in his present capacity as head of a political party is permitted to attack successive cabinet measures, he may obstruct the necessary functions of the government. It is therefore loyally requested that Itō be commanded to relinquish his position as party president in exchange for an important post in the privy council. In this manner all the *genrō* may be united to lend their assistance to the cabinet. Nothing would be more conducive to the happiness of the State."

Yamagata continued, "Itō will not listen to anyone unless he receives a direct command from Your Majesty. Please grant him this." Emperor Meiji in his wisdom was constantly attentive to both sides of any issue, so at the end of Yamagata's petition, His Majesty saw through the plot conceived by Yamagata and his followers to remove Itō as party head and was displeased. It was said that His Majesty then made a blunt inquiry: "I have listened to what you have to say, but what will you do if Itō accepts the presidency of the privy council but opposes leaving the party presidency? How would you know what Itō thinks?" Yamagata, it is said, was taken aback at this. Yamagata pleaded that not only they, but Itō's own man, Itō Miyoji, and others, were of the same mind. His Majesty then summoned Itō Miyoji, who respectfully presented himself. In response to the emperor's questioning he submitted his firm resolve: "Should Itō not accept Your Majesty's command, I promise to ensure that he and I will both take our lives. I shall see to it that he accepts your instruction." His majesty smiled at this and then at last granted the imperial order.

On July 6, the emperor summoned Itō and granted him an audience in an inner room of the palace. According to reliable sources, the emperor spoke to Itō as follows: "We must today negotiate with Russia over the Korean and Manchurian issues. This is a grave matter whose outcome is unpredictable. Therefore I wish you to be counted among the privy councilors and advise on these and other important matters of the state. Please give this your devoted attention and follow my wish."

Itō was surprised by these unexpected words and withdrew, pleading for a few days' grace to contemplate this development. As Itō had still not responded, in August the emperor sent his master chamberlain to the inn where Itō was staying. The chamberlain handed him a written transcript of what the emperor said to him the previous month.

"In view of the present state of affairs," ran the document, "I have decided to call again upon your enlightened services and to charge you with the heavy responsibilities of the Privy Council, so that you may attend to and advise on essential matters of the state. Moreover, much is still to be done to complete the undertakings begun by you within our country and overseas since the Restoration. I am desirous that you should complete what you have set out to do in your years of devoted service."

At first the emperor had been greatly displeased on perceiving what Yamagata and his men thought, but it was true nonetheless that national unity was now required in the face of diplomatic developments. While it was necessary to retain Katsura as prime minister, the assistance and advice of Itō were also earnestly desired. And whereas the emperor expressed no objection to Itō serving as party president, he must have pondered the possible difficulty of Itō's advising the throne while acting as a party chief. At times, Itō might find it difficult to act on his own behalf as a party president. These and other considerations, I believe, resulted in the imperial writ.

Itō was at first indignant at what Yamagata had done, but, when he realized what was on the emperor's mind, he understood what he had to do and decided respectfully to obey the imperial order. For Itō, leading a political party or serving the emperor in an advisory capacity both were contributions to the development of constitutional government.

In describing how Itō came to join the privy council, I have leaned most heavily for the details on Watanabe Ikujirō's account. It was the combination of conspiracy on the part of Yamagata and those under him, concern on the part of Inoue Kaoru and others for Itō, and the emperor's wish to have the prince assist him that made Itō decide to leave the Seiyūkai and assume the presidency of the privy council. Also, the success of Yamagata's conspiracy was only possible because of the extraordinary times, which found the nation on the eve of war with Russia. If these had been normal times, Itō would not have been so easily enshrined in the privy council.

On resigning from the presidency of the Seiyūkai, Itō recommended Saionji as his successor. Without Saionji, most of the former government officials who joined the party with Itō might have left again when he did. Under the wise and lucid leadership of Saionji, the Seiyūkai enjoyed greater unity than it did under Itō. Party business was mainly attended to by Matsuda Masahisa and Hara Takashi.

1. Ozaki in his prime. Photograph of September 1, 1937.

2. Ozaki with his wife, Yei Theodora, and daughters Shinaye and Yukika. Photograph taken at Karuizawa summer home, 1922.

3. Ozaki with dogs at his Zushi residence, 1935.

4. Ozaki speaking in the Imperial Diet, February 7, 1937.

5. Ozaki addressing a Shimbashi crowd, April 18, 1947.

6. Ozaki addressing a Shinjuku crowd in support of his long-time associate Tagawa Daikichiro during the Imperial Rule Assistance Association elections ordered by the Tōjō government in 1941. Later in the campaign Ozaki was arrested and briefly imprisoned, but not convicted, on charges of lèse majesté.

7. Ozaki, ninety years old and invited to America by the American Council on Japan, at a New York banquet held in his honor in 1950. On his right is Joseph Grew, U.S. ambassador to Japan from 1932 to 1941.

The Era of the Russo-Japanese War

I BECOME MAYOR OF TOKYO

After leaving the Seiyūkai over my difference of opinion with its president, Itō Hirobumi, I decided to remain an independent and take life a little more easily for a while as my nerves had been under considerable strain. Then out of the blue some old friends, Maruyama Masana of the Shimpotō and Nakahachi Yoshiaki of the Seiyūkai, came to see me to ask if I would like to be mayor of Tokyo. I had been involved in the city administration as a member of the standing committee of the Tokyo prefectural assembly, but that was before the separation of the city and the prefecture. Since then I had performed no official duties for the city and had paid little attention to its affairs.

I was surprised by the unexpected offer and inclined to refuse on account of my health. I told my two friends that I was frankly in no condition to take on a burdensome post. However, they assured me that as my deputies they would attend to all the onerous affairs of the city. All I had to do was to come in for the council meetings, which met two to three times a week. I need not even come to the office every day. They made it sound so easy that I took their word for it and accepted the offer without much thought. After all, I was an unemployed *rōnin* with few means of survival, which in itself was not the best thing for my health. It seemed a heaven-sent opportunity if the job was reasonably well paid and as undemanding as my friends intimated.

One might legitimately ask why I, with few connections, had been offered the job. I soon found out that it was entirely the work of men who had been close to Hoshi Tōru. As I said earlier, Hoshi had wanted to collaborate with me toward the end of his life. Even after his death, his men were often supportive.

"You must be joking," I said to them. "Why do you come to me when you know very well my principles lie elsewhere?" I asked Kawakami Yukiyoshi, one of Hoshi's more notorious blackguards. "No sir, it's not a joke. We mean it," he answered. "The old man (Hoshi) would never accept bribes. He wasn't that sort, sir. We must clear him of his bad name, and how better than for him to be associated with a person as famous for his honesty as you. Anyway, toward the end of his life Hoshi used to say the best thing for him was to work with you. This is why we want you to be mayor." I realized then that Hoshi had been serious when he said he wanted to work with me.

Thanks to Hoshi's group, who brought over most of the city assemblymen to our side, and by joining forces with the group of independents, I became the choice of the majority. In fact, with the Hoshi people's almost unanimous endorsement, I was sworn in as the second mayor of Tokyo on June 29, 1903.

With the prospect of a new job, I looked forward to the more relaxed and less stressful life that awaited me. I soon found out that I was poorly qualified for many of the tasks required of me at the city office, and that there was a never-ending river of trifling matters that awaited the mayor's decision. I realized too late the error of my hasty decision.

When I attended my first council meeting they were in the middle of debating the price of lumber and the cost per *tsubo* of a lane flanked by chestnut trees, things with which I was totally unfamiliar. I remembered I had once come across the English proverb "Knowledge is power." Now I realized what it meant. For instance, Nonoyama Kōkichi, who had always struck me as a very mediocre person, knew everything there was to know about the price of stone and lumber. Moreover, he was aware that he could use his knowledge against me. If I always allowed him to have his own way I was sure to be criticized as the know-nothing mayor. Fortunately, I thought, among the councilors were old friends like Ōishi Masami, Ōoka Ikuzō, Kōmuchi Tomotsune, Ebara Sōroku, Okuda Gijin, and Watase Torajirō. Of these, Ōishi especially had been like a brother to me, and I secretly expected Ōishi and Kōmuchi to back me up. I found I was wrong, though, when they sided with my critics.

It was too absurd for words, and I was sorely tempted to resign. The only thing that made me hesitate was the knowledge that I would be a laughing-stock if I stepped down without achieving anything. It was not long, however, before the council adopted a resolution of no confidence in me as mayor. I realized I could not resign at that point, even if I wanted to, because my honor was at stake. Had they not faced me with a no-confidence resolution, I might have stepped down, but not after that. I would have to fight it out with all my resources. Instead of what I had hoped would be a pleasant post, I was thrust into an arduous occupation and into fighting disagreeable battles even against my old friends.

People from Another World

The city council expected that a no-confidence vote would be enough to force a short-tempered person like me out of office. Seeing that I had no intention of leaving, they turned to meaner tactics, the sort mothers-in-law might use against their daughters-in-law. At almost every council meeting they would ask me questions about the cost of stone, or lumber, or of cleaning the sewers. They then proceeded to take over functions that were supposed to be part of the mayor's job. As it happened, therefore, I was quite content to give up such trivial duties.

At the time the city council was not a decision-making body, but an administrative office. The mayor was simply a civil servant who carried out resolutions of the council and possessed little authority. Strictly speaking, every chore, from the appointment and dismissal of janitors to the purchase of trivia for all the city offices, was the prerogative of the council. In reality, however, the appointment and dismissal of civil servants below a certain level and the purchase of goods below a certain price were, by referral from the city council, the happy duty of the mayor. I did not grieve deeply at the loss of these privileges. Secretly, I hoped that this avalanche of trifling issues would try the patience of my critical colleagues. I saw it as a sort of counterattack.

Now that the council members had burdened themselves with having to attend to every mundane detail, they were obliged, as I had gleefully foreseen, to increase the number of their meetings. After a while they became desperate and wanted to return these commissions to the mayor. But it was my turn to play, and I refused. In the end this juvenile episode was settled by having the mayor's power expanded. The councilors still continued, however, to use every trick they had to make trouble for me.

To my great surprise, reinforcements appeared from an unexpected quarter. Ezaki Reiji, who operated a photo studio near Asakusa park, was a man of enormous vitality and forceful character, and who for some time was involved in city government. He put the following question before the council: "The mayor is elected by the city assembly as are members of the council. Now, on the grounds of what article of the city regulations did council members feel empowered to recommend the resignation of the mayor, or to adopt a resolution of no confidence against him?"—Needless to say, there was no such article anywhere in the city regulations.

Ezaki continued, "If a satisfactory explanation is not forthcoming, then the council members will do well to offer the city assembly an apology for having overstepped their mandate. If they choose otherwise, they will have to be asked to resign." This was a cause of great embarrassment to the council members. Ōishi Masami and Kōmuchi Tomotsune and some others were weary of their unimportant jobs anyway and took the opportunity to resign. Ōoka Ikuzō secretly apologized to the city assembly and retained his seat. After this, there was a reshuffle of the council, and the mayor's authority was expanded.

Ezaki and his associates had not, however, acted to support the mayor out of any altruistic sense; they had their eyes on the council seats that had been opened as a result of their tactics. When a by-election was held to fill the now-vacant seats, they were duly elected.

Since I first took office as chief editor of the *Niigata Shinbun* late in 1879, twenty-three verdant springs and as many rainy autumns had passed. During these years I had met many types of people from the political world, bright and resourceful ones, as well as scoundrels. I thought I knew more or less all the varieties, but one of the surprises I encountered as mayor was the discovery of completely different kinds of people, people I had never seen or even imagined. They might have been from a different planet.

They spoke and led their lives in ways that often were not, by the standards I knew, admirable. And to my amazement they had a strange energy that prompted them to act at every opportunity without reservation or courtesy. There were men who had come to Tokyo from the countryside, intending to make a living with their bare hands, but some of them did well by bullying everyone unlucky enough to be in their way. They did have astonishing vitality and courage, however, and they had real ability, but they were also capable of trying cheap tricks to advance themselves. Confident to a fault, they treated the old veterans and rascals of the political world without respect like *bocchan*—spoiled sons from good families. Even Ōishi and Kōmuchi, veterans of many battles, were treated like children by them, and found themselves at the mercy of those used to the downtown *shita-machi* neighborhoods—the rough and vulgar parts of town where instinct was law and might was right. As a result, Ōoka felt obliged to offer apologies to Ezaki and his group.

How is it that people like this could get the better of well known and experienced politicians? It was because they simply had no respect for the moral standards that are observed in our society. To put it more starkly, they had no standards of any sort. An educated person, however experienced and cunning, possessed certain standards. Something prevented him from easily speaking or acting contrary to such standards. If he were tempted to do so, his conscience would bother him, a situation that gave his opponents the opportunity to exploit the weakness he thus betrayed. Uneducated but resourceful people used to making their own rules maintained no standards. They moved with wanton freedom to suit their convenience. The educated person moved in spheres where the standards he knew existed. This was why even the veterans of the political world often found themselves put at a tactical disadvantage by uneducated and mercenary commoners. Being mayor taught me that there were all sorts of unfamiliar and interesting people in our society.

REVISING TOKYO CITY BOROUGHS, WATER, AND DRAINAGE

The years flew by and before I realized it I had spent nearly ten years as mayor. During this time I worked on various projects, and gradually accumulated a fair amount of knowledge. Although I was out of national politics, local government was after all an essential aspect of constitutional democracy. Let me therefore refer quite briefly to this period.

The first project I was involved in was replanning. The improvement of the various municipal administrative districts had been a pending issue for some time, but in the past only makeshift redevelopment had taken place in areas ravaged by fire. Since the project had always been limited by a very tight budget, the years went by with little progress or any great improvement. For example, when a major fire broke out between Shinbashi and Kyōbashi in the early Meiji years, it resulted in buildings being rebuilt in brick. For a time it was a model district of wide streets and roofs built to new standards. The busy district between Kyōbashi and Manseibashi, however, remained much the same as it had always been during the Tokugawa period. After the Ginza Street was rebuilt, traffic congestion became extremely bad and there were many injuries to both people and horses.

"Why is something not done about it?" I asked, and I was told that land there was too expensive for the city to purchase. Apparently a *tsubo* of land cost two hundred to three hundred yen. This seemed very cheap to me. Anyway, it would have been much to our advantage in the long run had we gone ahead with redevelopment then rather than later. I therefore had something like fifteen million yen worth of foreign bonds issued to finance the re-planning of the municipal districts. The idea was to start with the area between Kyōbashi and Manseibashi, where the land was most expensive, and then to extend the project to other parts.

When the project actually began, land in the Kyōbashi–Manseibashi area cost less than originally budgeted. In fact, as I recall, there was a considerable amount of money left unspent. When the city plan was redrawn, the land I had purchased for a hundred yen a *tsubo* immediately shot up to eight hundred yen. All the main parts of the Tokyo municipal area were successfully redrawn in this way.

The idea of financing the Tokyo districts redevelopment project with foreign bonds had the support of Tsunoda Shinpei from the beginning. Tsunoda had not been favorably disposed to me at first, but he changed his attitude with his enthusiasm for the project. I knew that he was a talented administrator and decided to put him in charge. I was right to do so. As director-general in charge of municipal districts redevelopment, he worked diligently and sensibly.

Tsunoda had been an outstanding young member of Numa's group and a member of the Ōmeisha Society when it was pitted against our Toyo Giseikai in the early days of the Kaishintō. He liked to read haiku poems from an early age, and taking the pen name "Chikurei" produced some clever verses. Noda Taikai was one of his pupils. "Roasting Whitebait, a Product of Edo" was probably one of Chikurei's proudest works.

On the question of issuing foreign bonds to finance municipal redevelopment, I thought that having had to borrow so much myself due to my persistent poverty I was an experienced borrower. When I borrowed for myself, however, I could allow myself to borrow at high interest, but the same could not be said if I were to borrow on behalf of the city of Tokyo. Rather than begging for a lower interest rate I preferred to borrow from a loan shark and be done with it. For the sake of the city I now had to approach the business of borrowing from a very different angle.

Borrowing at low interest was, unlike borrowing at high rates, extremely difficult. Veteran borrower that I was, I thought I had earned myself a doctorate in borrowing, but I found myself faced with so many problems it was almost embarrassing. A slight difference, say of one-tenth of a percent in interest rates, would make a difference in interest payments on a loan of ten million yen amounting to hundreds of thousands. This attracted men, both Japanese and foreigners, to offer their services as agents. Those who were disappointed at not getting the job turned against those who did because of their success. This resulted in unexpected complications, due to which I thought at one time the whole project would fail, but it finally worked out.

During a municipal assembly meeting one day, commission became an issue. "Floating fifteen million yen worth of foreign bonds should have earned several hundred thousand yen in commission. What has the mayor done with the money?" The question was addressed to me. I was upset and not a little angered at this question, which I thought discourteous, and I indignantly retorted: "At no time in my thirty years of political life have I been asked such a vexing question. I do not even know what commission you are talking about. I therefore have no idea whether any such thing is due. I am quite sure there will be nothing of the kind. If the city ever does receive these hundreds of thousands of yen you speak of, I shall consult the questioner, who is evidently an expert on the subject, to decide how it should be dispensed." The chamber was silent, and the questioner had a very red face.

After redrawing Tokyo, the next project was to expand the city's water supply. I thought we had enough water, but following a long spell of drought there was now concern about a possible water shortage. Engineers often miscalculate.

Improving the sewage system was another challenge. When I assumed office there was no such system in the Yamanote upland district. Soiled water was freely discharged and left to dissipate underground. To correct the situation I had a system built to serve the district, but the effluent now drained into the Shitamachi low city districts. The canals became filthy, and those crisscrossing the Shitamachi district were so evil-smelling that it was almost unbearable there during summer. An increasing number of Western-style buildings made the situation even more intolerable due to the night soil discharged from their toilets.

The canal that ran behind the Imperial Hotel was called the *ohaguro mizo* or "black ditch," and presented a vile sight. This was a recurrent issue every time special guests were to be received at the hotel. The canal was so dirty that I had to take personal charge of the area, resulting in an imperfect proposal to fill the ditch to the brim with water to disguise its unsightliness.

In designing a sewage system the amount of flow was often miscalculated so that in places a gutter turned out in practice to be too narrow. What may have appeared to be trifling details in the planning stage sometimes became major problems later. The difficulties were compounded by an evil custom of dumping waste into the gutter, but the basic fault was miscalculation.

Tokyo had a meteorological observatory for some time, which enabled the city to compile statistics with regard to precipitation. As our engineer-designers used as their base the usual flow of a sewer and then added the maximum precipitation on record plus a little extra, the sewers should never have overflowed. Precipitation in those days, however, was measured from one to two o'clock or on some days from three to four o'clock in the afternoon. But the rain was not watching the clock. It could shower at one-forty in the morning and quickly stop or pour all night. It was irregular about when it started and stopped. While precipitation was faithfully recorded between certain given hours, the statistically measured precipitation for a specific period of the day and the actual amount of precipitation in that period on any particular day could be quite different. For this reason the new sewers were not very useful. I learned the hard way that, as the saying goes "Statistics are at once the most dependable, and the most treacherous of aids."

Tokyo still does not have a proper sewage system. Some areas have now been served, but many others are not. I realized that unless the sewage system was greatly improved we could not build a healthy city. During my years as mayor, I took considerable pains to expand the system, but it was a difficult job.

Improving Streets and Planting Trees

In those days, it would have been hard to find roads anywhere worse than those in Tokyo. When the weather was good, they were dusty and when it rained, the city streets were rivers of mud. Obviously the streets had to be improved and choices had to be made between roads of asphalt, bricks, pebbles, or wood. To test which was best I had every type of road built. Wood-paved side streets and an asphalted road in front of Tokyo University in Hongō and also in Kanda were examples.

There was an amusing story told about improving the streets of Tokyo. When I took office as mayor, it was in the Sōjurō-machi section of Ginza, I believe, that the heavily-trafficked side-streets received such a thick layer of gravel that it was difficult for carriages to pass, or even for people to walk, and the streets lost traffic, because the gravel had not been flattened with a roller.

I called in the engineer in charge and asked him why the gravel had not been rolled. The man coolly replied it was best if it was flattened by pedestrians, as this was the most economical method and was even good for the road. I turned to him in disbelief: "Why do you think we improve the roads? For cats and dogs? For horses? A road is made in the first place for the benefit of pedestrians. What kind of thinking is it to cause them inconvenience to improve the road that is made to help them?" The engineer was speechless. Technicians everywhere are apt to have this psychology. As long as their own bit of road is improved the convenience of its users is irrelevant.

I recommended to the city assembly that it purchase a steamroller. The engineers were loath to use it, however. One of the reasons they gave was that the heavy steamroller could not be driven over the bridges in various parts of the city. They feared that the bridges might collapse if the roller was forced to cross them. As they pointed out, there were apparently many such imperfect bridges. But any bridge that might collapse under the weight of a steamroller, I told them, was not worthy in this day and age to be called a bridge. Not convinced of the efficacy of my argument, however, I periodically prompted the engineer to use the roller.

Whenever I gave him orders to use it he would drive the steamroller noisily below my office window. Satisfied that my orders were being obeyed I would then turn to other matters, and by the time I next remembered to look the roller had been put away. Whenever I prompted him the same engineer would drive the machine under my window to make noise, but that was all it ever did. Before I realized what was going on, the city assembly had removed the operating cost of the steamroller from the budget.

The story smelled of irregularity so I had it checked. Among the members of the city assembly was a man who had made a large investment in a gravel company in Tamagawa. Unfortunately, this gravel pulverized when steamrolled, therefore it was not suitable for use on the roads. This would upset all those with vested interests. In fact it directly or indirectly affected both the engineer and the assemblyman, hence the cut in the steamroller's operating budget. So vested interests, in the form of the assemblyman's holdings in the gravel company, were the reason why the machine was never used. By the time I exposed this situation, it was too late, since the vehicle had deteriorated to the point where it could no longer be used anyway. Some years later, a scandal erupted over gravel procurement, the indirect causes of which may be traced back to this.

It was unimaginably difficult as a rule to convince citizens of the need for urban improvement. Since there was so much opposition even to improving the streets, I decided to take advantage of the British Japan fair, which was being held in London, to send a delegation of powerful assemblymen at the city's expense to inspect European cities. I secretly asked the guide to take them around so they would see as many fine streets as possible, anticipating that this would produce a salutary educational effect, and I looked forward keenly to their return with a new enthusiasm for road improvement.

Contrary to my expectations, the assemblymen reported that there was no need for road improvement. The reasons they gave were quite unbelievable. "Oriental civilization and occidental civilization are completely different," they reported, "Western civilization being in the main simple, and oriental civilization essentially complex. Westerners wear shoes at all times, whatever the weather. And since they do not take their shoes off in their homes, it is necessary to maintain clean roads to keep their houses clean. In the orient, in contrast, particularly in our country," they explained, "The culture is far more complex and refined. If the weather permits we use *setta* (leather-soled sandals) or *hiyorigeta* (low clogs for dry weather), and in the rain *ashida* (high clogs or rain clogs). We also use other varieties such as *komageta* (low clogs), *takageta* (high clogs), and *zōri* (straw sandals), all of which it is our custom to take off when entering the house. Our refined customs therefore do not necessitate the building of roads such as those in the West, where consideration is made for keeping one's shoes on in the home." This, more or less, was their line of argument, which was well received by most of their peers in the city assembly.

"Exactly!" exclaimed one assemblyman. "If the roads were improved as the mayor suggests, then thousands of clog shops in Tokyo would go out of business. Road improvement is not in the interest of the citizens." Ridiculous as this kind of reasoning is, this was the sort of city assemblyman I had to deal with—and not just where roads were concerned but in everything I tried to do. It was tiresome, to say the least.

At the same time as my attempts at road improvement, planting trees along the avenues was, for the most part, undertaken during my tenure. One would think at first that almost any trees would do, willows or flowering cherry trees for example, but this was not so. After years of painstaking research we finally imported seeds of roadside trees from the West, nursed them until the saplings were ready, and finally planted them along the streets.

While on the subject of tree planting, let me record also the circumstances leading to the presentation of flowering cherry blossom trees to the city of Washington. At the time of the war with Russia, the United States had shown enormous goodwill toward Japan. Jacob Schiff, a powerful American financier, was particularly helpful with regard to the issue of our foreign bonds. I had always wanted to express fitting appreciation for this kindness.

At the time, however, as we in Japan were then feeling very pleased with ourselves at the thought of having single-handedly defeated Russia. I thought about presenting the cherry trees to the city of Washington, but kept my thought to myself, because I thought the time was not right and expressing them prematurely might impede rather than advance the project. Needless to say, it was the government that should have offered gratitude to the U.S. for its kindness during the war, but there was no one in the Katsura government who thought of this. I knew that it might seem improper to have the suggestion come from the mayor of Tokyo, but nevertheless I was convinced that it was something that should be considered.

Then by good fortune I learned of a plan to plant Japanese flowering cherry trees along the Potomac River in Washington on the initiative of Mrs. Taft, the wife of the president. It occurred to me that this was an excellent opportunity to present the trees from the city of Tokyo to the city of Washington so that Americans need not buy them. I therefore proposed the idea to the city council as well as to the municipal assembly, both of which were in singular agreement. It was decided to present three thousand young cherry trees of from seven to eight feet in height, and experts were commissioned to take the necessary measures. The American Embassy was pleased and offered assistance.

However, upon inspection by officials of the U.S. Department of Agriculture on their arrival on the west coast of America, the trees were found to be infested with harmful insects and their eggs as well as various types of bacteria, and consequently they all had to be destroyed. The acting U.S. ambassador told me exactly what had happened. But he looked somewhat troubled, so to cheer him up I said, "To be honest about it! It has been an American tradition to destroy cherry trees ever since your first president, George Washington! So there's nothing to worry about. In fact, you should be feeling proud!" I was of course referring to the famous incident of Washington and the cherry tree. The acting ambassador withdrew, looking very relieved.

I had no idea then, but I later learned that there was not a single field in the whole of Japan that was not infested with pests or microbes. That was why trees grown in Japan usually had to be drenched with toxins.

If I did nothing further Americans would not learn of our goodwill, so I decided that cherry tree seeds should be planted in sterilized beds under the jurisdiction of the Ministry of Agriculture and Commerce. In this way we could nurse a new batch of cherry trees. After three years the saplings were ready, and they were then duly shipped. This time they passed inspection and were planted along the Potomac.

I have visited Washington two or three times when the cherry blossoms were in bloom and noted how well they have grown. Nowhere in Japan can one find such a concentration of three thousand trees in a single location. Not even in Yoshino are there so many. Today, the cherry trees in Washington have become a special feature enjoyed not just by Americans but by people from around the world, attracting hundreds of thousands of viewers and contributing to the prosperity of local hotels and restaurants.

Flowering cherry trees are generally short-lived and so they may not last long. However, since they are being so well cared for by the Americans they may well last much longer than in Japan. The blossoms themselves are normally short-lived too, but I learned that Americans spray them so that they keep their petals longer.

After the outbreak of the Pacific war I read in our newspapers that the trees had all been cut down, but I did not believe it. While the Americans must rightly have been angered by the surprise attack on Pearl Harbor, I did not think that they would do such an insensitive thing. As I believed, the trees survived the war. During the war, however, they were apparently called "Oriental" rather than Japanese.

The presentation of the flowering cherry trees must have left a very good impression, for I still receive letters and telegrams of gratitude from all sorts of people. Last year, Mrs. Barnett, the wife of the former military attaché at the American Embassy in Japan, sent me a bottle containing water from the Potomac Basin. The previous year, she sent a telegram written in Japanese: "Sakura saita, arigatō" (the cherry blossoms are out, thank you). While in Japan she was a student of Japanese waka poems and is regarded as a friend of Japan.

MUNICIPAL ACQUISITION OF STREETCARS AND THE GAS COMPANY MERGER

The most important project I undertook while mayor was the purchase and operation of the municipal electric streetcar service. It was also the most challenging. It was generally regarded that I had been trapped into the scheme by Hoshi's men, some of whom were related to the streetcar company as well as economically powerful. Though many believed this to be the case, the situation was quite the opposite.

Hoshi's men in the city assembly used the trolley line companies to play financial tricks as if the companies were their private property. First, a rumor that the city was going to purchase the streetcar business sent the price of its shares rocketing up in the securities market. Another rumor credited to the company would send the same stocks plummeting downward. The fluctuation in share prices enabled these men at any given time to make money on the order of hundreds of thousands of yen, which they then used to manipulate city assemblymen and councilors. What was worse, they also used the money to intervene in the proceedings of the Imperial Diet.

No matter how competent the mayor might be, as long as they were able to continue to play these tricks, there was a limit to how independently I could conduct the city's business. At any critical moment, enormous sums of money were made available so that the group could manipulate members of the city assembly and council. This was the major cause of corruption in the city's administration.

"The city must take this box of tricks away from them," I thought to myself. Naturally, the Hoshi group was opposed to losing the privilege. Even if they were able to sell off the box at a high price, once sold, they would not be able to play their tricks any more. For this reason, important people involved with the streetcar company were all against the transaction.

In spite of these facts, the public believed that I was being used by individuals with vested interests. We say the world has as many fools as wise men. It is true that there is always something we don't know. The central government was also deceived by the group, and no matter how many times I brought their sinister scheme to its notice it always failed to take action.

Those of Hoshi's men who still operated around Tokyo collected behind To-shihmitsu Tsurumatsu to challenge me with their grandiose plot. There were two streetcar companies in Tokyo. They started out as rivals, but before long they were secretly colluding for high stakes. As time passed, they jointly acquired the Kinugawa Hydro-electric Power Company, the Tokyo Gas Company was manipulated by them, and the Keiō and the Keisei Railroad companies, though smaller, were under their power too. The Tokyo Electric Lamp Company, originally independent, was likewise controlled by them through the Kōshu faction. They even had a plan to establish a major bank as a banking agent for all these companies large and small.

If the power and influence of this group of companies and their bank were allowed to grow there was a real danger of the city of Tokyo falling into their hands and not being able to act freely. The Kōshu group, which was active in Tokyo, was already in communication with Toshimitsu. These being the circumstances, those generally believed to be major proponents of municipal operation of the streetcars were, in fact, not simply unenthusiastic about the idea of municipal ownership of their lines, but they actually opposed that plan and wanted to retain their ownership of the lines in perpetuity. The more they were opposed to the municipal streetcar project, the more determined I was, at the very least, to take the streetcar lines away from them. The situation became increasingly tense.

Around that time Japan's specie reserve was being depleted to a level that threatened to compromise the convertibility of the yen. A boost of a hundred million yen would give relief to the government, if only temporarily. I thought if I made the most of the opportunity, I might be able to get the government to welcome the issue of foreign bonds and thus support the city's acquisition of the streetcar service. My strategy was to exploit the need of the government to bolster its specie reserve.

As I had expected, the government thought well of the idea of raising money by issuing bonds abroad. Our objectives were different, but there was concurrence as far as our need for foreign currency was concerned. The government, which until then had been cool to my project, was now eager to assist it in many ways. The Ministry of Finance also put its shoulder to the wheel, contributing expertise and credibility. As all the arrangements related to the issue were now delegated to the ministry although the money involved was six times that of the earlier city district improvement project, there was little trouble in the way of competition or interference with intermediaries, and no embarrassment over commissions.

The sum involved was one hundred million yen and any mishandling of the money even for a few days would mean risking a loss of several hundred thousand, so as an amateur I took exceptional pains in handling it. I visited Yasuda Zenjirō then for the first time to consult him regarding the project and was deeply impressed at his extremely clear-cut answers. I thought to myself it was no accident that this man had made a huge fortune. At the same time I was astonished to find, contrary to what one would expect of a great man of business who would undoubtedly have many visitors and a great deal of paper work, that the entrance to his house was a picture of calm, and in his study not a single letter visible, his carefully dusted desk standing in a well-lighted place by the window as if he never did anything more arduous at it than composing poems. Yasuda was relaxed and detached, as if he had already abandoned the material world. One immediately noted how very different he was from other powerful businessmen. I was curious to know how he had achieved such distinguished success, but the seriousness of my errand did not allow me the satisfaction. There can be no doubt that in one respect at least he was a man of unusual virtue. During his last years especially, he replaced his earlier passion for wealth with wanting to share it with society, exemplified by his large gifts to the city of Tokyo and the Imperial University. If he had lived longer he would have gone on to do much more, but tragically he fell to an assassin's knife. I was very sorry for his sake but also for society's.[1]

Thanks to all this effort, I now had one hundred million yen to spend for the municipal transportation system. I was able to realize my long-held dream to purchase the streetcar company for the city. Some thought the price was too high and I have to grant that we did not underpay the companies. Be that as it may, I could not afford to let the program fail by bickering over the price, as then Tokyo would lose the battle now and forever. It would fall completely under the control of the consortium. That was why I was determined to purchase the streetcar service now and forestall their conspiracy before they had a chance to beat us to the post. As I expected, the city's acquisition of the streetcars put an end to the intrigues of the Toshimitsu group and Tokyo was finally able to shake off its dependence on private interest groups.

Prior to this I had submitted to the House of Representatives a city district improvement bill and by means of this had the City Council, which hitherto had been merely an executive organ, transformed to a decision-making body. This increased the power of the mayor considerably, especially now that the main threat to the capital's independent administration had been removed. This enabled my successors to be in a far better position to carry out their mandates.

The merger of the city's gas companies was another of the projects I undertook during my tenure. There were two gas companies, one old and one new. It did not make sense for the two companies to duplicate investment and install separate

---

[1] Yasuda, founder of one of the great prewar conglomerates, was assassinated in 1921 by a right-wing extremist who considered him an exemplar of capitalist and *zaibatsu* greed.

gas lines, which installations inevitably resulted in frequent disruption and additional hazard to the city's streets.

When the opportunity arose to merge the companies I implemented a measure that brought together their interests with those of citizens. If gas (and electric power) companies, by nature monopolistic, were allowed to provide competing services, the redundant capital investment would result in economic disadvantages, while a non-competitive situation could lead to monopolies. What was the best way to have a single company provide each of these vital public services while preventing it from arbitrarily increasing its charges? Of the many options, I thought the best would be to adopt a sliding scale familiar in the Western countries.

In an order to the newly merged gas company I set a ceiling to its dividends at nine *shu* a year; if the company wished to increase its dividends then it must bring down its charges, and conversely if it wanted to increase its charges, it would have to reduce its dividends. Adjustments were made between dividends and charges as needed.

With this method, if a company was profitable, citizens enjoyed cheap gas. If they were burdened by high charges, then the company also suffered by having to reduce its dividends. Previously things had worked in quite the opposite way: the company earned more profits when it sold gas at higher prices, and if it sold gas more cheaply the company suffered a loss. The sliding-scale system had the reverse effect.

The adoption of this scheme met with considerable opposition, but I was able to overcome the obstacles placed in my path, and got the measure through on grounds of shared interests for company and urbanites. For some reason, though, the city failed to carry this out after I resigned my office as mayor. Subsequently we learned that a major panic broke out, and I tended to credit this to the government bureaux that failed to carry out the sliding-scale system I had worked out; they were not carrying out the program I had begun.

Those were the principal projects I was able to carry out as mayor. I had other goals, notably the development of Tokyo port but I was unable to get that through, due to the disapproval of the Hoshi people. They dug in their heels and resisted, offering a deal if I would give up the streetcar lines project, and this I would not do. This had priority. The development of the port, which was about the only major city project I could not myself carry out, was really not so much mine as my deputy, Tagawa Daikichirō's. Nonetheless, it was at least begun in my time.

Tagawa and I found each other through a strange coincidence. After my return from abroad, the *Chōya Shinbun*, the newspaper with which I was then connected, went bankrupt and Inukai and I were forced to rejoin the *Hōchi Shinbun*, where our friends in the editorial department gave us a welcoming party. At one point Inukai and I were joined by one of our old friends, Emoto Nagatatsu, who by then had a good deal of sake under his belt. "You were once our superiors and the brains of the Hōchi," he began. "You realize, I hope, that now you have come back after failing everywhere else you will be expected to know your place." In jest, I replied, "That doesn't make any difference. You'll have to do as you're told, just as before." But the joke misfired and we all had a good-natured brawl over it. Having heard what had passed between us, however, one of the young journalists whom I did not know introduced himself. "Excuse me, sir," he said, very formally, "My name is Tagawa Daikichirō. If that is your attitude, I cannot possibly work with you. I excuse myself as of today." Thus declaring his resignation, he left.

Many years ago now, around 1886, my eye was caught by editorial columns that appeared from time to time in the *Hōchi Shinbun* signed "Chikusui." I was impressed both by the content and by the quality of the writing. I had wanted to meet the author, but somehow had never got around to it. Finally, on inquiring who he was, I was told he was a student from Kyushu studying at the technical school and was known to Yano. This "Chikusui" turned out to be the same Tagawa I had offended at the Hōchi party. I quickly got to like the man very much and we became close friends from then on.

So Tagawa eventually came to be my deputy when I was mayor. His plan to improve the port area was as follows. The passage from Haneda to Shibaura being too shallow for maritime traffic, Tagawa's idea was to deepen the canal to permit the passage of larger ships. Then the soil recovered from the dredging could be used to reclaim a wide stretch of land on the Tokyo Bay shore in Shibaura. Crisscrossing the reclaimed land with canals would substitute for building a new port. In time, Tagawa's dredging and reclamation projects were completed in an excellent manner.

One other project on which I was unable to embark was the long-pending transfer of the fish market at Nihonbashi to a more convenient location. A fish market had to be strategically located for good access by both sea and rail, but Nihonbashi did not have good communications by canal to the sea and a rail connection was close to impossible. Disappointingly, I was not able to come to grips with this before I resigned.

AN UNUSUAL WAY TO IMPEACH THE KATSURE CABINET IN 1903

I was able to accomplish a few things during the decade I served as mayor of Tokyo, but during that period I was almost totally out of the picture as far as national politics was concerned. I merely occupied my seat during Diet debates. As the newspapers of the day had it: "Gakudō is dead!" Then as soon as I became active in the constitutional movement following my resignation as mayor they wrote, "Gakudō has risen!" In fact, I had neither died nor risen. I was ever the same old Gakudō. Those who mistook me for dead must have been surprised to see me making a nuisance of myself again.

For about two years as a member of the Ōkuma cabinet, I was extremely unpopular with the newspapers. Now they wrote, "Gakudō is senile!" and again, in spite of the fact that I was palpably there, "He is dead!" And after leaving the government, as soon as I became involved in disarmament and universal suffrage, they brought me back to life once more. "Gakudō is resurrected!" In this way I was killed off and reborn a number of times at the hands of the press. I was not popular with the press during my years as mayor simply because I made no effort to be. Having worked as a journalist myself for a considerable length of time, I knew the inner workings of the press. It would have been relatively easy for me to placate them for my own purposes. This I did not wish to do. I never flattered reporters. I let things take their course. I knew that there were men in the city government who did flatter journalists, and there were some who used base ways to ingratiate themselves. These sycophants were written up well in the papers, while those who did not resort to such tactics and simply left the reporters to do their job were often dealt with unsympathetically. This was at least one of the reasons why I received negative treatment in the press throughout my term of office as mayor.

In any case I was completely occupied with city affairs and ignored other political issues to such an extent that, as I have recounted, the papers even wrote, "Gakudō is dead!" The only issue that roused me to make an exception to my general neglect of things outside my immediate area of responsibility was the impeachment of the cabinet by Kōno Hironaka, the Speaker of the House of Representatives in December 1903.

After leaving the Seiyūkai, I had created a small study group of like-minded-men called the *Dōshi Kenkyūkai*. Among its nineteen members, however, were prominent men such as Katō Takaaki, Hyūga Terutake, Mochizuki Kotaro, Ogawa Heikichi, Okuda Gijin, and Mochizuki Keisuke.

As I wrote in the previous chapter, the Katsura government had wheedled the Seiyūkai into going along with its crude and irresponsible measures, and since it had no strategy for the impending negotiations with Russia, people were becoming disenchanted with the government and increasingly critical of its spinelessness. We were in the forefront of the attack.

People were especially concerned about the worsening relations with Russia. The alliance with Great Britain was predicated on the expectation of war between Japan and Russia. I had not been at all in favor of the alliance, but now that it was in place we had to find ways to minimize injury to the empire in case war with Russia could not be avoided. Russia for its part was non-committal following the conclusion of the Anglo-Japanese Alliance, postponed negotiations, increased its armaments, and displayed unfriendly and aggressive attitudes in public, and yet our authorities seemed to have no particular policy.

We were appalled at how weak-kneed the Katsura government was in the face of impending national disaster, and felt that it would be unable to cope with the situation to the advantage of the state. Something had to be done. Akiyama Teisuke came up with the idea, to which Ogawa Heikichi gave his support, of impeaching the cabinet in the response of the president of the House to the imperial message at the opening of the new Diet.

It was customary at the opening ceremony of every Diet to receive an imperial message. Both houses would then respectfully submit their response, the drafting of which from the very first Diet had always been left to the president. It was also customary for the president's response to the imperial message to be endorsed unanimously by all members regardless of their party affiliation and political standing.

It was a highly original idea for pushing through the impeachment which would have little chance of success if attempted through normal procedures. On being consulted, the president, Kōno Hironaka, at first demurred, and I was then approached for my opinion. Now that I think of it, it probably was a bad joke, but when I first heard of the plan I thought it rather interesting. "It's a good idea. Go ahead!" I said. "If it succeeds, the government has only two options—to call for a dissolution or resign en masse. Whichever it chooses, it will be shock therapy to both the government and the people. It might well have very significant results." I gave my endorsement, and added thoughtfully, "Kōno may appear to be a slow mover but on important matters he has the power to make bold decisions and can be far more adroit than you would expect." On being approached a second time and learning that I was in favor of the plan, he decided to go along with us and play the game.

With Kōno in agreement, the remaining question was how exactly to play the game on the day. The only way to do it, we decided, was to express our approval with a loud burst of clapping the moment the president had finished reading the crucial passage. It was also agreed that we would somehow take care of members who were likely to object.

The opening ceremony of the short-lived nineteenth Diet took place on December 10, 1903. President of the House Kōno had his secretary draft the letter of response as was customary and, carrying with him in his inner pocket the letter into which the impeachment had already been inserted as secretly agreed, took his seat. With a certain degree of apprehension I watched the scene unfold with a degree of apprehension as Kōno conducted the business of the House with great composure and delivered the response he had himself written:

> Respectfully submitted. Under Your Majesty's gracious patronage your subjects are deeply honored to have received your message on the occasion of the opening of the Nineteenth Imperial Diet. Today our nation enjoys a unique and felicitous opportunity for expanding its power and prestige, yet at this auspicious moment, to our profound concern, the abilities of the ministers of your cabinet are not equal to their historic task, domestic policy is conducted on an ad hoc basis, and propitious opportunities are lost in foreign affairs. We beg Your Majesty to grant us your judgment. After carefully deliberating among your subjects entrusted with assisting your government we shall devote ourselves obediently to your gracious will and faithfully live up to the mandate of our people. Respectfully submitted by your loyal subject Kōno Hironaka, Speaker, the House of Representatives.

Kōno delivered the response impressively, his voice resounding on the four walls of the House. All the members present, believing without much thought that this was the customary bland response to the emperor's message, endorsed it with the usual acclaim. The Speaker, also as was the custom, asked for confirmation: "No one opposed?" and the members unanimously answered with a hearty cheer. Alone among them, Mochizuki Kotarō, reputed for his brilliance and quick-wittedness, seemed to realize that something was wrong and called out, "Mr. Speaker! Mr. Speaker!" But Kōno firmly bade him be quiet and wound up the day's business with perfect finesse.

I was astonished at Kōno's uncharacteristically commanding presence and the unsuspected gift for drama with which he played his role. His acting could readily be compared with the memorable performances of the great actors Danjūrō the Ninth and Sadanji in the famous Kabuki drama *Kanjinchō*.

The members of the ruling party were aghast on rereading the text which they and the rest of us had just approved, for it was nothing short of an address to the Throne for their own impeachment. They were in a state of panic. Some ran to the Speaker's chair, seizing him and accusing him of foul play. "You have sat in the House since the first Diet as a party leader," they shouted at him, "You cannot claim ignorance of its customs." Kōno was not the least ruffled. "I did what I believed to be correct," he replied coolly.

At a quickly convened ad hoc meeting, the cabinet decided to dissolve the House before the Speaker's text was addressed to the Throne. The Diet was dissolved and our object of disciplining the government had been served. This was remembered as Kōno's surprise impeachment when Speaker Kōno framed the government by including its impeachment in his response to the imperial message.

A rumor then began to spread that it was I who had initiated Kōno's surprise impeachment, and the word even went around that the draft of the response had been written on city office stationary. The truth was that when Akiyama came to ask my opinion about the plan the draft had already been written. All I did was to correct a few words here and there. I was only peripherally involved in the incident. I must admit, though, that if I had not agreed with the plan Kōno might not have gone ahead with it. To that extent, I suppose I am guilty of bearing some of the responsibility in the matter.

The Parliament and the Russo-Japanese War

On February 6, 1904, Japan and Russia severed diplomatic relations and the emperor's declaration of war was issued on the tenth. As the Diet had been dissolved thanks to the fine performance by speaker Kōno Kironaka, the ninth general election took place on March 1. But people paid it little attention since by then we were already at war, and the result hardly differed from the situation which existed prior to the dissolution. With the outbreak of war we desisted from pressing our attack on the government. Faced with a foreign enemy, as at the time of the war with China, there was an undeclared political truce on the home front.

On March 16, just before the opening of the twentieth Diet (March 18–30, 1904), the Seiyūkai adopted the following resolution:

The present cabinet has failed in its domestic as well as in its foreign policies, and much concern is to be felt for the future of constitutional government. This meeting was originally called to identify those responsible for this situation. However, by imperial command a declaration of war against a foreign enemy has been issued and our nation faces unprecedented challenges. In recognition of the priority of military matters, this convention hereby postpones all usual business until a later date, and is resolved to support the military spending necessary to achieve the objectives of the war.

This represented the general feeling of the people. On the same day the Kensei Hontō also held its convention and apart from issuing warnings to the government on diplomatic and fiscal matters, adopted a resolution to approve government wartime measures.

During the twentieth Diet the government submitted a special military budget of 576 million yen, partly to be financed by public bonds, partly by extraordinary taxes and tobacco revenues. The House approved all government bills without revision save for minor amendments on details.

The House also adopted a resolution to enlist national support for future military spending.

The war has but begun and while we rejoice at the successes of our fleet, there will be a long and arduous path to travel before we can ensure victory in all theaters of conflict and regain peace in the orient. We will not begrudge the cost. The House particularly admonishes the ministers of the cabinet to strive their utmost to ensure that the noble cause of the empire shall prevail, to seek every opportunity to turn the vicissitudes and fortunes of battle to our favor, and expeditiously to bring the war to a victorious conclusion.

This declaration, representing the will of the people, was adopted by the House. How could the people have made their will known at home and abroad without the parliament? This response to the emergency demonstrated the value of constitutional government.

Throughout the twenty-first Diet, which met from near the end of 1904 to early in 1905 (November 1904–February 1905), the war with Russia was in progress and our forces were claiming victory at sea and on land. To sustain the war effort the government presented an additional budget of seven million yen to supplement already approved military spending. The main source of financing was again expected to be procured from the issue of public bonds. In addition, however, the government sought to revise the emergency special tax law to increase tax rates on ten items including real estate, and instituted new taxes including traffic tolls. It also nationalized the salt monopoly. The House passed the bill with only slight amendments.

Most encouraging were the favorable developments at the front. I had believed that war against Russia could never be won and therefore should be avoided. I was proved quite mistaken, however, and this was fortunate for the nation.

As the twenty-first Diet was about to close, President of the House, Matsuda Masahisa, made a speech in which he attributed our victories in the war to the existence of constitutional government. He pointed out that when one compared our circumstances with those of the enemy, an obvious correlation was to be observed between the existence or absence of good government and the rise and fall of national fortunes. He concluded that we must continue to defend and nurture constitutional government so that it would fulfil its great promises. It was an argument very pleasing to the ear.

When the country plunged into total war with a world power, the political parties suspended their own political war, as I stated earlier, and our people pulled together as one. In contrast, Russia made light of Japan and its fighting will was not vigorous. Moreover, its humiliating military reverses helped to fuel widespread discontent against Russia's autocratic government and the rise of a revolutionary movement obstructed its war efforts. Abuse of the autocratic government was everywhere visible, political strategy and the exigencies of war were constantly at cross purposes, and the tsar himself seemed less than eager for the battle.

It was much to the advantage of our country that the other powers sympathized with Japan in the war with Russia. Britain as our ally naturally sided with Japan, but even Germany and France, which in the past had teamed up with Russia to dispossess Japan of its acquisitions gained after the war against China (the Triple Intervention), wanted a Japanese rather than a Russian victory. The United States of America, especially, its unique humanitarian spirit stirred by the spectacle of the small but gallant island nation hurled into war with its giant neighbor, loudly praised the courage of the Japanese people, and its sympathy towards Japan was boundless.

Few, however, in America or Britain predicted victory for Japan. According to reports reaching Japan, our forces had been faring unexpectedly well both on land and at sea, and our people were euphoric. The powers were not so optimistic. The government in Tokyo, no less than our fighting forces in the field and at sea, far from being complacent about victory, nevertheless spared nothing in the struggle against Russia, which they knew very well was one of the mightiest of the great powers.

One day, a mysterious character by the name of Iino Kichisaburō came unannounced to the city office. He lived in Onden Aoyama and later came to be known as "the monk of Onden." For reasons unknown to me he had many friends in uniform who consulted him on all sorts of matters. He told me he was on his way to Manchuria. I asked him why. "Kodama is discouraged and I am going to encourage him," was his reply. General Kodama Gentarō was the chief of the general staff and in command of our forces. He did not believe that we could win, and was thinking only of how to end the war without loss of face. Apparently he had told Yamagata and other friends and acquaintances, "There is nothing more to do. Only pray to the sun."

Army strategists had made serious miscalculations. For example, it was thought that Russian reinforcements and heavy weapons would be slow in coming due to the fact that the same railway rolling stock would have to be sent back across Siberia each time a fresh batch of troops or guns was to be brought to the front.

In fact, they came in greater numbers than ever, because, as it was later learned, instead of returning the trains to Europe each time, the Russians simply sent more trains. Our side, on the other hand, suffered both from a shortage of fighting men, with the average age of reserve soldiers sent to replace those lost in battle steadily increasing, and from a short supply of arms and ammunition.

I was at first puzzled when asked to deliver a vote of thanks as mayor of Tokyo at a foundry where pots and pans were manufactured. I asked why, and was told that the factory was supporting the war efforts by making bullets. I was curious, and asked if it was true that a saucepan foundry could really cast bullets. In reply, I was told it mattered little whether they actually worked or not, but bullets had to be sent anyway so as to avoid loss of morale among the soldiers at the front.

It was in these circumstances that the government was looking for an opportunity to sign a peace treaty at the earliest possible date. The chance came on May 27, when the Russian Baltic fleet was all but destroyed in the Battle of Tsushima Straits, and the Russian will faltered. The Japanese government secretly sought the good offices of President Theodore Roosevelt as a mediator. Representatives of Japan and Russia subsequently met in Portsmouth, where a peace treaty was signed on September 1. However, Russia did not agree to cede any of its territory or to pay war damages. Japan's acquisition of the southern half of Sakhalin was due to Britain's good will. It was an unexpected windfall. Shidehara Kijūrō was to write of this later in his *Fifty Years of Diplomacy*.

The public was not so easily pleased. When the conditions of the Portsmouth Treaty of Peace were made known, there was a nationwide outcry accusing the government of cravenly accepting humiliating terms, forfeiting the fruits of victory, and wronging the country. The unpalatable truth of the military situation had not been told either in Japan or abroad, and so this reaction should not have been unexpected. The government unwisely attempted to control the people's anger by repressive means, which only aggravated an already volatile situation, and numerous cases of arson erupted in the capital. The situation went from bad to worse when the government mistook these isolated incidents for a general uprising. Now groups of angry citizens coalesced into mobs. Bent on violence, they set fire to the official residence of the home minister and burned trains, provoking the police into drawing their swords and killing and injuring demonstrators at random. In the end a state of emergency was decreed throughout the capital.[2]

The Katsura government could not avoid accepting responsibility for the outbreak of arson, and on September 10, requested an imperial judgment. The emperor in his generosity chose not to chastise the government, which then, feeling protected by the imperial grace, simply dismissed the home minister and the chief of police, who were the most convenient scapegoats, and remained in power.

---

[2] On September 5, 1905, riots broke out when police attempted to forestall a rally organized by an antitreaty group headed by Kōno Hironaka and scheduled to meet in Hibiya Park to protest the terms of the Portsmouth Treaty as insufficiently gainful for Japan. In several days of rioting, seventeen people were killed, 70 percent of Tokyo's police boxes were burned, and fifteen streetcars were de-

By then, however, the government had lost its confidence. When the twenty-second Diet (December, 1905–March, 1906) was about to convene, the government's situation among members of the House had become much worse. The main complaints leveled against the government were the conclusion of a humiliating treaty and the oppression of the people. Prime Minister Katsura, no doubt judging that it was better to go, seeing he would soon be embattled, led his entire cabinet to resign before the Diet had a chance to air its grievances. He recommended Saionji Kinmochi, the president of the Seiyūkai, as his successor.

Katsura himself, nonetheless, was elevated from count to marquis in recognition of the nation's victory in the war. It was the proudest moment of his boastful career. Katsura's pride was one thing, and of no very great moment, but it was indeed deeply to be regretted that my countrymen, all of a sudden priding themselves with unaccustomed arrogance on the illusion of having joined the club of first-class countries, had now started down a path that would lead to a great misfortune in the future.

SOME REMINISCENCES OF THE TIMES

One person whose memory will always remain vivid to me was Admiral Tōgō Heihachirō. There were welcome receptions for each of the senior officers of our victorious forces when they returned from the war with Russia, and as mayor of Tokyo I was always present on such occasions. Admiral Tōgō was unlike the others. His head modestly bent, he quietly gazed at the flowers on the table. His whole demeanor was of a loyal and reserved man, honest to a fault and devoid of even the slightest pride, for which he could easily have been forgiven, as a victorious admiral.

In preparation for the admiral's reception, the city assembly had had two elaborate campstools copied after one Tokugawa Ieyasu had used in the field. One was set for Admiral Tōgō to use and the other was placed in my room. Later, when Mr. William Jennings Bryan, a thrice-unsuccessful candidate for the United States presidency, visited Japan prior to his appointment as secretary of state by President Woodrow Wilson, I presented him with the second stool, saying, "This chair should bring you luck in the presidential elections," and he took it back with him to America. Not long ago when I visited the late. Mr. Bryan's home town, I happened to come across the same chair in the local museum. It was labeled "Present from Admiral Tōgō."

The visit of General William Booth, the founder of the Salvation Army, was another unforgettable event. The first part of the name of the organization was translated in those days as *saiseigun* (public welfare), and thinking this inappropriate I had it corrected to *kyūseigun* (salvation army), which is what it is

---

stroyed. There were also riots in Kobe and Yokihama and widespread complaints against government politics and tactics.

called today. When General Booth learned of this he was immensely pleased and thanked me. I have had occasion to hear him speak several times, and have always been impressed by his near-magical power to move everyone in his audience, including me.

Field Marshal Lord Kitchener (then General) was another whom I welcomed to Tokyo when I was mayor. He remained a bachelor all his life and was known for his extraordinarily fine character. When the city of Tokyo put on a banquet in his honor at the Kōyō-kan restaurant in Shiba, I learned that he could also be most unsociable. To every young waitress attending him that evening he asked, "Have you been to see the maneuvers?" Having come to Japan as the special envoy of the British monarch to take part in these maneuvers, he probably had nothing else on his mind.

As the host, I was next to the general, who sat imposingly throughout the dinner without saying a word except to ask the girls one after the other whether they had been to the wretched maneuvers, and since I was never the sort girls were much attracted to they naturally did their best to ignore us. At last the general turned to me and asked, "Why aren't the girls coming this way?" "I was advised that you didn't care for women," I joked, "so I told them to stay away unless they had to serve us," to which the general in all earnestness replied, "I do not dislike such women." I thought to myself it was not that the general disliked women, but that women disliked him.

That was about the time I lost my wife, who had shared my hardships for twenty years. She was a daughter of Tanaka Hanbei of Nagasaki. Her name was Shige. We were married in Tokyo and she accompanied me to Niigata when I took over as chief editor of the local newspaper. The Tanaka family had a substantial position in the community until the Meiji Restoration. My father-in-law enjoyed having guests, and some four dozen Satsuma and Chōshū political leaders, some of whom were later to become important national figures, had stayed at the house at one time or another.

After returning to Tokyo from Niigata in 1881 and becoming a government official and member of a political party, I was usually poor, as I have already said. In spite of this, I always had one or two secretaries and at times five or six. As if this were not enough, I raised my younger brother and sister, all of which burdened my wife with many hardships. Inconsiderate and indifferent, I gave her little money to buy rice and salt and was constantly away from home on political business. As I reflect on it, I really gave her a miserable time. Probably because of these hardships, she developed tuberculosis about ten years after we were married. A doctor who knew me well recommended that we live separately, but I did not follow his advice. Accepting her illness as our fate, I lived with her for another ten years until her death. All that time she took care to use different utensils so that I would not catch her disease, but I pretended not to notice in case it made her nervous and aggravated her illness. Little by little her condition gradually worsened, and she died in September, 1904, while I was still mayor of Tokyo.

I still lack words to mourn her loss
More than ten years lived in tears

Her death was a terrible blow to me, but I could not continue to live a bachelor's life forever. After a year I took as my second wife a woman born and raised in England. This was Theodora (Yei, her Japanese name), who later died in London in the seventh year of Shōwa, 1932.

Ozaki Saburō (no relative of mine), along with Inoue Kowashi, was reputed to be the most talented of the young men in Itō's political entourage. His name was long familiar to me as our political enemy, for he had drafted many laws that made us suffer. The security ordinance under which I was ordered out of Tokyo was drafted by none other than Saburō.

Theodora was one of Ozaki Saburō's three children. Saburō had studied in London under William Morrison, and married his teacher's daughter. It was a strange twist of fate that I should marry a daughter of my political opponent.

In spite of their three children, Saburō and his English wife did not get along well and were divorced. The children remained in England and were cared for by their mother, but Theodora came to Japan when she was sixteen to look for her father. Due to differences in customs and habits, she preferred not to live in her father's home and lived alone instead, supporting herself by teaching English privately and at the primary school attached to Keiō Gijuku. Mrs. Fraser, the wife of the British minister, took a liking to her and Theodora became her secretary, traveling with her to different countries, including two years in Italy.

Mrs. Fraser was the sister of Marion Crawford, a noted American literary figure. She eventually also began writing, and produced several books of her own. Their brother, Mr. Crawford, spent most of his time in an old castle in Italy writing novels too. Marion Crawford, having resumed her maiden name, had gone to live with her brother for some time after her husband's death and often asked Theodora to tell her old fairy tales from Japan to while away the long evenings. Mr. Crawford, who often listened to the stories with his sister, encouraged Theodora. "People would like to read your stories, you know," he would tell her. "Try and write them down." Theodora did so and published a number of books, which even to this day are read in the West.

Since my wife was brought up in England, Western ways, needless to say, became part of my family life. I am still grateful to her for being so considerate of my health and caring for my diet and home. I began going to the cooler climate of Karuizawa every summer at my wife's recommendation, and following her advice I moved from Kitashinagawa in Tokyo to *Fūunkaku*, Villa of the Winds and Clouds, my present residence in Zushi. I feel I owe my longevity, in spite of having been born with poor health, to my wife and Miss Hattori (Fumiko), who became our housekeeper at my wife's urging.

However, my wife and I had difficult times, owing to our different customs. For example, when Prince Connaught was visiting Japan, I as mayor of Tokyo had to host a dinner in his honor. While it would have been a normal courtesy for the mayor's wife to be present at the dinner her husband was giving for the visiting prince, it was hardly to be expected that members of the city assembly and council would appreciate the same courtesy, and I therefore finally asked the wife of a certain Japanese prince to keep Prince Connaught company. My wife felt greatly insulted by my bad manners and suffered considerably.

Also, during my time as mayor, a young man named Ishikawa Takuboku[3] came to see me. Although I did not know him and although he had no letter of introduction, I met him anyway. The young man presented me with some hand-inscribed *tanka* (Japanese poems) "In dedication to Ozaki *sensei*." Shamefully, I had no appreciation of Japanese poems in those days and did not recognize Ishikawa Takuboku's brilliance. I recall lecturing him to give up writing poems and apply himself to more useful studies.

A few years later, shortly after I resigned as mayor, I read an article in the *Asahi Shinbun* titled "Poetic Genius, Short-Lived Ishikawa Takuboku."

> He had large white hands
> This man they said was so extraordinary

This poem is said to have been about me. I regretted not having treated the talented poet more kindly.

I had written some Chinese poems in my youth but had given up on Japanese poetry as being beyond me. Later when I had occasion to read those composed by Emperor Meiji I found to my surprise that I was able to appreciate the beauty of their lines and of the poet's heart. I decided to stop writing Chinese poems and try my hand at Japanese ones instead.

My poems, therefore, do not belong to any strict school. Perhaps my style is a little like Yoritomo's. Once when I visited Shiraito Falls at the foot of Mount Fuji in Susono I came upon an inscription of a poem by Yoritomo. It was badly written and argumentative just like mine, so since then I have thought that mine belong to his school too.

SAIONJI AND KATSURA

The first Saionji cabinet came into being on January 7, 1906. It was not what one would call a party cabinet. While negotiating the change of government, Katsura apparently turned to Saionji to make sure the latter understood his role. "I recommended you to head the government," said Katsura, "not because you are the president of a major political party, but because you command the respect of the aristocracy and the army, and because you are exceptionally gifted with insight and ability."

Given the developments in the House, Katsura felt he had to resign, if only temporarily, but he intended unfinished business to be carried out by his appointed replacement, Saionji, and he made this the condition of the transfer of power.

[3] Ishikawa, 1885–1912, a brilliant poet and essayist.

Saionji did not refuse, and in forming his cabinet, rather than consulting the leadership of the Seiyūkai, he consulted with Itō and Yamagata. Saionji's position was made quite clear when he announced his cabinet. The Seiyūkai was represented only by Matsuda Masahisa and Hara Takashi, and apart from Katō Takaaki, who held the foreign affairs portfolio and who could be counted as belonging to a political party, the rest were all drawn from among the clan bureaucrats. It could well have been seen as a camouflaged Katsura cabinet, for although not a part of it, Katsura maintained his hold by acting as its adviser behind the scenes.

Bored with the long dry reign of Katsura, the people felt refreshed by the emergence of the Saionji government, but it was not enough to quench their thirst.

The first time we had become aware of Saionji's views was following his return from overseas about the year 1880, when with Nakae Chōmin and Matsuda Masahisa he published the *Tōyō Jiyū Shinbun* (*Oriental Liberal Newspaper*). Much later, having become minister of education in 1894, he advocated "*sekaishugi*" (world-ism) through the writings of Takekoshi Yosaburō. This was met with much opposition at the time, but it was evidence of an extremely progressive mind.

Prince Saionji, besides being creatively gifted and of noble disposition, was a man of refined taste.[4] When I became minister of education in his wake in 1898 and occupied the minister's official residence, I found behind the main house a tea room of four and a half tatami mats, which had been put there by Saionji. It had a long charcoal hibachi and in no way matched the residence, which was of Western design. The tea room, in strange contrast to the image of the minister of education, was, as far as I can tell, Saionji's only achievement during his period of office. I think he left nothing else that could be called an accomplishment. Perhaps the little room still remains there even today.

In addition to writing both poetry and prose, Saionji composed and liked to sing his own songs, which were popular in the geisha houses he frequented in Shinbashi. This talented and noble artist was naturally no match for Katsura, who was all politics and power. Compared with the elegant and aristocratic Saionji, Katsura, with his mean and insufferably priggish character, was cast in a very different mold, but his political skills were not to be slighted.

One problem was the presence in government of military men turned politicians. Of course, ordinary politicians, if uneducated, were hard to deal with too. One could never hope to win them through reason. Itō and Ōkuma, for example, were very knowledgeable and outstanding strategists, and they could at least be counted on to use these resources within the limits of reason, so one could predict their course of action. Uneducated politicians, on the other hand, were harder still to handle, as they had no reserve or courtesy and did not play by established rules. Those with a military background, in particular, had nothing else in their heads except victory and defeat. Winning by any means at their disposal, however unscrupulous, was all that mattered. They equated military strategy with political strategy, and so made no moral or systematic distinction between war and politics.

---

[4] For a study of Saionji, who was to become the last *genrō*, see Lesley Connors, *The Emperor's Adviser: Saionji Kinmochi and Pre-war Japanese Politics* (London: Croom Helm, 1987).

It seemed to me that this lack of a battlefield instinct was Saionji's severest deficiency. He was among the brightest among his peers, and perhaps it was partly because of his brilliance that he could not passionately engage in anything. He did not have it in him to force his views on others no matter what. Generally speaking, brilliant people can see far and have an ability to put themselves fairly in other people's shoes, but they tend to lack intensity. It is the less farsighted who seem to have more decisive powers of action.

His government was in place, but even then Saionji did not exert himself to put his own philosophy into practice. He left Seiyūkai party business mostly to Matsuda Masahisa and Hara Takashi. It looked as though all he did, to put it pictorially, was to provide an empty bowl for Katsura to fill as he wished.

ACHIEVEMENTS OF THE FIRST SAIONJI CABINET

The Saionji cabinet, with the background I have described, did not have the freedom to carry out its own program even if it had wanted to. Therefore, there was nothing to do, but carry on with the policies of the previous cabinet.

One of the important decisions made during the twenty-second Diet was to establish a fund to reduce government debt by at least 110 million yen every year. The cost of the war with Russia was 2 billion yen, most of which had been financed by public bonds. Including the issue of public bonds to meet postwar needs, the empire was burdened with a debt amounting to 1.8 billion yen. The Saionji government sought to finance the cost of redemption by extending the term of the wartime emergency special tax. This special emergency tax that had very harsh measures had been enacted to meet the exigencies of the war. The people suffered it as a necessary wartime measure. They were told from the time it was first introduced that the tax would be abolished one year after the end of the war, but the government now proposed to make it a permanent feature of the tax system.

A group of parliamentarians called the *Dōkōkai*, to which I belonged at the time, joining with colleagues from the *Yūushikai*, set up a small organization called the *Seikō* (political exchange) Club. The Seikō Club, with the Kensei-Hontō, opposed the government fiercely over the planned tax, but in vain.

The other thing the government did was to pass a railway nationalization bill. The two houses endorsed the government's proposed investment of approximately 460 million yen to purchase private railway companies around the country. Foreign Minister Katō, who was uncompromisingly opposed to the plan, was forced to resign.

The twenty-third Diet was convened on December 28, 1906. One of the government's first acts was to present a bill abolishing the *gun* (county) system. Bureaucrats opposed this idea from the first, because they did not want to lose the control that the county chiefs gave them. Katsura, who had appointed himself the supreme adviser to the Saionji government, was also opposed to it, fearing that it would create a complicated political problem. Home Minister Hara Takashi, however, recklessly went ahead with the presentation of the bill. In order to protect the prestige of the government he probably could not have done otherwise, but in the process Katsura and his group were deeply angered.

From this moment on, dark clouds began to gather over the political world. The *Daidō* Club took the opportunity to sever the collaborative relation between Katsura and Saionji, in order to overthrow the cabinet.

The Daidō Club was a fledgling political party that had been organized by break-away elements of the Teikokutō, the Jiyūtō, and the Kōshin Club, and some independents in December, 1905. It had sixty-three members, and its leaders were Katsura Tarō, Ōura Kanetake, and other members of the bureaucratic group.

The Daidō Club took the Seiyūkai by surprise by its opposition to the bill abolishing the county system. The Seiyūkai then tried to get Katsura's support, but he instead encouraged the Daidō Club in its opposition to the bill. In the end, the government, by persuading some moderate members of the Daidō Club to support it, managed to gain a narrow victory for the bill in the Lower House, only to have it crushed in the House of Peers.

The twenty-third Diet survived the threatening clouds, but the relations between the Katsura group and the Saionji cabinet did not. I feared that, depending on the way their relations developed, the future of the government could be dark, and this time the government set itself afire. It ignited during the budgetary process. Minister of Communications Yamagata Isaburō demanded appropriations for expanding rail operations. The demand was peremptorily dismissed by Finance Minister Sakatani Yoshirō, who said there was no way an exception could be made for the railways, let alone for such a huge sum as that called for by Minister Yamagata, when even projects endorsed by the Diet were being postponed in line with the government's commitment to tighten fiscal expenditures.

Prime Minister Saionji attempted to mediate, but the two ministers were adamant. Consequently, the prime minister was forced to submit the resignation of the cabinet on account of the disunity within its ranks. This time, however, Emperor Meiji accepted only the resignations of the two ministers, Yamagata and Sakatani, and rejected those of the others. The cabinet thus earned a breathing space, but it was no more than that, and the end of the Saionji government was nearing by the hour.

The tenth general election took place on May 15, 1908. This time the Seiyūkai won 193 seats, surpassing their strength of 180 in the preceding Diet. This notwithstanding, the Saionji cabinet resigned en masse before two months had passed. The visible cause lay in the failure of the government's fiscal policy, but it was the Katsura group that engineered it. In a manner of speaking, then, one could just as well say that the underlying reason was the break-up of the collaboration between the Saionji government and Katsura.

In the light of postwar financial requirements, Katsura knew only too well that a tax increase was inevitable. He knew that he could not win the support of the House if it were proposed by his cabinet, which had already lost its credibility. Cleverly, therefore, he passed the cabinet to Saionji before the House had to confront the tax issue, scheming that Saionji would have to take responsibility for the increase, which was sure to earn the people's resentment, and that when the crisis had passed he could take the cabinet back into his own hands. His strategy was certainly adroit.

The Saionji cabinet had fallen into the trap, but not so inescapably that it was obliged to relinquish power. It could have hung on if it had so wished. Had it been Katsura and not Saionji, he might have found ways to survive and last for another year or two. Saionji, however, did not crave power, and, despite opposition from ministers Matsuda and Hara and executives of the party, he insisted on the cabinet's resignation. The unexpected capitulation aroused discontent and criticism within the party as well.

THE MAKEUP OF THE SECOND KATSURA CABINET

The second Katsura government was established on July 14, 1908. The composition was more or less the same as the first. Without a single member of a political party it was a pure non-party government. The only novelties were that Prime Minister Katsura also took for himself the finance minister's portfolio, and that Gotō Shinpei, who was then serving as president of the South Manchurian Railway, was chosen to be minister of communications as well as governor of the railroad agency.

The major issue facing the country was still financial. Governmental spending had been excessive as a result of the war with Russia and the ensuing readjustments, and there was an urgent need for a drastic reform of fiscal policy. The fall of the Saionji government was popularly termed a "violent death" or "poisoning," but its underlying cause was the mismanagement of its economic policy. As soon as the new cabinet was formed, therefore, Katsura took the finance portfolio for himself with the idea of managing it according to his prescription for streamlining spending and living up to the nation's expectations.

Katsura's self-confidence was obvious to everyone. As an administrator, he was best at things like financial retrenchment. Most of the cabinet members were veteran bureaucrats and rather shop-worn and uninspiring, though the addition of Gotō Shinpei made it seem that the second Katsura cabinet was somehow fresher than the first had been.

Gotō was indeed unusual for a Meiji man. He was a physician. When Itagaki was attacked by an assassin in Gifu in 1882, it was Gotō, the head of a Nagoya hospital, who was called to attend him. Gotō was still a handsome young man. The older men surrounding the wounded Itagaki were skeptical about what this youth could do to help. Gotō was not in the least perturbed. "I must have a look at his wound. Take his clothes off," he ordered. Itagaki was lying on a rattan sofa. His frock coat had been removed but he still wore his fur vest. "We can't undress a wounded man," said one of Itagaki's men. "You can, if you're careful not to hurt him," replied Gotō firmly. And so saying, he took a pair of surgical scissors and cut open Itagaki's shirt from the sleeve. "Well, here's a rare fellow!" said one of the men, impressed. The incident made a quick name for Gotō quite early in his life. Once his brilliance was recognized it was not long before Gotō was invited to join the staff of the sanitation bureau in the home ministry, eventually becoming its director-general. A director-general today is regarded as belonging to a lower echelon of the civil service, but in those days it was a powerful position and Gotō was the target of considerable envy, particularly as he was still quite young.

However, as a result of his involvement in the notorious[5] Sōma incident and the fact that he sided with Nishikiori Gosei, Gotō was tried and spent some time in jail. It was a disaster that profoundly affected his life at the time, but it also spread his fame as "gallant Gotō." While he was forced to give up his position as head of the sanitation bureau he was not a man to rust away. In the meantime, the war with China broke out, and his success as head of the quarantine bureau when the soldiers returned victorious from the battlefield won him the attention of General Kodama, who selected him to be the civil administrator of Taiwan. Several before him had filled the post but all had been unpopular. Under Gotō things apparently went better than they ever had. He was successful in governing the new territory as well. Gotō was in a sense too talented and often did things that were unusual. He was a stallion that needed a good rider to hold the reins and check him from going astray. In Taiwan, General Kodama had a firm hand on the reins. But Gotō had no one to restrain him when he made that mistake over the Sōma incident.

During the second Katsura government I was still mayor of Tokyo and often visited the prime minister at his official residence over the question of the trolley system purchase. On one such occasion, Katsura politely asked me to wait in another room for a few minutes because something had cropped up and he had a visitor. I asked who it was. It was Gotō, the minister for communications, I was told. After a while I was asked to rejoin Katsura, but hardly ten minutes had passed when a secretary interrupted us saying, "Minister Gotō is at the front door wishing to see you, sir." Katsura laughingly told the secretary to show him in. "Didn't Gotō just leave?" I asked. Katsura replied amusedly, "This sort of thing happens often. On his way home, he gets an idea and comes back. Sometimes he returns three to four times. Every time he comes with a different idea. Out of three or four there is sure to be one good one, so I try to see him each time." This was a new insight into Gotō from the mouth of Katsura.

Gotō was a sort of genius. He may not have been a deep thinker, but from time to time he had an inspiration. Then he would act on it without much thought and often ended up with impractical results. While Katsura was there to hold him back things were not allowed to get out of hand, but after Katsura's death Gotō felt he could get away with anything, often with unfortunate consequences. Yet it was from about this time that Gotō became lionized by the people. Interestingly, like Itō, he too retained his simplicity until his death.

---

[5] A sensational, decade-long dispute centering on the Sōma, a retainer family of the former daimyo of Nakamura, that became publicized and politicized.

The Katsura government separated the railways from the Ministry of Communications, and Gotō was appointed their first governor. Soon after his appointment, he ordered uniforms made for station masters and all railway employees. He even had a governor's uniform made for himself. It looked much like the uniform of a naval officer, and Gotō became a familiar sight in it, wearing a short sword at his side. He reminded one of Itō, who did the same when he was resident-general of Korea. Gotō was exceedingly pleased when he was decorated with the Second Class Order of Merit. It was said that he was so proud of it that he wore it on his chest and walked around his room all night with it on. Strangely, this simple, unaffected manner won him mass popularity.

Apart from Gotō there was no outstanding figure in the second Katsura ministry. Nonetheless, after he had signed the Anglo-Japanese alliance during his first term of office and with the Russo-Japanese war over, no one called Katsura's second cabinet a deputy cabinet.

THE REFORMERS' STRUGGLE WITH THE ESTABLISHMENT

This was a period of appeasement between the clan bureaucrats and the political parties, with the government changing hands by prearrangement between Katsura and Saionji. This compromise between the *hanbatsu* and the party politicians lasted for some ten years, with the first Katsura cabinet preceding the first Saionji cabinet which was followed by the second Katsura and then the second Saionji cabinets. While Katsura was at the helm the Seiyūkai was the ruling party, and whenever Saionji headed the government Katsura's bureaucrats were in support.

We had had our share of bitter experience in the Matsukata-Ōkuma cabinet when we had to suffer for our party's appeasement of the *hanbatsu*. Since then we had known better than to let that happen again. The Matsukata-Ōkuma cabinet had been an arrangement between the *hanbatsu* and political party members, and its collapse was caused by internal conflicts. This time, the *hanbatsu* bureaucrats and the political party made arrangements to take turns creating different cabinets and thus remained alternating in power for ten years and more.

As the politics of appeasement developed in their new guise, the bureaucrats under Katsura rapidly consolidated their strength as recounted in earlier sections, but the Seiyūkai also expanded its power remarkably. At the time of the twenty-first Diet the Seiyūkai commanded 139 seats, in the twenty-second it had 149, in the twenty-third 171, and in the twenty-fourth 180. Under the Saionji cabinet following the general election of May, 1908, the Seiyūkai commanded 193 seats and an absolute majority. This naturally tended to make the party increasingly despotic. Inevitably there was a reaction against this., and as might have been expected the central counter-force was the Kensei Hontō.

Under pressure from the burgeoning Seiyūkai the Kensei Hontō was losing its strength by the day, and in order to reverse its fortunes impetus was given to plans for the merger of the nongovernmental political parties. This led to the emergence of two groups, which represented opposing reactions to the Seiyūkai, one against the arbitrariness of the *hanbatsu* bureaucrats, and the other against the high-handedness of the Seiyūkai.

To compete when Itō organized the Seiyūkai, the Kensei Hontō invited Ōkuma Shigenobu to be its president. But the real power of the party after I left fell naturally to Inukai Tsuyoshi, who enjoyed close relations with Ōishi Masami and worked with him to manage party affairs. Inukai's mind was focused solely on destroying the *hanbatsu*. If an alliance were to be made he wanted it to be with the Seiyūkai and to be aimed expressly at attacking the *hanbatsu* fortress. He had no appetite for striking an alliance with the Daidō club, which was friendly with the *hanbatsu* bureaucrats.

Pitted against Inukai's group, however, there existed a party within the party called the Yarai Club. It was often referred to as the Manan-gumi, as it chose to meet at the Man'an Club. Hatoyama Kazuo[6] and Takada Sanae were among its leaders. The group's general affairs were administered by Inukai, Ōishi, and (though less popular than the others) Hatoyama.

There was another group called the Hamano-ie-gumi, which was led by Hiraoka Kōtarō, the hero from Fukuoka. Hiraoka greatly disliked the Seiyūkai and was therefore opposed to Inukai's alliance of the popular parties. These two groups, in league with rank and file party members, formed yet another, the Kairakuen-gumi following the general election of March, 1903.

The three together, with an approximate membership of fifty-six, constituted the so-called reformist group. Their three principal objectives were an open policy, public election of officers, and the establishment of a new party. The Inukai group considered itself the mainstream.

The conflict between the reformists and the mainstream lasted a long time. The first victory marked by the reformist group was its success in wooing Ōishi Masami to its side. "Whether to pit ourselves against the *hanbatsu* or the Seiyūkai, that is the question. While it seems logical philosophically to strike at the *hanbatsu*, this would in the end give undue advantage to the Seiyūkai. The best option therefore is to work with the *hanbatsu* to defeat the Seiyūkai." It was with this reasoning that Ōishi was successfully converted to the reformist group.

The group's plan was to establish a new party with Katsura as its president and to launch a united attack against the Seiyūkai. As long as Ōkuma was president he would be an obstacle, and as long as Inukai held power he would be opposed. Therefore, the so-called rebellion against party executives amounted to nothing but the expulsion of Ōkuma and Inukai. At a meeting of the group's elected representatives on December 24, 1906, the reformists appointed new House officials, reducing the number of floor leaders from seven to five and of party whips from two to one, naming Ōishi Masami to the post. At the council meeting that followed on January 19, 1907, the party rejected the draft declaration prepared by its president Ōkuma as being disadvantageous to party strategy, adopting instead a drastically altered policy declaration. It also passed party regulations that abolished the select general affairs committee and replaced it with a standing commit-

---

[6] Father of Hatoyama Ichirō, prime minister from 1954 to 1956.

tee. As a result of the election of standing members of the fifteen-member committee, six were chosen from the mainstream group and nine from the reformists, the latter thus securing control of the party executive organ and celebrating their second victory. By now, Ōkuma realized that his convictions were not respected by the party, and with a representative council system replacing party management through the general affairs committee, he saw that as party president he was also redundant. Recognizing that these developments were tantamount to his expulsion, Ōkuma delivered a touching but grand farewell and took his leave as party president. Inukai was also driven from his key position as floor leader and found himself reduced to being one of the fifteen standing members of the committee.

Ōishi alone was triumphant as leader of the majority in the standing committee and the only floor leader. By then, Hiraoka Kōtarō had died due to illness, and Hatoyama Kazuo, the initiator of the reformist group, had left them for the Seiyū-kai, leaving Ōishi to be their nominal as well as their veritable head.

The Rikken Kokumintō
(National Constitutional Party) Established

For a year or two Inukai suffered not only from the bitter disappointment he felt at this turn of events but also from a painful and life-threatening gallstone condition. It looked as though he might end his days in adversity. However, following the general election of May, 1908, the course of action taken by the newly-elected representatives changed the situation for him. These newcomers to the Diet were concerned about the division within the party and tried at first to mediate between Inukai and Ōishi, but when their efforts fell on deaf ears within the reformist group, they ended up siding with Inukai. At the meeting of the Diet members on December 20, they voted both floor leaders, Inukai as well as Ōishi, back in. The reformists were naturally opposed, and a deadly pall hung over the meeting, but the group pushing for the re-election of the two prevailed. This time, Ōishi tendered his resignation as floor leader, leaving Inukai alone in the post.

The reformists, however, were victorious at the convention, seizing eleven out of fifteen places on the standing committee. On February 24, 1909, the new committee discussed the possibility of forming a new party. Inukai criticized it forcefully, taking pains to explain the duties of a political party and pointing out the evils of allying with a house party of the clan group, but to his great vexation the committee passed the motion to establish a new party. It did not stop there. The reformists, flushed with victory, demanded of Ōishi that Inukai be expelled. They said they would first recommend Inukai's voluntary withdrawal from the party, and expel him if he did not comply. Inukai brushed off the threat, saying "I have no reason to be expelled. I therefore have no intention of complying." In this way the internal conflict of the Kensei Hontō reached its climax.

The Diet members' group, furious at the violence of the reformist-dominated standing committee, passed the following resolution by acclamation: "The Diet members' group continues to have confidence in Inukai Tsuyoshi, the floor leader." It also passed another resolution, averring, "The Diet members' group recognizes that Ōishi Masami has already resigned as floor leader." The party convention then passed a resolution recommending the resignation of the standing committee, holding it accountable for what had happened. It also passed with loud acclaim another, stating, "The party convention rejects the expulsion of Inukai Tsuyoshi carried out by the standing committee." Inukai's ordeal had revived him and given him an opportunity to regain his hold on power and overcome the internal conflicts of the party. When at last these conflicts within the Kensei Hontō had been settled, Inukai commenced working to realize his long-standing ambition of merging the popular parties. In 1910 he proposed an alliance—first of all, with the Matashinkai group.

Since I had left the Seiyūkai, the small study group I had started, called the Dōshi Kenkyūkai, had evolved in turn into the Dōkōkai, the Seikō Club, the Yuyo-kai, and then the Matashin-kai. Every year the name had changed, but its membership had grown to forty-four as it merged with smaller groups sharing the same convictions.

By this time I had rejoined the Seiyūkai, leaving me as an observer with regard to the merger with the Kensei Hontō. For twenty years my political life had been determined by what I had believed to be my moral duty. In the last few years, however, I had permitted myself to move without any such pretext. So it was with my decision to rejoin the Seiyūkai. If a reason must be found, I suppose it was that I felt a need to strengthen the party, and in turn the House of Representatives, against the power of the Peers. I set no conditions for my return to the Seiyūkai. It was as if I checked into an inn called the Seiyūkai, where I had stayed before, signing my name at reception. For the Seiyūkai, it was simply a case of adding another name to the list: Ozaki Yukio, (room so-and-so).

While I remained an observer, Inukai's party alliance movement sent huge ripples over the political waters. At the time, the Matashinkai, like the Kensei Hontō, was composed of both popular party members and others who had come over from the bureaucratic groups. When it was approached by Inukai regarding a possible merger, the party split, and members of one faction of the popular party formed their own group, calling it the Mumeikai (nameless group).

Meanwhile, the *hanbatsu* bureaucrats were striving for a major realignment among the non-Seiyūkai groups in order to establish a new party. The reformist faction within the Kensei Hontō having lost its strength, and the so-called "popular party group" having moved out of the Matashinkai, the grand alliance had become a lost cause. The bureaucrats now embarked on a strategic campaign to form an alliance within their own group. This proved an instant success. On March 2, 1910, the Chūō Club was founded, adding to the entire Daidō Club a majority of the members of the Ishin Club and a number of ex-bureaucrat politicians who belonged to no group.

At about the same time, the authentic popular party (Mintō) group were conferring to create their own party, resulting, on March 13 of the same year, in the birth of the Rikken Kokumintō (People's Constitutional Party), amalgamating the whole of the Kensei Hontō, the whole of the Mumeikai, most of the Matashinkai members, and the remaining members of the Ishin Club.

Kōno Hironaka, Shimada Saburō, Sakamoto Kinnya, and Sakurai Kazuhisa joined from the Matashinkai, with Sengoku Mitsugu and Kataoka Naoharu coming from the Ishin Club. Inukai and Ōishi from the old Kensei Hontō, together with Kōno as representative of the new Diet members, were elected to run the general affairs of the new Kokumintō.

The political map was extremely clear. There were now three parties: the Seiyū-kai with 204 seats, the Kokumintō with 92, and the Chūōtō with 50.

POLITICAL MERGER "A COINCIDENCE OF SENTIMENTS"

The establishment of the Kokumintō dealt a severe blow to the Katsura ministry. At its inception, the cabinet announced a platform of impartiality. It would collaborate with any political party with which it shared similar views; it was, however, prepared to fight, however many times it had to dissolve the House, with any party that tried to ride rough-shod over opposition through sheer weight of numbers. Being a cunning man, Katsura had a secret understanding with Saionji to secure the collaboration of the Seiyūkai. The reformist faction within the Kensei Hontō, on the other hand, remained a formidable force, and there was still a chance of a successful alliance among the non-Seiyūkai groups. Katsura had positioned himself well for either option. However, for the reasons described above, the non-Seiyūkai alliance failed and the existence of the opposition Kokumintō party left the government with only the support of the Chūō Club with its fifty members.

While the Kokumintō actually had a strength of fewer than a hundred, it constituted a potentially formidable fighting force under Inukai's leadership. Its establishment was thus a major threat to the Katsura cabinet. Inukai, seeking to make the most of the situation, secretly met with Viscount Akimoto Yoshitomo of the Seiyūkai and proposed that the two parties work together to put up a fight against the government. Akimoto agreed and communicated his understanding with Inukai to Saionji and the two party executives, Matsuda and Hara. Hara Takashi did not go along with the idea; he did not think the time ripe, and Inukai's plan was stillborn. However, there were those among the Seiyūkai who were unhappy at the prospect of close collaboration with the Katsura government, so Inukai's proposition for an alliance, although it never materialized, shook the party. Inukai and his men skillfully encouraged the dissent, and the situation within the Seiyūkai was becoming increasingly precarious.

At just this time the Kōtoku Shūsui[7] Treason Incident took place. And the issue of a four per cent rate of interest on the public debt became a cause for public dissatisfaction. Political instability increased.

---

[7] Kōtoku (1871–1911), a well-known socialist who turned anarchist and, together with ten others, was executed for complicity in a plot to assassinate Emperor Meiji. Because the records of the trial have never been made public, it is often assumed that the case against him was weak.

At the beginning of the twenty-seventh Diet, against a background of these events, the Kokumintō submitted a vote of no confidence. The motion was rejected by a vote of 201 to 96, but this did not conceal the dark shadow which loomed over the Katsura ministry. Even Prime Minister Katsura himself could not remain calm, and in January, 1911 he visited Saionji at his residence to publicly request the assistance of the Seiyūkai. In fact, the two princes had met quite frequently, and with a tacit arrangement already made the talks on collaboration proceeded without difficulty. This was not to be a matter merely of collaboration at the policy level, but a much more comprehensive partnership, based on a "coincidence of sentiments." On January 29, the prime minister with his cabinet ministers hosted a banquet to which Seiyūkai members were invited at the Seiyūken restaurant in Ueno, to declare publicly their newly agreed alliance. "In the year 1911 it is no longer appropriate to insist upon the old notion of a transcendent cabinet. It is expected that politicians change with the times." And with this, the Katsura cabinet abandoned its so-called "transcendental posture."

In reply, Saionji said, "The government and Seiyūkai are of one mind and our collaboration should complete the task of perfecting the constitutional government. It is to this end that I lead the Seiyūkai. I express my deep respect to the Prime Minister for his broad-mindedness in embracing this historic opportunity for the political development of our nation." In this way the Katsura cabinet and the Seiyūkai struck a compromise. It soon came to light, however, that there was considerable dissatisfaction among the party members and that incidences of serious infighting had taken place. Be that as it may, Katsura did give up his long-cherished design of "transcendency" by acknowledging the self-assertion of the political party. I believe that by then he had already made up his mind. The organization of the Dōshikai later could not have been an accident.

The Katsura government was able to survive the twenty-seventh Diet thanks to its collaboration, known as the "coincidence of sentiments," it enjoyed with the Seiyūkai, but suddenly, on August 25, Katsura relinquished power, calling it a "voluntary resignation." According to the announcement issued by the government, most of the political commitments that had been announced at the time it came to power had been fulfilled.

THE SECOND SAIONJI CABINET

Following Katsura's petition before the throne to be relieved of his office as prime minister, Saionji, who was vacationing in Ikaho, was summoned to the palace and asked to form a cabinet. The second Saionji cabinet was born on August 30. Regarding the formation of the cabinet, departing from convention, the *genrō* elders were not consulted, and the imperial mandate fell on Saionji with only Katsura's recommendation. For his part, Saionji did not consult others outside the Seiyūkai in making his choice of cabinet members. Although only four of the cabinet seats—Prime Minister Saionji, Home Minister Hara Takashi, Minister of Justice Matsuda Masahisa, and Minister of Education Haseba Sumitaka—went to genuine Seiyūkai members, the other cabinet members, with the exception of the armed forces representatives, were more or less related to the Seiyūkai, so one could say that it was virtually a Seiyūkai party cabinet.

The Saionji ministry adopted an austerity policy from the beginning and introduced plans to retrench administrative and fiscal spending. In spite of the opposition of some party members, the cabinet postponed various costly public works projects including the improvement of local port facilities. The navy ministry compiled a seven-year armaments expansion program with a budget of approximately 350 million yen, which the minister tendered to the cabinet, while the army ministry also submitted a seven-year program with a budget of 50 million yen. However, the cabinet reached a passive decision to postpone even these armament expansion programs.

This was the policy with which the Saionji cabinet faced the twenty-eighth Diet. The Kokumintō and the Chūō Club, which was the direct retainer of the previous cabinet, were actively opposed to it, but there was nothing they could do since the Seiyūkai commanded an absolute majority in the House of Representatives.

In the meantime the House completed its term and the eleventh general election took place on May 15, 1912. The results, which leaned heavily towards the Seiyūkai, gave the party 211 seats, while the Kokumintō garnered 95, the Chūō Club 31, and independents 44.

After more or less successfully initiating administrative and tax reforms as it had intended, the Saionji cabinet unexpectedly ran aground over the 1913 budget. General Uehara Yusaku, the army minister, proposed an expansion of the army by two divisions, declaring that in the event the cabinet refused his request he would not be able to draw up a retrenchment plan under the auspices of the army ministry.

An additional two divisions had long been demanded by the army. Such a plan had been submitted in 1910 during the second Katsura ministry, but it had been refused by Katsura, who then was doubling as prime minister and finance minister. The army subsequently made the same demand to the Saionji government, but the cabinet for reasons of fiscal strain failed to adopt it, postponing the question instead to the 1913 fiscal budget, with the promise only that if revenue could be obtained as a result of administrative retrenchment and tax reform it would be used towards the cost of the two divisions.

And when the time came for the preparation of the 1913 budget, coinciding ominously with fiscal destitution, the expansion of the army became a major issue affecting the very survival of the cabinet.

At this critical moment for the Saionji ministry, Katsura suddenly announced plans to travel abroad. Katsura explained that he was only realizing what had been his heart's desire for many years, but in view of the timing it caught the attention of the entire political world. In addition to Katsura's, there were three other explanations that went around.

The first explanation held that Katsura's foreign travels would enable him to sever his relations with the Saionji cabinet. It was Katsura's dream to become prime minister three times, but if the Saionji cabinet deadlocked while he was in the country he would, out of a sense of indebtedness, have to give it a helping hand. That meant he had to share the burden of responsibility. So he chose to travel abroad to avoid doing so.

The second explanation was related to the plans he had for Russia—in other words, to inherit the unfinished business of Itō, who had fallen at the hands of an assassin at Harbin Station, and open the way to amicable relations with Russia, thus effecting a shift from the diplomacy of the past centered around Britain. The proof of this analysis was said to have been Katsura's decision to visit Moscow and to have Gotō, who was well versed in Russian affairs, accompany him.

The third was that his true intentions lay in preparing for the organization of a new party. Even Katsura, who was considered to be a master at manipulating political parties, would have come to realize through his experience of organizing two cabinets that smooth management of government cannot be achieved without a political party base, and to learn from the wisdom of Itō's organization of the Seiyūkai how to form his own political party and supported by its strength to be active on the political scene. His foreign travels would enable him to observe examples of advanced societies and thus help to prepare him for the realization of the intention of which he had already informed the emperor, who had responded favorably.

I do not know which of the three was nearest the truth. Most likely there was some truth in each of them. Katsura was not a man of simple motives. In any event, on July 6, 1912, Katsura left for the West, accompanied by Gotō Shinpei and Wakatsuki Reijirō.

But no sooner had the little group of travelers set foot in Moscow than Katsura received the sad news that Emperor Meiji had fallen ill, and he immediately set out to return home. Despite the prayers of the whole nation, His Majesty died on July 30. It is with awe that we recall the illustrious virtues of His Majesty in promoting the cause of constitutional government. And so we said farewell to the beloved era of Meiji and entered that of Taishō.

I, for one, committed myself to what I believed in the depths of my heart to be my most important trust as a subject of the late beloved emperor, which was to devote myself utterly to the great enterprise bequeathed by His Majesty—that of completing the establishment of constitutional government in our country.

MY SECOND TRIP ABROAD

In 1910, two years before Katsura set out with great commotion to Moscow, I made my second trip abroad, this time to Europe and America. My main purpose was to attend the Inter-Parliamentary Union conference to be held in Belgium as a member of the legislature. Other legislators might have attended these conferences in previous years, but I believe this to be the first time the House of Representatives of Japan sent an official delegate.

I left Tokyo on May 11 and boarded a steamship in Tsuruga for Vladivostok. After a dismally uneventful journey on the Siberian Railway I reached Moscow and then St. Petersburg, where I was most taken by the palace. As might be expected of an autocratic country, the magnificent palace glittered with dazzling gold.

I was granted an audience with the tsar. Judging from the magnificence of the detached palace where the audience was to take place, I expected the meeting to be very formal. As I entered through the main door, a military chamberlain met and escorted me. He stopped not far from the entrance before a smaller door, which he opened, then stood aside to let me pass. Presuming it to be a waiting room or ante-room of some kind, I entered without ado. And there was the tsar. Had I known the room was His Majesty's I would of course have saluted him more formally. I was amazed at the room's simplicity.

When the chamberlain closed the door behind me, I was alone with His Majesty. We talked without ceremony for some fifteen minutes. It seemed that in such circumstances one could raise any subject. I imagined that the lack of formality was somehow intended to make up for the autocratic nature of the country. In China, when K'ang Yu-wei arrived unbidden from somewhere by the Southern Sea[8] and sought an audience with the emperor, he was not only granted this, but soon given employment as a teacher. In Japan, the family of the Tokugawa shoguns maintained a stern façade, but there was the case of the paper hanger's errand boy who won favor in the household and, having gradually ascended in rank among the servants, wielded great power for a considerable time afterwards.

Another thing that astonished me was the fact that the magnificent palace was open to the general public, and even peasants from rural villages were permitted to enter. What was more, I spotted among those allowed in a man who looked suspiciously like a beggar and carrying what I thought was a ragged red blanket. I supposed that this must be intended to show the dignity of the imperial house on the one hand and to make its subjects love and respect it on the other. In any case, to separate the house from its subjects is not desirable for the sake of the state. Even in such an autocratic country as Russia measures were well taken to make its subjects love the imperial house rather than allow it to intimidate them.

In England, I was granted an audience with the king in the audience chamber with ambassador Katō, and, as I recall, a couple of chamberlains were in attendance. His Majesty shook my hand very graciously and was most sociable. The gentleness of his manner and conversation put me at ease and made me feel as though refreshed by a light spring breeze. In the West the monarchs and other members of the royal families take much care to give a good impression and are trained in courtesy and conversation as it is incumbent on them to be paragons in matters of social intercourse. In China the monarch is expected to make people feel awed, but in the West a monarch is expected to put them at ease.

[8] K'ang (1868–1927), who styled himself Nanhai (South Seas), was well known for his opposition to the Treaty of Shimonoseki, for his reinterpretation of the classics to portray Confucius as a reformer, and for his advocacy of reforms comparable to those of Meiji Japan before he was received in audience by the Manchu emperor, Kuang-hsu, in June 1898. He was the architect of the abortive "Hundred days of reform" of that year.

His Majesty was standing, as was the case in most audiences I experienced in the West. In Europe one follows the lead of the monarch even in such matters as taking one's leave. One first waits for an eye signal or suggestive gesture. Among ordinary people it is considered good manners to leave before overstaying one's welcome, but in the case of royalty one must wait for the royal command. It is all too easy to make a mistake. With the best intention, one could take one's leave when one's royal host wished to continue the conversation.

I also recall that in England quarters in the detached palaces are granted as a privilege to meritorious subjects. I thought this a particularly good way to extend favors to those who have served the state with distinction but had fallen on dire circumstances, and I therefore was moved to study this custom myself and if appropriate to propose its application upon my return.

It is not that we do not also treat our meritorious subjects well, yet there are times when they are ignored. Itagaki Taisuke, for example, was one of the outstanding veteran statesmen of the Restoration period and his contribution had materially assisted the restoration of the imperial rule. After the Restoration, he served in the cabinet with unswerving loyalty. However, because he was not ambitious in money matters, Itagaki descended into poverty and lived a most pitiable life, but neither the government nor the ministry of the imperial household took any steps to help him. Worst of all, there were some who even sneered at his honest poverty. As witnessed in such things this can be a most tragic nation. I believe the state owed that man at least as much as to ensure that he would live out his life in comfort. In England, by contrast, when General Wolseley[9] went bankrupt due to an undeserved misfortune, the royal court promptly gave him a residence in a wing of one of the palaces and a respectable pension. It is not proper for a state to neglect its worthy servants, pretending ignorance of their condition. This can be a model for the nation of indifference and ingratitude toward good and needy people.

During this tour I mainly visited scenic areas to shake the dust from my mind, which had long been burdened with practical concerns. I also availed myself of the opportunity to visit various parts of the Continent, where I found the culture and various institutions to have undergone great changes since the last time I had been in Europe twenty-odd years before. Naturally I had expected to see marked progress and pronounced changes, but I was still more impressed by what I saw. It made me think that while Japan had also progressed, there was no comparison. In matters of urban administration, for example, I was able now to observe with quite a practiced and discerning eye, but the scale was so different. I was reminded that nothing new can be achieved without change. The differences between the West and Japan were all too clear, and yet I did not feel as overwhelmed this time as on my earlier tour. I put this down partly to a blunting of my sensitivities.

There was nothing memorable to tell about the Inter-Parliamentary Union conference. Following the conference and my tour in Europe I crossed the Atlantic

---

[9] Presumably Ozaki refers here to Garnet Joseph Wolseley (Baron Wolseley, 1st Viscount, 1883–1913).

to America. Although I traveled not as mayor of Tokyo but as one representative among others, I was welcomed very warmly everywhere I went, not only in England but also in the United States of America.

One day I visited the head office of Watermans on Broadway in New York. The store manager welcomed me cordially and presented me with two fountain pens, one each for my wife and myself. In the West, mayors are respected and popular, so I thought the gesture might after all have been to use me for publicity. I changed my mind when President Taft invited mayors of nearby cities and cabinet secretaries who were on vacation to a banquet he hosted in my honor, at which the band played a piece of music called "Mayor of Tokyo." I deeply appreciated the generous and friendly reception I received as mayor of the capital city of our victorious nation.

On November 18, we arrived back in Yokohama.

The Movement to Protect Constitutional Government

Katsura Makes a Bad Decision

On August 13, following his return from the Russian capital on learning of the demise of the Emperor Meiji, Katsura was appointed to the important positions of lord keeper of the privy seal as well as grand chamberlain and adviser to the new emperor. These appointments aroused intense public criticism. Reflecting this, Inukai made a particularly penetrating remark. It was imperative, he insisted, that the offices of lord keeper of the privy seal and grand chamberlain be filled by persons of the highest qualities such as those found in Tokudaiji and Iwakura Tomosada, men of true patriotism and loyalty to the throne, who transcended political strife. Regrettably, Katsura's record up till now showed him to be of very different caliber. If the prince would henceforth put himself outside the power struggle of which he had hitherto been a part and instead devote himself to carrying out these new duties, it would be a blessing for the empire. And if the prince were sincerely to change his attitude, Inukai conceded, he would drop the issue. However, Inukai could not overcome his misgiving that it would not be long before the prince, ruled as he was by lust for honor, power, and money, would assume an unchallenged position as regent.

Yamagata, the old leader of the Chōshū clan, it was not difficult to see, had plotted Katsura's appointment to these high offices even before Katsura's return. Katsura's appointment was seen as Yamagata's way of perpetuating his own power base among the ranks of the army and the government. Inukai, however, saw it otherwise. According to him, "When Katsura learned of the demise of the former emperor, he quickly realized that there was no one to compete with him where his record of distinguished military and civilian services was concerned. He therefore wasted no time conspiring with the forces he had planted in the palace so as to take full advantage of the moment to outshine Yamagata and advance his plan to seize the premiership." Inukai believed that Katsura's appointment to these high posts would bring about a change in the political geography. And when the time for such change came, it was likely that Katsura would emerge from the palace to organize a government.

Unfortunately, this prophecy was only too accurate. Katsura by this time had been granted the title of *kōshaku* (prince, or duke) as a reward for the annexation of Korea. He had risen to the highest station accessible to His Majesty's subjects, while in politics he had served as prime minister and within the palace as lord keeper of the privy seal and grand chamberlain. On top of this he held the rank of general of the imperial army. Katsura was at the height of his glory.

Had Katsura possessed a more civilized mind he would have used it now to do some prudent thinking. This was a time to proceed with modesty. However, hardly four months had passed since he was appointed lord keeper of the privy seal when he volunteered to organize a new government following the fall of Saionji. "If not Katsura, who would take care of the people?" he asked as he proceeded to form the third Katsura cabinet. In so doing he compromised the boundary between palace matters and government affairs and brought criticism upon himself. The circumstances were as follows.

In November 1912, the Saionji government was in the process of compiling the budget for the following year. It had seen fit to cut administrative and fiscal expenditure and defer nonessential works. Army Minister Uehara, as has been noted, insisted on an increase of two army divisions, scheming to divert all the money that would be saved from retrenchment for the purpose. Finance Minister Yamamoto Tatsuo flatly refused, whereupon Prime Minister Saionji stepped in, arguing that spending cuts and enlarging the army were two separate issues. The cabinet, he said, should decide first on the retrenchment and then discuss the other at its leisure. However, the army minister would not yield and submitted his resignation on December 2, not to the prime minister but directly to the palace. No amount of solicitation would make him retract.

Saionji requested Yamagata and Katsura to find a replacement for Uehara as army minister, but to no avail. The powerful Chōshū clique within the army was uncooperative, and no one would fill the post. And since there existed an official rule that the two service ministers should be sought from among generals and lieutenant generals on the active list, Saionji was at a loss to find a candidate to take Uehara's place. There was no other course for the prime minister but to submit his resignation with his cabinet.

At that time the Seiyūkai had a majority of two hundred in the House of Representatives. The public was surprised that it could so easily be brought down by a single army minister and through him by the Chōshū military clique.

The reins of government had recently been passing back and forth smoothly enough between Katsura and Saionji. But this time Saionji did not recommend Katsura to the palace as his successor because the latter's name had been tarnished by association with the Chōshū clique.

The *Genrō Kaigi* conferred quickly and advised Prince Saionji to stay in office, but the prince would not. Matsukata was the next to be approached, but he too declined. Hirata Tōsuke, Yamamoto Gonnohyōei, and Terauchi Masatake were asked in turn. but none would take on the task of forming a government. During these confused days the *Genrō Kaigi* met eleven times, while the government fell into extreme disarray. The outcome was Prince Katsura's reemergence as prime minister.

The criticism that was leveled against Katsura's return to the premiership could be said to have been equally directed at the Chōshū group and its strongman Prince Yamagata. Apparently Katsura had anticipated that he would be the object of criticism for confusing the line between the palace and politics. He therefore attempted to justify himself by requesting the emperor to issue an imperial rescript in his favor. This only worsened his position before the public.

Those who held grudges against a government that let itself be run by cliques and bureaucrats now rose together to condemn Katsura and the insidious ways of the cliques. Crying for the protection of constitutionalism, these forces gathered momentum in the early days of Taishō era.

THE EMERGENCE OF THE CAMPAIGN TO PROTECT CONSTITUTIONAL GOVERNMENT

A few months prior to the birth of the Katsura government—that is to say, at the beginning of June, 1912—I invited the most powerful members of the factions in the Tokyo city assembly to the speaker's room and expressed my intention to resign as mayor. I wanted to devote all my energies to national affairs as a member of the House of Representatives. My resignation officially took effect on June 27. Now that I was freed from my mayoral responsibilities I felt my burdens lightened.

I was then a member of the Seiyūkai and was very indignant at the action taken by Katsura. But as I knew the Seiyūkai would never stand up to the government I did not commit myself to leading the charge. I had, after all, had the bad experience with the Seiyūkai of being betrayed by our own president, Itō, when he compromised with Katsura during the latter's first cabinet. Out of self-respect I was not going to let this happen a second time.

The Seiyūkai, however, allied itself with Inukai's Kokumintō, its longtime foe. Putting their old bitterness behind them, the two parties agreed to work together to challenge the government. The public was supportive. Seeing this, I felt reassured that the Seiyūkai would not back out in mid-stream this time. I took up my spear.

It began with a political meeting at a restaurant called the Seiyōken in Tsukiji on the evening of December 14. It had been organized by some young politicians and members of the Kōjunsha and a number of journalists. From the Seiyūkai, I, Okazaki Kunisuke, and thirty others were present, and from the Kokumintō, Inukai was there with several of his colleagues.

Hara and Matsuda, the real power holders within the Seiyūkai, did not turn up. Nor did Ōishi or Kōno of the Kokumintō. It was at this meeting that the term *kensei yōgo-kai* (Association to Protect Constitutional Government) was coined as we decided to call a convention on December 19.

The *Kensei yōgo-kai* convention took place at the Kabukiza theater in Kyōbashi. The opening address was delivered by Seki Naohiko of the Kokumintō, and Sugita Teiichi of the Seiyūkai was elected chairman. In naming the initiators of the convention, Inukai demanded that Matsuda and Hara be included on the Seiyūkai list. The party instead asked the Kokumintō to content itself with Ozaki, Okazaki, and Sugita. As a quid pro quo, Inukai insisted that the phrase "resolutely reject compromise" be inserted in the text of a formal declaration, to guard against possible reneging by the Seiyūkai in the future.

Remembering the earlier debacle, I was wary of going too far this time, and asked if it would not be enough simply to say "reject compromise." The last time I had found myself in a comparable situation, my own president, Itō, as I have already mentioned, caused me to lose face by coming to terms with our opponent, Katsura, so that in the end I was forced to leave the party to save my honor. Okazaki Kunio promised to stand up for me if the use of the harsher term should cause me any embarrassment, so in the end I decided to give in on this point. Later, when I did leave the party, Okazaki kept his promise and left with me. Okazaki, however, got back on board at the first small excuse.

Finally, the following resolution was unanimously adopted. "The rampant tyranny of clan government has reached its height and a crisis in constitutional government is imminent. Resolutely rejecting compromise, we will stamp out clan government and protect constitutionalism."

I took the rostrum on behalf of the Seiyūkai. Inukai followed, representing the Kokumintō, and then Honda Seiichi as spokesman for the press corps. The *Kensei-yōgo-kai* (Association to Protect Constitutional Government), as we decided it should be called, voted to establish its headquarters at the Seiyōken restaurant and appointed committee members. Spirits rose sky-high and the place shook with exuberant applause. The movement to protect constitutional government had been launched.

On the twenty-seventh a huge friendship meeting was organized at the Seiyōken and resolved:

1. to organize branch, multi-party Protect Constitutional Government Associations in every part of the country, and
2. to work for the election of Association supporters in the event of a Diet dissolution.

The resolution was distributed to all Seiyūkai and Kokumintō branches the following day.

"Protect constitutional government!" "Down with cliques. Up with the people!" Ardent calls in support of the campaign rang throughout the country. It caught on swiftly as a true national movement and public opinion ignited on a single issue as never before.

Time after time Inukai and I mounted the rostrum together. The crowds, who had cheered us as partners in earlier days, were delighted to see us together again and greeted us with the greatest excitement. Around this time they began to refer to us as the two champions of constitutional government.

The pace and fervor of activity grew stronger constantly as the first year of Taishō led to the second. On January 12, 1913, a coalition convention, at which I spoke from the same platform with Inukai, was held at the Youth Hall in Osaka's Tosa-bori. On the same day in Tokyo representatives of eighteen union organizations met at the Matsumotorō in Hibiya Park. On the sixteenth nonparliamentary members of the Seiyūkai and the Kokumintō held a convention in the same location. On the seventeenth a national convention of journalists took place at the Seiyōken. On the eighteenth a second informal meeting was held there by members of the Kensei-yōgo-kai, and on the twenty-fourth Tokyo Kyōbashi's Shintomiza theater was the venue for the *Kensei-yōgo-kai's* second convention. Public meetings and conventions took place in quick succession, giving ever greater momentum to the surging constitutional movement.

On all these occasions I was always there with Inukai. In fact we two were the center of the whole movement. Whenever we appeared voices from the audience called out for everyone to take their hats off to salute us. So enthusiastic was the welcome everywhere we went that it was often hard for us to make ourselves heard. But when at last we were allowed to speak there was dead silence and each one in the audience was with us.

On February 9 a huge convention was organized by the non-parliamentary members of the two parties at the Kokugikan National Sumō Pavilion at Ryōgoku in Tokyo. Even that mammoth pavilion was unable to contain the twenty thousand people who clamored to get in. Inukai and I both addressed the immense crowd, and the spirit of the people was at its peak.

The Formation of the Dōshikai

Seeing that the demand for constitutional government was spreading like wildfire throughout the country and his authority in the Diet became more threatened day by day, Katsura finally decided to organize a major political party himself to bolster his position. Gotō Shinpei, Sugiyama Shigemaru, and Akiyama Teisuke lost no time in presenting themselves at Katsura's political headquarters.

The thirty-four-member Chūō Club could be counted on to join the new alliance as it was led by Ōura Kanetake, a confidant of Prime Minister Katsura. He also had many so-called reformist members planted in the Kokumintō. Therefore, he planned on making these two groups the nucleus of his new political party, to which he would add a splinter faction from the Seiyūkai.

On January 20, 1913, Katsura invited the representatives of the major news agencies to his private residence in Mita and, with Gotō in attendance, announced the formation of a new political party. Sure enough, the Katsura men lying in wait in the Kokumintō promptly rose. The very next day, Ōishi Masami, Kōno Hironaka, Shimada Saburō, Minoura Katsundo, and Taketomi Tokitoshi, five of the leading members of the Kokumintō, abandoned the party and joined Katsura's bandwagon. At a meeting of its elected members quickly called at party headquarters the Kokumintō decided that no replacements would be appointed for Ōishi and Kōno and that Inukai alone would remain as leader in the House.

But "like-minded people" continued to go over to Katsura's coalition, so that in the end, with forty-six of its members having defected, the Kokumintō was reduced to a minor party of forty-one with Inukai as its leader. With most of his old-time comrades snatched away by Katsura, Inukai must have been deeply embittered.

I was hardly aware of the signs as these events unfolded, but in retrospect it is evident that Katsura must have nursed this plan long before the event. The predecessor of the Kokumintō was the Shinpotō or Progressive Party, whose precursor in turn was the Kaishintō. That is to say that most of those who defected to Katsura now were old comrades of mine too, men alongside whom I fought shoulder to shoulder in the past. It even turned out that Akiyama Teisuke, who had been Katsura's closest confidant, had apparently planned to include me in the plot.

It was in the summer of 1912 that Akiyama brought his wife and stayed with me for a week at a rented villa in Karuizawa. I had been a good friend to him. At one time we had belonged to the same group in the House. On one occasion that I remember when Akiyama was publicly accused of spying for Russia, I devoted myself to clearing him of dishonor. However, we had never visited each other's homes. I rarely visited people in their homes, even those with whom I happened to have cordial relations. Consequently I had extremely little social life.

However, when the Akiyamas stayed with me at Karuizawa we talked day and night of many things. There was some mention of a plan by Katsura to organize a political party but I let it pass as small talk. I expressed no opinion about it, one way or another. I have normally had little compunction when it came to expressing a critical opinion about others. The fact that on this occasion I kept my peace might have led Akiyama to believe that I was a sympathizer who would join them once the party was launched. I was not aware of this at the time, but what took place later led me to believe this might have been the case.

One evening in the winter of that year Akiyama visited me at my home in Shinagawa to try to talk me into joining them when the new party was launched. He tried to persuade me by saying that if I agreed to join them they would without question follow my guidance. It was my usual style to work with anyone who would act on my advice, but I could not believe from what I had so far of seen of Katsura that he would be so accommodating. Without hesitation I declined.

Akiyama was most reluctant to take no for an answer and continued to press me tenaciously. He was quite carried away by his own fervor. I did not know how to get rid of him. It was at least three in the morning before he finally left without achieving his objective. I was under considerable strain in those days and had not stayed up so late for many years. I promptly came down with a wretched cold and was forced to take to my bed for several days.

Katsura must have been made to believe through Akiyama that he would have my assistance. So he must have been very much surprised, and Akiyama even more so, when I led the Seiyūkai in defying them. In the end, the new party was able to muster eighty-six members in all—thirty-four from the Chūō Club, forty-six defectors from the Kokumintō, and six others.

On February 1, the new party established an office in the Imperial Hotel and was in a hurry to inaugurate itself. Katsura left the organization work up to Ōura, Gotō and the five ex-Kokumintō leaders. At a meeting of parliamentary members on the fifth, Ōishi and Kōno were appointed as the floor leaders. When Katō Takaaki joined, the party had five party leaders: Katō, Ōura Kanetake, Gotō Shinpei, Ōishi Masami, and Kōno Hironaka.

The new party was called the Rikken Dōshikai, or Constitutional Association of Like-Minded Friends. On February 7, a declaration was released in the name of Katsura Tarō, chairman of the inaugural committee. It stated: "In recognition of the many courtesies extended to me personally, I shall consult with like-minded people throughout the land, establish a public party, include powerful figures within the Empire, represent the just opinion of the people, exercise enlightened government, secure the foundations of the imperial rule, and thereby ensure constitutional government for the Empire."

Katsura Succumbs

On January 21, the Diet resumed following the New Year recess, but the public would not be satisfied until it had brought the Katsura government down. The prime minister therefore requested fifteen days' adjournment to give him time to organize the new party.

At the time the constitutional movement was born, Matsuda Masahisa and Hara Takashi, the strongmen of the Seiyūkai, were not yet committed. Hara was said to have coolly stated that, regardless of allegations, he was by no means a lackey of the clan cliques. Coincidence of sentiment did not mean surrender. On the contrary, Hara said *he* was using *them*. A political party develops only when it seizes the reins of government. By means of compromise, Hara boasted, he had cultivated the political foundations of the party as well as expanded its influence within the government. Without power nothing could be done. The opposition would continue to use the vote of no confidence as their tool no matter how many times the House might be dissolved. It was a poor tactic. The important point was to remain in the majority after each dissolution. Then, he said, it would be the enemy's turn to come to terms with the majority. What mattered, Hara said, was to be in power; nothing of note could be accomplished until then. If this fundamental compromise was acceptable, Hara continued, he was willing to collaborate.

As our movement gained momentum, the party leaders began to come around. The Speaker of the House, Ōoka Ikuzō and Hara's confidant, Yoshiue Shōichirō, turned up at the second informal gathering. When the second public convention was held on the twenty-fourth, Matsuda Masahisa showed up. And at the "white vote" gathering on the evening of February 5, the white-haired Hara Takashi was there in person.

On February 5, when parliament reconvened after the extended recess, we submitted a vote of no confidence against the cabinet. It was cosponsored by Motoda Hajime, Inukai Tsuyoshi, Seki Naohiko, Matsuda Masahisa, the leaders of the Seiyūkai and Kokumintō, and myself and supported by a majority of two hundred and ninety-nine.

The Seiyūkai was now the principal force pitted against the government and so was forced to fight the Katsura regime on the main stage. Matsuda, Hara, Motoda, and I discussed what would be the best strategy. Hara argued in favor of questioning the government before making a direct challenge. Motoda supported the idea. I was for launching the attack immediately as I thought we were unlikely to get any verbal commitment from the government. It would only dilute our focus. I was the minority in this as the others were all for a less confrontational approach. I said I would not ask questions but would wait and see how things evolved.

As it turned out, Motoda did not get far with his questioning. In fact, the prime minister made a mockery of him and used the opportunity to put on a most triumphant pose. I was disgusted and indignant. As I had feared, the questioning tactic had backfired and compromised the Seiyūkai stand.

My original thought was to present a strong argument for the government's impeachment, but couched in restrained language, and I had prepared a speech based on reason intended to choke the cabinet politely. When Katsura answered Motoda's questions in his condescending way, however, I was enraged. Mounting the rostrum in great fury, I completely forgot my prepared text and lashed out at the prime minister. Particularly objectionable was the way Katsura had slighted the imperial rescript, claiming he was not to be held responsible for it. Knowing that he held Germany in awe as though it were his guardian deity, I asked Katsura if he was aware that Prince Von Bülow when he was chancellor had publicly held himself responsible for every word of the Kaiser's. A prime minister must be accountable for all things, even for his sovereign's words. For Katsura to disclaim responsibility for the rescript showed his gross lack of understanding of a basic principle of constitutional government.

Katsura was visibly nonplussed. My tone hardened and the remainder of my speech devolved into an emotional torrent. "They pay lip service to loyalty and patriotism, as if these were their monopoly," I denounced the government, "but just look how they behave. They hide behind the throne, lying in wait to ambush their political foes. They have made the throne their breastplate, and the rescript their bullets to destroy their enemy!" The Dōshikai men were booing, but the more they booed the more my rage possessed me as I hurled my attack at Katsura.

Then an absurd thought flashed into my mind. If I suddenly pointed my finger at Katsura he might try to avoid it and fall off his chair! It was only a few steps from the rostrum to where he sat. Addressing the prime minister with great vehemence, I took a couple of steps forward, pointing directly at him. Carried away as I was at the moment with my own oratory the details may escape me now, but I could have sworn his face turned green. Unfortunately, Katsura did not fall off his seat.

After speaking for twenty minutes or so I left the podium feeling deflated. The short speech had taken much more out of me than usual. Having abandoned my prepared text, I returned to my seat discouraged. To my surprise, not only my colleagues but many who were not normally so friendly came running to congratulate me. Regaining my self-esteem, I felt better. Still, it was an unusual speech.

Apparently, a Frenchman who was in the gallery that day jumped to his feet with excitement when he heard me speak and was ordered out of the chamber by a guard. Dr. Mābē (phonetic spelling), chief editor of *The Outlook*, also happened to be there. When I met him later in Kamakura he asked me why I had spoken so violently. He did not understand the language, but must have been startled by my attitude and tone of voice. When emotionally provoked one can act quite outrageously.

General Terauchi Masatake, who was seated next to Katsura in the ministers' row, apparently believed that I had cast a spell on him. (Later, when it came Terauchi's turn to head the government, he would not allow me to take the floor. The day I was to make a speech impeaching his government, dissolution was called the moment I reached the rostrum.)

Prince Saionji and I

Katsura attempted to defend himself, and when Shimada Saburō was about to speak, the prime minister, fearing Shimada was going to pour salt on the wound, called for a five-day recess. Katsura was trying urgently to establish his new party, but our solidarity was firm, and the government continued to lose ground steadily. On February 8, Katō Takaaki was sent to Saionji to seek a way out of the difficulty, but in vain. The following day, Saionji was asked to the palace. Emperor Taishō asked him to exercise his good offices to assist in bringing order to the confused situation. Saionji promised to do what he could.

As soon as Saionji left the palace, he summoned Matsuda Masahisa, Hara Takashi, and me and told us what had passed between the emperor and himself. As Katsura was the cause of the political impasse, I could not, despite Saionji's intervention, agree that he should remain prime minister. I reasoned with the prince that he should not so easily have allowed himself to be put in this position even though it was the emperor's wish, and that as a true subject he should have spoken his mind. Saionji was adamant that he had already given the emperor his word and it could not be changed.

The four of us argued back and forth but could not bring ourselves to submit to the views of our president. Nor could we get the prince to take his words back. Time was passing and we were at a complete loss as to what to do. At length I spoke. We were in this disgraceful dilemma simply because we were members of parliament. A possible way out was if we were all to resign. Matsuda agreed. It was one way, he said. But no one was prepared to act on the suggestion immediately. And it was no use my being the only one to resign unless many others did so too. The idea got nowhere.

As we carried on inconclusively it became late. Inukai and others who had appointments with Saionji were calling. In these circumstances I could not face meeting Inukai, so I decided to take my leave. Matsuda and Hara remained with the prince. Before I left I told them that having openly challenged the government there could be no turning back. If Saionji insisted on my giving up the cause I would resign as floor leader.

Later a certain Komatsu Roku wrote about our meeting with Saionji and reported that the prince had scolded me. That was not true. Saionji was extremely troubled and was in no position to scold. For my part, no one except my own parents had ever scolded me. But it could well be that I am unfamiliar with the notion of being scolded because of my insensitivity. Possibly Saionji may have said something to me like, "That's going to be a problem." For a well brought-up person it could have been meant as a scolding, and so was reported in that way. If that were the case, it is all the more interesting as it gives an inkling of the aristocratic way of doing things.

Be that as it may, on my way home to Shinagawa from the prince's mansion in Surugadai, I noticed that the Seiyūkai headquarters in Shiba was lit as bright as day in spite of it being close to midnight. It looked as though quite a few people were waiting there to learn the outcome of the meeting at the Saionji residence. I continued on my way home without stopping, thinking that whatever I said would make little difference unless Saionji was prepared to act with us.

Soon after I got home the telephone rang. It was Matsuda asking me to go over to headquarters. Most of the men there were opposed to Saionji's decision and were determined not to budge no matter what the president might say, Matsuda informed me. He begged me to join him there. But it was already late and I was not convinced that any good would come of it. I stayed at home that night.

First thing in the morning, unconvinced as I was, I nevertheless drove over to headquarters. The men, many of them with bloodshot eyes from not having slept all night, were very excited. Some even wept as they announced their difficult decision. They would not follow the orders of their president. Seeing their resolve, I thought we could put up a fine battle. Eventually Saionji arrived. I told him that he would find most members opposed to his views and agreeing with mine. I would therefore retract the resignation I had offered on parting the previous night. There was no need for me to resign, he replied. If the majority of the members were opposed to his views there was nothing for him but to resign. I concurred.

A general meeting was held on the spot. Saionji repeated what he had said to the lord keeper of the privy seal and, in a departure from his usual proud manner, appealed to the members to come to his rescue. As I have recounted elsewhere, the prince seldom expressed himself with much emotion. It probably was the first time he had so earnestly argued on his own behalf.

However, the majority of the members, in spite of the passionate appeal of their president, could not bring themselves to agree with him. Instead, they resolved to challenge the government with a vote of no confidence. Saionji begged His Majesty's pardon for not being able to carry out the imperial will, and resigned from the presidency of the Seiyūkai and the political world.

The Yamamoto Government

On the morning of February 10, the public in tens of thousands converged upon the Diet to demonstrate in favor of democracy and constitutional government. Elected members belonging to the Protect Constitutional Government faction, each with a white rose in his lapel, entered with their heads held high as the crowd cheered.

The government braced itself, calling out three thousand police and three units of mounted special police. The sight of them only helped to turn an already excited crowd into a mob. "Down with tyranny and oppression!" they yelled. The capital was convulsed with rioting. The *Miyako Shinbun*, *Kokumin Shinbun*, *Yamato Shinbun*, *Yomiuri Shinbun*, and *Ni Roku Shinbun*—those newspapers that were sympathetic to the formation of Katsura's Dōshikai—were sacked, torched, or destroyed. Police stations were set on fire. Seventy separate locations were targets of violence, resulting in deaths and injuries among the rioters. More than two hundred rioters were taken into custody. Director-General Kawakami of the metropolitan police was forced to request the garrison commander for an emergency dispatch of troops to maintain security. The Diet was forced to recess for a third time, for three days until February 12.

In Osaka on the eleventh, members of the Osaka Youth Club held an inaugural meeting at the Youth Center in Tosa Shinbori. When police prohibited their leaders from speaking, the six hundred members present were enraged. As dusk fell they destroyed branch offices of the *Kokumin Shinbun* and *Hōchi Shinbun* and assaulted the private residences of three members of parliament: Mitani, Shichiri, and Takeuchi. By the time the growing crowd reached the Osaka Chōhō Press they numbered five thousand. Similar riots broke out in Kyoto, Kōbe, and Hiroshima.

Under the circumstances even the flexible Katsura had to take responsibility. On February 11, he summoned his ministers to his official residence and submitted the cabinet's resignation. In fifty days from its formation, it had achieved the record for the shortest stay in office in Japanese parliamentary history.

Before long, Katsura died. To all appearances he had been in fine fettle the day I attacked him so vehemently in the Diet, which made some speculate that my speech had hit him so hard it destroyed his health. It was also whispered that on his deathbed he said, "Ozaki killed me!" I doubt that I had anything to do with his death, but I might have to admit to having blunted his vanity.

With the fall of the Katsura cabinet, we expected to realize our avowed aim of eradicating clan influence and installing a constitutional government, with Matsuda Masahisa, if all went well, as the next choice for the premiership. With these expectations we were quietly advancing preparations. We were almost ready when our luck ran out. To succeed Katsura the *genrō* recommended Saionji, but as has already been stated the prince declined due to his feeling of guilt for having failed to follow the emperor's wishes, and instead he recommended Yamamoto. The *genrō* agreed, the emperor ruled accordingly, and Saionji soon after retired from politics. Naturally I was opposed to a Yamamoto cabinet. Because he was a towering figure in clan politics, a cabinet appointed by him could not fail to be precisely what we sought to abolish, no matter what excuses were made. Even Katsura had surrendered to the need for establishing a political party of his own. The next government had to be organized by the Seiyūkai or in coalition with the Kokumintō. I felt most strongly that the Seiyūkai, having felled Katsura who had himself at last come to acknowledge the inevitability of party government, could not and should not condone the creation of a Yamamoto cabinet, which had nothing to do with any political party.

Matsuda and Hara, however, let Yamamoto know that they would be prepared to participate in a coalition on condition that all ministers, with the exception of the prime minister and the foreign, army, and navy ministers, would join the Seiyūkai. At first, reaction to this initiative within the Seiyūkai was strongly negative. The members insisted that Yamamoto himself join the party, otherwise they would uncompromisingly oppose the formation of a non-constitutional government. They went so far as to threaten that any member who joined the cabinet would be expelled from the party. It took Hara Takashi's warning to make them change their minds. Hara foresaw that if they were slow to act, Katsura might well move to have a special decree issued to enable him to remain in office. In the event, an irregular coalition government was formed with Matsuda Masahisa, Hara Takashi, and Motoda Hajime included in the cabinet. Other cabinet members—Takahashi Korekiyo, Yamamoto Tatsui, Okuda Yoshito, and Tokonami Takejiro, governor of the national railways—joined the Seiyūkai.

With this development, I had no choice but to leave the Seiyūkai. Twenty-four members of the party left with me. Every time I took on the government from within the Seiyūkai I ended up leaving the party. The truth is that I had seen warning signs from the beginning, and I was right again, as things proved. As soon as Katsura fell, the Seiyūkai fell into line with the clan government of Yamamoto and declared that the Protect Constitutional Government movement was over.

There were suspicions that Yamamoto and Hara Takashi had been colluding secretly even before the collapse of the Katsura government. On the morning of February 10, when both the Katsura government and the Seiyūkai were on tenterhooks over whether the cabinet would stand or fall, Yamamoto appeared uninvited at Katsura's residence. Without removing his coat and hat and with his cane still in his hand, he walked straight into the house and told Katsura he should step down. The public was criticizing the way Katsura had maneuvered the new emperor in order to take power and had bestowed benefits at will. Geniality and bonhomie were Katsura's fortes. They had helped him win many victories. He had earned the nickname "*nikopon*," or backslapper. Now, however, the discourtesy and abusive language of his visitor infuriated Katsura. He insisted that he was in no way attached to the premiership. If there were someone who would take it on he would yield at any time. "Why don't *you* take it on?" he challenged Yamamoto, "If you have the stomach for it, do it yourself!" Later Katsura was to acknowledge that he had handled himself badly that morning. Words fly faster than the wind. As soon as he had drawn these words out of Katsura, Yamamoto went straight to Seiyūkai headquarters and told Saionji that Katsura was willing to step down and had recommended him as successor. As might be expected, this caused a stir among the leaders of the Seiyūkai.

Yamamoto returned to Katsura's residence. By then Katsura had regained his composure. He told Yamamoto that he must be unaware of the situation and explained to him in detail how Saionji had received the imperial rescript and was even then doing his best to unify the views of the Seiyūkai. Was it not improper for Yamamoto to intervene in the process, he asked? It was like fishing in troubled waters, and could well stain Yamamoto's reputation. Yamamoto apparently then sent a messenger to Saionji retracting his words. These episodes suggest that the way had been paved to form a coalition between the clan clique and the Seiyūkai with Yamamoto as beneficiary.

I Stay in the Fight to Protect Constitutional Government

In a sense, it probably was wise of Katsura to have given in to pressure for the cabinet to resign without dissolving the House. Had he insisted on holding out, he might have invited a frontal attack and extremely troublesome consequences. We would then have been able to score a decisive victory over the clan government. The momentum behind the movement for constitutional government would have been hard to resist.

However, Katsura, who was always quick to seize an opportunity, had dodged at the last minute. As usual, we had missed our chance. The Yamamoto government followed. When the Seiyūkai sought to compromise with it, the constitutional movement lost a lot of steam. Nonetheless, I continued the fight for constitutional government even after leaving the Seiyūkai, for the simple reason that I was committed to establishing the foundations of democracy after destroying the roots of clan government. It was not my purpose merely to bring down the Katsura government.

Following my departure from the Seiyūkai I organized a small group called the Seiyū Club. It was composed of twenty-six men who had resigned from the party in protest at the unprincipled political compromise of those at the top. However, Okazaki Kunisuke and Takekoshi Yosaburō returned to the folds of the Seiyūkai shortly afterward. Subsequently, we joined with the Shigakukai of Hanai Takuzō and formed the Chūseikai, thereby increasing our seats in the House to thirty-seven.

On the other hand, the Rikken Dōshikai had not yet been formally inaugurated when Katsura died suddenly. Following his death, the group suffered from internal dissension, prompting Gotō Shinpei and Nakakogi Ren to leave. Finally on December 22, 1913, the party held its inauguration ceremony, naming Katō Takaaki as its president. At the time it had a parliamentary membership of ninety-two.

Now that the Seiyūkai had compromised itself by allying with the Yamamoto government, our parliamentary capability had declined, but on the other hand there was still a great deal of fervor for our cause throughout the country. At a public meeting held on March 16 at the Nakanoshima Public Hall in Osaka, it was estimated that 50,000 people had tried to get in. The extent of public enthusiasm was reflected partly in the healthy number of newspaper subscriptions. Usually, newspapers suffered a ten or twenty percent reduction in subscriptions during the summer months. That summer, with the constitutional movement still vigorous, they did not experience the usual lull. Probably in an effort to ward off the seasonal downturn, major papers in Tokyo and Osaka quoted even my slightest remarks. It was about this time that the *Osaka Mainichi* published my essays daily in a series entitled "Gakudō's Memoirs."

In those days the fight for constitutional government took me to many parts of the country. Newspapers sent reporters to record my informal remarks during my stay at an inn or while traveling by train. Printing such trifles evidently helped to raise the reputation of a newspaper. Such was the continued impact of the movement on the nation.

An amusing episode occurred during this time when I traveled around the country making speeches. I was in the San-in region having lunch when they insisted on my having a drink. In jest I said drinks and women were for evenings. Taking me at my word, they were ready with both at dinner time. By then I had all but stopped drinking and did not touch alcohol at dinner. My hosts took it that I preferred women, and when I returned to my room that night I found a professional entertainer waiting for me. She followed me even inside the mosquito net that hung round my bed. Embarrassed, I ordered her home, but she would not leave, saying that she had strict orders from so and so. Traveling with me at that time was Kikuchi Taketoku, who was known for being a veteran in the field, so I went to him for advice. He said I should keep her if I liked her or otherwise send her home. I did not go to him for that. I had secretly hoped that he would quietly remove her from my room. He would not help, so I had to do it myself and sternly sent her home. She left sobbing. I often have to suffer for my own bad jokes.

After a banquet one evening in Kyoto during the same campaign, an entertainer from the Gion district followed me as I left. Not wanting to invite an incident I let her talk, and learned that the woman, who was no youngster, had gained some fame as a dancer who was known as "Democracy Geiko" for her love of politics. She was a devoted supporter of the pro-democracy movement and wore a white rose whenever she attended a banquet. Apparently she was an admirer of mine, for she joked that she would have forced herself on me had I not already remarried. In fact, she already had a generous patron, she told me. When I was appointed minister of justice in the Ōkuma cabinet several years later, she sent me two short congratulatory poems:

> A radiant mind has risen like our nation's sun
> Allowing us at last to see how freedom's won.
>
> He gives his whole life to this land
> There's a blossom on the freedom tree.

After this she campaigned for her patron and unfortunately was jailed for violating campaign regulations. With many others, she was granted a pardon on the occasion of Emperor Taishō's enthronement. The pardon was issued in the name of Ozaki Yukio, the minister of justice. She told me over and over again that it was the most joyful moment of her life.

I campaigned the length and breadth of the country for democratic government and the elimination of clan rule, including that of Yamamoto, whose government did in fact act on some of our demands. One of these was to broaden the qualification for ministers of the army and navy and governors general of Korea and Taiwan to include reserve officers, where hitherto these appointments had been strictly limited to officers on active service. While this was some sort of progress, it was a far cry from achieving equality between civilians and the military and I was not satisfied. The government also did see to it that all its ministers, save the prime minister, foreign minister, and army and navy ministers, joined the Seiyūkai, and so to this extent something a little closer to a party cabinet came into being. Due to these limited advances our objectives were thus somewhat narrowed.

However, since the birth of the Yamamoto cabinet, Inukai and I were no longer in step. For Inukai, the Protect Constitutional Government movement was a battle for revenge against Katsura, who had stripped him of half the members of his Kokumintō. He may have felt repaid when the Katsura cabinet was brought down, but my purpose went well beyond revenge. It made no difference to me whether the government was headed by Katsura, Yamamoto, or anyone else, so long as it was a clan government. Inukai, as we have seen, was most hostile to the Chōshū clique headed by Katsura. He must have thought that the most effective way to crush it was to use the powerful Satsuma clan headed by Yamamoto. This led to criticism being leveled against him for opposing army expansion while being partial to the navy, with which the two factions respectively were closely connected. People suspected that he had an unwritten contract with Yamamoto, and that his failure to attack the government when it was most at fault was evidence of collusion between them. In any event, intentionally or naïvely, Inukai had sowed the seeds for a later appointment in the second Yamamoto government. Meanwhile, he had been hinting at a wish to merge with the Seiyūkai. He must not have been surprised when I left the party.

Inukai's decision not to join the Ōkuma government and instead to be part of the Yamamoto government, and his decision later to join the Seiyūkai should be taken not so much as sudden or disconnected developments, but rather as a crystallization of a political strategy that he had been toying with for some time.

Leaving the Seiyūkai also represented for me a parting of the ways with Inukai, and pitted me in an uphill battle against the Yamamoto cabinet. It was then that the Siemens incident occurred, drastically changing the circumstances.

THE SIEMENS AFFAIR

The Siemens affair began with a typist at the Tokyo branch of Siemens-Schückertwerke Gmbh stealing essential documents relating to an order from the Japanese navy and using it to blackmail the company. When she did not get what she wanted, she sold the information to Andrew M. Pooley,[1] a journalist at Reuters,

---

[1] Pooley was the author of *Japan at the Crossroads* (London: Allen and Unwin, 1917), and *Japan's Foreign Policies* (London: Allen and Unwin, 1920). He also edited Hayashi Tadasu's *The Secret Memoirs of Count Tadasu Hayashi, G.C.V.O.* (New York and London: G. P. Putnam's Sons, 1915).

who in turn blackmailed the company and succeeded in extorting from them a quarter of a million yen. During the investigation that followed, it was discovered that the company had paid bribes to high-ranking Japanese officials. Prime Minister Yamamoto, Navy Minister Saitō, Foreign Minister Makino, Interior Minister Hara, and Justice Minister Okuda, among others, tried to bury these revelations, but a cable from the London office of Jiji Press exposed the story.

The affair became a major scandal involving Prime Minister Yamamoto and Navy Minister Saitō, who had long exercised power with regard to navy affairs. An excellent opportunity was thus provided for the non-Satsuma clansmen to expose abuses by the Satsuma people, against whose despotic manners they routinely held a grudge. The Siemens affair attracted so much publicity that it took the place of the Protect Constitutional Government movement in commanding public attention.

Naturally I took up the case in parliament. I held nothing against Yamamoto as an individual, but since he was the head of the clan clique, I led the attack against him. The Dōshikai, which until then had been my bitter foe and had most loudly obstructed my speech against Katsura, now became my supporter. Yesterday's enemy became today's friend over the Siemens scandal when Shimada Saburō led the Dōshikai to join my struggle. Since I was now alone politically this was not unwelcome. Once we found ourselves on the same side it was as easy as dealing with my own party, for many Dōshikai members were among my oldest friends.

It was now the Seiyūkai's turn to lash out against us. There was a great deal of heckling from the Seiyūkai benches, especially during the budget session when the question of the proposed navy expansion was deliberated. Inouye, for one, was obliged to cut short his speech because of the raucous interruptions by members of the Seiyūkai. I was next to speak. But before I took the floor I called on the speaker and asked if he had the ability to manage the floor. Offended at my question, the speaker, Ōoka Ikuzō, said he was under no obligation to respond to rude remarks and proceeded to give the floor to the next speaker.

I persisted, however, and finally got him to declare that he indeed had the ability to officiate. I then took the floor, saying I would exercise my right to speak only on the condition that the speaker was able to carry out his duties. In this way I more or less succeeded in gagging the Seiyūkai at the outset. Each time they attempted to abuse the power of their numbers to make a disturbance while I spoke, I played to the audience, threatening to sit down if the speaker lacked the authority to perform his duty to control the confusion and if the stenographers were unable to record my speech. Mr. Ōoka, a member of the Seiyūkai himself, had to shout at the members of his own party for quiet. In this manner I could deliver what, at least in my opinion, was a masterly speech calling for the reduction of the naval expansion budget. I must admit that this was one of the sweetest experiences of my parliamentary life.

Our attack on the Yamamoto government gradually gained momentum and spread even to the House of Peers. One Murata Tamotsu spoke at length, even quoting a bad joke I had made by twisting the pronunciation of the prime minister's first name, to the effect that prisons were full of fellows named "Gonbei." I had to remind myself once more that I really must refrain from making silly remarks.

Eventually Inukai, who up until then had been sympathetic to the naval expansion, expeditiously revised his Kokumintō party platform and joined forces with us. This created a potentially uncomfortable coalition between the Dōshikai and Kokumintō, which to that point had been at complete odds with one another. There is a saying, however, that personal sentiments must yield to what is right. I therefore took it on myself to mediate the collaboration between the two parties, concluding a Dōshikai, Kokumintō, and Chūseikai triparty front ready to mount a full-scale attack on the Yamamoto government.

As I took the floor against the Yamamoto government I glimpsed the magisterial figure of the prime minister. He was a formidable adversary. One would think that personal appearance ought to matter little so long as a person has a noble spirit. It would be better to have both nonetheless. In the case of a country's prime minister, especially, a poor appearance might have a negative influence on the nation's prestige. In Japan I feel this is particularly so when, for example, the prime minister must greet foreign emissaries at an accession ceremony. For the most part, successive prime ministers since the Meiji era have unfortunately been unimpressive to look at. The Saigō brothers and Ōkubo had uncommon features, but they did not become prime ministers. The most impressive was undoubtedly Yamamoto. He not only had a dignified face but possessed an imposing build for a Japanese. In addition to his physical appearance there was something quite intimidating about Yamamoto that could strike terror into one's heart. Even a man of such a caliber as Yamagata seemed to treat the count with awe.

Back in 1898, the Ōkuma-Itagaki coalition government had decided to reduce the budget demanded by the navy. It was said that the navy minister at the time, Saigō Tsugumichi, stated with embarrassment that, speaking for himself, he could readily go along with the cut, but that Yamamoto Gonnohyōe was the problem. He was often a bit of a nuisance, said Saigō, who then asked if the prime minister would mind talking him into accepting the cut. When I first heard this, I took it simply as another of Saigō's stories, but apparently there was more to it than that. Yamamoto had already been given the sobriquet "Minister Gonnohyōe" by the press even when he was still only a director-general.

Soon afterward, I attended a reception at the Ōkuma residence, where Yamamoto was present. There was no doubt about it, he did have a fine countenance. It amused me to imagine Navy Minister Saigō, ordinarily such a resourceful and self-possessed person, at a loss as to how to handle his subordinate. Looking now at the imposing figure of Yamamoto in the prime minister's chair, it occurred to me that it would be very gratifying if I could make his face turn green as I had with Katsura. I raised my voice to a fitting roar and glared at the prime minister. Unlike Katsura, however, Yamamoto merely stared coldly back at me and did not flinch in the least. He was certainly no common adversary.

Katsura may have been a man of wisdom but hardly of courage. Of the two attributes, Yamamoto was more a man of courage. I had contempt for Katsura from the beginning, but had always recognized Yamamoto's excellence. This difference in their natures must have had many consequences.

The Yamamoto government, already weakened by the Siemens scandal, now had to face a major cut in the budget for the construction of new warships. That was as politically damaging as a vote of no confidence. Yamamoto's government was not to last much longer. Although Yamamoto was totally cleared of the allegations against him, the prime minister nonetheless seemed unnerved by the affair. Perhaps his political ambitions were dampened. In any event, it was some time before he was seen again on the political stage.

The Ōkuma Cabinet Era

Marquis Ōkuma Receives the Great Command

With the fall of the Yamamoto cabinet, the three *genrō*, Yamagata, Matsukata, and Ōyama, met to choose a successor and invited Saionji to accept the premiership. When they failed to persuade him they turned to Tokugawa Iesato, the president of the House of Peers. On March 29 Prince Tokugawa was summoned to the palace and received unofficial instructions to organize a cabinet, but he too declined. The *genrō* finally decided to recommend Kiyoura Keigo, who, on March 31, received official instructions when he presented himself at the palace.

Kiyoura, with the assistance of his special advisor, Munekata Masashi, the governor of Dan-no-ura, immediately began to form his cabinet. Kiyoura, after consulting Yamagata, Yamamoto, and Navy Minister Saitō, foresaw no difficulty in finding someone suitable for the navy portfolio. He therefore concentrated on filling other posts. The formation of the Kiyoura cabinet did not promise to be easy, but it went unexpectedly smoothly, and most of the members had already been nominated when quite unpredictably it foundered on the military and naval portfolios.

The selection of the army minister did not seem to present any difficulty since Yamagata had already agreed, though informally. The army, however, had decided to see what the position of the new cabinet would be on the issue of the two additional divisions before agreeing to provide a service minister.

Rear Admiral Katō Tomosaburō, who had been approached for the post of navy minister, paid a visit to Kiyoura and officially put to him the following conditions:

1. To convene an ad hoc Diet session to vote an annual allocation of 9.5 million yen for the naval replacement program, and to support subsequent replacement demands.

2. If this presented problems, the prime minister was at least to vouch for the 9.5-million-yen allocation.

Kiyoura wasted no time in refusing the offer. The top officials in the navy ministry conferred and, judging their cause to be irretrievably lost, informed the prime minister of their refusal to fill the navy portfolio. It was clear that the announcement reflected not only Admiral Katō's personal opinion, but also the wish of the navy as a whole. In short, there was no way a navy minister could be found. Kiyoura was compelled respectfully to decline the premiership. This was known as the "aborted cabinet" of Kiyoura.

Earlier the Saionji cabinet had fallen as a result of its opposing the army's unconditional demand for two new divisions. This time the Kiyoura government was stillborn because of the united and uncompromising position of the navy regarding its replacement program. Once again the *genrō* met, and at length they decided to urge Ōkuma to come forward.

In a democratic country such as England the incoming cabinet is normally formed from among those who have been most responsible for toppling the preceding government, but this is not the case in Japan. Neither Shimada Saburō nor I, who were the main force in bringing down the Yamamoto cabinet, had the prominence or the caliber to be asked. In this situation, the *genrō* decided to bring back Ōkuma, who had by then already retired.

The marquis had long since ceased to be politically active. As he was also over eighty years old no one seemed to take the idea too seriously in the beginning, but since no other qualified contender had emerged, the idea of an Ōkuma government had gradually taken root. Those who had simply been playing with the idea began to take it seriously. There had been many changes of government since the Ōkuma-Itagaki coalition had fallen, but in all that time there had not been so much as a whisper of Ōkuma's return. It was indeed seventeen years or more since Ōkuma's name had been mentioned for the prime minister's post.

No one was more active on Ōkuma's behalf than Mochizuki Kotarō, who was a *kagemusha* behind the scenes pulling strings for Ōkuma. Some people tended to take him lightly, but in certain areas and in certain ways his ability to scheme was unmatched. It was particularly useful at this time that he been able to put himself on extremely good terms with Inoue Kaoru. Inoue, who by nature tended toward extreme reactions, had at one time apparently ordered his household "not to allow Mochizuki inside the gates." By this time, however, he had Mochizuki with him night and day, and had him called for every sort of occasion. For some decades Mochizuki had also been in favor with Yamagata. One way or another Mochizuki was thus able to convince Inoue that the situation could not be resolved without Ōkuma. The two men had long been estranged, but they had been colleagues in the days when they both belonged to a group that used to meet at the Ryōzanpaku (a gathering place of ambitious men) in the Tsukiji district of Tokyo, at which time Inoue lived at Ōkuma's residence. For his part, Ōkuma had always defended Inoue, even when the two were political enemies, saying, "Inoue was not a bad man, even though he might have done wrong." Neither harbored any personal ill will toward the other. After listening to Mochizuki's opinion, Inoue agreed and, in the end, took the initiative to convince Yamagata and all other necessary persons, so that the imperial mandate finally came to Ōkuma.

CONTROVERSY OVER FORMATION OF THE CABINET

While accepting the imperial mandate, Ōkuma, who as we have seen had been absent from the political world for some time, did not seem to want to run the government as its nominal as well as its actual head. After the death of Katsura, the Dōshikai, in a joint decision by its five managing directors—Katō Takaaki, Ōura Kanetake, Gotō Shinpei, Ōishi Masami, and Kōno Hironaka—chose Katō as its president. The ingenious Gotō Shinpei, ever the politician, seemed to be the one enemy mole within the party, opposing its new president. Soon after the decision had been made, however, Gotō left the Dōshikai. With him gone, unity among the party members improved and on December 23, 1913, the party held a ceremony to inaugurate itself officially, installing Katō as its president and Ōura, Ōishi, and Kōno as its general managers.

It seemed that Ōkuma intended to organize his cabinet with the Dōshikai as its main strength, leaving all practical matters to Katō, while for his own part he would assume a post of nominal leadership as prime minister. With this evident purpose, Ōkuma, after accepting the imperial command at the palace, called at Katō's residence to work with him on whom they would name to ministerial posts. Only after the cabinet's membership was more or less decided did he invite Inukai and me.

I was amazed. If anyone was to be consulted, then I should have been the first, having worked so hard to bring down the previous administration. At the very least, if Ōkuma intended to face the Seiyūkai (206 strong) with a coalition of the Dōshikai (92), the Kokumintō (39), and the Chūseikai (35), then it would have been natural to consult with the three of us, Katō, Inukai, and myself. Instead, Ōkuma had first consulted Katō, who, as a satellite of Katsura, had not yet quite recovered from the heavy blow that worthy had suffered, and had made decisions on key positions, albeit informally, before consulting me. I could not help being astonished at the way Ōkuma had proceeded.

Inukai was not only in a position that rendered him incompatible with the Dōshikai, but it was obvious to me that his extremely poor relations with Katō from the very beginning declined even more. "This Ōkuma cabinet is really a Katō cabinet," he declared to me. "I am going to refuse to join because in such a crowd we would have no chance to carry out our own views." I did my best to persuade him. "It isn't as hopeless as all that," I urged. "I intend to stick to my opinion. If the two of us joined, we could make it *our* cabinet." But Inukai persisted: "As long as Katō is there it will never be like that." He would not give in. Inukai appeared to know much more than I about the relationship between Ōkuma and Katō. Since I was not so well informed, I thought that Ōkuma was not necessarily the kind of person to be Katō's puppet. I believed that he would support our opinions if we were right. Inukai apparently did not agree.

At my first meeting with Ōkuma on the formation of the cabinet, I spoke my mind. "If this were England," I said, "the imperial mandate would have been given to me. You did nothing to bring the Yamamoto cabinet down. Your being asked to organize the cabinet was due to peculiarly Japanese circumstances and was hardly likely to have been based on either reason or justice. I will seriously consider your proposal if you wish to consult with me in organizing the cabinet. I will decline if you ask me to join it after the main posts have been allocated."

Ōkuma proposed that I select any post other than those of foreign, home, or finance minister. I insisted that I would not join the cabinet under those conditions. Ōkuma appeared astonished to hear this from a man whom he had brought up almost like a son and whom he probably still considered a son even then. He must have thought my comment intolerable or perhaps that I had lost my mind. I was, for my part, quite composed and meant every word I said.

I left him thinking that this had gone far enough and nothing more would come of it. However, having learned of what I had said, two men, Asabuki Eiji and Nagai Ryūtarō, came to talk me into softening my position. They came separately, but both sought to open the conversation by implying that they saw my opinion as not unreasonable: "If you were to be consulted over the cabinet posts, what would you say? Do you have any specific suggestions?" The specifics to me were self-evident. "I do not say that Ōkuma should not be prime minister," I replied, "nor would I say that Katō should not be foreign minister. Mr. Wakatsuki can have the finance portfolio. I cannot agree, however, to making Ōura home minister. As for the rest, if it is all right with Inukai let him have finance. I have no other suggestions."

I realized after being thus consulted that I had qualms only over the appointments of the home and finance ministers, so it all really boiled down to problems with only these two ministries. Asabuki and Nagai took their leave, hopeful that there was room for negotiation. The upshot of all this coming and going was that Ōkuma took under his own wing the home ministry, the post to which Ōura had been informally appointed, while the Ōura was relegated to the ministry of agriculture and commerce. I was more or less satisfied.

For my part, I wanted no particular post. I would tackle whatever job the prime minister wanted to give me. I therefore asked him what post he would have me fill. He said that if I had no particular preference he wanted me to take on the justice portfolio. It was interesting to reflect that at the time of his first cabinet, which he shared with Itagaki, he had likewise initially wanted me to be justice minister.

Unlike the previous time, Ōkuma might have calculated that my occupying the justice post would ensure a full and complete investigation into the Siemens scandal, which was just then preoccupying the public. Be that as it may, the public appeared to welcome my appointment as a significant gesture. In fact, I had no such intention. I had simply responded to Ōkuma's request and accepted the post.

In addition to the Siemens scandal there was a bribery case involving the Honganji Temple. A former minister of the Imperial Household Agency, Tanaka, and the present incumbent, Watanabe, were implicated. A number of other well-known personalities were also reputed to have received similar bribes. For all these reasons considerable attention was given to my appointment to the justice ministry.

THINGS EVOLVE CONTRARY TO MY INTENTIONS

So it was that the Ōkuma cabinet was sworn in on April 16, 1914. Its members were Ōkuma Shigenobu, prime minister and home minister; Katō Takaaki, foreign minister; Wakatsuki Reijirō, finance minister; Oka Ichinosuke, army minister; Yashiro Rokurō, navy minister; Ozaki Yukio, justice minister; Ichiki Kitokurō, education minister; Ōura Kanetake, agriculture and commerce minister; and Taketomi Tokitoshi, posts and telecommunications minister. Inukai held out and did not join the cabinet. However, the Kokumintō Party declared its intention to assist from without, stating that it was prepared to offer support insofar as the policy of the new cabinet did not go against the party line. Inukai was not impressed. "You can put whatever name you like as the prime minister. Any other will do just as well as Ōkuma. It is a totally bureaucratic cabinet whose old head, Katsura, has simply been replaced by Ōkuma with an infusion of Ozaki," he complained.

Now that I had joined the cabinet I felt skeptical. I must admit I was rather dismayed at my own lack of foresight. For one thing, I had believed that once I joined the cabinet I would be able to realize my own aspirations. In reality, however, none of my views in which I so ardently believed was accepted. In contrast, Katō's opinions were regularly approved. At length I realized, as Inukai had warned, that this was in fact a Katō cabinet. Moreover, it was my doing to have Ōura switched from the home portfolio to that of agriculture and to have Prime Minister Ōkuma double as home minister. With this setup I had thought that Ōkuma would look with favor on my opinions regarding major political issues. Again I was proven wrong. It was only in name that Ōkuma doubled as home minister. There appeared to have been a secret promise to the effect that the work of the home ministry would actually be supervised by Agriculture Minister Ōura. Even such matters as deciding on the budget for the secret service appeared to have been left to Ōura's discretion. Under these circumstances I recognized how foolhardy my trust had been and keenly felt that one should never let down one's guard to a politician even if he is one's own mentor. I had demanded that Ōura not be put in charge of the home ministry. In reality, however, he had been assigned two ministries—those of the home and of agriculture—instead of one.

I had never dreamed that my mentor, who was like my own father, would do this to me. It was too late now. If I had known, I would not have joined the cabinet, but by the time I realized the truth there was nothing I could do about it. There was some advantage, however, in having Ōkuma double as home minister. The status of justice ministry officials was improved.

Since police officers were required to undertake criminal investigations and other duties to uphold the law, it was only reasonable that their appointment should reflect the opinion of the justice ministry. Laws were passed and the system of government was designed accordingly. In time, however, it had become customary for local police chiefs to be appointed at the sole discretion of the home ministry without giving the chief public prosecutor any chance of interfering in their promotion or demotion. This was not only a violation of the regulations governing the civil service but it was also extremely irrational. If it suited the interests of the home ministry, one could break the law with impunity. And if the police were not answerable to the same laws, prosecutors obviously could not do their jobs properly. Ordinarily, to be fair, the police would accommodate a prosecutor's requirements, but not if these conflicted with the wishes of the home ministry. Unless this situation was rectified, the power of the judiciary was a fiction. I therefore asked the prime minister-cum-home minister to spell out rules covering the functioning of the civil service clearly and to issue a directive before a joint meeting of local officials, justices, and prosecutors to the effect that "assignment of police officers to the judicial department must be made in consultation with the chief public prosecutor." In other words, that the existing rules covering government organization should be obeyed. Ōkuma made an eloquent speech to this effect. I was satisfied and so was the staff at the justice ministry.

This nevertheless developed into a major issue. A group within the home ministry led by the de facto minister Ōura fought back. At first, Ōkuma did not take them too seriously, saying that things were all right as they were. Eventually, however, he was forced to cancel his earlier directive at another meeting of local officials.

What had at first appeared a promising formula ended in my defeat. The recourse to doubling the office of prime minister with that of home minister came to nothing after all. Thus my initial hopes were thoroughly betrayed. There was nothing more to be done. I was forced to conclude that it would be better after all to hold Ōura accountable by making him minister rather than have him exercise real power from behind the scenes. When the House was dissolved I therefore had him moved to the home ministry and my friend Kōno Hironaka brought in to fill the post of agriculture and commerce minister.

JAPAN ENTERS WORLD WAR I

Soon after the Ōkuma cabinet was formed, World War I erupted in Europe. Our ally, Britain, entered the war when Germany violated Belgian neutrality. With our ally at war it was a matter of obligation for Japan to follow suit in accordance with the treaty of alliance. Foreign Minister Katō and I clashed over the question of how this was to be done.

It was then I learned that there were times when even the most surpassing qualities would not avail a man unless he had been tempered in adversity. Katō Takaaki had a fine mind and a strong will, and with honest application had the makings of a great man. Because of his circumstances, however, he died without realizing his potential. It was not that he suffered from insuperable misfortunes, but rather, in plain words, that he simply had too many advantages.

Katō had always been an excellent student. After graduating, he married into the main branch of the Iwasaki family. I do not know whether it was Iwasaki[1] himself who discovered his admirable qualities or whether he was introduced by some other person, but the fact remains it was his enduring good fortune that Katō was always in demand and never had to face the adversities of life. This marriage may well have been the root of his failure. He had advantages enough without being married to an Iwasaki girl.

When Katō went to London to study, Mutsu Munemitsu took him under his wing and made it his job to show him around. The count was a good judge of

---

[1] Iwasaki Yatarō (1835–1885) founded the Mitsubishi enterprises.

people. Indeed, anyone who had made a name for himself in Meiji times was likely to have had some contact with him.

In addition to the patronage of Mutsu, Katō enjoyed as well that of Matsukata, who was of Satsuma origin and related to the Mitsubishi commercial empire, and was at the time a candidate for the premiership. Ōkuma also had his eye on Katō. As foreign minister in the Kuroda cabinet, Ōkuma was in fact the first to offer him a position, as a secretary in his office. Later, Itō too demonstrated his confidence in Katō by appointing him to Ōkuma's former post.

Young Katō, ignorant of the real world, found himself in great demand among the statesmen of the time. Mitsubishi's Iwasaki was partly to be blamed,[2] but because of these circumstances Katō allowed himself to believe that he was a great man and was unable to imagine a side of life other than that to which he was so accustomed.

In later years, unlike Inukai or Hara, Katō had the advantages of a formal education and long experience as a diplomat, but he had not learned the hard realities of professional diplomacy. Diplomacy at times demanded tough negotiation and the ability to make tactical moves with an eye to a larger strategy. It was astounding that Katō, for all his intelligence and savoir-faire, understood only the technicalities but not the art of diplomacy.

To Katō, diplomacy meant correct protocol and getting the minutiae right. He was extremely adept at drafting diplomatic documents and entertaining foreign emissaries. He knew little about the main issues. Thus, when the question of how Japan should enter the European war was debated in the cabinet, Foreign Minister Katō suggested that Germany should be asked if it would be willing to "hand over Kiaochow Bay to Japan for the purpose of returning it eventually to China," and that if Germany failed to respond within a given period, Japan should enter the war on that pretext.

I was opposed to such a procedure. "It is unreasonable," I protested, "to expect Germany to give up the Bay of Kiaochow it presently occupies to a country that has nothing to do with the matter. We might be justified in asking Germany to return the bay directly to China, but not to surrender it to Japan on the basis of an unverifiable promise to give it back eventually to China. This would be like asking a man to give us his mistress with the vague promise that we will return her eventually to her husband. The proposal is not only intrinsically absurd; it would not please China either to have our favors imposed upon her. Germany would not agree to such a proposition. Instead of taking this unreasonable course, a single announcement declaring Japan's entry into the war in accordance with the Anglo-Japanese Alliance would be much more to the point. This is the only correct way to proceed."

Unfortunately, the other ministers did not agree with me and instead favored Katō's senseless proposal, which was later to become an obstacle in our negotia-

---

[2] Katō (1860–1926) rose rapidly in the Iwasaki firm of Mitstubishi, was sent to study in England, married Iwasaki Yatarō's eldest daughter, entered the foreign ministry, and served five years as minis-

tions with China. So the phrase "for the purpose of returning it eventually to China" found its way into our negotiations with Germany, and later, as I had predicted, when Japan offered to return Kiaochow Bay to China the latter was in no mood to show appreciation. The territory would have been a fine present from Japan to China had we not anticipated obtaining it in this way but had instead entered the war simply on the strength of the alliance, captured the bay, held it, and returned it. I suspected the other ministers thought it would make the foreign minister lose face if they had followed my urging and rejected his proposal. In any case they opposed me and the result is well known to all of us.[3]

THE EARLY PHASE OF WORLD WAR I

Another point on which I took issue with Katō was his insistence that the British government be consulted over our entering the war—although, since Japan was allied to Britain, Katō's position was undeniably in line with the formalities. At that time, not even politicians in Europe had any idea that the war would escalate as it did. Hostilities had just broken out and the British government had not yet perceived the extent of the danger. Rather, it was a time when they would rather not have Japan's influence stretch over the China Sea and the Chinese mainland.

"We would do well to consult Britain," I asserted, "were we ready not to enter the war should Britain so advise, but not if such advice did not suit our purpose. Consulting Britain might be appropriate so far as diplomatic protocol is concerned, but it would be better not to consult Britain because doing so, should Britain then advise against it, would most probably make our entry into the war impossible. If it is our decision to enter the fray, then it is enough for us to announce our intention to do so on the strength of the Anglo-Japanese Alliance."

Once more my opinion did not prevail. The other members of the cabinet were too willing to follow the foreign minister's view, and the decision was taken to consult Britain as he had proposed. Just as I had foreseen, the British government consulted its minister in China and the commander of the Far Eastern Fleet and must have received a negative response to the prospect of Japan's participation in the war. Japan's entry would extend its influence over the Chinese mainland and the China Sea. This extension of Japanese power must have been seen as commensurately diminishing that of the British fleet and the minister himself. In any event, the government in London replied in a disguised negative by agreeing to Japan's entry—but a little later.

---

ter to London. He served in three cabinets before becoming, as Ozaki has noted, a leading figure in the Dōshikai.

[3] The lease of Kiaochow Bay in Shantung, which Germany had secured as a sphere of interest in the imperialist moves of 1898, was incorporated in Japan's "Twenty-one Demands" on China in 1915 and control of the bay was not returned to China until 1922, by which time the issue had helped inflame Chinese nationalism and direct it against Japan.

Since the Japanese government had already begun preparations for war, the British reply embarrassed Katō. He was now put in a position where he had to explain that Japan could not wait as public opinion was already too aroused. The British government reluctantly accepted. Rather than being appreciated, we were now indebted. Once we had made up our mind about entering the war, we would have been sufficiently justified in doing so on the strength of the alliance. Our insistence on observing unnecessary protocol created for us an unwelcome reputation for aggressiveness.

For the British part, they underestimated the gravity of the war and at first were loathe to have Japan join them, while in Japan the army had prejudged the war to end in a German victory. Therefore, many considered it extremely dangerous for Japan to risk making an enemy of Germany for the mere sake of honoring a treaty with Britain. Yamagata, who behind the scenes was the army's real head, held this view particularly strongly. It was especially ironic that those among the army leaders thought to have the most information did not until the moment of the Kaiser's flight abandon their firm belief in the victory of the Germany army. As a member of the cabinet and an elected representative of the people, I often heard these men speak, but on many important matters they failed to see the forest for the trees. It was deplorable, to say the least, that an amateur like myself was able to understand the European war from its outbreak to its end better than our best military experts.

The outcome of particular battles was naturally beyond my grasp, but I had my own general view of the war. Even if Germany were to succeed in vanquishing the whole of continental Europe it would eventually come to the same sorry end as Napoleon's empire. At that time Britain was isolated in Europe, and the United States was, if not a foe, certainly not a friend. America was still in its infancy and having it as an ally would not have amounted to much of an advantage for Britain. In the end, in spite of many adversities, Britain achieved final victory over Napoleon. And now, so long as Germany could not defeat the British on the high seas, its army would not conquer Britain either.

Unlike in Napoleon's time, however, the United States of America was now an extremely powerful country, and under certain circumstances it could be driven to enter the fray against Germany. At the very least, it could be counted on to maintain its neutrality. This would favor Britain much more than Germany. Even without America's participation, the situation was far more advantageous to Britain now than it had been a century before, and of course it would be much more so if America were to pitch in. Therefore, Germany would be defeated in the end.

This was how I saw the war. I discussed it with a number of army officers but none agreed with my view. Some members of the cabinet saw a measure of reason in it, but they never said so in as many words. Most were concerned enough, though, to listen to what the army officers had to say. I listened to them too, but most of what they said was professional observation on various aspects of the hostilities. When it came to general reflections on the war there was nothing that impressed me in the slightest.

Even more unlike the heyday of Napoleon, Britain could now count among its friends, in addition to America, its colonies Australia, Canada, and South Africa. They would all willingly dispatch large armies to stand by the mother country in its time of crisis. Moreover, Japan would support Britain as an ally. There was not the slightest doubt that Germany would finally suffer defeat even if it won on the continent of Europe.

TWENTY-ONE DEMANDS ON CHINA

The major diplomatic failure of the Ōkuma administration was over the "Twenty-One Demands" made on China. After the fall of Tsingtao to Japan, there were a number of issues pending over Kiaochow Bay, the Kwantung concession, and the South Manchurian railroad. Foreign Minister Katō therefore instructed the Japanese minister in China, Hioki Eki, to negotiate with a view to settling all pending issues at a single stroke.

On January 18, 1915, Minister Hioki presented twenty-one demands in five sections to the Chinese president, Yuan Shih-k'ai. After meeting twenty-odd times with Lu Chao-hsiang, the Chinese foreign secretary, Hioki had acceded to a number of Chinese requests. Having made revisions in accord with these requests to the Japanese demands, Hioki presented the final document on April 26, requesting China's agreement.

I was opposed to these so-called "twenty-one demands" from the outset, and disagreed emphatically, saying that for Japan to make such demands of China at that time was tantamount to announcing to the world that Japan was an aggressor. I ended up by yielding and placing my chop on the document only after minister Katō and other members of the cabinet insisted that the object of the exercise was in having *some* of the demands met. It was one of the great mistakes of my life.

I deeply regretted my lack of firmness, and as an act of atonement announced that thenceforth I would never again join any cabinet. Indeed I had a number of opportunities to join subsequent cabinets, but I rejected them all and remained till the end a plain member of the House of Representatives.

Generally I am known to be a strong-willed and obstinate person, but by nature am quite weak and docile and easily acquiesce. As a proof, according to the recently developed science of blood typing, I am type A, signifying a typically weak personality. It would be difficult for someone like myself, quick to submit to the views of others, to become a great statesman or soldier. I thought to myself that this would not do justice to myself as a man, and since boyhood worked on myself to improve my character. As a result I am now regarded as a headstrong person. Nonetheless, since I am submissive by nature, though I might make an effort to assert myself I still often end up agreeing with others and commit terrible mistakes as a result. Putting my stamp of approval on the "twenty-one demands" was a product of my weak and compliant nature.

As I had feared, the "demands" gave rise to accusations at home and abroad that the government was taking advantage of the war to put pressure on China with a view to establishing Japan's influence. What was more, the foreign minister exposed his bureaucratic character. Of the five sections and the twenty-one articles they comprised, Katō did not communicate to Britain the last seven articles of the fifth paragraph. These seven were couched as wishes rather than straightforward demands. He kept these articles secret as they concerned railroad matters and were to Britain's disadvantage. It should have been obvious that we could not get away with such a petty deceit, since once they were presented to China it was clear that the British minister in China would without delay notify his home government. It was only to be expected that it would arouse extreme suspicion as soon as it was exposed that we had kept that part of the document secret when the powers were notified of our government's intent.

On May 4 a joint conference of the *genrō* and ministers of the cabinet was held, followed on May 6 by a meeting in the presence of His Imperial Majesty. Finally an ultimatum was issued. The meeting attended by the emperor was considered of great importance, with the three *genrō*, Yamagata, Matsukata, and Ōyama, as well as ten ministers and the chief of the army staff, General Hasegawa, and the chief of the naval staff, Admiral Shimamura, attending.

So when the Chinese Deputy Foreign Secretary Tsao visited the Japanese legation, Minister Hioki refused to see him, saying that there was no need for a meeting. The choice was either to accept the document in toto or refuse it.

This was little short of laughable, because the compromise Tsao had brought with him was far more advantageous to Japan than the ultimatum. In fact, the compromise rejected only one of the seven articles in the last section, which was considered to be the most difficult for the Chinese to accept. The net result was that the Japanese, having presented them with a strict ultimatum, ended up by making good on only four of the original twenty-one points and reserving their decision on two, while the fifth section was totally deleted, thereby virtually forcing the Chinese to accept a version that gave us far less benefit than that which they had offered of their own accord. To accommodate the reactions of the *genrō* to the accusations at home and abroad, the original "demands" were thus ridiculously watered down. Things had come to a strange pass indeed.

Minister Katō habitually miscalculated, especially on matters concerning Chinese and European relations, my predictions usually proving more accurate than his. However, since Katō was the foreign minister, the other members of the cabinet supported him and my opinion was not taken seriously. In the end Katō became fed up with my chronic opposition, and he would get other ministers to agree with him before he presented any of his views in the cabinet. This became a formality with no other purpose than to let me know what had already been decided.

During the period when Katō served as foreign minister the Ōkuma government made many mistakes in diplomacy, but the blunder over the "Twenty-One Demands" was the worst and for long afterwards it sorely injured our relations with China. The Chinese government, after receiving the Japanese ultimatum, accepted the demands and notified us of its acceptance on May 8. On May 25 the treaty was signed. The Chinese boycotted Japanese goods and designated May 9 a Day of National Humiliation, publicizing their bitterness on all printed matter throughout the country. They organized an "Association to Vindicate the Nation" and encouraged a save-the-nation fund to help exonerate themselves of their dishonor. Relations with China deteriorated thereafter to the point where the Japanese eventually felt that they could not be solved short of war. The cause lay originally in our intemperate demands.

In addition, the trust and authority that Japanese foreign relations had previously enjoyed with the powers suffered tangibly. The loss of this intangible asset was immeasurable. As a member of the cabinet at the time I was overwhelmed with shame for not having the power to prevent this development.

Army Expansion Dispute Results in Diet Dissolution

The major problem the Ōkuma government had on its plate was a controversy over increasing the strength of the army. This had to be resolved. The building of two new army divisions had been a pending issue for some time but had not materialized. I, for one, had been opposed to the idea, as had some other members of the House. The second Saionji government had fallen on account of it.

While I personally was opposed to the army buildup, Russia was still seen by most as Japan's adversary. I believed, however, that it was in Japan's fundamental interest to have good relations with Russia and to work for peace in the Orient. Therefore, any military expansion that would excite the other party should be avoided. This is why I strongly opposed it from the beginning.

Although I have usually been considered a persistent champion of arms limitation, my views on the subject have always started from an assessment of what is necessary for national defense. As a youth I even wrote a piece entitled "Up with Militarism"; and later, when I was in China as a correspondent for the *Hōchi Shinbun* and saw that Chinese soldiers were not to be feared, I wrote another entitled "On Conquering China." This startled not only the Japanese officials and military men in China but the government and opposition parties at home. In the event, when war did break out between the two countries, Japan had an easy victory.

When the question of creating two more divisions came up, Japan's relations with Russia were quite tense, so I opposed the move. Essentially, I believed that sufficient armament was a relative matter and should be determined with a potential enemy in mind. When relations with another country are tense, any build-up of one's military forces will be met with a corresponding increase by the other. This will only result in diminishing one's military capability vis-à-vis the potential enemy. This is why, in contrast to the general mood, I opposed an arms build-up at the time when relations with Russia were strained. However, these relations had gradually improved since the war of 1904–1905, and by the time of the Ōkuma government there was an agreement already in place between the two nations that should have served to quell any misgivings Russia might have about a build-up by Japan. The only remaining issue with regard to the proposed military expansion was its cost. There was no longer any reason to oppose it and so risk dividing or destroying the government.

I had been in the forefront of the opposition, so when I came around to supporting the expansion, the cabinet was able to reach consensus. The situation in the Diet did not look very promising, however, and the members of the cabinet, having reached agreement on adding the two proposed divisions, could not now decide among them what strategy to adopt to convince parliament. Should parliament oppose the government bill, I maintained, we should go to the country to seek the will of the people. Instead of dissolving the House, however, the other cabinet ministers wanted to find ways to pass the bill.

This meant that the number of government supporters in the Diet had to be increased. The first target was the group led by Gotō Shinpei. At the time, Gotō commanded considerable strength in the House, and it was calculated that if half his group supported the bill it would probably be passed. Ōura therefore sent a deputation to Gotō to seek his support in persuading the members of his group to vote in favor of the bill. Gotō promptly agreed, and the members of the cabinet felt optimistic about the early realization of their plan. But it failed because Gotō was unable to convince his group to support it.

Yamamoto Kenjirō was Gotō's first protégé. The plan was to persuade Yamamoto to agree and then to get him to convince the others. Gotō called in Yamamoto and, after explaining that their assistance had been requested by Ōkuma, he asked for Yamamoto's help. Contrary to expectations, Yamamoto refused.

"I have consistently opposed the military increase," he declared, "and I cannot change my position now even to meet your wishes, Mr. Gotō—much less ask others to do so. However, I cannot say no either, since you have been kind to me. I must therefore find some other way out of the dilemma." Shortly afterward, Yamamoto announced he would resign from parliament. It was a fine decision true to his convictions.

With the failure of the Gotō strategy, the plan to add two divisions to the army was buried in the thirty-fifth Diet by a vote of 213 to 118. Thereupon the government was forced to beg for an imperial edict to dissolve the House. As will be told, this development, which led Ōura Kanetake to seek to buy members of parliament, resulted in his fall.

A SWEEPING VICTORY IN THE GENERAL ELECTION

Following the dissolution of parliament, a general election was held on March 25, 1914. General elections in Japan have habitually assured an overwhelming victory for the government party and a huge defeat for the opposition. This election was no exception. The Seiyūkai, which went into the election with the most members, was practically halved. This sort of outcome is generally ascribed to government intervention, but even without it such results are almost guaranteed in Japan.

Naturally, I abhor intervention in elections. Whether in or out of government, I have always opposed any intervention. However, with Ōura as home minister I felt there was no guarantee that his men then serving as local officials would not intervene. I was therefore prepared to use the state's powers of prosecution to arrest those who violated the law. With this in mind, I openly declared to Ōura at one cabinet meeting that if local officials intervened in the election I would have them arrested. In order to check on any possible intervention, I saw to it that special Ministry of Justice funds were set aside to defray the cost of the added duties that I intended to give the prosecutor's office. The fund was distributed to the courts, which ordered to have policemen—or in case they refused, those employed especially for the purpose—arrest violators and any persons intervening in the election. No special consideration was to be given government officials.

At the same time I felt the need to inform the people that the government was determined to pursue this matter and would ensure that any candidates willing to support the government would have to be elected fairly. With this object, I took to the country and devoted as much time as I could in between my public obligations to campaign in support of the fair election of government sympathizers.

The campaign lasted for about forty days. During all that time I slept in comfort on tatami no more than six or seven nights. All the other nights were spent on the move in trains or cars or on ferries. While campaigning for the election, I also inspected jails and courthouses and attended welcome parties jointly sponsored by the government and private sector groups. It is hardly an exaggeration to say that I was kept on the go for the forty days without decent sleep or rest.

I forced myself to persevere, but by the time the campaign was over, since I have a weak constitution, I was exhausted and running a fever. On returning to Tokyo I had myself examined by a doctor, who told me, "This is a sure way to kill yourself. You are risking your life as much as a soldier going into battle." I suppose he was right.

During this election campaign, even Prime Minister Ōkuma toured the country. His supporters participated actively too. Ōkuma, as I have often mentioned, was a big-hearted man. He was not given to bothering over trifling matters. Now that he was past eighty and beginning to show signs of senility, he had added indifference to his character. This led him not infrequently to support the two incompatible sides of an issue at the same time.

To cite just one example, Ōkuma had provided a similar letter of recommendation to two opposing candidates standing for election in the city of Fukui. When the train in which he was traveling stopped there, supporters of both candidates turned up to welcome him. Most people would have been at a loss for words, but the marquis thrust his head from the window and delivered an impromptu speech exhorting both sides to win. He was nothing if not flexible.

As a result of this election, the Seiyūkai, which had tyrannized the House with its absolute majority, suffered a miserable defeat. Seats held by the various parties before and after the election were as follows.

	Before	After
Dōshikai	95	150
Seiyūkai	185	104
Kokumintō	32	27
Chūseikai	36	35
Independents	33	65

When the special session was convoked on May 20, 1915, the government side was extremely strong. On June 1, a supplementary budget was passed as a package and the bill on the two new army divisions, which had been the cause of the dissolution, was passed with a majority of 232 votes to 131.

On June 3 the Seiyūkai in desperation submitted a resolution to impeach the government on grounds of mismanaging foreign policy and a second resolution on June 5 to impeach Home Minister Ōura. Neither resolution was passed, however, and the session was brought to a close. Until the previous Diet, there had been nothing that the Seiyūkai could not carry out, but now its decline was pitiful. At this time the party was no longer headed by Saionji but by Hara Takashi. In fact, Saionji had made known his intent to resign for some time, but could not carry out his resolve because of the difficulty of choosing a suitable successor. The Seiyūkai possessed two outstanding senior politicians. One, Matsuda Masahisa, had no rival in terms of career and moral influence. The other, Hara, was without peer for his competence and resourcefulness of mind. It was difficult to give the leadership to one and not the other. The dilemma was solved by the death of Matsuda Masahisa on March 5, 1914, after which Saionji did not hesitate to recommend Hara as his successor, which permitted him to resign as party president. On June 18 Hara was officially elected president.

In a certain sense, Hara was a lucky man. Although he had steadily climbed within the ranks of the Seiyūkai as he gradually eclipsed his seniors, his reputation never quite matched that of Matsuda. Had Matsuda lived longer, Hara would not so easily have attained the party presidency. Once he became the Seiyūkai's leader, however, his hidden brilliance flourished, and in time he became a president beyond compare. However, Hara's argumentative and quarrelsome disposition, which had dogged him since childhood, did not help him to get along well with people. He hated to admit that he was wrong, and would insist on having his own way even on issues that did not matter one way or the other. He showed the same obstinacy even as a young secretary to Mutsu Munemitsu. Rather than obey an instruction of which he did not approve, he would say, "I shall do as the minister says, though I do not agree with his reasons." On such occasions Mutsu made it a point to assure him it was an order.

One day Matsuda, Hara, and I were sitting together discussing Seiyūkai party matters. As usual, Hara was sticking to his point and we could not come to any conclusion. Matsuda, who was well known for his patience, did not oppose him even though Hara was plainly in the wrong. Since I had only returned to the

Seiyūkai a short time before, I too restrained myself and expressed my views mildly. Eventually, the easy-going Matsuda appeared to have run out of patience with Hara's stubbornness. He excused himself to go the men's room and then beckoned to me from behind the *shōji* paper screens and whispered into my ear: "We've had enough of this, don't you think?" I promptly agreed, and when we returned we refuted Hara's argument two to one.

However, after I parted company with Hara, that left him as the single most powerful person within the Seiyūkai, and when he then became the party's president his argumentative nature underwent an amazing change. From a predisposition to stick to his guns against all reason and quarrel with just about anybody, he acquired an uncharacteristic tolerance for other people's opinions and would now listen genially to what anyone else had to say. Until then I had always thought it was impossible for someone to change his innate personality. After witnessing this transformation in Hara I came to believe that with greatness it is indeed possible for a man to achieve a radical change of character even at an advanced age. To be sure, there were others who on attaining high office changed for the better, but not to the same extent as Hara. It may have been the Seiyūkai defeat in the general election of 1915 that was the catalyst that molded the man's character.

THE ORIGINS OF THE ŌURA AFFAIR

The Seiyūkai, having been dealt a crushing defeat at the polls, was hard pressed to find irregularities that they could pin on the government and, after searching diligently, they concocted a charge of corruption on the part of Home Minister Ōura. Shirakawa Tomoichi, a successful candidate from Marugame in Shikoku, had offered Ōura a campaign contribution of ten thousand yen. It was charged that Shirakawa's real motive was to reward Minister Ōura for his efforts at conciliation between Shirakawa and Kaji Mankichi, who was his competitor in the election. To begin with, the money was offered as a straightforward campaign donation. Moreover, since it was found that Ōura had refused to accept it, the charge lacked grounds and came to nothing. During the course of the investigation of the alleged corruption, however, evidence of bribery of politicians was exposed. This involved the use of confidential funds to bribe Seiyūkai members to support the passage of the bill authorizing the two-division army buildup during the thirty-fifth Diet, which preceded the general election.

To tell the truth, I was not at first favorably impressed by Ōura. He had started as a police officer in the Metropolitan Police Department and was gradually promoted to positions of responsibility. From the early days of the Diet he employed his exceptional powers of persuasion, augmented by money, to corrupt members of the Diet. He frequently even went so far as to harass members of my own party, earning the nickname "The Viper." It was an understatement to say we were not fond of him. As I came to learn more about Ōura from those close to him, I realized that in his own way he had a certain charm. As a police officer he used to attend Mishima Takayasu, who apparently had some dealings with the demi-monde. Ōura was often sent as a messenger to geisha. On such occasions Ōura, being a handsome young man, was apparently showered with flattery but was never distracted from his duty. In such circumstances it is not easy for a red-blooded young man to conduct himself as Ōura did. Later he was promoted to a post in Osaka where there was an incident involving violent soldiers. Seeing that the situation was getting out of hand, it was said, Ōura quickly changed into military uniform (since he ranked as an army second lieutenant), went straight into the brawl, and in no time brought the soldiers under control. It was a resource-ful act in response to an emergency.

By the time I first actually met Ōura, having heard these stories about him, my initial bad feeling toward him had been somewhat diluted. He was then minister of agriculture and commerce in the Katsura government, and as mayor of Tokyo I had to see him on business. I was led into an imposing room where a sword was on display, all rather splendid, and Ōura, when he came in, was polite and digni-fied. I was sufficiently impressed that now the ill feeling I had harbored was almost erased. However, while recognizing his many fine points, I was on my guard from the beginning when we both served in the Ōkuma government against the possibility of his interfering in elections and buying members to influence voting. For this reason I fiercely opposed his becoming home minister. As I had feared, Ōura did get himself involved in a matter of no small consequence.

A number of politicians belonging to the Tōkai-gumi of the Seiyūkai were among those offered bribes. Probably at their own suggestion, feeling that it would be risky to meet Ōura alone, these members requested that I should also be present. They probably wished to cover themselves by finding out first where I stood on the military build-up proposal. I readily accepted their offer and met them with Ōura. They asked me whether I favored increasing the number of army divisions. I said I did. Among those present at the meeting were even some of my own close followers, who no doubt wished to be sure of my views before making up their minds. Most, however, were probably looking for my tacit support to go ahead with accepting bribes. Their self-conscious manner of speaking led me to suspect that something was wrong. I therefore said clearly that their support was welcome if for reasons purely of national policy they were prepared to endorse the govern-ment opinion unconditionally, but if they were seeking to obtain anything in return it would be a criminal act. Ōura motioned to me not to take such a strong line, but I firmly repeated what I had said. Until then, it had not really dawned on me that Ōura was seeking to buy the members, but his suspicious behavior prompted me to give them a clear warning. Perhaps it paid off. Among those negotiating with Ōura, the members of the Tōkai-gumi from Mie and Shizuoka districts left the group and were spared from committing crimes.

No sooner had Ōura had been charged with bribery by the Seiyūkai than the affair, of course, immediately became a judicial issue. I had never thought it would come to this, but I had had the matter investigated on account of Ōura's strange behavior, and found many irregularities. Ōura and his group claimed that no wrong had been done, but there was no way of evading the fact that Ōura had committed an offense in the eyes of the law. I was sorry for Ōura, but for the minister to violate the law was a fundamental breach of official discipline. I had to decide that it could not be glossed over.

One day, a friend who occupied an important government post paid me a visit and said, "Is your excellency aware of the custom with regard to legal procedures involving members of the House? Everyone of course knows very well that it is wrong to buy politicians, but how many in past governments—or this—can you remember who have been blameless? I have decisive proof against Mr. Hara, for instance. But because I think it is a loss to the nation to deprive ourselves of the services of a great statesman over such a trifling matter, I keep it to myself." To this I replied, "It is the natural obligation of the state to punish those who have committed crimes. If you have proof, please provide it. I shall have any accused person arrested, whether it is Mr. Hara or anybody else." Apparently this friend of mine went to Prime Minister Ōkuma and said, "Ozaki is being unreasonable. Ōura was not acting out of self-interest. What sort of minister is he to arrest a fellow member of the cabinet?" There was nothing I could do about it. I had made up my mind that Ōura had to be dealt with.

THE SOLUTION PLAN TEMPERS JUSTICE WITH MERCY

I was resolved to deal with Ōura, but he was, after all, home minister. Within the permissible range of justice I had a strong wish to protect a colleague. Laws are enacted not merely to punish people. I therefore thought to consult with Hiranuma Kiichirō,[4] the public prosecutor general and his deputy Suzuki Kisaburō to reach an appropriate solution. After studying various possibilities, the justice ministry reached the conclusion that if Ōura decided to retire from politics he would not be arrested. There were enough precedents of this kind in which tens of thousands of minor offenses escaped arrest every year on record at the ministry. And if those arrested and found guilty proved themselves sufficiently repentant, they could often earn a stay of penalty. There was, however, simply no precedent for a man of Ōura's prominence being arrested and charged.

The basic objectives of the criminal code were not to punish but to prevent crimes and to provide a deterrent for the future. From this point of view our decision regarding the Ōura affair allowed for generosity on the one hand while taking adequate measures to discourage similar wrongdoings. All the same, I felt sorry for Ōura. He held a very prominent post and had built a reputation which, had all gone well, might have taken him the whole way to the premiership. To force him into political retirement would be a severer punishment for him than for an ordinary person to be sent to prison. From the standpoint of my personal feeling for him this caused me much anguish, but I could not allow my sympathy to compromise my duty. The final decision of the ministry, I believe, gave due consideration to both justice and mercy. When I put my decision before the cabi-

---

[4] Prime minister, January to August 1939.

net it was met with strong opposition. It was argued that the plan was too harsh on Ōura. The other members of the cabinet claimed that if I were to push this through in spite of their opposition there would be no choice but for the cabinet to resign.

It appeared that some bureaucrats belonging to clan cliques thought it was permissible to violate the law if it were done in the national interest. Ōura himself did not appear to consider what he had done either unlawful or morally wrong. Ōura had sensible people and lawyers under him such as Shimooka Tadaji and Isawa Takio, but they too were victims of the same kind of bureaucratic reasoning and apparently advised him that his actions did not constitute a crime. Perhaps encouraged by their advice, Ōura, who had remained quiet up to the point where the cabinet became deadlocked over how to deal with the situation, stood up with his head high and declared: "Well then, let us fight it out openly and fairly in the courts." "What are you going to fight openly and fairly?" I asked, unable to hide a faintly malicious smile. The other ministers found this amusing and made a point of frowning silently. The whole point of offering the solution I did was because of the certainty that Ōura's actions would be judged criminal if the matter went to court.

As I have said, Ōura evidently did not think he had done anything wrong. But in a law-abiding country one cannot be allowed to act as though absolutely anything is justifiable if it is done for the country's sake. Apparently the bureaucrats did not share this view. As a person, Ōura appeared a typical respectable warrior, but because of his bureaucratic, or rather his clan background, his thoughts and feelings were often totally alien to mine. The affair was concluded in line with what I had suggested; in other words, in return for his retirement from political life, Ōura was not prosecuted. Others were, however. Apart from those who had actually taken bribes, these people had acted not for personal aggrandizement or out of greed, but for the sake of what they thought was good for the country. I felt truly sorry that they had to be dealt with in a way that gave them no future. Even today, those whose minds are set in a bureaucratic mold carry out as a matter of course many things that are not permitted in a law-abiding country. It is unconscionable that there are those in power who consider such behavior routine.

The decision in the Ōura case was criticized as too harsh by those who were close to Ōura and those trapped in bureaucratic thinking, but it was praised as a wise judgment by those with common sense. There was even criticism that the conclusion was too lenient on Ōura.

ŌKUMA CABINET RESHUFFLE

When the time came for Home Minister Ōura to resign as a penalty for having bribed members of the House, Foreign Minister Katō and other cabinet members from the Dōshikai suggested that instead the cabinet should take joint responsibility and resign as a body. As I remarked earlier, this Ōkuma government was actually Katō's in all but name. Ōkuma, who had at first left everything to Kato, began to enjoy running the government and gradually became his own master. This did not endear him to Katō and his followers. They must have thought the Ōura affair an excellent opportunity to get rid of Ōkuma and pressed the cabinet to take joint responsibility for Ōura's indiscretions and then to reshuffle under Katō's leadership.

Navy Minister Yashiro and Education Minister Ichiki also joined the Dōshikai members in urging the cabinet to resign. I was now alone in opposing the idea. I stated my position thus: the act of bribery in this case had never been deliberated by the cabinet, and was committed by Ōura alone. None of us knew of the affair until it was publicly exposed. It was bad policy to take responsibility in matters in which we had not been involved. Naturally we should have been considered jointly accountable had the issue been referred for cabinet deliberation. But as it was the individual act of a minister he had to be held solely responsible. Theoretically, the prime minister might be regarded as accountable on grounds of neglecting to carry out adequate supervision of his ministers. He, it should be borne in mind, was accountable only to His Majesty. This case, however, was not grave enough to require the prime minister's resignation.

Such was the gist of my argument. The other members of the cabinet nonetheless signed their names to a letter of resignation prepared by the chief secretary. Prime Minister Ōkuma himself was prepared to submit his resignation. Katō Takaaki in his usual supercilious way sneered at me: "Well, Mr. Ozaki, will you run the cabinet alone? There is a precedent, of course—when Mr. Watanabe Kunitake was put in your position after the mass resignation of the Itō government." I finally signed my name, but only after explaining my position. "I will not resign on account of any joint responsibility; I shall do so only because the prime minister is tendering his resignation, in which case I believe all ministers should follow. The circumstances that provoked this situation hardly differ from an informal resignation by a minor official, which is customarily not accepted. The prime minister should of course not resign on account of joint responsibility either. It is up to His Majesty's pleasure: if he decides that there is no need for the prime minister to resign, then of course Ōkuma should humbly accept His Majesty's wish and reorganize the cabinet."

Navy Minister Yashiro turned to me scornfully: "What's come over the champion of constitutional government [as I was called]?" "The responsibility of the champion of constitutional government is to explain clearly the locus of accountability," I retorted. I am afraid this was a childish exchange. Ōkuma, usually a man of many words, kept silent.

The cabinet resigned en masse, although for my part I did so for different reasons from my colleagues. In a cordial decree, His Majesty dissuaded Ōkuma from resigning. In the event, it was Foreign Minister Katō, Finance Minister Wakatsuki, and Navy Minister Yashiro who tendered their resignations, and the cabinet was then reshuffled. The result of the reshuffle more or less totally reflected my opinion. It may well have been that Ōkuma had similar thoughts and that the convergence was merely coincidental.

Ōkuma apparently expected that I would demand the home ministry portfolio but instead I recommended Education Minister Ichiki for the post. Ichiki Kitokurō was extremely reserved and conscientious. He had attended a private school run by Okada Ryōichirō, a friend of my father's, and I had heard that his excellent qualities already showed themselves in those early days. For this reason I had always been interested in him. So when I found that he had earned a good reputation as a government official after working for some time as a university professor, I asked Kōmuchi Tomotsune what he thought of him. Kōmuchi was an unimpressive person, much like a sober Shinto priest at first sight but betraying in his facial expressions an intelligent and enlightened mind. He had an unusually discerning eye where people were concerned. Responding to my question, Kōmuchi said: "He is someone just like you."

While Ichiki was in the cabinet, the price of rice plummeted and it was decided that the government should purchase rice in order to readjust the price. Ichiki agreed to this but reported at the same time that he had sold all the rice he had. Knowing that the government intended to purchase rice from the market, it was an opportunity for some officials secretly to buy rice for profit. But for the very reason that he knew that if the government purchased rice the price would rise, Ichiki had come to the cabinet meeting only after selling all the rice he owned. This single incident accurately attests to the man's integrity. Even I thought that he need not have sold his rice, as there was nothing to be ashamed about if its price were to rise. Since Ichiki was such a self-denying and modest person, I thought that as home minister he might not achieve much but that he would be sure at least not to commit any blunders.

With Ichiki responsible for home affairs, I put Takada Sanae to succeed him at his post in education. Taketomi Tokitoshi was replaced as minister of post and telegraphic services by Minoura Katsundo and assigned the finance portfolio. Navy Minister Yashiro was replaced by Admiral Katō Tomosaburō and Ishii Kikujirō was appointed to succeed Foreign Minister Katō.

For the first time a cabinet had been created that would carry out some of my views. Not only were there in the cabinet men who shared our vision, but Ōkuma himself was practically a second father to me, and I had to a great extent been tutored by him. I enjoyed a relationship with him in which I could feel that my wishes, if he saw nothing wrong with them, would, for the most part, be granted without demur.

The Ōura affair was most unfortunate and it was disappointing to have lost such powerful cabinet ministers as Katō, Wakatsuki, and Yashiro as a result of it. With supplementary appointments to fill the vacant portfolios smoothly achieved, I felt that the Ōkuma government could now do much more. While Katō and Wakatsuki had resigned, the relationship between the Dōshikai and the Ōkuma government had not been severed.

THE GRAND CEREMONY OF ENTHRONEMENT, AND YAMAGATA

Following the cabinet reshuffle, I had the honor to serve in the grand ceremony marking the accession of Emperor Taishō. Kyoto in mid-November is generally rather chilly. At first light on the day of the Great Thanksgiving Festival (Daijōsai) following the enthronement there was an unusually heavy frost and I was chilled to the bone. I sympathized with the Son of Heaven, who also must have been feeling the cold. I often went hunting and was in good health, but that day I wore many warm clothes and five strategically placed body warmers under the full court dress. I was still cold. I was concerned for His Majesty lest he catch cold this bitter night when even the lamps seemed to freeze.

At times such as this the question of ennoblement was sure to come up. With the enthronement we had celebrated the birth of a new era, the first world war was over for Japan, and honors were being awarded for meritorious service. Had Katsura's generous ways prevailed this would certainly have been an occasion for the conferring of peerages. A certain number of elevations were in fact made within the Ōkuma cabinet. Both the army and navy ministers were made barons, and Katō Takaaki, despite the brevity of his service as minister of foreign affairs, was raised from baron to viscount. It would have been perfectly reasonable for other members of the cabinet to be considered too.

In my case, however, I had committed myself to lifetime service in the House of Representatives. I would have to leave the House if I were to receive a peerage in the imperial honors list. I therefore had a private talk with Ōkuma to make sure this would not happen. If this led indirectly to others being disappointed it could not be helped.

His Majesty would have been pleased to grant Fukuzawa Yukichi a title posthumously, but Fukuzawa's former followers in Mita learned of the move and tried to convince those in authority that they would rather decline the honor on behalf of their late mentor, who would not have wished it. Apparently they were told that they could hardly decline an imperial gift. When I heard about this I conferred with those in charge. In the end, Fukuzawa was not named a peer.[5]

Koizumi Yakumo (Lafcardio Hearn) too, who had taken Japanese nationality, had never been recognized in spite of the great contribution he made to the country through his writing. I had raised this matter with the authorities on a number of occasions in the past but had always been frustrated as invariably some had not even heard of Hearn. As a Japanese I thought I should at least meet him to express my gratitude, and I asked for an appointment through Takada Sanae. Koizumi was known to dislike interviews, but uncharacteristically agreed not only to meet me but also offered to make the visit himself. We had agreed on the date.

A few days before our appointment, however, he suddenly cancelled the appointment. I found it odd that he should so suddenly change his mind, and asked

---

[5] Fukuzawa had died in 1901.

Takada to make inquiries. Koizumi, it appeared, had heard of an "Ozaki who had married an Englishwoman, treated her cruelly, and divorced her," and on the strength of this had declined to see me. Takada, taking it on himself to vindicate my honor, explained to him that that was a different Ozaki and that Ozaki Yukio had out of sympathy married a daughter of the divorced woman. Koizumi apologized for his carelessness and renewed his promise to visit me. But soon thereafter he fell ill and died, so I never did have an opportunity to meet him in person after all.[6]

It pleased me enormously to be involved in recommending people for the peerage at the time of the enthronement. His Majesty had actually wished to grant other awards in addition to peerage titles, but this was not to be. Thinking of the enthronement, I am reminded of a story about Yamagata. During the banquet in the Kyoto palace my wife was seated between Yamagata and Matsukata. My wife was able to keep up the conversation in English but felt quite uncomfortable having to entertain the high-ranking and older men in her inadequate Japanese. So taking a queue from an English proverb, "The way to a man's heart is through his stomach," she apparently started talking to them about food.

Bread sold in the towns in those days was generally poor and many foreigners baked their own at home. We did too. Apparently my wife had promised Yamagata she would bake him some homemade bread, so she had some wrapped and delivered by one of our servants. The Yamagata household staff, evidently afraid that it might contain a bomb, promptly turned the parcel over to their security police. Carefully unwrapping it and finding only bread, the guards had it checked for poison just to be sure. Had my wife consulted me I would have written a note to go with the parcel, instead of provoking unnecessary apprehension. Nevertheless, the incident provides a good illustration of Yamagata's cautious character.

Yamagata was a scrupulously careful person who, it was said, always made doubly and triply sure of things. Itō and Ōkuma were equally gifted, but perhaps on account of their rapid rise through the ranks they were inclined to be negligent in their later years and often made decisions without due thought or consideration. But not Yamagata, who remained cautious to his death. He therefore made few blunders and was apparently proud of this.

Yamagata, it goes without saying, was far and away the most powerful member of the military clique, and remained my political enemy throughout most of his life. As such, I had few opportunities to come into direct contact with him and with rare exceptions only observed my enemy from a distance. But when Ōkuma was prime minister Yamagata and Inoue provided support, albeit indirectly. Under the circumstances, it was necessary for me to visit the Yamagata residence three or four times.

On one such occasion when I visited Yamagata in Odawara the two of us were taking lunch in a small room when Terauchi arrived to pay a visit. The prince instructed one of his staff to tell the count to come back another time as he was occupied with a guest. He must have been doing his best to show me hospitality.

---

[6] Hearn died in 1904, and it is strange that Ozaki enters this here.

When I told him I loved horses, he responded by recounting to me the following episode, which occurred during a dinner with the Emperor Meiji.

The emperor, in an unusually merry mood, called for an amusing story. A certain general ventured: "How's this, Your Majesty? The other day Yamagata fell off his horse!" The emperor, enormously pleased, grinned broadly. "What!" he exclaimed, "Yamagata fell, did he?" and glanced at Yamagata, who was seated diagonally across from him. The marshal, sitting bolt upright, declared firmly, "Nothing of the sort, Your Majesty!" spoiling the merriment. When the dinner was over and Yamagata was about to take his leave, the same general came up to him and said accusingly, "How could you tell such a barefaced lie to His Majesty and disgrace me like that?" to which Yamagata, with an imperious look, replied: "You must know that the honor of a military man cannot be compromised."

A crafty old fellow like Yamagata is very difficult to deal with. I recall an important meeting on national affairs at which a certain minister opposed the prince head on. He had logic on his side, and I watched with amusement to see how pressed Yamagata would be for an answer. The prince gazed at the ceiling and said simply, "Well, but that is just a theory." That was all he said. If the argument was on his side he would attack his opponent mercilessly, and when his adversary had the stronger argument he would merely gaze at the ceiling and complain that it was an unworkable theory. What a crafty old rogue he was.

THE EXPEDITION AGAINST YUAN SHIH-K'AI

After the Sino-Japanese War showed how weak the Manchu dynasty was, revolutionary movements sprang up in many parts of China. In October of 1911, the revolution in Wuchang succeeded. With Huang Hsing as generalissimo, Sun Yat-sen became president. The following February, the Ch'ing dynasty was overthrown after 277 years in power, and the imperial government was replaced by the Republic of China.

The revolutionary party, lacking the strength to govern the whole country, compromised with Yuan Shih-k'ai, who had been the real power behind the Ch'ing throne, and made him president. Yuan Shih-k'ai, with both civil and military power now in his hands, became exceedingly arrogant and claimed the imperial throne, ambitiously hoping to pass it on to his descendants.

I could see trouble brewing. If Yuan Shih-k'ai became emperor, I reasoned, China would most certainly be thrown into disorder. Civil war in China while the World War I was in progress would be a major event with grave repercussions for the whole world, and not merely a threat to neighboring Japan. Yuan somehow had to be dissuaded from pursuing his ambition. If Japan advised China against reinstating the imperial system, it might be hoped that Great Britain, the United States, and France would follow suit. Our foreign ministry had never taken the leadership among the powers, having so far only followed the lead of the Europeans and Americans and having always agreed to their proposals. It would not be a bad idea to have a little practice in leadership, since Japan was hoping to establish an independent diplomacy of its own. I shared this thought with other members of the cabinet, but the newly appointed foreign minister, Ishii, was on his way back to Japan to assume his new responsibilities and there was no one to support the idea.

The following day, Vice-Minister Shidehara and Director-General Koike from the foreign ministry attended the cabinet meeting to report on their activities. Taking the opportunity to test their reaction to my idea, I suggested that if we were to advise opposing Yuan Shih-k'ai's ascendancy to the imperial throne, Great Britain, the United States, and other countries would be likely to follow. At the same time, it would make Japan, the traditional follower, a leader for a change. And this would be in the interest of the world. "What do you gentlemen from the foreign ministry think of this?" I asked. The cabinet ministers were all listening.

The ambitious Director-General Koike spoke first: "Yes, if Japan takes the initiative I believe the powers will follow." Vice-Minister Shidehara expressed a similar view. Then the ministers who had not agreed with me before changed their tune. "Well, it's an interesting thought," they said. "Let's give it a try."

In this way it was more or less decided that Japan would take the initiative in issuing a notification opposing the re-adoption of the imperial system in China. Koike met Ishii en route to Tokyo and explained the whole issue. It was finally decided that the proposal would be submitted to the full cabinet as an opinion of the foreign ministry.

The cabinet readily adopted the proposal. When it was presented to Great Britain, the United States, and France, they promptly agreed with our point. Even Italy said it would participate in issuing a joint notification. This dealt a huge blow to Yuan's campaign for the imperial throne.

The move must have surprised Yuan Shih-k'ai. The wily Yuan had no doubt studied the minds of the two *genrō* statesmen, Yamagata and Inoue, as well as that of Prime Minister Ōkuma, and felt satisfied that quarter would not oppose his going ahead with his strategy. So he must have wondered where things had gone wrong. In fact, not only Yuan but Yamagata too appeared at a loss as to what had happened and apparently bitterly chided both the prime minister and the foreign minister about this.

However, Mr. Jordan, the British minister in China who was known to be unfriendly toward Japan and who was perhaps motivated by a desire to claim distinction for himself, secretly counseled Yuan Shih-k'ai to execute his plan despite instructions from London to the contrary. This put at risk the cooperation of the powers on which we were counting. Under the circumstances, I insisted that if a representative of any of the powers jeopardized his country's cooperation, we should request his home government serve him a serious warning. The British foreign office was accordingly notified of Jordan's attitude and, yielding to our misgivings, instructed the minister in China that henceforth on issues regarding relations with China he must take no unilateral action without consulting Britain's ally, Japan. The Japanese government was duly informed of this.

This may seem trivial, but it was a turning point in the diplomatic histories of both Japan and Britain. It was through this that Japan for the first time took the leadership among the powers. Great Britain had traditionally held the dominant position in China, but now it had recognized Japan's preeminence and agreed to consult with us. Japan had increased its diplomatic stature, whereas Britain had compromised its long-held primacy. It is to be hoped that those in charge of our foreign relations will long remember this and take care never to forfeit the diplomatic recognition that Japan had now secured.

Yuan had suffered a temporary setback to his quest for the throne, but being no common man he would not give up easily. There were still many strings he could pull in Japan. Of particular use to him were his relationships with members of the *genrō* circle from whom he indirectly sought support for his accession. The *genrō* differed from the government's view and expressed opinions in support of Yuan's pretensions. This was soon made known to Yuan, who was now in a hurry to take the throne.

Just as one feared, as soon as Yuan Shih-k'ai took new steps to advance his cause, relying on support from the *genrō* and others, punitive campaigns were launched against him throughout China, thrusting the country into turmoil. Within Japan, *genrō* statesmen Yamagata and Inoue were applying pressure on the government to ease its policy toward Yuan. At the time, the *genrō* and the members of the cabinet were all gathered in the former capital of Kyoto for the grand ceremony of enthronement, and meeting each other daily in the palace. Whenever they met, apparently, Yamagata would remind Foreign Minister Ishii that he was in favor of easing Japan's policy. Gradually, Ishii and other ministers began to relent, and in the end Prime Minister Ōkuma was forced to declare that he thought it was time they ended the matter. There was little one could do under the circumstances. I determined to resign. I scribbled my final position on a scrap of paper and presented it at a cabinet meeting.

"If you decide not to go through with what has been decided," I wrote, "and by heeding the words of the *genrō* abandon the country's position of leadership we have secured, I will resign here and now, leave government service, and fight it out in the court of public opinion." Seeing my determination, they accepted my proposal after considerable debate. The government would pursue its Yuan policy as decided. I believe my scribbled memo is still kept in the archives of the foreign ministry.

Meanwhile, Yuan Shih-k'ai died and the controversy was quickly resolved. Some people tell me that Yuan Shih-k'ai would not have died in that fashion had it not have been for me. I never met Yuan Shih-k'ai nor do I know much about his career. It would seem that he bore a striking resemblance to our Katsura for his lack of good taste and classical knowledge, and for having similar worldly and vulgar predilections. I disliked both men. This part of my character is referred to as disagreeableness.

In the whole world there have been only two men whom I so heartily disliked: Katsura of Yamato and Yuan of Cathay. The following short satirical poem honestly described my feelings at the time. Both Katsura and Yuan died not long after I began to attack them. There was a strange feeling that I might have had something to do with their demise.

> I should not hate; those hated seem to die.
> Thus Yuan and Katsura, triumphant in their time

I thought they might well use their vulgar powers to train the demons of hell to avenge them when I get there. But I will probably go to heaven rather than hell. Thinking of this I wrote another little poem.

> How laughable that they should await me with their demons
> For they will not see me, since we tread different paths.

Organizing the Kenseikai; The Cabinet Resigns

When the grand ceremony was safely over, the *genrō* no longer disguised their attempts to unseat the Ōkuma government. As I have mentioned, they kept their eye on the government's every move concerning the China policy. Seen through the eyes of the clan cliques, the mission of the Ōkuma government had been completed now that the Seiyūkai, which was instrumental in bringing down the Katsura government, had been deprived of its voting majority. Now they harassed the government at every turn to bring about its downfall.

The eighty-year-old Ōkuma seemed weary and ready to resign. He bitterly resented the despotic ways of the *genrō* and their coterie and complained from time to time that he would like to resign but for lack of a successor. So one day I said to him, "A successor does not come by chance. He has to be nurtured. Katō Takaaki could be your natural successor if he could first be installed as president of a political party with an absolute majority. It would be difficult to find a suitable successor in today's framework of a three-party coalition." Ōkuma seemed agreeable to this. I had one condition, however.

"It is not enough just to create a major party," I went on. "It will require at least a year or so of training before it can do a proper job. If you are prepared to stick it out for another year, I will support the amalgamation of the coalition partners into a major party and see that Katō is put at its head. I will need a minimum of half a year. If you intend to step down as soon as the parties merge, I will not support the plan and the organization to which I belong will not be party to it."

"All right," agreed Ōkuma, "no one can predict political developments, but all things being equal, I can promise to stay on for a year or so after the organization of a new party. Please go ahead."

With this understanding, I began organizing a major political party by consolidating Katō's Dōshikai, the Kōyū Club affiliated with Ōkuma, and my own Chūseikai. On visiting the Imperial Palace to report to the throne on government affairs, Ōkuma confidentially expressed his wish to resign due to old age. At an appropriate time in the future he would beg to be relieved of his post and recommend Katō as his successor.

Meanwhile, the organization of the new party was proceeding well. The Dōshikai approved the move as a body, and the entire Chūseikai with 67 members and about half of the Kōyū Club joined the new party, which with 199 members immediately commanded an absolute majority.

At first there were voices urging that Ōkuma himself should lead the new party, but because of the history of its development it was decided to install Katō, the president of Dōshikai, as its head. It was suggested that the party be called the Rikken kyōdōkai (Constitutional Cooperative), but it was decided instead to call it the Kenseikai (Constitutional Government Party).

With the Kenseikai more or less successfully organized, Katō and the members of the old Dōshikai, weary of waiting, became impatient to organize their own government. Certain members of the cabinet therefore urged Ōkuma to step down and some ministers close to him threatened to resign if he did not. At the same time those outside of government suggested that if he stepped down amicably he would be appointed a *genrō*. And once a *genrō* he would almost certainly outlive Yamagata, and as virtually the sole *genrō*, things would go his way. By offering such inducements they hoped to work on his family too. I, however, was against Ōkuma becoming a *genrō* under any circumstances and repeatedly advised him to firmly decline any such invitation. Caught in the middle of this crossfire, pushed by some of his own ministers to resign and lured by others with the *genrō* carrot, he seemed understandably confused.

Yamagata, in the meantime, having learned from Ōkuma of his earlier confidences to the emperor, secretly planned to reject the birth of the Katō cabinet and conspired with his men to snatch the reins of the incoming government. The plot was watertight in typical Yamagata style. It would have to be carried out before the Kenseikai organization was complete. Members of Yamagata's group therefore did all they could to prompt the prime minister to step down immediately.

The endless intrigue and subterfuge that surrounded him eventually told on the normally optimistic Ōkuma. With the inauguration ceremony of the Kenseikai scheduled to take place on October 10, he went to the palace on October 4 and submitted his resignation—and then told me what he had done. I was most indignant. But the resignation had been submitted and there was nothing one could do about it. My objective in amalgamating the parties was destroyed completely.

When the cabinet thereupon tendered its resignation as a body, Ōkuma recommended Katō as his successor, while Yamagata countered by putting forward Terauchi Masatake. The contest ended in Ōkuma's defeat. The character of the two men was well reflected in the way they conducted themselves throughout.

What in fact happened was that Ōkuma, who seemed to enjoy the full confidence of Emperor Taishō, formally recommended Katō as the best man to succeed him and left the palace satisfied. Yamagata, hot on his heels, then recommended General Terauchi and took his leave of the emperor, but remained at the palace until after the imperial approval was announced.

From what I learned afterward, Yamagata had confided to those close to him that he had "no intention of leaving until the imperial sanction was given, even if it meant waiting till midnight or dawn." This was the difference between Ōkuma and Yamagata. It was only natural that the marquis should lose. A few hours after he left the palace, the imperial mandate was awarded to Terauchi. Naturally this reflected the personal recommendation of the *genrō*. But the cabinet members had not yet actually tendered their resignation, and there was wide criticism of the despotic conduct of the *genrō* and the unconstitutionality of the Terauchi government.

The members of the old Dōshikai were served a crude surprise, for they had helped to precipitate Ōkuma's retirement with the express object of paving the way to create a cabinet of their own.

The State of Domestic and Foreign Policy
after the War

FIGHTING THE TERAUCHI GOVERNMENT

On coming to power Terauchi unapologetically declared: "For the successful achievement of national unity (kyokoku itchi) it is not appropriate for government to be ruled by a political party agenda. My government, therefore, will transcend all political parties. Where political views differ among factions and parties the government will be open-minded, represent the public interest, and maintain a proper balance among them." This is the famous declaration, "Represent the public and maintain the balance." There was no way that this sort of supra-party government could be implemented in 1916, the fifth year of the Taishō era. The people were embarrassed by the pretext and dismissed it with contempt.

For many years we had fought to break the despotism of the clan governments, but even after the constitution was promulgated and the Diet opened, the clan cliques continued to wield formidable power. Eventually Terauchi was forced to realize that it was impossible to ignore the popular will represented by political parties, and he abandoned his quest to introduce supra-party government.

Every clan strongman had different ways of working with political parties. Yamagata freely dispensed money to undermine political parties. He was successful to a point, but his tactics incurred the heavy price of corrupting constitutional government.

Itō manipulated political parties with great resourcefulness, but when in difficulty he had the bad habit of hiding behind the throne. In the end he established the Seiyūkai, saying, "Mercenaries are not dependable. I have to have my own troops."

The tactless Matsukata had a head-on collision with the political parties and squandered his chances by his notorious intervention in the election. In the subsequent administration he set up a coalition with the Shinpotō, or Progressive Party, but this was another failure.

Katsura compromised with the Seiyūkai, and instead of establishing a coalition under his own leadership took turns at the helm of government with Saionji, an arrangement that lasted for some time. Yet in the end, even this master of conjuring with other political parties was forced to organize his own.

Yamamoto Gonnohyōe barely managed to form a cabinet by getting most of his ministers to join the Seiyūkai. The Ōkuma cabinet followed in its wake.

Following this period of political turbulence it was one thing for the Terauchi government to declare itself above such things but quite another to perform accordingly. As a matter of fact, in organizing his cabinet Terauchi sought a compromise with the Kenseikai's president, Katō Takaaki, but when his overture was rejected, Terauchi aligned himself with the Seiyūkai. Meanwhile, holding a deep-seated grudge against the Kenseikai, Inukai's Kokumintō was negotiating with the cabinet behind the scenes. What emerged was in effect a Terauchi-led coalition covertly incorporating both the Seiyūkai and the Kokumintō under the folds of the ruling party in order to fight the Kenseikai in the House.

With this objective the Terauchi government tried to undermine the Kenseikai during the thirty-eighth session of the Diet by disclosing the China diplomacy of the Ōkuma administration. I attempted to describe the weakness of the Ōkuma cabinet in diplomatic matters in the previous chapter. In any case, the exposure was a poor tactic.

Gotō Shinpei, the home minister and de facto vice-premier, had, while a member of the opposition party, supported his denunciation of the Ōkuma administration's China diplomacy by circulating a secret document. The Terauchi government inherited this ploy and continued to carp at the shortcomings of the previous administration.

The content of the document was so trifling that its exposure would do little harm. However, since it had originally been circulated in confidence, the government first convened a secret meeting to consider it and then launched their attack on the Kenseikai. I lost no time in mounting a counterattack.

"It is to the advantage of the previous administration that the document is now exposed," I reasoned. "If the present government of Mr. Terauchi contends that the conduct of its predecessor was improper, it is surely inappropriate for it to retain the army and navy ministers, who were parties to the impropriety. Why does the government not dismiss the two ministers? And why do the two ministers not take their leave?" This silenced the government and its supporters. Our friends were in high spirits over this and the enemy abandoned the chase.

Confident that the Terauchi government would suffer great loss of face, I left for home like a general exulting over his humbled foe. But I left too soon. The next day's paper carried no word of my counterattack. Worse still, the report of the proceedings in the Diet indicated that the previous administration was in dire straits as a result of having its China policy exposed. Overnight the government had successfully pressured the newspaper to create an artificial public opinion diametrically opposed to the facts.

Once more I repented for not having administered a coup de grâce and for allowing myself to be prematurely elated over my apparent victory. Hindsight is not foresight. As I left the scene triumphantly with my colleagues, Tagawa Daikichirō alone had warned me that our departure was premature. "If only we had given them the coup de grâce, the Terauchi government would never have been able to recover from the blow," he said with chagrin. My generalship is quite good but my weakness is in not seeing the battle through to the end, so that all too often defeat springs from the jaws of my victories.

I Am Attacked by a Thug While Speaking

No sooner was the Terauchi government established than we launched a campaign to thwart the clan cliques once and for all. We organized assemblies and adopted resolutions and arranged forums to inform the public. The campaign kept up its momentum into the new year and lasted until the spring of 1917.

In the past, gangsters had frequently been employed in politics, but much less had been seen of them lately. With the emergence of the Terauchi administration, however, the thugs began to stalk again. They were at every public speech. I was attacked a number of times. They were not necessarily in the government's pay, but as can only be expected under a military régime they clearly operated with its tacit permission. This government was certainly resourceful. It was, however, a strange act of providence that the very government that had connived with such ruffians would fall later due to the rice riots that sprang up in some fifty places throughout the country.

On January 24, 1917, the atmosphere was charged from the very beginning at an antigovernment public meeting we put on at the Meiji-za kabuki theater. Even the presence of several hundred policemen failed to quell the mob that engaged them in running battles. One of the thugs even fell from the upper circle onto the actors' central stage walkway (*hanamichi*).

I had been on the rostrum for some time when suddenly a thug ran onto the stage. In his right hand he held a seven-inch knife aimed directly at my chest. Had I run away I would certainly have been wounded. Instead, I dodged to the side so that the man staggered forward with the knife. Morimoto Kazuo (later mayor of Tsuruga), who was at my side, leaped forward and held him firmly under his arm.

The hall was in disorder. The stage immediately filled with people as some sprang onto it from the floor of the theater and as others came running on from backstage. Some began quarreling noisily, and no one had any idea what was happening.

I was wrestled to the floor and dragged into a small room. I had no way to tell if these people were for or against me. I feared they were my enemies, and I let them do with me as they pleased. Suddenly one of them called out, "Sensei, stay put here, please," and I knew they were on my side. Eventually order was restored and I returned to the stage when a friend sent word that I could resume my speech.

I shall quote from an article in the magazine *Yūben* (Oratory) written by a friend, Ishikawa Hanzan, who was in the audience that day, since it is likely to be surer than my memory.

> When the mob had cleared the stage, members of the audience called out to ask after Mr. Ozaki, concerned for his safety. "Mr. Ozaki is all right," came voices from the four corners of the hall. We decided that an announcement should be made to reassure

the audience about his safety. Mr. Nakajima Kisō therefore asked for their attention and told them, "Mr. Ozaki is unharmed and will shortly return to resume his speech." At this, the crowd cheered and shouted exuberantly, "Long live Ozaki!" three times. Amidst wild cheering Mr. Ozaki returned to the stage perfectly composed. He betrayed no sign of stress and addressed the crowd in his usual low and calm voice. Immediately he launched into criticism of the Terauchi government, and not a word was wasted on the incident that had occurred only minutes earlier. In a speech I made just before Mr. Ozaki's return, I drew loud applause when I told of a similar incident, and fully expected Mr. Ozaki to refer in one way or another to what had passed when he spoke. Contrary to my expectations, he remained completely calm as if nothing had happened and continued his speech with the same voice and expression on his face as when he had been so violently interrupted. I was deeply ashamed of my own performance and felt limitless respect for his character. After thirty minutes or so another thug tried to run up onto the stage. This time he was immediately restrained by a number of brave men who were guarding Mr. Ozaki on both sides of the rostrum. As before, Mr. Ozaki watched the scene with perfect composure, apparently not at all shaken by the incident. When it was all over he resumed speaking where he had left off, without a word of what had happened.

Ishikawa Hanzan went on to describe how President Roosevelt had continued a speech after he was shot and wounded, and praised me for being no less courageous. To tell the truth, I was surprised myself. Even to this day I recall with a strange sense of wonder how I remembered my exact words when I was interrupted in mid-sentence and was able to start there again as if nothing had happened. Convinced that I am a coward by nature, I had never dreamed myself capable of such a thing. I am still amazed at myself, and I am not at all sure I could behave the same way if faced with a similar situation again.

INUKAI'S SEDITIOUS PLOT

During the thirty-eighth session, the Kokumintō with Inukai at its head introduced a motion of impeachment against the Terauchi administration. Fundamentally, the Kokumintō opposed the Kenseikai and supported the Terauchi government, and it seemed odd for a friendly party to seek to impeach the government. But this was a ploy on the part of Inukai Bokudō to divide the enemy ranks. The Kokumintō's impeachment motion had to be supported by the Kenseikai willy-nilly. It was an ingenious stratagem by Inukai to dissolve the House and thus deal a major blow to the Kenseikai.

I saw right through this. I did my best to avoid playing their game but could do nothing to change the situation. I knew that if we joined in the charade it would cost us dearly, but I have a habit of easily falling in with a just cause. So knowing all too well the folly of supporting an insincere motion for impeachment, I played along. It seemed logical that if the government had decided to dissolve the House it would do so sooner or later anyway, with or without the passage of the impeach-ment resolution. If that were the case, I could at least try to change the false impeachment bill into a true one.

The motion impeaching the Terauchi government was introduced on January 25 with 28 signatures from the Kokumintō, 198 from the Kenseikai, and 18 from the Kōseikai, a total of 241 [sic] or two-thirds of the House. Inukai of the Koku-mintō introduced the bill. Motoda Hajime of the Seiyūkai stated his opposition to it, and following the defense by Prime Minister Terauchi it was my turn to speak.

As I was walking to the platform the government produced an imperial rescript calling for a dissolution. In the normal course of events I should have been al-lowed to deliver my impeachment speech, then a vote would have been taken and the call for dissolution would have followed. But on this occasion I was not permitted to speak. Later I heard the following explanation as to why a snap dissolution had been called as I walked to the platform. Having witnessed my impeachment of Katsura, Terauchi decided, in his own words, "not to let Ozaki speak, as he might use hypnotism or some sort of magic, and it would be a terrible disgrace if I were to fall victim to it and collapse in my seat." I had no proof of the story's authenticity, but one did sense the panic of the government when Arimatsu Hideyoshi, director-general of the cabinet legislation bureau, dropped the package wrapped in a purple *furoshiki* containing the rescript for dissolution. In any event it was a most cowardly performance.

The general election was scheduled for April 20, and in the preceding weeks, following precedent, I spent forty days and nights campaigning for my colleagues. And, as usual, three days before the election I ran a fever and could not move.

This time I gave as many as eight speeches in twenty-four hours. I had once been told by a Chinese that one's tongue could be sore from talking, and I had read of this phenomenon too, but now I experienced the real thing. In fact, the tongue does not get sore but one becomes almost incapable of speech due to toothache.

The government mounted an attack on the Kenseikai, claiming a desire to "break up the unnatural majority." Apparently this slogan was the brainchild of Gotō Shinpei, the home minister. They dispatched bureaucrats who encouraged intervention on the pretext of regulating the election, and, as if this were not enough, they abused their political power by mobilizing veterans associations, local autonomous bodies, schoolteachers, and civil servants to support the ruling party.

As a result of the election, the Seiyūkai increased their seats by 55 to 165, leaping into the position of the largest party. The Kenseikai lost 76 seats, being reduced to a mere 121. The Kokumintō increased their representation from 28 to 35. In addition, 60 independents gained seats.

As was usual, the election ended in a major victory for the government party and the defeat of the opposition. Inukai's seditious plot was successful. What a mischievous trick he had played on us.

THE FOREIGN AFFAIRS INQUIRY COUNCIL

A transcendental cabinet is one without allegiance to any particular party. It is an old trick for achieving nonpartisan support for the ruling party in the guise of national consensus. The Foreign Affairs Inquiry Council was an attempt to bring this about.

General Miura Gorō[1] had held that matters of defense and diplomacy should be above party politics. During the Ōkuma government the so-called three-party summit met at the general's residence. It consisted of Hara Takashi, president of the Seiyūkai; Katō Takaaki, president of the Dōshikai; and Inukai Tsuyoshi, head of the Kokumintō.

There was much conjecture concerning the meeting of the three party heads. According to his press briefing, General Miura had originally planned that the *genrō* participate, but finding that impossible, he was content to bring the three party leaders together in an attempt to forge a national consensus.

I do not know whether Terauchi's proposal had any connection with that earlier meeting, but the prime minister invited Katō, Hara, and Inukai, the heads of the same three parties, on June 2, 1917, and conferred with them about setting up an ad hoc study group on foreign affairs. Hara and Inukai promptly endorsed the idea, but good old Katō temporized, saying that he would need to think about it.

Some of the leaders of the Kenseikai felt that it would be good for president Katō to be part of the study group. I was of course opposed. To keep foreign affairs above party politics was a fine-sounding excuse, but in reality if this were not as gratuitous as gilding solid gold it was at any rate a device to gag the political parties.

Katō considered himself a leading expert on foreign affairs, so secretly he was displeased at being invited to be a member of the study group with amateurs. He and I had opposite views on many things, but strangely we saw eye to eye on this one thing—that he should not become a member of the study group. Perhaps this was the only time after all these years of sitting in the same cabinet or being a member of the same political party that we shared the same opinion.

The study group on foreign affairs was set up, therefore, with President Katō of the Kenseikai missing. Prime Minister Terauchi chaired the group, with Foreign Minister Motono, Home Minister Gotō, Navy Minister Katō (Tomosaburō), and Army Minister Ōshima as members from the cabinet. Hirata Tōsuke and Count Itō Miyoji also joined, in addition to Hara, the Seiyūkai president, and Inukai, president of the Kokumintō.

With Katō absent there would be an inevitable void in the national consensus, but as far as the Terauchi government was concerned it more or less achieved its

---

[1] Miura (1846–1926), a maverick Chōshū militarist, served in the early Meiji genrōin, commanded government troops in the Satsuma rebellion, rallied opposition to Ōkuma's treaty reform attempt in 1889, was appointed minister to Korea in 1895, and was imprisoned but not convicted for complicity in the murder of Queen Min that year, before returning to the political world in support of the Protect the Constitution Movement at the outset of the Taishō era.

original objective . Although the Seiyūkai was now the largest political party as a result of its success in the election, it did not command the strength to control the House by itself. As for the Kokumintō, it lacked a good enough excuse to change its tune and support the government after, even for strategic reasons, it had just sought to impeach it.

The signal success of the study group meant that the Seiyūkai (with 160 members) and Kokumintō (with 35) could publicly support the Itō government. Moreover, the members of the Kōseikai who had been in opposition during the previous session of the Diet and the newly-elected independent members joined to form the Ishinkai (Restoration Group) and with 42 members crossed over to the government side. The Terauchi government was now on very solid foundations with 237 seats and enjoying an absolute majority.

A bill introduced by the Kenseikai in the thirty-ninth special session to impeach Home Minister Gotō and a resolution to question members of the ad hoc study group on foreign affairs were defeated because of insufficient support.

The Kenseikai again had to fold when its government impeachment bill submitted during the fortieth session was defeated due to the opposition of the Kokumintō and the Seiyūkai. Noteworthy during this session was the number of revisions submitted on the House election law. A bill put forward by the Kenseikai proposed larger electoral districts and the enfranchisement of those taxpayers who were assessed five yen in direct tax. It also envisaged adding to the voters' pool intellectuals with private incomes regardless of the amount of tax they paid. The Kokumintō made a similar proposal to that of the Kenseikai but it set the tax ceiling at three yen. The Seiyūkai proposed setting the tax rate at five yen but preferred to return to a small electoral-district system. The government favored maintaining the status quo insofar as electoral district and tax requirements were concerned,[2] but proposed to add forty-five seats by revising other stipulations. Of the four revisions, the government bill was withdrawn first, followed by the Seiyūkai's, and the remaining two bills were promptly voted down.

THE SIBERIAN INTERVENTION

The Siberian expedition, having poured 600 million yen worth of national sweat and blood into the wastelands of Siberia and having sacrificed 2,500 of the 75,000 men from the imperial army it sent to the northern battlefields, brought Japan nothing but dishonor.

Sending an expeditionary force to Siberia was a product of the Terauchi government. The members of the study group on foreign affairs all endorsed the venture, however, and they were not alone; virtually the entire country supported it. Almost everyone I met was for it except for those who had no interest in national matters.

---

[2] Since 1900, the direct tax requirement for male suffrage, which began in 1890 at 15 yen, had stood at 10 yen.

I alone opposed it from the very beginning. My reading of the situation was as follows. The prima facie objective of the Siberian expedition was to dispatch troops in response to the U.S. suggestion to support the Czechoslovakian forces. I was afraid that while it might seem all right at the time to share in such a venture with a humanitarian and idealistic country, it might put us onto a collision course for the future. I could not speak for the distant future, but unlike the past, at least in the circumstances following the Great War, world public opinion would no longer condone nations taking advantage of the defenseless.

If Japan were strong enough to deter the powers when the whole world turned against it, we might realize the objective of the expedition. In the absence of such strength, taking advantage of the defenseless situation of Siberia in the hope of a windfall was, to say the least, ill-advised. We might raise a little dust, but it was inevitable that we would not only fail to achieve the objective but be forced in the end to pull out in disgrace.

Convinced of this analysis of the situation, I most strongly opposed the intervention. I tried to reason logically with politicians in and out of government and I raised the issue frequently within the party, but those among them who by then were eager to dispatch the expeditionary force could not understand.

I then decided to go outside political circles and engage people with analytical minds and discerning views. I therefore requested the Kōjunsha[3] to pull together twenty or thirty people at a time from academia, business, and other circles who were actively concerned with national matters, and shared my views with them. Contrary to my expectation that these people would support me, the majority disagreed with me. Almost everyone thought that the expedition into Siberia was a once-in-a-lifetime opportunity.

But one person I could count on was Yamagata. A friend of mine, Mochizuki Kotarō, was an ardent proponent of the Siberian expedition, and no matter how much I tried to convince him otherwise, he would not listen. Finally he went to Yamagata to get his support, but when he returned he was terribly downhearted. I asked him what had happened. "Yamagata is dead against the Siberian expedition," he sighed. "He said one should never draw a sword without having thought how it would be sheathed. It was one thing to send men to Siberia, but where was the plan to withdraw them? No, he was just terribly opposed to the whole thing." I felt greatly relieved. If Yamagata, the one strong man the army had, was opposed, I believed the plan would not be carried out no matter how many feverishly favored it.

Soon afterward, Yamagata changed his mind and agreed to the expedition. I learned this again through Mochizuki. The reason for this swift turnaround was the successful persuasion of Tanaka Gi'ichi.[4] I do not know what means Tanaka

---

[3] An association of several thousand of Fukuszwa's Keiō graduates, first organized in 1880, that brought men in various professions and occupations together and published its own journal.

[4] Tanaka (1864–1929), who figures importantly in Ozaki's story below, was a protege of Yamagata and the army's Russian expert, having been sent to Russia to study in 1898 and figuring importantly in Manchurian affairs at the time of the Russo-Japanese War. By this time, he was assistant chief of staff of the imperial army, and he would soon be army minister.

used to persuade this rigidly principled and normally unyielding man. I could only imagine, but I suspected that instead of trying to reason with him he simply played the part of a little boy presuming on the love of his grandfather. The most obstinate old man in the world would not refuse a loving grandson. I was impressed that even a very strict man like the prince could be moved by that technique.

I have elsewhere referred to the fact that Yamagata was strongly attached to his own men. It was at the same time his strength and his weakness. During his student days Mochizuki had studied in England for seven or eight years with the assistance of Yamagata and had developed a strong bond with him. When Mochizuki returned from Europe, the prince apparently treated him generously, paying him as handsomely as most ministers in the cabinet. For some reason, however, Mochizuki chose not to take the prince's side and joined with us in attacking the military cliques.

It is human nature to want to have nothing more to do with a person who has betrayed you, but Yamagata apparently continued to entertain good feelings toward Mochizuki, particularly in Mochizuki's old age. It was admirable of the prince, not only for not rejecting Mochizuki because of his ungrateful opposition, but also for always treating him kindly. This, presumably, was his attitude, not just toward Mochizuki, but toward all those under him, so it is easy to understand how dedicated to him they were. For a man so kindly disposed even to one who had turned his back on him, it was not surprising that his cautious and even formidable strictness would be undermined by a favorite son.

In any event, due to the conversion of Yamagata the matter of the Siberian expedition was abruptly settled. Japan dispatched an even larger force than that originally planned. Once the Czechoslovakian soldiers were relieved, the United States pulled out in accordance with its declared intention. The Japanese force stayed behind but, failing to achieve anything militarily, found itself stalled in one place and unable to advance. The eventual cost to Japan was 600 million yen, and thousands of men dead or wounded in the massacre at Nicholaevsk, for which the government could not even get an apology. The humiliated survivors were eventually pulled out. In every respect it was a deplorable episode, not to speak of the utter folly of throwing away 600 million yen only to experience disgrace.[5]

THE FALL OF THE TERAUCHI GOVERNMENT

The Great War in Europe that began in 1914 developed into a world war with the entry of the United States. It ended in victory for the allies, and an armistice was signed on November 11, 1918. The world was at peace again, but the four years of the Great War had profound consequences on the politics and economics and

---

[5] From February to May in 1920, Russian partisans killed several hundred Japanese soldiers, sailors, and civilians at Nikolaevsk, a town near the mouth of the Amur river. The incident prolonged Japan's occupation of the area and of northern Sakhalin, which the imperial army occupied in a demand for satisfaction that proved futile.

the very ideals on which nations stood. Toward the end of the war the revolution led by Lenin changed the face of Russia, in Germany the monarchy fell with the abdication of the Kaiser, and political upheavals convulsed Italy. Owing to the great distance from the battlefield, the impact of the war and its aftermath was comparatively slight in Japan, but spiraling prices caused the people great hardship.

On September 4, 1917, the government issued a strict antiprofiteering ordinance. It also issued small-denomination notes and other ordinances including one regulating shipping so as to ease the effects of runaway inflation. But it failed to achieve its purpose. People's livelihoods became increasingly threatened, and a nervous apprehension gripped the country. To contain the growing sense of panic the government suppressed freedom of speech, which increased rather than lessened the people's insecurity.

As we entered the year 1918 prices were at an all-time high, the price of rice in particular rising without pause. On April 16 the government ordered all rice exchanges to suspend spot and medium-term transactions, but this did not work. In late July the price spiraled to over fifty yen for one koku (approximately five U.S. bushels) of rice or triple the price during the Ōkuma administration.

And so the so-called rice riots broke out. On August 6 a group of housewives in a fishing village in Toyama prefecture went to the authorities to petition for relief, but this soon turned into a riot. It touched off escalating riots in Kyoto, Osaka, and Hyogo prefectures in which rice merchants were assaulted and wealthy farmers threatened.

Rice riots engulfed the whole country, including Wakayama, Nara, Okayama, Hiroshima, Yamaguchi, Fukuoka, Kōchi, Kagawa, Mie, Aichi, Shiga, Gifu, Shizuoka, Kanagawa, Yamanashi, Niigata, Miyagi, and Fukushima like a gale churning the autumn leaves. Finally on August 13 rioting broke out even in the imperial capital and was barely suppressed with the aid of the army.

At this time the imperial family made a gracious personal gift of three million yen toward the people's relief, while the government for its part spent ten million yen from the national treasury to buy foreign rice and make compulsory purchases from farmers' stocks. As low-priced rice became available the riots finally subsided.

After what had occurred Prime Minister Terauchi had no option. On September 21 on the pretext of poor health he led the resignation of the cabinet, taking responsibility for the failure to adjust rice prices and for the nationwide riots. With the fall of the Terauchi government, a conference of the *genrō* was convened in the emperor's name. The *genrō* again wanted Saionji to take charge, but the prince declined and recommended Hara Takashi, president of the Seiyūkai. Hara duly received the imperial command to appoint a cabinet, which he did on September 29, 1918.

This was the first government to be led by a commoner. It was an overwhelmingly Seiyūkai government. Apart from the army and navy ministers, the only non-Seiyūkai minister was Uchida Yasuya, who was given the foreign affairs portfolio. Even so, Uchida had a bureaucratic background and was raised in the diplomatic world with Hara. They had both worked as secretaries for Mutsu, and although Uchida was not formally a member of the party he was practically one of them.

Earlier, the Seiyūkai had always been forced to compromise with either the bureaucracy or the military clique and could not carry out its professed policies. At last, now that they were able to appoint a cabinet of their own, I was satisfied that they would do what they said they would do, and I decided to take a well-disposed position of neutrality.

I had until then attacked every government we ever had—with the sole exception of this Hara government. For this reason alone the Seiyūkai frequently showered me with appreciation. It is unusual to be thanked merely for not reproaching others, but I suppose when one is known to be abusive it must be a relief to be spared. That is probably the advantage of being considered a harping critic.

Despite the fact that I broke my routine by refraining from my usual scolding and maintained my positive neutrality, the Hara administration did not implement its professed intentions. The government aggressively increased spending here and there and showed a welcome tendency to breach official rules; otherwise it was no different from others. I was disappointed.

EUROPE AND AMERICA IN THE AFTERMATH OF THE GREAT WAR

From about the time the war's end could be seen coming, and spurred by the signing of the treaty of peace at Versailles, democratic ideas were gaining strength in Japan. This released increasingly strident calls for equality, and conflict between labor and management flared.

It was the time of a major ideological turning point worldwide. It seemed to me that ideas and feelings in the West had already undergone enormous changes. What would become of the postwar world? How would the war trauma be healed? And how should Japan prepare for it? To find answers to these important questions I left for Europe on March 17, 1919, with my son Yukiteru, and Tagawa Daikichirō, Mochizuki Kotarō, Suzuki Shōgo, Yokoyama Yūi, and Morimoto Kazuo.

By chance we were on the same boat crossing the Pacific as China's Wang Ching-wei.[6] He was a large but refined gentleman, of noble and aristocratic bearing. I found his hand as soft as a woman's. It seemed strange that he should be an expert on explosives. He was still young and it was no small achievement to have made a name for himself at that early age.

After a voyage of sixteen days we landed safely at San Francisco and crossed the country by rail directly to New York, where we stopped only briefly before continuing our journey to London. We stayed in London until early October. Since

---

[6] Wang (1883–1944), Chinese revolutionary associate of Sun Yat-sen, studied in Japan and first gained fame for a bold plot to assassinate the Mahchu prince regent. In the 1930s, he was to fall out with Chiang Kai-shek and end his days as a collaborator with Japan, head of the puppet government at Nanking.

the peace conference was then in progress, the British capital was a convenient place for our purpose, as all information reached there.

This was my third trip abroad. The first time I was an exile driven from my country by the security ordinance of 1887. The second time, when I was doing double duty as mayor of Tokyo, I attended the 1910 conference of the Inter-Parliamentary Union in Brussels. The first trip was more exciting than the second, and the second more so than the third. The scenes I had thought unforgettable thirty years before did not seem so extraordinary this time. Shaking hands with Gladstone on my first trip had felt like an electric shock. Just setting foot on English soil was exciting enough. Twenty years later neither Georges Clemenceau nor David Lloyd-George impressed me particularly. The feeling, or lack of it, was even stronger this time. One seems to lose sensitivity with age.

There was much confusion in Japan before we left because of the many new ideas that were flooding in. Coming to the West I realized that what seemed new to us in Japan was already old elsewhere. These ideas seemed new only because we in Japan had built a wall around ourselves and prevented foreign thought from penetrating. The socialist philosophies of Ferdinand Lassalle and Karl Marx were already some seventy years old. After these there seemed to have been nothing new. This was, to be honest, a little disappointing.

On the other hand, how these ideas were being implemented was another matter. I was surprised to find that socialistic tendencies in the West were much stronger than I had expected. I had thought myself quite a progressive in Japan, but in Europe I felt rather behind the times. Here I had a strong impression that socialism had really taken root. It seemed clear that whether we liked it or not socialist principles would be central to the workings of the world for some time to come. If only to realize that Japan had to find its own way through the turbulence that lay ahead, our trip seemed worthwhile.

What had precipitated this movement? No doubt it was the world war. Governments now saw more clearly than ever that they would have to depend on the power of the majority—the proletariat. On their side, the proletariat realized the enormous power of being in the majority. Their discovery of this was by far the greatest factor giving impetus to the ideas of Marx and Lassalle.

On Sunday afternoons in Hyde Park one could listen to people making ardent speeches on all sorts of subjects to curious passers-by. They were free to say anything they liked and they attracted a lot of attention. Here a man was delivering a sermon in front of a cross bearing the figure of Jesus while an atheist preached close by. There a speaker was upholding the monarchy while another argued for a republic. Hearing each other's voices, the orators often engaged in argument, and the audience shifted from one to the other.

With freedom of speech guaranteed, people can express themselves as they will and have the satisfaction of appealing for public support. In fact, it is difficult to win supporters unless you have something worthwhile to say, but at least you have the comfort of having made your point. By contrast, if freedom of thought is not guaranteed and freedom of speech suppressed, the pent-up frustration will one day explode. If people are not permitted to express their beliefs freely they will turn naturally to other means and eventually to violence.

While in London, I visited the offices of *The Daily Mail*. Thirty years earlier when I visited a newspaper company they were typesetting with what looked like piano keyboards. This time they were still using pianolike machines, but words like "Yukio Ozaki" were preset on blocks of lead. This convenient way of printing could never be duplicated in Japan, where thousands of *kanji* (Chinese characters) are used.

We do not realize how much we stand to lose because of our dependence on *kanji*. Compare Japanese children who go to school in the United States and those brought up in their home country. Those living in Japan are a full year behind their peers in America in terms of knowledge. Granted that it is not easy to abolish the use of *kanji*, but we would do well to teach our primary-school children Esperanto or some such foreign tongue as a second language.

THE INDESCRIBABLE SCARS OF THE WAR

On July 19, following the signing of the peace treaty in late June, a national celebration took place in Britain. The whole of London was decked with flowers. It was an impressive event.

I went to Trafalgar Square and found it packed with people. The entire place was in a state of commotion uncharacteristic of the English, who were ordinarily as undemonstrative as oxen. They were behaving quite brazenly, the men and women dancing in each other's arms and singing at the tops of their voices. The war had made the women as bold as the men, unlike those of bygone days.

For fifty cents apiece they were selling a stick with a feather attached at one end, which their purchasers used to freely tickle passers-by. I myself was assaulted with one of these by a large lady and ran for cover to an underground station. It was hilarious, however, to watch a six-foot-tall bobby tickled in the face with one of these, simply eyeing the offender and not a least ruffled by the indignity. And there were rattles that made a deafening sound as people twirled them right beside your ears. Others showered you with colorful confetti, which they carried in their pockets. With all formality gone everybody behaved like children. From observing the normally self-possessed English behaving with such abandon it was not difficult to imagine the depth of their suffering during the war.

The royal family had suspended their annual garden party during the war, but now the war was over and once more they welcomed their guests to Buckingham Palace. The event was held over three days in August with three thousand guests attending each day. I was invited on a day reserved for foreign envoys.

As the guests lined the narrow path leading from the palace to the garden behind, Their Majesties the King and Queen exchanged a few words with each of us. We all then drifted around the garden, mixing and mingling at random.

It was then that I ran into Gotō Shinpei. I asked after his health since I had learned that he had suffered a bad case of food poisoning from the prawns he had consumed en route. "Thank you," he said, "I am much better now." This was the substance of the so-called meeting between Gotō and myself, no more and no less.

Gotō left Britain before we knew it. In America, during the course of our return home, we learned that the count had delivered a speech there not long before. The most memorable part of his speech as recounted to me went as follows: "A Shinto priest and a Buddhist monk were arguing over their different concepts of heaven and hell. The priest was criticizing the monk for confusing people with his idle sermons. 'Now, tell me,' demanded the priest, 'where exactly is your hell?' The monk had a prompt answer: 'Alongside the Plains of High Heaven' (the Shinto equivalent of Olympus). Traveling through Europe this time, I found democracy to be lying adjacent to militarism." Gotō was fond of witticisms. But I suspect he must have meant "back to back with" rather than "adjacent to."

In mid-September we set out to see the battlefields of France and Belgium. Twelve of us traveled as a group in three cars organized by Cook's Tours. Observing the battlefields, so recently stilled, I felt that no artistic or literary masterpiece could ever convey the grimness of the scenes we saw. It would hardly be too farfetched to compare them with Pompeii after its destruction. Pompeii, of course, was a prosperous port and agricultural center of thirty thousand people when it was totally buried in a cataclysmic eruption of Vesuvius almost two thousand years ago. A corner of the ruins was discovered by accident seventeen centuries later during the drilling of a well. On a previous trip I had been to see the excavation work then in progress. Houses and roads were being exposed intact just as they were when the disaster occurred. Some of the buildings were found with their signboards still legible. I saw the remains of human bodies and dogs lying where they had suffocated to death. It was a terrible sight. But here I was overwhelmed by the horror of the battlefield, worse by far than the gruesome vestiges of Pompeii.

In one place, according to our guide, an entire town had disappeared from the face of the earth. No trace or shadow remained. Not a single foundation was in sight. All that was left was a bare field. It was hard to imagine that the place had once been a city with a name. Tagawa Daikichirō, who was travelling with us and who had fought in both the wars with China and Russia, swore that the devastation created in those wars was child's play compared to what lay before our eyes.

Verdun is surrounded by hills topped with historic fortresses. The hills were once covered with thick forests. During the war they were all cut down to ragged stumps a foot or so high by shellfire. Helmets and swords were scattered everywhere. Brass shell-cases that would make fine flower vases lay all around. Visitors were collecting them as souvenirs. Trenches and barbed wire scarred the plains as far as the eye could see. Only tanks would overcome trenches and barbed wire in this terrain. The English invented them.

The battlefield was a vast opencast mine of iron, copper, and lead. The landscape was a scene of utter desolation. I was struck by the fact that the bodies of all the dead had been removed. I walked the battlefield for three days and found not a single body left anywhere.

No natural disaster could be so catastrophic. I tried vainly to express in verse what I had witnessed:

> Angels in heaven and fiends in hell must quake
> At man's dread power to kill for country's sake.
> Destroying all with powers dread,
> He kills and kills until he's dead.
> For he's too vain to realize
> That every time he kills he dies
> A little, and his country's name
> Forevermore must bear his shame.

I did not have words for what I felt. I was aghast. What fools we humans are to create such destruction in the name of nations, heedless that it is part of the process of destroying our own country and with it all mankind.

What we saw in Belgium proved to be quite the opposite of what we had heard about the Germans in Japan. They must have chosen to appease Belgium, for they posted guards at the palace and would not even permit themselves to occupy it. One would have expected them to establish their headquarters there but they did not even shame it with the German flag.

In Japan we had heard that the invading German army had taken all the brass and other metal fittings from hotels and homes. This was certainly not the case at the Hotel Astoria, where we were staying. It is true that the Germans might have replaced them, but I thought it unlikely from my recollection of the hotel the last time I had stayed there.

This brief tour of the battlefield and my observations of postwar society gave me sufficient evidence to conclude that Europe was in a state of turmoil and far from regaining normality. Even the English, known for their thriftiness, were increasing their expenditure by creating departments of health and transportation instead of attending first to the settlement of their war debts.

The original budget submitted by the chancellor of the exchequer, Chamberlain,[7] showed a shortfall equivalent to 2.5 billion yen. I have never been good at reading budgets, but it was clear enough to me that the deficit would only get worse. In three months or so, as it happened, the budgetary deficit soared to 4 billion yen, which warranted a warning statement from the chancellor of the exchequer. The British people, who had been optimistic only three months earlier, were becoming very insecure.

The situation resembled the sea after a hurricane. The next menacing wave was visible but not the one behind it. Conditions in the ocean beyond were less discernible still. Many visitors, glancing during a momentary lull in the storm, judged the sea to be calm. But even then the currents were strong; the sea was far from calm.

---

[7] Apparently a slip by the author. Neville Chamberlain assumed this office in 1923.

I was enjoying the opportunity to judge for myself what was going on in Europe and wanted to stay longer, but I could see that it would take at least another six months to a year before things really settled down, as the situation was not that simple. I could ill afford to stay away that long, so I decided to return to Japan. It had been well worth the trip. I resolved to do what little I could to promote arms limitation, international peace, and cultural progress.

THE JAPANESE GET LEFT BEHIND

It was early October when we left London for America. I kept thinking as we were crossing the Atlantic. Human beings are exasperatingly unteachable. One would have expected that we would learn from the Great War, be wiser after all the suffering we had gone through, and change our worst habits. I was surprised to find that in spite of everything there was little change.

Until now it had been taken for granted that while even the very existence of a nation defeated in war would be endangered, the victors were bound to become stronger. But this time, because of the enormous developments in modern warfare, not only were the vanquished nations, Germany and Austria-Hungary, reduced to ruins, but as for the winning side, Russia was destroyed, France was in crisis, Italy was in turmoil, and Britain had lost its traditional glory. This was due to a fundamental change in the organization of the world. Their economies were no longer the sovereign preserve of the nations but now had to be shared. The world had become smaller and the nations were interdependent as never before. In other words, the world had become a single body. This was to say that if an arm of this body hit its foot with a hammer it was not just the foot that would feel pain but the whole body, and even the offending arm itself.

Long ago the world was like a great rock. You could have struck it on any side and done it no harm. As life and human society developed, it evolved into a plantlike organism. If you cut off a branch on the right, another would grow on the left. Such was the world as we knew it until quite recently. Nations that lost their wars would wither and those that won them would prosper. But with the march of civilization, the world became at length a single body like a living creature. Now the whole body—the arms, the legs, the head, and every part—shared in the pain and comfort of all. One country in ruins would bring injury to the whole world.

Ignoring civilization's advance, some of us believed that victory would bring good to our country and threw all our resources into fighting the Great War. The victory was earned, but without the benefits that were supposed to accompany it. The victorious nations were still suffering from the terrible destruction that was its price.

The architecture of the world had changed but not the lunatic designs of men. Even after fighting a war whose reasons were still unclear and after killing and wounding millions of good people and bringing down immense misfortune on the whole world, there were men who still considered it an honor to have served in it for their country's glory. There was not the slightest sign of remorse. The folly of it all was beyond comprehension. It was disgusting. I had come all the way to Europe and America to see the boundless folly of man.

I arrived in America weighed down with these thoughts. On an earlier visit to the country, as I have mentioned, I had been presented with a fountain pen at Waterman and Company's head office in New York. I called there again this time to have the somewhat bent nip replaced. Twenty or so female assistants were serving customers at the counter. I showed one of them my pen. She said there was no need to buy a new one and she would have it fixed in three minutes. My pen was carried off to another part of the building where repairs were performed, and within a few minutes it was returned in perfect order as she had promised. I asked what I owed her. Nothing, she said. Waterman and Company apparently had a policy to repair their nibs at no cost, even for a pen that was ten years old. I was very impressed.

By contrast, Japanese products were mass-produced and of abominable quality. The worst were children's toys. They replaced those of German manufacture in American stores when enemy products were boycotted, and the Japanese toys were sold widely, not just in the cities but throughout the country. But they broke easily and quickly lost their color. Americans who were kindly disposed toward Japan turned the situation the other way around: "Our children must be much rougher than yours," they would tell me. "They're always breaking their toys. Your children must be so gentle." I did not know what to say.

I thought this was quite deplorable. American children's first recollections would be of the poor quality of Japanese goods. A man who worked for a railroad company once said to me, "Children should be allowed to travel free on the trains because once a child has been on a train he will be hooked for life." Japanese toys were having exactly the opposite effect on American children.

I had similar experiences in Britain. Bond Street was where the finest quality goods were sold. Yamanaka had a shop there too. On this latter visit I found that many more shops were unwilling to display Japanese goods than when I was there before. I met a Japanese man who had a curio repair business in London. I suggested to him that he might open a shop in Bond Street, where I thought his fine scrolls and screens deserved to be seen. He said without hesitation that Japanese goods would not be accepted there.

However, Chinese goods sold well both in Britain and America. Unlike Japanese products they were better and more solidly made. Not only their goods, but the Chinese people themselves had a better reputation than the Japanese. In terms of history and literature China had more to boast about than we did. Perhaps it was because of this, I had observed during my first trip abroad, that the overseas Chinese tended to be proud of their home country and to stick to their traditional cuisine and customs. As a result they had tended to make themselves unwelcome. But this time I found it was the Japanese who were conceited. By now, in contrast, the Chinese had lost their arrogance, had better language skills, and mixed more easily with other Americans. They had shown much more adaptability. So while the Japanese were not popular, the Chinese now were liked. Japan and China had reversed their positions in the thirty years since I had made my first visit abroad.

THE FORMIDABLE CHARACTER OF AMERICANS

After leaving Washington, D.C., at the end of November, we traveled via Chicago, Salt Lake City, and Portland to the West Coast. There we visited Tacoma, Vancouver, and Seattle. The Japanese citizens in Vancouver organized a welcome reception and speaking engagements for me. After one speech, the chairman unexpectedly turned to the audience and said that he had hoped to be able to present a commemorative gift to me, but since there had been insufficient time to prepare it he asked those who wished to leave a gift of money, which he afterwards presented to me.

I was asked to speak in Seattle too. Here fifty cents, the equivalent of one Japanese yen, was charged. Unless fees were charged people came in droves and were often destructive. In Vancouver the hall was damaged. In Seattle there was an audience of twelve hundred or so. After subtracting for expenses the organizers presented me with a thousand yen.

In the United States prominent people were paid for making speeches. William Jennings Bryan probably earned more giving speeches than he had received from his modest salary as secretary of state. Politicians must be accountable for their campaign funds. The most straightforward way is to collect only small amounts of money from the people. In Japan we used to charge for our speeches. My colleagues Numa Moriichi and Shimada Saburō used to charge ten sen per person and had quite an income from this. Yano Fumio, Inukai Tsuyoshi, Minoura Katsundo, and I used to do the same, but after the opening of the first parliament and politicians had to face elections the practice was stopped. Not only did we not take money but we had to beg people to listen to us.

Those were the days of prohibition in the United States, and since no liquor was served at receptions there was much useful talk. In Japan one was expected to drink at receptions so there was rarely an opportunity for serious talk. I enjoy a drink, but not drunkards, so I never drink to the point where I lose sobriety. Therefore I am always a bore at such occasions.

I was impressed at the decisive way in which the Americans carried out prohibition. Billions of dollars must have been lost as a result of it. The U.S. administration did not pay compensation. If such a measure were taken in Japan, those with vested interests would certainly demand reparation. I inquired of a certain American why no one was demanding compensation. He answered: "Because it is sinful to make and sell liquor. There is no need to compensate a person for losses incurred in abstaining from sin." I thought to myself that if we banned brothels in Japan the government would surely be expected to pay compensation.

It was not just prohibition that was notable. Americans are remarkably resolute people. They do not appear to mind risking their lives. In the Great War they spent an enormous amount of money and lost many lives, but they seem to regard war as being rather adventurous and exciting. Men and women routinely carry guns and use them against each other, often fatally. It is a great mistake to think the women are weak.

The Americans will do something if they think it right and stop doing it as soon as they realize it is wrong. That even goes for the way they conduct their foreign affairs. Manners and protocol matter very little to them. When they think it is necessary to assist Czechoslovakia they invite Japan to send troops to Siberia. When they think the job is done they withdraw, almost childlike, without consulting anyone.

Another thing that struck me most forcefully was that since the Great War the United States had become a truly formidable power. I do not mean this only in material terms but also spiritually. At the last peace conference Britain and France were all for demanding reparations from Germany and dividing its warships among the victors. But the United States declared it would not take a cent's worth of reparations. The battleships should be destroyed if we were serious about building an ideal world.

Quite apart from the merits of the argument, its spirit was lofty enough to inspire the world. The United States neither vacillated nor fell back into conservatism. This might partly be explained, I thought, by the vast undeveloped areas it encompassed which encouraged enterprise and innovation and attracted diverse races, and so was a constant source of stimulus to its people. I had thought myself to be above jealousy either for myself or my country, but in America I was often assailed by a tremendous sense of envy.

Japan was full of decisiveness until 1877, the tenth year of the Meiji era. This was because of the underlying progressive spirit that animated the Restoration. However, by the twentieth year of Meiji a backlash of conservatism neutralized our passion and made us incapable of decisive action. New things were considered dangerous and shunned; new ideas were regarded with deep suspicion and were suppressed. One can prevent an influenza epidemic by inoculation, but cannot prevent the spread of ideas, which are not germs one can inoculate against. We have, however, not changed since. I thought this was profoundly regrettable for the newborn Japan.

With these thoughts I left Seattle on the *Suwa Maru* and reached Yokohama on the last day of the year.

The Suffrage Movement and Arms Control

AFTER RETURNING from Europe in October I found society in Japan quite confused, but not to the degree that I had in Europe. Not having really experienced the war, the Japanese had profited nicely from the hostilities and now were drowning in the eddies of a superficial peace. I saw all too plainly a frightening undercurrent pulling at the fabric of the nation. While spiraling prices threatened the people's very survival, labor-management confrontation was intensifying by the day and the ensuing social unrest was now beyond the powers of the Hara government to solve through its social policies.

What surprised me most was the mounting opposition to the parliamentary form of government riding the wave of the so-called new ideas. This was particularly strong among labor organizations. They were opposed to the parliamentary system and wanted to achieve their objectives through direct action. Trade union organizations represented the more moderate forms of direct action, but these could easily turn toward violence in the hands of the temperamental Japanese. I felt it most dangerous for them to attempt to achieve their objectives by such methods.

This tendency had to be checked at all costs. After contemplating the options, I came to believe that the only way was to give the people the vote so they could decide issues for themselves. Universal (male) suffrage had been advocated since the opening of the first Diet. It was not debated, however, until February 26, 1902, during the sixteenth session, when representative Nakamura Yaroku jointly presented a bill with independent member Hanai Takuzō and with Kōno Hironaka and Furuhata Gentarō of the Kensei Hontō, with the support of other sympathetic members of the House, including Mochizuki Keisuke, Nemoto Tadashi, and Hamana Shimei of the Seiyūkai.

Until then the suffrage bill had not officially been put on the parliamentary agenda. Consequently, no party had officially opposed it. The bill, however, was promptly defeated when it was presented in committee. Since then the bill had been presented every year from 1905 to 1910. During the twenty-seventh session in 1911 it passed with a comfortable majority, but it met with fierce opposition in the House of Peers. Its advocates were duly discouraged. The flame had been thoroughly quenched, it seemed, and no one dared to rekindle it. Not until 1918 did it once more show signs of life. However, while suffrage had been an issue since the opening of parliament and some of my friends had been backing it for some twenty years, I had not joined their struggle.

Naturally I favored the franchise in the sense that it gave everyone equality. But actual implementation of universal suffrage would take time. I had my own views on the realities of national elections. I had a pretty good idea of the public's level of commitment toward voting, as I had had personal experience in waging elections for many years. Giving voting rights to people with little or no knowledge of constitutional government could result not only in a failure of the system, but there could be abuses and other inherent risks as well. For these reasons I believed that rather than introducing an unrestricted popular vote prematurely, the people should be educated about the obligations that went with that right. It would be far better and safer if they were first enlightened sufficiently to demand and win the right for themselves. I considered this the best approach toward developing a basis for true constitutional government as well as for the cause of suffrage itself.

After returning from Europe and observing the situation in my country I felt there was no time to waste. A dangerous tendency to resort to direct action was gathering momentum, threatening the fortress of the constitutional government. Direct action involved the danger of violence and civil war. Only popular participation in government could prevent it. But I knew full well that the people did not yet have it in them to demand their rights. All right, I thought, so let them have them and use them. Let us see what happens. If, after exercising their rights and seeing they had not achieved their aim, they then turned to other measures, one could do little to stop it. It would be a pity, however, for them to rush into direct action without even trying the parliamentary system. I thus changed my previous position. Popular voting could no longer be deferred. I would be in the front line of the battle for it.

Naturally, I was not so optimistic as to imagine that the mere fact of writing suffrage into law would immediately improve government. Popular participation in government could even make matters worse. It required careful preparation, and even after the law was passed much would remain to be done by the government and individuals alike to promote the political education of the voters. With these reservations I was now fully involved in the battle for popular suffrage.

STRANGE MASS PSYCHOLOGY

By 1919 the campaign for popular suffrage was becoming heated. The thirtieth anniversary of the promulgation of the Constitution fell on February 11. Three thousand students from universities in the capital held a mass rally in Hibiya Park and presented to the forty-first Diet a petition demanding for adult men the right to vote. The campaign triggered a nationwide movement and changed the character of the national debate overnight. Workers who until then had been somewhat cool toward politics began to demand political participation.

The forty-second Diet convened on December 26 of the same year, by which time the demand for popular suffrage had reached a fierce pitch both in and out of the Diet. It was Inukai who leaped to capitalize on this opportunity. All of a sudden the Kokumintō tabled a specific proposal: to accord voting rights to young men on reaching their twentieth birthday.

The Kenseikai caused a temporary log-jam due to the opposition of its president to the Kokumintō's proposal, but sensing the general mood, it finally drew up a so-called executive plan providing for the granting of voting rights to men above the age of twenty-five and possessing an independent livelihood—but to come into effect after 1925. Shimada Saburō and I promptly challenged the plan and demanded that "1925" should be replaced by "immediately" and the independent livelihood requirement deleted. The Kenseikai appeared for a time to be on the verge of division owing to internal disagreement over this issue. Finally, at a meeting of their elected representatives it was decided to replace "1925" with "the next election" and otherwise to stick to their original proposal. It was then the turn of a popular suffrage promotion group called the Fusen Jikkōkai (Society to Implement Suffrage), who filed a third proposal.

Three suffrage bills issuing simultaneously from the Kokumintō, the Kenseikai, and the Jikkōkai came as a tremendous shock to the political world. Mass rallies promoting popular suffrage held at Ryōgoku's Kokugikan, the national sumo pavilion, on February 1 attracted some 50,000 people. They held lanterns and paraded in long files to demonstrate their resolve.

In the grounds of Shiba Zōjōji, the temple of the shoguns, a constitutional workers council named the Rikken Rōdōkai was inaugurated. At Nihonbashi's Tokiwa Club, a meeting was held of the Zenkoku Fusen Rengōkai, the National Suffrage Alliance. In Ueno Park, blood was shed when a national rally clashed with police. Workers demonstrated in Shiba Park, and 50,000 people turned out for a rally in Hibiya Park. Even Buddhist monks joined the suffrage movement. The cry for the right to vote swelled like a tidal wave.

On February 11 another huge rally in Hibiya Park brought together many like-minded organizations. I had made it a personal rule not to participate in such events, but later in the day, thinking the crowd would by then have largely dispersed, I went to the park to have a look. Someone spotted me, however, and soon I was surrounded by a mob. I thought that, being short, I could lose myself in the crowd, but by then some newspaper photographers had found me and were taking pictures.

I did not know what the people had in mind and I doubted very much at the time if they did either. But when they followed me I turned to one of those nearest to me and said, "Won't you please all leave me alone?" "Not until you speak to us!" was the reply. At least I now knew what they wanted. They suggested we walk over to the Imperial Hotel, so I turned in that direction. As soon as we were within its gates they demanded that I speak to them there and then.

But the hotel was very busy that day and I did not want to cause any inconvenience, so I suggested we move again to a park. "How about Sukiyabashi Park?" a voice called, and off we all went once more. In the park was a cenotaph to the war dead, and the crowd wanted me to speak to them from there. Some people were already occupying the monument, but they came down quietly when the crowd demanded that they do so.

When I climbed onto the base of the monument, someone shouted, "Hats off to Mr. Ozaki!" and they all took them off. But it was a cold and windy day and I suggested that we keep them on. So everybody put their hats on again. Then another man called out, "Let Mr. Ozaki keep his on, but hats off the rest of us!" and they obediently complied. But I insisted they keep theirs on, so they went back on again.

After I had finished speaking I made to leave, but the crowd pressed in upon me. Twice they parted to let me through when one among them called loudly to let me pass, and twice they closed in again. When at last I managed to make my way out of the park many were following me still. I repeatedly tried to tell them that it was time they went their way, but there were still sixty or so with me when I finally reached Shimbashi station. The other people at the station must have wondered what was going on with all the commotion and cheering.

It was the first time I had personally experienced this sort of situation. Crowd psychology is a very strange thing. While the individual is not easily swayed, put him with others in a crowd and he will do whatever he is told. It seems almost as though they have been incorporated into a single body, and each member behaves with no more individuality than a finger. People appear no longer to have control over themselves.

This is extremely dangerous. It was fortunate for me that on this occasion the mob was cheerful; but things might have been very different had they been in a sour or ugly mood, in which case they might have turned to arson or looting.

EXPELLED FROM THE KENSEIKAI AGAIN

The demand for popular suffrage seemed to be winning the day, but the Seiyūkai and the Hara government were obstinately opposed. The Seiyūkai had originally evolved out of the Jiyūtō, or Liberal Party, while the Kenseikai and Kokumintō were offshoots of the Kaishintō (Progressive Party). When we organized the Kaishintō we represented the gradual and moderate forces in contrast to the radical stance of the Jiyūtō. The political landscape had completely reversed. The liberal Seiyūkai had become the conservatives while the Kokumintō and Kenseikai had become the radical parties.

This was a result of the unusual development of society. At the beginning many of the Jiyūtō members were sons of old clansmen. They proclaimed a policy of decentralization and established centers of power in the farming villages. By contrast, the Kaishintō was organized by government officials, academics, and intellectuals who favored centralized government. They had their power base in the urban areas. As a result they tended to be more moderate in their approach and preferred gradual change.

With the remarkable social progress of the previous four decades, however, capitalistic industrial civilization had taken firm root in the cities, and the cities were hotbeds of socialistic ideologies. The rural districts tended by nature to be conservative. This was as true in Japan as in other societies. In this way the Seiyūkai, whose power base lay in the rural districts, had turned conservative while the urban-based Kenseikai had became the radical political force.

With the conservative Seiyūkai and the Hara government expressing outright opposition, the suffrage bill was unlikely to pass the forty-second Diet, even with Kenseikai, Kokumintō and Jikkōkai sponsorship. And while the people gave us tremendous support by staging mass rallies and demonstrations the bill died in the committee stage and was fated for burial in the plenary session.

Before the bill had a chance to be put to a plenary vote the government abruptly dissolved the House. With the bill doomed anyway, why did the Hara government call for a dissolution? This can be explained by the fact that at that time there was a small electoral district system in place and the prime minister hoped to gain an absolute majority by calling a snap election.

While the prime minister was criticized for staging what the public thought was an unjustified dissolution and an abuse of power, the Seiyūkai won an unprecedentedly large victory in the general election of May 10, 1920, just as he had hoped.

As a result of the election, the Seiyūkai increased its strength by 119 seats and seized an absolute majority of 281. By contrast, the Kenseikai lost ten of its 118 seats while the Kokumintō was reduced from 31 to 29.

It had always been known that small districts were more vulnerable to intervention. So it was that in this election Dr. Imai Yoshiyuki, who was known as "the god of the suffrage movement," lost his seat in Osaka, and Katō Seinosuke, Fujisawa Ikunosuke, Machida Chuji, and Kataoka Naoharu, all leading figures in the Kenseikai, also lost unexpectedly.

When the forty-third Diet was convened on July 1, the Hara government, given the overwhelming majority it enjoyed in the House, had no effective parliamentary opposition, but the opposition parties maintained a high profile outside the Diet. The public had become disenchanted with the government after almost two years of mismanagement. Mass rallies were held in Ueno and Hibiya parks as well as on the reclaimed lands of Shibaura, and resolutions to impeach the government were adopted. In almost every instance the public clashed with the police.

Inside the Diet, however, the suffrage bill was killed by a vote of 286 to 155, as had been expected. A motion to impeach the government suffered a similar fate.

On one occasion during a special session of this Diet my colleague Shimada Saburō introduced an inquiry into the corrupt practices of the ministers of state. This pricked the government at its weakest point. The ruling Seiyūkai was angered and, under the pretext of defending the honor of parliament, tried to expel Shimada from the party.

I was so enraged when I learned about this that I had Shimada's inquiry copied and filed in my name with the intention of obliging the government to expel me as well as Shimada. The Seiyūkai had not expected this and in the end had to withdraw the decision to expel Shimada. Some may think this was a bit childish of me, but I must say it is rather gratifying to be able to put a party with an absolute majority into disarray.

In the nearly fifty years of my parliamentary life there have been three occasions when I was able single-handedly to bend the will of the majority. The first was when Hoshi Tōru and Sassa Tomofusa attempted unsuccessfully to trap me on a question concerning the expenses of the imperial household. The second was when the Seiyūkai tried to prevent me from speaking on the naval build-up issue during the Yamamoto government. This was the third.

I would not make a good general commanding great armies in the field, but I think I would be rather good at leading a small unit to confuse the enemy's ranks or single-handedly cutting through the defenses on his flank. I flatter myself that I would never have lost a duel, but leading big armies was beyond my powers. As Kusumoto Masataka aptly pointed out, a general would not look right if he had a drawn spear in his hand instead of his baton of command. No doubt this was mainly due to the smallness of my own capacity, but it had also to do with my political fate to constantly find myself part of a minority party.

Inukai, unlike myself, was a brilliant and resourceful man. However, he too appeared to be more comfortable at the head of a few troops in hand-to-hand combat. And he belonged, as I did, to the Kaishintō, and had grown up in a small universe. Upbringing rather than birth appear to make the deepest imprint on one's character, as indeed they say.

I managed to prevent Shimada from being expelled but got myself into the same stew over the suffrage bill.

The suffrage bill, which was presented before the forty-second Diet, was doomed even before it had any chance of being deliberated as no one had a major stake in its survival. But an idea whose time has come is undefeatable, and the bill resurfaced during the forty-fourth Diet. Having submitted it, however, the Kenseikai did their best to draw its teeth by insisting that a potential voter should have independent means and that he should be at least twenty-five years old. This reflected the secret thoughts of the president, Katō Takaaki, who was really not in favor of the bill but was only giving it lip service. The Kokumintō bill was not much different.

These bills were mere exercises in rhetoric, emasculated even before they could be voted on by the conditions attached to them by the proposing parties. On February 3rd the Kokumintō bill was defeated. Therefore, the Kenseikai bill, owing to its similarity to the Kokumintō bill, should have been automatically precluded by Article 39 of the constitution. I reminded the speaker, Mr. Oku, of this procedure through Tagawa Daikichirō but he did not accept this advice. So I repeated the advice myself and shortly afterward left the House.

This became an issue within the Kenseikai. Tagawa was promptly dismissed from the party for compromising its discipline, while I, because of my seniority within the party, was merely asked to withdraw from it. I did not follow the party recommendation, however. Instead, I pleaded that, as the initiator of the idea, I should be the one to be expelled and not Tagawa—as indeed I was when I did not heed their recommendation to resign from the party of my own accord.

Being expelled and resigning from political parties have been my lot. I was expelled from the Kaishintō we organized and from its successor the Shinpotō. The Seiyūkai did not actually expel me, but I left it of my own volition on two occasions. Had I not done so I would probably have been expelled anyway. I have always been an ardent party politician, but I could never live with a party that bound my conscience. Having been thus expelled from the Kenseikai gave me the freedom to campaign for arms limitation, and this suited me admirably. It was probably in the better interest not only of myself, but of the country and the world at large.

Such experiences had made me painfully aware that the Japanese political soil produced factions and not true political parties. I therefore came to the conclusion that I should abandon my penchant for creating political parties and concentrate on developing the raw materials for them—namely, men. I felt that given the circumstances it was fruitless to try to build more political parties. I would have to start from the basis of making men fit for political life. Since that time I have kept myself free from associating with parties and have remained an independent.

It was easy to blame the political parties for all their wrongs, but it was not so easy for people to see that the blame should lie with individuals. Politicians made up political parties, but it must be remembered that it was the people who had elected them in the first place. If politicians were no good, then the people who elected them had erred. It was difficult for one to accept that the fault for others' sins was one's own.

Our people failed to elect those who would work for their interests and they paid the price of electing instead those who worked against their true interests, involving them in wretched wars. It was like entrusting a robber with guarding one's safe and giving him the key. Unless this fundamental weakness was overcome we would have only factions in Japan, never true political parties.

The Proposal to Limit Armaments

One's idea of nationhood depends on where one perceives it in a spectrum spreading from narrow to broad. At the narrow end rests extreme xenophobia of the kind that existed in pre-Restoration Japan, when unwelcome foreigners were welcomed with the sword. With a little tolerance, provided it was a time of peace, one might go so far as to call other nations brethren of the four seas and permit commerce and intercourse with them, only to open fire without further ado the moment it seemed one's immediate interests so required. While the latter was admittedly to be preferred to a state of outright xenophobia, it too has already become too narrow a definition for today's changing times.

As the world becomes smaller with the development of the various modes of transportation and our interests increasingly converge with the internationalization of the economy, our concept of nationhood must be broadened to reflect our recognition of these changing realities. Until now the nation state has been the most efficient structure to ensure people's security and well being, but with the progress of civilization and the evolution of the world's institutions a narrow definition of nationhood would henceforth compromise rather than ensure human happiness. Without the narrow nationalism that is its product we would not have fought the world war; without it the war would not have lasted so long or spread so wide. The attachment to anachronistic ideas was the cause of so much misery.

If such a war were ever to be waged again with the latest weapons of destruction and last for many years we would end up destroying ourselves. The concept of the nation must be recast to be in harmony with the evolving structure of the world.

In the years immediately following the Great War the government urged the building of a so-called "eight-eight" fleet consisting of eight battleships and an equal number of cruisers, which would constitute the nucleus of the imperial navy. With this fleet, they contended, our sea defenses would be complete. I was skeptical of this.

National defense is a relative matter. If our country increased its armaments the effort would be in vain if a potential foe responded by building up its own even more. Moreover, the effectiveness of our defense would become more uncertain, not less. On the other hand, if we reduced our arms and the reduction were matched or exceeded by the other country, the result would be the opposite and our defenses would be relatively strengthened.

A child should be able to follow this reasoning, but not our public. Many held to the naïve notion that an arms build-up would of itself render the country safe.

Within a year after embarking on the "eight-eight" fleet program the navy had spent almost 500 million yen. Added to the army's expenditure of 260 million yen, the country had put out over 750 million yen on defense, which represented Japan's total tax revenues at the time. The nation's entire tax revenue was to be spent on defense, while all related administrative and operational expenses were to be borne by income from public enterprises, national monopolies, and public debt issues. This was an extremely dangerous fiscal policy.

Government revenue for 1921, including extraordinary accounts and a brought-forward surplus of 200 million yen, amounted to a mere 1.56 billion yen. Excluding the brought-forward surplus, it stood at around 1.3 billion yen. A defense expenditure of 750 million yen would chew up half the total revenue if the services had their way. I was horror-struck by this budget.

It did not matter whether the navy or the army was spending more. The point was that Japan might well increase its armaments, but if it provoked the other side into exceeding that increase we would only be spending money to endanger our own national security. The navy, especially, was a visible measure of the nation's economic strength and shipbuilding capacity. Unfortunately, Japan was deficient in both. By these criteria, the navy's rivals, Great Britain and the United States, possessed five times the capacity. If we attempted to compete in a naval arms race against the combined power of the two nations, our sea defenses would only be weakened.

Nevertheless, if we neglected to strengthen our arms while the other party was doing so, our security would obviously be jeopardized. Fortunately for Japan, both in England and America the momentum for arms limitation as a result of the war was great. The prevailing mood therefore favored arms reduction, if that could be achieved. It was opportune for Japan to take advantage of this momentum.

Forewarned, forearmed. If Japan took the initiative to propose arms limitations, England and America would most certainly follow. If we could get them to agree to limit their navies, we could achieve national security without further effort and without building another warship. At the same time, we would save ourselves from national bankruptcy and ensure the well being of our people.

Moreover, it was clear that even without Japan calling for arms limitation, sooner or later Great Britain and the United States would offer the same. If Japan chose then to refuse to agree to arms limitation and was unilaterally determined to strengthen its navy, it was certain that the two powers would form an alliance, and build up their navies beyond Japan's capacity to match them. Unless we were prepared for this we could not abstain from participating in the arms limitation conference. Anticipating this, if we were in any case prepared to follow the British and American lead by attending the arms limitation conference and agreeing to arms limitation, it would be far wiser for us to take the initiative ourselves in proposing arms limitation. This is what one calls independent diplomacy. It would ensure an agreement that was far more advantageous to our nation.

This is why I advocated a naval limitation agreement. At the time, however, there was hardly any support for my proposal, whether within the walls of parliament or without. Before I was dismissed from the Kenseikai I brought up the issue within the party, but no one supported me. With all the statistics I mustered to press my argument, still no one would agree.

However, it was clear to me that before long the powers would bring up the issue and ask Japan to participate. Soon after my dismissal from the Kenseikai I submitted a draft resolution on arms limitation to the forty-fourth Diet. The resolution called for:

> 1. Limitation of the empire's naval strength through negotiation with Great Britain and the United States.
> 2. Consolidation and reduction of our land forces on the basis of the Charter of the League of Nations.

In submitting the resolution to the plenary session on February 10, 1921, I took the floor for two hours explaining my reasoning to the other legislators.

In my speech I expounded on the relative nature of national defense, and on the need for arms limitation if only from the budgetary point of view. I declared that it was quite possible to come to an arms limitation agreement, but only if Japan would not stand in its way. Without any such agreement, Great Britain had not built any new warships during the previous five or six years, and France and Italy also had unilaterally suspended construction.

The gist of my concluding argument was that that now left two countries: Japan and the United States. Already in America powerful senators and congressmen had declared themselves in favor of an agreement on limitation, and the issue had passed the foreign affairs committee of both houses. After the new president had settled in, most probably by late April or early May, it was expected that he would invite Japan to join an agreement. "I believe that already you have decided in your hearts that you would wish to accept this invitation," I continued, and when the time comes there is most unlikely to be anyone in Japan who would refuse. Indeed, we have said we would be prepared to attend such negotiations two to three months from now—the prime minister and foreign minister have both made clear statements to that effect in the House of Peers as well as in the House of Representatives. Under the present circumstances, it is the profound belief of this legislator that it would be in the best interests of the nation publicly to state its intention of taking the initiative for arms limitation, for our country's sake, for world peace, and for justice and righteousness. I therefore plead that with level heads and free from bias you will in the national interest adopt the resolution.

At first it seemed from their reaction that I had succeeded in winning my audience over unanimously. But in reality there were few supporters among them. I warned my colleagues that they might disagree with me that day but that within a year they would have to change their minds; that they should act now so that they would not have to be ashamed later. When the resolution was put to the vote it was rejected 285 to 38, with almost the whole House opposing. The Kokumintō under Inukai supported it in the name of world peace, but both the Kenseikai and Seiyūkai opposed it.

Perhaps this was the only time that the Kenseikai and the Seiyūkai, the two major parties, which normally fought like cats and dogs, acted hand in hand. A certain member of the Kenseikai who abstained confessed later, "When the speaker prodded me to vote, I felt my face burn with shame. This was the first time in all my life that I voted the same way as those Seiyūkai people. I had never felt so strange." I had to smile wryly at the peculiar workings of party psychology.

A CRAFTY EXTREMIST

The speech on arms limitation was one of the most energetic I had made in my forty years of parliamentary life. Faced with its summary defeat in the House, I resolved to appeal to the people directly, asking them to vote one way or the other and in this way prove to the world that our public opinion was in favor of arms limitations.

With this intention I immediately left the capital and by the end of June had covered about 9,400 ri (23,000 miles), addressing a total of 73,000 people, including audiences at Tokyo Imperial University and thirteen other universities, four organizations, forty-nine cities, and twenty-three towns. I had also attended twenty-three tea discussion groups. With the exception of the speech at Tokyo Imperial University, I had had postcards given on each occasion to members of the audience on which to record their vote for or against arms limitations.

Out of the 31,519 who returned their postcards 29,250 or 92.8 percent were for arms limitations. In contrast to the votes in the House of Representatives (38 in favor and 285 or 88 percent against) the result seemed to me strange. Of course there was no way of knowing the views of the other 40,000 people who did not send in their postcards, but the exercise gave me grounds to assume that the vote in the House did not represent the will of the people.

I was the first in Japan to undertake a solo tour of the nation to ask the people for their opinion on an issue. At the same time I attempted two other novelties. One was to charge an admission fee to my speeches and the other was to take questions from the audience.

Charging an admission fee for a political speech is not done very much even today. However, if it was natural for one to express one's views in writing and sell books, it should not be considered out of order to charge an entrance fee for a speech. I charged from ten sen to fifty sen depending on the location. In Osaka we charged fifty sen and the place was packed.

Now that we were charging a fee I felt that the halls were much more animated than on earlier occasions when we had not done so. At least one can say with certainty that the audiences, apart from whether they were for the issue in question or against, seemed much more earnest than those who were admitted free.

Answering questions from the audience also proved quite effective. One could never be sure if the audience understood one's drift when one spoke and they just sat and listened. It was both disrespectful to the audience and irresponsible on the part of the speaker. In the course of this tour I therefore decided to take questions and answer them courteously and to the best of my knowledge.

During the campaign things got a bit hot at times. A would-be assassin who had been after me was caught, and on another occasion a dozen ruffians broke into the hall where I was speaking and injured several policemen in the ensuing fracas.

I believe it was also during this tour that a leader of the Kokusuikai in Nagoya, an ultra-nationalist organization that had the support of Tokonami Takejirō,[1] had made it known that there would be trouble if I were to go there. The Kokusuikai boss always carried a gun, but it was said that he only shot people in the legs. This was a comforting thought. A clever man, I said to myself. He knew that shooting one in the leg would probably not be fatal so he would get off lightly, but it would achieve the desired objective all the same.

I had been warned in advance that the fellow was after me but I went to Nagoya anyway. However, as soon as I arrived I was taken ill and could not leave my room on the second floor of the inn where I was staying. I was running a high fever and was in no condition to make a speech. The man arrived at the inn with a dozen of his henchmen and demanded to see me. I sent a message that I was not feeling well enough to see anybody, but he insisted on coming up. I heard the sound of footsteps on the stairs. As soon as the man entered the small room he gave me a ghastly look and snarled, "Get ready to die. I have come for your head!"

---

[1] Tokonami (1866–1935) was a home ministry bureaucrat and rightist politician who was active alternatively in the Kenseikai and the Seiyūkai.

I remained silent. Suzuki Shōgo, who was beside me, said something like, "What on earth are you talking about?" whereupon the man lifted the heavy brazier in its paulownia wood box and hurled it at me. As I was in my nightclothes I quickly pulled the futon over me. Ash and embers scattered around the room singeing the futon and tatami mats, but I was unscathed. To my surprise, Suzuki, with a little help from me, quite easily subdued the man.

Hearing the commotion, people started up the stairs. Among them were a number of policemen whom I asked to stay outside the room while I invited my assailant to talk. I sat down and he did the same. As we talked, the man must have found something in me to make him change his mind, for it was not long before he was calling me his elder brother and saying he wanted to invite me out. I told him I was taking it easy for the night and asked him to leave.

I suppose he admired me for calmly inviting him to talk instead of turning him over to the police as he well deserved. Later, I was told by Shimozono Sakichi, who had attended the memorial service for Tokonami Takejirō, that my new acquaintance had spoken to him of the incident and confessed he had never been so ashamed.

In my long years of political life I have encountered a number of dangerous moments, but though rather a reckless person by nature, I have always escaped danger. On this occasion I was saved because I was in bed. Not being religious I do not put this down to divine intervention but superstitiously think of myself as having been born under a lucky star. In the past I have had my share of misfortune, but it was self-inflicted and never anything that could not have been avoided. Any potential tragedy that came my way was usually attended to in some providential way without any interference from me.

I Sharply Attack the Army's Misguided Expansion

Soon after I returned from my speaking tour of the nation, the United States, as expected, approached the Japanese government with an offer to host a naval limitation conference in Washington, D.C. Having soundly voted down my resolution, the government should logically have rejected it. Instead, the Hara government sent word it was delighted to accept the American invitation and dispatched Navy Minister Katō Tomosaburō, Speaker of the House of Peers Tokugawa Iesato, and Japan's ambassador to the United States, Shidehara Kijūrō, as its representatives with full powers. The members of the delegation were well chosen.

The naval limitation conference opened on November 12, 1921, with the eventual agreement setting a ratio of 5:5:3 for the naval powers of Great Britain, the United States, and Japan, respectively. Accordingly, Japan suspended the eight-eight fleet program and was thus able to save the nation an annual naval shipbuilding cost of 500 million yen.

A shrewd business acquaintance turned to me at the time and pensively remarked, "How were you ever able to predict that? If we businessmen could make a prediction like that just once in our lives we would make a fortune!" to which I replied, "It wasn't anything to do with inspiration or prediction. All I do is read the same papers you do and try to interpret the news from abroad correctly."

The most ironic part of it all was that both the government and the people, rather than rejoicing that the naval agreement had enabled us to save an annual national expenditure of 500 million yen, shouted "national crisis!" and "national shame!" because we were limited to a ratio of three against the British and United States shares of five. They called me by such abusive names as "traitor" and "hireling of America."

After this, assassins constantly followed me, and the police had to provide me with a bodyguard. Even with this arrangement thugs occasionally forced their way into our home in Kita-shinagawa, injuring policeman and others present.

On one such occasion three thugs rushed in while I was at home (in Shinagawa). Quickly, I slipped outside with Yukika, my youngest daughter, and hid behind the house. The thugs were overcome by the police and arrested. The father of one of them learned of the incident and came later to offer his apology in person. I appreciated this and wrote a thirty-one-syllable *tanka* poem then and there and presented it to him, after which he took his leave, encouraged by my verse.

> If it was patriotism that drove the young man
> My would-be assassin deserves honor for it.

With the country crying "national crisis!" I published a booklet titled "Good Fortune Has Befallen our Nation," in which I explained that arms limitation was the way to save Japan—that far from being a national crisis this was a most felicitous turn of events.

At the convening of the forty-fifth Diet, as though they had forgotten that they had vetoed my resolution not long before, the Seiyūkai, the Kenseikai, the Kokumintō, and the Kōshin Club submitted a joint proposal promoting arms limitation and reducing the power of the army and navy.

The proposal read in two parts as follows:

A. A proposal concerning the curtailment and reduction of the army. The government proposes to reduce the period of service in the infantry to one year and four months and to integrate various military units, thereby saving an annual expenditure of forty million yen.

B. A proposal concerning the revision of government regulations on the appointment of service ministers. The government wishes to abrogate the present regulation, which restricts the appointment of service ministers to generals and lieutenant generals and admirals and vice-admirals as this restriction is no longer appropriate.

What this amounted to was that a majority of parliamentarians had done a complete volte-face in less than a year, from a position opposing arms limitation to one now supporting it. For my part, I felt that a saving of 40 million yen was not sufficient. I submitted a revision demanding a reduction of 100 million and took the floor again for a full two hours to make my point.

Leading off from the reply of the service ministries to the four-party proposition, the thrust of my argument addressed fundamental concepts regarding national defense. I put it this way. "The fact that the army cannot even say whether it is in favor of or against the apparently unanimously endorsed proposal reflects a fundamental difference between the attitudes of the two services regarding national defense. The navy has decided that defense is relative, but the army takes the position that defense is an absolute matter. It seems to me that the army is wedded to a strange compulsion to defend even in the absence of an enemy, to wage a one-man sumo wrestling fight without an opponent."

From conversations with officers in the military I had learned that the army was scheming to take advantage of the turmoil on the continent to deploy twenty-one Japanese divisions in China. Exposing this plan, I berated the army for seeking to build up its forces for such a purpose, the object of which could never be achieved anyway, while paying lip service to Japan-China goodwill. To meet reasonable requirements for national defense six or seven divisions would be enough, I argued, and ten divisions would ensure a comfortable margin. I went on further to demonstrate the disadvantages to the country of maintaining super-abundant military forces. I really gave the army a piece of my mind.

> The alienation of our country from the civilized nations of the world and our descent into a situation of almost utter isolation is substantially due, while there are other contributing causes, to the excessive size and reckless adventures of our army. The difficulties in which this country finds itself today in the Orient, as well as the difficulties it is experiencing in its diplomatic relations with the Western countries, are all a consequence of our slide into a dual diplomacy as a result of the army gaining ascendancy over the foreign ministry and conducting its own irrational foreign policy. Our present national defenses are defending us only in name. The truth is that they actually constitute a prime source of danger to the empire.

The army's outdated weaponry was also the object of my criticism. "It does not take a military expert to know whether in the modern world one can fight a war with guns that fire a single bullet at a time. Today's wars in Europe are fought with heavy and light machine guns. Our popguns belong in museums, not on today's battlefields."

It is my conviction that the surest way to guarantee national defense lies in making friends and not enemies.

> It takes more than a strong army to defend a country. Our defense will never be assured if we continue to make enemies, three today and four tomorrow. We should have profited from the lesson of the Triple Intervention of 1895: that one can only cope with a hostile alliance by belonging to another. But what has our army done? It sent troops into Siberia and made an enemy of Russia. It dispatched forces to meddle on the mainland and infuriated China. It angered the Western countries by opposing consultations on military force reductions. It has created enemies to the left and enemies to the right. It has thrust the country into dire circumstances where it cannot easily find a friend.

The Untimely Death of Hara Takashi

As noted earlier, breaking my rule, I took the edge off my attack on the government and assumed a neutral attitude with regard to the Hara cabinet. Nonetheless, I was unconvinced by the way it handled things. Especially since its unprecedented and overwhelming victory in the general election, it had driven in high gear and often acted senselessly.

It was Hara Takashi's resourcefulness more than anything else that had built up the Seiyūkai into the power it had become. For this, the party revered Hara. His leadership style was very much like that of Hoshi Tōru, with whose own undoubted qualities his all-round ability compared favorably.

Someone had given me a book full of boastful accounts of his own career and experiences. In it he describes the farewell gifts he received from Katsura and Hara when he left for overseas, apparently during the time of Japan's war against Russia. Katsura reportedly told him, "I would like you to help procure war funds when you reach the United States. I shall accordingly assist you with your travel expenses." In spite of the grandiose announcement, the Katsura gave him a paltry eight hundred yen.

Some years later when Hara was prime minister, the same man was again planning to go abroad. He was not particularly close to Hara, but when he learned of the trip Hara, without being asked, presented him with three thousand yen. The author concluded thus: "Katsura and Hara were worth eight hundred yen and three thousand yen to me, respectively. In other words, there was a difference of 1 to 4." Well, that is one way of looking at it.

Some of my closest friends belonged to the Seiyūkai. According to what they told me, Hara was a generous giver. During the general election he would give 15,000 yen if he was asked for 10,000 yen and 30,000 yen if asked for 20,000, always more than had been asked, taking into consideration the position and personality of the asker. Not surprisingly, all these people became his ardent admirers and eulogized Hara.

Hara, like Hoshi, had no attachment to money. He rewarded himself little and lived in his small house in Shiba even after he became prime minister. It was the same house he had acquired when serving as secretary to Mutsu. Most people starting out as somebody's secretary and advancing to the prime ministership would move into a finer house, but Hara continued to dwell in his modest home even at the height of his career as prime minister. It is a proof enough that he was man of little affectation and pecuniary interest. On the other hand, he lavished money on members of his party and sometimes even tipped them off to opportunities for advantageous concession rights. Small wonder that he was held in such esteem by his fellow party members.

However, Hara could hardly hope to continue like this without causing trouble. Hoshi in his later years realized this and was in the process of changing his ways when he was assassinated. Hara used the same tactics to rise to the presidency of the Seiyūkai and then to the prime ministership. Admittedly, he was not as blatant about it as Hoshi, but I felt he could not continue to get away with it indefinitely.

Hara seemed secure, given the absolute majority of the Seiyūkai in the House and the steadfast support of the Kenkyūkai in the House of Peers. His foundations seemed rock solid. However, I warned a good friend of Hara's, "It is time for Hara to step down. For him to continue longer in office will do him no good in the future. It may even endanger his life. He should step down now and start again." My advice was not heeded. As a matter of fact, public opinion was clamoring to be heard on the issues of suffrage, inflation, and foreign relations. In addition, there were reports on the government's mishandling of three major investments, the Manchurian Railroad, and the opium issue.

After three years in power the Hara government had lost its initial luster and was the object of increasing resentment. To a visiting correspondent from the *Asahi Shinbun* I remarked, "If he continues as he is doing, Hara is going to be murdered one of these days." The *Asahi* published this as if it were their own revelation. Five days later Hara was stabbed by an unknown youth in Tokyo station. The newspaper came under suspicion of having been in communication with someone who was privy to the plot. After investigation it became known that the *Asahi* had only repeated the remark I had made to their correspondent. The matter was thus cleared up and dismissed as a product of my imagination.

Very often I have this sort of inspiration. Unfortunately, my presentiments often come to pass. Hoshi acknowledged his mistake before he met his death. I do not know if Hara realized his errors before he died.

THE TAKAHASHI KOREKIYO CABINET

With the untimely death of Hara, Takahashi Korekiyo was lucky enough to inherit the government but, unable to hold its reins, was ousted after only six months. Takahashi was a man of unusual personality. In a sense he was without a peer in all Japan. Having served long as minister of finance, he was, as expected, well versed in matters of finance and the economy. The fact was that though he had a good general grasp of his field he was indifferent to trifling matters. To be kind, one might say he was big-hearted; on the other hand, one could also say he was unconcerned and irresponsible.

Takahashi was said to have had a difficult boyhood and to have known hardship while studying in America.[2] After his return to Japan and by the time he became minister of agriculture and commerce he was deep in debt. I was also used to being poor and sometimes resorted to borrowing from a loan shark because of my reluctance to have to bow my head to ask friends to help me out. Loan sharks were often after both Takahashi and me. Observing his state of poverty in those days, I felt encouraged to know I was not the only one.

---

[2] Takahashi (1854–1936) was born the son of a shogunal artist, and was adopted by a Sendai samurai, who sent him to America to study finance. On his return, he rose to high positions in the Yokohama Specie Bank and the Bank of Japan, before undertaking the first of a series of ministerial posts, chiefly as minister of finance, in the Yamamoto cabinet in 1913, at which time he joined the Seiyūkai. He was assassinated in the Young Officers Rebellion of February 26, 1936.

Takahashi's insouciance and carefree attitude fascinated me. When working for the ministry of agriculture and commerce, he was caught up in a messy silver mine operation, which resulted in his resignation from the civil service. For some time afterward he went about carrying a *shamisen* for a geisha.

From bureau chief, as he was then, to shamisen-carrier—carrying a musical instrument for a geisha—granted that he had to make a living somehow—was not the kind of situation others could easily put themselves in, particularly in light of the unsympathetic public gaze to which he was subjected. When Takahashi took over the highest office in the government after Hara Takashi was slain, I wondered which he preferred, being prime minister or carrying a beautiful geisha's *shamisen*. He probably enjoyed neither. These cameos of the man reveal a good deal about his unusual caliber.

Takahashi and I were long-time associates in both our private and public lives, sometimes politically on the same side and at other times political foes. Had he been a less extraordinary person he would probably have found it difficult not to betray some strain in our relations when our political fortunes separated us. But not he. His demeanor was little affected by his political ups and downs, and he would carry on as though nothing had come between us as old friends. He was always pleasant to deal with and I have no doubt he showed the same cordial manner to all. He was free from prejudice too, and in that respect he probably had no equal in the country.

I often wondered how he could remain jovial and carefree when life had treated him so badly. Then I read the autobiography he dictated, which was carried serially in the *Asahi Shinbun*, and learned that he had had the same character since birth.

According to his own account, Takahashi was born into a family of low status. On one occasion, when there was a gathering with families of high feudal status, Takahashi, still a child, had none of the others' restraint and went right up to his feudal lord's wife, who promptly picked him up and held him in her arms to the consternation of those present. She gave him a little present and termed him "an interesting child." This anecdote helped me to understand that Takahashi was quite indifferent to matters of social status. He must have felt the same when as a small boy he climbed onto the lap of the wife of his feudal lord as later when he became an employee at a geisha house.

For the Japanese, who are normally bound by convention and formality, Takahashi was a rarity. Such a man would not be thrown into raptures by public praise or cast into despair by criticism. Later, this trait helped him to earn acclaim as a "national treasure" for managing the vital issue of the nation's finances. But as Hara Takashi's successor as president of the Seiyūkai and as prime minister he was an utter failure.

In those days the Seiyūkai had become a mammoth organization. This was largely to Hara's credit and he was the only one who could manage the party properly. After his untimely death the Seiyūkai became as unruly as the Taira family following the death of its strongman, Kiyomori.[3] No one could manage it, much less the big-hearted and carefree Takahashi.

---

[3] Taira no Kiyomori (1118–1181), late Heian period warrior chief, whose brief ascendancy was followed by the first (Minamoto) shogunate established by his foes.

The problem began during the closing days of the forty-fifth Diet when Naka-hashi Tokugorō, the education minister, came under fire in the House of Peers for his effort to raise the status of technical schools and was pressed to resign. Taka-hashi tried to ride this out by issuing a statement that the cabinet would stand or fall as a unit. Then, when Nakahashi was shown guilty of duplicity, Takahashi reversed himself and wanted Nakahashi and Railroad Minister Motoda, who was also under fire, to resign together so that he could replace them with Yamamoto Teijirō and Ogawa Heikichi. But the two ministers refused to resign, insisting that the whole cabinet share responsibility.

The dispute was saved from developing into a cabinet reshuffle as a result of the good offices of Saionji, but the veiled enmity between the two groups contin-ued. In early June Prime Minister Takahashi attempted another cabinet reshuffle, but again without success. With the disunity among the members of the cabinet plainly in view, the Takahashi government finally resigned on June 6. This was the root cause of the split of 1924 when the Seiyūkai broke up into two groups, the second calling itself the Seiyū Hontō or "real Seiyūkai."[4]

While the Takahashi government was being shaken up, the opposition resumed the campaign for an expanded male suffrage with redoubled energy. When the Kenseikai dropped its long-standing condition of requiring a voter to be of inde-pendent means before he was given political rights, the suffrage group gained momentum as never before.

On December 26, 1921, the three groups convened at the Seiyōken restaurant in Tsukiji to renew their solidarity. On January 22, 1922, a national convention was organized in Akasaka's Sannōdai. Journalists from Tokyo and Osaka formed a *fusen-dōmei*, a popular suffrage alliance, and organized nationwide mass dem-onstrations on February 5 and 11 (National Foundation Day).

Popular suffrage songs, like the one that follows, were written to be sung to the tune of "The River Amur."

> At last the people have awakened
> To the call for a second Restoration,
> For equal political rights
> And suffrage for all.
> Graciously did the late Emperor
> Take the Imperial Oath.
> Has the government forgotten?
> Has the Seiyūkai forgotten?
> Let us swiftly bring down
> The government that obstructs suffrage.
> Enemies of political freedom,
> Let us defeat them now!

The suffrage bill was submitted to the House on February 23, 1922, and with fifty or so members clamoring to speak either for or against the issue, deliberation

---

[4] The Kaishintō, it may be recalled, had suffered the same terminological split in 1898.

lasted three days. I was finally given the floor to speak on behalf of the motion on the last day of the debate, February 27.

From a unique position, leaning neither toward the Kenseikai nor toward the Seiyūkai, I emphasized that suffrage was inevitable since one could not close off a country to foreign ideas in a kind of ideological seclusion policy, and I also stressed the importance of having a safety valve for popular sentiments. From time to time the House was enlivened with hurrahs and boos.

The suffrage bill was again defeated due to the opposition of the Seiyūkai. During my intervention I addressed not only the need for popular elections but also shared my thinking generally on constitutional government. Since the beginning of the formation of the Kaishintō, I had exerted my best efforts for the sound development of political parties, sometimes from within and at other times from without. Now, however, I could not help but deplore the state into which those parties had fallen.

From Taishō to Shōwa

THE KATŌ TOMOSABURŌ CABINET

Following the fall of the Takahashi government, no adequate successor could be found. It was at this point that Katō Tomosaburō returned from Washington, D.C., where his political skill had been widely acknowledged. He was asked to accept the premiership.

The Katō government had the support of the Seiyūkai, but it was a supra-party government that ran counter to the times—so much so that the Kenseikai and the Kakushin Club organized a pro-constitution movement. The government, however, functioned quite well.

Katō, unlike Katsura, showed neither political preference nor special acumen. He was, in effect, a purely military type. During the Russo-Japanese War, he demonstrated exceptional leadership qualities as chief of staff to Admiral Tōgō, particularly during the Battle of Tsushima Straits. Subsequently, he was appointed vice minister for the navy by Yamamoto Gonnohyōe, who had recognized his abilities.

In those days as mayor of Tokyo I hosted receptions for foreign military attachés and on occasion assisted at diplomatic functions. In that capacity I frequently met and so became friendly with Katō. I thought him then to be an interesting and sensitive person. But he was a man of few words, so all we did was eat what was put before us without saying much. Nonetheless, I had the impression that he was well disposed toward me.

While in England on my way to Belgium to attend a conference of the International Parliamentarians' Union, I stayed with the family of a good friend of my wife's. The old man of the family, a former officer in the Royal Navy who once spent some time in Japan as a naval instructor, asked me if I knew an officer by the name of Katō, "a man of awesome qualities." After returning to Japan I observed Katō more closely and found him to possess quite exceptional intelligence.

Because of this, I recommended him for the post of naval minister to Ōkuma when he was in the process of organizing his cabinet. He was not appointed at that time, however, because Katō Takaaki urged that Admiral Yashiro, who came from the same old feudal domain, be given the office. When the cabinet was reshuffled following the Ōura incident, both Katō Takaaki and Admiral Yashiro resigned. Again I recommended Admiral Katō, but those around Ōkuma were not enthusiastic. After all, they said, Katō had already been invited once by Kiyoura to join the cabinet but had declined, and due to this the Kiyoura cabinet was stillborn; it was no use, therefore, inviting him to join the waning Ōkuma cabinet. I thought I had a better case and insisted, and Ōkuma readily agreed. Perhaps this was because of the familiarity of our relationship, but it seemed somewhat surprising at the time.

Katō was installed as navy minister in the Ōkuma cabinet and retained the portfolio in the successive Terauchi, Hara, and Takahashi governments. Eventually he was to enjoy acclaim as one of the three most able navy ministers along with Yamamoto Gonnohyōe and Saitō Makoto.

During his long tenure as navy minister he undertook two major but conflicting projects. One was the notorious naval expansion program known as the "eight-eight fleet build-up." The other was the naval limitation negotiations in Washington. He made the most of the two labels, one favoring military expansion and the other military reduction. Either way he was popular with the public. It was a strange record, albeit reflecting the ambiguities of the times.

When a young Russian diplomat asked the secret of collecting materials for reports, the famous General Ignatiev answered simply: "It's easy. When there is little to say, you report unsupported facts. The next time you make corrections. This way you have materials for two reports. The foreign minister receiving the reports will without fail commend you for your diligence." It is not that I think Katō shared Ignatiev's duplicity, but somehow this anecdote comes to mind when I think of Katō's skillful handling of both military expansion and reduction. At the same time, had it not been for Katō, regardless of his civilian or military background, it would not have been possible to perform this feat while coping successfully with opposition from within the navy.

Katō's skills were recognized and he was called eventually to organize a cabinet. The Kenseikai was bitterly opposed to the government, because the Seiyūkai had given Katō its support. I took a strictly neutral position, however. I had by then dissociated myself from the Kenseikai, and knowing Katō's outstanding qualities I wanted to see him perform. I did not of course support the government but neither did I oppose it. The suffrage bill was again submitted to the forty-sixth session of the Diet under the Katō (Tomosaburō) cabinet. It was immediately voted down due to the opposition of the Seiyūkai.

Prime Minister Katō's handling of questions in the Diet was splendid. Of the successive prime ministers I can think of none who rivaled him—not even Itō and Ōkuma, while others of course never came close. If heaven had willed that he should live longer he might well have left his mark as a great statesman. Unfortunately, though, after a he was year in office, failing health jeopardized his efforts. On August 24, 1923, he died as his cabinet faded away like a flickering candle. It was very regrettable.

THE YAMAMOTO "EARTHQUAKE" CABINET

After Katō's death, the imperial command was issued on August 3 for Yamamoto Gonnohyōe to organize a cabinet. Yamamoto had remained out of power for the previous ten years following his earlier resignation as prime minister over the Siemens scandal. After ten years out in the cold, it was again time for him to head a cabinet. Unluckily for him, the disastrous Kantō earthquake of September 1 struck while he was in the process of selecting the members of his cabinet, foreshadowing difficulties to come. Yamamoto had intended to form a national cabinet by inviting the best and bravest minds of all parties to join it. Takahashi Korekiyo, president of the Seiyūkai; Katō Takaaki, head of the Kenseikai; and Inukai Tsuyoshi, who headed the Kakushin Club, were at the top of the list of illustrious men. In addition, Ōishi Masami, who was without a party post, had also been invited. I was probably the only one not invited among the more well-known of the political figures. Takahashi and Katō declined. In the end the cabinet was not as grand as the impressive list of candidates.

Inukai entered the cabinet as post and telecommunications minister and education minister, notwithstanding the negative decisions of both Takahashi and Katō. This was not really surprising. About a year before this, Inukai had dissolved the Kokumintō to join our independents and the seven who had quit the Kenseikai to form the Kakushin Club. We were given to believe that Inukai had accepted the portfolios because he had been promised by Prime Minister Yamamoto that the suffrage bill would be passed whatever the odds.

Yamamoto stood out with his fine and spirited character. I well recall his behavior at the time of our negotiations with the first Katsura cabinet. Though a mere naval minister then, he would call Katsura by his name without a title even in our presence. He even had the presumption to answer for the prime minister before the latter had a chance to speak. He was always in high spirits.

During his first cabinet, as an advocate of constitutional government, I was Yamamoto's foe. He proved a formidable adversary and a brave warrior. He had a very powerful presence. Even Yamagata seemed to be diminished by comparison with him.

Considering his impressive background, I had high expectations for Yamamoto when he was called to organize the government. But no one can fight the aging process. By now showing signs of senility and no longer his former energetic self, he did not act boldly enough. Like the aging Ōkuma, for whom I grieved secretly when I served as a minister in his second cabinet, Yamamoto was definitely showing signs of age.

What amused us was the way Yamamoto spoke. He made an imposing figure when he spoke in the House, but his vigorous rhetoric was without substance and it was difficult to recall afterward what he had actually said. He nonetheless succeeded in impressing his audience with the prolixity of his speeches.

Few can express themselves so pithily and to the point that their speech is entirely free of meandering and obfuscation. I can think only of Takekoshi Yosaburō and Tagawa Daikichirō. My own speeches bore even me with their redundancy and formlessness.

The first thing I expected the Yamamoto government to do was seize the opportunity the earthquake had provided to drastically reform the city of Tokyo. Since I had the experience of serving the city as its mayor for close to ten years, I submitted some suggestions regarding its future.

I believed that the concentration of political, economic, and academic functions in one city was fraught with danger. The capital had proved to be prone to major earthquakes. It would be all the more vulnerable if we were to find ourselves at war with a foreign power. Unlike in the past, bombs could be dropped from the air so that entire cities could be devastated overnight. Man now had the power to inflict destruction greater than any earthquake. If there were separate administrative, economic, and academic cities, total ruin could be avoided because some would surely be spared.

Granted that it was not practical to disperse Tokyo in three different directions, I wanted at least to remove academic activities from the secular and crowded city environment. Since the Imperial University had been burned down this presented no great difficulty. The university would simply sell its land in the capital and acquire an appropriate site elsewhere. It could be transferred easily without burdening the national treasury. I discussed this idea with people at the university and had the support of its younger and more imaginative members but not of the establishment. In the end the university would be rebuilt on its old premises.

The streets were a carry-over from the old days. As a result of Gotō Shinpei's reconstruction plan, the roads were somewhat widened but the houses flanking them were much higher than in the past. That is, if the roads were, for example, twice as wide as before and the houses on both sides were three times as high, then the roads in effect were now one third narrower. As the Great Kantō earthquake had proved more devastating than the Ansei quake of 1855, we must be prepared for an even greater disaster in the future.

I had great expectations of the Yamamoto cabinet, which was notable for its high concentration of ministers, each powerful enough to be prime minister in his own right. Prominent among them was Gotō, who had earned the nickname "big furoshiki" (big talker), having served not only as mayor of Tokyo but also in important posts in Taiwan and Manchuria. It was in the work of reconstructing the city that the government revealed its true colors.

The session, later to be called the Reconstruction Diet, was convened on December 1, 1923, and lasted until December 23. But the Seiyūkai succeeded in compelling th government to cut the reconstruction budget by 129 million yen, and the government's powerlessness was exposed.

After this, no one expected the Yamamoto cabinet to last very much longer. On December 27, the first day of the forty-eighth Diet, there took place in the Toranomon district an unprecedented and treacherous attempt on the life of the crown prince. Yamamoto took responsibility and tendered his resignation. His government had lasted merely four months.

DIVISION OF THE SEIYŪKAI

After the resignation of the Yamamoto cabinet, Home Minister Hirata, after conferring with the *genrō* Matsukata and Saionji, submitted the name of Kiyoura Keigo, chairman of the Privy Council, to the palace, and on January 1, 1924, the command to form a cabinet was handed down to him by the palace. I thought Kiyoura was a good man, intelligent, flexible, and not fussy about trifles.

When Kiyoura was working in the Justice Ministry I used to visit him with Katō Seinosuke. Kiyoura, Katō and Yokota Kuniomi were good friends and seemed to talk with each other a great deal. In those days Katō was well off, but the other two were without private means and lived like poor students.

Kiyoura and Yokota once taught in primary schools in Saitama Prefecture, while Kiyoura apparently had also read Buddhist scriptures and delivered sermons on behalf of monks. He must have trained his voice from youth, for when he became prime minister he was a good orator and his policy speeches were succinct and clear. Kiyoura had long been a favorite of Yamagata and served as minister of justice in 1896 during the Matsukata-Ōkuma coalition government. He held the same portfolio in the second Yamagata government and the first Katsura government. In the latter he served as minister of agriculture and commerce and as home minister in addition to the justice portfolio. He handled his responsibilities well but he was prone to be used by people because of his background.

The Kiyoura cabinet was heavily weighted with titles. People called it the "government of the privileged" as it was based on the four factions of the House of Peers. But I was optimistic about this nonparty government, hoping that it would be above giving favors to this party or that faction and would conduct a general election in a most fair manner. And if it were to resign in favor of the party that enjoyed the greatest majority it would have played its part well. I believed Kiyoura to have this intention and was secretly supportive of him.

As far as the political parties were concerned, it was no small blow for them that the government had been organized by nonpolitical parties for two years during the three successive governments of Katō Tomosaburō, Yamamoto, and Kiyoura. The frustration of the Kenseikai must have reached extraordinary levels for it had been out of power for some time. Popular demand for the passage of the suffrage bill had been mounting every year and party president Katō was finally forced to withdraw his long-held condition that there should be no vote for those lacking financial means. This mounting popular demand became the main force of the second constitutional movement.

What attracted the most attention was the attitude of the Seiyūkai. It was still a large political party with a membership of 278. If the Seiyūkai were to support the Kiyoura government the movement to protect the constitution would have no chance, however hard the Kenseikai might try. As might be expected, the agents of Kiyoura reached out to the Seiyūkai, and this became the direct cause for the party to split up.

From the very beginning reformist and non-reformist groups within the Seiyūkai were continuously in conflict. When Kiyoura appointed his cabinet, Nakahashi and Motoda, who had earlier been expelled, were in high dudgeon. They complained that the Seiyūkai, which was the largest party in the House of Representatives, should have received the imperial command to organize the government. It had not because of the incompetence of its president, Takahashi. Nor would it in a hundred years if it did not change its president and other leaders.

A meeting of the Seiyūkai's supreme executive was held at the residence of the president to determine the party's position on the Kiyoura government. After six hours of contentious deliberation, it was finally decided to leave the matter up to the discretion of the president. It was then Takahashi's turn to speak.

"I believe," he said, "that the party should decide not to support the government. At this important juncture, as an old man, I dedicate what remains of my life to the service of the country." As proof of his commitment, he would resign his peerage and stand as a candidate in the forthcoming lower-house election. He asked that the others appreciate his position and act with him.

Takahashi was an enterprising man who had gone from being bureau chief of a government agency to a geisha's *shamisen* carrier. It seemed to me that it was not such a heroic decision for such a man to give up his peerage, join the ranks of us ordinary mortals, and fight an election. Nonetheless, his decision moved those present, and it was said that some quietly wiped away tears. In this way it was decided that the Seiyūkai would oppose the Kiyoura cabinet.

Nakahashi, Motoda, and their people decided to try an alternative strategy. This was to split the party by showing support for the government. The chairman of the General Affairs Section of the party, Tokonami Takejirō would have to be invited to join them, as he was thought to have a charismatic personality. The move proved successful. The group broke with the Seiyūkai and created a splinter party called the Seiyū Hontō. With 149 members defecting to the Seiyū Hontō and 129 remaining with the Seiyūkai, the large party split neatly into two.

THE SECOND "PROTECT CONSTITUTIONAL GOVERNMENT" MOVEMENT

With the division of the once-mammoth Seiyūkai, the political map became clear. The government had the support of the 149-strong Seiyū Hontō, while the anti-government side could count on the 129 who remained with the Seiyūkai, plus 103 in the Kenseikai and 43 from the Kakushin Club, for a total of 275. Under the circumstances, the opposition of the Kōshin Club (23 members) and independents (14) was hardly significant.

The three opposition forces now decided to join hands and fight a common battle for constitutional government. The Kenseikai, which had fought and lost the first constitutional battle, would spearhead the attack with the Seiyūkai and the Kakushin Club at its side.

From the beginning, I had no intention of being involved in this battle against the Kiyoura government. For one thing, it did not seem worth it, and anyway I thought that the people involved were not sincere. While all this was being thrashed out in one room, I was in an adjoining anteroom with Inukai. We both agreed that the Kakushin Club was not a political party, and when Akita Kiyoshi and Furushima Kazuo, who were in the anteroom with us, asked us to join them in the struggle, we were adamant about not joining.

The Save Constitutional Government movement had been all about breaking up the clan cliques and divesting the military of its privileges so that it would be on a par with other government agencies. It also had been about perfecting constitutional government. In other words, the whole point of it was to undertake institutional reform, but not to bring down the government. It seemed, however, that the real intention was to force the Kiyoura cabinet out. If that were their motive it would be difficult to come to an agreement over the formation of the next cabinet, and all the more so to implement the kind of policy needed to truly defend the principle of constitutional government. No, I was going to have no part of a movement that was out to seize political power in the name of defending constitutional government. But Akita and Kojima kept insisting in spite of my frigid response. They probably felt that they would not be taken seriously without my blessing. Even after that, old friends from the three parties stubbornly took turns to try to talk me into at least making an appearance.

I demanded that they first give me their word that I would be free to speak my mind about constitutional government. The main purpose would not be served by personal attacks, whether against Katsura or Kiyoura. They gave me their word, and I finally relented and joined them. The first meeting took place in Ueno at the Seiyōken restaurant. It was decided at the meeting that Takahashi, Katō, Inukai, and I would be the central figures of the movement.

I took the occasion to remind my three colleagues that it was easy to talk about defending constitutional government but that they should not misuse the term. I reminded them that the whole purpose of the movement had been to reform the structure of government, but that it was not enough to put on only one act of a play. In any event, the Save Constitutional Government movement came to an abrupt end once the Katsura government fell, and Inukai, who had been in the forefront of the movement, withdrew to the other side to support the Yamamoto government. If we were to put on another play, I insisted, we had better act it out to the end.

They took my reprimand in good spirit and insisted that I join them at a convention in Osaka. The four of us went down together and appeared at the meeting in a public hall. I took the opportunity to state my position before the public so as to avoid any perverse misinterpretation of the movement as a power grab. The three party chiefs listened grudgingly, but not the crowd. They were ecstatic.

Many friends of mine were in the Kenseikai. They spent a lot of time attacking the Kiyoura government, calling it a "government of the privileged." I told them that the Kenseikai was more "privileged" than the Kiyoura group. Most of them, I reminded them, were married to daughters of the zaibatsu. Katō, the president, was more aristocratic than Kiyoura for a start.

When an election was finally called they claimed that the Seiyū Hontō was an avowed enemy and that its members were unfit to be called comrades. I confided to them that I disliked the party as much as they but that that was not the way to build positively for the future. Unfortunately, the three parties that combined to fight under the slogan of protecting constitutional government eventually proved to be principally interested in seizing power as soon as the Kiyoura cabinet had been forced out.

THE FORMATION OF A "SAVE CONSTITUTIONAL GOVERNMENT" CABINET

When the three parties to the movement achieved unity the Kiyoura government was driven into a corner. In a similar predicament, the Katsura had submitted a general resignation, but Kiyoura found an excuse to dissolve the Diet on January 31, 1924.

Actually, on the very day the House was dissolved, I was to question the government on "the use of supreme power and the organization of the cabinet." My seven-point question covered political intervention by the imperial household bureaucrats, censure of Imperial Household Minister Makino, censure of Home Minister Hirata, criticism of insolence of the *genrō*, the need to abolish the *genrō* system, the need to transfer the supreme power, and the resistance of certain government bureaucrats to imperial commands. I had it in mind to deliver a forceful coup de grâce, as I had done to bring down the Katsura government.

According to reliable sources, the Kiyoura government, perturbed when they learned of my intended speech, had made up their mind in advance to dissolve parliament. In the event, the government denied me the opportunity to take the floor and requested the imperial command to dissolve the House. They needed an excuse, and used the unconvincing pretext of claiming that they were taking precautions against the intrusion of undesirables.

So the Kiyoura government fell, not as a result of my speech, but owing to their defeat in the general election that followed. While the Seiyūkai was reduced from 129 seats to 101 and the Kakushin Club from 43 to 29, the Kenseikai increased its membership from 103 to 154, which gave the three antigovernment groups a combined strength of 284. For their part, the Seiyū Hontō tumbled from 149 to 114.

Kiyoura visited Saionji at the latter's Kyoto residence, Seifūsō, and informed him of his intent to resign. The cabinet resigned on June 7. As Kiyoura's successor, Saionji recommended Katō Takaaki, president of the Kenseikai, now the largest political party and core of the three Protect Constitutional Government movement forces. The Imperial order was thus given to Katō to organize the government.

I was against a coalition government from the beginning. From my own experience I knew it was not easy to maintain a coalition. It was like three not-so-friendly people living together who find it difficult to agree on trivial matters. When one of them is dying to drink sake, one of the others is sure to want a bowl of sweet shiruko. At every mealtime they would be forced to put up with each other's disagreeableness. Similarly, the coalition would hang together for a while, but not for long. As time passed it was sure to break up from within. I thought the collaboration of the three groups would last longer if the Kenseikai were to form a cabinet, with the Seiyūkai and the Kakushin Club supporting it from the wings.

Apparently Katō had secretly intended to form a single party government anyway. He could not refuse to work within the coalition unilaterally, however, just because it was he who had been called upon to organize the government. He therefore employed the strategy of consulting Takahashi and Inukai armed with conditions that would make it just too difficult for them to join the cabinet.

If Katō had been serious about forming a coalition government then he should have consulted the presidents of both the Seiyū and Kakushin parties from the beginning. However, he had already made up his mind that his own party, the Kenseikai, would fill the portfolios of home minister and finance minister and that his own brother-in-law would be given that of foreign affairs before he asked Takahashi and Inukai to join the cabinet.

This was a blatant case of discourtesy, to say the least. Under the circumstances it would have been difficult to form a coalition even if there had been such an intention. It was like inviting a visitor into one's house while concealing a ten-inch dagger and then threatening to use it if he refused to enter. The option Katō gave the two was in effect an invitation to become ministers without portfolio in his cabinet, or otherwise to support him from the outside. If they could not accept this, Katō would challenge them by dissolving the House. This simply made it too difficult for anyone to join. At least I would not.

Disappointingly, Takahashi and Inukai agreed to join the cabinet in spite of the flagrant discourtesy to which they had been subjected. I did not understand what Inukai had in mind. In the past he had refused a similar invitation from Ōkuma, and here he was agreeing without demur to join the Katō cabinet along with the Seiyūkai's Takahashi, whom he asked to go in with him. I assumed that Inukai, being a resourceful person, had seen through Katō's scheming and had acted to undermine it. In a public speech I intimated that it would only be a matter of time before Inukai stirred up turmoil within the cabinet. As I expected, after about a year, the cabinet began to evince signs of discord. Inukai went about it in such a clumsy way, though, that in the end it was he who was the one to lose. Far from overthrowing the Katō government, he and his followers were forced to resign.

Takahashi aside, I was bitterly disappointed over the whole affair, having expected Inukai and Okazaki to be a little more tactful. To this day I cannot imagine what Inukai was thinking when he staged a merger of the Kakushin Club with the Seiyūkai under the patronage of General Tanaka. This time, he schemed to overthrow the Katō government and ended up destroying himself. It really was a very stupid business. Perhaps it was a case of an old giraffe unable to keep up even with a mule. The following is an account of what ensued.

REORGANIZATION INTO A ONE-PARTY CABINET

In the cabinet the Kenseikai provided, in addition to Katō Takaaki as prime minister, Wakatsuki Reijirō as home minister, Hamaguchi Yūkō as minister of finance, and Sengoku Mitsugu as railways minister. The Seiyūkai contributed its president Takahashi Korekiyo as minister of agriculture and Yokota Sennosuke as minister of justice. On Yokota's untimely death Ogawa Heikichi replaced him, and when the Ministry of Agriculture and Commerce split up into the Ministries of Agriculture and Forestry and of Commerce and Industry, Takahashi combined both portfolios. The Kakushin Club's Inukai was appointed post and telecommunications minister. Takarabe Takeshi filled the position of navy minister and Ugaki Kazushige that of army minister. Katō's brother-in-law Shidehara Kijūrō became foreign minister and Okada Ryōhei minister of education. Apart from the three ministers from the Seiyū and Kakushin parties, the cabinet had a strong bureaucratic flavor. It probably reflected Katō's personal preference. To Katō this must have felt like carrying bombs close to his bosom.

Although the Katō government contained these alien elements it adopted an austere policy in opposition to the Seiyūkai's extravagance. It tended to suffer from a lack of decisiveness but its direction was in keeping with the times. The main achievement of this government was in drafting the suffrage bill, which had been a long-pending issue. It was primarily Inukai, as post and telecommunications minister, who was responsible for writing the text.

The Seiyūkai betrayed some hesitancy because of its past history but it could not oppose the bill. It was therefore submitted to the fiftieth session of the Diet and, with the support of the three coalition parties, passed the House of Representatives smoothly and was referred to the House of Peers.

I recalled that when a bill proposing suffrage was first submitted to the House of Peers at the twenty-seventh session of the Diet in 1911, it was immediately aborted as the peers declared that they would not allow the bill to pass their gates. But the times had changed and even the peers could not swim against the tide. This time, with minor revisions, the Upper House quickly voted in favor of the bill, and since the proposed revisions were not ones of principle agreement was easily reached after consultation between the two houses of parliament and the bill became law. The Japanese people were immensely pleased in anticipation of an imminent general election for which they had until now long awaited.

One would naturally assume that once a law was passed, and particularly such an important one as this, the government would act on it with the greatest possible haste as soon as preparations were in place. The Katō government, however, was not sincere about going through with it. They readily acquiesced when the Privy Council demanded that restrictions be placed on its provisions, and showed no enthusiasm for its rapid implementation. One would hardly have expected otherwise of bureaucrats-turned-politicians.

When the fiftieth session was concluded, Takahashi Korekiyo resigned as president of the Seiyūkai and recommended General Tanaka Giichi as his successor. The fuse was finally lit on the bomb that Prime Minister Katō had been carrying. On April 13, 1925, the Seiyūkai called meetings at its headquarters of its advisory and consultative committees followed by a plenary session of its members to elect a new president. With the resignation of Takahashi from the Seiyūkai presidency and simultaneously as minister of commerce and industry as well as of agriculture and forestry, the prime minister called on Tanaka to ask him to join the cabinet in the place of Takahashi. Tanaka refused. It must have been a premeditated move. In the end, however, the Seiyūkai's vice-president, Noda Utarō, took over as minister of commerce and industry, and Okazaki Kunisuke as minister of agriculture and forestry. The bomb did not explode. On May 10 the Kakushin Club merged with the Seiyūkai. The plot had already been hatched when Tanaka was invited to head the latter. As it turned out, the plotters were evidently taken by surprise by Takahashi's unexpectedly sudden resignation and were obliged to change their plans. From the outset I was critically opposed to the merger of the Kakushin Club with the Seiyūkai. At the plenary meeting on May 10, however, the majority decided to go with Inukai after he gave them his account of the circumstances. I left the Kakushin Club with eight like-minded colleagues, and at the end of that month, with some members of the Chūsei Club and a number of independents, I organized the Shinsei Club.

It made no sense for Inukai to join the Seiyūkai with the old Kokumintō members. Inukai was a sympathetic man, but, to put it bluntly, he had strong emotions of love and hate. It is for this reason that he never had more than a small contingent of men around him. At this time his political strength was waning under pressure from the more powerful Seiyūkai on one side and the Kenseikai on the other. He probably felt sorry for those who remained loyal to him. I believe that it was purely because of his feelings of compassion for his followers that he abandoned his principles and joined the Seiyūkai.

Inukai probably knew only too well that joining the Seiyūkai spelled the end of his political life. So, to coincide with joining the party, he announced he was retiring from politics. But his electorate in Okayama would hear nothing of it and he returned to political life. Inukai himself was unable to achieve what he had set out to do, but his men were all able to gain significant posts. Akita Kiyoshi and Hamada Kunimatsu in turn became speaker of the House, and without exception the men he took in with him were given important party positions in the Seiyūkai.

Not unexpectedly, membership of the Seiyūkai under Tanaka grew to 139 with the addition of most of the Kakushin Club members and some from the Chūsei Club. Choosing an appropriate time, Inukai resigned as post and telecommunications minister. Apparently, the original plan was to withdraw from the Katō cabinet all ministers belonging to the Seiyūkai and Kakushin Club so as to rob the government of its identity as a constitutional coalition, and after overthrowing it to replace it with a Seiyūkai government led by Tanaka. This bomb did not explode either. Adachi Kenzō of the Kenseikai simply replaced Inukai in his cabinet seat.

By then, relations between the Kenseikai and the Seiyūkai were becoming tense. On June 20, about a thousand Seiyūkai members including its president Tanaka held an ad hoc assembly and adopted a resolution banning any change to the party charter in order to collaborate with other parties. Predictably, the two parties clashed over a tax bill when it came up for debate in the cabinet. The Seiyūkai favored conferring on local autonomous bodies the right to collect land taxes with the objective of assuring them an independent revenue base, but the Kenseikai would not compromise on their scheme to reduce the tax by twenty percent.

Prime Minister Katō apparently called Okazaki and Ogawa aside and highhandedly asked what they would do now that there was no consensus on such an important issue such as the tax. One could interpret this as an implicit suggestion that they resign.

The two ministers avoided answering there and then, but on the following day at an extraordinary cabinet meeting they stated that after giving the matter due consideration they would not resign. The prime minister then declared that it was very regrettable there was no agreement on the issue and that he was resigning since there was no way he could carry out the mandate given him. Other ministers said they would follow him. Okazaki and Ogawa agreed that they too would resign as the prime minister had decided to step down. This appears to have been the story behind the mass resignation of the cabinet.

Once again the emperor commanded Katō to take office. This time the Kensei-kai single-party government was born. Three Seiyūkai ministers were replaced: Egi Tasuku, the cabinet secretary, took over as minister of justice; Hayami Seiji, the parliamentary vice-minister for finance, became minister for agriculture and forestry; and Kataoka Naomi, the parliamentary vice-minister for home affairs, was appointed minister of commerce and industry.

PARTY MERGERS: SEIYŪ HONTŌ MANEUVERS WITH SEIYŪKAI AND THEN WITH KENSEIKAI

Having schemed to purge the *goken* coalition cabinet of the other parties, the Seiyūkai was relegated to the opposition as the single-party Kenseikai cabinet was formed. Its plan had failed.

When we created the Kaishintō, both we and the Jiyūtō were fighting against the clan government. It seemed only natural for political parties to be in the opposition. Yet once a political party has held the reins of government its leaders thenceforth seem to resent being out of power even for a single day. This was especially true of the Seiyūkai, which had been close to political power for a long period, for when it did not actually hold the premiership it colluded with the government to retain power. Having become so accustomed to rule and now finding itself forced into opposition it seemed to suffer from an extreme depression. The Seiyū Hontō shared the feeling. Ever since the collapse of the Kiyoura government it had had to endure the cold wind of obscurity. The members of the old Seiyū Hontō, used to enjoying an absolute majority in the House of Representatives, were tired of the adverse situation in which they had found themselves since the party broke up. By this time some members of the Seiyūkai and the Seiyū Hontō would remind each other of the golden days of power whenever they met. Embers of old love were being rekindled. A momentum gradually gathered force for the two parties to rejoin each other. This culminated when President Tanaka of the Seiyūkai called on President Tokonami of the Hontō. The result was a promise to collaborate in the fifty-first session of the Diet with the object of forming a government. The planned merger of the Seiyūkai and the Hontō broke down, however, over disagreement as to who should occupy the post of standing committee chairman once the house went into session.

It was amusing to see how quickly talk of collaboration between the Hontō and the Kenseikai began, to all appearances quite smoothly, once the Seiyūkai and Seiyū Hontō plans collapsed. However, a hardcore group in the Hontō party headed by Hatoyama adamantly opposed collaboration with the Kenseikai, and a twenty-six-member group left the Seiyū Hontō to return to the Seiyūkai.

This brought the Seiyūkai's strength to 160—just four short of the Kenseikai's total of 164. During all this jockeying for partners, Prime Minister Katō Takaaki died from a sudden illness, leaving the political balance more uncertain than ever. Often I have premonitions about people and their lives, and, embarrassingly, it is the ominous ones that seem more often to hit the mark. Elsewhere I have told how my forebodings about the deaths of Hoshi (Tōru) and Hara (Takashi) came true. It was the same this time with Katō.

It seemed to me that Japan was reliving the history of the late Tokugawa period. There was a repeat performance of the great Ansei earthquake and even of the assassination of the senior shogunal minister, Ii Naosuke. Ii Naosuke was assassinated over a combination of domestic and foreign-policy issues: the Ansei Purge and the conclusion of international treaties. Unfortunately, no one now could come close to the caliber of Ii. I imagined, therefore, that if Hara were to be assassinated on a domestic issue and Katō over foreign policy, the two deaths would be equivalent to Ii Naosuke's. I often shared this rather ignoble thought with others.

We met by chance one day not long before his death when Katō came up to Karuizawa during the summer vacation. I thought he looked very weak and I was left with the impression that he might drop dead of his own accord before an assassin could get to him. Out of sympathy, I warned his family and friends that in the interest of his health he should really get more rest. Apparently Katō learned of this and was furious. He boasted that he wanted those who worried about the state of his health to know that he was fit for anything except perhaps to run in a marathon. This was reported in the newspapers. In spite of Katō's bravado, I still believed he would not have much longer to live if he were to remain burdened with the stressful responsibilities of his office. For what it was worth, I offered my counsel to the members of the Kenseikai to encourage him to take a rest. It fell on deaf ears, of course. The people around him could not see the truth as plainly as I, because of their own wishful thinking, obsequiousness, or personal ambition.

WAKATSUKI'S WINDFALL CABINET

With the untimely death of Prime Minister Katō, Wakatsuki Reijirō, then home minister, collected both the presidency of the Kenseikai and the prime ministership. He was without doubt a child of fortune. Wakatsuki had an extremely fine intellect. He was outstanding in managing departmental affairs. I was all for recommending him as prime minister. In fact, when the Kenseikai was in utter confusion over the election of a successor to Katō, I lost no time in going to the party headquarters to urge an early decision in favor of Wakatsuki, as things might get out of hand if they tarried.

He might well have been made party president without any help from me, but before long Wakatsuki was chosen to be the president and prime minister. Yet I was to be utterly disappointed at the way he conducted himself in that post. One publication, referring critically to him, quoted the following proverb: "A mean man proves a disgrace to an enviable position." Wakatsuki had a fine intellect but a base attitude. Granted that people can improve with training, he might eventually have grown into the job. As it was, however, he behaved not as a prime minister, but like a little errand boy.

It was by sheer chance that Wakatsuki came into the office of prime minister. In real life one has to go through a lot of red tape to prove ownership of an item in the "lost and found." If this applies to any object of little value left on the bus, it must be all the more true of a large windfall such as a cabinet. When Hara was assassinated it was Takahashi who had the benefit of this windfall. In order to make it his own, Takahashi attempted to reshuffle the cabinet he had inherited. In the process, the cabinet collapsed. What could Wakatsuki do to make this windfall cabinet his?

Wakatsuki became prime minister on January 30, 1926, during the fifty-first session of the Diet. The suffrage bill had already been passed by the House and written into law. Its implementation was the biggest issue at the time. It was a heaven-sent opportunity for Wakatsuki to have dissolved the parliament and conducted a popular election and in that way to have made the cabinet his own.

I had expected him to do this and had indirectly advised him accordingly, but he did not go through with it. Instead he managed to hold the government together by courting the Kenkyūkai and Dōseikai groups in the House of Peers and aligning with the publicly avowed archenemy Seiyū Hontō in the House of Representatives.

With the fifty-first session behind him, Wakatsuki seemed to have initiated negotiations with the Seiyū Hontō for a prospective coalition. When he succeeded Katō as prime minister he kept the portfolio of home minister for himself. And since Sengoku Mitsugu, the minister for railways, had expressed a wish to resign, this gave Wakatsuki two ministerial posts with which he could tempt the Hontō into a coalition government. The Seiyū Hontō had already lost twenty-six members during the last session over a bungled compromise, and as a consequence had slipped to the position of third-largest party instead of the second. They now feared they would lose even more members if they went into the proposed coalition, which left them unsure as to whether they could retain the strength necessary to have a significant impact on the political scene. For this reason the coalition never materialized.

Instead, Wakatsuki decided to have a small cabinet reshuffle. Hamaguchi Yūkō was moved from the ministry of finance to home affairs; Hayami Kenzō, the agriculture and forestry minister, was given Hamaguchi's former post; and Machida Chūji, the executive general affairs manager of the Kenseikai, was given Hayami's. Wakatsuki also invited Inoue Kyoshirō to the railways ministry with a view to strengthening his relations with the House of Peers.

For my part, I returned to my electoral district of Mie to report on what had happened during the fifty-first session, which had just ended. Unfortunately I caught a cold. In the beginning I thought it was the usual sort of cold that would soon go away, but the fever persisted. Because of this I had to call off my speaking engagements and spend some time in a hospital in Yamada city before I felt well enough to return to Tokyo.

For some time I had been planning to visit Suō and Nagato, which are Chōshū provinces. I had been three times to Satsuma, Ōsumi, and Hyūga, and had spoken there attacking clan cliquism. In Chōshū I had only been to one town called Shimonoseki and its vicinity and never to the interior. I therefore wanted to tour the area and to speak to the people about the contributions their forefathers had made as well as about their faults. I took the planning of my conquest of Chōshū seriously. This was enemy territory and I could not afford to become a laughing stock by falling ill there. I took the precaution, therefore, of asking Doctor Nishino at Keiō University Hospital to give me a check-up. The doctor after a thorough examination told me I had no business travelling. Inflammation of the middle ear (tympanitis) was at a stage where it required hospital care. He would not even let me go home. As good as his word, he kept me in the hospital for the next few weeks. My conquest of Chōshū had to be canceled. After this operation, my hearing deteriorated and my ears were no longer of any use to me. I did have the occasion later to do a speaking tour of Yamaguchi Prefecture, but something intervened to force me to return without covering a wider area. I put this down simply to karma.

I Advise the Prime Minister to Resign

As far as the Wakatsuki government was concerned I had decided to take a positive but neutral position, but as the so-called Matsushima incident evolved I eventually felt obliged to advise him to step down.

The Matsushima incident was a scandal that developed in the process of moving the Matsushima licensed quarters. A member of parliament, Minoura Katsundo, under investigation for fraud, accused Prime Minister Wakatsuki of perjury.[1] Here was a prime minister charged by a personal friend and senior politician with no less a crime than perjury. It shattered me to learn about this in confidence from a very reliable source. Concerned at the undesirable repercussions this would give rise to in the nation, I realized that the best and only course of action had to

---

[1] The Matsushima affair came up in February 1926, when a developer who planned to acquire and then move the Osaka brothel area requested the help of highly placed politicians, including the Seiyūkai's Iwasaki Shō and the Kenseikai's Minoura Katsuhdo. The matter became an issue in the Diet on March 2, and by November, Prime Minister Wakatsuki's honesty was being questioned. Minoura (1864–1929), educated at Keiō, became editor of the *Hochi Shinbun*, entered politics at the time of the Ōkuma cabinets, becoming minister of communications in 1915; he was active in railroads and other enterprises. Although he was cleared of the charges in the Matsushima affair, it ended his public career.

be the prime minister's resignation. Promising and requesting confidentiality, I discreetly advised the prime minister through a mutual friend to resign. Unfortunately, the prime minister not only failed to listen to my advice but he did not respect the confidentiality I had asked for and let it be known publicly that I, a member of the ruling party, had recommended his resignation.

Advising someone to resign is normally taken as an expression of ill will or even of hostility, but in my case I had only good will and sympathy for Wakatsuki. My motivation for this decision was to show by the resignation of Wakatsuki the moral importance of the office of prime minister and thereby to protect its authority. Secondly, by making certain that there was no room for suspicion against the exercise of the sacred power of the judiciary, I was convinced that this would give an unparalleled opportunity to fight corruption and arouse social consciousness.

At the same time I thought such an action would be a godsend for all parties concerned. For Wakatsuki, the resignation would prevent his character from being tarnished, and the Kenseikai would be able to break the impasse that now hobbled it.

Instead, Wakatsuki replied that he would not step down because he did not have a guilty conscience. I could not believe this. He probably did not understand the meaning of my advice. In other words, Wakatsuki seemed incapable of understanding the position he was in. It was not on account of his guilt that I had advised him to step down. If he were guilty then he was obviously a criminal before the law, and there would be no question of whether or not he should resign. It was to be presumed that he was not guilty. It would be shocking if he were.

Above all I was concerned about the position of prime minister. Today's prime minister was the regent or chancellor of earlier days. He had to be a gentleman and a man of virtue. This is clear from the requirements for high office set out in ancient works like *Shokugen shō*[2] and *Shokkan shi*. If there were no eligible person endowed with these qualifications, then the position would be left vacant. Nowadays, the post of prime minister has to be filled notwithstanding the total absence of a qualified candidate. It was my belief nevertheless that the moral accountability of a person holding this position should be at least equivalent to that required of the highest officials of past times.

The office of prime minister should be a dignified symbol of the nation. It was a prestigious post whose incumbent should be a paragon of national character and discipline, and not just the country's managing director. That a country's prime minister should be accused of perjury, and by a man who had been senior to him in the party and furthermore his close friend, a man with unchallengeable character prior to his involvement in this affair, was unthinkable. Whether or not the prime minister had actually been guilty of a crime seemed to me relatively unimportant. If for no other reason than that he had been accused of untruthfulness, he owed His Majesty and the people a sincere apology. It was up to him to resign

---

[2] A manual for administrative reform laid out for Emperor Go-Murakami by Kitabatake Chikafusa in 1340.

gracefully and by so doing make abundantly clear the inescapable moral responsibility of a prime minister.

Wakatsuki might have thought that it was all right for him to be prime minister just so long as he was not guilty of a crime in the eyes of the law. If this base attitude was to characterize the prime minister and first minister of His Majesty, it would be no wonder if the ordinary people were given to corruption and decadence.

It could not be expected of a petty official who had studied law, successfully passed the civil service examination, and climbed the long ladder to the top to be conscious of the dignity that comes with achieving the supreme station in government. I had hoped that the task would make the man. It is lamentable indeed that there are so many unworthy men occupying the highest offices in our country.

Had Wakatsuki resigned as prime minister and proved his innocence as a private citizen, he could have vindicated his honor and probably reentered political life. What I worried about was the inevitable loss of integrity of the judiciary if he remained at his post while standing accused and then, however deservedly, gaining acquittal.

The case could not so readily be dismissed. Exoneration does not necessarily mean innocence. Many lawbreakers have been acquitted for political reasons in spite of indisputable proof of guilt. This I have discussed in detail with reference to the Ōura affair.

The question of whether or not the prime minister's testimony constituted perjury from a legal standpoint is a trivial matter compared to its significance from the point of view of political accountability and moral responsibility. What made me feel sorry for Wakatsuki was the inescapable discrepancy, which before God would clearly be judged a lie, between what he had stated before a judge as a witness to the Matsushima scandal and the answer he had given as home minister in response to an enquiry by Minoura, who was one of the proponents of moving the Matsushima licensed quarters. Why did he not tell the judge what had actually transpired and relieve Minoura from the shame of being accused of fraud? Whether the law would regard this as perjury is another matter. I felt that it was weak of Wakatsuki to have expressed himself so equivocally with the intention of deceiving the public.

True, there were those who feared that it would create a bad precedent if the prime minister were to step down over such an issue. My answer to them was this: "This disreputable affair is without precedent in our long history. Hopefully there will be no more like it. We can ill afford to have our prime ministers accused of perjury by their long-time colleagues, however elevated they may be in party rank. The resignation of the prime minister might indeed seem to be a bad precedent to those who foresee the frequent recurrence of such scandals. From where I stand, quite apart from the actual facts of the case, it would create a healthy precedent for the prime minister to step down with good grace in order to defend the dignity of the position and ensure the sanctity of the judiciary." There was little more I could do as Wakatsuki did not listen to my advice.

COLLAPSE OF THE WAKATSUKI CABINET

Wakatsuki was extremely fortunate to have inherited the office of prime minister. And fortune appeared to breed fortune, for while the cabinet pitched and tossed with every ripple for lack of a solid keel, it nonetheless survived for some time.

In the first place, the government benefited from the absence of any focused opposition. It was also fortunate in that General Tanaka Giichi, the president of the Seiyūkai, who was better placed to succeed to the premiership than Wakatsuki, did not have the confidence of the public because of his involvement in many political scandals, including those concerning the alleged misuse of secret service funds and the so-called three-million-yen incident.

It was to the government's advantage too that the third-ranked party, the Seiyū Hontō, was too weak to assume the reins, on top of which its leader, Tokonami Takejirō, had also been summoned to testify in the Matsushima affair and had thus lost the confidence of the people. In brief, the Wakatsuki government was destined to collapse sooner or later anyway, and it only survived as long as it did for lack of a credible successor.

It was during this government that Japan suffered a great loss with the death of Emperor Taishō. The era now changed from Taishō to Shōwa. At the beginning of the new Shōwa era, Prime Minister Wakatsuki met with his rivals Tanaka and Tokonami and arranged with them to suspend political warfare and reach a compromise. It was typical of the way Wakatsuki conducted affairs.

The compromise between the two parties, which were known to have a cat-and-dog relationship, could not last long. The arrangement became a dead letter, and the Seiyūkai sharpened its fangs and charged at the Wakatsuki government. Wakatsuki sought to repel the charge by forging an alliance with the Kensei Hontō, but it was clear to everyone that the life of the government was ebbing by the day.

The financial outlook at the time was dire and it appeared that without tactful measures it could precipitate a serious crisis. Under the circumstances, the Wakatsuki government introduced a bill in 1927 providing for the issue of special notes in the guise of earthquake relief with the real object of realigning financial circles. There was considerable opposition to the bill.

The opposition challenged the government that the bill was a ruse for bailing out certain banks and a few merchants who had political friends at the taxpayers' expense. They charged that this was an outrageous case of political favoritism and demanded that the government disclose the details. The government thrust aside their argument by saying that banks which had suffered loss from the issuance of earthquake disaster notes deserve to be bailed out, as otherwise it would eventually be the people who would stand to lose. The bill, the government claimed, was not intended to save certain capitalists, but it found itself in no position to disclose details because of the grave repercussions this would have on the business world. This time the government was able to defend itself because of the solid support of its allies in the Kensei Hontō.

However, because of the foolish remarks made by the finance minister (Kataoka) during the deliberation on the subject in the Diet, the uncertainties of the financial world, far from being put to rest, were if anything worsened. In the event, the financial world fell into extreme confusion following the stoppage of on-call funds by the Bank of Taiwan and the closure of the Suzuki Shōten. The government attempted to manage the crisis by issuing an emergency imperial order to salvage the Taiwan Bank. This move proved to be a submerged rock on which the government foundered at last. The Privy Council rejected it on the grounds that it did not constitute a measure covered by the terms of Article 7 of the constitution. This time the government was driven into a corner.[3]

Once more Wakatsuki exposed his inborn weakness. As a long-time bureaucrat he must have been only too used to caving in to the scoldings of his superiors, and now, notwithstanding his earlier defiance of opposition in the Diet, he surrendered the government and ran for cover at the first murmur of complaint from the Privy Council. As a responsible politician he should have put up a battle by first stating his convictions and putting them to a vote of confidence in the House. In the beginning I had secretly harbored kind thoughts for this government, but this incident was enough to make me disgusted. So the cabinet resigned en masse on April 17, 1927, and the imperial command passed to Tanaka Giichi, president of the Seiyūkai, to form the next cabinet.

THE TANAKA SEIYŪKAI CABINET

Tanaka Giichi was irresponsible as a politician and often up to no good, but as a person he was broad-minded and quite amusing. I recall two occasions when I found him cause for amusement. The first time, he was then probably head of the Military Affairs Bureau. Field Marshal Uehara from the Satsuma clan was army minister. It was learned through Tagawa Daikichirō that the minister wanted me and some others to accept his plan to expand the army to twenty-five divisions. Diet-member Hanai Takuzō, Tagawa, and I met with the minister at a restaurant to discuss his plan. Field Marshal Uehara had brought Tanaka along with him, and introduced him by saying, "I have told you more or less what I have in mind, but this fellow—the general referred to him thus—is more knowledgeable. Please ask the fellow to explain." And Tanaka stroked his chin and kept taking sips of

---

[3] These events were more complicated than the Ozaki text suggests. The banking crisis of 1927, triggered by the collapse of the Bank of Taiwan and the Suzuki Trading Company, led to a run on the banks so severe that hastily printed one-sided notes were stacked at tellers' windows so as to reassure people anxious to withdraw their savings. Relief was hampered, not only by problems of constitutionality, but by discord between the Bank of Japan and the Ministry of Finance, further complicated by the anger of conservative Privy Council members over the "weak" China policy followed by Foreign Minister Shidehara in dealing with the Northern Expedition of Chiang Kai-shek. See Thomas Schalow, "The Role of the Financial Panic of 1927 and the Failure of the 15th National Bank in the Economic Decline of the Japanese Aristrocacy" (Ph.D. Dissertation, Princeton University, 1989).

sake without venturing any explanation. He must have realized from looking at our faces that it was not worth the trouble.

It was quite a while before I saw Tanaka again. During the Ōkuma government, there was to be a visit by a Russian prince. We had planned for the prime minister to give a reception, at which time the prince would be enlightened as to recent developments in East Asia. The foreign office evidently had no one who spoke Russian, since Tanaka Giichi was produced as an interpreter.

As Ōkuma eloquently delivered his brief, Tanaka interpreted for him with well-disguised ignorance of the Russian language. I knew not a word of it myself, but it was painfully evident to me that Tanaka was totally unable to interpret faithfully for the prime minister. It was almost unbearably comic. He seemed not to notice the embarrassing situation in which he was placed. He had a funny look on his face while continuing to talk what must have been pure nonsense. I thought he must have a quite remarkable sense of humor.

Earlier I referred to the nonchalant manner of Takahashi Korekiyo. Tanaka, with his relaxed way of doing things, rather resembled him. It would not bother Tanaka in the slightest simultaneously to be implementing measures that were diametrically opposed to each other. In his relations with China, for example, he saw no problem in assisting the northern side while at the same time helping the south. It is just plausible that he was deliberately helping both sides so as to be in good stead with whichever side emerged victorious.

Granted the undoubted merits of being a carefree, broad-minded, and amusing man, I had thought from the beginning that it was just too risky to have Tanaka occupy such a responsible position as that of prime minister. From the start of his government I felt I must be cautious.

When Tanaka took over the government, he inherited from his predecessor a commitment to restructure the nation's finances. In fact, when his cabinet was inaugurated the financial world was in a depression. In order to take appropriate measures to meet this emergency Prime Minister Tanaka called on Takahashi Korekiyo, who was then close to retirement. Takahashi rallied to the call and served under him as finance minister.

In Japan, where things normally come about in a formal and prescribed way, it was perhaps unusual for a man who had previously served as prime minister to serve in the cabinet of another. For Takahashi this was nothing extraordinary. As soon as he was sworn in as finance minister Takahashi had three emergency bills drafted, including one deferring payment by banks. Once the proposed package was endorsed by the privy council, he carried out emergency measures to stabilize the financial world. Three bills intended to bail out the financial sector were passed in the ad hoc session of the Diet convoked on May 3, 1927. The cabinet was able to ride the threatened depression.

With the financial sector successfully restructured and the 1928 budget drawn up and adopted, Takahashi stepped down, recommending Mitsuchi Chūzō, the minister of education, as his successor. This was in keeping with Takahashi's style.

In the meantime, there was progress in the discussions between the Kenseikai and the Seiyū Hontō regarding their merger. On June 1, a new party was formed erasing their names forever from our parliamentary history. In their place a new party, the Minseitō, was born. Hamaguchi Yūkō was put forward as its president. The former presidents of the Kenseikai and the Seiyū Hontō, Wakatsuki and Tokonami, with Yamamoto Tatsuo and Taketomi Tokitoshi, would serve as advisers to the new Minseitō party and assist its president, Hamaguchi.

With the birth of the Minseitō it was now clear that the opposition held the absolute majority, and it was strongly suspected that the House would be dissolved during the fifty-fourth session of the Diet. As anticipated, the dissolution was brought about on February 22, 1928, just as the members returned after recess. As the Tanaka government had been geared to fighting a general election from its very start, there was much interest in the outcome.

The result of the election was as follows: 218 seats for the Seiyūkai, 217 for the Minseitō, 4 for the Jitsugyō-dōshikai (Businessmen's Club), 3 for the Kakushin (Progressives') Club, 7 for the new proletarian parties, and 15 independents. Thus the Seiyūkai not only was unable to gain an absolute majority but ironically achieved a margin of only one seat ahead of the Minseitō. Home Minister Suzuki Kisaburō boasted that he would increase the number of Seiyūkai seats to 250 by the time the special session was held, hinting at buying over some members of the House and splitting the opposition.

Observing how the Tanaka government had conducted its affairs from the beginning, I had reason for serious concern. When it was in opposition, the Seiyūkai had frequently attacked the Kenseikai for its passive attitude. It was interesting, therefore, to see what policies it would carry out once in power. However, it appeared that all it cared about was to win the election and that it had no time to worry about anything as trivial as making policies. What was worse, they were so eager to expand the party's power that they were not in the least deterred from meddling in the very first general election following the passage of the suffrage bill. These were causes for great alarm.

During the ad hoc session I urged the government and the political parties to do some soul searching. I warned them of an impending national crisis of serious proportions in the three areas of ideas, politics, and the economy. The resolution was placed before the Diet on April 28, 1928.

No Appreciation of the National Crisis

Following my statement explaining the reasons for tabling the resolution on "the three national crises," the House was ordered recessed for three days. As the situation still appeared unlikely to change, a further recess of three days was ordered on May 1. By this time, Home Minister Suzuki had to accept the fact that there was no other way out of the political situation than for him to resign. When he finally did so, the wording of the resolution, particularly at the end of the first section where it referred to the political crisis, was changed to reflect the new circumstances. It now read, "The House therefore trusts that in the future no such irregularities will be repeated," replacing the old line, which read, "The House therefore impeaches the minister and urges his resignation." With the amendment duly made, the resolution was passed. The only outstanding issue was the vote of no confidence submitted by the Minseitō. As the motion was submitted on the last day of the session it was never deliberated and the fifty-sixth session was adjourned.

My resolution on the three national crises was generally perceived to be an attempt to impeach the home minister, but of course my intentions were not that simple. I was genuinely concerned about the crises referred to in the resolution and felt strongly that things would turn seriously against Japan unless the government, the political parties, and the people all woke up to realities.

My motives for insisting on the resignation of Minister Suzuki as the man directly responsible for government meddling in the election were based on two considerations: the first simply on the basis of political morality, and the other based more on a naïve wish that political strife should not be permitted to intensify on the eve of the coronation. From a purely strategic vantage point based on party interests, I saw clearly that the Tanaka government might resort to calling another snap election if it found itself cornered by a no-confidence vote.

I therefore advised my Minseitō friends thus: "Content yourselves with getting Suzuki and be forbearing with the others. The cabinet will be sufficiently traumatized by this that they will eventually expire without further help from you. But if you cut off their line of retreat and go for a final coup de grâce they will fight like cornered rats and, however unreasonably, dissolve the house once again." The Minseitō leadership did not appear to even understand the merit of this simple tactic. Neither the defender nor the attacker understood the art of war and were aimlessly mauling each other at the expense of the political system they pretended to uphold.

In the midst of all this I was not personally affected either by the attitude of the Minseitō or by the criticism of the public. I simply set out to do what I believed had to be done. My first move was to talk to the prime minister about the need to dismiss Suzuki, who had committed an extremely grave offense as home minister in the first universal suffrage election. I pressed upon him the advisability of this measure as proof of his commitment to constitutional government. Prime Minister Tanaka followed my advice. In fact, he had no other choice but to listen to me, because in view of the numerical vulnerability of the ruling party he needed my support, without which his government's very existence would be at risk. My vote was as good as forty-five, and we held the balance of power. For the prime minister, Suzuki was an important and dependable resource. Dismissing him was tantamount to driving a dagger into his own belly. Tanaka took that difficult step— a step which an ordinary man would have taken pains to avoid. Only an exceptionally broad-minded man could have done that.

I was not averse to helping out the prime minister if he was willing to listen to me. Since my son-in-law Sasaki Kyūji was an elected member belonging to the

Seiyūkai and knew Tanaka well, I said I was prepared to meet him at the Sasakis' and offer what advice I could about the future.

Prime Minister Tanaka came as invited despite the press of parliamentary business. For an hour or so I lectured him on what needed to be done to overcome the three national crises. He offered agreement on every point. "If you agree, you must act immediately," I told him. "If you're that nervous about it, I'll be in trouble," were his words as he took his leave. As I said, he was an amusing man. He did, however, give me his word that he would obey to the letter the resolution on the three national crises.

I let the Tanaka government off with nothing more than the dismissal of Home Minister Suzuki, because finding a solution to the country's present predicament was far more important to me than toppling another government. But I could not help reflecting how strangely the public behaves at times. They would readily idolize me for some small feat, and yet ridicule and scorn me for the work of the last two weeks during the ad hoc session of the Diet, which I was convinced did more good for the country than the previous fifty years of my political career combined.

I suppose this was because the public did not share my sense of urgency over the crisis. The only reason I prescribed unpopular remedies was because I wanted to start the country back on the road to health before it was too late. It made me sad to think that perhaps my people would only come to their senses when they were finally on their deathbeds. To ridicule and dismiss my warnings about the impending national crisis was no better than getting drunk and singing the gagaku song "Blessed Peace" in one's coffin. I tried this and that, but my words fell on deaf ears both in and out of the House. If a patient is willing to be seen by a doctor, the doctor has a chance to help him. There is nothing the doctor can do when sick men both in and out of government will not take the medicine they need.

THE FLUX OF THE FORMATION AND SPLINTERING OF POLITICAL PARTIES

As I recounted earlier, Prime Minister Tanaka promised me personally that he would definitely carry out the recommendations of the crisis resolution. His promise notwithstanding, the government not only failed to act on it but continued to behave disgracefully. It struck me in those days that it was perhaps attributable to the nature of political parties or to the declining quality of politicians that the prime minister's behavior gave such cause for concern. The political parties were notorious for their deep immersion in scandal and graft taking. Under the circumstances they were not fit to be given the mandate of government. I thought that there was no other way but for the political parties to be left out of power until such time as they regained their senses. For this reason I would have nothing to do with the attempt to form a third political party in the early spring of 1928. When I was approached by its proponents I turned them away, saying that it would do no good to form more political parties as we knew them.

Meanwhile, there was more meaningless merging and division of political parties. Then, on August 1, 1928, Tokonami Takejirō announced out of the blue that he was quitting the Minseitō and notified president Hamaguchi of his intentions. This sudden resignation took everybody by surprise, as Tokonami had shown exemplary commitment to the party since its inception and had exerted more efforts than other faction chiefs during the spring general election. Informed sources were quick to point out that this was just another manifestation of Tokonami's penchant for power. He had taken this course of action, they alleged, when he arrived at the conclusion that there was no chance for the Minseitō to succeed the Tanaka government.

With the departure of Tokonami an undercurrent of dissatisfaction within the Minseitō welled to the surface, encouraging the disenchanted members to voice dissent against the party leadership. On being disciplined with expulsion from the party, they formed the Kensei-ishin kai (Constitutional Renovation Club). This group of seven members joined forces with the government, which gave the Tanaka régime confidence to muddle through the forthcoming fifty-sixth session.

On June 4, 1928, the Manchurian war lord, Chang Tso-lin, was killed in an explosion. The truth was never made public. The event was merely referred to as "a certain grave incident," and when the issue was taken up during the fifty-sixth session the government offered hardly any explanation. Because of this the Tanaka government found itself in a precarious position. The resulting no-confidence vote introduced by none other than President Hamaguchi Yūkō of the Minseitō suffered defeat by the wide margin of sixty-four votes. Shortly afterward, however, the Tanaka government fell due to its treatment of the "grave incident."[4] On July 2, 1929, it was Hamaguchi of the Minseitō who received the imperial command to organize a new cabinet.

Seeing that Hamaguchi had now won the premiership, Tokonami led his small party to join the Seiyūkai. The last change of government had shown that the third-ranking party would have no chance of acquiring power, and since political isolation would have meant assured self-destruction for the party there probably was no alternative for Tokonami other than to take the course of action he did. Thus ended the party peregrinations of Tokonami Takejirō who impressed one as being a stray child of the political world. On his return with his followers to the Seiyūkai six years after he left it in 1923, the map of the political world at last became clearer. The "certain grave incident" was the veiled reference to the fact that Chang's murder was the work of staff officers of Japan's Kwantung Army, and Tanaka's resignation was the result of young Emperor Hirohito's anger at his failure to deal with the issue of discipline.

On the one hand, the Hamaguchi government, seizing the opportunity offered it by the disenchantment of the public at the bad government of its predecessor,

---

[4] Chang Tso-lin was the victim of an explosion arranged by Colonel Kōmoto Daisaku, staff officer of the Kwantung Army, who hoped the act would lead to the army's seizure of Mukden—as the explosion on the South Manchurian Railway tracks three years later led to the Manchurian Incident. Emperor Hirohito questioned Tanaka about rumors of army involvement in Chang's murder and was

appeared to be doing everything in its power to improve its image by launching a ruthless house-cleaning. Home Minister Adachi in particular carried out a full-scale dismissal of local government officials, replacing them with an invincible legion which he boasted would return the party with an absolute majority in the House of Representatives if and when it were to be dissolved. On the other hand, the Seiyūkai was gradually getting into a mood to replace its president when, on September 29, 1929, Tanaka died suddenly of angina. It was now a matter of great urgency for the party to find a new leader.

There was a faction that supported Tokonami, and a second that rallied round Suzuki to push Inukai. The two factions negotiated behind the scenes and eventually the Kuhara and Nakahashi factions joined forces to back the Inukai-for-president movement. On October 12, with the old Seiyūkai factions falling into line as well, Inukai was finally named to assume the presidency of the Seiyūkai. President in name he was, but in Inukai's case he was a tenant; needless to say, somebody else owned the house.

The fifty-seventh session was convened according to schedule, and as expected the House was dissolved on January 21, 1930. The second universal suffrage election took place on February 20 with the Minseitō gaining 273 seats and the Seiyūkai 174. As planned, the government party gained an absolute majority.

HAMAGUCHI, THE LEONINE PRIME MINISTER

Hamaguchi Yūkō and I were widely separated by age, and in fact not close at all. The first time I came across him was during the Ōkuma cabinet when he served as administrative vice-minister of finance under Wakatsuki. Every time the cabinet met I would see him in the anteroom. "Who is that man who always waits here?" I inquired of Wakatsuki's secretary, and learned that the man with a face like a lion was the vice-minister. "What's he doing here?" I asked, and was told that he wanted to be on hand in case he could be useful to the minister during cabinet meetings.

I had heard of Hamaguchi when he was a young and junior bureaucrat as a man of rare honesty and reliability. I had not met him until now, but he certainly seemed to be living up to his reputation. Unlike Katō, Hamaguchi was not born with a silver spoon in his mouth, and intellectually he was no match for Wakatsuki. Plainly stated, he was slow, but it can be imagined that he himself knew that, since he was reputed to have worked hard at school. At one time during his college days he competed for top honors in his class with Onozuka Kiheiji, who later became president of the Imperial University. This must have cost him desperate effort, made possible no doubt by his physical endurance and natural diligence.

Subsequently I had the opportunity to hear Hamaguchi's views on finance and economic matters. None were unusual and his predictions were not particularly

---

promised an investigation. When Tanaka, under pressure from the army, failed to carry through, the emperor reprimanded him sharply, leading to his resignation. He died shortly afterward.

accurate. His integrity was unquestionably a qualification for the premiership, but I do not believe for a moment that he qualified on grounds of intellect. Of all our prime ministers, the one least remarkable for his intellectual powers was Matsu-kata, followed by Hamaguchi.

Being a serious and responsible politician, Hamaguchi might well have been capable of leading the government in this time of crisis if he had had loyal and competent people around him. I recalled, however, that when he was finance minister he had overworked himself and was taken seriously ill. I feared now that he might die from the far greater strain of being prime minister. He was a bureaucrat trained in the ministry of finance, so he could always somehow get by in that field. But he did not have the capacity to carry the heavy burdens of the prime minister's office, and I had a premonition that his health would not even last out the year.

I was wrong. His health did not give out. It occurred to me that he was perhaps so elated at being prime minister that he had forgotten how great was his responsibility. Hamaguchi succumbed not to ill health, but to a bullet.[5] It was a shame that the life of this well-meaning man should be cut short by an unknown young tramp. More sinful than the assassination attempt was the petty bickering and partisanship that finally finished off the wounded man.

Even after the attack Hamaguchi managed to put in an appearance in the Diet for the remaining one-third of the fifty-ninth session. But it was hard to face a man so drawn and haggard, and decency discouraged anyone from asking questions, which he probably did not have the strength to answer.

It is expected of a statesman in any constitutional democracy to be prepared if necessary to risk his life and to speak his convictions before his parliamentary peers. I queried, however, whether this was truly the intention of his appearance in the House. Did he come with the genuine intention of tackling major national problems? It was not at all clear. I could not help thinking that it was almost undemocratic and unconstitutional for him to make an appearance two-thirds of the way into the session and then to discourage deliberations by playing on the pity and sympathy of the House.

At a personal level I deeply regretted what it was now my duty to do, but I had to accept the harsh truth of the situation. Hamaguchi's presence in the Diet not only undermined his function as prime minister, but was a disgrace to the parliament. Therefore, with the objective of presenting a resolution delicately urging the prime minister's resignation so that he could have time to rest and recuperate, I sought the agreement of the various factions.

One might call it heaven's mischief, but before I managed to present the resolution it was ironically I who almost died of illness. The resolution was never presented. Fate works in strange ways.

---

[5] Prime Minister Hamaguchi came under attack by the services, the Privy Council, and civilian nationalists who charged that in pushing through Japan's agreement to naval limitations worked out at the London Conference he had violated the emperor's right of supreme command. He was shot by a young rightist at Tokyo Station in November 1930 and died the following August.

Japan in the Storm

MY FOURTH TRIP ABROAD

In the spring of 1931, though I had been fighting a heavy cold since March 8, I forced myself back to the Diet to present a resolution recommending Prime Minister Hamaguchi's resignation (the details of which I explained in the previous chapter). On March 18 I suddenly ran a high fever. It was diagnosed as pneumonia, and I was rushed to Keio University Hospital. Many worried that pneumonia would be too much for a seventy-three-year-old man. At a certain point I too feared that I would be taking a free trip, either to hell or to heaven. Fortunately or unfortunately, I returned to the transitory world halfway through the trip.

Up to this time I had been quite proud of myself for keeping my health through decades of rigorous political strife. However, having quite recently suffered an inflammation of the middle ear, and now pneumonia, I felt advancing age catching up with me. I told myself, though, that as long as the heavens were willing to give me life I must continue to work for the political rebirth of my country.

That summer I received an invitation from the Carnegie Institute to visit the United States. The institute had been established with a bequest by Andrew Carnegie to promote international peace. One of its activities was to invite men of distinction from various countries to exchange ideas. As my wife had been receiving medical care in California since May, I decided to accept the opportunity thus afforded to travel to America and visit her at the same time.

I was thinking in those days that while the progress of civilization had made the world smaller, at the same time it had made the individual larger in some senses and more broad-minded. Once, for instance, it was impossible to travel all the way around the globe. When we were finally able to do so it took us months and years. Early in the Meiji era Jules Verne intrigued us with his novel *Around the World in Eighty Days*. Today the world has shrunk to the point where we can do it by air in no more than a week or so.

In contrast, the power of the individual has grown so that today one man can move the planet. Thomas Edison and Henry Ford were such men. Even ordinary merchants who want to do business on a large scale must deal with the whole world.

Because of this paradoxical development of the world and the individual, man is now forced radically to change his political life. In an age when the individual was small and the world large, he depended for all things on his life in the village and on its chief for his safety and happiness. With the advance of civilization he found himself living under the rule of a feudal lord, and then as time passed and the nation state came into being, under his king. Since then the world has become ever smaller, to the extent that the four seas are like one large lake. Under the circumstances, it has become inconvenient and even disadvantageous for the big powers such as the United States, Russia, and China to close their borders. Now they must trade with the whole world.

However, so used have we become to living in our own little countries that it is hard for us to relinquish the habits of mind that this has fostered. We still cling to our old isolationist tendencies even when the contemporary world no longer permits us to seek security and happiness neatly within our national borders. This is to say that modern man is becoming progressively unable to live in harmony with the world as it evolves around him. International conflicts and global distress are simply the results of the mismatch between the state of the world and the state of the human mind. It is difficult for us to overcome Japan's present dilemma by ourselves. We must find a way together and in harmony with the other nations. There are many informed people in the world who recognize this and are endeavoring to act accordingly. If we can only manage to imbue the League of Nations with a large enough vision the world will be able in the future to overcome its present political and economic difficulties. If on the other hand, I thought, the nations continue to be pitted against each other as they were before the Great War, the civilization we have striven for for so long will eventually be destroyed and we will be thrust back into the Dark Ages.

In this frame of mind, therefore, I wished to meet with other thinking people and to contribute what I could to leading the world out of its existing state of national wrangling and into one of international collaboration. In this way I might hope to find a solution to Japan's internal and external difficulties. Such was the purpose of my fourth trip abroad.

I wanted a hand in strengthening the League of Nations as a means of achieving these objectives so that all international conflicts, whether economic, political, or ideological, would be resolved by discussion, or if necessary by due process of international law, rather than, as was still the preferred method, by military force. In other words, I wished to transform the present state of international anarchy into something akin to a domestic situation. In addition, I wanted to do what I could to improve relations between Japan and America.

It was with these thoughts that I set sail from Yokohama with my two daughters Shinaye and Yukika on August 13, 1931. On our arrival in America I was pleased when the customs officer put stickers on all our luggage saying "Passed Without Inspection," recalling that on my second overseas trip when I was on my way home from England via New York, a less helpful officer had insisted on inspecting all my belongings, despite the fact that I was mayor of Tokyo. The special treatment was a kind gesture that I appreciated. I learned later that my wife had written from her sickbed to a friend in the State Department informing him of my arrival, and that U.S. Customs had subsequently been instructed by Washington to give me this courtesy. Later, when I reached Europe, these same stickers made the already kindly disposed English customs officer even more polite. Since it is our hope to welcome an increasing number of travelers our customs officers will do well to exercise discretion taking into account the position and dignity of our guests from abroad.

The first thing my daughters and I did on our arrival was to visit my wife at the hospital in San Diego. Then before traveling on to New York with my daughters I gave a series of talks to Japanese residing on the West Coast.

A Speech to Test the Waters

The situation in Manchuria was already perilous even before I left Japan but it exploded into what was called an "incident" with the bomb blast at Liut'iaokou, a rail location, on September 18, 1931. The fire that had been smoldering now burst into flame.

In New York I shared my thoughts at a "friendship dinner" to which I had been invited. Statesmen present at the dinner included former U.S. secretary of state Frank Kellogg, co-author of the Kellogg-Briand Pact; former Italian prime minister Orlando, who had been his country's chief representative at the Paris Peace Conference; the German Ambassador; and me. Field Marshal Robertson, chief of the British Imperial General Staff during much of the Great War, and General Pershing, commander of the U. S. Expeditionary Forces during the war were also there. [Note: The *New York Times* of October 22, 1931 reported that because General Pershing was unable to attend General James Harbord came in his stead.] Also present were Colonel Charles Lindbergh, famous for his solo flight across the Atlantic; Admiral Byrd, the polar explorer; and Dr. Eckener, who circumnavigated the globe in the *Graf Zeppelin*.

There were three hundred or so tables with over a thousand guests. The most prominent of these entered the banquet room one by one preceded by their country's flag to the strains of their national anthem. I have attended a number of these banquets but this was the grandest of them all.

At the banquet I made a speech to test the merits of my world trip. It was not long after the Manchurian dispute and Japan's position was bad, but I ventured to express my opinion quite frankly along these lines:

> At a time when we are troubling our friends all over the world with the unfortunate incidents in Manchuria, I feel rather awkward talking about peace and friendship among nations. However, the Sino-Japanese conflict is only a temporary question, while what I want to say concerns something of much longer duration.
>
> The United States of America is the richest and perhaps the most powerful nation in the world at present. Every country must be either jealous or afraid of you, however warm and true the friendship you extend to them. In the present state of our civilization, no nation can have a true friend. If it is weak, it is despised; if it is strong, it is feared. Hence all kinds of armaments, alliances and double-dealings arise.
>
> Japan was much poorer and weaker at the end of the last century than it is today. Though it might have been despised by them in their hearts, still it was made much of by America, admired by China, and courted by both Russia and Great Britain,

which resulted in the Anglo-Japanese alliance. We never stood in a better position internationally than at that time. Now that we have made some progress in industries and armaments, we have no true friend among the nations. The United States wants to defend Hawaii and the Philippines, and England is building a naval base at Singapore to defend India and Australia—but to defend them against whom, if not Japan? Such is the fate of a nation! If you blame Japan for being militaristic, I do not hesitate to remind you that it was the Occidental nations that made Japan militaristic.

On this occasion, which is dedicated to cultivating friendship, I might be allowed to speak with complete frankness instead of in diplomatic language. While we were peacefully composing poems, practicing flower arrangement, and burning incense— in a word, while we were addicted to things artistic and beautiful—you did not give us a place even among third-rate powers. It was only after we had built a navy on the English model and an army on the German model and had won wars against the two biggest nations in the world that you Americans and the Europeans accepted us on an equal footing. I say this only to speak the truth. It is not meant as criticism.

All empires and nations are founded on might instead of right. Unless this fundamental condition for the existence of nations is reformed, the unamiable spirit that governs their relations will never be eradicated. Let us try to make all the nations of the world stand on a moral basis by accepting the authority of the International Court of Justice and by ceasing to teach narrow nationalism to their citizens. International relations should be based on friendship and goodwill instead of on jealousy and antagonism. Peace and security can only be obtained through friendship. Canada and the United States share a border more than 3,000 miles long with virtually no defenses on either side, yet they have no fear of each other and they feel secure. This good example can be followed by the other nations of the world.

When the world was larger owing to the absence of many kinds of communication that we have today, one nation could prosper at the expense of another. But now that the world has become very much smaller—perhaps one-tenth of what it used to be at the beginning of the present century—and destructive weapons of war are a hundred times more effective, no nation can live and prosper by being the enemy of others. But as long as human beings are brought up with the doctrine of narrow nationalism instead of internationalism, the sentiment of true friendship can never properly grow. Even the most upright and kind people become selfish and unreasonable when they are governed by nationalistic sentiments. This fact was amply proved by Christian dignitaries who prayed only for the victory of their own nations during the war. Nationalism was very useful in a time now past, as feudalism was useful in a still earlier age before it. But now that the world has become so small, that narrow kind of nationalism is out of date. It must be fundamentally redefined, though not abolished altogether like feudalism. Everything is becoming internationalized except the human heart. Real friendship among the nations can only be nurtured in a spirit of true internationalism.

During the dinner Eckener was behind us, but I talked with Admiral Byrd and Orlando, who were on either side of me. Byrd was the youngest American admiral and was much respected. Years afterward when he was in the Antarctic, members of his party put Western names to landmark sites. The admiral knew that Lieutenant Shirase of Japan had explored the area long before him and given Japanese names to natural features, and had them changed back to the original Japanese.

At the banquet the public was seated on a lower level. My two daughters too were seated among them. Apparently they were looking at me from time to time as I spoke. Admiral Byrd wanted to know if they were acquaintances of mine. When I told him they were my daughters, he got up from his chair saying he would pay them his respects. When he came back he was full of praise for them. "How do they compare with their father?" I asked in jest. Byrd seemed at a loss for words. "Favorably?" I suggested. He agreed, with a friendly smile.

When the admiral visited England on his return from an earlier expedition to the Arctic he was given an enthusiastic welcome wherever he went. He was often asked by women where was the coldest place in the world. It is said that he answered "English bedrooms." It is true that going from centrally heated American homes to England you will find the bedrooms uncomfortably cold. I myself found this to be the case. Japanese bedrooms are worse, of course.

AFTER THE MANCHURIAN INCIDENT

The speech summarized above was apparently well received by the guests at the banquet. The *New York Times* the following morning commended it in its editorial as the best speech of the evening. The good reception revitalized my wavering spirit and gave me new hope that I might well be able to achieve the purposes of my trip. This was a temporary respite, however, as Japan's international standing was to deteriorate from then on.

At the outbreak of the Manchurian "incident," Americans were somewhat surprised at the sudden development but did not foresee any far-reaching consequences. Particularly since the Japanese government had their trust, the American administration and most of the diplomats in Washington believed him when a member of the Japanese embassy under instructions from the home government declared that Japan "had occupied Mukden but had no intention of attacking Chinchow." The minister in the embassy of a certain country who had long resided in Tokyo and was a friend of mine said he thought that the incident would probably remain a local conflict. I thought it would not be good for the future of Japan to let this misapprehension pass and felt obliged to reply, "Now that Mukden has been occupied Chinchow is hardly likely to be spared. The incident could very well expand." But the minister in question protested, "The Japanese government has always kept its word. If the government makes a definite assertion that Japan will not assault Chinchow, it won't." Secretly I feared that while the Japanese government now enjoyed such trust from the powers, soon, lamentably, it would lose that trust.

During the early stages of the incident there were apparently powers favorably disposed to our country and wanting to resolve the issue in Japan's interest. Since the end of the Great War, however, the American and European powers had been promoting, in place of their time-honored tradition of solving international disputes by force, the idea of resolving all such matters by international treaty and consultation with the result that the world had flocked to sign the antiwar pact. Under the circumstances, Japan met with opposition from fifty-odd states in the League of Nations and stood alone.

In this situation I could not possibly voice the purpose for which I had quietly studied and which I had fostered as my contribution to my country and mankind. All I felt I could do now was to try to better Japanese-American relations, and so I offered my humble opinion here and there to improve the education and attitudes of Japanese born in America.

The growing prejudice of mainstream Americans toward those of Japanese origin and the insular attitudes of mainland Japanese involved in the education of second-generation Japanese-Americans were jeopardizing the position of the first-generation Japanese-Americans and even threatened to have a detrimental effect on bilateral diplomatic relations. Though I did my best therefore to change the attitudes of both, I must admit my efforts had little impact. Yet it seemed to me that if something were not done to arrest this trend the position of the *nisei* too would become increasingly difficult and that especially in Hawaii serious political difficulties might result.

The Death of Inukai

While crossing the Atlantic I learned that Inukai Tsuyoshi had become prime minister. I wrote a congratulatory cable, but thought better of it. Knowing Inukai's aspirations, I decided it was not such an honor for him to become prime minister after all. What was more, while he was officially the president of the party he was in reality little more than a lodger in the house of the Seiyūkai. A lodger turned prime minister in the name of his landlord could do very little to carry out his own intentions. While the world might congratulate Inukai on the honor, I was not at all sure that this was really good for him. In fact, I began to feel increasingly that his appointment might do more to soil his honor than enhance it, and so decided against dispatching the wire.

It was not long after my arrival in England that I received news of the assassinations of Inoue Junnosuke, a former minister of finance, and Dan Takuma of Mitsui. While abroad and separated by thousands of miles from the events unfolding in East Asia I sensed the violent confusion of thought rocking Japan since the Manchurian incident. In fact, when the incident erupted I could not help feeling that even an unimportant person like myself might be killed if I spoke up with sincerity for the sake of the country. It may seem cowardly now but I changed my original plan to return to Japan by the end of 1931 and decided instead to remain abroad for the time being to watch the situation. I was not particularly afraid of dying but I felt I would be betraying my mission as a politician if I were to lose my life before saying what I should.

I took the time therefore to travel to Germany and other European countries and immersed myself in the study of politics for the new age. In May more bad news reached me. My good friend Inukai had been assassinated at the prime minister's official residence. I was filled with deep emotions. On learning of his untimely death I wrote this poem:

> That my friend was murdered seems a dream
> I pray it is not so.

As a man, Inukai Bokudō was a person of great sagacity and eclectic interests. He was unusually versatile. Whatever he undertook he was able to do better than most other men. There was nothing he could not successfully turn his hand to given his intelligence and knowledge. His calligraphy was admired even by Chinese who prided themselves on their art. He was a first-class player of *go*. He was also an authority on swords and a skilled judge of them, and was much respected as well for his knowledge of inkstones.

Inukai's broad interests and encompassing intellect showed frequent flashes of genius. Usually, genius is thought to be effortless proficiency in all things. I too used to think like this and envied his natural talents, until one day his wife begged me to "counsel him as he has recently taken so ardently to the study of swords that he has hardly slept for two or three nights and I worry that it will undermine his health." I learned then that when he undertook anything he worked at it without sleep. His many skills and impressive wisdom may have come from a natural ability to understand the whole of things from learning a little of them; on the other hand they may have been the fruit of efforts unknown to others. "Genius is hard work." The Western adage puts it well.

Inukai was also a very kind man, or rather I should perhaps say he was a man of deep emotions. He offered his friendship without reserve particularly to his old friends, and he was sincere to all. If I were to force myself to identify any weakness in this intelligent and warm-hearted man, then it would perhaps be the extent of his strong feelings of love and hatred. When Inukai was kindly and favorably disposed to a person he was not averse to patronizing, protecting, and assisting even someone of little consequence. On the other hand, he would refuse to deal with people however great their importance and position if there was anything about them of which he did not approve.

As a politician Inukai was warm-hearted, kind, and chivalrous and had a charm that strangely attracted people. In spite of his fearless and confident features he was loved by young and old alike. He appeared to possess a centripetal force that attracted people to him, unlike myself, as I seem to have a centrifugal force that dispels rather than attracts people. He also possessed a characteristic, probably due to his great discernment, that enabled him to think lightly even of his seniors. For example, he and I were taken into Ōkuma's favor more or less at the same time, but, unlike myself, Inukai was unawed by Ōkuma and called him a "schemer" behind his back. This was not meant maliciously but was simply a caustic remark considering the Ōkuma's ability always to have a plan for everything.

We had a mutual mentor in Yano Fumio. It was said that whenever Inukai wished to borrow money from him he (Inukai) would always start an argument before making a direct request for a loan. This anecdote illustrates both Inukai's audacity toward his seniors and his ability as a tactician.

When it came to political parties and party politics, Inukai and I had different views and ways of going about things. Inukai had a strong will combined with abundant resourcefulness and an indefatigable power of action. He was by nature combative. As a politician, therefore, he was a man of action rather than one of principles and belief. In contrast, I believed that the first commandment for a politician was to carry out his principles, which often led Inukai to criticize me, saying, "Ozaki is not a politician. He is a scholar."

It followed that Inukai and I did not always fight on the same side. But the differences that at times separated us were like those between two travelers, one of whom travels by rail and the other by sea. We parted company sometimes, but we always came together again. If I were asked who was my oldest and dearest friend, Inukai would be the first to come to mind. For this reason I felt his death all the more deeply.

I wrote the following two short poems when I paid my respects at Inukai's grave on my return to Japan:

> I visit your tomb
> Thinking: you have gone ahead
> Where I too must go

> Still in this new age
> There are ruffians just like those
> Who struck down Sakuma and Yokoi.[1]

MY WIFE'S ILLNESS

As a consequence of international censure over its meddling in Manchuria, Japan was obliged to withdraw from the League of Nations. I was hardly in a position, therefore, to press my thoughts of reforming the League in the interest of world peace, at least for the time being. The swelling right-wing tendency in Japan made it all the more difficult for my dreams to come true, both at home and internationally.

In the early 1920s, I had occasion to warn my countrymen of the striking parallels between Japan in the years beginning in the latter part of the Meiji era and prior to the Restoration in the late Tokugawa period. Regrettably the situation current then appeared to support my fears. The cause of this lay in the utter self-

---

[1] Sakuma Shōzan (1811–1864) and Yokoi Shōnan (1809–1869), both Restoration activists, were assassinated by zealots who considered them proforeign.

conceit and arrogance of the people. Conceit checks progress, and a tendency to isolationism is a product of it.

In the speeches and actions of the time one could hear disquieting echoes of those last Tokugawa years. If those who held dissenting views were to be cut down as they murdered Sakuma Shōzan and Yokoi Shōnan, the country would be in peril. At a time when we were short of leaders, we might then have only awakened after we had done ourselves irreparable harm. It seemed that in our country we made it a practice to kill off great men. We were more or less self-sufficient during the late Tokugawa period so that problem was largely limited to the military. In the 1920s, however, we were on a path toward economic disaster. In that kind of world even a person of so little importance as myself had to fear death if he spoke his mind for the sake of the country. In fact, friends wrote to tell me that it was dangerous for me to return at that time. Perhaps, I thought, my enemies will not bother to murder me if they consider me too old to be a threat either as a poison or an intellectual antidote. However, I decided that it was not too early for me to prepare for death since it could come at any time as I traveled around the world at my age.

My loving mother taught me that I should die smiling. So that I would not forget her lesson I used to have hanging on the wall of my study a scroll, which read, "Go cheerfully from life to death." I have forever been thankful to my mother for this apt lesson, and especially so after I reached three score and ten, since from that age death begins to loom larger than life. Since the opening of the first parliament in 1890 and particularly around the time of the war with China (1894–1895) when political divisions were most bitter, I never left home in the morning expecting to return safely at night. The circumstances were very different now, of course. But for a man in his seventies traveling around the world it seemed that the odds were better on dying than on living. In the circumstances, I felt that it would not be too soon to think what kind of tombstone I would like.

I did not want it to be an ordinary stone or bronze column. Instead of a tombstone I decided I would write down my thoughts as a guideline for a second much-needed reform of my country.[2] It would defeat my purpose to return home before my admonitory piece was completed, so I decided to take advantage of my stay in safe England to perform my last service. With this in mind I rented a house in Campden Hill Court in Kensington, London, and began writing.

For some time my wife's health had been deteriorating. She had traveled to America to enroll our daughter Shinaye in school, and had taken the occasion to pay a visit to her mother in London. While on the boat she slipped and fell, hurting her shoulder. On her return to Japan she was treated in the orthopedic department of the Imperial University Hospital, but complained of more pain after the treatment. She then transferred to St. Luke's International Hospital, where she received radiation therapy. There was no visible improvement, however.

[2] The Meiji restoration being the first.

In the meantime, I had come down with an acute mid-ear infection and was hospitalized at Keiō University Hospital, where my wife came to see me almost daily. There was a young orthopedic surgeon there who enjoyed a high reputation, and following the advice of friends we asked him to see my wife. His diagnosis was that her pain was not the result of a fracture. Shoulder bones are solid and do not fracture easily by falling. He suspected that the cause was a bacterial infection.

On the initiative of the president of St. Luke's International Hospital three top doctors were asked to make a joint diagnosis. Their combined opinion was that my wife had a sarcoma for which there was not yet any cure. They said that perhaps some treatment was available in America or Germany, but there was none yet in Japan.

It so happened that a widow of the former American secretary of the treasury was visiting Japan just then. She was interested in literature and became a good friend of my wife. She told her there was a good hospital near where she lived, and urged her kindly to go there for treatment. It was in this way that my wife traveled to America with this woman and entered a hospital there.

As already recounted, I was planning to travel at about that time too, but she went ahead. By the time I finally started out, she had had an operation and the prognosis was good. She was allowed to make short visits outside the hospital, but the doctor advised that she was not yet ready to make a long journey. It was thus that I left her and went on to England with our two daughters.

As time passed my wife's health improved considerably and she was able to travel. Taking the boat alone from the west coast to avoid the long overland train ride, she reached England about half a year after me. She had put on weight and was not able to get into her old clothes. We were all very happy at her good recovery but eventually she complained of pain in her side. The cancer had metastasized to her lungs and heart and surgery was impossible. The English doctor did not tell my wife this, but advised instead that she should enjoy life and live as usual.

What was so shocking was the ignorance of the Japanese doctors. The doctors at the Imperial University Hospital treated her injury as a simple fracture after she told them that she had broken a bone. No wonder she did not get better. The doctor at Keiō University Hospital knew there was more to it than a broken bone, but did not know the disease. He could not be blamed as no one in Japan knew of it at that time. I used to think that Japan was in many aspects underdeveloped compared to the West, but I still thought our military and medical science were two areas that were not far behind. But I was proven wrong. In the West ordinary nurses knew how to treat sarcoma patients.

The same applied to military matters. During my third trip abroad I realized that the West, having come through the trial of the Great War, possessed advanced tanks, airplanes, guns, and even poison gas. In comparison, Japanese arms were much inferior. Only after I returned to the country and brought this to the government's attention did they finally request a budget for the study of new arms. If we are not careful we will fall greatly behind in all matters. There is nothing more to fear than arrogance and negligence.

Setting that aside, my wife was doing very badly. She remained in bed hardly able to move. More than anything else she wanted to return to Japan. Her longing became even stronger after she received a wire from one of the imperial princesses wishing her a speedy recovery. I wanted to do what my wife so desired even if it meant she might not survive the trip. I asked one of the two nurses who were looking after her to accompany her until we reached Japan. This is one reason why I decided to return before my "admonition" was completed. But as we were getting ready, my wife died in the home we had temporarily rented in London, in late 1932.

I Am Reelected in Absentia

I have had a long political life. I do not know how long it will continue but I am determined to serve my county as long as I live. Looking back at the time of the first election when I was so much younger, it seems like a dream. I was now the oldest active member of the Diet. I thought about these things while I was in England. My British friends appeared surprised to learn that I was such a veteran. To be sure, this was partly because I looked young for my age.

In general, Westerners are polite, so they are very respectful when encountering Orientals. But I think they do not really respect us that much. I fancy it is particularly the case with someone like me who is physically small and homely. I cannot help feeling it when I am introduced as one of the most outstanding men of Japan. Surely they must wonder how such an unimpressive man can be that important. I was particularly sensitive to this during my second trip abroad. In my boyhood I used to think that if I failed to be respected it was because of my youthfulness. If only I were older, then things would be different. Consequently, I did my best to look like my seniors, and from about my eighteenth year until I was twenty-five or so I managed to appear two or three years older than I was. As time passed I no longer needed to pretend, and by the time I was forty or fifty I behaved quite naturally.

Nonetheless, I still was usually considered to be younger than I really was, particularly in the West. Toward the end of the Meiji era when I traveled abroad as the mayor of Tokyo, I was often referred to as "the young mayor." Even on my fourth trip no one took me for an old man of seventy. Quite a few in fact reckoned me to be no more than fifty.

While I was in Britain there was a general election in Japan and I was successfully reelected. Election in absentia is a formidable challenge. When my friends learned that I had achieved this feat, they were genuinely surprised. They were even more surprised to know that I had held a seat without a break ever since the first parliament—for over forty years, that is, as Lloyd George had done. Since they had assumed I was about fifty, it would have meant that I had first been elected before puberty. No wonder they were surprised.

It is a tradition in England to show respect to the member who has served the longest by referring to him as "the father of parliament." By British standards, therefore, I was the father of the Japanese parliament. In fact, now that Inukai had been assassinated I became the sole member of the House of Representatives remaining from the first parliament. I felt somewhat lonely.

I recognize that one's looks and character are not immutable. They are perfectly malleable, depending on one's station and effort. A glance at my picture when I was about ten will tell you that I was an exceptionally ugly child. My younger brothers were handsome but not I. I do not know why but I was born ugly and my mother minded this. Because of my misaligned teeth I could not close my mouth. The noses of all my brothers had imposing bridges, but mine had practically no bridge at all. My nostrils opened to the sky and people teased that the rain would collect in them.

As I entered my teens I felt ashamed of my looks and tried hard to change them by emulating the fine features of my friends. I could hardly hope to win any contests but somehow I was able to close my mouth and make my nose look down.

I am by nature extremely timid and cowardly and I tended as a youth to be passive. If I were to achieve my ambitions I resolved that I must overcome this handicap. Thus I worked on changing my character at the same time as my looks. As a result, while I was not able to alter my features satisfactorily my other efforts were more successful. By the time I entered Keiō Gijuku and later at Kōgakuryō my peers thought me obstinate and unyielding. If people see in me an obstinate and strong-willed person, this was my intention. Apart from whether it was a good thing or bad, it is a fact that I developed quite the opposite character from the one I was born with. If instead of taking so much trouble to reform my character I had kept my original affectionate and submissive nature, I might perhaps have had more success in life. Looking at it another way, I need not have put myself into the predicament in which I find myself today.

In any case, my own experience is proof that with enough determination one's nature and features can to some extent be altered. One need only look at those who serve as ministers in the cabinet. After being in the post for two or three years they generally improve their looks only to degenerate again when they step down.

"In Lieu of My Tombstone"

There was no mistaking that the future of Europe was in the balance. If the existing situation were to persist, it would end up in another war. If the continent should again become a battlefield, the European powers would be virtually destroyed because of the extremely powerful weapons that they now possessed; their civilization would go into decline and they would find themselves back in the middle ages.

All the civilized countries were at a crossroads. In a few years' time we would know in which direction they would go. The sole reason for my persevering at my advanced age was that I might live until then so as to contribute what I could to the creation of a new world.

> I dreamed I would find a way
> For the peoples of the five continents
> To live in peace

What burdened my mind above all was the future of my country, Japan. Seen from afar, Japan, in the guise of pursuing an "independent diplomacy," appeared to be shifting from a policy of international collaboration to one of isolationism. If Europe were ever to be engulfed again in a great war and if Japan could remain uninvolved and completely neutral, then beyond any doubt our country would be able to hold its own among the richest and strongest of the civilized powers and enjoy unparalleled happiness. I felt it vital that bound as they still were by their feudalistic instincts my countrymen should master them.

With these thoughts, I devoted myself to writing an essay entitled "In Lieu of My Tombstone." I appealed to the world to cultivate an undivided love for all humanity and to extinguish single-minded patriotism and anachronistic nationalistic ideologies. We should abolish all armaments from the face of the earth so that we might avoid forevermore the calamities of war in which a handful of generals and politicians earn honor at the sacrifice of millions. In addition to offering ways of avoiding the threat of impending war, I addressed the following thoughts to Japan:

The world's land and resources should be used for the benefit of all mankind. The earth was not created only for the Asian peoples, any more than for the Europeans. We are beginning to understand this truth, and as we progress we will understand it better. The greatest obstacle to attaining this global perspective is the narrow-minded ambition of nations that seek to prevail over others by the exercise of wealth and power. So long as nations are dominated by this ambition there will be no progress toward equality among them.

This is most significant when considering the future of a country such as Japan, which has neither sufficient wealth nor strength. It would take one or two painful centuries for Japan to match the resources and territories of other powers. It is therefore in the interest of this country to pursue internationalism and collaboration with others and to do everything possible to encourage acceptance of the principle of using the world's land and resources for the benefit of all mankind.

Isolationism and a closed-door policy might be feasible for Britain and the United States, or for the Soviet Union and China, which have vast territories and enormous resources, but these are not appropriate for Japan, whose situation is entirely different. It is more advantageous for this country to be the pioneer of an open-door policy and to promote the global exchange of wealth and people. In order to achieve this objective we must inject into Japan a noble spirit and sense of purpose. In this way our country will take the honorable path of speaking for all small and weak nations.

This is the way to save not only the world but also Japan. Japan's future depends on whether it succeeds in taking this direction. It is a choice between life and death. Will Japan lead the smaller nations on the road to equality and survival? Or will it stumble along a narrow path with the great powers of the world and share their fate?

If the world's wealth and people are allowed to move freely, economic recovery will be spurred and the gap between the rich and the poor will be bridged. To secure this, the abolition of arms will annihilate the difference between the strong and the weak countries and bring about global equality, which means security and happiness for all mankind.

Collaboration or isolation? Open doors or closed? Which will it be? You who read this, wherever you are in the world, I beg you to ponder these lines and choose wisely.

"In Lieu of My Tombstone" first appeared in the monthly magazine *Kaizō*; later, part of it was translated into English and published in London as "Japan at the Crossroads."

I RETURN HOME IN THE MIDST OF A STORM

As safe a place England was, I could not remain there forever. I had a country. And that country was in the midst of a storm. During the year and a half I had been away there had been one incident after another, including the one in Manchuria. When one is abroad, one never really knows the truth about events occurring at home. It is a politician's duty to study the causes of all such events and to do his best for his country in any crisis. As I had made considerable progress with my writing I felt I was now ready to lay down my life for my country, and I sailed from London for Japan on January 13, 1933, carrying with me the remains of my late wife.

During the voyage I continued writing "In Lieu of My Tombstone," and on February 21 the *Terukuni maru* reached the port of Kōbe. That day heavy security at the Kōbe docks warned me that something unusual was afoot. I soon learned that an article I had written for a newspaper while in London appealing to my countrymen to take the course of international cooperation had met with opposition from the radical right wing and that they planned to obstruct my return, hence the heavy security arrangements.

I had been abroad for over two years and under the extremely stormy conditions of the period I had become a "traitor" to the country. I was threatened by one ruffian when I slipped ashore just to take lunch. I did not particularly mind being called a traitor. Japan is eternal. I knew that someday my countrymen would come to understand my true concern. However, not wanting to embarrass the authorities, I decided against disembarking at Kōbe and continued by sea to Yokohama. It was February 25 when I finally arrived home in Zushi.

Even after my return the Home Ministry assigned a security guard to accompany me wherever I went. He followed me to Karuizawa. He even followed me on the walk that I habitually took every day in order to be able to sleep well at night. Apparently my life was judged to be in danger without the guard. I could never understand why I was the target of assassins but now that I had guards to defend me the thought frightened me all the more. Without the guards I could probably have forgotten the danger but with them around me day and night, far from feeling safe, I was more afraid than I would have been without them. When I was younger, the government considered me a dangerous character and assigned someone to tail me. Now they sent guards to protect me. I could not help being impressed at the extent of the changes that had taken place.

I returned to the country prepared for the worst but I was still alive, thanks perhaps to the government guards. The truth is that since the outbreak of the crisis in China people were more concerned about that and had forgotten my existence. Even the guards who had watched over me day and night eventually disappeared one by one, perhaps because they were called to join the forces dispatched to China. Now guards only kept watch from a distance at railroad stations and for the first time in four or five years I was free to walk alone.

In the meantime, the military had assumed power in Japan. After the assassination of Prime Minister Inukai, political parties were reduced to a peripheral and auxiliary existence and were no longer in effective control of government. The Inukai cabinet was succeeded by one headed by Admiral Saitō Makoto. This was followed after two years by one headed by Okada Keisuke, another admiral. The political parties had obviously ceased to govern. I reflected that if politicians were estranged from government it might have the salutary effect of giving them the opportunity to repent of their corrupt ways. At first I even thought that in order to force them to examine their consciences it might after all be a blessing in disguise if they were not allowed to form the government for the time being. In any event, not only did they fail to show any remorse, but within the political parties arose forces willing to appease the military, and this led eventually to the promilitary members coming to power.

Taking advantage of the situation, both the army and the navy drew up huge military budgets, which they tried to justify by arousing alarm about the impending "crisis of 1936." They argued that the Washington naval limitations treaty was to expire in 1936 and the nation should build up its armaments in order to prepare for the unrestrained naval shipbuilding race that would surely follow. I tried in vain to counteract their propaganda by pointing out that the danger came not from outside but from within.

The government sent a representative to the preliminary naval arms limitation conference in London in October 1934 to demand a level of armaments for Japan equal to those of Britain and the United States, which caused the conference to fail. On December 29 of the same year the government sent Ambassador Saitō to notify Secretary of State Hull of Japan's abrogation of the Washington naval arms limitation treaty.

Since my return to the country I had been quietly observing how things were evolving, and I came to feel that I would be betraying my trust as a member of parliament if I were to let the situation develop any further without intervention of some sort. On March 20, 1935, soon after the sixty-seventh session of the Diet opened, I presented a number of questions concerning national defense, to which I received no response from either the government or the military. To be sure, the government could not have answered my questions.

These consisted of the following seven points:

1. Of the army and the navy, which does the government intend as the mainstay of the nation's defense?

2. Does the present government consider that spending 46 percent of the country's total revenue (over 70 percent of ordinary revenue excluding public bonds) is an appropriate price to pay for national strength?

3. In the whole wide world there is no country that would not invite financial and economic bankruptcy if it spent so much on its military forces. What grounds does the government have for believing that the imperial state is the exception?

4. Does the government believe that it can satisfactorily develop other national projects with the kind of budgetary allocations that have been made in the past few years?

5. Does the government have the will to rectify the imbalance in the distribution of the budget at the earliest possible opportunity after next year? If the government will allow ministers other than those from the army and navy to freely voice their opinion, none is likely to approve the recent pattern of allocations.

6. The present government has demanded at the London preliminary conference that Japan be accorded the right to equal levels of naval armaments as the other powers, and apparently intends to do the same at the forthcoming naval limitation conference. How does it intend to implement its claim if both Britain and the United States are agreeable to it?

7. Should the next naval conference unfortunately end in failure, does the government believe that it can maintain national security better than at the current level? If so, on what grounds?

I concluded my questions with the following remonstrance:

In life one should guard against the time, more than any other, when one is at the height of success. Ancient warriors taught that one should tighten one's armor when victorious. We should heed them. Today the military churns out prime ministers one after the other and half the nation's revenue is spent on arming itself. This is worse than the days of the Satsuma and Chōshū clan governments. It is not without reason that the military men have come to believe that there is nothing to prevent them from doing as they will. They are even having their say now in economic organizations and academic theories. This is the time when you people most need to be cautious. If for any reason young officers neglect this precaution, it is the obligation of their seniors to reprimand them. . . .

Never since the promulgation of the constitution has freedom of speech been so suppressed as it is today. I do not know who suppresses it but there seems to be no freedom of speech even within parliament. This must be why both houses of peers and representatives have accepted the government budget without deliberation. Publishers cannot print any newspaper or magazine or book that contains any criticism of the military. Those that dare to try have the offending passages removed. Military men, who should not be involved in politics in the first place, and their followers are the only ones who enjoy complete freedom of speech. It is a sad proof of how freedom of speech is suppressed when an academic theory publicly endorsed throughout the Meiji, Taishō, and Shōwa eras all of a sudden becomes the victim of political and social sanctions.[3]

At a time when no one can express his views publicly and everyone is worried about the direction the country is taking, those in power should attend to their duties with great caution. Public opinion formed under such circumstances cannot be counted on to last. I earnestly plead with the military men to ponder this.

At that time I thought a great deal about assassination. I believe few countries' politicians' lives are in such danger as ours are in Japan. Too many fine politicians have fallen to assassins. Since the Meiji Restoration there have been quite a few whom I have personally known. Ōmura Masujirō was assassinated in the early years of Meiji. He was one of the finest among the leaders of the Restoration. Hirosawa Saneomi too was assassinated. He was a leader, a councilor, a contemporary of Itō and Yamagata, and a man of great distinction. Later Ōkubo Toshimichi too was assassinated. There was a time when he alone shouldered the burden of Japanese politics. Next Mori Arinori was murdered. Hoshi Tōru and Itō Hirobumi were killed by Koreans. Hara Takashi, Hamaguchi Yūkō, Inoue Junnosuke, Inukai Tsuyoshi, Mutō Sanji, Saitō Makoto, and Takahashi Korekiyo were murdered as well. Among those lucky enough to be spared but who almost lost their lives were Iwakura Tomomi, Itagaki Taisuke, and Ōkuma Shigenobu, and more recently, Okada Keisuke, Makino Shinken, and Saionji Kinmochi.

Military men are fond of saying, "We risk our lives for society." I hope this means that they risk their own lives rather than someone else's. Men in uniform should have this attitude. It is indeed a fine attitude to have. In reality, however, men in uniform cannot offer themselves as targets for the enemy except in wartime. And when it does come to war, many rank-and-file soldiers and junior officers die, but very few colonels. Generals have even fewer opportunities to risk their lives. If my memory serves me correctly, there were two major-generals killed in the wars with China and Russia. None of the higher-ranking generals lost their lives. We can see, therefore, that even military men, particularly those of higher rank, who professionally offer their lives in service have few opportunities to die in war.

In contrast, the higher a politician's office the greater his chance of meeting an unnatural death. Looking back, I think one can safely say that since the Restoration there have hardly been any politicians equivalent to four-star generals and field marshals who have not become targets of assassins. The list even includes Wakatsuki Reijirō and Suzuki Kisaburō.

---

[3] The reference is to the long-standard work of the political scientist Minobe Tatsukichi, to the effect that the emperor was an "organ of the state," which was now repudiated as lèse majesté. Books were burned, and Minobe resigned the seat he had been given in the House of Peers as an imperial appointee.

In Japan it appears that politicians rather than military men, as they achieve senior rank, must "risk their lives for society." Death on the battlefield has a certain glamor about it. It is even a source of honor to meet death fighting the enemy, and then death is meaningful. But politicians are murdered by our own people and often for unclear reasons. There is no honor in such a death. There is no meaning.

Ordinary people abound but fine men are few. Those who were murdered, especially, were national treasures. Many of them were as valuable as tens of millions of ordinary people put together. The death of these men has caused immeasurable loss to the country.

My Harsh Words at an Award Ceremony

Sixty years of political warfare. It has been a long battle. There is a saying: 'The longer one lives, the more one has to be ashamed about.' As for myself, my life has been poor but I do not think I have done anything to be ashamed of. But seeing the kinds of failures that have occurred recently in political society I do feel rather ashamed. I recall how earnestly we attended the early sessions of the Diet.

Having said this, I must hasten to add that I do not mean that earlier times were necessarily better. Old men tend to say 'things were better in the good old days'— but that is false. I happen to know what it was like in the 'good old days' that the old men refer to, and if one compares the past with today, present times are a lot better. Our people have been taught by the Chinese to believe that things were better in the past and that they are getting progressively worse. This is a big mistake.

If things had been deteriorating as the old men claim, we should by this time all be cavemen again, and we are not. Of course we should not forget the past but it is clear we cannot return to it. We must always look ahead, see what is happening all over the world, adopt what is good and move forward.

By this logic I tell myself that the mistakes of the past are lessons for the future. What is happening today in the Diet is heartbreaking. I share in the responsibility for this, and cannot place all the blame on others. The thought makes me feel all the more wretched.

In spite of these, my intemperate words, the House of Representatives on March 16, 1935, when we celebrated the fiftieth anniversary of work starting on the constitution, passed a resolution congratulating me on my contribution to constitutional government from the very first parliament. The original mover of the resolution had intended that I alone should receive the award, as I was the only member who still survived in the House from the first parliament. There were friends who said to me, "You deserve the grandest ceremony as there can never be another member who will have served the country continuously from the first parliament." However, I did not think this was right because we would be celebrating a mere accident of longevity. Instead I made a counterproposal consisting of the following two points:

1. All members who have served twenty-five or thirty years should be honored, and

2. Members of parliament have not been the only contributors to the cause of constitutional government. A thorough study should be made, therefore, by the fiftieth anniversary of the opening of parliament to identify persons within and without parliament, living or dead, with the objective of recognizing them appropriately.

I presented my proposal to the speaker, Hamada, and through him to the Diet steering committee. Probably as a result of this a few others besides myself received the honor.

When the resolution of appreciation was adopted I took the floor. "My happiness would be many times greater," I began, "were I to be given this honor because we have a situation in which the political parties, including the two leading ones, have matured to the point where they can take their turn in government." I went on to examine the reasons for the loss of credibility of the political party system. "The parties themselves are largely responsible for the gradual loss in credibility of the parliamentary system, though the people themselves are responsible too. Those in government bear the greatest responsibility of all."

I pointed out that there was an extreme lack of equilibrium between the legislature and the administration. "I am somewhat embarrassed to talk about myself, but as you have just heard I have served for more than forty years as a senior member of the legislature. For having served no more than two or three years as a junior minister in the administration I was awarded the First Order of Merit with the Grand Cordon of the Rising Sun and appointed to the third court rank— but the state has never seen fit to offer me any recognition for my forty years of service among my distinguished colleagues in the House."

I criticized the evil custom of glorifying officials while playing down the importance of private citizens. The intrinsic cause of the corruption of the political parties, I asserted, was the use of incorrect methods of gaining power and money. I cited unconstitutional acts condoned by the government to ensure victory in general elections. "Our people do not know how to conduct themselves in these circumstances," I argued. "They do not vote if one does good. But they will vote for the politician who abuses money and power by wrongdoing. In other words, the parties expand their influence if they commit wrong and lose strength when they do good. It is fair to say that political party leaders, knowing only too well that they cannot serve their country without power, risk social censure to collect the wrong kind of money and to misuse it for all sorts of questionable purposes."

I ended my unusual address by concluding thus: "I did what I could, but it was to no avail. I therefore took what I considered to be the last resort: that is, I thought that the parties might repent if they were deprived of the power to organize a government. You must be aware that for the last ten years or so I have with much regret appealed that political parties not be given this privilege. It is my conviction that proper constitutional government is possible only when there are proper political parties and that it is not in keeping with this principle to hand over the government to political parties when they are doers of wrong as they are today. Every one of my colleagues has opposed me. As it happened, however, and in a manner with which I could least agree, the party constitutionally in power was toppled and the Seiyūkai despite its absolute majority failed twice to form a cabinet. I believe you must know what I am referring to . . . Those with any conscience must ask themselves how this occurred . . . If you the members of the two leading parties will be contrite and set yourselves on the right way I pledge to support you until my death."

The February 26 Incident

It was admittedly out of the ordinary to chide the parliament rather than to thank it for the recognition it was giving me. In spite of my reproaches, however, the political parties were not inclined to feel any remorse. They took refuge in lethargy, and the government allowed itself to be bullied by the hard-core faction of the military into sending notification in January 1936 of Japan's withdrawal from the London arms limitation conference.

Not long thereafter, on February 26, young military officers rose up in arms against the political leadership. It was a full-fledged coup d'état. Those who were targets of the assassins included Okada Keisuke, the prime minister, Saitō Makoto, Takahashi Korekiyo, Watanabe Jōtarō, Makino Shinken, Suzuki Kantarō, and Saionji Kinmochi. Of these, Saitō, Takahashi, and Watanabe lost their lives. Strangely, not until a few days later was it learned that Prime Minister Okada was still alive. For some time thereafter it remained a mystery how he had survived. Unknown to me, as it happened, I was distantly connected with it. My eldest daughter Kiyoka was married to Sasaki Kiyūji, who was a close friend of Okada. The prime minister's secretary, one Fukuda, who was instrumental in saving his life, had been introduced to him by Sasaki. The vehicle used in the escape was Sasaki's own, and it was at the Sasaki residence that the prime minister took refuge after the incident.

I too had assumed Okada was dead, when my daughter Kiyoka said to me, "Father, did you know Okada is still alive?" "Where is he?" I asked in amazement. "In my home!" replied Kiyoka. I then learned how it had all happened and eventually saw Okada himself.

The story of the escape is quite extraordinary. Sasaki, being a close friend of the prime minister and taking him for dead, paid a visit to Okada's residence a day or two after the incident with the intention of paying his respects and burning incense. He parked his car in front of the house and went in, lit incense before the funeral altar, and came out to find that his car had gone. Obviously, somebody had taken it. Sasaki was in very poor humor when he returned home and told this to his wife.

"Okada is here!" said Kiyoka, to her husband's astonishment. While Sasaki was in Okada's house, his secretary Fukuda had cleverly used the opportunity to disguise the prime minister swiftly by both hiding his lower face behind the kind of cloth mask worn in winter by people with colds and by putting on him a pair of tortoise shell-rimmed sunglasses. He then whisked him off in Sasaki's car.

Apparently, when the attempted coup occurred, the prime minister hid in a maid's closet and had the maid bring him food until his escape. In any event, this was quite unbecoming for a man who was a navy admiral. For some time after the incident Okada appeared crestfallen and was extremely courteous even to me, as though to atone for some mortifying sin. When I met him again a few years later his attitude had changed and he was once more acting normally.

The military leaders claimed that the two incidents which took place on May 15 and February 26 were caused by the corruption in political circles. If that were the case, they should have assaulted the real culprit, not Inukai Tsuyoshi, Saitō Makoto, Takahashi Korekiyo, Watanabe Kintarō, Okada Keisuke, Makino Shinken, Suzuki Kantarō, or Saionji Kinmochi. They were all faithful ministers who had served in three imperial eras and were most remote from the so-called political corruption. The men the military should have sought to replace were people altogether different from those they targeted.

How can one expect to correct political corruption by murdering outstanding people and replacing them with inferior ones? Even the killers cannot fail to understand this. It is clear, therefore, that the motive for their crime had nothing to do with what the military leadership claimed. Moreover, corruption in the political sphere should be no excuse for the military to commit crimes. There were other times after the Restoration when political corruption was even worse than in the Shōwa era, but there was no incident like that of February 26. Perhaps this can be explained by the fact that military discipline had never been so lax.

The military leadership should have realized the gravity of their responsibility. Yet in the Hirota cabinet that was formed following the incident with the important mandate of rebuilding order in the military, the army minister Lieutenant General Terauchi Hisaichi issued a statement attacking liberalism.

ASSASSINATION AND CONSTITUTIONAL GOVERNMENT

In a society that claims to be founded on the principles of constitutional government, those causing harm to their country should be challenged by exposing their alleged wrongdoing and submitting them to due process of the law. To murder people for no other reason than that one did not agree with them was customary in an age when feudal lords held the lives of the common people at the mercy of their swords. These evil and anachronistic habits must surely be changed. Moreover, most assassinations are the result of immature and peremptory judgments. When one hears out assassins in court one finds that they have hardly any fact or reason to lean on, and most come to regret their action later. It is a totally absurd situation.

One may think a certain public figure is dishonest. To presume to judge him is the first stage of exceeding one's powers. To take it on oneself to inflict actual punishment is out of the question. Particularly for young people unversed in worldly matters, to assassinate prominent national figures of whom one disapproves is an act of gross disloyalty and is unpatriotic. If removal of a certain person from public office is claimed to be necessary for the good of the country, then the case against him should be publicly stated and submitted to the judgment of the nation. And if a certain person in public office commits irregularities in one case, but is useful to the country in other ways, it may still be a national loss to remove him. To give him room for penance and an opportunity to serve his country better is the recourse of a true and loyal patriot.

"Action before words" may in some circumstances be an admirable personal maxim, but when applied in public affairs it is more than likely to lead to unconstitutional and unpatriotic acts. Since the world is full of people who talk a great deal but do little or nothing, a man of deeds and few words is respected. But the constitutional way and the one least conducive to error is to talk first and then take action—in other words, to appeal first to public opinion, evaluate it, increase one's support base, and then take the desired action.

When we brought down the clan autocracy it was through the power of the spoken word. We would not have been successful in subjugating the Satsuma and Chōshū forces had we attempted to do so by feudalistic means, that is to say through military power. Had we tried to defeat them militarily we could not have succeeded even in fifty or a hundred years, since the Satsuma-Chōshū government had decisive influence over the army, the navy, and the police and possessed plentiful military funds.

The Satsuma-Chōshū clan autocracy monopolized the most important posts, not only in all the armed forces and other areas of the national government, but also in most of the major private businesses. We attacked them from the front with only the power of the spoken word and the pen and without deploying a single platoon. The result showed up in the ballots. With every election an increasing number of those who were against the Satsuma-Chōshū clan government were elected. All the buying and all the interventions they resorted to only diminished their support until finally we could claim victory.

It was not bombs and guns that overthrew the Satsuma-Chōshū forces but the power of speech and the ballot. If we who had so little strength could do this much, then when more powerful persons have the courage of their convictions and resort unambiguously to the constitutional weapons of freedom of speech and universal suffrage anything should be possible. To convince the public, particularly the young, to believe this is the surest way to eradicate assassination forever as a political expedient.

All over the world and throughout the ages, the assassination of public figures has been de rigueur, especially in the more backward countries. As a nation's culture develops and its dignity increases assassinations become less frequent. From this point of view, the current situation of our people affords little cause for rejoicing.

If one were to name those parts of Europe in which assassination is still as much in vogue as in Japan, one could only cite backward countries such as Spain, Portugal, and the countries of the Balkan Peninsula. Even in Germany and France there have recently been far fewer assassinations than before. Britain experienced a few long ago, but hardly any in recent times. There were people in Germany and elsewhere, it is true, who were murdered for voicing opposition to the government during the war. The British, however, left Ramsay MacDonald alone although he publicly opposed the war. He was thus able to serve his people on three occasions as their prime minister from the first Labour government in 1924.

Assassination is accepted in Japan because the majority of our people are still enslaved by feudal thought and sentiment. As proof, people not only evince little indignation at the killing of men who may be considered national treasures, but tend to be sympathetic toward the killers. In such circumstances we shall continue to be plagued with many more criminals. There are enough murderers in this country without making heroes of them; if things do not change there will be many more. Unless this evil tendency is corrected, great men of our nation may expect to be struck down one after the other. To remove the danger of assassination from becoming a vogue we must at ordinary times guide our people to respect the constitutional system of government. A few of us are exerting ourselves in every way we can to disseminate the principles of constitutional government in order to enlighten the feudal minds of our people, but this is easier said than done.

It is hoped, therefore, that the old policies will be changed and that all schools, starting at the primary and secondary levels, will seriously endeavor to inculcate constitutional thinking in the minds of the young. Outside the schools, thoughtful people should work daily to diffuse this attitude wherever they can. This is one of the most important among the righteous things that a loyal patriot must do.

My Three Farewell Poems

Following the February 26 incident, Hirota Kōki came to power in the wake of the luckless prime minister Okada. One of the first things the Hirota cabinet did was to restore the practice of appointing military ministers exclusively from the pool of officers on active service. This was a reversal of our earlier successful efforts in 1913 to have the Yamamoto cabinet expand the pool from which military ministers would be drawn to include officers in the second reserve.

From this time on, military intervention in political matters became increasingly undisguised. The military now involved itself directly in diplomatic affairs, and in November 1936 the government signed the Japan-German Anti-Comintern Pact with the excuse of expelling communism and defending the national polity (*kokutai*). The pact subsequently evolved into a tripartite pact with the addition of Italy.

Ironically, at the same time as constitutional government was in the process of being undermined, the vastly expensive new Diet building was completed in time for the opening of the seventieth Diet. I finally had to say goodbye to the old building that had never been out of my mind, even in my dreams, for forty-odd years. It was a joy to move to the magnificent new parliament building, which fittingly symbolized the growing prosperity of our nation, but there was nonetheless an unbreakable attachment to the old one. It had been our battlefield, after all, for some forty-four years.

> I bid farewell in silence to my home
> Bearing the scars of half a lifetime

The seventieth Diet reconvened after a break. From the outset the government was split between those who favored dissolution and those who supported one side or the other in the so-called "harakiri mondō" (suicide debate)[4] between Hamada Kunimatsu and Army Minister Terauchi. Prime Minister Hirota was unable to mediate and resigned on January 23. General Ugaki Kazushige received the imperial mandate to appoint a cabinet but failed because of opposition from within the army. In the end, General Hayashi Senjūrō became prime minister.

I could not overlook these despotic actions on the part of the military. I felt that I would not be doing justice to the country as a member of parliament if I remained silent. It also occurred to me that I might be killed if I spoke out, but I could not remain silent. I turned to my friends who advised against it, saying it was dangerous. A politician has to discharge his duty even at the cost of his life. I made up my mind to face death and took the floor of parliament with a death poem in my breast pocket.

The gist of the speech I delivered was as follows:

> What unavoidable reason accounts for the increase in defense spending? Is this inescapable threat expected to come from within the country or from without? If it is to come from without, will it come from the continent or from across the ocean?
>
> If the government claims that defense is necessary to guard against possible eventualities both from continental and maritime powers, then it would mean that we must be prepared to meet either or both. Possibly, we may have to engage not just two powers, but three or four. Is our country strong enough for this?
>
> Defense implies defending and protecting the country from other parties. Is the government satisfied that our army and navy are capable of competing with enemy powers with comparable or superior strength? If so, justify the grounds for such a claim.
>
> Military armament is generally identified with national security. This can of course be true, but in contrast a high level of armament can undermine national security. National defense must be considered in relation to the strength of the other party. So if he arms more heavily than we do, our national defense will be commensurately threatened.

[4] In January 1937, after Hamada Kunimatsu of the Seiyūkai gave a speech bitterly critical of military arrogance, Army Minister Terauchi demanded an apology, charging the honor of the imperial army had been called into question. Hamada offered to commit ritual suicide if the House found him in contempt, but went on to suggest the army minister might want to consider the same step if it did not. Terauchi remained silent.

And now, has the government considered the impact of the Anti-Comintern Pact? The possible repercussions from Russia must be the prime concern. Is there no danger that the Pact will bring about irredeemable consequences?

I concluded my speech with the following question.

Where does the current government intend to take the country? This is not clear to me. . . The empire has to make great strides, but the government must have a clear strategy as to whether the national development is to be made mainly through the use of military power or the economy. Given time it may be possible to develop both military and economic strength, but this is seldom achieved. Even if it were indeed the intention to strive for both there must at least be a stated national policy, a guide-line from the government as to which of the two will be given priority. What is the government policy with regard to this? In other words, in developing a fixed axis for national policy does the government envisage expansion toward the north or the south? Which will the empire choose, the continent or the sea? Without a clear policy on these issues the government is like a sleepwalker; it wanders toward the north and then the south, sets its hand on the continent and then stretches it over the sea. In this way the nation can hardly achieve its objective. I ask the government to explain its central policy with regard to this.

You may laugh that I must have been out of my mind to produce a death poem just to make a speech like this. But I did it because I am a coward at heart and was full of fear. There are people who seem to take me for a brave and strong man. In fact, newspapers repeatedly wrote: "Ozaki took the floor prepared for death. What audacity!" The shameful truth is that I am a coward. I was born with a weak, meek, and submissive character. Early in my youth I realized that this was not good and worked to change my personality. As a result I am often mistaken for a strong-willed, bold, and obstinate person. Because of my basic timidity, what others may be able to take in their stride is often to my mind a fearful venture at the risk of my life.

Inukai, unlike myself, was from childhood much more audacious by nature. Right up until his death, therefore, it apparently never occurred to him that he might be assassinated. I think I may be murdered. This is the difference between a cowardly person and a naturally brave one. It may well be because of my own cowardice, but I lament the fact that one had to write a death poem if one were to make that kind of speech.

I wrote two short poems on that occasion. One should have been enough, but somehow I thought two were needed.

> Let His Majesty hear what I have to say
> Even at the risk of my life.

> With the determination of Masashige
> I mount the rostrum.

Many newspapers throughout the country wrote of how daring I was to have made that speech. To be honest, I was afraid for my life. I survived, as it happened, but with the feeling that my death poems had somehow been wasted. The incident reminded me of an experience I had fifty years earlier.

When I traveled to Britain for the first time, I followed the common practice and insured myself against accident. However, on returning home unscathed I felt I hadn't got my money's worth. I now had a similar feeling of having wasted my death poems when I came off the rostrum unharmed.

The next time I broke my silence was following the resignation of the Hirota cabinet. The military government of General Hayashi was short-lived, and was to have been succeeded by one led by General Ugaki. I presented my questions in writing. As this promised to be even more dangerous than my previous attempt, I again produced a poem.

> I would not have lived in vain
> If I could but die a shield for my emperor.

I was sure that this time they would do it. Apparently, about twenty right-wing groups were conspiring against me. The police department increased the number of my guards. But instead of killing me, my enemies accused me of lèse majesté. I myself had attacked the military on the grounds of lèse majesté because they had gone against the imperial will in preventing General Ugaki from forming a government. They responded by indicting me for the same crime. I thought my time had come, but it was not yet to be. Once more my death poem was wasted.

In the meantime, the two parties seemed set to pass a large budget and tax increase of 2.8 billion yen, claiming that there was no other way in the current external and internal circumstances. Would this measure solve the country's problems? The minister of finance said he "could not vouch for the future." No one with any sense of responsibility could let this sort of thing by, but none spoke up.

I had to make another resolve and produce another farewell poem. The pity of a coward is that he cannot do a man's job without being prepared for death. This time it had to be a true farewell. I wrote the following poem and submitted a written question to the government.

> From the pure blood I shed will be born an army of spirits
> To defend my country.

I called it a question but in fact it was a personal statement. It contained nothing that the government could answer.

Days passed and no one came for my head. For the third time my farewell poem was wasted. I am still alive today. I do not know how long I will be able to live but I am prepared for death. I do not wish it but I am prepared. If anyone wants my head, let him take it. Every drop of blood I shed will become a living spirit that will work loyal deeds and check those who would wrong the country. I fervently will it so.

After preparing myself for death and having written several farewell poems, it is strange and even amusing to find that I am still alive. I wrote these lines reflecting on the irony of it.

> Each time my farewell poem has been in vain.
> I ask myself, is this a blessing or a curse?

When an acquaintance warned me on a later occasion that an assassin was after me, I wrote in self-mockery:

> I am a scoundrel for having given again and again
> The only life I have, and still be here.

A scoundrel can also mean a good-for-nothing, and I am one. In fact, I am a "gokudō" (scoundrel), rather than a "gakudō" (learner).

Because of my natural tendency toward cowardice, I prepare myself for death whenever there is a major undertaking. I think my state of mind after any desperate decision is something akin to what monks call enlightenment.

When one makes up one's mind to give up life, the most important thing that even a cowardly person such as I finds is that there is nothing left to fear in the world. Basically one is afraid because of the fear of losing one's precious life. When one has made up one's mind to face death at any time fear is irrelevant, and even a born coward like myself shares the same mental state as a bold person.

When I arrived at this state of mind everything became much easier. I felt as though I were transported into a cloudless day or a clear moonlit night. In today's terms one might say things looked a lot brighter. The renowned scholar Fujita Tōkō[5] is said to have faced the danger of death three times in his life, but I faced it three times in the course of two months. Since then, I can honestly say that life has become refreshingly straightforward. I can tolerate things that used to bother me. I am patient over trying matters. These are the result of my being extremely cowardly. But now that I have faced up to it, people commend me for my audacity. It is interesting. The individual, like society itself, is a circle. Where its strength is least and where it is most are often indistinguishably close.

Political Situation During the "China Incident"

The political parties finally gave consent to the huge budget proposed by the Hayashi cabinet in spite of my best efforts to prevent it. But the cabinet pulled a surprise by dissolving the Diet on March 31 when both houses completed deliberation of all items on the agenda, and the seventieth session came to a close.

I simply do not understand the reason for the dissolution. People were appalled and, harshly criticizing the cabinet for having a feast without paying the bill, called it a "bilking dissolution." In the general election that followed, the antigovernment forces gained strength, with the Minseitō securing 79 seats, the Seiyūkai 175, and the Shakai Taishūtō (Social Mass Party) 35. On May 31, the Hayashi cabinet, unable to live with this turn of events, resigned.

On June 4, 1937, following the fall of Hayashi, a government was formed by Konoe Fumimaro. A little more than a month later, on July 7, the "China Incident" occurred. At first the government insisted that it was adopting a policy of "nonexpansion." Eventually, however, it was dragged into the fighting throughout the

---

[5] Fujita (1806–1855) was a leading theorist of imperial loyalism of the Mito domain.

whole Chinese theater of war, but the cabinet closed the way to resolving the conflict by refusing to negotiate with Chiang Kai-shek.

With things as they were I felt that any advice from me would be wasted, and I kept my silence for a while. But on the so-called Nishio issue, I could no longer contain myself. On March 16, as the seventy-third session of the Diet was nearing its end, Nishio Suehiro of the Social Mass Party was about to be expelled from the House of Representatives on account of a speech he had delivered on the national mobilization bill, a subject the Diet had adopted as its main topic for deliberation.

Nishio had not opposed the bill itself, but with the intention of encouraging the Konoe cabinet had expressed himself carelessly: "As Hitler has done, as Mussolini has done, and as Stalin, I feel we should boldly go where Japan is destined to go." The government considered this cause enough to subject Nishio to disciplinary action. Notwithstanding the fact that when some members of the House called on him to withdraw his statement Nishio had promptly obliged, the Seiyūkai and Minseitō parties succeeded in pushing the resolution through on the strength of their majority.

I did not know Nishio personally, nor had I any relationship with his Social Populist Party. But I felt it necessary to intervene on principle. It would be ethically suicidal for a parliamentary government to rob one of its members of the freedom of speech. There would be no future for constitutional democracy if the party in power could arbitrarily expel any member it so willed. This sort of unreasonable expulsion could not be permitted.

Unfortunately, I am an old man and hard of hearing. I knew I could not argue my point successfully in the chamber. So I had myself appointed as a member of the disciplinary committee and asked for the floor. I repeated in both the plenary session and before the committee the exact words that had been the undoing of Nishio. But unlike Nishio I did not withdraw them. Instead, I challenged them, saying, "If Nishio's words were so offensive as to deserve his expulsion, then I should deserve it all the more for my refusal, unlike Nishio, to withdraw those very same words. Gentlemen, I am afraid you will have to expel me before you do the same to Nishio."

In the past I had successfully saved Shimada Saburō from expulsion by resorting to the same method. This time it did not work. A majority of the members made an unreasonable distinction between us, contending "Ozaki and Nishio are different persons altogether" and, ignoring my challenge, proceeded to expel Nishio. Political parties timidly submit to the strong but use violence against the weak. If this were the case there was no way the parties could be reborn.

Prior to this incident in the House, some of my colleagues had taken the initiative to have a bronze statue of me placed prominently within the new Diet building. It would have been done had I not now chastised them, saying, "Rather than have a bronze statue made of me, I would ask that the honorable members reflect on their conscience, return to their calling and cancel the disciplinary action against Nishio."

A year before the conflict broke out in China, Hitler had announced the remilitarization of the Rhineland and abrogated the Locarno Treaty. The German army advanced openly into the Rhineland. Italy and Britain were at odds over Ethiopia. The rift between Germany and France had prompted closer relations between France and both Britain and the Soviet Union. Simultaneously, Germany and Italy were drawing rapidly together. Europe was split between the German-Italian camp and the forces of the three other powers. It was on the verge of another major war.

In November 1937, Italy joined the Anti-Comintern Pact Japan and Germany had signed one year earlier. A war in Europe would be likely to develop into a world war. I had cause to worry over possible developments for Japan under these circumstances and found it difficult to sleep at night. But whatever I said fell on deaf ears within the government and the military. When even the political parties refused to listen I had no choice but to remain silent.

It seemed to me that the whole nation had gone crazy. Sometimes I would pinch myself to see if I was the one who had gone mad. But no, it was not I but the people who had lost their mind. By this time very few people would take the trouble to listen to me. Of the numerous Gakudōkais (Ozaki support groups) scatttered throughout the country, the most committed was the Nagoya Gakudō-kai, which organized general meetings faithfully twice a year and asked me each time to address them. Even they held their last general meeting in the spring of 1939, after their leaders were cautioned by the civil and military police that they would be reprimanded if they heard me out.

At that last general meeting in Nagoya I shared my thoughts on China and Europe, which were in the main as follows. It was my last public speech until the end of the Pacific War.

No one knows at this time how our present relations with China will be resolved. They could be settled if we put our mind to it, but it appears that few seriously so intend. For example, it would seem that the majority in this country are not disposed to deal with Chiang Kai-shek.[6] Peace, however, is of no use unless it is made with the party with which one is at war. There is no way to put the quarrel to rest if we say that we will not make up with our adversary but with someone else. For reasons known only to them our people say they do not wish to deal with Chiang Kai-shek. Yet for three years they have fought against him. How can there be a settlement in these circumstances? If things are to continue in this way, a settlement seems remote.

Yet a godsend may be forthcoming from another quarter. By this I refer to the state of things in Europe. . . . A major war in Europe would help greatly to settle the Chinese problem. Not only this, but Japan would also be in a position promptly to regain the ten or twenty billion yen it has lavished on its involvement in China. Money would come falling from heaven. All you have to do is recall the last great war in Europe. . . .

---

[6] In January 1938 Prime Minister Konoe, in a fateful decision, announced that Japan would refuse to deal with the Chinese government and looked forward to the establishment of a new regime. Japan was now committed to the total destruction of the Chiang government.

And if war should indeed break out in Europe, Japan must think hard whether it is better for it to join Germany and Italy or to be on the side of Britain, France and the United States.

The United States may be expected to join in the war sooner or later. If Japan were to join Germany and Italy and make an enemy of Britain, France, and the United States, Japan, unlike in the last world war, would have to fight the Anglo-American navies alone. This would be a formidable task. Even were we to win, it would be at the expense of enormous sacrifice. . . . What would be gained by victory at such a cost?

On the other hand, if we were to join the British, American, and French forces against Germany and Italy, just as in the last war, Japan would still remain more or less disengaged, since there would be no need to dispatch our army or navy to Europe. It would in fact cause immense complications if we tried.

If we remained neutral, however, the Anglo-American and French forces would humor Japan so as not to have the security of their bases in the orient undermined. And Germany and Italy would do their utmost to please Japan in order to persuade us to oppose their enemies.

If Japan were to maintain its neutrality in the case of war in Europe, it would be well-positioned to become a main actor in the Orient—indeed in the world. With this god-sent opportunity, we would have to be mad to want to share the destruction that will befall Europe. . . .

CHALLENGING THE IMPERIAL RULE ASSISTANCE ASSOCIATION (TAISEI YOKUSANKAI)

The conflict with China was unresolved and the threat of a second world war loomed ever larger in Europe. On January 5, 1939, Prime Minister Konoe resigned after only a year and seven months in office, and a new government was formed by Hiranuma Kiichirō, chairman of the Privy Council.

At that time, Hiranuma was considered to be the very symbol of the right wing. I knew his character well as he was serving as the chief prosecutor when I was minister of justice in the Ōkuma cabinet. My impression was that he was an extremely indecisive sort of bureaucrat, rather than what he was generally feared to be.

As was expected, the cabinet met a dozen times or so and still could not make up its mind about allying itself militarily with Germany. Meanwhile, when Germany signed a nonaggression pact with the Soviet Union, the cabinet resigned, saying lamely, "The European situation is singularly unfathomable and strange."

The next man to receive the imperial appointment was General Abe Nobuyuki. His government lasted some four months. And on January 15, 1940, the responsibility passed in turn to Admiral Yonai Mitsumasa.

The Second World War had broken out the year before with Britain and France declaring war on Germany. The Japanese government had not even been able to resolve the conflict with China and the country's relations with Britain, the United

States, and the Soviet Union were becoming increasingly tense. By now the political parties were not only completely debilitated, but some members even talked of their dissolution. In the end both the Seiyūkai and the Minseitō were in fact dissolved.

In the middle of all this, the Yonai cabinet submitted its resignation on July 16 and the second Konoe cabinet was born. The Konoe government strengthened the Anti-Comintern Pact, my advice to maintain the country's neutrality notwithstanding, and on September 27 it signed a military alliance with Germany and Italy. Thus was Japan committed on the side of Germany in the Second World War. The government had led Japan onto the path I had most feared since the beginning of the incident in China—that is to say, to commit suicide with Germany and Italy.

As the government pressed on forcefully with its mistaken foreign policy, it rationalized the suppression of public opinion and was set on taking the road to dictatorship. On October 12 the government established what it called the Imperial Rule Assistance Association, with the prime minister naming himself its president. By declaring the organ an integral part of the government, it gave it virtually unrestrained access to the country's financial resources.

To my further amazement, the Imperial Rule Assistance Association established within itself a parliamentary division charged with securing the subservience of the Diet. Members of parliament became the handmaids of the association, totally neglecting their position and responsibilities under the constitution. It is true that the weakness of the political parties had invited this. But the apathy of the party members was what was most to be lamented in the interest of constitutional government and the nation.

There was another thing that escaped my understanding. This was the change of government four or five times in the course of the major conflict with China. A politician called to serve the nation as a minister in the cabinet should serve it as long as he lives. There is no excuse whatsoever for him to resign when the nation is at war. But they all seemed to think nothing of their responsibilities as they came and went at will. I find it impossible in my conscience to explain how anyone can be serious who so readily abdicates his duty.

The manner in which ministers can so casually resign their appointments is simply not acceptable. If they have no resources to continue their service to the nation they should take it upon themselves to end their political lives. In fact they should be prepared to spend the rest of their days as dead men, never to reappear in public. It is indeed the height of irresponsibility that they continue shamelessly to occupy public positions after their resignation from ministerial office.

I believe there is no other country in the whole world whose leaders can match ours for fickleness. It would be an obvious anachronism today, but in feudal times a public servant would take responsibility for not being able to live up to the rigors of his office by taking his own life with a sword to his stomach. This is no time for *harakiri*, but it is my conviction that such a person should at least have a sufficient sense of responsibility to disappear altogether from public life. Everywhere else, prime ministers are risking their lives in the service of their countries. It is deplorable that in Japan they can so fecklessly resign.

I could not let the Imperial Assistance Rule Association go unchallenged in the Diet. Nor could I let pass without protest the axis pact, which was driving Japan onto such a perilous road. So when the seventy-sixth Diet was convened I submitted the "Question concerning government leadership in the changing situation." In taking the floor I was once again prepared to face death.

From the way things were developing at that time I could see that the country would go to war against Britain and America whatever I said. At the outbreak of war it was only too possible that some ruffian would kill me as his war cry. It could happen any time. I would take the rostrum and state my thoughts fully prepared.

But when my question was submitted in writing, a majority of the ministers of the cabinet and of my fellow members of the House prevented my taking the floor. In order to take the floor at a plenary session one had to have twenty-five or more supporters. I spent three days trying to win the required support but failed to find the necessary numbers. It had never before happened in all my fifty-odd years in the Diet that members of parliament thus suppressed the parliamentary activities of a man who had served the House since its beginning.

The main motive of those who did not support me was to protect themselves. They feared that I would be attacking the government and the military and even the majority among them in the House. Many may also have thought that they might find themselves in a difficult situation if they supported my taking the floor, since they would be branded as opponents of the military. There were some too who did not support me because they were concerned for my safety. If I were to state my views honestly I would not be permitted to return home without incident. I would lose my life either on the rostrum or on my way home. They could not allow this. I appreciated their thoughtfulness, but I was frustrated at having been prevented from carrying out my intention. In short, I was not permitted to rise.

The Pacific War and Its Aftermath

EARLY VICTORIES AND A STAGED ELECTION BY THE IMPERIAL RULE ASSISTANCE ASSOCIATION

After the conclusion of the Tripartite Pact between Japan, Germany, and Italy in September 1940, American sentiment toward Japan deteriorated. As the strain in Japan-U.S. relations intensified, consultative talks were begun between the two governments at the end of 1940 with a view to adjusting relations. Official negotiations began in April 1941 and a basic understanding was reached.

Within the Japanese government, however, there were pro-Germans such as Foreign Minister Matsuoka Yōsuke, who schemed and manipulated. Overseas, the Japanese Army had advanced into Indochina. American public opinion against Japan worsened and the U.S. administration began to distance itself from Matsuoka. As a result, Prime Minister Konoe Fumimaro submitted the resignation of the whole cabinet to force Matsuoka out, and subsequently received the imperial mandate to organize his third cabinet.

The third Konoe cabinet attempted to resuscitate Japan-U.S. relations, and a conference was held at the White House beginning November 17. But within the cabinet, Army Minister Tōjō Hideki, with the backing of the Army, insisted forcefully that negotiations with the U.S. be suspended. Prime Minister Konoe and Army Minister Tōjō were at loggerheads. Finally, Konoe was forced to resign and the Tōjō cabinet was born.

So it was that on December 8 Japan launched the Greater East Asia War (later to be known as the Pacific War) against Britain and America. The news was greeted with nationwide rapture due to the unexpected success of the surprise attack on Pearl Harbor.

At that time I occupied a room in Rakuzansō Villa in Ikenodaira, Niigata, which was managed by my son-in-law Sasaki Kiyuji. What worried me most on learning that Japan was at war was the jubilant response of the people. I expressed my reaction in the following verses:

> Forget not how the arrogant victor of Okehazama [Nobunaga]
>   was taken by surprise at Honnōji
>
> How foolish to deceive oneself into thinking one will prevail in a game of chess
>   without any possibility of checkmate.

On December 17 the Tōjō government called the seventy-eighth Special Session of the Diet, which was followed on December 26 by the opening of the seventy-ninth Ordinary Session. The main objective of both was to approve emergency defense expenditure.

In April 1942, five months after the war had begun, the Tōjō government held a general election that was to have taken place the previous year under Konoe. But Konoe's government had extended the current political term by one year saying that it was undesirable for the nation to indulge in an election while at war.

By this logic, with the country pitted against the combined might of Britain and America, a far more formidable foe than China, the general election should have been postponed further, but the Tōjō government forced it, claiming that it had been called in obedience to the will of the people. The government's claim to respect the will of the people sounded plausible, but in fact the ruling military clique simply found it an expedient tactic to seduce the people when they were drunk with the unexpected victories on the battlefield, and to elect puppet politicians who would meekly endorse the government's conduct of the war.

It was an unreasonable scheme. In view of the fact that there had been argument even over the war with China, it was irrational to suppose that the government could elicit the full support of the people for a war against the Anglo-American peoples. There was no way of knowing what the outcome would be if a general election were to be carried out under normal procedures.

As it was, the government had General Abe Nobuyuki from the Army, which had earlier recommended General Tōjō as prime minister, hastily put together a political organization called the Imperial Rule Assistance Association. Having named it the ruling government party, they then called the election.

Historically, our elections have been distorted by the superstition that success requires three *ban*: *kaban*, *kanban*, and *jiban*—a briefcase (full of money), a signboard (publicity), and influence (political base). With these criteria, the party in power has the advantage every time.

As if this were not enough, the Imperial Rule Assistance Association gave its exclusive endorsement to a slate of candidates it designated "important national figures." With the connivance of the government, these "recommended candidates" were given every convenience. Those of us who did not fall into this category, the "non-recommended candidates," not only had to fight the election without such assistance, but had to suffer official pressure and bureaucratic intervention as though we were "undesirable national figures." The result of the election was clear before it was fought.

Needless to say, the election would accurately reflect public opinion and the people's will only if it were absolutely fair and free from intervention by the government. With the government abusing its power to influence the outcome, true public opinion was silenced and the people's will suppressed. An election manipulated to suit the government in power would misrepresent the people's will and lead the country astray.

I was enormously fearful of the evolving situation. While the society at large, terrorized by the special police, kept its criticism of the government in check, I felt I had to do all I could to protect the Imperial Constitution, the basic law of the country, which would ensure the enduring respect of the Imperial Family and the happiness of the people. I therefore sent the following open letter to Prime

Minister Tōjō asking him to rethink his course of action and cancel the Imperial Rule Assistance election.

To His Excellency Prime Minister Tōjō

Your Excellency,

I write this letter for our country's sake and yours.

Surely Your Excellency must appreciate that the Imperial Constitution was granted by His Majesty, the Meiji Emperor, after painstaking labor and out of consideration for the good of the Imperial Family and the people, and that with regard to its application the emperor has time and again called upon successive prime ministers not to stray from the true meaning of constitutional government.

I must lament for your own sake that, in spite of the above, the Imperial Rule Assistance Association (Yokusankai), over which Your Excellency presides and which functions at colossal expense to the nation, has intervened in the general election directly and indirectly even so far as to recommend candidates.

This is nothing less than electoral manipulation and a flagrantly unconstitutional act which is but a step toward the appointment of parliament by government.

This is a situation, moreover, which could compromise the present painstakingly earned state of national unity and trigger conditions leading to disunion and strife.

While I believe the best course of action for the country and for yourself would be to withdraw the prerogative of the Imperial Rule Assistance Association to recommend candidates for election to the Diet, let us for the time being set this aside. I earnestly pray, therefore, that you will sternly instruct the association and government officials throughout the country never to interfere in elections but to assume a strictly just and neutral attitude thereto.

Ozaki Yukio
April 1942

Postscript:

While the above refers only simply to the subject, I wish you to know, since it touches on the principle of constitutional government, that I intend to have it treated as an open letter.

It was quite an unpretentious letter and did not exceed the bounds of common sense in the way in which it referred to constitutional government, yet even this was risky at that time.

I AM INDICTED FOR LÈSE MAJESTÉ

As I was at the top of the list of hated "undesirable persons" from the point of view of the Tōjō government, I was obliged to stand as a non-recommended candidate. I expected the government to apply particularly strong pressure against me. In these circumstances, I feared I might even lose the election this time after retaining my seat for fifty consecutive years since the opening of the parliament.

I thought to myself that should I lose the election it might at least arouse the people. Since they were so used to my being returned to the House, their attention would be drawn if I were to lose. They might even ask why.

I was eighty-five years old by Japanese counting, and I fought the campaign as if it were my last. A statement I prepared titled "Consulting the voters about my last service to the nation" began with a poem.

> For the cause of good government
> I am prepared to die fighting within these walls.[1]

I explained that the purpose of my candidacy was to protect and promote the constitution.

Even this explanatory letter was mauled by the government censorship to such an extent that it hardly made sense. For instance they deleted the sentence, "Our so-called constitutional government has gradually become so distorted that the lives of the common people, for all it avails them, might as well still be at the mercy of the samurai."

The following paragraph was also deleted: "Who would in all sincerity wish to oppose freedom, which is to invite non-freedom—in other words slavery and life in prison? One should think before one speaks. In the past, when the alliance was made with liberal Britain, the Meiji emperor so much approved of this that he granted a peerage or advanced the rank to all members of the cabinet of the time. Later, Emperor Taishō sent his son, His Highness Prince Chichibu, to study in England, that country of liberalism. Are not they who speak ill of liberalism in effect finding fault with these actions of the Meiji and Taishō emperors?"

This statement too was cut: "I am firmly of the opinion that beyond proper provision for national defense armaments should be kept to an absolute minimum."

And this: "Constitutional government has gradually receded to the point where we are about to establish a House of government-elected representatives. If things are permitted to continue in this way, there is a danger that the political system which the great Emperor Meiji strove to give the nation as his life's work will be reduced to nothing but a name."

Similar deletions were made so ruthlessly to the campaign speech I had recorded that it was no longer of any use. My open letter to Prime Minister Tōjō was banned from public disclosure. I immediately made a strong protest to the home ministry but to no avail. They merely avoided the issue.

But my resolve was not so easily broken. I was getting on in years but still relatively healthy and I was determined to fight the election out. The government, it was obvious, would keep a close watch on me and take every opportunity to put obstacles in my path. However, they could not prevent me from speaking.

In these extremely disadvantageous circumstances I planned to make a series of campaign appearances in my electoral district over a period of about two weeks beginning on April 14. Before setting out, however, I delivered my first speech

---

[1] I.e., the newly constructed Diet building.

in support of Tagawa Daikichirō, a long-time comrade, who was standing as a candidate in the Third District of Tokyo (Nihonbashi, Kyōbashi, and Asakusa).

The campaign speeches were to be made between April 11 and 13 at five places, including the Arima Kokumin Gakkō in Kakigara-machi, Nihonbashi-ku, and at the Teppōzu Kokumin Gakkō in Nagisa-cho, Kyōbashi-ku.[2]

I took the rostrum following Tagawa and explained how the Tōjō cabinet's dictatorial character was going against constitutional government, and the so-called Yokusan election was a serious breach of the constitution. I went on to say that if the people were so little suspicious of the government's actions, it was because, as the generations passed from the Meiji into the Taishō and Shōwa eras, we had forgotten the tireless efforts of Emperor Meiji, who laid down the constitution, and those of our forefathers who had striven to give us constitutional government. To illustrate this I quoted from a *senryū* (satirical poem): "Uriye to karayō de kaku sandai me" (the fortune gathered by the first generation is squandered by the third). In warning that for the country and the individual alike the words and deeds of the third generation are most telling, I appealed to our Shōwa generation to take heed, as "two generations, Meiji and Taishō, have already passed since the constitution was promulgated".

A number of policemen were present in the meeting halls and from time to time would call out to me to "be careful" (of what I said). On the night of April 13 they ordered me to stop during my speech at the Teppōzu School. I had more or less said what I had intended and was about to leave the rostrum, so the interference did little harm. Nonetheless, it appeared to have had left a deep impression on the audience, for after the meeting had finished they surrounded the car I was in, crying, "Long live Ozaki sensei!"

After completing my speeches for my friend, Tagawa, I left Tokyo station by a night train on April 13 and did a campaign tour of my own district. On April 20, as the campaign was winding up and with the election day close, I received a call from the director of the special police division of Mie Prefecture urgently requesting a meeting. When I met him the following day in Isobe, he showed me a summons from the Tokyo Prosecutor's Office ordering me to appear. I requested that the superintendent of the public prosecutor's office in the city of Tsu be permitted to substitute for the Tokyo Prosecutor's Office, but my request was refused.

I was therefore compelled to cancel my election engagements and call off scheduled speeches. On the morning of April 23 I appeared at the Tokyo Prosecutor's Office and was questioned by a man who claimed to be an assistant prosecutor. The charge against me was based on a farfetched and forced interpretation of something I had said during my speech in support of my friend, Tagawa. I was accused of recklessly criticizing the imperial family. In particular, my quotation from the *senryū* suggesting that the third generation was spendthrift, he claimed, was a deliberate innuendo directed against the present emperor.

---

[2] By this time, all public schools had been renamed *kokumin* (people's) schools, a word with strong overtones of belonging.

It was getting late by the time the questioning ended. Just then a friend brought me a box lunch, but assuming that I would soon be allowed to leave, I told him to take the lunch back as I would not be needing it. However, the prosecutor told me to accept it as I would not be having dinner at home. I was curious as to what other business there might be, but I obeyed the prosecutor and waited after consuming the lunch. At length, after making a fair copy of the record of the interrogation, the prosecutor pronounced, "You are to be charged with lèse majesté. Go directly to the preliminary court as your case has been referred to the preliminary judge."

Stunned, I reached the preliminary court at around 8:30 p.m. After a couple of questions, a young judge pointed to a short document and asked me to affix my seal to it. It contained a sentence to the effect that I had "recklessly criticized the undertakings of Emperor Meiji and thereby referred disrespectfully to Emperor Taishō and Emperor Shōwa." I said I had not "recklessly criticized the undertakings of Emperor Meiji," I was prepared to put my name to the document if the sentence were changed to read "respectfully commended the illustrious virtues of Emperor Meiji." The preliminary judge consented willingly and changed the sentence as I had asked. That much was fine, but I was surprised, to say the least, when he then said, "The Prosecutor's Office has made arrangements for a car and other provisions with the intention of sending you to Sugamo prison for custody."

If the charge was one of lèse majesté, it hardly called for such urgency. There was no danger of a candidate such as myself absconding while the election campaign was in progress. If destruction of evidence was what worried them, the only evidence they were likely to want were the stenographic notes of the assistant prosecutor, and there was clearly no way I could destroy them. It was a strange action indeed to hold in custody someone like myself who posed no danger of running away or destroying evidence.

I imagined to myself that the charge had been invented by the judiciary at the request of the government, who were bent on sabotaging my election and that of the candidates I supported. If I had allowed myself to be conceited, I might have supposed that perhaps the government and their circle saw me as a formidable foe and had acted to remove this nuisance.

Thinking that I would be executed if the offense were found to be grave, and considering I would probably be held prisoner until after the election, I spent the night in Sugamo prison, where General Tōjō and others were later to be detained.[3] By then as a result of government control the newspapers had no backbone left and reported an event like this only very briefly and in an unobtrusive and insignificant manner. However, while this was true of the domestic press, foreign newspapers gave the case considerable prominence. The government of Chiang Kai-shek even used the event for anti-Japanese propaganda.

Whether it was because of this I shall never know, but I was discharged after one day in detention and was able to return to Mie Prefecture and continue with

---

[3] As A Class war criminals prosecuted by the International Military Tribunal for the Far East. Tōjō and others condemned were hanged in Sugamo.

my campaigning. Once back in my constituency, I found the situation extremely unsettled due to malicious propaganda: "Only a traitor would vote for Ozaki, who has been imprisoned for lèse majesté," "A vote for Ozaki will be wasted, as he will have to resign his seat once his charge of lèse majesté is proved," and even, "Those who vote for a person charged with lèse majesté will also be charged with lèse majesté." While there was a great deal of restlessness, I was nonetheless returned to the House. My constituents had trusted me even under these circumstances.

The government was no doubt vexed that its plot to defeat me had failed, but there was nothing more even they could do against me. They even seemed to find it troublesome to proceed with a trial, but they had no choice, having charged me in the first place. A public trial was at last opened in the Tokyo District Court in September, almost half a year after the original indictment.

Even before the trial began I had constantly reminded my family and friends not to say or do anything that would in any way be seen to solicit pity from the officials of the judiciary other than taking appropriate measures to request a fair trial. In fact, I secretly welcomed the opportunity offered by a public trial. As things were at the time, one could not speak freely even in parliament, and I judged that the courts were the only place left for free speech.

As it turned out, the trial was public only in name. It was a secret trial at which only relatives and a few friends were allowed in the gallery. But before they could sentence me they would require the emperor's consent. Believing therefore that the proceedings of the trial would have to be seen by His Majesty, I stated to my heart's content things I could not say even in parliament.

After stating my convictions I begged to be served a severe punishment as an admonition to posterity if indeed my words and deeds were found truly disrespectful. I received a two-year suspended sentence of eight months in prison with hard labor. The sentence was unexpectedly light considering that the trial was held with imperial consent. In fact, the outcome had probably been anticipated since it was a trumped-up charge in the first place, but my friends seemed enormously relieved.

They had urged me to abide by the decision, saying it would do me no actual harm. But I disagreed. Since I was accused of an offence against the imperial family, I had to insist on my innocence. I was absolutely convinced of it, of course, but if the court had decided that I had truly committed an act of lèse majesté then it was not normal that the punishment should be so light. The greater the unreasonableness and unlawfulness of the authorities, the greater the eventual consequences to them would be. An old man like myself whose days were numbered would serve the cause better if he were given an unreasonable punishment.

I therefore protested, saying, "If I am guilty of the serious crime of lèse majesté, then the punishment is too light, and I should be served the maximum penalty provided for by law."

As a result, on June 29, 1943, the grand court commenced factual proceedings, and on June 27 of the following year revoked the earlier judgment in favor of a verdict of not guilty. While the decision was only what it should have been all along, it was nonetheless welcome in a society where the right way was not always appreciated as such. I was pleased. Our judiciary had proved itself independent, if just barely, of the executive in the military dictatorship which our country had become.

JAPAN SURRENDERS SOONER THAN I ANTICIPATED

No sooner was the general election over than the Imperial Rule Assistance Association established the Yokusan seiji kai (Imperial Rule Assistance Association Political Wing). As with few exceptions most parliamentarians joined this group, the Tōjō government considered them to be on its side and went ahead with the senseless war. The Society, which later evolved into the Dai Nihon seiji kai (Great Japan Political Society) with Army General Minami Jirō at its head, attempted to establish one-country/one-party rule.

Soon after the Yokusan kai was established, the eightieth Special Session of the Diet was convened and promptly, during a brief two-day session, approved the fiscal 1942 supplementary budget and three other bills. The newspapers praised the feat, saying "it was a realization of the unity of the whole country." It was no more than a foregone conclusion, this so-called unity of the whole country, which meant simply that the Diet was now the acknowledged servant of the government.

During this session, some members planned to expel me from the House under the pretext that I had been indicted for lèse majesté. This was highly irritating. While many former members of parliament lost the Yokusan kai election, it appeared that more than two hundred had been successfully returned. These same members only four or five years previously had unanimously resolved to have my statue placed in the Diet building and to give me some kind of award. They could not now turn around and support a move to expel me just because I had been indicted on a charge from which I had since been exonerated. Without their support, an expulsion resolution requiring a two-thirds majority of members present could not be passed.

With this in mind I could allow myself some optimism. Thinking, however, of the last election, which had been conducted in a totally illegal and unethical way, the likes of which I had never once seen during my fifty-odd years of parliamentary life, there was no guarantee that members thus elected would not commit every sort of perfidy. The thought of this drove me to indignation and disgust.

While I had escaped condemnation and dishonor for a crime I did not commit, I could not function as a politician in opposition having been robbed of my freedom to speak and write. With the series of unpleasant incidents that accompanied the charge of lèse majesté, the establishment of the Yokusan kai, and the move to expel me from the House, an attack of my old neuralgia hit me and caused me many sleepless nights.

Among the very few who showed me deep understanding and sympathy in these difficult circumstances was the late Iwanami Shigeo, the founder of the

Iwanami Publishing House.[4] Iwanami invited me to his newly built villa in Atami shortly after I returned to Tokyo following the election and gave me a most royal welcome. Here I was able to spend a few restful days before going on to Raku-zansō in Ikenodaira. In parting I presented Iwanami with the following poem:

> Having experienced a night in prison
> I find myself now sleeping in a palatial bed.

Rakuzansō was an inn for skiers managed by my son-in-law, Sasaki Hisaji, who ran it more or less as a hobby. For a few years I had been living there in one of the rooms at my daughter Kiyoka's invitation. In winter I enjoyed skiing, and every morning from spring to autumn I walked in the neighboring hills and valleys, collecting wild fatsia (Japanese angelica) and butterbur to complement our diet, which was increasingly wanting for shortage of food.

In those days I often presented people who would visit me in the mountain villa with the following poem:

> My reward for living so meagerly for eighty-five years
> Is a daily bowl of rice with butterbur.

(The poem was a play on words. Butterbur, *fuki* in Japanese, could be written to mean "wealth and honor.")

As for the war, as I had feared and expected, the situation turned against us before the first year was out. By 1944 it had further deteriorated and our command of the sea had been greatly compromised. The government could not indefinitely cheat the people with propaganda and lies, and finally had no choice but to report the withdrawal of our forces from the islands of the South Pacific. In June, the U.S. troops began landing on Saipan. With its fall, Prime Minister Tōjō was compelled to admit the truth publicly: "The empire is in an unprecedentedly critical situation." On July 18, 1944, he and his cabinet resigned en bloc.

The Tōjō cabinet was succeeded by one headed by Koiso Kuniaki, but it too tendered its resignation when U.S. troops landed on the main island of Okinawa less than a year later. The Suzuki Kantarō cabinet, which followed, was born with the mandate of saving the situation and finding a way to terminate the war.

Hardly had the Suzuki cabinet been sworn in when a huge fleet of B-29 bombers raided the imperial capital, destroying countless homes and causing fires in parts of the imperial palace, the Akasaka detached palace, and the Meiji shrine. At about the same time, news reached us that our ally, Germany, had been invaded on both eastern and western fronts. On April 23, Soviet forces penetrated Berlin and on May 1 Hitler committed suicide. Four days later the entire German army surrendered unconditionally.

With the end of the war in Europe, Japan found itself alone against the whole world. Already, Saipan, Iwo Jima, and Okinawa had been occupied, and the major

---

[4] Iwanami (1881–1946) was a publisher whose inexpensive paperback editions of Japanese and Western classics became so popular they sold in large volume and created the phrase "Iwanami culture," a symbol of Japan's interwar years liberal culture.

cities of Tokyo, Osaka, and Nagoya and numerous lesser cities had been bombed, reducing many parts of Japan to ashes. Millions of our people were suffering from a shortage of food, clothing, and shelter. Nothing, it seemed, could prevent the situation from worsening day by day. It did not take much intuition to foresee that sooner or later the noose would tighten and we would face catastrophic defeat.

Even in these dire circumstances our leaders declared that we would fight on, as if there were any chance left of victory. By fighting on, they meant only to prevent enemy troops from successfully landing on the mainland. But even if one assumed that we were able to completely repel the invading troops, it was obvious the enemy would not so easily lose the will to fight. The United States would most likely cooperate with the United Kingdom, China, Russia, and France to drive the whole country to a state of total exhaustion. They might even launch a second and third invasion. They had ample reserves even if they could be defeated on the coast, but our people were already suffering great hardship and could only expect the worst.

The outcome of wars is determined not by victory or defeat in local battles but, in the final analysis, by either the ability to force the enemy to surrender or to be forced to capitulate by losing the most important strategic point.

Now that things had come this far, our civilian and military bureaucrats could do what they might to bluff the people into a courageous stand, but there were in reality only two choices left, surrender or be destroyed. Finally, the people, cheated for so long into believing the myth of Japan's invincibility, were shaken. And even then the government failed to find a way to bring the war to an end. They only surrendered after most of our cities were bombed and Hiroshima and Nagasaki sacrificed.

Mistakenly, I thought we might last for six months or so after the German defeat. But now that Germany had surrendered it was clear the war had to be ended as early as possible. For this, Japan must take the initiative to declare a cease-fire in order to escape the dishonor of surrender. I wrote two papers after researching the idea.

One was titled "Cease-Fire and the Creation of a New World Initiative" and the other, "Requirements for Building a Peaceful New World." The two papers were written not just for Japan but for the whole world.

Before the two papers were published our country had surrendered. *Yamato aamashii* (the Japanese spirit) was weaker than I had thought.

Mass Resignation of Parliamentarians Proposed

On August 15, the day the emperor broadcast to the nation the decision to surrender, the Suzuki cabinet submitted its resignation. On the following day Prince Higashikuni Narihiko received the imperial mandate to form a cabinet.

The eighty-eighth session of the Diet was convened on September 11 with Higashikuni as prime minister. I attended the session since when the war ended I had returned after a considerable absence to my home, Fūunkaku (abode in the winds and clouds), in Zushi.

Parliamentarians who had schemed to oust me and journalists who had mostly ignored me during the war approached me as if they were giving a triumphant welcome to a returning general. Wishing to reprimand their frivolousness and insincerity, I rebuked them sharply, saying things like, "Shouldn't you bear most of the guilt for our defeat?" Newspapers found even these remarks noteworthy and they printed them daily.

Major reforms were carried out under General MacArthur and in almost no time voices praising democracy rang throughout the country. I wrote the following poem to protest the current of the times:

> My hopes for my country have been answered
> But, sadly, by someone else.

Now that the country had surrendered, there was an urgent need for a program of national reconstruction. I thought that in order to save Japan we had to save the world. In a world that had shrunk so small due to the progress of civilization and developments in transportation and other amenities, it was as difficult to save this country alone as it would have been to save an isolated prefecture after the new administrative units were mapped out in Japan following the conversion of the feudal domains into prefectures. The primary responsibility for international instability lies with nations bound by old concepts that have not kept up with the progress of civilization, in brainwashing their peoples with anachronistic and amoral ideologies.

With the convening of the new session of the Diet, I submitted to the government through the speaker, Shimada Toshio, the following written statement on which to build a policy position for the peace negotiations, based on a plan I had been working on for some time.

1. Given that civilization and war are not compatible, the building of a new world in which wars are eradicated must begin with the current peace negotiation.

2. While, conventionally, peace negotiations were conducted in consideration of the relative military might of the victor and the vanquished, in other words based on force, this time when we come to peace negotiations, they must be based on the concept of a world in which war will be eradicated.

3. While the expense of war and other losses are usually greater for the vanquished than the victor, compensation to the other party was conventionally the burden of the vanquished. Such an unreasonable act of force should be completely abolished.

4. Taiwan, Korea, and Manchuria, being regions acquired by military force, should, without awaiting the meddling of other countries, be liberated at our own initiative and allowed to determine for themselves by the free will of their inhabitants how or with whom to cast their future. If we initiate this proposal, the United States must similarly treat the Philippines, and the United Kingdom, Hong Kong, and Burma.

5. Other problems should be resolved on a basis of morality and reason, having discarded old emotions, and of letting bygones be bygones.

6. If another country makes demands not based on reasonableness but on power, we must never accede. If another country tries to press its demands by military force, we will not meet it with force, rather we shall offer no resistance but will let the world know of this.

7. We shall not only advocate building a new world but will cordially welcome experts to study ways of achieving it, to reform education and erase narrow-minded nationalism and statism, and to educate and train people to serve the new ideology of a universal brotherhood of the whole world under one roof.

Would the nations come to an awakening after experiencing the two major calamities of the century? Or traumatized with wartime fatigue and preoccupied with the difficulties of postwar management, would they adopt isolationist policies such as self-sufficiency, forgetting the need for fundamental improvement in national education as we did in the years following the First World War? This is a crossroads of life and death for the nations and all humankind.

In this context, while the Second World War had ended with Japan's surrender, the causes that could prompt a third had not been removed. As mentioned earlier, I had drafted two papers just prior to the end of the war, and this document, which I submitted to the House of Representatives, was essentially a summary of them.

The Higashikuni government received many instructions from the General Headquarters of the occupying forces, covering among other things reform of the administrative system and the election law, but they were unable to carry them out as speedily as expected. On top of this, some of the emperor's ministers were accused of war crimes, and on October 5 the cabinet resigned abruptly. Shidehara Kijūrō was called on to form its successor.

I am inclined to think that whereas it is quite a large undertaking to create a new age, producing people appropriate for it should be relatively easy, just as we wear lighter clothes in summer and heavier ones in winter. Often the masses do it by themselves without waiting for guidance from farsighted leaders. This is evident from the experience of our own country following the conversion of the feudal domains into prefectures, which witnessed how loyalty to the clan was transformed in a short time into patriotism for Japan.

Now that we had lost the war and were setting out with a fresh philosophy to create a new Japan, we should not depend only on foreign instructions but must have a suitable design of our own. However, problems were likely to arise if the old leaders remained in their positions. It was an urgent duty incumbent on all responsible persons in government and opposition, in the civil service and the military, who contributed in any way to inviting the current national crisis and the betrayal of the Meiji emperor's great achievements, to examine themselves and find sincere ways to atone for the past.

For myself, with regard for the responsibilities of office and in order to uplift people's minds to a new level, I believed that we members of the House of Representatives should all tender our resignations and not stand as candidates for the next four years. On December 3, I put this thought in writing and submitted it to the speaker. Not one member, however, was willing to resign in agreement with my opinion. Rather, most of them were secretly preparing to stand as candidates in the next election as all-time believers in democracy.

In the meantime, it was decided that members of parliament who had served as officers in the Imperial Rule Assistance Association and those elected as the Association-recommended candidates were to be divested of public office and would be disqualified from running in the next election. Again, as in the case of the democratic development of the country, my opinion was implemented with help from without.

Quite soon after that I was summoned to the imperial palace for an audience with His Imperial Majesty, the Emperor. It was only three years earlier that I had been branded an "unpatriotic person" and indicted for lèse majesté with the imperial sanction, and here I was summoned to the court. I found this change of circumstances extremely interesting and wrote the following poem which I showed to the emperor:

> Today, summoned to the palace, yesterday in prison,
> What will tomorrow hold for me, heaven or hell?

The audience lasted for about forty minutes, but the emperor had nothing particular to say. As for myself, there were many things I wished to tell him, but in the event I did little more than pay him my respects since I was not sure how much he would understand.

I had thought that the emperor would show the strain he must have felt at being placed in such unprecedentedly painful circumstances, but I was surprised to find that he had a healthy-looking face, which did not show any mark of anguish. He was moved to laughter by the little satirical poem I showed him.

THE ELECTION OF THE SPEAKER OF THE NEW DIET

With the end of the war many political parties were established and a call for democracy was raised by the Socialist and Communist Parties. Yamakawa Hitoshi, acting as a go-between, visited me at the Iwanami villa in Atami, where I was resting, to ask for my cooperation. He was followed by Nosaka Sanzō of the Communist Party, who had recently returned to the country after spending the last sixteen years in exile. Already I was beginning to feel a bit frail and could not be as active as I would have liked, so I promised to do what I could from the outside.

This democratic front shared the same roots as the democratic principles (jiyū-minken no shisō) I have all along espoused. The secret, I believe, lies in treating people as human beings, in line with the changing times. At the time of which I write, the Japanese race stood between life and death. Solutions to problems regarding the Tennō (Emperor) system and the constitution, concerning which different groups had their own opinions, could be deferred, but survival could not be delayed. At this vital juncture in our history, all parties from the progressives to the communists should stand together. All groups should work as one to free the Japanese people from their slave mentality and make whole human beings of them. This is what I understood as the democratic front. Therefore, I decided to support the democratic movement of Yamakawa and others, so long as it fell in line with the tenor of my own views.

As a first step toward Japan's democratization, it was resolved to hold a general election on April 10, 1946. I decided not to run. Since it was my opinion that all those who had served as members of parliament during the war should resign, I intended to bid farewell to my fifty-six years of political life since the establishment of the Diet.

However, in my constituency in Mie Prefecture, my candidacy had meanwhile been registered at the recommendation of the Gakudōkai (Ozaki support group), and I had been elected in my absence with the largest number of votes. I declined to accept, but when a representative of the Gakudōkai traveled to the capital and then to Atami, where he stayed several days trying to persuade me to change my mind, I finally gave in. On April 16 I agreed to represent them.

About that time I was informally asked if I would agree to become an adviser to the Privy Council. This I refused firmly. Also, I had been designated Shosanmi, Kun Ittō (senior grade of the third Court rank and Order of Merit, first class), for no better reason than that I had served twice as a minister in the cabinet. After the end of the war I had asked to be allowed to relinquish these privileges. On May 4, I was officially notified that I had permission to do so. So I became once more plain Ozaki Yukio.

To mark the occasion I shaved off the beard I had cultivated as a reminder of my detention in relation to the lèse majesté case under the Tōjō government. Afterwards, I dropped the familiar nom de plume "Gakudō" in exchange for "Sotsuō" (grand old man of ninety), simply because I had attained ninety years of age. The Chinese character for *sotsu* (ninety) doubled as an abbreviation for soldier, so "sotsu-ō" could be taken to mean "starting all over again as a rank-and-file soldier."

The Shidehara cabinet continued in office until the general election, and then resigned. Hatoyama Ichirō, president of the Liberal Party, which won a majority of the votes, was deemed to be the most powerful candidate for prime minister, but he was purged from public office by the occupation forces for having allegedly extolled despotism in his book *Sekai no kao* (Faces of the World). Foreign Minister Yoshida Shigeru was then invited to head the Liberal Party, and as its new president automatically became prime minister to succeed Shidehara.

Prior to the inauguration of the Yoshida cabinet, the ninetieth Special Session of the Diet was convened. I had some expectations for the new Diet, which should have been reborn with the general election, but the progressives, that is to say the Socialist and Communist Parties, behaved rashly, and the conservatives, that is the Liberal Party and the Progress Party (Shinpotō), made no attempt to change their old and reckless ways.

On May 16, the day the Diet was convened, there was a general scramble for the offices of speaker and vice-speaker of the House. Finally, after consultation, the two conservative parties decided to appoint Miki Bukichi of the Liberal Party and Kimura Kozaemon of the Shinpotō as speaker and vice-speaker, respectively, and attempted to push these appointments through on the strength of their majority.

I have for some time believed that the election of the speaker and vice-speaker should be divorced from party interests and strategy, and that it would be better to choose a man of integrity from the minority party. On the day the new parliament was convened and with the opportunity this offered for starting afresh, I thought it was a good time to carry out my idea. Therefore, I went to the Diet rather early that morning and attempted to speak before voting for these offices began. Some within the Liberal and Progress Parties did not agree with my proposal, but they could not prevent me from speaking. It was the first time in ten years that I had taken the floor.

I urged that the members of parliament should be the first to correct the principle and custom of putting the government above the people, and referring to the election of the speaker, declared: "Regardless of the size of the party or the abilities of the individual, the most important quality required of the speaker is his character. He should be extremely wise and extremely fair, and use his office neither to obstruct his rival nor to favor his friend. Such is the role of a speaker. For this, the election must put character above all other considerations.

"If there are candidates of character from both the majority and minority parties, it is better from the point of view of ensuring impartiality," I advised, "that he be selected from the minority party."

"In the present circumstances," I continued, "when Japan's future is in the balance under the occupation, the whole country should be united to save us." I went on to argue that the mass demonstrations conducted not infrequently by the Communist and Socialist Parties were unconstitutional: "It is shameful indeed that the masses rally in front of the Imperial Palace over the heads of their representatives in parliament."

After I stepped down from the rostrum, the election of the speaker took place. Secretly I had hoped that there would be many in the Diet that day, especially among the newcomers, who would listen to my advice, but when the time came they elected Miki as speaker and Kimura as vice-speaker as they had schemed.

I was deeply disappointed that the new Diet had not heeded my words. But several days later Miki Bukichi was purged. Once again, ironically, my proposal was carried out by the occupation forces.

THE REVISION OF THE CONSTITUTION AND THE
GENERAL STRIKE OF FEBRUARY 1

The ninetieth session, which had been recessed following the speaker's election, was reconvened on June 20. On June 24 the constitutional revision bill was submitted.[5] However, after four days of questioning in the plenary session, the bill was referred to the constitutional committee chaired by Ashida Hitoshi. It was not until two months later on August 24 that it was reintroduced to the plenary.

As stated earlier, it was my belief that the revision of the constitution should be undertaken when the nation was more settled. I therefore kept my silence even during the deliberations. On the day when the bill was expected to pass, however, I took the floor in response to a strong demand that I do so.

I first of all expressed my approval of the text of the proposed constitution. Then, in explaining my belief that what was most needed with regard to a constitution was not so much the suitability of its provisions but the virtuousness of its operation, I ventured: "The unprecedented national disgrace we suffer now is the result of our failure to comply faithfully with the former constitution, which, compared to the one proposed today, was far inferior. If the old constitution had been properly implemented, we would never have had to face today's humiliation. As I have said, the constitution that is about to be adopted today is far superior to the old. But we must be prepared to recognize that the loftier the constitution, the more difficult will be its implementation given the low level of education and morality of our people. It will be a serious mistake if you pass this bill believing disingenuously that a good constitution will make a good country. If a constitution could save a country there would have been none destroyed. It is easy to write a good constitution but it is very difficult to enforce it."

At this point, referring to the relative positions of the legislative and administrative branches of the government on the floor of the House, I said: "If you truly wish to practice democracy, the seating must first of all be rearranged. The ministerial benches and special seats for government delegates should be abolished and made into seats for the elected members." I stressed that it would take at least two to three generations to correct the evil custom of putting the government above the people. And to those members who wore a triumphant look on their faces for having brought down the government, I offered advice, referring to the example of the loyalists of the Meiji Restoration.

"All of you, compared to them, are far richer in knowledge and experience. To my regret, however, you are bound by the bad habit of glorifying the government and of lacking respect for the people who elected you. Because you do not aspire to be responsible for the country, you meddle in petty affairs, and think you have done your job if the cabinet falls. It is no great feat to topple cabinets. Unarmed, we were able to overthrow the clan governments with their armies even in those turbulent times. The people did not support us—in fact, many were even against us. We could do it in spite of all those odds—and not because we had power. It was because we had a cause, and we could see far ahead."

[5] Ozaki omits discussion of the process of drawing up the new constitution, which was carried out in the Government Section of General Headquarters before being submitted as an amendment to the Meiji Constitution. Those events can be followed in Theodor McNelly, *The Origins of Japan's Democratic Constitution* (New York: University Press of America, 2000), and in broader compass in Richard B. Finn, *Winners in Peace: MacArthur, Yoshida, and Postwar Japan* (Berkeley: University of California Press, 1992).

I went on further to offer a critical view of the past and present of party government in Japan, especially the wrong perception of political parties held by most members. Finally I ended my speech by calling on members to address the existing critical situation with national unity.

"You will be making a terrible mistake if you think that what we have today are true political parties. You mimic political parties but you are really bands of conspirators. Party members, when told to be bound by party decisions, obey them without conscience or any thought of right and wrong. The recent election of the speaker is a case in point. Repeated disgraces do not seem to make you any wiser.

"We will make the same mistakes over and over again unless we rid ourselves of this hypocrisy. I do not give the warning lightly. The political parties are so full of themselves that they pretend they have great purposes and the right to form the government the moment they find themselves with a majority of seats. And shamefully, whomever it is these Liberal and Progress Party politicians make their chief, after fishing among the veteran bureaucrats since they are unable to find a fit leader among themselves, they are bound to install as their president. You are profoundly mistaken if you think these are real political parties. This sort of thing is possible because you are all opportunists. True political parties would be ashamed to behave like this."

Miki, who had been elected speaker in spite of my counsel, was purged and the violent demonstrations I had advised against were suspended, not as a result of my warnings but by order of General Headquarters. As a Japanese, I felt this was very shameful. Another general strike, commonly referred to as the "2.1 strike" as it had been scheduled for February 1, 1947, was banned by General MacArthur's order just prior to being carried out.

I was deeply perturbed by the fact that after the war not just workers but civil servants and teachers too would readily abandon their duties to strike, and at every opportunity I called on our people to find other constitutional means of protest. This, I thought, was because they had never been taught what is good and what is bad. Accordingly, I proposed a readily understandable standard: "What increases happiness for oneself and others is good. What diminishes it is bad." I urged that all actions be judged against this simple standard.

This is to say that the rightness or wrongness of an action is determined by whether it will increase or decrease the happiness of the majority. Those who foment strikes against government and other public institutions particularly, since these exist to serve the people, are themselves enemies of the people.

Railroads and telecommunication services are nationally managed in this country. If their workers go out on strike, everybody suffers inconvenience. In order to serve the interests of a minority of tens of thousands or a million workers, eighty million people can be disturbed. This is an action that wrongs the nation.

Moreover, if you ask if by increasing wages the lives of workers will be improved, the answer regrettably is no. There is no gold in Japan to back up the extra money put into circulation, so there is no other way but to over-issue bank notes, and the value of our money will decline. This does nothing to improve the lives of workers. Just because strikes are permitted in Western countries does not mean that this would necessarily be good for Japan. We must stop this careless imitation of others.

In a despotism an action is considered wrong only if it violates the law. In a democracy any act that damages the interests of the many for the benefit of a few is wrong. Regardless of whether punitive laws exist or not, such acts undermine the foundations of democracy. Strikes in public institutions of all kinds are bad because they violate the interests of the many for the sake of defending those of a few.

I spoke on this subject and wrote about it in the newspapers. No one took any notice of what I said and a general strike was about to take place. I could barely sleep for several nights before the day of the intended strike. I was only able to sleep well again when it was put down at the last minute by MacArthur's headquarters. From the point of view of a Japanese nothing could be more shameful. I knew that our people had little education and morality, but I did not think it to be this bad.

I WARN THE POLITICIANS ABOUT EVILS OF PARTY RIVALRY

Following the ban on the general strike, the government was instructed by MacArthur's headquarters to hold a general election. Accordingly, the Diet was dissolved at the end of March with a general election slated for April 25.

As the new constitution was to be promulgated on May 3, it was decided that an election would also be held for members of the House of Councilors created in lieu of the House of Peers. Governorships formerly appointed by the government were also to be filled in public elections, which would likewise take place in May around the time of the election for prefectural and municipal assemblies.

In advance of these elections I submitted to the Diet the following draft resolution on electoral reform: "Elections to be called in the near future will choose officers who will be in charge of building a new Japan. While all elections are grave events as they concern the fate of the country, the most important is that which elects members of the House of Representatives. Members of this House, therefore, have a special duty to endeavor to remove conventional bad habits by cooperating on every issue. The House hereby resolves to show its sincerity by abiding by these principles."

To explain the purport of this resolution I took the floor on March 13 and spoke as summarized below.

Today we are no longer living under such circumstances as in the past when clan, military, and bureaucratic cliques held sway while freedom and the rights of the great majority of our people remained oppressed. Sovereignty is now the possession of us all. That is to say, Japan belongs to all the Japanese people. In this situation, while there may be differences of opinion among us there can be no group that we regard as a bitter enemy.

However, in the Diet today one sees that each party and faction is wrangling with the next as if it were an irreconcilable foe, exposing each other's weaknesses and defects and hindering the effectiveness of the whole body. As a result, damage is inflicted on the entire nation.

Even the United States, which we fought with arms until two years ago, has adopted an attitude of mutual aid and assistance and is endeavoring to meet the food, clothing, and housing needs of our people. Yet among ourselves we are dividing into parties, splitting into factions, obstructing each other's usefulness, and making life more difficult than ever. Unless we repent of this fundamental error and change our direction, the present sad state of affairs in which we labor will only worsen.

Pondering what can be done to prevent this, encourage mutual conciliation among our people, and surmount the national crisis that is upon us, I can find no better course than the voluntary dissolution of the confrontational political parties and factions until such time as the nation's life is stabilized.

Now that Japan is a democratic country, it is incumbent upon the elected members of this House to set an example and provide leadership. They must show the way by abandoning their adversarial attitude and predilection for strife during this time of peace, and inspired with a spirit of shared love of country dissolve the political parties and organize a government of national unity until our people's lives are more secure.

It would be unreasonable to make such a request at an ordinary time, but at a time when the nation teeters between life and death I strongly urge that you sincerely consider the merits of this proposal.

In other words, I believed that instead of being true political parties the existing groups were no better than cabals. Their members' actions were no different from those of the old Seiyūkai or Minseitō and were based solely on party policies. For the time being they should be disbanded. I therefore urged that the way to save the nation was to do away with parties and factions for some time to come.

Because of the serious and controversial nature of my statement I expected that most of the members affiliated with one or other of the political parties would oppose me. In fact I was secretly prepared for some to invade the rostrum in order to prevent me from speaking. Strangely enough, however, the resolution was adopted almost unanimously with only two or three members opposing. I felt somehow deceived and at the same time uncomfortable at my proposal's easy passage.

The last motion I filed concerned the election of the speaker. By then I hoped to have the House's the full support, but whereas the resolution I had expected to be opposed was almost unanimously adopted, this time my proposal was met with solid opposition. This demonstrated our politicians' frightening degree of shamelessness and lack of conscience. The only explanation I can find is that they see parliament as some kind of sport.

What did they have in mind by supporting my recommendation to dissolve the political parties? If they did not intend to implement what they had formally agreed in the House, that was an act of fraud. They could only have meant to ridicule me personally. This was the first time in more than fifty years that I had felt distinctly uncomfortable at having my views supported.

As the election neared, each political party waged its campaign on a policy platform, while the newspapers urged voters to vote not for the individual candidate, but for the party. I believed, of course, in voting for the candidate with the greatest personal integrity, truthful to the assertion I had made in the Diet. When candidates asked me to endorse them, I did so only after getting them to promise to abide by the following ten conditions.

1. I agree to the dissolution of political parties and factions until national independence is recovered and people's lives are more or less settled, and will do my utmost for national recovery on a basis not of confrontation and rivalry, but of mutual conciliation and assistance.

2. I understand that a member of parliament should accept his mandate only in response to the free wish of the members of his constituency, and that a candidate should not beg voters to support him.

3. I shall do my utmost not to violate the foregoing principle even in the event it cannot be fully obeyed.

4. I shall not run in any election in a way to aggravate inflation by the extravagant use of campaign funds.

5. I shall strive to abolish the use of *kanji* (Chinese characters) and improve the Japanese language.

6. I shall exert myself to correct bad habits such as drinking, smoking, and frequenting prostitutes.

7. If I am elected, I will make my decisions according to my conscience and what is right and in the interest of the nation.

8. It must be known by all that the parliament is a place for consultation and deliberation on behalf of our people and the nation, and not merely for debate, let alone for wrangling and squabbling. Any act of violence whether inside or outside the Diet should be severely punished.

9. I shall strive to make my words and deeds obey the standard of what is good and what is bad: that which increases happiness for myself and others is good, what diminishes it is bad.

10. I will correct the bad habit of submitting to the decision of the party or union against my own conscience.

It appeared I was almost alone in emphasizing personal character over party in voting in this election. The occupation General Headquarters also seemed to be pushing the principle of voting for a party. So when I was asked to make a broadcast, I accepted only on condition that I be allowed to air views other than those of General Headquarters. Permission was granted, and I urged the people to vote on the basis of the candidates' personal character.

In England and the United States, where there are two major parties, it makes sense to vote on the basis of party policies and platform. But not in countries with many small parties, as in Japan, where votes cast for parties will be mainly wasted. It is for this reason I asserted that votes should be cast for worthy individuals.

At this time, with minor parties competing, no single political party could win the reins of government. Government therefore would necessarily be by a coalition of parties. But no coalition would be formed if each party persisted in pressing its unique and superior policy. They would have to compromise. In other words, parties would be obliged to bend their policy platforms and slight their election promises if they were to reach a consensus and be able to cooperate with their erstwhile political opponents. As a result, people who voted on the basis of policy would be bound to feel cheated.

Such ineptness was advocated by all, including those in high places, because they knew nothing of the rudiments of constitutional government. The political situation in Japan was different, and to emulate blindly the way things were done in Britain and America might well not work here. Fundamentally, it was true, constitutional government was to be learned from Western examples rather than by going out of our way to develop a uniquely Japanese model. All the same, we had to understand what we were learning, so as not to go wrong.

In the end, the election gave the Socialist Party 143 seats, the Liberal Party 131, and the Democratic Party 124. The name of the parliament was changed from "Imperial Diet" to "National Diet" and the first session was convened on May 24.

The Yoshida cabinet resigned. But due to fierce rivalry among the parties, the Diet wasted the first day unable to decide who was to be either speaker or prime minister. Late in the evening of May 21 they finally picked a speaker and the following day the prime minister.

Matsuoka Komakichi of the Socialist Party was elected to be the speaker, Tanaka Manitsu of the Democratic Party the vice-speaker. Katayama Tetsu, president of the Socialist Party, became prime minister.

Katayama immediately embarked on forming the cabinet. He encountered numerous difficulties, and not until May 31 was he finally able to put together a coalition cabinet composed mostly of Socialists and Democrats.

I was appalled at the ugly political rivalry and the scramble for the offices of speaker and vice-speaker. Through the newly elected Vice-Speaker Tanaka, whom I had known well, I issued a warning addressed to all members.

> If there is a fire in a large city, we must not waste time discussing how it should be put out. We must all pitch in and do what we can to put it out each in his own way. If we spent too long debating who should do what and what method to use, the city would be burned to the ground.
>
> And if two political parties can bend their doctrines and policies to successfully organize a coalition government, then it should be possible for three or four parties to form a united national coalition government. And how much more so at this time when the fate of Japan is in the balance. One mistake could send the country to its death. We can talk about party doctrines and policies after the country has recovered, but not when it is in process of being revived
>
> Much time is spent today arguing about such things as whether the prime minister should come from the largest party or if ministerial posts should be allocated to corre-

spond with the number of members in each party. There will be plenty of time to worry about these things after the country has revived and it is spring again. This is a fateful time in our history. We have more important things to think about.

I offered this advice not once or twice, but three times. My warning, however, was not heeded and the factions continued to wage their ugly contest for power. Correspondents from the United Kingdom, the United States, and France all condemned the outrages of our parliament.

THE STORM OVER MY PEACE RESOLUTION

The Allied occupation had almost completed its second year when it was learned that some British and American figures had a strong wish to promote peace with Japan. On June 15, occupation General Headquarters announced that as of August 15 private trade would be authorized.

Talk of a peace treaty meant the beginning of the process for a defeated and occupied Japan to enjoy the glory of independence once again. At the same time it was an opportunity for the world to return to peace. However, depending on how the treaty was negotiated and on its content, Japan's independence could still be compromised and world peace only a sham. It could even trigger another war.

As I have mentioned elsewhere in a number of places, I had certain thoughts on peace even before Japan's surrender. I therefore summarized my thoughts in the form of the following resolution and with an accompanying explanatory statement I intended to submit it to the Diet in the hope that it would be put before the world as my country's policy.

Whereas usually in the past the main consideration at a peace conference was the relative military strength of the victor and the vanquished, this approach if adopted now will not put to rest the specter of a third world war. With unlimited progress in the development of weapons of mass destruction and methods of killing foreseeable in the future, most of the civilized world would be totally destroyed. In order to prevent this catastrophe, the House, desirous that this peace conference be unlike any in the past and that it be conducted not on the basis of strength or victory but on one of reason befitting civilized man, hereby resolves:

1. Taiwan, the Ryukyu Islands, Korea, and Manchuria should be placed for the time being under the auspices of the United Nations so that their independence or affiliation may be determined by plebiscite at such time in the future as the inhabitants are ready and so desire.

2. Reparations should be paid to cover the difference of losses sustained by all the parties concerned after fair calculations have been made.

3. If victorious nations demand excessive and unreasonable reparations, we shall oppose this on logical and mathematical grounds and will not cooperate in their collection.

The draft resolution stirred extraordinary commotion in and out of the Diet and eventually outside Japan as well. Perhaps for this reason, while the document was distributed to all members, the speaker, Matsuoka Komakichi, did not take steps to have it put formally before the House. The statement accompanying the resolution was neither distributed to the members nor printed in the newspapers.

Through the agony of her defeat Japan acquired the precious gift of democracy, but for the reason that it was not fought for but given it still had ragged and untrimmed edges. In spite of the fact that the new constitution contained provisions to insure freedom of speech, assembly, and association, certain resolutions, recommendations, and bills were still under the control of General Headquarters and were expected to be submitted and deliberated under certain guidelines.

For a country under occupation, perhaps this could not be helped. What was more disconcerting to me was the extremely servile attitude, the same kind of opportunistic appeasement displayed to the military during the war, that the government and the majority of the members of parliament now showed toward the occupation forces.

When I questioned Speaker Matsuoka on his handling of my draft resolution, he indicated that having sounded out General Headquarters on the issue he was "counseled" against introducing the resolution. "If it were merely 'counsel,' we should have the freedom to follow it or not," I told him. In fact, I demanded that the speaker confirm the exact intention of General Headquarters. To this he admitted that he had received "orders" not to introduce the resolution. I finally gave up, knowing that if it were an "order" it had to be obeyed so long as Japan was under the occupation.

The draft resolution and the accompanying statement were censored by General Headquarters and were almost totally ignored by the press. I do not know by what accident it was but the *Jiji Shinpō* printed it. Perhaps for this reason it was immediately translated and carried with a summary of the statement in foreign newspapers.

Most, however, mistook my proposition as aggressive and condemned it on the basis of their own national sentiments. Chinese newspapers particularly expressed strong criticism.

This brought home to me that the world at large was still bound by nationalistic bigotry, which blinded others from understanding my true intentions.

The New York Times international weekly of August 3, for instance, drew on the coverage in *The Christian Science Monitor*, to comment that: "The terms of the Draft Resolution are extreme, but are representative of views widely held in Japan and are based on the assumption that Japan is in an advantageous position because of its strategic importance to the U.S. as a base against Russia. It is widely believed that working out a peace treaty with the present government, led by a Christian socialist prime minister who is working to further economic recovery, offers prospects of nipping in the bud the vastly erroneous thoughts held by the Japanese."

While the Diet was in session, I escaped the heat in early July, thanks to the kindness of a friend, to a villa called Rakujusō by Lake Yamanaka near Mount

Fuji. The villa was named by Tokutomi Sohō, who later became a war criminal, who had used it every summer. Tokutomi, rather than enjoying happiness and fortune as the villa's name connoted, now had to endure life in Sugamo prison.[6] Rakujusō appeared to have been named for me.

After spending two months at the villa, I returned to Zushi in mid-September. The Diet was still in session. This first session was originally convened for fifty days, but was prolonged four times and met altogether for a record 240 days until the second session was convened on December 10. It accomplished little, however.

During the second session the Katayama government fell and was succeeded after four weeks by the Ashida government on March 10. The Ashida government was in power only for about seven months when it resigned over the Shōwa Electric scandal while the Diet was in session.

On the night of October 14, the Diet called for a ballot to decide who was to head the next government. First, the House of Councilors backed Yoshida Shigeru with an absolute majority of 144 votes, but he failed to win a majority in the House of Representatives. A subsequent deciding vote of 185 to 1 gave Yoshida victory.

However, since the Socialist Party and most of the members of the Democratic Party cast blank ballots, 213 of the 399 eligible votes, a larger number than the votes actually cast for Yoshida, were abstentions. On October 15, on the result of this ballot, Yoshida became prime minister.

Efforts to Avoid Dissolution Prove Futile

After ten years away, I went up to Karuizawa in early July, but because of a boil on my stomach I spent the summer mostly in bed. Since I remained there during the third Diet it was through the newspapers that I learned with horror how the prime minister's nomination had come about.

As 185 votes out of 399 were obviously short of a majority, it was a clear violation of the principle of democratic government according to which all matters are decided by majority vote. The whole affair was strange: for Yoshida quietly to slip into the premiership in this manner, for the media meekly to accept the violation without any attempt to challenge it, and for the entire country and everyone in it to appear totally indifferent.

I was so excited I could not sleep at night. At first I thought to myself that perhaps I had lost my wits for being so excited. But no matter how I looked at it, 185 out of 399 was not by any manner of means a majority. I had to conclude that my countrymen could not even count.

---

[6] The facts are somewhat different. Tokutomi (1863–1957), a prolific writer who became head of the patriotic writers' organization during World War II, was initially charged with being an A Class war criminal, but he was placed under house arrest in Atami instead of being incarcerated. In 1947, charges against him were dismissed.

At that time a village elder visited me, so I put to him: "Have you ever adopted a motion as a majority decision when it was only supported by a minority?" "No," he answered, and gave me a curious look. What a strange question, he must have thought!

I returned to Tokyo immediately and took the issue up with Speaker Matsuoka, who had reported the minority decision as a majority to His Majesty the Emperor. Matsuoka said it was done in accordance with the view of a chief secretary who had taken it upon himself to consider the 213 blank ballots to be abstentions and decided on the election of Yoshida with his 185 votes.

Although this was a clear case of ignorance and malfeasance on the part of the chief secretary, the first mistake, however, was for Speaker Matsuoka to have reported the minority vote to His Majesty as a majority. The second mistake was for the emperor to have accepted it as it was reported to him. The third mistake was for Yoshida to have taken office as prime minister. In other words, the Yoshida government was born as a result of three mistakes.

If one subtracted the 213 blank ballots out of the total of 399 eligible votes, 185 would constitute a majority of the balance. But that does not constitute an election. It is out of the question to consider present members who cast blank ballots as absentees. There are two possible explanations why a member fails to vote due to absence. He may not want to vote or he is ill. By contrast, there were two possible motives for members who were present on this occasion to cast blank ballots: either they wished to indicate their view that there was no need for a prime minister at all, or they were opposed to Yoshida.

It would be a serious matter if members of parliament considered a prime minister unnecessary. It would be tantamount to saying there is no need for government and no need for a state. I could only be aghast that what is so clear could have escaped both Ashida and Katayama, both of whom had served as prime minister. It must be assumed that the blank ballots were cast to passively indicate opposition to Yoshida. This is evidence that no one in the country understands democracy.

Since the blank ballots of present members should obviously not be regarded as the nonexistent votes of absentees, the correct procedure would have been to repeat the election as often as necessary until the house elected someone with a clear majority as prime minister. The third Diet, having nominated Yoshida to head the cabinet, then recessed. It was reconvened on November 8. When the plenary session of the House of Representatives passed with a majority a resolution demanding a policy speech from the prime minister on November 15, Yoshida declared that before any other business he intended first to dissolve the Diet as his government was in a minority.

The government had taken pains to forestall criticism by advertising that a government had the right to dissolve the Diet in accordance with the provisions of Article 7 of the constitution. The Yoshida cabinet was born of falsehood and for it now to dissolve the Diet was simply preposterous.

The constitution provided that sovereignty resided with the people and that the Diet was the highest organ of national power. For the government to dissolve the

Diet was comparable to an employee beheading his master. It was an outrageous act, which could not have been carried out even under the old constitution.

I therefore made an emergency interpellation, protesting that: "No article or chapter of the constitution states who possesses the right to dissolve the Diet. There is insufficient evidence to conclude that Article 7 of the constitution gives the government this right. Article 7 merely refers to the official announcement of dissolution. If the Diet passes a vote of no confidence in the government, the whole cabinet must resign. The government, however, cannot dissolve the Diet."

The Yoshida government, wanting to dissolve the House within the year, claimed that it had the right to do so. The opposition supported my protest with a show of hands, for though they considered dissolution unavoidable they wished to delay the date as long as possible in order to deal a bigger blow to the government. Both positions were based on party interests and tactics.

From my long experience I was convinced that it was unreasonable for the government unilaterally to dissolve the Diet and, besides, that frequent elections bore harmful results. For these reasons I wished somehow to stop the Yoshida cabinet from making this mistake.

However, most people, seeing the issue only in the short view, were sold on the idea of dissolving the Diet. Most of the newspapers too were veering toward that opinion. Even Saitō Takao asserted that it was the proper constitutional procedure to dissolve the Diet when the government was in a minority.

Wishing to correct the misapprehension of the people on this issue, I attempted to have my views published in the newspapers and magazines, but with public opinion already decided in favor of dissolution my manuscripts were being returned. However, it became clear that General Headquarters was also opposed to the right of dissolution based on Article 7 of the constitution as asserted by Prime Minister Yoshida, and that in its view the government could not dissolve the House of Representatives unless a situation as prescribed in Article 69 occurred.

In any case, it appeared that the dissolution was inevitable. Under the circumstances, I proposed that if dissolution was indeed unavoidable it should be brought about by a resolution of the House itself.

I approached Inukai Ken, who was then an adviser to the Democratic Party, in the hope of having him guide the party to circumvent the dissolution.[7] If Inukai agreed with my reasoning and acted accordingly, I calculated that about half of the Democratic Party members would relinquish their antigovernment position and decide to cooperate with the government. And since there could be no dissolution on the basis of Article 7, it would thereby be averted.

Through a mutual friend I asked for a meeting with Inukai. He came to see me at Zushi. I explained the unreasonableness of the dissolution and the evil effects of holding a general election, and sought his support. Inukai, freed from the postwar purge, had just been reinstated to public life, but had no seat in the House. In case he felt that he would not have an opportunity of regaining a seat in the House without an election, I offered to resign so as to give him an opportunity to

---

[7] Inukai Ken was the son of Ozaki's long-time associate Inukai Tsuyoshi.

run successfully in a by-election in my constituency with my support, and pressed strongly for his decision. Inukai took his leave without giving me an answer. His subsequent actions showed that he was not going to follow my urging.

In addition, I tried to solicit the help of the *Yomiuri Shinbun* newspaper through Baba Tsuneo, who was a good friend. I communicated my opposition to the dissolution through Isa Hideo, who was then working in the editorial section of the newspaper and even visited Baba in person, but to no avail. So this effort proved futile as well.

Consequently, when the fourth Diet convened on December 1, the opposition submitted a vote of no confidence in accordance with the provisions of Article 69. It passed with 227 votes for and 130 against. The House of Representatives was dissolved the same day.

AN UNEXPECTED TRIP TO THE UNITED STATES

The general election held on January 23, 1949, returned the former government party with an absolute majority, and the Yoshida cabinet was formed with Yoshida receiving the nomination of both houses. Immediately after the fifth Special Diet was convened in the wake of the general election, I headed for Hiroshima with my son Yukiteru and Dr. Itokawa. The night train was unheated and I caught a cold. By the time we arrived at Hiroshima it had developed into pneumonia and I was hospitalized.

Luckily, I recovered with the help of a penicillin injection. In late April I returned to Tokyo and in July I went again to Karuizawa. Toward the end of September I left Karuizawa to visit my constituency in Mie Prefecture after a long absence, and lectured in ten or so places.

The year passed and in the spring of 1950, when I was ninety years old, my daughter, Yukika, brought me news that a certain Tsukada Kazuhei, who had lived in America for fifty years, wished to invite me there. I enquired for what purpose and learned that he wanted me to see the cherry blossoms I had presented to the city of Washington forty years earlier. Other than that there was no particular reason to go. I declined, saying that I appreciated his kindness but did not wish to accept a private invitation.

Earlier, Yukika had asked me if I would respond to an invitation from the MRA (Moral Re-Armament) headquarters inviting me to attend a European conference. I had declined this too, explaining, "I haven't the slightest understanding about God or Buddha. My presence at such an assembly would be a nuisance to them."

I thought that the question of travels abroad had been settled when, while stopping in Kawagoe during a three-day lecture tour of Saitama Prefecture, I received a telegram from Fūunkaku (my home in Zushi). It referred to a cable that had arrived from the American Council on Japan,[8] an institution founded by Joseph

---

[8] This organization is described in Howard B. Schonberger, *Aftermath of War: Americans and the Remaking of Japan, 1945–1952* (Kent: Kent State University Press, 1989).

Grew, who had at one time served as American ambassador to Japan, and William Castle, inviting me to America. Later, Yukiteru arrived with the original.

After giving it thought overnight, I decided to accept the invitation. I would firstask Isa Hideo and Hattori Fumiko, a nurse, to accompany me, and also Yukiteru and Yukika.

We left Haneda on the morning of May 16. The plane made brief stops at Wake Island and Hawaii and arrived in Los Angeles on the evening of the following day. It was a more relaxed and pleasant trip than the one I made by train to Hiroshima two years earlier.

Of our forty days in America, we spent twenty in New York and eight in Washington. Everywhere we received a great welcome. In New York I was given a suite with a large sitting room at the Waldorf Astoria. One night a banquet was held in my honor attended by 250 distinguished personalities, including Grew and Castle and Dr. Yukawa, at which I was invited to speak. My speech went something like this:

> A hundred years ago Japan was awakened from its imagined seclusion by the visit of Commodore Perry. Today it is being taught liberation from narrow nationalism to a broad globalism by General MacArthur.
>
> Joined now instead of separated by the Pacific Ocean, the United States of America and Japan are bound by an inseparable destiny. Our two countries must be ever more closely linked in the future. I would like to call it a moral alliance.
>
> The Second World War was a result of three mistakes. The first was Japan's role in the Manchurian Incident, the second was America's abstention from the League of Nations, and the third was England's failure to take decisive action either against Japan's provocations in Manchuria or Italy's invasion of Ethiopia. The roots of these mistakes lay in the fact that all these countries were preoccupied with their own ethnic and national interests and in educating their people for nationalism.
>
> Today this error must be rectified. We must especially discard narrow nationalism and statism and adopt a philosophy of globalism. And this is not so difficult.
>
> America has had the experience of successfully building today's big and strong federation by integrating peoples of different customs and cultures in an age when transportation and communication facilities were less developed than now. For their part, the Japanese have built a nation by integrating three hundred or more small and divided independent states. If America and Japan will capitalize on these achievements and apply their experience worldwide a federation of the whole world can be created.

The cherry blossoms round the Potomac Basin had fallen by then but I was photographed under the trees as requested by the press, and I spoke to America on television. In Washington we stayed at the Shoreham Hotel, which was like a palace in the woods in contrast to the Waldorf Astoria. Our days were filled with meetings with journalists reporting on foreign affairs and attending luncheons with commentators, or one hosted by the Library of Congress. Senator Alexander Smith of New Jersey and Mr. Castle gave cocktail parties in our honor, and the

Japanese living in America hosted a welcome reception. We were taken on a tour of both chambers of Congress.

The *Washington Post* twice published editorials welcoming me and criticizing the city authorities for not giving sufficient courtesy to the man who had presented the capital with its cherry trees. The following three verses reflect my thoughts in New York and Washington.

> Am I awake or do I dream
> > So generous the welcome here?
> Are these attentions what they seem
> > Or shadows that will disappear?

> With song beneath this fleeting cloud
> > Intoxicated by Potomac's moon
> Beneath the blossoms' snowy shroud
> > I'd gladly sing my life's last tune.

> But if 'tis written that my span
> > Shall keep me here a hundred years
> I'll yield what's left of this old man
> > To earth—and moon and snow and flowers.

When we visited the Library of Congress I saw that they had put on an exhibition of my books and short poems with explanations and a brief biography. I asked if the exhibition had been specially arranged because of my visit, and learned that the library regularly exhibits writings by parliamentarians and advocates of democracy from all over the world. My visit happened to coincide with a week during which my works were exhibited.

At Congress we received a wonderful welcome, particularly in the Senate, where they invited me onto the floor and adopted a Senate resolution of welcome. I shall quote from the correspondence Isa sent to the *Yomiuri Shinbun* newspaper following this event.

The elder statesman was led personally by Senator Alexander Smith to a seat next to the Senator's own. . . . After the old gentleman had sat down, Vice President Alben Barkley stood and, after speaking briefly of his life and achievements, introduced him to the full Senate. Senator Smith then rose to express a welcome on behalf of the whole Senate and their gratitude for the gift of cherry trees. He then proceeded by proposing that the Senate express its delight at the statesman's visit in the form of a special resolution. Senator William Knowland of California seconded the motion and the Senate responded with thunderous applause. The senators came up one by one to shake hands with the old gentleman while the speech was still continuing. He seemed happy and left the Senate with Senator Smith's hand on his shoulder. A veteran journalist who claimed to have covered the U.S. Congress for thirty years expressed amazement, saying it was the first time in his experience that the Senate had shown such friendliness to a foreign national.

I had intended to have an operation in New York after the scheduled itinerary had been completed and had arranged to be taken in at an ear, nose, and throat hospital in Manhattan. However, New York was already getting hot as midsummer approached and a quick decision was made to return home. We left on June 15. On our way home we spent three days in Los Angeles and a week in Honolulu, receiving a warm welcome from the local Japanese in both places.

We left Honolulu on the morning of June 24 and arrived safely at Wake Island that afternoon. About thirty minutes or so after our departure at six that evening, however, the plane turned back to Wake because of engine trouble, and we were forced to spend thirty hours on that scorchingly hot island. We arrived at Haneda two days late on the morning of June 27. I wrote the following verse in the plane.

> Apparently I have come to no harm
> After flying to and from America

POSTSCRIPT BY ISA HIDEO

At this point the memoirs come to an end, but the old gentleman survived four more years until at last he died in peace on October 6, 1954. For half of these last years he was too frail to leave his bed. He no longer attended the Diet and received few visitors.

At Keiō Hospital in Tokyo in November the year after his return from America, Ozaki underwent the eye operation that he had planned to have in New York. The forty days in the hospital must have taken a great toll on his old body, for his health deteriorated thereafter and he no longer had the vigor he had before the operation. However, he was heartily glad to be able to read newspapers and magazines again as a result of the operation, and he kept his attention on domestic as well as overseas news and commentaries, and whenever he had visitors he spoke of the need to reform the national language and build a world federation. Often he would still take up offers to speak.

In mid-January of 1952 he caught cold and was forced to take to his bed. His condition was critical. The newspapers and radio reported daily as his strength ebbed and flowed. After twenty days his condition improved sufficiently that his relatives and friends who had been staying with him at Füunkaku could go home relieved. At the advanced age of 93, though, it was difficult for the old gentleman to recover completely. That autumn, he ran in the general election from his sickbed.

Fortunately, he was returned due to the faithful campaigning of the members of the Mie Gakudōkai and other friends and followers. He was thus able to extend his world record of being reelected for twenty-five consecutive terms. Due, however, to political uncertainty, the Diet was dissolved in March of the following year, 1953, and, in the general election held in April, Ozaki lost. For the first time he found himself without a seat in the parliament he had served without a break for more than sixty years since 1890.

The House of Representatives immediately conferred on him the title of Honorary Member. The following year the House enacted a law intended probably to be applied only to him, authorizing an annual allowance equal to that of the living members. The Tokyo Metropolitan Government created the title of Honorary Citizen and made Ozaki the first.

Not enough was done to reward the old gentleman as a veteran fighter for democracy. Following the news of his defeat in the April election, he would say little when he had visitors. He hardly ever again spoke about political affairs, and lay silently in bed giving himself to the care of Hattori san and Sasaki Kiyoka, his elder daughter.

This routine continued for another year. Occasionally there were days when he felt better, but he could no longer stand up because of his prolonged illness. He became totally deaf. His only enjoyment was to be taken out into the garden in his wheelchair when the weather was fine.

The wheelchair had been given to him by Kitajima Tōjirō at my request. In the heat of the summer, however, it even became difficult for him to sit in it. By August he was weakening perceptibly, and he barely survived the summer. At 9:22 p.m. on October 6 he went peacefully to sleep, forever.